Preaching the Crusades to the Eastern Mediterranean

Preaching was an integral part of the crusade movement. This book focuses on the efforts of the first four Avignon popes to organize crusade preaching campaigns to the Eastern Mediterranean and on the role of the secular and regular clergy in their implementation. Historians have treated the fall of Acre in 1291 as an arbitrary boundary in crusader studies for far too long. The period 1305–1352 was particularly significant for crusade preaching, yet it has not been studied in detail. This volume thus constitutes an important addition to the flourishing field of late medieval crusade historiography. The core of the book deals with two interlocking themes: the liturgy for the Holy Land and the popular response to crusade preaching between the papacies of Clement V and Clement VI. The book analyses the evolving use of the liturgy for the crusade in combination with preaching and it illustrates the catalytic role of these measures in driving popular pro-crusade sentiments. A key theme in the account is the analysis of the surviving crusade sermons of the Parisian theologians from the era. Critical editions of these previously neglected propagandistic texts are a valuable addition to our corpus of papal correspondence relating to the crusades in the later Middle Ages. This book will be of interest both to specialized historians and to students of late medieval crusading.

Constantinos Georgiou earned his PhD from the University of Cyprus (2015). He is currently an A. G. Leventis Postdoctoral Fellow in the Department of History and Archaeology of the same university.

Preaching the Crusades to the Eastern Mediterranean

Propaganda, Liturgy and Diplomacy, 1305–1352

Constantinos Georgiou

LONDON AND NEW YORK

First published 2018
by Routledge
2 Park Square, Milton Park, Abingdon, Oxon OX14 4RN

and by Routledge
711 Third Avenue, New York, NY 10017

Routledge is an imprint of the Taylor & Francis Group, an informa business

© 2018 Constantinos Georgiou

The right of Constantinos Georgiou to be identified as author of this work has been asserted by him in accordance with sections 77 and 78 of the Copyright, Designs and Patents Act 1988.

All rights reserved. No part of this book may be reprinted or reproduced or utilised in any form or by any electronic, mechanical, or other means, now known or hereafter invented, including photocopying and recording, or in any information storage or retrieval system, without permission in writing from the publishers.

Trademark notice: Product or corporate names may be trademarks or registered trademarks, and are used only for identification and explanation without intent to infringe.

British Library Cataloguing-in-Publication Data
A catalogue record for this book is available from the British Library

Library of Congress Cataloging-in-Publication Data
A catalog record for this book has been requested

ISBN: 978-1-138-74370-0 (hbk)
ISBN: 978-1-315-18165-3 (ebk)

Typeset in Times New Roman
by Deanta Global Publishing Services, Chennai, India

To Anastasia and Gregory

Contents

Acknowledgements ix
List of abbreviations xi

Introduction 1

1 Clement V's and John XXII's organization of preaching campaigns and the clergy's role in their implementation 20
Ad recuperandum imperium Constantinopolitanum proficisci: *French plans for the recapture of Constantinople – the promotion of Charles of Valois's crusade* 21
Verbum vivifice crucis publicare: *Organising the preaching campaign for the Hospitallers' passagium to Rhodes* 25
Crux per prelatos et alios viros ydoneos per totam christianitatem predicaretur: *The Council of Vienne and the epilogue to Clement V's crusading organization* 32
Statum miserabilem Terre Sancte considerans: *Papal endeavours to reinvigorate the crusading zeal for the Holy Land, 1316–1322* 36
Cruxque universaliter predicaretur tam in suis quam aliis regnis et terris: *The crusade preaching campaigns in the context of Franco-papal crusade negotiations, 1322–1328* 40
Committimus predicande concedendeque crucis officium: *Between Avignon and Paris, crusade planning and propaganda during 1331–1334* 46

2 Organising and implementing preaching campaigns under Benedict XII and Clement VI 67
Contra Agarenos verbum crucis predicari: *The continuation of the 1334 naval league and the promotion of Philip VI's crusade – from initial support to final abandonment* 67

    Ad succurendum Christianis in Romanie partibus: *Pope Clement VI,*
       the preaching for the anti-Turkish league and the capture of Smyrna,
       1342–1344   73
    Filium Imbertum Dalphinum Viennensem, ducem et capitaneum
       exercitus contra Turcos deputandum: *Dauphin Humbert II of*
       Viennois' leadership of the Christian armada against
       the Turks, 1345   75
    Pro efficatiori succursu Christianorum verbum crucis vivifice
       mandavimus predicari: *The preaching of the second phase*
       of the Smyrna Crusade   82

**3 Preaching the crusades: Propaganda, liturgy and popular
reaction in the early fourteenth century**   **97**
    Crusade propaganda and liturgy: Preaching testimonies in the
      chronicles of the early fourteenth century. The liturgy for the
      liberation of the Holy Land as a component of crusade
      propaganda   *97*
    Popular responses to preaching   *108*

**4 University trained clergy and the preaching
of the crusade, 1305–1333**   **134**
    Crux penitentie predicatur et imponitur volentibus transfretare
      de Egypto in Jerusalem: *The crusade sermons for the Fourth*
      Sunday in Lent   *135*
    Stimulating Philip VI to assume the cross: *Pierre de la Palud's*
      sermon on the feast of the Exaltation of the Holy Cross, 1331   *141*
    Crusade propaganda and diplomacy in the framework of the
      Franco-papal crusade negotiations, 1332–1333: The sermons of
      Pierre Roger, Archbishop of Rouen   *153*
    The crusade sermons in the first half of the fourteenth
      century: An overview   *168*

    Conclusion   *188*
    Appendix I   *193*
    Appendix II   *196*
    Appendix III   *201*
    Appendix IV   *227*
    Appendix V   *259*
    Bibliography   *269*
    Index   *288*

Acknowledgements

I owe a great debt of gratitude to numerous people whose encouragement and assistance, both on an academic as well as on a personal level, enabled me to embark on this exciting journey and finish this book. First and foremost, I would like to thank my supervisor during my PhD studies at the University of Cyprus, Professor Chris Schabel, whose enthusiasm, relentless advice and patience during our long palaeographical meetings helped me shape my research and form my general approach to history. His kind support, including the generous grant of his professorial funds for research, allowed me to work ceaselessly on the final stages of the book. Among the people at the Department of History and Archaeology of the University of Cyprus whose advice and support I have enjoyed, I must especially thank Associate Professor Angel Nicolaou-Konnari for her assistance and generous provision of source materials and books from her personal collection during the writing of this book, and for giving me the chance to be part of the 'Prosopography of Medieval Cyprus' research programme. I would also like to thank to Dr Christina Kaoulla and Mr Apostolos Kouroupakis, friends and former fellow doctoral students, for their support and comments. Many thanks are also due to the two anonymous readers for their constructive comments that have made this book much better, as well as to Mr Michael Greenwood and Mr Michael Bourne, Editor in History and Senior Editorial Assistant in History, respectively, at Routledge Publishing.

In addition, I am indebted to those people who have helped me with various aspects of this book: Dr Monica Brinzei (Institut de recherche et d'histoire des textes, CNRS) for her valuable comments and for kindly providing copies of several sermon manuscripts from different libraries in Paris; Professor Nicole Bériou (former Director of the Institut de recherche et d'histoire des textes, CNRS) for helpful suggestions on crusade sermons and for her hospitality during my stay in Paris; Dr Christoph T. Maier (Universität Zürich) for his encouragement and constructive comments on my work, Dr Simon Phillips for his invaluable advice on the Knights Hospitallers of Rhodes; Dr William Duba (Université de Fribourg) for advice regarding aspects of this book (I would also like to thank Dr Duba for bringing to my attention this book's front cover illumination of Pierre Roger preaching before Pope John XXII); and Dr Savvas Neocleous for his help with obtaining source material during his postdoctoral fellowship at the Pontifical

Institute of Medieval Studies, Toronto. My gratitude is also due to Professor Helen Nicholson, Dr Nicholas Coureas, Dr Irene Bueno and Dr Jessalynn Bird, all of whom provided me with copies of their work.

Many thanks for hospitality and services beyond the call of duty go to the staffs of the University of Cyprus Library, the British Library, the Institute of Historical Research, the Bibliothèque nationale de France and the Bibliothèque Sainte Genevieve. I am also grateful to Bibliothèque nationale de France for providing permission to reproduce the illumination on the front cover of this book. I must especially thank Mr Robert Petre (Archivist at Oriel College, Oxford) for his guidance and overall assistance; Ms Jayne Ringrose (Deputy Keeper of Manuscripts at University Library, Cambridge) for her help during my research visit to the Cambridge University Library; Dr Wolfgang-Valentin Ikas (München, Bayerische Staatsbibliothek); Ms Anne Laurent (Institut de recherche et d'histoire des textes, CNRS); and Mrs Evie Antoniou-Ktori (Interlibrary Loan Department, University of Cyprus Library) whom I continuously bothered with far too many requests.

I also want to deeply thank the University of Cyprus, which awarded me a generous Junior Research Scholarship during the academic year 2013–2014. I also had the privilege of working as a postgraduate researcher in the University of Cyprus programme on 'Sources for Cypriot History', which afforded me the opportunity to work with Chris Schabel on the *Bullarium Cyprium III*. I am also extremely grateful to the Department of History and Archaeology, University of Cyprus, for fully covering the expenses of my research visits to London, Cambridge, Oxford and Paris during my doctoral studies.

Finally, I would have been unable to finish my PhD without the firm support of friends and family. I would like to thank my parents, Pantelis and Eleni, and my brothers, George and Loucas, for their love. My closest friends, Dr Anthi Andronikou and Dr Eleni Kefala, have been supportive and exceedingly patient, listening for hours to my thoughts and concerns on popes and crusaders. Many thanks are also due to Mr David Porter, who proofread the final version of the book.

Last but not least, I reserve my greatest thanks to my wife, Anastasia, without whom I would have been unable to write this book. Her moral support, patience, love and helpful comments were invaluable, often rescuing me from deadlock. I am lucky to have her by my side. The birth of our son, Gregory, made this journey much more pleasing at its final stages. I am proud to dedicate this book to them.

Abbreviations

AIME	*Antiquitates Italicae medii aevi*, ed. L. A. Muratori, 25 vols. (Milan: Typis Michaelis Bellotti, 1723–1896).
Annales Ecclesiastici	*Annales Ecclesiastici ab anno 1198 usque ad annum 1565*, eds. A. Theiner, *et al.*, 37 vols. (Paris-Freiburg-Bar le Duc, 1864–1867).
ASV	Vatican City, Archivio Segreto Vaticano
Reg. Aven	Registra Avenionensia
Reg. Vat.	Registra Vaticana
BEFAR	Bibliothèque des Écoles françaises d'Athènes et de Rome
Cartulaire	*Cartulaire general de l'ordre des Hospitaliers de S. Jean de Jerusalem 1100–1310*, ed. J. Delaville Le Roulx, 4 vols. (Paris: Leroux, 1894–1906).
John XXII, *Lettres Communes*	*Lettres communes du pape Jean XXII analysées d'après les registres dits d'Avignon et du Vatican*, ed. G. Mollat, 16 vols. (Paris: BEFAR, 3e séries, 1904–1947).
Benedict XII, *Lettres Communes*	*Lettres communes du pape Benoît XII*, ed. J. M. Vidal, 3 vols. (Paris: BEFAR, 3e séries, 1903–1911).
Benedict XII, *Interessant … les pays*	*Lettres closes et patentes du pape Benoît XII intéressant les pays autres que la France*, eds. J. M Vidal and G. Mollat (Paris: BEFAR, 3e séries, 1913–1950).
Clement VI, *Lettres Rapportant à la France*	*Lettres closes, patentes et curiales du pape Clément VI se rapportant à la France*, eds. E. Déprez, *et al.*, 3 vols. (Paris: BEFAR, 3e séries, 1901–1961).

xii *Abbreviations*

Benedict XII,
Lettres ... Rapportant à la France — *Lettres closes, patentes et curiales du pape Benoît XII (1334–1342) se rapportant à la France*, ed. G. Daumet (Paris: BEFAR, 3e séries, 1899–1920).

John XXII,
Relatives ... à la France — *Lettres secrètes & curiales du pape Jean XXII (1316–1334) relatives à la France*, eds. A. Coulon and S. Clémencet, 3 vols. (Paris: BEFAR, 3e séries, 1900–1967).

MGH:S — *Monumenta Germaniae Historica: Scriptores Rerum Germanicarum. Nova Series,* eds. G. H. Pertz, *et al.*, 38 vols. (Hanover: Hahn, 1983–).

RBMAS — *Rerum Britannicarum medii mevi scriptores*, ed. H. R. Thomas, *et al.*, 2 vols. (London: Longman, Eyre and Spottiswoode, 1863–1890).

Clement V, *Regestum* — *Regestum Clementis papae V: Ex Vaticanis archetypis sanctissimi domini nostri Leonis XIII pontificis maximi iussu et munificentia*, ed. Cura et Studio Monachorum Ordinis S. Benedicti, 10 vols. (Rome: Typografia Vaticana, 1885–1892).

Schneyer,
Repertorium 1150–1350 — *Repertorium der Lateinischen sermones des Mittelalters für Die Zeit von 1150–1350*, ed. J. B. Schneyer, 11 vols. (Munster-Westfalen: Aschendorffsche Verlagsbuchhandlung, 1973–1995).

RHGF — *Recueil des historiens des Gaules et de la France*, eds. M. Bouquet, *et al.*, 24 vols. (Paris: Imprimerie Impériale, 1737–1904).

RIS — *Rerum Italicarum Scriptores: Raccolta degli storici Italiani dal cinquecento al millecinquecento*, ed. G. Carducci, *et al.*, 33 vols. (Città di Castello: Ex Typographia Societatis Palatinae in Regia Curia, 1900–1979).

VPA — *Vitae Paparum Avenionensium*, ed. G. Mollat, 4 vols. (Paris: Librairie Letouzey et Ané, 1916–1928).

Introduction

The Western Church applied preaching as the principal means of mass communication in the Middle Ages for the doctrinal and moral catechesis of the clergy and the laity. By the end of the eleventh century, preaching had become the medium for the transmission of a special message to Western Christianity, the papal summons for the conduct of a new religious war for the liberation of the Holy Land. A century later the papacy expanded its crusading agenda to European fronts. The Church soon recognized the significant role preaching could play in recruiting crusaders, in raising money for the crusade and in inspiring crusaders to prepare for battle. For these reasons, beginning in the twelfth century, the papacy paid considerable attention to preaching campaigns prior to each crusading expedition, and the popes commanded preachers to accompany the crusading armies into battle. The Church profited from the rhetorical flair of several preachers who developed ideas that underpinned the crusade as a 'just war' against the enemies of the faith and for the defence of the Church.

The first crusade sermon was delivered by Pope Urban II at the Council of Clermont in 1095. Urban's rousing speech inspired great popular enthusiasm for the proposed military undertaking and marked the beginning of the crusading movement, which would have a profound impact on European society throughout the following four centuries. The idea of crusading was built on strong theological foundations, thus enabling its supporters, the papacy and many Christian kings to transform the Western concept of holy war.

Although not all Urban II's successors were personally involved in preaching the crusade, they all supported the proclamation of a new crusade with crusade preaching. The papal summons of Eugene III for a new crusade in response to the fall of the County of Edessa, during Christmas 1145, established a pattern for the conduct of crusade preaching that remained in place until the end of the twelfth century. Pope Eugene entrusted the business of preaching the Second Crusade almost entirely to the Cistercian Bernard of Clairvaux when, in March 1146, the pope commissioned Bernard to preach the new crusade throughout France and Central Europe.[1] In 1187, Pope Gregory VIII ordered Henry, Cardinal-bishop of Albano, and Baldwin, Archbishop of Canterbury, to preach the crusade in France and Germany and in England, respectively.[2] The French theologians Peter of

Blois and Allan of Lille also contributed to the preaching of the crusade with their sermons.[3]

The dearth of well-educated parochial priests able to preach the crusade while performing their pastoral duties, in conjunction with the abstention of local bishops from regular preaching in the twelfth century, may have forced the papacy to rely extensively on highly educated theologians, especially Cistercians, for the propagation of the crusade.[4] The papacy's dependence on one or two papal legates for the management and execution of crusade preaching meant that the success of the preaching would hinge on the preacher's rhetorical abilities and charisma. As Penny Cole rightly observes, 'the dominance of one personality' in the preaching of the crusades emerged in the twelfth century.[5] This entangled the preachers in lengthy preaching tours, and the expansion of their preaching across vast geographic areas created communication difficulties between preachers and their audiences in different territories.[6] Furthermore, by relying on one or two preachers, the crusading message did not reach more isolated and rural areas, as twelfth-century preachers limited their activities to populated urban centres.[7]

This changed with the elevation of Lotario dei Conti di Segni to the Holy See as Pope Innocent III at the dawn of the new century. The previous pattern of the deputation of one or two charismatic preachers for the propagation of crusades and their expansive preaching tours was superseded by numerous individual preachers. Pope Innocent designated two cardinal legates for the preaching of the Fourth Crusade: he commanded various high prelates from the secular clergy in England, France and Italy to execute diocesan and provincial preaching and assigned a great number of individual preachers from the monastic orders to preach in England, France, Germany, Italy and the Low Countries.[8] The engagement of local prelates in crusade preaching helped the Church communicate its crusade message to audiences across Europe in their native languages. Unlike previous preaching expeditions, the use of numerous preachers for the Fourth Crusade accelerated the transmission of crusading propaganda. Nonetheless, the distinct style of each preacher and the different understanding each had of the crusading idea meant that there were considerable variations in the messages these preachers communicated.[9] This gradually changed after the first quarter of the thirteenth century.

The growth of the urban centres of Europe during the twelfth century brought about the reform of people's religious lives, as the principles of moral theology were disseminated to a broader segment of society. A circle of distinguished Parisian theologians around Peter the Chanter developed such ideas, inaugurating the movement of pastoral reform at the turn of the twelfth century: Peter sought to make the theological teachings of the cathedral schools accessible and comprehensible to the diocesan clergy to make the clergy more effective in the execution of its pastoral duties;[10] this was intertwined with the revival of pastoral theology and popular preaching by well-trained preachers.

The statutes of the Fourth Lateran Council of 1215 reflected the Church's desire to counter the pastoral inefficacy of the diocesan clergy and disseminate the word of God. During the council the Church addressed the pastoral incapacity of the parish clergy and the need for the systematic conduct of preaching in the growing urban centres. In 1215, Pope Innocent III introduced new initiatives for the education of the lower clergy, encouraged the proliferation of theology manuals and preaching aids and prescribed the engagement of local bishops in preaching and in the administration of the religious and moral life in their dioceses.[11]

The ideals of the pastoral reform movement found practical expression at the University of Paris, which emerged as the centre for the academic, moral and philosophical instruction of master-preachers; many of the most prominent crusade preachers of the thirteenth and fourteenth century studied, and even taught, at the university.[12] Graduates of Paris were well-educated theologians who could lecture effectively and dispute theological issues convincingly: they were connoisseurs of the techniques of preaching. Apart from the training of learned theologian-preachers, the University of Paris became renowned throughout Europe for the production and diffusion of written manuals for use by other preachers.[13] The thirteenth century actually saw the proliferation of different genres of preaching aids: *exempla* collections; *distinctiones* and *florilegia*; different types of *summae*; treatises on the technique of preaching (*artes praedicandi*); and collections of model sermons.[14] These preaching aids included advice for the right conduct of preaching, explained how to give a proper sermon and provided preachers with illustrative material for their own sermons.

Several preaching aids, especially model sermons and *exempla* collections, were devoted to crusade preaching. As Christoph Maier shows, crusading themes first appear in the late twelfth century in a *de cruce* sermon – a model sermon intended for preaching on the feast days of the cross – by Allan of Lille.[15] Other crusade preachers, including Eudes of Châteauroux in the thirteenth century and Pierre de la Palud and William Bernard in the fourteenth century, included passages concerning the crusade in their *de cruce* sermons. The *sermones quadragessimales* (sermons for Lent) are another group of model sermons in which the theme of crusading is also prevalent. It seems that the penultimate Sunday in Lent (Palm Sunday) and the *Laetare* Sunday (the Fourth Sunday in Lent) were fitting for crusade preaching because of their penitential aspect, while the Stational liturgy of the cross in Jerusalem was, for the crusaders, a devotional commemoration of Jesus carrying the cross; examples of such sermons are the *Laetare* sermons by the Dominicans, William Peyraut and James of Lausanne, and the Augustinian, Henry of Friemar.[16] Sermons preached on special occasions also featured crusading themes, such as the two sermons by Eudes of Châteauroux in memory of the deceased crusaders at Massoura in 1249 and the sermon of Pope Clement VI on the appointment of Dauphin Humbert II of Viennois at the head of the Christian fleet against the Turks.[17] A different category of sermons not arranged by liturgical themes or the Church's calendar and addressing the crusade exclusively belong to the genre of the *ad status sermones*, model sermons addressing special social groups. The great majority of preserved crusade sermon texts from the thirteenth century derive, in reality, from *ad status* collections, but it has been impossible to date to identify any from the fourteenth century. There are two distinguishable types of crusade *ad status* sermons, one addressing those who were already crusaders (*ad crucesignatos*), wherein the preaching was meant for their moral instruction before setting out for battle, the other for those who would become crusaders (*ad crucesignandos*).[18]

The thirteenth century also witnessed the creation of different collections of *exempla*, including fabulous popular stories taken from folk culture, the lives of saints, legends and miracles, and biblical episodes with a moral message, all of which served as tools for crusade preachers.[19] Following the example of the Cistercian monks of the twelfth century, the Dominicans, James of Vitry, Stephen of Bourbon and Humbert of Romans, collected and thematically arranged a great number of such illustrative stories;[20] these collections from the thirteenth century included several suitable *exempla* for the preaching of the cross.[21]

Apart from sermons and *exempla* collections there are two crusade preaching treatises from the thirteenth century. The first is the *Brevis ordinacio de predicatione sancte crucis in Anglia*, a short handbook for the preaching of the cross, probably written in the early thirteenth century for an English audience, as the title reveals.[22] This short manual provided crusade preachers with simple and easily remembered material from a wide range of authorities, as well as techniques for successful popular preaching.[23] Nevertheless, there remains a question as to its use by crusade preachers in England and as to the influence it exerted on the fourteenth-century English Dominican, John of Bromyard, on the chapter he devoted to the preaching of the cross in his *Summa predicantium*.[24] The other, longer tract for the preaching of the crusade was written sometime between 1266 and 1268 by the Dominican, Humbert of Romans. In the *Liber sive tractatus de predicatione crucis contra Sarracenos infideles et paganos*, Humbert collected and systematically arranged a great wealth of preaching material to facilitate the success of future preachers in any conditions and before any type of audience.[25] Humbert's *De predicatione* was highly esteemed by fourteenth-century crusade preachers and became the inspiration for the compilation of their crusade sermons.

The great number and variety of preaching tools, in combination with the emergence of the mendicant orders in the 1220s, formed the basis for the transformation of medieval popular preaching in general and of crusade preaching in particular. The consolidation of the Dominican and Franciscan Orders provided the papacy with well-educated friar-preachers who made good use of preaching tools and properly preach the crusade.[26] The mendicant students at the University of Paris also proliferated preaching aids, while prominent mendicant master-preachers compiled collections of their sermons and wrote new preaching manuals for other preachers.[27] The wealth of written manuals of instruction in the mid-thirteenth century and their broad circulation, as well as the increasing reliance of crusade preachers on these manuals for the compilation of their sermons, effected the gradual amalgamation of the crusade message, as we see in the preserved sermon texts of the fourteenth century.

In 1234, Pope Gregory IX engaged the mendicant friars in preaching the crusade in different parts of Europe; thereafter, all of his successors throughout the thirteenth and fourteenth centuries largely relied on Dominican and Franciscan friars for broadcasting crusade propaganda. Beginning in the early 1340s, the Avignon papacy also summoned the Augustinians and the Carmelites to contribute to the preaching of the cross with increasing frequency. The mendicant friars offered reliable support, and their emphasis on preaching the cross made crusade preaching systematic in the later Middle Ages.

The conscription of the mendicant friars as crusade propagandists during the thirteenth century and their role in the evolution of crusade preaching have sparked the interest of a number of modern historians. Different scholars in France and Germany made the first sporadic approaches to the topic in the nineteenth and early twentieth century,[28] and studies of mendicant preaching of the crusades in the 1980s and the early 1990s outnumber those of pre-mendicant preaching or anti-heretical crusade preaching. Despite Ferdinand Delorme's survey of the documentary and manuscript sources available for the study of mendicant preaching of the crusades, the topic lay buried for several decades.[29] The revival of academic interest in the preaching of and about the crusades, which began in the mid-1970s, illuminated various aspects of the topic and demonstrated that crusade preaching by the mendicant friars was quite significant. In 1974, the erudite Franco Cardini published an article on the idea of spiritual crusade in the preaching of Saints Bernard, Francis and Bonaventure, and another on the Franciscan Gilbert of Tournai in 1975.[30] John Freed's *The Friars and German Society in the Thirteenth Century*, published in 1977, examines the presence of the mendicant friars in the urban centres of Germany and Prussia and discusses their crusade preaching during the anti-Hohenstaufen and anti-pagan crusades in the Baltic region.[31]

Thereafter, during the late 1970s and particularly in the 1980s, a number of outstanding studies of the crusades appeared, which assessed the important role of the friars as crusade preachers. Jonathan Riley-Smith, in *What Were the Crusades?*, demonstrated the significant role the mendicants had in the dissemination of the crusading message.[32] Norman Housley has repeatedly illuminated the prominent position the mendicants occupied in the propaganda machinery of the papal Italian crusades between 1254 and 1343.[33] Christopher Tyerman proved that Dominican and Franciscan friar-preachers in thirteenth- and fourteenth-century England regularly preached the crusades,[34] while Benjamin Kedar, in *Crusade and Mission*, studied the missionary efforts of mendicants in lands with Muslim populations and the growing emphasis of these mendicants on promoting the crusade.[35]

This scholarship has expanded the research on thirteenth-century mendicant preaching to include the pre-mendicant crusading era and other, different crusade preaching disciplines. The engagement of crusade historians with crusade preaching reached its apogee in the final decade of the twentieth century, when Jaap Van Moolenbroek wrote about Oliver of Paderborn's preaching of the Fifth Crusade in Frisia in 1214 and Moolenbroek undertook a detailed analysis of Oliver's account of the miraculous appearance of crosses in the sky, which Oliver shared to promote the crusade.[36] In 1991, Penny Cole published the first full-scale study of crusade preaching since Valmar Cramer's extended 1939 article on the subject during the thirteenth century.[37] Cole's *The Preaching of the Crusades to the Holy Land, 1095–1270* offers a survey overview of crusade preaching from Urban II's sermon at Clermont in the late eleventh century to the preaching campaign for

Louis IX's second crusade in the second half of the thirteenth century. Cole examines developments in the organization and conduct of preaching campaigns in the first two centuries of crusading history, and analyses several crusade sermons and other preaching tools. Since the publication of Cole's study, no other scholar has dealt systematically with the evolution of crusade preaching as it applies to both the sermons and their preachers between the eleventh and thirteenth centuries, until 2012 when Jean Flori published a study of crusade preaching between the eleventh and thirteenth centuries.[38] The recent publication of the collective volume, *Legati, delegati e l'impressa d'Oltremare (secoli XII–XIII)/ Papal Legates, Delegates and the Crusades (12th–13th Century)*, sheds new light on the preaching efforts and diplomatic relations between the different clerks and prelates commissioned by the popes to organize and lead the crusades in the twelfth and thirteenth centuries.[39]

In his monograph, *Preaching the Crusades: Mendicant Friars and the Cross in the Thirteenth Century*, Christoph Maier studies how, during the thirteenth century, the papacy involved the Dominican and Franciscan Orders in the preaching of the cross. Maier reveals the important role the mendicants played in the organization of recruitment campaigns for the crusades;[40] Maier also analyses three crusade sermons, which he has edited, preached by Cardinal Eudes of Châteauroux in Apulia in 1268 and 1269 in support of the crusade against the Muslim colony of Lucera.[41] Maier's literary contribution to the topic continues with a volume in which he summarizes seventeen *ad status* crusade sermons that he himself has translated and edited.[42] In 2001, Maier published another article in which he compares descriptions of crusade preparations made by Louis IX of France and Henry III of England as described by the chronicler Matthew Paris.[43]

Prominent individual crusade preachers, such as Humbert of Romans and Eudes of Châteauroux, continue to hold the attention of crusade historians. In his article, James Brundage discusses the strategies of persuasion in Humbert of Romans's handbook for the preaching of the crusades, while Penny Cole, more recently, examines the history of the surviving manuscripts of *De predicatione sancte crucis* and analyses its content.[44] In his PhD thesis, Valentin Portnykh provides a historical analysis and a critical edition of Humbert's *De predicatione sancte crucis* text, which was prepared after intensive examination between a manuscript from Madrid (Madrid, Biblioteca Nacional de España, ms 19423) and one from the Vatican (Biblioteca Apostolica Vaticana, ms. Vat. lat. 3847).[45] Portnykh's further contribution to the study of Humbert of Romans and the discovery of a shorter version of his treatise on the preaching of the cross continued with articles in *Studi Medievali* and *Revue d'histoire ecclésiastique*;[46] Portnykh's commitment to the theme led, more recently, to the full critical edition of this treatise.[47] Penny Cole, David d'Avray and Jonathan Riley-Smith discussed two sermons by Eudes of Châteauroux – both edited by Cole in her book – on the defeat at Massoura (1250) and the death of Robert of Artois, as well as Eudes's sermon on the death of Pope Innocent IV.[48]

The preaching of Bernard of Clairvaux for the Second Crusade has also attracted significant scholarly attention. Giles Constable studied a *reportatio* of a sermon preached by Bernard after the disaster of the Second Crusade.[49] Bruce W. Holsinger revealed the biblical background of crusading ideology in Bernard's sermons on the *Song of Songs*, while Jonathan Philips assessed the importance of Bernard's preaching tour of the Low Countries as it pertained to the crusaders' capture of Lisbon.[50] More recently, John R. Sommerfeldt and Sylvia Schein discuss Bernard's crusade preaching and sermons:[51] Sommerfeldt argues that Bernard hoped a just war in the East would reduce unjust fighting in the West, and that Bernard's preaching was part of a wider plan for the reform of the Church. Beverly Kienzle wrote an extensive survey of the preaching of the cross in the patristic era and the early Middle Ages, showing how this affected the model sermons for the cross (*de cruce*) compiled by Bernard of Clairvaux and Humbert of Romans, which in turn form basic sources for subsequent crusade sermon production.[52]

Crusade preaching in the pre-mendicant period has also stirred the interest of a number of scholars. The preaching of Pope Urban II for the First Crusade is the main subject of a John Cowdrey article from the early 1970s, while a number of recently published articles discuss issues arising from Urban II's preaching at Clermont.[53] Peter the Hermit's preaching during the First Crusade was the main subject of Léon Paulet's research in the mid-nineteenth century and for Coupe's article appearing in *Nottingham Medieval Studies* more than a century later;[54] James MacGregor also examined the role of clerical preaching in the emergence of the militant knightly piety ideal on the eve of the First Crusade.[55] Sophia Menache has also published an article on the transmission of the crusade message and the main communication channels for the message between the First and Third Crusades.[56] Shmuel Shepkaru examined the atrocities of crusaders and locals against the Jews following Urban II's crusade appeal; Shepkaru interpreted the mechanism of anti-Jewish violence through the investigation of a number of contemporary Latin accounts and Jewish reports.[57]

Other scholars have dealt sporadically with crusade preaching in the late twelfth and early thirteenth century. Peter Edbury evaluates the written evidence in the *Itinerarium Cambriae* of Gerald of Wales for remapping the preaching tour of Wales by Baldwin, Archbishop of Canterbury, in support of the Third Crusade; Edbury also examines crusade preaching in the twelfth century more generally.[58] Kathryn Hurlock studies the use of crusade propaganda and popular reaction to it in Wales between 1099 and 1280, while Matthew Phillips analyses the sermons of Allan of Lille intended for the promotion, in France, of the Third Crusade.[59] Two articles on Pope Innocent III assess the importance of his pontificate in the reform of crusade preaching and examine Fulk of Neuilly's role in the preaching of the Fourth Crusade.[60] William Purkis, in a recent article, describes Caesarius Heisterbach's *Dialogus Miraculorum* as a depository of memory for the preaching of the Fifth Crusade,[61] and Edouard Baratier examines the instructions to the secular clergy in Marseilles for the organization of crusade preaching as commanded in a bull issued by Pope Honorius III in 1224.[62]

A number of scholars of medieval preaching have investigated and edited several sermons for the preaching of the crusades against the Albigensian heretics in Southern France. In volume 32 of the *Cahiers de Fanjeaux*, Nicole Bériou, Beverly Kienzle and Carolyn Muessig analyse the sermons of different clerics and Cistercian monks in Occitan for the crusade against the Albigensians; they assess the role of the Cistercians in anti-heretical preaching before the emergence of the mendicants, papal attitudes to Catharism and the differences among preachers in their conception of heresy;[63] Beverly Kienzle also explores Pope Innocent III's initiatives to engage the Cistercians in the fight against heresy and examines in particular three individual Cistercian preachers.[64] Jessalynn Lea Bird has analysed and edited two anonymous sermons found in a miscellany from the Abbey of Saint Victor in Paris for the preaching of the Albigensian crusades and the Fifth Crusade, and she has written an article on the justification provided by some Parisian theologians for the anti-heretical crusades.[65] Bird also offers a synoptic presentation of the collection of sermons included in Paris, Bibliothèque nationale de France, ms nouv. acq. lat. 999, which were delivered in preparation for recruitment for the Fifth Crusade;[66] her investigation of the Palm Sunday sermons of the Paris masters and the Victorines who preached the crusade revealed Palm Sunday as a distinct day on the Church's liturgical calendar when preachers preferred to call their audiences to participate to the crusade.[67] Moreover, in a more recent article, Bird elucidates the different forms of memory of the crusades in their preaching and explains how this memory gradually transformed the thematic variety of the crusade sermons.[68] In addition to these articles, most of them about crusade preaching in France, other scholars have recently turned their attention to crusade propaganda in the Iberian Peninsula.[69] Jeannine Horowitz looks at the main themes in thirteenth-century *exempla* intended for the preaching of the cross in the collections of *exempla* by James of Vitry, Stephen of Bourbon and Humbert of Romans, while James MacGregor identifies references to the First Crusade in the crusading *exempla* of the thirteenth and early fourteenth centuries.[70]

There has been growing interest in the use of biblical exegesis in crusader sources, especially papal appeals for crusading, crusade sermons and propaganda. In the early 1990s, Penny Cole first demonstrated the evolving use of Psalm 78.1 in crusade propagandistic documents from the period 1095–1188 in support of the theme of religious pollution of the Holy Places by Muslim occupation.[71] Cecilia Gaposchkin recently observed the revelation of Joshua as a king in holy war and as a symbol for crusade in sermons for the crusade before the departure of Louis IX for the East. Gaposchkin examines the parallels between episodes from the story of Joshua at the glazing cycle of Sainte-Chapelle and Louis IX's crusading ambitions,[72] while Douglas Earl studies the evolving importance of Joshua as a significant exemplar for the conduct of Christian holy war between the twelfth and late thirteenth centuries.[73] Nicholas Morton explores the use of Maccabean exemplars in crusade preaching and crusading during the twelfth and thirteenth centuries: Morton demonstrates how the memory of the Maccabees in such sources led to the gradual consolidation of the idea of crusading.[74] Elizabeth Lapina studies the connections between the city of Antioch and the Maccabean warriors and demonstrates their resemblance to the crusaders in the narratives of the battle of Antioch written in the aftermath of the First Crusade.[75] The use of the Bible in crusader sources is further discussed in a collective volume of 19 articles published in 2017.[76] Thomas Smith, among others in the volume, examines the use of the Bible in the *arengae* of Pope Gregory IX's crusade letters, while Jessalynn Lea Bird demonstrates how biblical quotations in the sermons delivered during the preparations for the Fifth Crusade shaped the course of this particular expedition.[77] Lydia Walker examines the apocalyptic ideas in the *ad status* sermons of James of Vitry and the role of the Book of Revelation in modelling visionary descriptions in crusade preaching.[78]

Unlike the preaching of the crusades in the period before the final loss of the Holy Land, the preaching of the crusades held little fascination for historians of the 'Later Crusades'. Norman Housley has assessed the role of the Avignon papacy in the organization of propaganda campaigns and the prominent position of the mendicants for the execution of preaching for crusading to the Holy Land, Iberia and elsewhere;[79] Housley has also examined the degree of papal control over the preaching, the management of indulgences, the popular reaction to the preaching and obstacles to crusade preaching. In *The Invention of the Crusades*, Christoph Tyerman makes brief references to crusade preaching during the papacy of John XXII.[80] Beattie Blake recently analysed the sermon preached by Cardinal Bertrand du Pujet at the papal chapel in Avignon, during Lent 1345, for the promotion of the crusade against Christian rulers in Italy whom the papacy considered enemies of the faith.[81] In their more recent articles, Nicholas Coureas and Maria Paschali discuss the emergence of the Carmelite friars as crusade propagandists in the mid-fourteenth century.[82] Finally, Timothy Guard's research on the English diocesan registers offers a representation of clerical responses to papal directives for crusade preaching in fourteenth-century England, but his treatment of the subject is limited in scope;[83] in his article 'Pulpit and Cross', Guard provides more evidence of the English experience of the propagation of the crusades and the production of crusade preaching aids in fourteenth-century England, but the portrait still remains unfinished.[84]

One reason the preaching of the cross has received little consideration is the notion among some historians of the 'Later Crusades' that the standardization of crusade preaching and the consequent absence of originality in the crusading message made crusade propaganda less effective in the fourteenth century. Nonetheless, one must remember that people at the time would not have recognized any originality in the preachers' crusade messages. Christopher Tyerman explains that the lack of spontaneity in preaching and originality in crusade messages accounts for 'the absence of enthusiasm and the hesitation of the masses in the sense of recruitment'.[85] Nevertheless, the three distinct, massive outbursts of popular zeal during or shortly after a general crusade preaching, within fewer than four decades during the first half of the fourteenth century, suggest otherwise. Norman Housley, another historian of the 'Later Crusades', claims that 'the fourteenth century had no Peter the Hermit or Fulk of Neuilly, indeed it had little place for them', and that the quality of preaching was less important than it had been in the previous century.[86] Housley presumably makes this assertion because of the scarcity of written records naming popular crusade preachers, or referring to their preaching and the impression their words made, rather than because adequate individual preachers had disappeared by the fourteenth century. Nonetheless, there is ample evidence in narrative and documentary sources testifying to the inspiring preaching of Cardinal-priest Nicholas of Fréauville, papal legate in the Kingdom of France, on the Île-de-la-Cité during Pentecost of 1313, and to that of Peter of Pleine Chassagne, Latin Patriarch of Jerusalem, and Peter of Courpalay, Abbot of Saint-Germain-des-Prés, in the Sainte-Chapelle on 23 July 1316.[87] The most distinctive stirring, popular crusade preacher from the first half of the fourteenth century was the Dominican friar, Venturino of Bergamo: Venturino's preaching of the crusade against the Turks in 1344 sparked an outbreak of popular enthusiasm for the crusade in Italy; Venturino's eloquence even impressed Pope Clement VI.[88]

New socio-economic and political conditions in Europe during the first half of the fourteenth century forced the royal powers to set new priorities and compelled the Avignon popes to convince the Christian kingdoms of Europe, especially the French Crown, to contribute to the implementation of the crusade to the Holy Land; this in turn resulted in the emergence of court-bound crusade propagandists, all prominent figures of the high clergy and famous Parisian theologians, who compiled a number of crusade sermons, all preached in the context of crusade negotiations at the papal and French royal courts. These sermons constitute an important source for the study of the preaching of the crusades in the first half of the fourteenth century. Such sermons reveal the Church's anxiety over securing the participation of powerful lay individuals in its crusading plans and exposed the general disinterest of the latter in crusading. The court crusade sermons delivered during crusade negotiations between 1331 and 1333 (see the list of crusade sermons from the fourteenth century in Appendix I and the editions in Appendices III and IV) reflect social, political and economic complexities, all of which hindered the execution of a general crusade, none of which Western Europe could resolve.

The Lenten and *de cruce* sermons, which include crusade addresses, must be added to the court crusade sermons (see Appendices I and II). That these sermons were compiled to serve a dual purpose, to reveal the religious message of the feast day on which they were to be delivered and to communicate symbolism that would inspire crusade enthusiasm, makes locating them a difficult task. Unlike the court crusade sermons, in which the compiler or a later hand often defines the preacher and the occasion of the preaching of the sermon, there is no distinguishing feature to help us determine which Lenten and *de cruce* sermons included crusade addresses; these sermons were included in manuscript collections arranged by liturgical dates to suit regular preaching throughout the ecclesiastical year and did not belong to a specific liturgical day.[89] The only way to identify these particular sermons is to review the entire text of every Lenten and *de cruce* sermon from the fourteenth century; that such texts are found in thousands of manuscript collections of sermons arranged by liturgical dates makes this an enormous and daunting task.

Given that the preachers had to be prepared to preach crusade sermons at any time of the year, the field of study becomes even broader, demanding many years of research in manuscript collections for the identification of other crusade sermons. In this effort, Johann Baptist Schneyer's *Repertorium* of medieval sermons remains an invaluable tool, despite its omissions; in his voluminous *Repertorium*, Schneyer lists more than one hundred thousand sermon incipits in a great number of sermon collections in the principal manuscript libraries of Europe.[90] Schneyer's monumental opus offers the student of medieval preaching a detailed inventory of manuscript sermon collections in different libraries, but it is no substitute for a folio-by-folio reading of the manuscripts themselves.

It became possible, however, to identify 11 crusade sermons from the first half of the fourteenth century. Some of these sermons were delivered on particular occasions. The three sermons of Pierre Roger/Clement VI, preached in 1332–1333 and 1345, consist a harmonious blend of masterly diplomacy and development of pro-crusade discourse. The majority of these sermons were preached on specific feast days or Sundays of the Church's season as their symbolism fitted crusading very well. The sermons for the Exaltation of the Cross by the Dominicans Pierre de la Palud and William Bernard of Narbonne and those for the Fourth Sunday in Lent (*Laetare Jerusalem*) by James of Lausanne, Henry of Friemar and the two anonymous sermons from Avignon are distinctive examples of crusade sermons from the fourteenth century which were identified in the context of this book. To these examples can be added two other sermons by William Bernard and James of Lausanne for Lent and the First Sunday after the Epiphany respectively.

Narrative sources constitute another important source for the study of crusade preaching in the first half of the fourteenth century. The abundance of printed editions of annals, chronicles and memoirs in collections such as *Rerum Britannicarum medii aevi scriptores, Monumenta Germaniae Historica, Recueil des historiens des Gaules et de la France, Antiquitates Italicae medii aevi, Rerum Italicarum Scriptores, Vitae Paparum Avenionensium, Recueil des historiens des croisades: Historiens Occidentaux* and other individual editions of chronicles adds a wealth of knowledge to the study. The different chroniclers, despite their diverse narratives, social status, levels of credibility and proximity to the recounted events, often included details about various crusade preaching occasions in their accounts: they usually name the preacher and give the date and the location where the preaching took place, as well as the audience, although their narratives fail to report the preacher's actual words. Nonetheless, these narrative accounts are the main source for testimony to popular reaction to crusade preaching in the first half of the fourteenth century.

Of significant importance to this study are the papal letters from the Archivio Segreto Vaticano, especially those in the *Registra Vaticana* and *Registra Avenionensia* collections. Significant portions of the registers of papal correspondence (John XXII, Benedict XII, Clement VI) relevant to this study have been summarized or published in full by the Bibliothèque des Écoles françaises d'Athènes et de Rome. Since these publications are not complete, it has been necessary in some cases to consult the original documents in the manuscripts. The Benedictine monks have done further work in the field by publishing a significant part of Clement V's registers in the late nineteenth century. The registers of the Avignon popes are essential for understanding papal attitudes to the preaching of the crusades. Unlike many thirteenth-century crusade bulls, the letters of the Avignon popes do not instruct the clergy about what should be said in their sermons, but instead outline detailed plans for the organization of preaching and liturgical campaigns for the crusade. The correspondence of the Avignon papacy constitutes an integrated representation of the papal administration of crusade preaching, offering invaluable data on commissions to preach, the names of preachers and the areas of their operation, sometimes even revealing anticipated obstructions to the normal conduct of preaching.

In this context, the present book attempts to shed new light on the organization of crusade preaching campaigns and the evolving use of liturgy for the Holy Land during the pontificates of the first four Avignon popes, and to investigate the 11 identified crusade sermons and their preachers during this period. The first two chapters focus on the efforts of the Avignon papacy to organize preaching campaigns for the crusade to the East between 1305 and 1352, and the role of the clergy, secular and regular, in implementing papal aims. More specifically, Chapter 1 deals with the reigns of Clement V and John XXII, 1305 to 1334: it opens with Clement's attitudes vis-à-vis Constantinople and the organization of crusade preaching in support of Charles of Valois's crusade for its recapture, followed by an examination of the preaching campaign introduced by Clement V for the promotion of the Hospitallers' *passagium* to Rhodes in 1309; it also discusses the crusade preaching at the Council of Vienne (1311–1312) and the *crucesignatio* of Philip IV of France. The chapter continues with a historical overview of the political and economic situation in the West during the *interregnum* between the death of Pope Clement V in April 1314 and the election of Jacques Duèze, Cardinal-bishop of Porto e Santa Rufina, as Pope John XXII in early August 1316, and it outlines John XXII's endeavours to reinvigorate crusading enthusiasm for the Holy Land in France. The chapter then describes the organization of the crusade propaganda campaign in the context of papal negotiations with King Charles IV of France. In its final section, this chapter discusses the years 1331–1334, maybe the most intensive period of crusade planning and the production of crusade sermons during the Avignon papacy.

Chapter 2 explores the period of the last two Avignon popes related to this study, Benedict XII and Clement VI, 1334–1352. This chapter begins with the papacy of Benedict XII and details how the pope's initial enthusiasm for the promotion of the planned crusade of Philip VI of France ended in a fiasco with the cancellation of the crusade in 1336. It then examines the intensification of crusade preaching for the organization of the anti-Turkish crusade for the capture of Smyrna in 1344 under Pope Clement VI, followed by an explication of the immediate papal reaction to news of the slaughter of the crusade's leaders and the preaching for the second phase of the Smyrna Crusade. Finally, it presents and analyses the crusade sermon preached by Clement VI on the assignment of Humbert II, Dauphin of Viennois, as leader of the Christian armada to defend Smyrna.[91]

The largest part of Chapter 3, which is based on testimonies in the narratives of chroniclers from France, England, Italy and Germany, investigates actual preaching events in the early fourteenth century and examines developments in the performance of the liturgy for the Holy Land that the Avignon popes introduced between 1305 and 1352. This chapter further offers an analysis of popular responses to crusade propaganda, highlighting the excessive impact crusading propaganda and liturgy made on people's pro-crusade feelings. The redemptive message of crusade propagandists and the prospect of Church protection in a period of economic turmoil in Europe prompted the outburst of the People's Crusade in 1309, the Pastoureaux in 1320 and the massive reaction to the preaching for the second phase of the Smyrna Crusade in 1345.

Chapter 4 examines the content and structure of the identified crusade sermons compiled between 1305 and 1352, presenting a comparative view with regard to sermons and treatises for the preaching of the cross from the thirteenth century. The chapter opens with a presentation and thematic analysis of the preserved fourteenth century sermons, with crusade appeals, for the Fourth Sunday in Lent, followed by an examination of the *de cruce* sermon that was delivered by Pierre de la Palud, Latin Patriarch of Jerusalem, and stimulated French royal interest in crusading to the East. Finally, the chapter analyses the preserved sermons preached by Archbishop Pierre Roger, French royal envoy at the papal court in Avignon, in the context of the Franco-papal crusade negotiations, which lasted from 1332 until 1333.

In addition to these four chapters, the book's appendices provide a list of 11 crusade sermons from the fourteenth century, the critical editions of James of Lausanne's *Laetare* crusade sermon, the text of the two sermons preached by Pierre Roger/Clement VI during the Franco-papal negotiations for the crusade and, finally, the sermon Pope Clement VI delivered on the appointment of the Dauphin Humbert II of Viennois as the leader of the Christian fleet for Smyrna.[92] The inclusion of previously unknown or little-known sermon texts is a valuable addition to the corpus of papal registers relating to the crusades in the later Middle Ages. James of Lausanne's *Laetare* sermon with crusade appeals (Appendix II) is the longest, best-organized and most sophisticated exemplar of a crusade sermon for the Fourth Sunday in Lent; James's dependence on Aristotelian syllogism distinguishes his *Laetare* sermon thematically from the other fourteenth-century exemplars. The sermons of Pierre Roger/Clement VI (Appendices III–V) demonstrate his rhetorical flair and his quality as a diplomat; both rendered him the most prominent figure of early fourteenth-century crusade propaganda. Appendices III and IV offer the reader a distinctive interpretation of the crusade from the perspective of a clergyman in the service of a secular ruler, while the final sermon in Appendix V has much to tell us about his interpretation, now as pope, of the Smyrna Crusade and, in particular, the controversial appointment of Humbert II as its leader following the death in action of Henry of Asti. In these cases, there are grounds for an argument that these sermons take us to the heart of Pierre Roger/Clement's thinking, as he almost certainly wrote them himself.

Notes

1 Sylvia Schein, 'Bernard of Clairvaux's Preaching of the Second Crusade and Orality', in *Oral History of the Middle Ages: The Spoken Word in Context*, eds. G. Jaritz and M. Richter (Budapest: Central European University, Department of Medieval Studies, 2001), 188–195; Jonathan Philips, 'St Bernard of Clairvaux, the Low Countries and the Lisbon Letter of the Second Crusade', *Journal of Ecclesiastical History*, 48.3 (1997), 485–497.
2 Penny Cole, *The Preaching of the Crusades to the Holy Land, 1095–1270* (Cambridge, Massachusetts: The Medieval Academy of America, 1991), 65, 71. For a full account of the preaching tour of Archbishop Baldwin in Wales see Peter W. Edbury, 'Preaching the Crusade in Wales', in *England and Germany and the High Middle Ages*, eds. A. Haverkamp and H. Vollrath (Oxford: Oxford University Press, 1996), 221–233; Kathryn Hurlock, 'Power, Preaching and the Crusades in *Pura Wallia* c.1180–1280', in *Thirteenth Century England*, eds. W. Bjorn, B. Janet, *et al.* (Woodbridge: Boydell, 2007), 94–108.
3 Jean Flori, *Prêcher la croisade, XI–XIII siècle. Communication et propaganda* (Paris: Perrin, 2012), 162–173.
4 Beverly Kienzle, *Cistercians, Heresy and Crusade in Occitania, 1145–1229: Preaching in the Lord's Vineyard* (Rochester, New York: York Medieval Press/Boydell Press, 2001).
5 Cole, *The Preaching of the Crusades*, 78.
6 For more details over this see below Chapter 1, pp. 31–32.
7 Cole, *The Preaching of the Crusades*, 42–56; 65–72.
8 Cole, *The Preaching of the Crusades*, 82–84, 88–95; Flori, *Prêcher la croisade, XI–XIII siècle*, 183–205; Andrew Jones, 'Fulk of Neuilly, Innocent III, and the Preaching of the Fourth Crusade', *Comitatus*, 41 (2010), 119–148.
9 Cole, *The Preaching of the Crusades*, 96–97.
10 Nicole Bériou, *L'avènement des maîtres de la parole. La prédication à Paris au XIIIe siècle*, 2 vols. (Paris: Institut d'études Augustiniennes, 1998), i, 30–46; Cole, *The Preaching of the Crusades*, 113–115; Christoph Maier, *Crusade Propaganda and Ideology: Model Sermons for the Preaching of the Cross* (Cambridge: Cambridge University Press, 2000), 4–6.
11 Siegfried Wenzel, *Latin Sermon Collections from Later Medieval England: Orthodox Preaching in the Age of Wyclif* (Cambridge: Cambridge University Press, 2005), 229–231; David d'Avray, *The Preaching of the Friars: Sermons Diffused from Paris before 1300* (Oxford: Clarendon Press, 1985), 20–21; Cole, *The Preaching of the Crusades*, 117; Flori, *Prêcher la croisade, XI–XIII siècle*, 239–244.
12 James of Vitry, Eudes of Châteauroux, Gilbert of Tournai, Humbert of Romans, Bertrand de la Tour, James of Lausanne, Pierre de la Palud and Pierre Roger, important crusade preachers and compilers of manuals for the preaching of the cross in the thirteenth and fourteenth centuries, were all educated at the University of Paris.
13 d'Avray, *The Preaching of the Friars*, 273–286.
14 Siegfried Wenzel, *Medieval Artes Praedicandi: A Synthesis of Scholastic Sermon Structure* (Toronto, Buffalo, London: University of Toronto Press, 2015); d'Avray, *The Preaching of the Friars*, 64–85; Maier, *Crusade Propaganda and Ideology*, 6.
15 Maier, *Preaching the Crusades*, 112.
16 For more examples and details on these sermons see Chapter 4 and Appendix II.
17 Cole, *The Preaching of the Crusades*, 235–243 (appendix D).
18 Maier, *Crusade Propaganda and Ideology*, 4.
19 Claude Bremond, Jacques Le Goff, Jean-Claude Schmitt, *L'"Exemplum"* (Turnhout: Brepols, 1982), 37–38; Cole, *The Preaching of the Crusades*, 115.
20 For the twelfth-century Cistercian collections of *exempla* see Stefano Mula, 'Twelfth- and Thirteenth-Century Cistercian *Exempla* Collections: Role, Diffusion, and

Evolution', *History Compass*, 8.8 (2010), 903–912; *The Exempla or Illustrative Stories from the Sermones Vulgares of Jacques de Vitry*, ed. T. Frederick Crane (London: The Folklore Society, 1890); *Anecdotes historiques, légendes et apologues tirés du recueil inédit d'Étienne de Bourbon*, ed. A. Lecoy de la Marche (Paris: Société de l'histoire de France, 1877); For Humbert of Romans see Simon Tugwell, *Early Dominicans: Selected Writings* (New York: Paulist Press, 1982), 371–383.

21 Jeannine Horowitz, 'Les *exempla* au service de la prédication de la croisade au 13e siècle', *Revue d'histoire ecclésiastique*, 92.2 (1997), 367–394.

22 'Ordinacio de predicatione sancte crucis in Anglia', in *Quinti belli sacri scriptores minores*, ed. R. Röhricht (Geneva: Publications de la société de l'Orient Latin, 1879), 2–26; Maier, *Preaching the Crusades*, 114.

23 For full structural and content analysis of *Ordinacio de predicatione sancte crucis in Anglia* see Cole, *The Preaching of the Crusades*, 117–126.

24 John of Bromyard, *Summa predicantium doctissimi viri fratris Johannis Bromyard, Ordinis Predicatorum* (Basel, 1485); Timothy Guard, *Chivalry Kingship and Crusade: The English Experience in the Fourteenth Century* (Woodbridge: The Boydell Press, 2013), 149–153; Timothy Guard, 'Pulpit and Cross: Preaching the Crusade in Fourteenth–century England', *English Historical Review*, 129.541 (2014), 1328–1345.

25 Maier, *Preaching the Crusades*, 114.

26 William A. Hinnebusch, *The History of the Dominican Order*, 2 vols. (New York: Alba House, 1965–1973); John R. H. Moorman, *A History of the Franciscan Order from its Origins to the Year 1517* (Oxford: Clarendon Press, 1968); d'Avray, *The Preaching of the Friars*; John Freed, *The Friars and German Society in the Thirteenth Century* (Cambridge, Massachusetts: The Medieval Academy of America Publications, 1977).

27 d'Avray, *The Preaching of the Friars*, 98–99, 160–163.

28 Reinhold Röhricht, 'Die Kreuzpredigten Gegen den Islam: Ein Beitrag zur Geschichte der Christlichen Predigt im 12. und 13. Jahrhundert', *Zeitschrift für Kirchengeschichte*, 6 (1884), 550–572; Georg Wolfram, 'Kreuzzugspredigt und Kreuzlied', *Zeitschrift für deutsches Altertum*, 30 (1886), 89–132; Albert Lecoy de la March, 'La prédication de la croisade au treizième siècle', *Revue des questions historiques*, 48 (1890), 5–28; Ferdinand M. Delorme, 'Bulle d'Innocent IV pour la croisade (6 février 1245)', *Archivum Franciscanum Historicum*, 6 (1913), 386–389; Ferdinand M. Delorme, 'Bulle d'Innocent IV en faveur de l'empire Latin de Constantinople', *Archivum Franciscanum Historicum*, 8 (1915), 307–310; A. Van den Wyngaert, 'Frère Guillaume de Cordelle O.F.M.', *La France Franciscaine*, 4 (1921), 52–71.

29 Ferdinand M. Delorme, 'De praedicatione cruciate saec. XIII per Fratres Minores', *Archivum Franciscanum Historicum*, 9 (1916), 99–117.

30 Franco Cardini, 'Nella presenza del soldan superba: Bernardo, Francesco, Bonaventura e il superamento spirituale dell'idea di crociata', *Studi Francescani*, 71 (1974), 199–250; Franco Cardini, 'Gilberto di Tournai. Un Francescano predicatore della crociata', *Studi Francescani*, 72 (1975), 31–48.

31 Freed, *The Friars and German Society in the Thirteenth Century*.

32 Jonathan Riley-Smith, *What Were the Crusades?* (London: Macmillan, 1977).

33 Norman Housley, *The Italian Crusades: The Papal-Angevin Alliance and the Crusades Against Christian Lay Powers, 1254–1343* (Oxford: Clarendon Press, 1982); Norman Housley, *The Avignon Papacy and the Crusades, 1305–1378* (Oxford: Clarendon Press, 1986); Norman Housley, *The Later Crusades: From Lyon to Alcazar, 1274–1580* (Oxford: Oxford University Press, 1992).

34 Christopher Tyerman, *England and the Crusades* (Chicago, London: The University of Chicago Press, 1988).

35 Benjamin Kedar, *Crusade and Mission: European Approaches Toward the Muslims* (New Jersey/Princeton: Princeton University Press, 1988).

36 Jaap J. Van Moolenbroek, 'Signs in the Heavens in Groningen and Friesland in 1214: Oliver of Cologne and Crusading Propaganda', *Journal of Medieval History*, 13 (1987), 251–272.

16 *Introduction*

37 Valmar Cramer, 'Kreuzzugspredigt und Kreuzzugsgedanken von Bernhard von Clairvaux bis Humbert von Romans', *Das Heilige Land in Vergangenheit und Gegenwart*, 1 (1939), 43–204; Cole, *The Preaching of the Crusades*.
38 Jean Flori, *Prêcher la croisade, XI–XIII siècle. Communication et propaganda* (Paris: Perrin, 2012).
39 *Legati, delegati e l'impressa d'Oltremare (secoli XII–XIII)/ Papal Legates, Delegates and the Crusades (12th–13th Century)*, eds. M. P. Alberzoni and P. Montaubin (Turnhout: Brepols, 2014).
40 Christoph Maier, *Preaching the Crusades: Mendicant Friars and the Cross in the Thirteenth Century* (Cambridge: Cambridge University Press, 1994).
41 Christoph Maier, 'Crusade and Rhetoric Against the Muslim Colony of Lucera: Eudes of Châteauroux's *Sermones de rebellione sarracenorum Lucherie in Apulia*', *Journal of Medieval History*, 21.4 (1995), 343–385.
42 Christoph Maier, *Crusade Propaganda and Ideology: Model Sermons for the Preaching of the Cross* (Cambridge: Cambridge University Press, 2000).
43 Christoph Maier, '*Civilis ac pia regis Francorum deceptio*: Louis IX as Crusade Preacher', in *Dei Gesta per Francos: Etudes sur les croisades dédiées à Jean Richard*, eds. M. Balard, B. Z. Kedar, J. Riley–Riley Smith (Aldershot: Ashgate, 2001), 57–63.
44 James Brundage, 'Humbert of Romans and the Legitimacy of Crusader Conquests', in *The Horns of Ḥaṭṭīn: Proceedings of the Second Conference of the Society for the Study of the Crusades and the Latin East, Jerusalem and Haifa, 2–6 July 1987*, ed. B. Z. Kedar (Jerusalem: Yad Izhak Ben-Zvi, 1992), 302–313; Penny Cole, 'Humbert of Romans and the Crusade', in *The Experience of Crusading: Western Approaches*, eds. N. Housley and M. Bull (Cambridge: Cambridge University Press, 2003), 157–174.
45 Valentin L. Portnykh, 'Le traité d'Humbert de Romans, O. P., De la prédication de la sainte croix contre les Sarrasins (XIIIe Siècle). Analyse historique et édition du texte' (PhD diss., Novosibirsk, Novosibirsk State University, 2011).
46 Valentin Portnykh, 'An Unknown Short Version of the Treatise *De predicatione sancte crucis* by Humbert of Romans', *Studi Medievali*, 2 (2015), 721–738; Valentin Portnykh, 'Le traité d' Humbert de Romans (OP) 'De la prédication de la sainte croix'. Une hypothèse sur son utilisation dans les guerres saintes du XV siècle', *Revue d'histoire ecclésiastique*, 109.3–4 (2014), 588–624.
47 Valentin Portnykh, 'The Short Version of Humbert of Romans' Treatise on the Preaching of the Cross: An edition of the Latin Text', *Crusades*, 15 (2016), 55–115.
48 Penny Cole, David d'Avray, Jonathan Riley-Smith, 'Application of Theology to Current Affairs: Memorial Sermons on the Dead of Mansurah and on Innocent IV', in *Modern Questions about Medieval Sermons: Essays on Marriage, Death, History and Sanctity*, eds. N. Bériou and D. d'Avray (Spoleto: Centro Italiano di studi sull'alto medioevo, 1994), 217–245.
49 Giles Constable, 'A Report of a Lost Sermon by St. Bernard on the Failure of the Second Crusade', in *Religious Life and Thought (11th–12th centuries). Collected Essays of Giles Constable* (Variorum Collected Studies Series, 89) (London: Variorum Reprints, 1979), 49–54.
50 Bruce W. Holsinger, 'The Color of Salvation: Desire, Death, and the Second Crusade in Bernard of Clairvaux's Sermons on the Song of Songs', in *The Tongue of the Fathers: Gender and Ideology in Twelfth–Century Latin*, eds. D. Townsend and A. Taylor (Philadelphia: University of Pennsylvania Press, 1997), 156–186; Jonathan Philips, 'St Bernard of Clairvaux, the Low Countries and the Lisbon Letter of the Second Crusade', *Journal of Ecclesiastical History*, 48.3 (1997), 485–497.
51 John R. Sommerfeldt, 'The Bernardine Reform and the Crusading Spirit', *Catholic Historical Review*, 86.4 (2000), 567–578; Sylvia Schein, 'Bernard of Clairvaux's Preaching of the Second Crusade and Orality', in *Oral History of the Middle Ages: The Spoken Word in Context*, eds. G. Jaritz and M. Richter (Budapest: Central European University, Department of Medieval Studies, 2001), 188–195.

52 Kienzle M. Beverly, 'Preaching the Cross: Liturgy and Crusade Propaganda', *Medieval Sermon Studies*, 53 (2009), 11–32.
53 John Cowdrey, 'Pope Urban II's Preaching of the First Crusade', *History*, 55 (1970), 177–188; Giles Constable, 'Charter Evidence for Pope Urban II's Preaching of the First Crusade', in *Canon Law, Religion, and Politics: Liber amicorum Robert Somerville*, eds. U.–R. Blumenthal, A. Winroth, P. Landau (Washington: Catholic University of America Press, 2012), 228–232; Kangas Sini, 'A Great Stirring of Hearts or Papal Inspiration? Contesting Popular Authority in the Preaching of the First Crusade', in *Authorities in the Middle Ages: Influence, Legitimacy, and Power in Medieval Society*, eds. K. Sini, M. Korpiola, T. Ainomen (Berlin: De Gruyter, 2013), 55–68; Christie Niall and Gerish Deborah, 'Parallel Preachings: Urban II and al–Sulamī', *Islam and the Medieval Mediterranean*, 15.2 (2003), 139–148.
54 Léon Paulet, *Recherches sur Pierre l'Hermite et la croisade* (Paris and Bruxelles: Ve J. Renouard, 1856); M. D. Coupe, 'Peter the Hermit– a Re-assessment', *Nottingham Medieval Studies*, 31 (1987), 37–45.
55 James B. Macgregor, 'The Ministry of Gerold d'Avranches: Warrior-Saints and Knightly Piety on the Eve of the First Crusade', *Journal of Medieval Studies*, 29.3 (2003), 219–237.
56 Sophia Menache, 'The Communication Challenge of the Early Crusades, 1099–1187', in *Autour de la Première Croisade: Actes du colloque de la Society for the Study of the Crusades and the Latin East (Clermont–Ferrand, 22–25 Juin 1995)*, ed. M. Balard (Paris: Publications de la Sorbonne, 1996), 293–314.
57 Shmuel Shepkaru, 'The Preaching of the First Crusade and the Persecution of the Jews', *Medieval Encounters*, 18 (2012), 93–135.
58 Peter W. Edbury, 'Preaching the Crusade in Wales', in *England and Germany and the High Middle Ages*, eds. A. Haverkamp and H. Vollrath (Oxford: Oxford University Press, 1996), 221–233.
59 Kathryn Hurlock, 'Power, Preaching and the Crusades in Pura Wallia c.1180–1280', in *Thirteenth Century England*, eds. W. Bjorn, B. Janet and P. Schofield (Woodbridge: The Boydell Press, 2007), 94–108; Matthew Philips, 'The Thief's Cross: Crusade and Penance in Allan of Lille's *Sermo de Cruce Domini*', *Crusades*, 5 (2006), 143–156.
60 Jessalynn Lea Bird, 'Reform or Crusade? Anti-Usury and Crusade Preaching During the Pontificate of Innocent III', in *Pope Innocent III and his World*, ed. J. C. Moore (Aldershot: Ashgate, 1999), 165–185; Andrew Jones, 'Fulk of Neuilly, Innocent III, and the Preaching of the Fourth Crusade', *Comitatus*, 41 (2010), 119–148.
61 William Purkis, 'Memories of the Preaching for the Fifth Crusade in Caesarius Heisterbach's Dialogus Miraculorum', *Journal of Medieval History*, 40 (2014), 329–345.
62 Edouard Baratier, 'Une prédication de la croisade à Marseille en 1224', in *Economies et sociétés au Moyen Age: Mélanges offerts à Édouard Perroy* (Paris: Publications de la Sorbonne, 1973), 690–699.
63 Beverly M. Kienzle, 'Hélinand de Froidmont et la predication Cistercienne dans le Midi (1145–1229)', in *La prédication en pays d'Oc (XIIe– début XVe Siècle)*, Cahiers de Fanjeaux 32, (Toulouse: Privat, 1997), 37–67; Carolyn Muessig, 'Les sermons de Jacques de Vitry sur les Cathares', in *La prédication en pays d'Oc (XIIe– début XVe Siècle)*, Cahiers de Fanjeaux 32, (Toulouse: Privat, 1997), 69–83; Nicole Bériou, 'La prédication de croisade de Philippe le Chancelier et d'Eudes de Châteauroux en 1226', in *La prédication en pays d'Oc (XIIe– début XVe Siècle)*, Cahiers de Fanjeaux 32, (Toulouse: Privat, 1997), 85–109.
64 Beverly M. Kienzle, 'Innocent III's Papacy and the Crusade Years, 1198–1229: Arnaud Amaury, 'Gui of Vaux–de–Cernay, Foulque of Toulouse', *Heresis: Revue d'hérésiologie medieval. Edition des textes*, 29 (1998), 49–81.
65 Jessalynn Lea Bird, 'The Victorines, Peter the Chanter's Circle, and the Crusade: Two Unpublished Crusading Appeals in Paris, Bibliothèque Nationale, MS. Latin 14470',

Medieval Sermon Studies, 48 (2004), 5–28; Jessalynn Lea Bird, 'Parisian Masters and the Justification of the Albigensian Crusade', *Crusades*, 6 (2007), 117–156.
66. Jessalynn Bird, 'Crusade and Reform: The Sermons of Bibliothèque Nationale, MS noun. acq. lat. 999', in *The Fifth Crusade in Context: The Crusading Movement in the Early Thirteenth Century*, eds. E. J. Mylod, G. Perry, T. W. Smith, J. Vandeburie (London: Routledge, 2017), 92–113.
67. Jessalynn Bird, 'Preaching the Crusades and the Liturgical Year: The Palm Sunday Sermons', *Essays in Medieval Studies*, 30 (2015), 11–36.
68. Jessalynn Bird, 'Preaching and Crusading Memory', in *Remembering the Crusades and Crusading*, ed. C.-W. Megan (London: Routledge, 2017), 13–33.
69. Marisa Costa, 'In praedicatione crucesignatorum. Estratégias ducentistas de incitamento à cruzada', *Cuadernos de investigación del monasterio de Santa María la Real*, 22 (2006), 6–40; Peter Linehan, '"Quedam de quibus dubitans" on Preaching the Crusade in Alfonso X's Castile', in P. Linehan, *Historical Memory and Clerical Activity in Medieval Spain and Portugal* (Farnham: Ashgate, 2014), 129–154.
70. James MacGregor, 'The First Crusade in Late Medieval "Exempla"', *The Historian*, 68.1 (2006), 29–48; Jeannine Horowitz, 'Les *exempla* au service de la prédication de la croisade au 13e siècle', *Revue d'histoire ecclésiastique*, 92.2 (1997), 367–394.
71. Penny Cole, '"O God, the Heathen Have Come into Your Inheritance" (Ps. 78.1): The Theme of Religious Pollution in Crusade Documents, 1095–1188', in *Crusaders and Muslims in Twelfth-Century Syria*, ed. M. Shatzmiller (Leiden: Brill, 1993), 84–112.
72. Cecilia M. Gaposchkin, 'Louis IX, crusade and the promise of Joshua in the Holy Land', *Journal of Medieval History*, 34 (2008), 245–274.
73. Douglas S. Earl, 'Joshua and the Crusades' in *Holy War in the Bible: Christian Morality and an Old Testament Problem*, eds. H. A. Thomas, J. Evans and P. Copan (Illinois: Inter Varsity Press, 2014), 19–43.
74. Nicholas Morton, 'The Defence of the Holy Land and the Memory of the Maccabees', *Journal of Medieval History*, 36 (2010), 275–293.
75. Elizabeth Lapina, 'The Maccabees and the Battle of Antioch' in *Dying for the Faith, Killing for the Faith: Old Testament Faith-Warriors (1 and 2 Maccabees) in Historical Perspective*, ed. G. Signori (Leiden: Brill, 2012), 147–159.
76. *The Uses of the Bible in Crusader Sources*, eds. E. Lapina and N. Morton (Leiden: Brill, 2017).
77. Thomas W. Smith, 'The Use of the Bible in the *Arengae* of Pope Gregory IX's Crusade Calls', in *The Uses of the Bible in Crusader Sources*, eds. E. Lapina and N. Morton (Leiden: Brill, 2017), 206–236; Jessalynn Bird, 'Preaching and Narrating the Fifth Crusade: Bible, Sermons and the History of a Campaign', in *The Uses of the Bible in Crusader Sources*, 316–340.
78. Lydia Walker, 'Living in the Penultimate Age: Apocalyptic Thought in James of Vitry's *ad status* Sermons', in *The Uses of the Bible in Crusader Sources*, 297–316.
79. Norman Housley, *The Avignon Papacy and the Crusades, 1305–1378* (Oxford: Clarendon Press, 1986).
80. Christopher Tyerman, *The Invention of the Crusades* (London: Palgrave Macmillan, 1998).
81. Beattie Blake, 'A Crucial Sermon by Cardinal Bertrand de Poujet', *Medieval Studies*, 67 (2005), 75–98.
82. Nicholas Coureas, 'Philippe de Mézières' Portrait of Peter Thomas as a Preacher', *Carmelus*, 57.1 (2010), 63–80; Maria Paschali, 'Crusader Ideology, Propaganda, and the Art of the Carmelite Church in Fourteenth Century Famagusta', in *The Harbour of all this Sea and Realm: Crusader to Venetian Famagusta*, eds. M. Walsh, T. Kiss, N. Coureas (Budapest: CEU Medievalia, 2014), 135–150.
83. Timothy Guard, *Chivalry, Kingship and Crusade: The English Experience in the Fourteenth Century* (Woodbridge: The Boydell Press, 2013).

84 Timothy Guard, 'Pulpit and Cross: Preaching the Crusade in Fourteenth-century England', *English Historical Review*, 129.541 (2014), 1319–1345.
85 Tyerman, *The Invention of the Crusades*, 72.
86 Housley, *The Avignon Papacy*, 127.
87 *Les Grandes chroniques de France*, ed. J. Viard, 10 vols. (Paris: Société de l'histoire de France, 1920–1953), viii, 287–290; *Chronique Latin de Guillaume de Nangis de 1113 a 1300 avec les continuations de cette chronique de 1300 a 1368*, ed. H. Géraud, 2 vols. (Paris: Imprimerie de Crapelet, 1843), i, 396; 'Prima Vita Clementis V', in *Vitae Paparum Avenionensium*, ed. G. Mollat, 4 vols. (Paris: Librairie Letouzey et Ané, 1916–1928), i, 21–22; *Chronique parisienne anonyme du XIVe siècle*, ed. A. Hellot (Nogent-Le-Rotrou: Société de l'histoire de Paris, 1884), 25–26; 'Chroniques de Saint-Denis depuis 1285 jusqu'en 1328', in *Recueil des historiens des Gaules et de la France*, eds. M. Bouquet, *et al.*, 24 vols. (Paris: Imprimerie Impériale, 1737–1904), xx, 698–699.
88 ASV, Reg. Vat. 137, fol. 166^v, ep. 584: 'Nos attendentes scientiam, et eloquentiam, zelumque ferventem dilecti filii Venturini de Pergamo ordinis fratrum Praedicatorum'.
89 Maier, *Crusade Propaganda and Ideology*, 6.
90 *Repertorium der Lateinischen sermones des Mittelalters fur Die Zeit von 1150–1350*, ed. J. B. Schneyer, 11 vols. (Münster–Westfalen: Aschendorffsche Verlagsbuchhandlung, 1973–1995).
91 The same critical edition of this sermon as it appears in the Appendix V of this book, was first published in the journal *Crusades*. See Constantinos Georgiou, 'Ordinavi armatam sancte unionis, Clement VI's Sermon on the Dauphin Humbert II of Viennois' Leadership of the Christian Armada Against the Turks, 1345', *Crusades*, 15 (2016), 157–175.
92 Georgiou, 'Ordinavi armatam sancte unionis', *Crusades*, 15 (2016), 157–175.

1 Clement V's and John XXII's organization of preaching campaigns and the clergy's role in their implementation

The death of Pope Benedict XI on 7 July 1304, was followed by an *interregnum* of eleven months, after which the conclave of cardinals elected Bertrand de Got, Archbishop of Bordeaux, as Benedict's successor.[1] Shortly after his consecration on 14 November 1305, the new pope, Clement V, set the business of crusading as an absolute priority. The Latin East, the Christian front in the Syro-Palestinian zone, had eroded after continuous defeats inflicted by the Mamluks in Syria during the 1260s and after the disastrous events of 1291; the new state of affairs in Syria, and the consolidation of Turkish power in Asia Minor, made the Christian frontier in the Aegean and Byzantium even more vulnerable. Clement's concern for the Christian enterprise in *Outremer* is evident in the encyclical issued two days after his consecration wherein, among other things, he urged the faithful to pray for the recovery of the Holy Land.[2] Clement was actively associated with the crusade even before he became pope; during Clement's time as Cardinal-bishop of Albano (1294–1297), Pope Boniface VIII sent him to the court of Edward I of England to negotiate peace between England and France for the success of a potential crusade to the Holy Land.

Clement's reign comprised a series of intensive efforts, instigated by the papacy, to launch a crusade. It is hard to delineate the elements of this policy: the causes must be attributed to 'no one single factor but rather to a complex set of interacting factors'.[3] A number of different issues, political and diplomatic, rekindled the papacy's hopes for a new crusade to the Holy Land. On 31 August 1302, the Treaty of Caltabelotta ended the war for Sicily between the royal houses of Anjou and Aragon.[4] The peace agreement between Charles II of Anjou and Frederick III of Sicily brought their long-term hostilities to a halt and provided the papacy with two potential allies for its crusading plans. Moreover, on 20 May 1303, the Treaty of Paris put an end to the struggle between Edward I of England and Philip IV of France over Gascony. This was followed by the termination of the Franco–Flemish war on 23 June 1305, which relieved Philip IV from another major worry in his borders. On 11 March 1307, Clement V sent a letter to King Philip and to his son, Louis of Navarre, explaining how beneficial the solidifying of peace between France and England would be for the 'happy and swift recuperation of the Holy Land'.[5] In 1308, Edward II (Edward I's successor) became Philip's son in law when he took Isabella as his wife.[6]

The relatively calm milieu in Europe relieved the most traditionally prominent supporters of crusading to the Holy Land of involvement in warfare in the West, thus generating new hope for the *Outremer* cause, and a number of Western rulers and men of arms favoured the idea of a prospective crusading expedition during Clement's pontificate. Still, it was only after the death of his wife, Joan of Navarre, on 2 April 1305, that the king of France considered setting off on a new crusade. Philip's change of heart meant the pope now had a proper ally in his endeavour to recover the Holy Land.[7] Moreover, the continuous dispatch of crusade plans – in the form of treatises and *memoires* of the Holy Land – to the papal curia, made Clement deliberate on a crusade to the East.[8] The nine years of his pontificate, 1305–1314, saw intensive efforts to recruit participants and launch a crusade to liberate the Holy Land.

Nevertheless, the papacy was to encounter insurmountable difficulties on different fronts as it sought to prepare the ground for a new crusade. These difficulties included the tenacious demands of the Spanish kings for papal financial backing of the *Reconquista*, the Venetian rebellion against ecclesiastical suzerainty at Ferrara, as well as the reluctance of the kings of France and England to go on crusade, despite their declarations in support of the venture;[9] a reluctance rooted in the domestic affairs of their respective kingdoms.[10]

Ad recuperandum imperium Constantinopolitanum proficisci: French plans for the recapture of Constantinople – the promotion of Charles of Valois's crusade

Two months after his coronation, Clement V issued the bull *In superne preeminentia* proclaiming the crusade of Charles of Valois, brother of King Philip IV of France, against Constantinople;[11] its participants were granted the same rights, indulgences and privileges as those fighting for the Holy Land. Despite proclaiming this eastern expedition, Clement's primary objective was to recapture Jerusalem, with the capture of Constantinople as a means to this end. One of Clement's arguments for an anti-Byzantine crusade was that a successful expedition to Constantinople would facilitate the recovery of the Holy Land: 'this will help the recovery of the aforementioned Empire [of Constantinople], which has been expected for a long time, and, through its recuperation, the business of the Holy Land'.[12]

Such a belief was not new: since 1204, Constantinople had been seen as the *medium* for the recapture of Jerusalem. Throughout the thirteenth century, to demonstrate and justify the crusades against the schismatics in Frankish Greece, the papacy aligned the control of Constantinople with crusading to the Holy Land, and in 1215, the Roman Church provided crusade validity to military expeditions on fronts beyond the Holy Land. In addition to the popes, notable crusade propagandists, such as the Cistercian Arnaud Amaury and James of Vitry, believed full Latin control over Constantinople would enable Western Christianity to provide effective support to the Latin kingdom of Jerusalem.[13] Ever since the Byzantine recapture of Constantinople in 1261, and especially after the fall of

Acre in 1291, the papal curia was convinced the reconquering of Constantinople by the Latins was a prerequisite for a general expedition to the Holy Land. The Franciscan, Ramon Lull, in his *Liber de fine* (1305), favoured a crusade against Constantinople even before Charles of Valois's official proclamation of his own crusade against it; during the period of Charles's deliberations, three other plans were drafted advocating the crusade against Byzantium.[14]

By reclaiming Constantinople, Charles of Valois bolstered Clement's pursuit of the city. Both men desired the revival of the Latin Empire of Constantinople, each for his own purpose. In 1301, Charles of Valois married Catherine of Courtenay, titular empress of Constantinople; thus, he became and remained titular emperor of Constantinople until Catherine's death on 11 October 1307. For the pope, this was a good occasion to entangle the French royal house in his crusading campaign and to revive crusading to the Holy Land; Clement was well aware of how beneficial the good will and financial support of Philip IV would be for the crusade in general for his brother's expedition specifically.[15]

Clement V followed the policy of Martin IV (1281–1285), preferring military action to restore Constantinople rather than a 'precarious entente with the Greeks'.[16] Indeed, in Charles of Valois's project, the pope saw an opportunity to jolt Western Christianity out of a lengthy crusading idleness. Moreover, the ideological and political criteria for the revival of the Latin Empire of Constantinople were supported throughout Western Europe. Charles of Valois's planned expedition against Constantinople had already received papal sanction in 1304, when Benedict XI granted full-scale crusade indulgences and levied tithes on the Church.[17] Thus Charles of Valois entered into negotiations, from the West to the Balkans, to create a network of alliances.[18] Clement also further expanded his plans by dispatching letters to Venice, to Genoa and to the whole body of ecclesiastical prelates in the Kingdom of France; he especially pressed Philip IV to offer financial aid to his brother from the biennial tithe granted him for the crusade.[19] On 14 January 1306, Clement addressed letters to the bishop of Senlis in Picardy and the bishops of Cefalù and Brindisi, papal collectors in the kingdoms of Sicily and Naples, respectively, granting indulgences and other privileges to those who offered financial help or *cum dicto comite* [Carolo comiti Andegavensi] *ad recuperandum imperium Constantinopolitanum proficisci voluerint*.[20]

Clement V was not content to solely proclaim the crusade against Constantinople; he continuously offered his support to its cause. The pope issued two letters, on 10 March and 3 June 1307, indicative of his fervour to bring Charles of Valois's plans to fruition. Clement commanded the general preaching of the crusade and, shortly afterward, announced the excommunication of the Byzantine emperor, Andronicus II Palaeologus.[21] The 10 March letter, dispatched to the Archbishop of Ravenna and to all bishops of the Romagna province, Clement extolled Charles's moral excellence and praised his enthusiasm for a new crusade and for the protection of the faith and the liberty of the Church.[22] For Clement, the purpose of a crusade against Byzantium was the protection of all Christianity; according to the pope, Byzantium was in grave danger from the Turks, the Saracens and other infidels, and the 'mother Roman Church and all the Christian religion' would receive serious danger and more serious disorder if the Empire slipped from Christian hands.[23] This, combined with reports the curia received regarding crucial conditions in the East and providing advice as to how to battle the infidels, aroused the concern and ire of Western Christianity and made the defence of Christendom's frontiers a crucial component of crusade making in the fourteenth century.[24]

The instigators of schism in Byzantium were against the idea of the union of the Churches, which they saw as offensive to divine dignity and a great threat to the Christian faith.[25] Clement wanted to send a clear message regarding the validity of the proclaimed expedition and thus, in his 10 March letter, he underlined that one of the main justifications for a crusade against Byzantium was the Schism and the return of the schismatic church of Constantinople to Rome;[26] Clement also advertized Charles's legal claim to the Latin Empire of Constantinople.[27] The rhetoric Clement V used to promote the Charles of Valois' anti-Byzantine crusade was rooted in thirteenth-century experience.

Clement V ordered the preaching of the Valois crusade in the kingdoms of Sicily and Naples, in the lands of Romagna, the March of Ancona, in the city of Venice and its provinces and, finally, in the diocese of Castellana. Obviously, the preaching was very restricted, in terms of geographical extent: unlike the extensive preaching campaigns of the previous century, the pope intentionally confined the preaching of the Valois crusade to a certain number of territories in Italy. During the thirteenth century, the preaching of anti-Constantinople crusades was normally authorized in the kingdoms of France and Hungary, but less frequently in England, Italy, Spain and Poland.[28] During the first half of the fourteenth century the Western Christian powers concerned with crusading in the Balkans confined the preaching of the Valois crusade to a strictly limited area.

The Romagna region and the March of Ancona were still under a certain papal influence, and the safe and efficient preaching of the crusade was assured therein. Clement expected the largest number of crusade contingents to come from the Guelph communes in Italy; as for the kingdoms of Sicily and Naples, kings Frederick III and Charles II of Anjou, respectively, were favourable to the Valois crusade.[29] On 24 January 1306, Clement V had sent letters to Frederick III and Charles II urging them to support Charles of Valois's crusade. Later that year, Philip IV reaffirmed the treaty of alliance signed four years earlier by Charles of Valois and Charles II of Naples.[30]

It was from Venice that Clement V had the highest expectations. Both Clement and Charles of Valois needed to secure transportation for their crusade,[31] and Venice and Genoa, the two principal maritime powers at that time, were therefore the most appropriate actors to meet such a challenge; each had a longstanding presence in Romania (the Frankish principalities founded in the lands of the Byzantine empire before the Fourth Crusade in 1204, including the Latin empire of Constantinople, the kingdom of Thessalonica, the principality of Achaia, the duchy of Athens and Thebes, the duchy of the Archipelago, and the Venetian lordships in the Aegean) and each derived immeasurable benefit from its commercial activities in the Aegean. On 24 January 1306, Clement dispatched letters granting indulgences to the doge and commune of Venice and to the potestà of Genoa, on the condition each joined the crusade.[32] Fourteen months later, however, when Clement announced the preaching of the crusade, he did not mention Genoa, and on 19 December 1306, Doge Pietro Gradonico and Charles of Valois signed a treaty '*pro defensione fidei et recuperatione imperii Romanie*'.[33] Venice would be one of the most important protagonists in the attempted recovery of Constantinople from the Greeks, and Clement was well aware of it. Genoa's alliance with Byzantium, since 1261, deprived the Republic of Venice of a dominant position in the Aegean and trade in the Black Sea.[34] This was underlined in the 1320s, when the front for crusading operations shifted to the sea with the formation of the naval leagues. The realization of any crusading venture in the East was closely linked to the commercial and economic interests of the Italian maritime powers;[35] consequently, the pope offered the same indulgences to them as he did to those crusading to the Holy Land, and he carefully commanded the preaching in all Venetian dominions, the only instance of preaching beyond Italy.

The geographical extent of the preaching campaign shows that the pope limited the preaching for Valois' crusade to the lands of those in favour of the enterprise, or who at least appeared to be. In his rhetoric, Clement tried to persuade Venice and the kings of Sicily and Naples to follow Charles of Valois to Constantinople:

> You courageous warriors and athletes of God, we pray, admonish, and urge you, imploring you attentively through the Lord Jesus Christ ... rising up under the cover of the right hand of God in eager support for the same count [Charles], to assist efficaciously and vigorously.[36]

Clement's objective was to secure allies for Valois's project, and thus he downplayed the need for financial commitments. Indeed, what was needed was a small force of capable warriors, '*ydoneos bellatores*', to be paid with church taxes in France, rather than a mass of armed men inspired by a major campaign of crusade preaching.[37] For this reason, Clement's exhortations to Philip IV to grant his brother all revenue arising from crusade legacies in the French kingdom, and from the redemption of vows, were the only evidence in addition to the tithes for the Holy Land of financial support he provided to Charles of Valois.[38] Clement was also ready to grant the income from the tithe imposed in Sicily and Naples to Frederick III and Charles II, respectively, under the condition '*si cum dicto comite ad recuperandum imperium Constantinopolitanum proficisci voluerit*'.[39] Beginning in 1308, Clement V folded a number of measures into his preaching campaign to secure the finances for the Hospitallers' *passagium*; the money was to be given to the Master General of the Hospital, Fulk of Villaret. This might have been why Clement refrained from commanding a general preaching for Valois, a practice he did initiate to secure economic resources for the Hospitallers' expedition to Rhodes.

The 10 March 1307 letter to the Archbishop of Ravenna and the bishops of Romagna, Clement urged the secular clergy to preach Charles of Valois' crusade.[40]

Unfortunately, this is the only surviving missive regarding this preaching, and it is poor in details. In his letter, the pope commands the secular clergy to preach and generally hand over the sign of the cross where the preaching for the Valois' crusade was to be implemented, but it contains no information as to how often the preaching was to be performed.[41]

The 10 March 1307 letter also lacks references to any contribution by the orders of friars in the conduct of preaching or the designation of any papal legate or papal nuncio responsible for the campaign.[42] It is impossible to know whether papal commands to the secular clergy were executed, or whether there was any popular response to the preaching, since neither the papal correspondence nor the narrative sources provide any such evidence. The papal orders for the Valois crusade do not provide us with adequate knowledge as to how the crusade was actually preached, and the language in which the preaching was conducted, and its audiences, are unknown to us.

As Norman Housley has remarked, 'In general the crusade bulls of the Avignon popes contain much more detail on the preaching and organization of the crusade than those of their predecessors'.[43] Clement V paid special attention to distributing detailed instructions for the preaching of the Hospitallers' crusade; this was not the case for the crusade against Constantinople. Despite this, the existing data for the preaching of Charles's crusade by the secular clergy and its geographic expansion illustrate Clement's priorities. Despite papal backing and the league of allies secured for Charles of Valois's Constantinople expedition, Charles's plans ultimately came to naught, and toward the end of 1308, the promotion of the Hospitallers' crusade was well underway. Western claims on Constantinople were revived in 1313 by the marriage of Philip of Taranto, son of Charles II of Naples, to Catherine, the daughter of Charles of Valois. Philip's efforts to recapture Constantinople, however, met the same fate as those of his father-in-law some years earlier.[44]

Verbum vivifice crucis publicare: Organising the preaching campaign for the Hospitallers' *passagium* to Rhodes

At the time of the proclamation of the Latin crusade against Constantinople, the situation in the Eastern Mediterranean was becoming increasingly precarious. The Christian kingdoms of Cyprus and Cilician Armenia were under continuous pressure, as their vicinity to Muslim territories left both kingdoms exposed to Saracen pirate raids from the sea, while Armenia remained vulnerable to Mamluk land incursions.[45] Such a critical situation required the presence of Latin military power in the region to defend both kingdoms, each a vital remnant of Latin territory, and Clement V summoned the masters of the Templars and Hospitallers to Poitiers to discuss a new crusade.

James of Molay and Fulk of Villaret, masters general of the Templars and Hospitallers, respectively, were both men of great military experience in the East.[46] There is a notable diversity of opinion among chroniclers, however, regarding the date the pope demanded their presence at the curia;[47] but a letter to Fulk of Villaret from the papal chancery on 6 June 1306, commanded the master of the Hospital to proceed to the papal court.[48] The great majority of the narrative sources agree on Poitiers as a meeting place, and that Fulk of Villaret was in the midst of a campaign for the conquest of Rhodes that had commenced in June 1306, which delayed his arrival at the papal curia. The master general captured some important castles and Lindos, on the southeast cost of the island, for the Hospital, before he left Rhodes in November for Limassol and Europe.[49] Amalric Augerii, author of the *Sexta Vita Clementis V*, asserted that in 1306, 'Fulk, the master of the military Order of the Hospital, with a great Christian army ... captured Rhodes which at that time was in the hands of the Turks under the dominion of the schismatic emperor of Constantinople'.[50] Bernard Gui, author of the *Quarta Vita Clementis V*, made no mention of Fulk but of the Hospitallers' adventure in Rhodes.[51]

Both Fulk of Villaret and James of Molay drafted crusade plans during 1305 and 1306, demonstrating their desire to undertake the crusade and impelling Clement to summon them to the curia.[52] The *Memorandum* written by Fulk of Villaret in 1305 is of particular interest, as it briefly deals with potential papal contribution to the preaching of the new crusade. Fulk refers to Pope Urban II's preaching of the First Crusade in Nîmes and Clermont; he does not mention prominent crusade preachers of the twelfth century, but he gives special preference to Pope Urban II, Peter the Hermit and Bishop Ademar of Le Puy, the first exemplars of crusade preaching.[53]

There are several reasons Fulk referred to Urban II's preaching. By emphasising that pope's impact on the crusading propaganda campaign, he wished to exert pressure on the Church, especially on the newly elected pope, in the hope that Clement V would personally contribute to a new crusade. The situation for the Hospitallers was critical, and cooperation with the papacy would benefit both parties. Fulk hoped Urban II's fervent preaching of the First Crusade might inspire Clement's personal involvement in preaching for a new crusade, and that Clement would designate members of the regular or secular clergy for continuing the preaching:

> Furthermore the lord pope, after he preaches the cross and does the things which have been described, shall appoint as legates good men, secular or regular clerks. These men will then proceed through the cities and provinces which are inhabited by the faithful, and will preach to them the cross and will give them indulgences, and will declare the fixed day [for the departure] and the passage's captains, in the same way as the lord pope did the above things.[54]

Preaching was undoubtedly important for the recruitment of people willing to commit themselves to the crusade; in combination with the redemption of vows for money, it would provide secure financial support for the *passagium*.[55] Fulk wanted the crusade set in motion soon after the conduct of the preaching, as recruits would be inspired to achieve its goals. Fulk understood the necessity of preaching the cross: it would encourage the warriors and prepare them morally for the crusade and its military action. He wrote in his *Memorandum*:

> Our lord the pope, wherever he may be, will preach the cross, exciting and exhorting the people of Christ with his sermons ... and he will declare the time of the departure of the *passagium*. As far as the time is concerned, we think it is useful to set [its departure] not long from now, because when much time goes by many impediments and obstacles get in the way and people are by nature more animated and fervent when they are closer to fulfilling their desires.[56]

Not paradoxically, Fulk stresses Peter the Hermit's role in the origins of crusade preaching; his citation of Peter the Hermit probably stemmed from a tradition built around Peter as the personage who inspired and guided the participants in the First Crusade.[57] By the thirteenth century, Peter the Hermit's reputation as the charismatic and inspirational preacher of the First Crusade had been established. There are scattered references to Peter in James of Vitry's *Historia Orientalis*, in the narratives of Oliver of Paderborn – who preached the Fifth Crusade in Frisia – and in the Dominican, Humbert of Romans's preaching manual, *De predicatione sancte crucis*.[58] In referencing James of Vitry's depiction of Peter, Fulk of Villaret wanted to remind Clement of Peter's quality.[59] The grand master considered it important to follow the example of the First Crusade, and Clement V adopted Peter's example for his ardent preaching of the new crusade. It is clear that the deeds of First Crusade participants were deeply ingrained in the historical consciousness of Western European society, and this made the First Crusade the *exemplum* for crusading activity thereafter.

Fulk of Villaret deals briefly with crusade-preaching issues in his plan: in his *Memorandum* he offers advice on the military aspects of the crusade, rather than rhetorical schemes for the preaching of the cross. As Leopold has argued, the different crusade proposals were dominated by more practical issues and were not designed to operate as preaching guides.[60] Moreover, their audience was restricted to the pope and the secular rulers in Western Europe, and those propagandists dealing with the promotion of the cross suffer from a lack of originality.[61] But since such proposals were mainly intended to serve as written advice to individuals on the military aspects of the crusade and not for popular preaching, the lack of originality in crusade preaching would have had little impact on public opinion. As the case of Fulk's *Memorandum* demonstrates, the objective was to induce papal support for the Hospitaller enterprise.

In the spring of 1307, almost a year after Clement's summons, Fulk finally left to join the papal curia at Poitiers, where he received papal support for the conquest of Rhodes;[62] in this the pope was greatly influenced by a second *Memorandum* by the master general of the Hospital and some other respectable men '*qui diu steterunt ultra mare*'.[63] The latter memoir supplements Fulk's first plan, in terms of crusade strategy, and provides a detailed proposal for its prompt implementation.[64] The importance of this document lies not in the originality of its proposals, but rather in the significance it places on Rhodes as a base for future crusade operations. It clarifies that the Hospitallers had not yet achieved the complete capture of Rhodes and declares their desire to achieve this.[65] When Clement V issued the bull *Exurgat Deus* on 11 August 1308, he ordered similar directives for the execution of the Hospitallers' *passagium*; the aims of these directives were analogous to the aforementioned Hospitallers' document.[66]

After 11 August 1308, a unique opportunity arose for Clement that would provide him with a most appropriate ally in his quest, the Hospitallers. The pope was aware Christian lands in the East were in critical situations, especially Armenia. He also knew a general crusade, led by the king of France, would require protracted, detailed organization and would face an uncertain future.[67] Clement had already experienced the complexity of the effort it took to bring different powers together for a crusade against Constantinople. This, combined with the Western Christian rulers' reluctance to crusade in the East, facilitated Clement's support for a small-scale expedition, one that needed a trusted force set in motion without delay;[68] in their *Memoranda* the Hospitallers had declared their readiness to prepare this force and embark for Rhodes.

This also presented the pope with an opportunity to shield the Hospitallers from the severe criticism they had come under for their alleged luxurious and sinful living, and from accusations they had been responsible for the Latin failure in Syria.[69] For both reasons, many had called for the two main military Orders of the Hospital and the Temple to be merged.

The Hospitallers were seeking a more suitable base. Cyprus, their headquarters at the time, was not an appropriate locale for the Order's long-term sojourn.[70] The knights wished to protect themselves from the king of Cyprus, and thus they sought to leave the island.[71] Rhodes was identified as an ideal location, most likely following Fulk of Villaret's accession to the leadership of the Order.[72] In 1292, Henry II of Lusignan, King of Cyprus, levied a two-bezant tax on the servants of all religious Orders, including the military Orders on the island, and he forbade the knights to arm their ships without royal permission.[73] In 1299, Pope Boniface VIII ended the levy and allowed the military Orders to arm ships, but Henry II in 1306 violated the agreement.[74] He also prohibited the acquisition of landed property in Cyprus by the Knights of St John and the Templars if they lacked a royal or papal license.[75] These provisions were included in the treaty of 1299 that governed the relationship between the crown and the island's two main military Orders.[76] Thus, as Schein states, the knights desired to remove their headquarters from Cyprus and build a naval force to make the Order competitive in maritime warfare.[77] The present milieu, combined with the persecution of the Templars, enabled cooperation between the papacy and the Hospitallers on Eastern Mediterranean crusading policy.[78]

The arrest of the Templars by Capetian authorities in France on 13 October 1307, could only be interpreted by Clement as a frontal attack on pontifical authority and the Church's prerogatives over the Order. Even though Clement tried to help the Templars and take control of the situation, by ignoring the brothers' alleged heresy and the temporary halting of the inquisitorial process in France, the declarations of heresy on the part of the Order's leadership and Philip's determination to bring down the Order left the pope no room to manoeuvre.[79] Consequently, on 12 August 1308, with the bull *Ad omnium fere*, the pope consented to the campaign against the Order and resumed the Trial of the Templars.[80] Clement's decision, a day after the proclamation of the Hospitaller expedition to Rhodes, cannot be construed as entirely accidental; his chief intention was to safeguard papal authority and protect the other main military Order, the Knights of St John, from the ravenous fury of the Capetian king. The successful outcome of the Hospitallers' *passagium* was the *medium* for the achievement of such aims, and Clement was well aware of it. By attributing his share to the process against the Templars, Clement at least gained Philip's good will for the unimpeded promotion of the Hospitaller expedition throughout the French kingdom. For this reason, on 20 September 1308, Clement called on Philip IV of France to facilitate preparations for the crusade by providing the knights with horses, arms and provisions, and by exempting them from any taxes. Clement also exhorted Philip not to delay.[81]

On 11 August 1308, a year after Fulk of Villaret arrived at the curia in Poitiers, Clement V issued a series of bulls proclaiming the Hospitallers *passagium particulare*, a harbinger of the general crusade.[82] To defend the kingdoms of Armenia and Cyprus, the pope offered spiritual rewards to those who gave subsidies or joined the crusade.[83] The chroniclers make reference to the magnitude of indulgences granted by the pope: the author of the *Annales Paulini* asserts, 'in that year [1308] the pope conceded indulgences for the sins and penalties, of such a sort that had not been heard for a century', while another chronicler emphasizes the grant of *indulgentia magna valde*.[84] This grandiose scheme of indulgences, offered in combination with an elaborate liturgical apparatus, was contrived to derive as much revenue as possible from the non-embarking faithful.[85] The pope considered these indulgences and the extensive preaching of the crusade as the primary means for an en masse recruitment and fundraising from the faithful.

The *Annales Paulini* testify to the arrival of the bishop of Nazareth in London on 25 January 1309, the day of St Paul's Conversion; the bishop had a particular right, granted to him by the pope, for the support of the Holy Land.[86] Clement further renewed the papal restrictions on commercial relations with the infidels and issued commands for wide-ranging preaching.[87] Already familiar with crusade politics from the first year of his pontificate, Clement V promoted the *negotium crucis* on a continual basis; Clement's efforts echoed those of Gregory X (1271–1276), whose leadership and vigorous organization 'left a lasting mark on how crusading would operate in the years to come'.[88]

The pope sent mandates to both regular and secular clergy to broadcast the preaching, and he passed liturgical measures in support of the Hospitallers' crusade. A series of letters from Clement also underlines his intention to use the mendicant friars as components of the papal propaganda machinery.[89] In a letter concerning the contribution to preaching, Clement included in his addresses the general priors of the Hermits of St Augustine and the Carmelites.[90] In this respect, Clement V differentiated from the thirteenth century tradition of designating members from the two main mendicant Orders, the Franciscan and Dominican,[91] as executors of preaching by also commanding the general priors of the Carmelites and the Hermits of St Augustine to contribute to the preaching. This continued throughout Clement V's reign and returned in intensified form under Clement VI. In his directives, however, Clement mentioned the Franciscans and Dominicans specifically and made general reference '*ac aliorum ordinum*' to friars from the other Orders. The pope assigned them to preach in every diocese for the Hospitallers' *passagium,* giving them full favour and urging them to give proper attention and devotion to their duty. On 11 August 1308, in bulls proclaiming the crusade sent to all Church prelates, Clement ordered:

> According to the prudence given to you by God, you shall effectively exhort all the ecclesiastical persons and the brothers of the Orders of Preachers and Minorites of your cities and dioceses who have the power to hear confessions and preach the words of the cross.[92]

On 20 June 1309, the Franciscan, Peter of Pleine Chassagne, Bishop of Rodez, was appointed papal legate and assigned the organization and expansion of crusading propaganda in the East.[93] Peter was to accompany Fulk of Villaret to the East, starting his journey from Brindisi in September 1309.[94] On 15 September 1309, Clement urged Peter to include the 'Dominicans and Franciscans and members of other Orders in the area of his legation or in the vicinity as he wishes'.[95] The friars were to hear confessions and give sermons during the celebration of Mass in every episcopal or parish church on Sundays and feast days, and on every other day, and the pope ordered the high prelates to permit the friars to preach in every place in his diocese.[96]

Clement hinted he was aware of the tepid and passionless efforts of some friars and other members of the secular clergy. Writing on 11 June 1309 to the master general of the Dominicans and the minister general of the Franciscans, and again a month later to all archbishops, bishops, abbots and other prelates, the pope wrote: 'In the effusion of the prayers they show themselves to be very tepid and remiss'.[97] It is unclear whether the preaching faced any clerical opposition, as the sources lack any evidence of such; the pope himself, however, expressed his eagerness for the prompt and efficacious promotion of the crusade on the Hospitallers' behalf. Clement V was aware that many of the lower secular clergy and some members of the friars were negligent in the execution of preaching because they were illiterate, and he viewed illiteracy as a destructive ignorance that prevented them from properly exercising their ecclesiastical duties.[98] This is most probably why Clement emphasized this point, particularly in a letter to the mendicant Orders.[99]

A second important reason may have impeded the regular and secular clergy from consistent preaching: the emergence, in the fourteenth century, of Western monarchs who, steadily increasing in strength, resisted papal authority and exerted more control over their subjects.[100] Both the crusaders and the clergy – especially the secular clergy, who had been responsible for the execution of the crusade preaching – were under the influence of powerful lay rulers, and the implementation of papal commands depended on their goodwill and cooperation. If a monarch found the crusade preaching in his lands to be unsuitable, he could prevent his lay vassals and the clergy from undertaking such a campaign. On 31 May 1307, Charles of Valois told Venice that as '*homo ligius regis Francie*', he could not leave France to crusade against Constantinople because of the tense situation between France and Flanders.[101] In early 1309, Philip IV obstructed preparations for the Hospitallers' crusade in his kingdom and expressed his discontent to Clement V that he had been excluded from this initiative.[102] The papal–Hospitaller project became a reality only through papal insistence and determination. Likewise, James II of Aragon variously hindered the Hospitallers' crusade by demanding the pope grant him the same privileges as he had those who fought for the Holy Land.[103] Royal resentment of the papal–Hospitaller plans has affected the unimpeded promotion of the Hospitallers' crusade in France and Spain; the only clear evidence for unhindered propagation is found in the registers in the English dioceses.[104]

The more educated members of the secular clergy, such as archbishops and bishops, had too much work to do within their dioceses to give the crusade preaching proper attention,[105] so the burden of crusade preaching fell on the shoulders of the lower, less-educated parish clergy, whose preaching was of questionable quality. The papacy paid special attention to how the preaching should be conducted: they believed the success of the crusading propaganda depended strictly on the preachers' quality, morality and charisma, as well on their enthusiasm and overall number.[106] The image of a fiery preacher giving all of his energy for the crusade was still alive in the western consciousness, as exemplified in Fulk of Villaret's *Memorandum*.[107] Clement V insisted that only with divine piety, devotion and *verborum levitate* would the preachers *fidelium aures* and *audientium cordibus inclinent*, convincing them to follow.[108] As Christoph Maier relates, to preach the crusade successfully 'required skill and circumspection to devise the right kind of sermon for each individual occasion'.[109]

Wishing to overcome linguistic barriers, Clement ordered oral preaching to be conducted in the vernacular language, with special prayers for the Hospitallers' *passagium* delivered in Latin. Clement commanded all high prelates to order the brothers of the Dominican and Franciscan Orders in their dioceses to make public the words of God *in vulgari cuiuslibet patrie*.[110]

The evolution of crusade propaganda under Clement V, on behalf of the campaign of the Knights of the Hospital, resembles the great preaching campaigns of the thirteenth century and demonstrates Clement's desire to extensively promote the Hospitallers' venture. Clement paid careful attention to the execution of preaching, which he strengthened through liturgical means, to derive as much a benefit as possible from the non-embarking members of the faithful and to prepare morally those who would then embark, as will be discussed in Chapter 3. Faced with a number of obstacles to the advancement of the crusade against Constantinople in Spain, and confronted by the unpleasant consequences of Philip IV's policy against the Templars, Clement put his full strength behind ongoing Hospitaller business in the Eastern Mediterranean, the accomplishment of which would spared the Order the fate of the Templars and would safeguarded papal prerogatives over the Hospitallers.

The consolidation of the Knights of St John in Rhodes was a result of this endeavour, and the Dominicans, Bernard Gui, Bishop of Lodève, and Amalric Augerii, prior in St Mary of Aspirano in the diocese of Elne, stressed the significance of the Hospitallers' achievement for the crusading movement. The two men argued that once Rhodes was captured, there would be more ports providing suitable passage for Christians to the Holy Land, to Acre and to Cyprus.[111]

Crux per prelatos et alios viros ydoneos per totam christianitatem predicaretur: **The Council of Vienne and the epilogue to Clement V's crusading organization**

On 12 August 1308, a day after the proclamation of the Hospitallers' *passagium*, Clement V announced – via the bull, *Regnans in excelsis* – a general Church council to meet in Vienne on 1 October 1310.[112] On 4 April 1310, however, the pope informed the clergy that the inauguration of the council was to be delayed, as the inquisitorial process against the Templars was incomplete in some locations.[113] The council eventually began on 16 October 1311: it was attended by a great number of Church prelates, King Philip IV of France and representatives of various monarchs.[114] The following matters were discussed during the council, as noted in the bull of convocation: the affair of the Order of the Temple, the crusade to and recovery of the Holy Land, and the reform of the Church.[115]

On 3 April 1312, the second session of the Council of Vienne commenced in the shadow of the first session. The disintegration of the Order of the Templars, in tandem with the intense political-economic proceedings before and during the first session, underscored the prominence of Philip IV in the political arena and his anxiety over obtaining sufficient economic resources for the royal treasury.[116] It was most likely for this reason that John, canon regular of St Victor in Paris, wrote of the Council of Vienne: 'it is said by many that the council took place with the purpose of extorting money'.[117]

Clement V opened the second session of the council, held in the presence of the French king and other members of the royal house of France, with a sermon. As the full text of Clement's sermon has not survived, and there are no other sources for this speech save for scattered references in various narrative sources, it is uncertain what Clement actually said.[118] Having as *thema* for his sermon the biblical verse (Proverbs 10:24) *Desiderium suum justis dabitur* (the desire of the righteous shall be granted), Clement expressed his deep desire for the recovery of the Holy Land and announced a new overseas crusade to the faithful: the intention of the king of France to embark on a new crusade to the Holy Land and the papal decision to grant a crusade tithe, dovetailed with the sermon's *thema*. At the end of his sermon, the pope urged Philip IV, his brothers and his sons to assume the cross within a year and then imposed a clerical tithe for the Holy Land for a period of six years.[119] After Clement concluded, the prayers *Flectamus genua* and *Levate* were read; the pope himself then recited the prayers *Confiteor, Precibus et meritis, Indulgentiam* and *Benedictio*.[120] These prayers, part of the apostolic blessing ritual and developed under Gregory X, confirmed Clement's willingness to grant crusade indulgences. While there is scant evidence of the actual words of Clement's sermon, he nevertheless exhorted Christendom to join the Church in its effort to liberate the Holy Land through the accomplishment of a *passagium generale* under the command of the French king. In sum, Clement summoned Philip IV to take the cross, announced the intention of the Church to sustain all expenses and defined a six-year tithe for the Holy Land.[121]

Following Clement V's appeals for advice at the convocation of the council, three *De Recuperatione Terrae Sanctae* proposals were presented, with another sent for consultation. The indefatigable Franciscan, Ramon Lull, submitted a proposal for the merger of the military Orders and for the establishment of schools for the study of oriental languages.[122] William of Nogaret, a lawyer and member of Philip IV's royal council, wrote a treatise in which he concluded that preparations for the crusade required ten to twenty years, and that its prospects for success were extremely unfavourable.[123] Nogaret positioned the French Crown as the predominant supporter of the promotion and conduct of the crusade, and declared his support for the French plan to conquer Constantinople prior to recapturing the Holy Land. He also discussed the financing of the crusade, explaining its significance as a prerequisite for its completion, and explicated the French king's priorities with regard to the crusade.[124]

The envoys of Henry II of Lusignan, King of Cyprus, delivered another crusade plan during the deliberations. Henry proposed economic warfare, with a naval blockade to be followed by a military expedition against Egypt.[125] The final proposal at the Council of Vienne was presented by William Le Maire, Bishop of Angers. Le Maire's proposal was the only one presented at the council that dealt with the spiritual issues of crusading, such as preaching and indulgences, since he believed that matters of a practical nature were best undertaken by men with military experience.[126] Bishop Le Maire, as a high prelate, was chiefly concerned with the responsibilities of the clergy, and he wished to establish ecclesiastical control over the crusade. Regarding the preparatory stage for a general passage, Le Maire argued:

> For that reason it seems to me that the starting point of a general passage should be now prefixed [so that it should begin] in ten to twelve years, as the pope and other wise men see fit. In the meantime the cross should be preached effectively and fervently by prelates and other worthy men throughout all Christendom, conceding a plentiful indulgence to those who will become crusaders.[127]

Like the others, Bishop Le Maire considered the realization of the general passage untimely, and he proposed a preparatory period of ten or twelve years. He persisted in emphasising the importance of preaching to recruit new crusaders, explaining to the council that the preaching in support of the crusade must be intense and of the highest quality, and that it should be conducted by prelates or by the most worthy of men. Finally, Le Maire advised the pope to grant such indulgences to all those who would take the cross and 'to all those who will offer alms and subsidies for the support and liberation of the Holy Land as he conferred for the Hospitallers at Poitiers'.[128]

In the end, the Council of Vienne ordered preparations for the launching of a general crusade be set in motion under the leadership of the King of France, and a six-year ecclesiastical tithe was granted to Philip IV for the economic sustenance of the expedition.[129] The outcome of the council was the organization of the first major crusade since the last Latin possessions in the Syro-Palestinian littoral zone were lost.[130] After the successful outcome of the Hospitallers' *passagium*, Clement was positioned to exploit the Christian bridgehead in Rhodes for the realization of a general passage for the complete re-conquest of the Holy Land. The decisions taken at the council, however, were under the shadow of Philip IV, who pressed for the dissolution of the Templars which, once achieved, would give Philip control over all Templar assets in France and make him the most powerful lay ruler who could lead and promote the crusade. The absence of any other Christian ruler in declaring the crusade was noteworthy; the pope had failed to achieve the general participation of Christendom in the crusade,[131] and over the next three decades the French royal house was the only lay power that played a prominent role in the papacy's crusading plans.[132]

The epilogue to the crusade decisions made at Vienne was the *crucesignatio* of Philip IV of France and other members of the royal family in the presence of papal legate Nicholas of Fréauville. On 5 December 1305, Clement appointed Nicholas of Fréauville, who was already the French king's confessor, Cardinal-priest of Sant'Eusebio in the first nomination of the Sacred College.[133] With a series of letters issued on 10 February 1313, Clement designated Cardinal Nicholas papal legate in the French kingdom, assigning him the preaching of the crusade everywhere in France and commanding him to give the cross to Philip IV.[134] The pope authorized Nicholas to employ the mendicant friars and the secular clergy in the kingdom of France to assist in the execution of his mission,[135] and he made Nicholas responsible for selecting the right places wherein the most appropriate persons should preach the crusade.[136] Finally, the legate was to hear confessions and to grant indulgences similar to those decreed at the Second Council of Lyon in 1274 by Pope Gregory X and, subsequently, by Boniface VIII.[137]

In 1313, the ground was prepared for a major crusade to the Holy Land. The preparatory stage of the crusade had enjoyed continuous papal support and, for the first time since 1285, enjoyed the direct involvement of the French king, one the world's most powerful men.[138] The collaboration between the Holy See and the French Crown seemed to be a *sine qua non* for Clement V to realize his ambition. These propitious circumstances collapsed, however, after the deaths of Pope Clement V (20 April 1314) and Philip IV (29 November 1314). The crusade had lost its mainstays, and the period of uncertainty that followed their deaths was a serious setback for the crusading movement. The Holy See remained vacant until 7 August 1316, when Jacques Duèze, Cardinal-bishop of Porto e Santa Rufina, was elevated to the papal throne as John XXII, while the instability of the French monarchy hindered rekindling any crusading initiatives. During the apostolic vacancy of 1314–1316, a fluid political landscape, economic deterioration and nutritional deficiency – due to continuous military operations and natural disasters – impoverished Western Europe and made the liberation of the Holy Land seem no more than a distant dream.

Indeed, by the end of 1314, the political situation in the French kingdom became tumultuous, as the last Capetian kings entered a vicious cycle of dynastic rivalries and upheavals. In the two years following the death of King Philip IV, the French throne was occupied by three different tenants, while the Capetian dynasty was confronted with the first of its succession issues. On 29 November 1314, Louis X succeeded his father, Philip IV, as the new King of France, until his death on 5 June 1316. On 15 November 1316, John, Louis X's infant son, was raised to the throne under the regency of his uncle, Philip the Tall, but the new king reigned for a scant five days, and his premature death caused succession problems as, for the first time in centuries, the King of France died childless. Philip the Tall, the second son of King Philip IV, managed a number of political manoeuvres and took the throne as Philip V on 20 November 1316. It was also during this political instability that the French Crown had to face renewed hostilities initiated by Robert, Count of Flanders, in 1316.[139] On 9 January 1317, Philip V, the penultimate monarch of the house of Capet, was crowned at Reims. The war with the Flemish would consume the royal house of France until 1320; it drained the royal treasury and cost many lives. It was followed by the death of Philip V on 3 January 1322.[140]

The Kingdom of England was similarly embroiled in political upheaval due to strained relations between some members of the baronage and the crown, by chronic financial problems and its war against the Scots that, after the Scottish victory at Bannockburn in 1314, pushed the kingdom to the verge of civil war.[141]

The situation in Italy was also complicated. The division of the local communities in the northern and central peninsula into Guelph and Ghibelline factions led to a protracted and often intense contest for power, and the ambitious policy of the German Emperor Henry VII (1308–1313) in Italy inflamed the rivalry between the Ghibelline and Guelph factions in Lombardy and Tuscany.[142] After the death of Henry VII on 24 August 1313, the German Empire began a long period of upheaval following the commencement of a struggle for succession. In 1313, the German princes split into pro-Hapsburg and anti-Hapsburg factions: after the death of Henry VII, the anti-Hapsburg princes elected Louis IV of Bavaria as Emperor, whilst the pro-Hapsburg barons rallied around Frederick of Austria of the House of Hapsburg.[143] The ensuing contest for sovereignty divided imperial power and pulled all parties into a destructive conflict that proved quite deleterious to the cause of crusade.

In addition to the imperial succession disputes in Central Europe, excessive rainfall from April to July 1315 destroyed crops across large areas of the continent. This was the first year of the Great Famine (1315–1322), and much of the continent and its kingdoms were afflicted by pestilence and high mortality rates.[144]

In the years between the death of Pope Clement V and the election of John XXII, nearly all Western Europe was mired in conflict, which made it nearly impossible for many of the key benefactors of the crusade to support it. At the same time, dynastic and political crises in the Empire, in England and in France proved that none of the involved parties were ready to set aside their domestic objectives for the crusade. In addition, Latin Europe remained in the grip of the Great Famine which accelerated economic decay throughout Europe and quelled any interest in crusading. The elevation of John XXII, however, would spark the resurgence of such efforts.

Statum miserabilem Terre Sancte considerans: Papal endeavours to reinvigorate the crusading zeal for the Holy Land, 1316–1322

On 6 September 1316, a day after his coronation, the new pope, John XXII, wrote to Philip the Tall, regent of the French Crown, about the concession his predecessor, Clement V, made to Philip IV of a six-year tithe on all ecclesiastical revenue in the French kingdom for the sake of the Holy Land.[145] John ordered papal collectors to continue exacting the tithe for the next two years and proscribed the use of this revenue for anything but the Holy Land, a policy the pope himself would abrogate in 1319.[146] John wrote again to Philip some days later, following the practice of his predecessors, to make clear from the outset of his pontificate his readiness to provide financial incentives for the reinvigoration of crusading enthusiasm and to involve the French royal house in his plans for the crusade. On 14 September 1316, the pope granted Philip a four-year tithe on all ecclesiastical benefices, both regular and secular, as well as the incomes from all vacant ecclesiastical benefices;[147] John sent Philip a second letter that same day explaining how Philip could obtain profits from the vacancies.[148] John XXII had great expectations for potential collaboration with the French Crown for the organization and launch of a crusade. To this end, at the dawn of his reign, the pope initiated a diplomatic effort to secure French partnership for his crusading schemes. Thus, all Holy Land crusade negotiations during the reign of Pope John became a Franco-papal affair, reaching their climax during the early 1330s. Christopher Tyerman argues that England's diminishing engagement in the crusade during these years proves 'the crusade had become almost a French monopoly'.[149] Indeed, the papal correspondence, even from the beginning of John XXII's reign, supports this contention. In an undated letter, with *terminus ante quem* 19 November 1316, wherein the pope refers to Philip as regent, the former exhorts the latter to conclude a peace with Flanders and turn to the business of the Holy Land. The pope referred to the historical role of the French crown in the crusading movement and in the fight against the opponents of the Church and the Christian cult. John also reminded Philip of the devotion of his father, Philip IV, to the cause of the crusade. John XXII prompted Philip to consider participating personally in the crusade, reminding him of his duty as *crucesignatus*.[150]

Writing on 17 November 1316 to a number of French aristocrats, John XXII demanded their obedience to Philip, arguing for the 'French power, whose aid is second only to that of God in the needs and expectations of the Holy Land'.[151] The growing involvement of John XXII in the political affairs of France, especially in the early years of his pontificate, inescapably led to the direct dependence of the potential success of crusade negotiations on the political priorities of the French throne, as the case of the Franco-Flemish war indicates. This conflict was the most significant obstacle to John XXII's effort to obtain the support of Philip V for his planned crusade to Jerusalem. The pope devoted much energy and time to resolving the Franco-Flemish conflict; he sent delegates to both France and Flanders to effect the suspension of hostilities.[152] Throughout his campaign for peace between France and Flanders, the pope made the crusade his central theme. John XXII was relying on the French monarchy to contribute significantly to the recovery of the Holy Land, and in his approach to peace in Flanders he did not hesitate to favour the King of France.[153]

The pope often described the miserable condition of the Holy Land in the hands of the Saracens in a dramatic tone and terms, and he vehemently declared his desire for the launch of a crusade for its recovery as soon as possible.[154] Thus it was that John recommended that Robert, Count of Flanders, reconcile with King Philip V: 'we, for the good of concord and on account of the intense desire and great affection that we had and have, and which we suppose without doubt that the king himself has, for the overseas passage, which because of discord of securities of this sort can very likely be delayed'.[155] On 26 August 1317, the pope wrote to Philip V: 'we should have been aware against the same rebels, and enemies and obstructers of the said passage', openly blaming the Flemish for distracting the French king from crusading affairs and for delaying his embarkation on a new crusade.[156] Similarly, John of St Victor, in his account, characterized the Flemish as *perjuros et impeditores passagii transmarini*.[157] John XXII expected to form an alliance with the French king for the *negotium Terre Sancte*; for John, the union of royal and papal power was a prerequisite for the revival of crusading to Jerusalem.[158] The emergence of central monarchies that were not inclined to set aside their political priorities for the sake of the crusade, however, combined with the diversion of papal attention to increasing conflict in Italy, created unstable ground for Franco-papal crusade negotiations.[159]

It is now appropriate to turn our attention to the crusade negotiations between the papal curia and Philip V and his nobles during the years 1316–1322. Soon after the death of Louis X and Philip the Tall's June 1316 seizure of the regency of the French kingdom, the first symbolic expression of crusading ardour took place in the Sainte-Chapelle in Paris, when Philip reaffirmed his support for the crusade following inspirational preaching by the new Latin Patriarch of Jerusalem, Peter of Pleine Chassagne, and by Peter of Courpalay, the abbot of Saint-Germain-des-Prés, on 23 July 1316.[160]

Soon after his coronation in January 1317, Philip V of France announced he would go on crusade once he established peace in his kingdom,[161] and, on 8 March 1317, he summoned a great number of barons and prelates to Paris to discuss the crusade.[162] In May of that year, an assembly was held in Paris to discuss crusade plans, and Philip made a gesture of devotion to the crusade by resolving his dispute with Charles of Valois and Charles of La Marche to remove a significant impediment to crusade preparations.[163] These proclamations of goodwill remained little more than proclamations, however, as domestic affairs demanded Philip's immediate attention and distracted him from the crusade until August 1319, when he settled his kingdom's Flemish troubles.[164]

In the meantime, Armenian appeals for military aid arrived at the papal curia, prompting John XXII to plead with Philip V to hurry his crusade preparations.[165] On 14 January 1318, the pope granted Philip a three-year tithe on all ecclesiastical revenue in the kingdoms of France and Navarre and in the county of Burgundy;[166] in March of that year the pope secured a new two-year tithe for the French king to pay off his debts and prepare for the crusade.[167] As crusade discussions between Avignon and Paris advanced, it seems both parties began to revise their general crusade plans as a smaller-scale military expedition. On 24 March 1318, the pope wrote to Philip 'that for reasons related to the usefulness of the aforesaid overseas general crusade and considering your own interest, it would become a *passagium particulare* at the present time'.[168] The next day, John commanded papal collectors to divert 100,000 florins to Philip V from the crusade tithe imposed by Clement V in 1312, collected in France, to aid Philip in preparing the *passagium particulare*, an order the pope renewed on 7 August 1318.[169] On 13 September 1318, at Longchamp-en-Lions, the French king designated his cousin, Louis of Bourbon, Count of Clermont, as captain general of the crusading army of the *passagium particulare* set to embark before his own *passagium generale*.[170] In 1319, a Franco-papal flotilla from Narbonne and Marseilles comprising ten galleys was ready to sail to the East, but political upheaval in Italy demanded papal intervention, and John XXII risked and ultimately lost the entire flotilla in a battle against the Ghibellines in Genoa.[171] The misuse of crusading resources for the conflict in Genoa underscores John XXII's concern for diminishing papal power in Northern Italy. Throughout the 1300s, the papacy, and particularly John XXII, used the crusade as a means to justify papal wars against the Ghibelline opposition and German imperial claims in Italy. John's political claims in Italy and the consequent struggles with Christian lay powers proved harmful for the waging of any crusade in the East; papal Italian policy emboldened the German Emperor to accuse John of disregarding the Mamluk threat to Armenia for the sake of his secular claims in Italy.[172]

After the naval defeat in Genoa, Louis of Clermont was desperate for new funds for his crusade, but Philip made it clear that it would be very difficult to prepare another preliminary crusade while the conflict with Flanders was still ongoing. John XXII was sceptical of French crusading motives, but he expected Philip's 'agreeable desire' to hasten the crusade's dispatch.[173] As early as March 1318, the pope had reprimanded Philip for having been extravagant and wasteful with the funds set aside for the planned crusade.[174] On 8 October 1319, however, Philip returned to crusade planning with a gesture of goodwill for the *negotium Terre Sancte* by summoning an assembly of nobles and prelates to Paris for Christmas to deliberate on the crusade.[175] This Christmas meeting was followed by a larger assembly, again in Paris, in February 1320.[176] Many prelates, nobles and crusade veterans, all of them associated with previous crusade plans, participated in this assembly, including Bishop William Durand of Mende, Louis of Clermont and Fulk of Villaret, the recently deposed master of the Hospital. William Durand of

Mende had been involved with crusading affairs since 1313 and, until his death in 1330 in Cyprus (while returning from an embassy to the Sultan in Egypt), he had held a dominant position in crusade planning and organization.[177] Louis of Clermont, *crucesignatus* in July 1316, had founded the confraternity of the Holy Sepulcher, and in 1318 he wrote a crusade plan for his prospective preliminary crusade.[178] Louis continued to play a significant role in French crusade plans until Pope Benedict XII definitively cancelled Philip VI's crusade in 1336. Of Fulk of Villaret, Marino Sanudo wrote, 'he knew better than anyone else in the world how to wage war against the infidel Turks'.[179] Fulk was involved in drafting two crusade treatises; he had been fighting the Turks in the Levant since early 1300s and was famed as the leader of the Hospitaller crusade of 1309–1310.

The assembly of February 1320 was followed by two others during Lent of 1320 and by a series of smaller ecclesiastical and lay assemblies over the next year,[180] but there is no documentary evidence of any crusade decisions made at these assemblies. Tyerman has observed that the only account from these crusade assemblies is the chronicle written by an anonymous Parisian author, an original and important source of the events in Paris from late 1316 until 1339.[181] This anonymous chronicler asserts that Philip V 'ordered all princes of his realm and all his seneschals and bailiffs and all the other officials to stop being superfluous and that finished the wars and restored the peace'.[182] This and other assertions help us comprehend John XXII's ongoing approach to Philip V and the latter's crusade. For the pope, peace in Europe and the sensible management of crusade finances were prerequisites for a crusade.[183] Pacification on the continent was finally achieved with the January 1320 treaty between France and Flanders.[184]

The retrenchment of royal expenditures seemed to be a precondition for papal concession of a new crusade tithe to Philip.[185] The ordinance for the curtailment of royal expenses was a diplomatic manoeuvre by John XXII, who had first rebuked the penultimate Capetian king for his financial policies since 1318 in an effort to force Philip to prove to the pope and to the French nobles his intention to use the crusade money for crusading; the same anonymous Parisian chronicler asserts that the King declared he would accomplish a crusade to the Holy Land, evidence of Philip's commitment to his crusade vow.[186] It is uncertain, however, if Philip's declaration was sincere, or if the King chose to comply with papal recommendations because he was in need of new funds, funds that would finally be guaranteed.

Pope John XXII, however, was convinced: he continued to support the French crusade plans, and, on 5 June 1321, he granted Philip V a new four-year crusade tithe for the preparation of a crusade to recover the Holy Land.[187] The pope reminded the French king of his promise to participate in the actual expedition[188] and commanded the following:

> Also, the cross will be preached generally both in your aforesaid kingdoms and in other kingdoms and lands in which it seems expedient. Beyond this, the aforesaid See shall assign certain persons in all kingdoms and areas for exacting, levying, collecting, and putting in a safe place all things bequeathed and left in testaments or last wills on the occasion of this overseas business. Furthermore,

in every single church there will be placed a hollow chest sealed with certain keys, in which the offerings and alms that the faithful give in support of the Holy Land should be stored. The profits of all these shall be directed to the support of the said passage at the judgment and arrangement of the Church. Moderate and limited indulgences will also be granted for the mentioned business.[189]

In 1321, John XXII ordered the general preaching of the crusade for the first time since his election. The pope did not offer details about the organization of the preaching campaign, but he ordered chests for offerings placed in churches and granted indulgences. That these measures had been fruitful during the Hospitallers' preaching campaign allows us to suppose that preaching was carried out by the mendicants, in cooperation with the local clergy, on Sundays and feast days. The scarcity of guidelines in John XXII's letter reveals that the procedure for the diffusion of the word of the cross was more than familiar to fourteenth-century clergy, rendering explicit instructions unnecessary. Similarly, on 5 and 20 December 1322 and on 5 December 1331, when John proclaimed the general preaching in support of Charles IV's and Philip VI's plans for the East, the pope was particularly concise in his directions. The crusade preaching apparatus had already been institutionalized, so only on special occasions did papal letters explain who was responsible for the conduct of preaching and when and where it would take place. It is noteworthy that papal correspondence from the beginning of the pontificate of John XXII increasingly summarizes papal instructions for the conduct of preaching. Apart from the Hospitaller preaching campaign, papal correspondence in the fourteenth century progressively gives more consideration to the liturgical measures to accompany the preaching campaign, rather than to the preaching itself. This is quite possibly related to the greater attention, toward the end of the thirteenth century, devoted to securing financial resources for the crusade. The placing of chests in every single church was the means for the Church to garner general contributions, through alms.

Philip's renewed crusade interest created the proper moment for John XXII to proclaim measures for the realization of a crusade. But the deterioration of the King's health, beginning in October 1321, and his death, on 3 January 1322, prevented another Capetian from fulfilling his crusading vow. John XXII's letter to Philip proclaiming the crusade and the pope's deep desire for it had assured the King, 'we supplicate humbly and pray insistently as to make your days greater by adding felicity', but by the beginning of 1322 the crusade had lost its champion.[190]

Cruxque universaliter predicaretur tam in suis quam aliis regnis et terris: The crusade preaching campaigns in the context of Franco-papal crusade negotiations, 1322–1328

When Philip V of France died on 3 January 1322 without a male heir, his younger brother, Charles, the third son of the late King Philip IV, succeeded him, according to Salic law. The new king was crowned on 21 February 1322 as Charles IV, the last king from the house of Capet. Pope John XXII, who had vested all his expectations for the leadership of a crusade for the liberation of the Holy Land in the French Crown, affirmed papal support for and goodwill towards the new king and called on Count Charles of Valois to 'protect and guide his nephew, King Charles'.[191]

In crusading matters, the pope looked to the new French king as his mainstay. In the first two years of Charles IV's reign, the papal curia and the French court entered into laborious crusade negotiations which, after 1323, fell into abeyance when both parties faced different challenges. According to Norman Housley, by this time Franco-papal 'cooperation was no longer fruitful, it hampered rather than forwarded the cause of crusade'.[192] Nevertheless, in the context of Franco-papal crusade negotiations, the Church initiated a preaching campaign and instituted liturgical measures of great intensity.

John XXII's first contact with Charles IV regarding the crusade was on 22 June 1322, when the pope informed the French king of the serious situation in the Kingdom of Armenia, the result of Saracen attacks and the loss of the important Christian port of Ayas.[193] Pope John wrote to King Charles at the beginning of August to inform him of the arrival of the royal delegates, the Bishop-elect of Viviers, Peter Gauvain, and Matthew of Varennes, at the papal curia to discuss the wretched case of Armenia and to respond to Charles's queries regarding the organization of the expedition.[194] The French king had asked about the overall number of men and horses necessary for the expedition, the required equipment and supplies and their transportation, the date on which the passage would start, its duration and how it would be financed.[195]

In December 1322, in response to Charles IV's enquiries, John issued a series of bulls proclaiming the preaching for the crusade, specifying the kind of financial aid the Church would provide for the fulfilment of the crusade and defining the indulgences granted to those hastening *pro subsidio regni Armenie*.[196] On 5 December 1322, John sent his own plan for the crusade to Charles, exhorting him to follow the example of his brother in assuming leadership of the overseas passage.[197] In his letter, the pope emphasized the necessity of the *passagium particulare* to aid the Christians in the East, a position strikingly dissimilar to the French plan for a three-strand crusade. Charles IV supported the idea of separating the crusade to the East into three parts: the *primum passagium*, the *passagium particulare* and, finally, the main crusading expedition, the *passagium generale*. The pope stressed the state of emergency in the Kingdom of Armenia because of the fierceness of the Mamluks, a situation requiring urgent military assistance from Western Christianity. Although the pope did not grant a new crusade tithe to Charles, he professed the Church's readiness to provide funds for the enterprise. Charles IV, like Philip V, fervently desired financial aid from the Church; the pope, however, was already suspicious of the French Crown because of Philip V's misappropriation of funds and extravagant spending.[198] John XXII was also reluctant to grant a new tithe to the French king because he needed to finance his war in Lombardy against Matthew and his son, Galeazzo I Visconti, the lords of Milan, and their Ghibelline supporters.[199] Nevertheless, on 5 December 1322, John XXII ordered:

> Also, the cross would be preached generally both in your kingdoms and in lands in which it seems expedient, and certain persons would be assigned by the same See in all aforesaid kingdoms and areas for exacting and collecting, and putting in a safe place all things bequeathed on the occasion of the said overseas business, and in every single church there would be placed a hollow chest sealed with certain keys, in which the offerings and alms that the faithful give in support of the said passage should be stored, all these were to be directed to the support of the said passage at the judgment and arrangement of the Church. Moreover, moderate and limited indulgences would also be granted for the mentioned business.[200]

Despite his disinclination to grant a new crusade tithe to Charles IV, the pope adopted a number of different measures to accumulate crusade resources on behalf of the French king, including crusade preaching and indulgences. John XXII also permitted the conduct of preaching beyond the Kingdom of France, thus ensuring revenue from churches outside France, and for this reason the Holy See took responsibility for the appointment of money collectors for legacies and bequests for the crusade; in this way the pope could control the flow of funds for Charles's crusade without burdening the French church and the kingdom's clergy with a direct crusade tithe. Additionally, by granting moderate indulgences, the pope stimulated the eleemosynary impulses of the faithful, ensuring extra money for the papal *camera* while enabling the Church to further its crusading plans. In fact, with the exception of the plenary indulgence for those fighting for the Holy Land, from 1184, indulgences were used rather moderately to convince people to fight against the infidel and to raise money for the crusade.[201] John XXII ordered the placement of chests in every church for alms, after the award of moderate indulgences, but this money was only to be used for crusade preparations. The concession of financial aid in advance of any crusading expedition, to secure the involvement of Charles IV himself, brought extra pressure to bear on the pope and was the predominant element of the Franco-papal negotiations of 1322–1324.

On 20 December 1322, in a separate letter – which in great part reproduced the bull *Ad pie matris communis* – to all Christianity, John XXII ordered the clergy to preach the cross and to grant crusade indulgences; John also renewed his 5 December command for general crusade preaching in the territorial possessions of the French king. He asked the following of the Church prelates:

> You and every one of you, by you or any regular or secular [clerics] whom you consider worthy to be assigned for this purpose, shall take care to receive reverently these [apostolic] letters whenever they happen to be delivered and presented to you; to read diligently through the word of preaching, according to the prudence provided to you by God, both the [letters] and the indulgences and remissions and other things contained in them publicly in your cities and

dioceses before the people, who are to be summoned especially for this when it seems expedient; and to publish them and put them into the vernacular.[202]

According to papal mandates, the high prelates had the power to choose members of the secular or regular clergy for the conduct of preaching according to their own judgment; instead of appointing a nuncio or legate to organize the preaching, the pope employed local French clergymen in his crusade preaching endeavour, which made the propaganda machinery more flexible and more effective. The secular clergy, especially those charged with pastoral duties in parishes and isolated rural areas, had very strong ties with local parishioners and could address their congregations in their vernacular. The encouragement of the vernacular preaching of the cross underlines the high expectations the papacy had for these preaching campaigns. Like Clement V in 1308, John XXII was aware of the need to use the vernacular effectively and persuasively to preach the crusade. The necessity of simple rhetoric – and even for the use of 'simple Latin' – for more direct contact between preacher and audience, had been apparent since the middle of the twelfth century.[203] In 1147, the Bishop of Oporto had to use an interpreter to preach to English contingents participating in the Second Crusade; Archdeacon Gerald of Wales, who accompanied the Archbishop of Canterbury, Baldwin of Forde, on his 1188 preaching tour of Wales, states in his autobiography that if the Archbishop 'had spoken in Welsh, I do not think that a single man would have been left out of all this magnitude'.[204] The papacy wished to shrink the language gap between the preacher and his audience. The unavoidable separation of status, class, experience and region could only be abridged if the preacher could communicate directly in the congregation's vernacular language.[205] The use of the vernacular for crusade preaching illustrates papal aspirations for the summons to crusade, that this call would reach every single member of the faithful. The regular clergy, especially the mendicants, had a strong presence in urban areas and, in combination with the itinerant nature of their mission, provided the Church an effective network for the diffusion of the crusading summons throughout France. With these measures in place, and following the commitment of Charles IV, John XXII expressed his ardent support for the crusade and worked to organize aid for Armenia.

Apart from the preaching for the dissemination of the crusading word, John XXII gave new prominence to the concession of indulgences, the liturgical practices and the remission of sins as a way of financing the coming crusade. Also on 20 December 1322, John issued a plenary remission of sins for all those who, within the next five years, would travel east to fight for the salvation of Armenia.[206]

In early 1323, Charles IV convened a crusade council in Paris. The council was attended by Charles of Valois, by French prelates and nobles, by the Venetian, Marino Sanudo Torsello, and by representatives from Armenia.[207] After discussing papal proposals, the council decided to gather and send a fleet to the Eastern Mediterranean to prevent westerners from trading with Mamluk Egypt and to garrison the Christian coastal cities against potential

Muslim attacks. This naval mission was to be the first stage of a planned tripartite crusade. During the council, news of Muslim threats to Cyprus reached Paris, and the critical state of affairs in the East prompted Charles to immediately appoint Amaury, Viscount of Narbonne, and Bérenger Blanc as captain and admiral of the Christian fleet, respectively, with an embarkation date of 1 May 1323.[208] The King declared he would bestow 20,000 *livres tournois* on the *primum passagium*, he asked for a general financial contribution within his kingdom, and announced certain measures for raising money for the crusade.[209] Charles also proclaimed that he would contribute 300,000 *livres tournois* for the implementation of the second passage, the *passagium particulare*, over the course of 1324.[210]

Despite these generous proclamations, Charles declared that the crusade was the business of Christ and, as such, the Church must pay most of its costs; this was a clear indication of the French throne's perspective, and financial support for the crusade and the use of funds collected for it dominated Franco-papal deliberations. Because of a series of calamities in Western Europe, the Holy See and the French monarchy were reluctant to lavish their money on a crusade, as it was superseded by their respective political priorities and domestic affairs. These were the main reasons for the failure of crusade negotiations from 1322 to 1324 which, once concluded, meant that no support was ever provided to the threatened Christian kingdoms of Armenia and Cyprus.

In March 1323, Louis, Count of Clermont, and the French royal delegation reached Avignon and presented the French crusading proposal to the papal curia.[211] Charles demanded all crusade money collected from legacies and the redemption of vows and almsgiving; he also announced his intention to replace the papal tithe collectors with royal ones. Needless to say, these French crusading schemes were rather unwelcome in Avignon.[212] John XXII and his cardinals were henceforth suspicious of Charles's motives, and the distrust between the two parties increased, damaging the preparatory stage of the crusade and delaying its departure.

In April 1323, the pope and the College of Cardinals discussed and considered all of the French crusade proposals. Seventeen of the cardinals presented their advice in written form – these were included as consecutive entries in the papal registers.[213] The cardinals expressed disparate opinions of Charles IV's crusade proposals: their statements, taken together, provide a valuable picture of how crusade preparation and conduct were discussed and organized by the high prelates of the Latin Church in the first quarter of the fourteenth century.

All the cardinals took issue with the French crusading proposals. They argued that 1 May was impossible as the date for the departure of the *primum passagium*, as there was not enough time for sufficient preparation. Many of the cardinals expressed doubts about the *primum passagium*, as they favoured the papal plans for a two-part crusade.[214] Most importantly, Charles's desire to gather all crusade subsidies under his control aroused much scepticism among the cardinals, all of whom were opposed to any plan that would vitiate their control. Beyond their reservations about the French king's proposals, the cardinals addressed the organization of the crusade, giving the pope advice on practical issues, rather than spiritual ones, such as the preaching of the crusade. The cardinals were primarily interested in financing the crusade, but they also considered how many crusaders were needed for the expedition and for how long, the number of ships required for their transportation, the leadership of the crusade and the role of the Christians in the East.[215]

In late April 1323, negotiations became even more complicated when Charles of Valois sent a crusade plan to the papal curia.[216] Charles, the uncle of the French king, would be the captain of the French crusading army for an expedition to commence in August 1325. Soon thereafter, Charles IV wrote John XXII to express his support for his uncle's project and to voice his approval of Charles of Valois as leader of the *passagium particulare* whilst also assuring the pope of his intention to command the general crusade.[217] Charles of Valois was eager for a prompt reply from the pope, but John sent his response on 25 May 1323, disappointing both Charles IV and Charles of Valois with both his delayed reply and his financial offering.[218] The pope appeared unwilling to make generous concessions; he only granted potential crusaders a two-year tithe on ecclesiastical revenue in the kingdoms of France and Navarre for preparation of the expedition.[219]

By autumn of 1323, the deliberations for the crusade had entered their most critical phase, with its financial issues the only matters under discussion.[220] Charles IV pressed the pope for a crusade tithe to be levied throughout Christendom, but John XXII was tenacious and unwilling to offer more than he had in his letter of 25 May. On 7 November 1323, John it clear that he would offer nothing more than he had in May; later that same month he informed Charles IV of the fifteen-year truce the Armenians had concluded with the Mamluks.[221] Even though the threat to Armenia had been eliminated, at least temporarily, on 23 December 1323, the pope still granted Louis of Clermont 25,000 florins for the preparation of the *passagium particulare* from the money collected in France.[222] Six days later, on 29 December, John XXII notified Charles IV of his payment to Louis.[223]

In August 1324, France went to war against England – this was the War of St Sardos, which followed the invasion of English-controlled Aquitaine by Charles of Valois. Despite the concession of a two-year crusade tithe to Charles IV in December 1324, the papal efforts to launch a crusade to the Morea against the Catalans and the Greeks and the granting of plenary indulgences to those fighting for the defence of Chios and the neighbouring lands against the Turks on 28 April 1325, the Holy See gained nothing for the crusade.[224] Crusading enthusiasm disappeared from French royal circles with the death of Charles of Valois on 16 December 1325. From 1324, John XXII was fully embroiled in Northern Italy and his strike against Louis IV of Bavaria, German Emperor, whose imperial claims threatened papal power in the region; by 1326, a preaching campaign guided by Bertrand of Poujet against the Ghibellines of Milan was in progress.[225] Charles IV, the last Capetian king, died in 1328, marking the end of crusade preparations between the house of Capet and the curia.

Committimus predicande concedendeque crucis officium: Between Avignon and Paris, crusade planning and propaganda during 1331–1334

The ascendance of Philip of Valois – the first king from the House of Valois – to the throne of France provided the papacy with one of the more persistent proponents of its endeavour to recapture the Holy Land. In the opinion of Norman Housley, the crusade project presented to John XXII by envoys of Philip VI in February 1332 'was the most important of all the French proposals in this period, and it involved the greatest degree of negotiations, crusade preaching, and taxation since the reign of Gregory X'.[226] The new king, the son of Charles of Valois, a crusade devotee, had been *crucesignatus* since 1313, when he took the cross from the hands of papal legate Nicholas of Fréauville during the cross-taking ceremony on the Île-de-la-Cité.[227] Philip's constant concern for the crusade brought him a step away from joining the Spanish in a crusade against the Moors of Granada in 1326. He continued to gaze towards the Iberian Peninsula until 1331, when the allure of an earnest, royal crusade for the recapture of the Holy Land drew his attention East.[228]

A likely explanation for Philip's shift of attention from Spain towards *Outremer* is the preaching of the Dominican Pierre de la Palud, Latin Patriarch of Jerusalem. In 1329–1330, after escorting Maria, the daughter of the Duke of Bourbon, to Cyprus for her marriage to Guy of Lusignan, the eldest son of King Hugh IV, Pierre de la Palud, the new patriarch of Jerusalem, along with Bishop William Durand of Mende, visited the Mamluk court to negotiate pilgrims' rights in the Holy Land. On his return to Avignon in the autumn of 1330, Palud relayed to John XXII the fruitless outcome of his diplomatic mission to Cairo.[229] In September 1331, according to the continuator of William of Nangis and the *Grandes chroniques de France*, Palud delivered a dramatic, rousing sermon before Philip VI and a large number of prelates and barons in which he exhorted the French nobility to embark upon a new crusade.[230] The sermon 'provided the spark which rekindled official French crusading enthusiasm'[231] and induced John XXII to set crusade preaching in motion that December. It was also in September 1331 that grave news from Armenia, where the situation had again become serious, reached the papal court. The pope informed Philip VI of the arrival of delegates from King Leo IV of Armenia and their petition for immediate Christian action to resist Mamluk pressure on the kingdom.[232]

On 5 December 1331, with the bull *Gaudemus et exultamus in Domino*, John XXII notified the high prelates of France of Philip VI's determination to go '*ad deliberationem dicte Terre Sancte de manibus infidelium*' and announced all measures in support of royal crusading initiatives.[233] The pope appointed Pierre de la Palud as papal-legate in France: Palud was responsible for the conduct of the preaching campaign in the kingdom, and the pope commanded all archbishops and bishops in France to assist the legate.[234]

But turning words into action required significant funds. The money collected from donations was insufficient, so the French Crown became involved in elaborate and detailed negotiations with the curia to secure the papal concession of a crusade tithe and to finalize the organization and launch of the crusade.[235] These discussions began in February 1332: the French demanded complete control of all crusading funds, and this issue dominated the negotiations until July 1333.[236] In late July 1332, in a meeting with his barons at Melun, southeast of Paris, Philip VI announced his determination to go on crusade;[237] three months later he reaffirmed his intention to travel to *Outremer*, and in March 1333, he instructed royal officials to secure commitments of financial support throughout the French kingdom.[238]

During this phase of crusade arrangements, Philip appeared more willing to make concessions to papal demands pertaining to the administration of crusade money. The King agreed to a papal request for the appointment of two French prelates to determine if the King had acted too slowly during the crusade's preparatory stage, and for the election of a body of delegates, all senior clerics, to oversee the collection of crusade funds. Philip also vested his emissaries to the papal court with full authority to affirm to the pope that the crusade would depart on 1 August 1336.[239] An agreement between the two parties regarding the course of action was finally reached on 24 May 1333,[240] and on 16 July 1333, at a consistory presided over by the pope, the French ambassadors – with Pierre Roger, Archbishop of Rouen, as the head of their delegation – swore in Philip's place the king would sail overseas *in propria persona*.[241] Pierre Roger delivered an inspirational sermon in which he stressed the importance of the crusade for the relief of the Christians in the East and warned of the ever-increasing danger of the Turks to Romania;[242] with his sermon, Archbishop Pierre Roger inaugurated a period of pro-crusade mobilization in Western Christianity and expunged any papal doubts about the sincerity of Philip's crusading aims. Ten days later John XXII issued a series of bulls appointing Philip VI rector and captain-general of the forthcoming crusade to the East.[243] The pope also imposed a sexennial crusade tithe on ecclesiastical revenues in support of Philip VI's crusade;[244] he defined indulgences for all the *crucesignati* and sent clergy across Europe and to the East with detailed orders for the conduct of a general preaching of the cross and the implementation of liturgical measures. The bull *Ad commemorandum recentius*, sent to high clergy throughout Christianity on 26 July 1333, delineates specific details about the preaching and liturgical campaign.[245] The pope urged the clergy, secular and regular, to take part in the crusade preaching, and he granted all clerics who hastened to preach indulgences of one year and forty days (partial remission of sins for a period of one year and forty days); those who heard the preaching and confessed their sins were granted 100-day indulgences, while those who chose to crusade enjoyed plenary indulgences (full remission of the penalties imposed by Church as consequence of sin).[246] On 15 September 1333, the pope made Archbishop Pierre Roger responsible for preaching the crusade in France and commanded him to assign Philip VI the cross:

> But because, as we have learned, the aforesaid king and with him many dukes, counts, barons and nobles, and many other persons of different social

status intend shortly and they desire intensely to be marked with the sign of the cross on the pretext of the said passage, we, considering your person to be pleasing to the king himself, and without doubt hoping that said king and the others noted above permit your speech and ministry for the sake and benefit of devotion, or rather for the effect that listening to it will bring, on the authority of the present letter we assign to you and we command that when and where you are asked concerning this by the same king, according to the prudence granted to you by God, you shall preach with fervour the word of the cross to him and the others mentioned above and put upon their shoulders the sign of the same cross. Furthermore we also commit to you the duty of the preaching and granting of the cross throughout the said kingdom, to be carried out by you yourself only outside your diocese.[247]

Following the papal exhortations of 1 October 1333, Pierre Roger delivered a crusade sermon in the Prés-aux-Clercs.[248] Roger's preaching campaign continued in France until March 1336, when Benedict XII cancelled Philip's crusade.

In the meantime, news of rising Turkish aggression and attacks on Latin possessions in the Eastern Mediterranean reached Western Christendom. Beginning in 1332, formal embassies from Cyprus, Armenia and Venice, and written advice from individuals with experience in the East, such as Marino Sanudo Torsello, William Badin and Andreas of Antioch, alarmed Avignon and Paris of the Turkish menace, prompting them to send military help.[249] A plan for joint naval action by France, Genoa and Venice gradually emerged alongside the Franco-papal negotiations for the *passagium generale*. The idea of united Christian action in the Aegean was imperative for Venice, since Venice had to confront cruel Turkish attacks on its Aegean dominions, and it was for this reason that Venice approached Philip VI in 1332 to discuss the formation of a naval league for immediate action in the Aegean. Despite the King's initial reservations, after the meeting at Vincennes of December 1333, concerning the Beatific Vision, John XXII pressured him to sign a final agreement for the formation of a joint Western naval league in March 1334. According to the terms of the alliance, a fleet comprising forty galleys from Venice, the Hospitallers, Cyprus, the Byzantine Emperor, France and the pope was to assemble at Negroponte in May and remain in the Eastern Mediterranean for five months. On 14 September 1334, a naval engagement fought in the waters near Adramyttion, a city in Asia Minor on the coast of Mysia, was a comprehensive Christian victory.[250] The Christian success at Adramyttion reduced the number of Turkish raids for a while, but it did not reduce the power of the different Turcoman tribes in Asia Minor, who resumed pillaging Venetian strongholds in the Aegean once conditions were again favourable for such raids.

The last years of John XXII's papacy saw continued Turkish attacks menacing the remaining Latin dominions in the Aegean. From the 1330s, as the naval league of 1334 evinced, the main crusading objective became the protection of the remaining Latin possessions in the Eastern Mediterranean, rather than the liberation of the Holy Land. Thenceforth, the theatre of conflict shifted from the Syro-Palestinian coast and Egypt to the Aegean Sea and the seafront of Asia Minor, and the crusade as a military expedition, originally intended as an offensive, became defensive.

The years between autumn 1331 and late 1334 were a period of intense diplomatic engagement between the curia and the French Crown. The clergy, as well as many officials and nobles, were involved in the crusade, as formal ceremonies, meetings, preaching and liturgy were consistently arranged, defined and discussed. The extensive dissemination of crusade propaganda by parochial and regular clergy helped secure funds for the crusade, but did little to recruit new crusaders. Through crusade preaching and liturgy, Western European congregations were exhorted to donate alms and leave bequests, and all those who would take the cross could redeem their oaths for money.[251] Pierre de la Palud and Pierre Roger, much like Peter of Pleine Chassagne and Nicholas of Fréauville before them, proved that the involvement of devoted, inspired and skilled preachers from the upper echelon of the secular clergy was crucial to an effective preaching campaign,[252] as their advanced education enabled them to contend with and triumph over the challenges inherent in their duties. Many high prelates, given their intimacy with different Western European monarchs, served as royal confessors and advisors or as delegates to the curia. These prelates influenced many in royal circles to take the cross, as Philip IV, Edward II and Philip VI did.

The reign of John XXII, the longest of the popes of Avignon, demonstrated the absolute papal dependence on the French Crown when it came to planning, organizing and launching a crusade to the Holy Land. John laid all his crusading expectations on the King of France, the *Rex Christianissimus*, and devoted all his energy to long-term negotiations with the last two Capetian kings of France and its first Valois king. Despite his allegiance to and need of the French Crown, John did not entirely accept French demands for crusade tithes and for full control of crusade funds: he rebuked Philip V and Charles IV for the extravagance of their royal houses and for their misuse of the money collected for the crusade and, unconvinced of the sincerity of Philip VI's crusading aims, appointed a committee, in September 1333, to investigate the King's preparations.[253] Indeed, the success of any papal endeavour for crusading to the East was entirely reliant on the goodwill and cooperation of the French monarchs. The death of Pope John XXII on 4 December 1334 prevented any further anti-Turkish action in the Aegean and complicated Franco-papal crusade negotiations even further, and in March 1336, Benedict cancelled the crusade.

Notes

1. After a brief pontificate of eight months, Benedict XI died in Perugia and his successor, Clement V, was elected as the new pope in the same place.
2. *Registrum Simonis de Gandavo diocesis Saresbiriensis, AD 1297–1315*, 2 vols. (Oxford, 1913–1914), i, 220–223; Sophia Menache, *Clement V* (Cambridge: Cambridge University Press, 1998), 17–18, 101.
3. Sylvia Schein, *Fideles Crucis: The Papacy, the West, and the Recovery of the Holy Land 1274–1314* (Oxford: Oxford Clarendon Press, 1998), 181.
4. For details on this treaty, see Kenneth M. Setton, *The Papacy and the Levant (1204–1571)*, 4 vols. (Philadelphia: The American Philosophical Society, 1976–1984), i,

140–162; Angeliki E. Laiou, *Constantinople and the Latins: The Foreign Policy of Andronicus II 1282–1328* (Massachusetts: Harvard University Press, 1972), 128–134.

5 'Collectio Actorum Veterum', in *Vitae Paparum Avenionensium*, ed. G. Mollat, 4 vols. (Paris: Librairie Letouzey et Ané, 1916–1928) [hereafter VPA], iii, 75: 'Inter sollicitudines nostras illa est temporibus istis precipua, quod inter carissimos filios nostros reges Francorum et Anglorum illustres pacis vinculum solidetur, quodque negotium passagii transmarine sic inchoetur ... ac recuperationem felicem et celerem Terre Sancte'.

6 'Annales Londonienses', in *Chronicles of the Reigns of Edward I and Edward II: Annales Londonienses and Annales Paulini Edited from Mss. in the British Museum and in the Archiepiscopal Library at Lambeth*, ed. W. Stubbs, 2 vols. (London: Longman, 1882–1883), i, 129, 152.

7 Sylvia Schein, 'Philip IV and the Crusade: A Reconsideration' in *Crusade and Settlement: Papers Read at the First Conference of the Society for the Study of Crusades and the Latin East*, ed. P. W. Edbury (Cardiff: University College Cardiff Press, 1985), 121–124; Schein, *Fideles Crucis*, 181.

8 For the crusade plans and memories of the Holy Land at the end of the thirteenth and the beginning of the fourteenth centuries, see Aziz S. Atiya, *The Crusade in the Later Middle Ages* (London: Methuen, 1938); Schein, *Fideles Crucis*; Antony Leopold, *How to Recover the Holy Land: The Crusade Proposals of the Late Thirteenth and Early Fourteenth Centuries* (Aldershot: Ashgate, 2000).

9 For crusading in the Iberian Peninsula see Norman Housley, *The Avignon Papacy and the Crusades, 1305–1378* (Oxford: Oxford Clarendon Press, 1986), 50–65; Norman Housley, *The Later Crusades: From Lyon to Alcazar, 1274–1580* (Oxford: Oxford University Press, 1992), 267–290.

10 Edward II was engaged in confrontation with the Scots, while Philip IV, despite the treaty in 1305 with Flanders, had to face, until 1309, the hostility of those Flemish cities that did not recognize the terms of the peace. From October 1307, Philip IV was also engaged in the prosecution of the Knights Templar. For England and the Crusades in the fourteenth century see Timothy Guard, *Chivalry, Kingship and Crusade: The English Experience in the Fourteenth Century* (Woodbridge: The Boydell Press, 2013).

11 Clement V, *Regestum Clementis papae V: Ex Vaticanis archetypis sanctissimi domini nostri Leonis XIII pontificis maximi iussu et munificentia*, ed. Cura et studio monachorum Ordinis S. Benedicti, 10 vols. (Rome: Typografia Vaticana, 1885–1892), nos. 243–248 [hereafter *Regestum*].

12 Clement V, *Regestum*, no. 248: 'quod predicti imperii [Constantinopolitani] recuperatio diutius expectata prestabitur ac per recuperationem ipsius Terre Sancte negotium'; *Annales Ecclesiastici ab anno 1198 usque ad annum 1565*, eds. A. Theiner, *et al.*, 37 vols. (Paris-Freiburg-Bar le Duc, 1864–1867), xxiii, 374–375 [hereafter *Annales Ecclesiastici*]. For more details on the papacy's plans for the conquest of Constantinople after 1261, see Deno John Geanakoplos, *Emperor Michael Palaeologus and the West, 1258–1282: A Study in Byzantine-Latin Relations* (Massachusetts: Harvard University Press, 1959), 335–364; Laiou, *Constantinople and the Latins*, 12–14; Schein, *Fideles Crucis*, 184.

13 Nikolaos G. Chrissis, *Crusading in Frankish Greece: A Study of Byzantine-Western Relations and Attitudes, 1204–1282* (Turnhout: Brepols, 2012), 42. Chrissis's major study offers an excellent overview of the development, in the thirteenth century, of the papacy's message regarding the legitimacy and the validity of crusade in Frankish Greece and the conquest of Constantinople. See also Nikolaos G. Chrissis, 'The City and the Cross: The Image of Constantinople and the Latin Empire in Thirteenth-Century Papal Crusading Rhetoric', *Byzantine and Modern Greek Studies*, 36.1 (2012), 20–37; Nikolaos G. Chrissis, 'Crusades and Crusaders in Medieval Greece', in *A Companion to Latin Greece*, eds. N. I. Tsougarakis and P. Lock (Leiden: Brill, 2015),

23–72; Nikolaos G. Chrissis, 'New Frontiers: Frankish Greece and the Development of Crusading in the Early Thirteenth Century', in *Contact and Conflict in Frankish Greece and the Aegean*, eds. N. G. Chrissis and M. Carr (Farnham: Ashgate, 2014), 17–41.

14 Leopold, *How to Recover the Holy Land*, 139–143; Chrissis, *Crusading in Frankish Greece*, 269; Chrissis, 'Crusades and Crusaders in Medieval Greece', 35.

15 Clement V, *Regestum*, no. 245.

16 Deno John Geanakoplos, 'Byzantium and the Crusades, 1261–1354', in *A History of the Crusades: The Fourteenth and Fifteenth Centuries*, ed. H.W. Hazard, 6 vols. (Madison: The University of Wisconsin Press, 1969–1989), iii, 27–69, 42.

17 Benedict XI, *Le registre de Benoit XI*, ed. C. Grandjean (Paris: Bibliothèque des Écoles françaises d'Athènes et de Rome, 1903), nos. 1006–1007; Mike Carr, *Merchant Crusaders in the Aegean, 1291–1352* (Woodbridge: The Boydell Press, 2015), 28; Chrissis, *Crusading in Frankish Greece*, 269.

18 For more details on Charles's preparations, see Laiou, *Constantinople*, 201–220, 229–242; Carr, *Merchant Crusaders*, 29–30; Henri Moranvillé, 'Les Projets de Charles de Valois sur l'Empire de Constantinople', *Bibliothèque de l'École des Chartes*, 51 (1890), 63–86.

19 Clement V, *Regestum*, nos. 245, 248.

20 ASV, Reg. Vat. 52, fols. 42ᵛ–43ʳ, ep. 220: 'usque cum itaque eius est ratione uxoris tue carissime videlicet in Christo filie Caterine et cetera ut supra usque ducti tibi et omnibus qui pro dicte terre sancte subsidio signum crucis nullatenus receperunt proficiscentibus tecum in expeditionem hoc modo negotii dicti imperii, et eis etiam qui propriis expensis illuc iuxta eorum facultatem miserint ydoneos bellatores, vel qui licet in allis expensis cum non possint suis in personis tamen propriis tecum curaverint proficisci, illam concedimus tui et ipsorum veniam peccatorum'; Clement V, *Regestum*, nos. 243–244, 246.

21 Clement V, *Regestum*, nos. 1759: 'Andronicum Paleologum, qui Grecorum imperatorem se nominat, tanquam eorundem Grecorum antiquatorum scismaticorum et in antiquato scismate constitutorum et per hoc hereticorum et heresis ipsorum ac scismatis antiquati fautorem de fratrum nostrorum consilio denuntiamus excommunicationis sententiam latam a canone incurrisse ac ipsius fore sentencie vinculo innodatum'; *Annales Ecclesiastici*, xxiii, 376, 387. On 03 June 1307, Clement issued the bull excommunicating the Byzantine emperor, Andronicus II Palaeologus.

22 Clement V, *Regestum*, no. 1768: 'Scimus enim, quod ab eiusdem comitis primordio iuventutis exaltationem ecclesie et fidei predictarum velut eiusdem ecclesie specialis alumpnus promovere sollicite studuit, assistens eidem ecclesie eiusque fidelibus temporibus oportunis et in hoc Dei negotium agi considerans... et suorum exposuit personas pro defensione sepedicte fidei et ecclesie libertatis'.

23 Clement V, *Regestum*, no. 1768: 'Profecto ad ipsum imperium de filiorum alienorum eripiendum manibus ipse fidei zelus debet corda fidelium velut ignis accendere, nam si quod Deus avertat prefatum imperium ad Turcos, Sarracenos et infideles alios, qui assidue Andronicum prefatum impugnant, devenire contingeret, grave discrimen et confusionem gravissimam reciperet Romana mater ecclesia totaque religio christiana'.

24 Norman Housley, 'Frontier Societies and Crusading in the Late Middle Ages', in *Intercultural Contacts in the Medieval Mediterranean*, ed. A. Benjamin (London: Frank Cass, 1996), 104–106.

25 Chrissis, *Crusading in Frankish Greece*, 45–47.

26 Clement V, *Regestum*, no. 1768: 'dum illud ab olim per quondam Michaelem Palaeologum tempore, quo vivebat, et post eius obitum per Andronicum, eius filium, ipsorumque complices et fautores scismaticos et ab unitate Christiane fidei deviantes, elevates superbie cornibus in divine maiestatis offensa, apostolice sedis iniuria et totius christianitatis obprobrio conspicimus dampnabiliter occupatum, multo nimirum

52 Clement V's and John XXII's campaigns

merore complectimur, trahimur in amara suspiria et diris vexamur angustiis et ad subveniendum ei de remedio, per quod ab ipsorum dominio, immo potius exterminio Deo propitio liberari et ad fidem reduci valeat orthodoxam, vias et modos libenter exquirimus ac sollicite opem et operam adhibemus'.

27 Clement V, *Regestum*, no. 1768: 'Cum itaque dictus comes [Carolus], qui ratione carissime in Christo filie nostre Caterine, imperatricis Constantinopolitane illustris, uxoris sue, ad eiusdem recuperationem imperii…intendere et ad id disponere vires suas'.

28 For the geographical expansion of the crusades in Frankish Greece during the thirteenth century see Chrissis, *Crusading in Frankish Greece*, 182–183, especially the maps in Appendix IV, 283–288; Chrissis, 'Crusades and Crusaders in Frankish Greece', 62–62.

29 Laiou, *Constantinople*, 204.
30 Laiou, *Constantinople*, 204.
31 Laiou, *Constantinople*, 204.
32 Clement V, *Regestum*, no. 248.
33 *Diplomatarium Veneto-Levantinum, sive Acta et Diplomata res Venetas, Graecas atque Levantis illustrantia a.1300–1454*, ed. G. M. Thomas, 2 vols. (Venice: Typis Marci Visentini, 1880–1899), i, no. 27, 48–53; Setton, *The Papacy and Levant*, i, 165–166.

34 Donald Nicol, *Byzantium and Venice: A Study in Diplomatic and Cultural Relations* (Cambridge: Cambridge University Press, 1988), 118–222.

35 For a very good account which supports this position, see Elizabeth A. Zachariadou, *Trade and Crusade: Venetian Crete and the Emirates of Menteshe and Aydin (1300–1415)* (Venice: Hellenic Institute of Byzantine and Post–Byzantine Studies, 1983); also see Carr, *Merchant Crusaders*.

36 Clement V, *Regestum*, no. 248: 'vos atletas Dei et fortissimos bellatores, universitatem vestram rogamus, monemus et hortamur attente obsecrantes per Dominum Iesum Christum … in promptum auxilium eiusdem comitis sub velamento divine dextere consurgentes "sic eidem" potenter et viriliter assistatis'.

37 Norman Housley, *The Later Crusades*, 55.
38 Clement V, *Regestum*, no. 243: 'redemptiones votorum omnesque obventiones preter decimas Terre Sancte subsidio deputatas, a personis in regno Franciae constitutis diligenter colligate, Carolo comiti Andegavensi ad expugnandum imperium Constantinopolitanum convertenda'; Norman Housley, *The Avignon Papacy*, 12–13.

39 ASV, Reg. Vat. 52, fols. 42^v–43^r, ep. 220; Clement V, *Regestum*, no. 1755: 'dictam decimam per biennium ex nunc proxime subsequens per te, quem deputamus tenore presentium ipsius decime collectorem, vel subcollectores tuos, quos ad hoc duxeris deputandos, colligi et exigi et conservari fideliter nostro et ecclesie Romane nomine volumus carissimo in Christo filio nostro Frederico, regi Trinacrie illustri, si cum dicto comite ad huiusmodi negotium prosequendum cum debita bellatorum comitiva, prout excellentiam decet regalem, voluerit proficisci, postquam prosequi negotium ipsum inceperit, alioquin eidem comiti pro dictarum expensarum subsidio assignandam'.

40 Clement V, *Regestum*, no. 1768.
41 Clement V, *Regestum*, no. 1768: 'de fratrum nostrorum consilio verbum vivifice crucis deliberavimus proponendum ac ministerium predicandi eandem necnon tradendi venerabile signum eius cunctis de regno, provinciis, terris, districtibus, et diocesi supradictis devote petentibus illud'.

42 For the role the papacy assigned to the Orders of mendicants, the Franciscans and the Dominicans, in particular, in the organization and conduct of crusade preaching from the thirteenth century, see Christoph T. Maier, *Preaching the Crusades: Mendicant Friars and the Cross in the Thirteenth Century* (Cambridge: Cambridge University Press, 1994); d'Avray, *The Preaching of the Friars*; Moorman, *A History of the Franciscan Order*.

43 Norman Housley, *The Italian Crusades: The Papal-Angevin Alliance and the Crusades Against Christian Lay Powers, 1254–1343* (Oxford: Clarendon Press, 1982), 121.
44 For details on crusading in Romania between 1313 and the death of Philip of Taranto in 1331, see Laiou, *Constantinople*, 237–242; Housley, *The Later Crusades*, 53–55; Chrissis, *Crusading in Frankish Greece*, 269–270.
45 Schein, *Fideles Crucis*, 194; Carr, *Merchant Crusaders*, 26–28.
46 For their long career in the East, see Jonathan Riley-Smith, *The Knights of St John of Jerusalem and Cyprus, 1050–1310* (London: Macmillan, 1967), 208–209; Malcolm Barber, *The Trial of the Templars* (Cambridge: Cambridge University Press, 1993).
47 Some sources assert Clement V invited Fulk of Villaret and James of Molay in 1306, while others argue this happened in 1307, see *Les Grandes chroniques de France*, ed. J. Viard, 10 vols. (Paris: Société de l'histoire de France, 1920–1953), viii, 257; 'Prima Vita Clementis V', in *VPA*, i, 6; 'Excerpta e memoriali historiarum, auctore Johanne Parisiensi, sancti Victoris Parisiensis canonico regulari', in *Recueil des historiens des Gaules et de la France*, eds. M. Bouquet, *et al*., 24 vols. (Paris: Imprimerie Impériale, 1737–1904), xxi, 647 [hereafter RHGF]; 'Continuatio Chronici Girardi de Fracheto', in *RHGF*, xxi, 28.
48 Clement V, *Regestum*, no. 1033; *Chronique Latin de Guillaume de Nangis de 1113 a 1300 avec les continuations de cette chronique de 1300 a 1368*, ed. H. Géraud, 2 vols. (Paris: Imprimerie de Crapelet, 1843), ii, 359.
49 Anthony Luttrell, 'The Hospitallers at Rhodes, 1306–1421', in *A History of the Crusades*, ed. H.W. Hazard, iii, 278–314, 283–285.
50 'Sexta Vita Clementis V', in *VPA*, i, 93: 'Fulko, magister militie Hospitaliorum, cum magno exercitu christianorum, cum magna sanguinis effusione ipsi ceperunt insulam Rodarum, quam tunc Turci sub dominio imperatoris Constantinopolitani scismatici tenebant'.
51 'Quarta Vita Clementis V', in *VPA*, i, 62: 'Hospitalarii cum exercitu christianorum obpugnare ceperunt insulam Rhodi cum circumadjacentibus insulis circiter quinque, que ab infidelibus Turchis inhabitabantur sub dominio imperatoris Constantinopolitani'.
52 Jean Petit, 'Memoire de Foulques de Villaret sur la Croisade', *Bibliotheque de l'École des Chartes*, 60 (1899), 602–610; For an English translation of Fulk of Villaret's Memorandum see Norman Housley, trans., *Documents on the Later Crusades, 1274–1580* (Basingstoke: Macmillan, 1996), 40–47; *Cartulaire general de l'ordre des Hospitaliers de St Jean de Jerusalem 1100–1310*, ed. J. Delaville Le Roulx, 4 vols. (Paris: Leroux, 1894–1906), no. 4681 [hereafter *Cartulaire*]; James of Molay, 'Concilium super negotio Terre Sancte', in *VPA*, iii, 150–154.
53 Petit, *Memoire*, 604; For accounts of Pope Urban's II preaching of the First Crusade see Jonathan Riley–Smith, *The First Crusade and the Idea of Crusading* (London: Athlone, 1986); John H. E. Cowdrey, 'Pope Urban II's Preaching of the First Crusade', *History*, 55 (1970), 177–188.
54 Petit, *Memoire*, 605: 'Preterea quod dominus Papa, postquam Crucem predicaverit et fecerit que premittuntur, ordinet bonos viros clericos seculares aut religiosos, profecturos legatos per civitates [et] provincias quas fideles colunt, predicaturos eis Crucem, daturos indulgentias et dicturos terminum ac capitaneos pasagii per eundem modum per quem dominus Papa fecerit supradicta'.
55 Petit, *Memoire*, 609: 'Item quod dominus Papa mittat litteras sue potestatis quocumque terrarum per predicaturos Crucem, quod transfretare non volentes pro pecunia possint redimere votum suum'.
56 Petit, *Memoire,* 604, 605: 'Dominus noster Papa, ubicumque erit, predicabit Crucem, excitando et inducendos plebem Christi cum suis predicationibus ... prefigetque terminum quando passagium suum incipiet viaticum. Et in quantum tangit terminum, nobis videtur utile quod brevis terminus assignetur, quia in longis terminis plura

impedimenta interveniunt et objecta, et naturaliter homines fiunt animaciores et fervidiores cum suum habere propinque desiderium prestolantur'.

57 Leopold, *How to Recover the Holy Land*, 61–62.
58 Christopher Tyerman, *The Invention of the Crusades* (London: Palgrave Macmillan, 1998), 64; James B. MacGregor, 'The First Crusade in Late Medieval "Exempla"', *The Historian*, 68.1 (2006), 29–48, 36, 47.
59 Tyerman, *The Invention*, 64, 144.
60 Leopold, *How to Recover the Holy Land*, 84.
61 Leopold, *How to Recover the Holy Land*, 84–85.
62 'Prima Vita Clementis V', in *VPA*, i, 10, 15; 'Excerpta e memoriali historiarum, auctore Johanne Parisiensi, sancti Victoris Parisiensis canonico regulari', in *RHGF*, xxi, 650; 'Continuatio chronici Girardi de Fracheto', in *RHGF*, xxi, 32.
63 The second memoir put forward by the Hospitallers is part of a manuscript in Paris (BnF, MS lat. 7470, fols. 172^r–178^v) and published by Benjamin Kedar and Sylvia Schein as 'Un projet de passage particulier proposé par l'Ordre de l'Hôpital 1306–1307', *Bibliotheque de l'École des Chartes*, 137 (1979), 211–226, 220–226. The memorandum is undated, but textual evidence suggests it was written between September 1306 and early summer 1307 when Fulk of Villaret was in Cyprus. See Schein, *Fideles Crucis,* 219; Kedar and Schein, 'Un projet de passage particulier', 215.
64 Kedar and Schein, 'Un projet de passage particulier', 216; Schein, *Fideles Crucis*, 219.
65 Clement V, *Regestum*, nos. 2148, 2693, 2351, 2352, 2371, 2387, 2614, 4986, 7427; *Cartulaire*, no. 4751; Luttrell, 'The Hospitallers at Rhodes, 1306–1421', 285; Norman Housley, 'Pope Clement V and the Crusades of 1309–1310', *Journal of Medieval History,* 8 (1982), 29–43, 31; Kedar and Schein, 'Un projet de passage particulier', 212–214; All the 'De Recuperatione Terrae Sanctae' treatises of Clement V's pontificate lacked original ideas, as Schein shows. See Schein, *Fideles Crucis*, 200–218.
66 Clement V, *Regestum*, nos. 2988–2989; Kedar and Schein, 'Un projet de passage particulier', 216.
67 Kedar and Schein, 'Un projet de passage particulier', 218.
68 For Clement V's deliberations with potential candidates for the leadership of the crusade, see Schein, *Fideles Crucis*, 187–193; Menache, *Clement V*, 103.
69 Menache, *Clement V*, 105; Housley, 'Pope Clement V and the Crusades', 31; Riley-Smith, *The Knights of St John*, 201–202; Anthony Luttrell, 'The Hospitallers and the Papacy, 1305–1314', in *Studies on the Hospitallers after 1306: Rhodes and the West* (Aldershot: Ashgate Variorum, 2007), 595–622, 595; Allan Forey, 'The Military Orders in the Crusading Proposals of the Late 13th and Early 14th Centuries', in *Military Orders and Crusades* (Aldershot: Ashgate Variorum, 1994), 318–331, 325; Norman Housley, *The Avignon Papacy*, 261.
70 Luttrell, 'Hospitallers and the Papacy', 596; Housley, *Avignon Papacy*, 266.
71 Norman Housley, 'Cyprus and the Crusades, 1291–1571', in *Cyprus and the Crusades*, eds. N. Coureas and J. Riley-Smith (Nicosia: Cyprus Research Centre, 1995), 187–206, 197–198.
72 'Chronique du Templier de Tyr (1242–1310)', in *Les gestes des Chiprois, recueil de chroniques Françaises écrites en Orient aux XII*e *et XIV*e *siècles*, ed. G. Raynaud (Geneva: Sociètè de l'Orient Latin, 1887), 319–320.
73 Boniface VIII on 13 June 1298 refers to the levy that was made six years earlier, so 1292 *Bullarium Cyprium 2: Papal Letters Concerning Cyprus, 1261–1314,* ed. C. D. Schabel (Nicosia: Cyprus Research Centre, 2010), 228–231; *Les régistres de Boniface VIII*, ed. G. Digard (Paris: Bibliothèque des Écoles Françaises d'Athènes et de Rome, 1884–1939), no. 2609; Riley-Smith, *The Knights of St John*, 201, 204.
74 *Cartulaire*, nos. 4420, 4727–4728; Clement V, *Regestum*, nos. 1247–1248; *Bullarium Cyprium 2*, 317–319; Riley-Smith, *The Knights of St John*, 201, 204.
75 *Cartulaire*, no. 4467; *Bullarium Cyprium 2*, 245–254; Riley-Smith, *The Knights of St John*, 204.

Clement V's and John XXII's campaigns   55

76 For an extensive English summary and full text edition of the treaty's document see *Bullarium Cyprium 2*, 245–254.
77 Schein, *Fideles Crucis*, 154.
78 For Papal-Hospitallers relations during Clement V's pontificate see: Sophia Menache, 'The Hospitallers During Clement V's Pontificate: The Spoiled Sons of the Papacy?', in *The Military Orders: Welfare and Warfare*, eds. M. Barber and H. Nicholson (Aldershot: Ashgate, 2000), ii, 153–162.
79 On 27 June 1308, seventy-two Templars carefully selected by Philip IV confessed the offences committed by their Order before Clement. See Menache, *Clement V*, 218–227; Barber, *The Trial of the Templars*, 116–122.
80 Clement V, *Regestum*, no. 3400; Menache, *Clement V*, 225.
81 Clement V, *Regestum*, no. 2986.
82 Clement V, *Regestum*, nos. 2986–2988, 2991–92, 3010, 3616.
83 Clement V, *Regestum*, no. 2987: 'Dilectis filiis magistro et fratribus hospitalis sancti Iohannis Ierosolimitani. Dignum et congruum reputamus, ut eos, qui ad Christi obsequia prosequenda se conferunt, specialibus gratiis honoremus. Intendentes igitur, ut passagium, quod per vos in subsidium Terre sancte providimus faciendum, tanto libentius personarum ecclesiasticorum fulciatur auxilio, quanto magis persone ipse favorem sibi senserint gratiosum, vestris supplicationibus inclinati vobis auctoritate presentium indulgemus'.
84 'Annales Paulini', in *Chronicles of the Reigns of Edward I and Edward II*, i, 266; 'Hoc anno papa … concessit indulgentias culparum et poenarum quales a saeculo non erant auditae'; 'Continuatio Chronici Girardi de Fracheto', in *RHGF*, xxi, 32.
85 Guard, *Chivalry, Kingship and Crusade*, 23.
86 'Annales Paulini', 266: 'Eodem anno [1309], die Conversionis beati Pauli, venit Londonias episcopus Nazareth cum privilegio domini papae in subsidium terrae sanctae'.
87 ASV, Reg. Vat. 56, fols. 198ᵛ–199ʳ, ep. 967; ASV, Reg. Vat. 55, fol. 128ʳ [there is a brief summary of these letters in Clement V, *Regestum*, nos. 4772, 2992]; Clement V, *Regestum*, nos. 2986–2989, 2994–2997, 4392, 4769–4773; 'Annales Paulini', i, 266; 'Continuatio Florianensis', in *Monumenta Germaniae Historica: scriptores rerum Germanicarum. Nova Series*, eds. G. H. Pertz, *et al.*, 38 vols. (Hanover: Anton Hiersemann Reprint, 1983–), ix, 752 [hereafter MGH:S]; 'Excerpta e memoriali historiarum Johannis a sancto Victore', in *RHGF*, xxi, 653; Giovanni Villani, *Cronica di Giovanni Villani a miglior lezione ridotta*, ed. G. F. Dragomanni, 8 vols. (Florence: Per il Magheri, 1823), ii, 137.
88 Philip B. Baldwin, *Pope Gregory X and the Crusades* (Woodbridge: The Boydell Press, 2014); Schein, *Fideles Crucis*, 182; Maier, *Preaching the Crusades*, 93.
89 ASV, Reg. Vat. 56, fols. 198ᵛ–199ʳ, ep. 967, fol. 140ᵛ, ep. 682; Clement V, *Regestum*, nos. 2989–2990, 3614, 4392, 4773, 4769.
90 ASV, Reg. Vat. 56, fols. 198ᵛ–199ʳ, ep. 967: 'Dilectis filiis magistro Praedicatorum et generali ministro Minorum necnon et generalibus prioribus fratrum heremitarum sancti Augustini et sancte Marie carmeli ordinum'.
91 Maier, *Preaching the Crusades*, 39–76; Tyerman, *The Invention of the Crusades*, 63; d'Avray, *The Preaching of the Friars*, 21.
92 ASV, Reg. Vat. 56, fols. 198ᵛ–199ʳ: 'Et nichilominus omnes ecclesiasticas, seculares et regulares personas … et Predicatorum ac Minorum ordinum fratres … vestrarum civitatum et diocesium confessiones audiendi et proponendi verbum Crucis potestatem habentes iuxta datam a Deo prudentiam studeatis efficaciter exortari'; Clement V, *Regestum*, nos. 2989–2990, 2995, 4769–4773; *Cartulaire*, no. 4876; Riley–Smith, *The Knights of St John*, 224.
93 Clement V, *Regestum*, nos. 4392: 'Venerabili fratri Petro episcopo Ruthenensi, Apostolice Sedis legato … te pro huiusmodi Christi negotio ad hoc providimus deputandum fraternitati tue in Alexandrino, Anthioceno et Ierosolimitano patriarchatibus necnon in regni Cipri adque Armenie minoris et insuli Rodi plene legationis officium

commictentes, ut auctore Domino evangelizes pro Christo populis verbum Crucis', 4494, 4496; *Bullarium Cyprium 2*, 366–369; Girolamo Golubovich, *Biblioteca Bio–Bibliografica della Terra Santa e dell'Oriente Francescano*, 5 vols. (Florence: Quaracchi, 1906–1927), iii, 128; Luttrell, 'The Hospitallers at Rhodes', 285; Riley-Smith, *The Knights of St John*, 223.

94 Golubovich, *Biblioteca Bio–Bibliografica*, iii, 131; *Annales Ecclesiastici*, xxiii, 446–447; 'Quarta Vita Clementis V', in *VPA*, i, 67; 'Sexta Vita Clementis V', in *VPA*, i, 98; 'Chronicon Auctore Bernardo Guidonis, Episcopo Lodovensi', in *RHGF*, xxi, 719.

95 *Bullarium Cyprium 2*, 371–372: 'Cum te etc. usque destinemus, et in desideriis nostris geratur ut, summotis impedimentis quibuslibet, huiusmodi negotia prosperum consequantur effectum, assumendi auctoritate nostra quandocumque et quotcumque volueris ex dilectis filiis fratribus Predicatorum et Minorum ac aliorum ordinum quorumcumque tue lagationis et partium vicinarum quos utiles fore prospexeris ad executionem officii prelibati'.

96 Clement V, *Regestum*, nos. 2989: 'Ideoque fraternitatem vestram monemus et hortamur in filio Dei patris vobis nichilominus in virtute obedientie districte precipiendo mandantes, quatinus tenorem et formam indulgentiarum huiusmodi Christi fidelibus eis proposito verbo Crucis singulis dominicis et festivis et aliis diebus, de quibus expediens fieri, in ecclesiis et locis vestrarum civitatum et diocesium in missarum solempniis et aliis horis congruentibus publicetis ac per rectores ecclesiarum et Predicatorum ac Minorum ordinum fratres et alios religiosos et personas ecclesiasticas earundem civitatum et diocesium in eisdem solemniis et horis faciatis solicite in vulgari cuiuslibet patrie publicari'.

97 ASV, Reg. Vat. 56, fols. 198ᵛ–199ʳ: 'Verum sicut nuper non sine mentis turbatione percepimus, nonnulli ex eis, quos increpandos exinde graviter fore conspicimus, in effusione orationum huiusmodi se reddunt nimis tepidos et remissos'; Clement V, *Regestum*, no. 4769.

98 Menache, *Clement V*, 298–299.

99 ASV, Reg. Vat. 56, fols. 198ᵛ–199ʳ, ep. 967: 'multi tamen vestrum [Predicatorum et Minorum ordinum fratres] pro ut omnino sine mentis turbatione precepimus ad exequendum exhortationis et publicationis huius pium opus exhibent se nimis negligentes, tepidos et remissos'.

100 This is pointed out in Housley, *The Avignon Papacy*, 84; Menache, *Clement V*, 82.

101 Housley, *The Avignon Papacy*, 85; *Diplomatarium Veneto–Levantinum*, v, 59–60: 'tunc nobis non liceret, durante vel imminente evidenter guerra, regnum dimittere, cum ad regis et regni defensionem simus astricti, et simus homo ligius regis Francie et per regni ratione comitatus Andegauensis, cui paritas est annexa'; Housley, *The Later Crusades*, 428.

102 *Cartulaire*, nos. 4831, 4841, 4860; Clement V, *Regestum*, nos. 3988–3991.

103 *Acta Aragonensia: Quellen zur Deutschen, Italienischen, Französischen, Spanischen, zur Kirchen–und Kulturgeschichte aus der Diplomatischen Korrespondenz Jaymes II (1291–1327)*, ed. H. Finke, 3 vols. (Berlin–Leipzig, 1908–1922), iii, no. 27, 207–211: 'Et licet passagio, quod dicti magister et fratres prosequi dinoscuntur, per concessionem a nobis faciendam de similibus indulgentiis'; Anthony Luttrell, 'The Aragonese Crown and the Knights Hospitallers of Rhodes: 1291–1350', *The English Historical Review*, 76 (1961), 1–19; Housley, 'Pope Clement V and the Crusades', 28–32.

104 Thanks to Timothy Guard's scrupulous research of the English diocesan registers it became evident the Hospitaller expedition received extensive promotion from the English diocesan clergy. Guard, *Chivalry, Kingship and Crusade*, 23–24, note 7.

105 Housley, *The Italian Crusades*, 115.

106 Maier, *Preaching the Crusades*, 4.

107 Petit, *Memoire*, 604.

108 ASV, Reg. Vat. 56, fols. 198ᵛ–199ʳ, ep. 967: 'et si quando aliqua circa ipsius passagii negotium ac exhortationem et publicationem huius proponere ipsos contingat illa sub

tali verborum levitate percurrunt, quod nullum in audientium cordibus circa passagium ipsum imprimunt devotionis affectum'; Clement V, *Regestum*, nos. 4769, 4392; *Cartulaire*, no. 4864.
109 Maier, *Preaching the Crusades*, 122.
110 Clement V, *Regestum*, nos. 2989, 2990.
111 'Quarta Vita Clementis V', in *VPA*, i, 68–69; 'Sexta Vita Clementis V', in *VPA*, i, 99.
112 Clement V, *Regestum*, nos. 3626, 3628–3629; *Conciliorum Oecumenicorum Decreta*, ed. J. Alberigo (Bologna: Istituto per le Scienze Religiose, 1972), 333; 'Secunda Vita Clementis V', in *VPA*, i, 31; *Annales Ecclesiastici*, xxiii, 407; Schein, *Fideles Crucis*, 221.
113 Clement V, *Regestum*, no. 6293.
114 *Conciliorum Oecumenicorum*, 333; Schein, *Fideles Crucis*, 239.
115 Clement V, *Regestum*, nos. 3626, 3628–3629.
116 For the Templar's interrogation and the reading of their depositions during the Council of Vienne see Anne Gilmour-Bryson, '"Vox in excelso' Deconstructed. Exactly What Did Clement V Say?' in *On the Margins of Crusading: The Military Orders, the Papacy and the Christian World*, ed. H. Nicholson (Farnham: Ashgate, 2011), 83–88; George Lizerand, *Clément V et Philippe IV le Bel* (Paris: Librairie Hachette, 1910), 312–323.
117 'Prima Vita Clementis V', in *VPA*, i, 19: 'Dicitur a pluribus quod pro exorquenda pecunia concilium fuit factum'; Schein, *Fideles Crucis*, 248; Menache, *Clement V*, 112.
118 *Les Grandes chroniques de France*, viii, 285–287; *Continuatio chronici Girardi de Fracheto*, in *RHGF*, xxi, 37; *Continuatio chronicis Guillelmi de Nangiano*, i, 389–392; 'Prima Vita Clementis V', in *VPA*, i, 19–20; *Chronique métrique de Godefroy de Paris*, ed. J. A. Buchon (Paris: Imprimerie d'Hippolyte Tilliard, 1827), 171–175; Franz Ehrle, 'Zur Geschichte des Päpsteichen Hofceremoniells im 14 Jahrhundert', *Archiv Für Literatur und Kirchengeschichte des Mittelalters*, 5 (1889), 565–600.
119 *Les Grandes chroniques de France*, viii, 286; *Continuatio chronici Girardi de Fracheto*, in *RHGF*, xxi, 37; *Continuatio chronicis Guillelmi de Nangiano*, i, 391; 'Prima Vita Clementis V', in *VPA*, i, 19; Franz Ehrle, 'Zur Geschichte des Päpsteichen Hofceremoniells im 14 Jahrhundert', 577–578; Menache, *Clement V*, 115.
120 Ehrle, 'Zur Geschichte des Päpsteichen Hofceremoniells im 14 Jahrhundert', 578.
121 Clement V, *Regestum*, nos. 8781–8783, 9983; Menache, *Clement V*, 115; Housley, 'Pope Clement V and the Crusades', 41.
122 Jocelyn N. Hillgarth, *Ramon Lull and Lullism in Fourteenth Century France* (Oxford: Clarendon Press, 1971), 127–128; Leopold, *How to Recover the Holy Land*, 34–35; Schein, *Fideles Crucis*, 248.
123 Leopold, *How to Recover the Holy Land*, 35; Schein, *Fideles Crucis*, 249; Menache, *Clement V*, 114.
124 Leopold, *How to Recover the Holy Land*, 35; Schein, *Fideles Crucis*, 249–250.
125 Leopold, *How to Recover the Holy Land*, 36; Schein, *Fideles Crucis*, 203, 212–213; Menache, *Clement V*, 114.
126 William Le Maire, 'Livre de Guillaume le Maire', ed. C. Port, in *Mélanges historiques: Choix de documents*, 2 (1877), 206–569, 474; Leopold, *How to Recover the Holy Land*, 36–37; Schein, *Fideles Crucis*, 250–251.
127 William Le Maire, 'Livre de Guillaume le Maire', 474: 'Idcirco mihi videtur, quod ex nunc prefigandus esset terminus passagii generalis ad decem vel duodecim annis, prout ipsi domino summo pontifici et aliis sapientibus videretur, et quod interim crux per prelatos et alios viros ydoneos per totam christianitatem predicaretur efficaciter et ferventer, concessa cruce signandis indulgencia copiosa'; Leopold, *How to Recover the Holy Land*, 36–37; Schein, *Fideles Crucis*, 250–251.
128 William Le Maire, 'Livre de Guillaume le Maire', 475: 'Item, quod omnibus elemosinas et subsidia prebentibus ad subsidium et liberatione Terre Sancte conferret dominus noster talem indulgentiam et tantum, qualem concessit Pictavis pro Hospitalariis'.
129 Clement V, *Regestum*, nos. 8781–8783, 9983; *Conciliorum Oecumenicorum*, 333.
130 Schein, *Fideles Crucis*, 246.

131 For discussion, see Schein, *Fideles Crucis*, 248; Menache, *Clement V*, 116.
132 For the Franco-papal crusade negotiations in the first thirty-six years of the fourteenth century see Christopher Tyerman, 'The French and the Crusades, 1313–1336' (DPhil diss., University of Oxford, 1981); Norman Housley, 'The Franco–Papal Crusade Negotiations of 1322–23', *Papers of the British School at Rome*, 48 (1980), 166–185.
133 'Quarta Vita Clementis V', in *VPA*, i, 61; *Annales Ecclesiastici*, xxiii, 369; Menache, *Clement V*, 83; Mollat, *The Popes at Avignon*, 6.
134 Clement V, *Regestum*, no. 9941: 'Dilecto filio Nicolao tit. Sancti Eusebii presbytero cardinali apostolice sedis nuntio ... Ad personam itaque tuam, quam dicto regi gratam credimus ac acceptam, nostre mentis oculos dirigentes illam, cuius nobis sunt note virtutes, quamve in magnis et arduis dicta sedes diversis vicibus est experta et de cuius operibus virtuosis fructus utiles provenisse conspicimus, ad imponendum eiusdem vivifice crucis signum regi, filiis, fratribus, baronibus et militibus supradictis nec non et quibuslibet tam de dicto regno, quam ad illud venientibus undecunque signum recipere volentibus supradictum et alias ad ipsius predicationis officium in regno predicto, que tibi presentium auctoritate committimus', nos. 9942–9963 (summaries).
135 ASV, Reg. Aven. 48, fols. 432^r–433^v: 'ad imponendum Crucis signum Philippo, regi Francie'; Clement V, *Regestum*, no. 9941: 'huiusmodi tibi onus devote suscipiens et personaliter ad regnum te conferens supradictum et in hiis iuxta datam tibi a Deo prudentiam procedens efficaciter et prudenter illa per te et alios, quos ad hoc ydoneos esse putaveris, presertim archiepiscopos et episcopos dicti regni, qui quidem archiepiscopi et episcopi etiam aliis, dum tamen ydoneis hec commitere valeant, exequi studeas diligenter'; ASV, Reg. Vat. 60, fols. 271^v–272^r: 'huius negotia prosperum sortiantur effectum iniungendi huius negotiorum tua prosecutione durante Predicatorum et Minorum ac quorumcumque aliorum ordinum fratribus ubicumque per regnum predictum constitutis quemcumque prosecutionem predictorum negotiorum videns expedire'.
136 ASV, Reg. Aven. 48, fol. 433^v; 'ad quemcumque volueritis loca ydonea et ibidem verbum crucis proponendi'.
137 Clement V, *Regestum*, no. 9942 (summary); Baldwin, *Pope Gregory X and the Crusades*, 137–142.
138 For the involvement of Philip IV in crusading, see Schein, 'Philip IV and the Crusades: A Reconsideration', 121–126.
139 *Annales Ecclesiastici*, xxiiii, 28–29; *Chronographia regum Francorum*, ed. H. Moranvillé, 3 vols. (Paris: Société de l'Histoire de France, 1891–1897), i, 233, 235, 237–242; 'Prima Vita Joannis XXII', in *VPA*, i, 108–110, 118–119.
140 For further details, see Georges Duby, *France in the Middle Ages 987–1460: From Hugh Capet to Joan of Arc* (London: Wiley-Blackwell, 1993); Elizabeth Hallam and Judith Everard, *Capetian France, 987–1328* (London and New York, 2001).
141 'Excerpta e Memoriali Historiarum, Auctore Johanne Parisiensi, Sancti Victoris Parisiensis Canonico Regulari', in *RHGF*, xxi, 659; 'Thomae Walsingham Quondam Monachi S. Albani Historia Anglicana', in *Rerum Britannicarum medii aevi scriptores*, ed. H. R. Thomas, 2 vols. (London: Longman, 1863–1864), i, 140–141 [hereafter *RBMAS*]; 'Johannis de Trokelowe Annales', in *RBMAS*, i, 84–85; 'Flores Historiarum', ed. H. R. Luard, in *RBMAS*, 3 vols. (London: Eyre and Spottiswoode, 1890), ii, 158–160; 'Prima Vita Joannis XXII', in *VPA*, i, 108; Andrea Ruddick, *English Identity and Political Culture in the Fourteenth Century* (Cambridge: Cambridge University Press, 2013). Christopher Tyerman, *England and the Crusades, 1095–1588* (London: University of Chicago Press, 1988), 244; Sophia Menache, 'The Failure of John XXII's Policy Towards France and England: Reasons and Outcomes, 1316–1334', *Church History*, 55.5 (1986), 423–437, 428.
142 For more details see 'Chronicon Parmense ab Anno 1038 usque ad Annum 1338', in *Rerum Italicarum scriptores: Raccolta degli storici Italiani dal cinquecento al millecinquecento*, ed. G. Carducci, *et al.*, 33 vols. (Città di Castello: Ex Typographia Societatis Palatinae in Regia Curia, 1900–1979), 9.9, 134–148 [hereafter *RIS*];

Giovanni Villani, *Cronica di Giovanni Villani a miglior lezione ridotta*, ed. G. F. Dragomanni, 8 vols. (Florence: Per il Magheri, 1823), ii, 188–198; Oscar Browning, *Guelph and Ghibellines: A Short History of Medieval Italy from 1250–1409* (London: Methuen and Co, 1893), 49–60; Carr, *Merchant Crusaders*, 57.

143 Peter Herde, 'From Adolf of Nassau to Lewis of Bavaria, 1292–1347', in *The New Cambridge Medieval History, c.1300–c.1415*, ed. M. Jones, *et al.*, 7 vols. (Cambridge: Cambridge University Press, 1995–), vi, 515–550, 537–538; David Nicholas, *The Evolution of the Medieval World: Society, Government and Thought in Europe, 312–1500* (London and New York: Longman, 1992), 620.

144 The Great Famine is reported by a great number of accounts throughout Europe: 'Excerpta e Memoriali historiarum', in *RHGF*, xxi, 662; 'Historia Anglicana', in *RBMAS*, i, 145–147; 'Johannis de Trokelowe Annales', in *RBMAS*, 92–94; 'Prima Vita Joannis XXII', in *VPA*, i, 114; *Chronographia Regum Francorum*, ii, 225; 'Continuatio Chronici Guillelmi de Nangiano', in *RHGF*, xx, 614; 'Annales Londonienses', in *Chronicles of the Reigns of Edward I and Edward II*, i, 236; 'Annales Paulini', in *Chronicles of the Reigns of Edward I and Edward II*, i, 279; 'Chronicon Parmense ab anno 1038 usque ad annum 1338', in *RIS*, ix.9, 143; Giovanni Villani, *Cronica*, ii, 198; 'Continuatio Chronici Girardi de Fracheto', in *RHGF*, xxi, 44–45; *Les Grandes chroniques de France*, ed. J. Viard, 10 vols. (Paris: Société de l'Histoire de France, 1920–1953), viii, 326; 'Fragment d'une chronique anonyme finnisant en M.CCC.XXVIII', in *RHGF*, xxi, 151; *Chronicon Galfridi le Baker de Swynebroke*, ed. E. Thompson (Oxford: Clarendon Press, 1889), 9; 'Adae Murimuth continuatio chronicarum', in *RBMAS*, ed. E. Thompson (London: Eyre and Spottiswoode, 1889), 24; 'Chroniques de Saint-Denis depuis 1285 jusqu'en 1328', in *RHGF*, xx, 698; Jordan W. Chester, *The Great Famine: Northern Europe in the Early Fourteenth Century* (Princeton: Princeton University Press, 1996); Jordan W. Jester, 'The Great Famine: 1315–1322 Revisited', in *Ecologies and economies in medieval and early modern Europe: studies in environmental history for Richard C. Hoffmann*, ed. S. G. Bruce (Boston 2010), 45–62; Michael Jones, 'The Last Capetians and Early Valois Kings, 1314–1364', in *The New Cambridge Medieval History*, vi, 388–421, 388; Carr, *Merchant Crusaders*, 56.

145 ASV, Reg. Vat. 63, fols. 4^v–5^r, ep. 14; John XXII, *Lettres secrètes & curiales du pape Jean XXII (1316–1334) relatives à la France*, eds. A. Coulon and S. Clémencet, 3 vols. (Paris: Bibliothèque des Écoles Françaises d'Athènes et de Rome, 3e séries, 1900–1967), i, no. 23 [hereafter John XXII, *Lettres ... Relatives à la France*]: 'felicis recordationis Clemens papa V, predecessor noster, statum miserabilem Terre Sancte pia meditatione considerans eique volens de oportuni succursus auxilio providere, decimam omnium ecclesiasticorum reddituum regni Francie convertendam in ipsius Terre Sancte subsidium'.

146 John XXII, *Lettres ... Relatives à la France*, no. 23: 'exigatur in dicte Terre subsidium et non in usus alios convertenda'.

147 John XXII, *Lettres ... Relatives à la France*, no. 27: 'fructus, redditus et proventus omnium beneficiorum ecclesiasticorum, cum cura vel sine cura, tam regularium quam secularium ... usque ad IIII annos inclusive vacare contigerit'.

148 John XXII, *Lettres ... Relatives à la France*, no. 29: 'clausula speciali de modo percipiendi fructus beneficiorum vacantium Philippo regenti concessos'.

149 Tyerman, *England and the Crusades*, 241.

150 John XXII, *Lettres ... Relatives à la France*, no. 74: 'Et quidem, fili, non te latet, cum fere sit orbi notorium, qualiter guerra illa Flandrie, procurante pacis emulo, satore zizanie, suscitata, dictum regnum tempore jam longo turbaverit que animarum pericula, quas strages corporum, quanta induxerit dispendia, ut jam idem regnum in se ipso videatur expertum, quod inimico familiari nulla pestis est efficatior ad nocendum... Nec ignoras qualiter gallicane potentie gladius in Christi blasphemos ad ipsius exaltationem fidei, et dilatationem christiani cultus limatus antea et acutus, propter commotionem et perturbationem hujusmodi habuit, pro(h)dolor, in effusionem christiani sanguinis acui et limari,

sic quod prefatus genitor tuus, qui, pie devotionis inflamatus affectus, ad ultramarinum an(h)elabat passagium personaliter prosequendum, circa prosecutionem guerre predicte distractus, intendere, dum vivebat predicto nequivit passagio, nec tu etiam qui ad passagium ipsum affici diceris, vivifice crucis signaculo propterea jamdudum assumpto'.

151 John XXII, *Lettres ... Relatives à la France*, no. 53: 'Gallicana potentia cujus auxilium post Deum singulariter expectat, et expectit Terra Sancta'; Norman Housley, *The Avignon Papacy*, 18.

152 John XXII, *Lettres ... Relatives à la France*, nos. 54–57, 67, 74–76, 189, 192, 196–199, 367, 706; *Chronographia regum Francorum*, ii, 233–242; *Les Grandes chroniques de France*, viii, 336; *Annales Ecclesiastici*, xxiv, 80–81; 'Prima Vita Joannis XXII', in *VPA*, i, 120–122.

153 Menache, 'The Failure of John XXII's Policy', 426–427.

154 John XXII, *Lettres ... Relatives à la France*, nos. 54–57, 67, 74–76, 189, 192, 196–199, 364, 366–367, 530, 667, 706, 800.

155 John XXII, *Lettres ... Relatives à la France*, no. 800: 'Quibus omnibus et singulis ac aliis etiam attendendis diligenter attentis, nos, pro bono concordie ac propter intensum desiderium et grandem affectum quem gerebamus et gerimus et regem ipsum gerere sine dubitatione supponimus ad ultramarinum passagium, quod ex discordia securitatum hujusmodi potest verisimiliter retardari'.

156 John XXII, *Lettres ... Relatives à la France*, no. 364: 'viderimus contra rebelles ipsos, et hostes ac impeditores dicti passagii'.

157 'Excerpta e memoriali historiarum', in *RHGF*, xxi, 667.

158 Menache, 'The Failure of John XXII's Policy', 434.

159 Tyerman, *England and the Crusades*, 229; Housley, *The Avignon Papacy*, 18; Menache, 'The Failure of John XXII's Policy', 433–434.

160 For more details on Peter of Pleine Chassagne's preaching in 1316 see Chapter 3. 'Continuatio Chronici Guillelmi de Nangiano', in *RHGF*, xx, 615–616; 'Chroniques de Saint-Denis depuis 1285 jusqu'en 1328', in *RHGF*, xx, 698–699; *Chronique Parisienne anonyme du XIVe siècle*, ed. A. Hellot (Nogent-Le-Rotrou: Société de l'histoire de Paris, 1884), 25–26; Paul Lehugeur, *Histoire de Philippe le Long, roi de France*, 2 vols. (Paris: Imprimerie Lahure, 1897), i, 196; Christopher Tyerman, 'Philip V of France, the Assemblies of 1319–20 and the Crusade', *Bulletin of the Institute of Historical Research*, 57 (1984), 15–34, 16, 22; Housley, *The Avignon Papacy*, 108–110.

161 Tyerman, 'Philip V and the Crusade', 17.

162 Paris, Archives de France, JJ 54A, fol. 14r, nos. 191–192.

163 *Chronique Anonyme Parisienne*, 27–28; Lehugeur, *Histoire de Philippe le Long*, i, 197; Tyerman, 'Philip V and the Crusade', 18.

164 Taylor, 'French Assemblies and Subsidy', 221. The Franco–Flemish treaty was signed on 22 August 1319 and was finally ratified in January 1320. See Lehugeur, *Histoire de Philippe le Long*, i, 152–155.

165 John XXII, *Lettres ... Relatives à la France*, no. 238a.

166 John XXII, *Lettres ... Relatives à la France*, nos. 471: 'duas juxta morem solitum integras decimas omnium ecclesiasticorum reddituum atque proventuum in regnis Francie et Navarre ac comitatu Burgundie, solvendas per triennium a proximo futuro festo Purificationis Virginis in antea continue numerandum', no. 505.

167 John XXII, *Lettres ... Relatives à la France*, nos. 512–515; John XXII, *Lettres communes du pape Jean XXII analysées d'après les registres dits d'Avignon et du Vatican*, ed. G. Mollat, 16 vols. (Paris: Bibliothèque des Écoles Françaises d'Athènes et de Rome, 3e séries, 1904–1947), no. 6664 [hereafter John XXII, *Lettres Communes*].

168 John XXII, *Lettres ... Relatives à la France*, no. 511: 'Porro ne Terre Sancte subsidium ad quod fervente afficimur et te indubie supponimus affici, sine aliquali remedio deserere videremur, actum invicem extitit, et tuo nomine acceptatum, quod ex causis tangentibus utilitatem prefati generalis ultramarine passagii et tuum concernentibus interesse particulare fieret passagium in presenti'.

169 John XXII, *Lettres ... Relatives à la France*, no. 531: 'mandavimus ut vos vel duo ex vobis quicquid collectum est, per vos aut deputatos a vobis, de decima pro generali ultramarino passagio per felicis recordationis Clementem papam V, predecessorem nostrum, imposita, pro anno videlicet preterito proxime, deductis inde primitus et retentis centum milibus florenorum in quoddam particulare passagium inter nos et gentes carissimi in Christo filii nostri Philippi, regis Francie et Navarre illustris, ordinatum pro Terre sancte subsidio fieri, convertendis, que deputandis super hoc a nobis vel apostolica Sede volumus exhiberi', nos. 672–673; John XXII, *Lettres Communes*, no. 6742.

170 *Titres de l'ancienne maison Ducale de Bourbon*, ed. M. Huillard–Bréholles, 2 vols. (Paris: Typographie de Henri Plon, 1867–1874), i, 259, no. 1509; 'notum facimus quod nos ipsum capitaneum, rectorem et gubernatorem generalem omnium dictorum gentium armorum quas ante dictum generale passagium per terram vel per mare duxerimus pro dicte Terre subsidio destinandas'; Housley, *The Avignon Papacy*, 21; Tyerman, 'Philip V and the Crusade', 19; Malcolm Barber, 'The Pastoureaux of 1320', *Journal of Ecclesiastical History*, 32 (1981), 143–166, 157.

171 John XXII, *Lettres ... Relatives à la France*, no. 983; John XXII, *Lettres Communes*, no. 10267; 'Excerpta e memoriali historiarum', in *RHGF*, xxi, 669; 'Prima Vita Joannis XXII', in *VPA*, i, 125–126; 'Continuatio chronici Guillelmi de Nangiano', in *RHGF*, xx, 624; Giovanni Villani, *Cronica*, ii, 219–221; 'Chroniques de Saint-Denis depuis 1285 jusqu'en 1328', in *RHGF*, xx, 702; Housley, *The Avignon Papacy*, 22; Tyerman, 'Philip V and the Crusade', 19; for the purchase and construction of galleys at Narbonne and Marseilles see Charles Bourel de la Ronière, 'Une Escadre Franco–papale (1318–1320)', *Mélanges d'archéologie et d'histoire*, 13 (1893), 397–418.

172 Housley, *The Italian Crusades*, 25–30, 79, 161, 254–255.

173 John XXII, *Lettres ... Relatives à la France*, nos. 1032, 933, 946, 1227, 667; 'tue beneplacitum voluntatis'; *Bullarium Cyprium 3*, eds. C. Perrat and J. Richard (in collaboration with Chris Schabel) (Nicosia: Cyprus Research Centre, 2012), 54, no. r–91.

174 John XXII, *Lettres ... Relatives à la France*, no. 513: 'Verum quia predictas decimas sic in tuum converti comodum cupimus quod eas prout assolet, in usus inutiles et extraordinarios non contingat expendi'.

175 See Philip V's letter of 8 October 1319 to knight Guy of Bauçay, Lord of Cheneché, calling for his presence at Paris on Christmas 1319 for 'finable deliberation sus le dit passage': *Archives historiques du Poitou*, eds. P. Guérin and C. Léonce, 14 vols. (Poitiers: Imprimerie Oudin, 1881–1958), xiii, 67–68; *Chronique Parisienne anonyme*, 43; Charles H. Taylor, 'The Composition of the Baronial Assemblies in France, 1315–1320', *Speculum*, 29.2 (1954), 433–459, 448; Tyerman, 'Philip V and the Crusade', 20; Barber, 'The Pastoureaux', 158.

176 The best analysis of crusade gathering in 1320 remains Tyerman's account on 'Philip V of France, the assemblies of 1319–1320 and the Crusade'. See also Taylor, 'The Composition of Baronial Assemblies in France, 1315–1320', 448–453.

177 For William Durand, Bishop of Mende, see Constantin Fasolt, *Council and Hierarchy: The Political Thought of William Durant the Younger* (Cambridge: Cambridge University Press, 1991); Leopold, *How to Recover the Holy Land*, 248–252; Tyerman, 'Philip V and the Crusade', 20–21.

178 Boislisle, 'Projet de Croisade du Premier Duc de Bourbon, 1316–1333', 246–255; *Chronique anonyme Parisienne*, 29–30; Tyerman, 'Philip V and the Crusade', 18, 21.

179 *Chroniques Gréco–Romanes*, ed. C. Hopf (Berlin: Imprimerie Gustave Schade, 1873), 167: 'che sapeva meglio metter guera, e discordia trà li Turchi infedeli, e lor Vicini, che tutti li Uomini del mondo'; Tyerman, 'Philip V and the Crusade', 23.

180 Tyerman, 'Philip V and the Crusade', 28–29.

181 Tyerman, 'Philip V and the Crusade', 26–27.

182 *Chronique anonyme Parisienne*, 43; 'ordonné de cesser de superfluitez ... et especialement dez princez de son royaulme et de tous ses seneschaux et balliz et tous aultrez officiers, et que guerres feussent ram[en]ez à paix'.
183 The peace issue as a prerequisite for the realization of a crusade to the Holy Land was the dominant idea in the papal correspondence with Philip V during the Franco-Flemish conflict. As for the management of the royal subsidies, it has been already noted above; see John XXII, *Lettres ... Relatives à la France*, no. 513.
184 *Les Grandes chroniques de France*, viii, 350–352; *Chronographia regum Francorum*, ii, 249–250; *Chronique anonyme Parisienne*, 49; Giovanni Villani, *Cronica*, ii, 226.
185 Tyerman, 'Philip V and the Crusade', 27.
186 *Chronique anonyme Parisienne*, 43: 'et yce leur dist begninement et devotement le roy à ce que la promesse Philippe le Beaux son pere, Louys son frere jadiz roy de France, et le voyage de la Terre sainte feussent faiz et accompliz'.
187 John XXII, *Lettres ... Relatives à la France*, no. 1262.
188 John XXII, *Lettres ... Relatives à la France*, no. 1262: 'volumus et quod, postquam passagium hujusmodi receperis in propria prosequendum persona et te ad id ut premittitur'.
189 John XXII, *Lettres ... Relatives à la France*, no. 1262: 'crux etiam universaliter predicabitur tam in tuis predictis quam aliis regnis et terris de quibus videbitur expedire. Preter hoc deputabuntur per Sedem predictam certe persone in omnibus regnis et partibus ad exigendum, levandum, colligendum et in loco tuto ponendum Omnia lega[ta] et relicta in testamentis seu ultimis voluntatibus occassione hujusmodi negotii transmarini. In singulis nichilominus ecclesiis singuli trunci concavi ponentur, certis clavibus consignati, in quibus oblationes et helemosine quas fideles in Terre Sancte subcidium fecerint reponantur, quorum omnium emolumenta ad arbitrium et ordinationem Ecclesie in subcidium dicti passagii convertentur; indulgentie quoque moderate et determinate dabuntur pro negotio memorato'. Moreover, John granted on the same day (05 June 1321) full remission of sins *in articulo mortis* in return for passing across the sea or contributing to the crusade by sending one warhorse every year. See ASV, Reg. Vat. 72, fols. 51^v, 53^r, eps. 852, 861; John XXII, *Lettres Communes*, nos. 13582, 13586. Mollat in his summaries from John XXII's *Lettres Communes* referred to the registers from Avignon, but I have been unable to read the manuscripts since folios 128^r and 130^r from in the register (Reg. Aven. 15) have been destroyed.
190 John XXII, *Lettres ... Relatives à la France*, no. 1262: 'supplicamus humiliter et precamur instanter ut dies tuos cum augmento felicitatis adaugeat'.
191 John XXII, *Lettres ... Relatives à la France*, nos. 1366–1367: 'hortatur ut Carolum regem, nepotis ejus, protegat et dirigat'.
192 Norman Housley, 'The Franco-Papal Crusade Negotiations of 1322–3', *Papers of the British School at Rome*, 48 (1980), 166–185, 166.
193 John XXII, *Lettres ... Relatives à la France*, no. 1431; Housley, 'The Franco–Papal Crusade Negotiations', 168–169.
194 John XXII, *Lettres ... Relatives à la France*, no. 1487: 'de casu flebili Armenie'.
195 John XXII, *Lettres ... Relatives à la France*, nos. 1487, 1562: 'primo de numero personarum tam pedestrium quam equestrium quem Vestra Sanctitas in hoc particulari passagio disposuerit transfretari. Secundo, de aparamentis; qualia, quanta, quando et ubi fient. Tertio quo tempore quod volet precise, supposita possibilitate, illos quos disponet passagium facere, aggredi dictum iter. Quarto, quanto tempore volet hujusmodi transfretantes in prossequtione predicti negotii remanere; Quinto, an et quomodo Vestra Sanctitas providebit quod numerus, secundum Sanctitatis Vestre dispositionem inibi transmittendus, si quocumque casu ipsum, quod absit, contingeret defalcari, durante dicto tempore debeat integrari; Sexto, quando, qualiter et unde et quanta ministrabitur pecuniapro aparamentis dicto passagio necessariis ordinandis et pro habendis, sustenandis et retinendis personis toto tempore quo in prossequtione dicti negotii disposueritis ipsas esse, et pro ceteris pro dicto passagio necessariis vel etiam

oportunis pro toto predicto tempore faciendis'; Housley, 'The Franco–Papal Crusade Negotiations', 169.
196 ASV, Reg. Vat. 74, fols. 3ᵛ–5ᵛ, eps. 7–10; John XXII, *Lettres ... Relatives à la France*, nos. 1562, 1571–1573; John XXII, *Lettres Communes*, nos. 18089–18092, 18141–18149, 18174–18175.
197 John XXII, *Lettres ... Relatives à la France*, no. 1562: 'Carolum, regem Francie, rogat ut, ad exemplum fratris eius, negotium passagii transmarini assumat'.
198 John XXII, *Lettres ... Relatives à la France*, no. 513: 'verum quia predictas decimas sic in tuum converti comodum cupimus quod eas prout assolet, in usus inutiles et extraordinarios non contingat expendi'.
199 For details of John XXII's war against the Visconti in Milan see Giovanni Villani, *Cronica*, ii, 238–240; Norman Housley, *The Italian Crusades*, 25–28, 59; Housley, 'The Franco-Papal Crusade Negotiations', 170.
200 John XXII, *Lettres ... Relatives à la France*, no. 1562: 'cruxque universaliter predicaretur tam in suis quam aliis regnis et terris de quibus expediens videretur, et per Sedem eandem deputarentur in omnibus regnis et terris predictis certe persone ad exigendum et colligendum et in certo loco ponendum omnia legata et relicta facta dicti occasione negotii transmarini, et in singulis ecclesiis singuli trunci ponerentur in quibus reponerentur oblationes et helemosine fidelium que fierent pro dicto passagio, certis clavibus consignari, que omnia ad cognitionem et arbitrium Ecclesie convertentur in subcidium passagii memorati. Et insuper indulgentie moderate et determinate concederentur pro negotio prelibato'.
201 Henry Charles, *A History of Auricular Confession and Indulgences in the Latin Church*, 3 vols. (Philadelphia: Lea Brothers, 1896), iii, 145, 152–155; Jonathan Riley-Smith, *What Were the Crusades?* (London: Macmillan, 1977), 60–65.
202 John XXII, *Lettres ... Relatives à la France*, no. 1572: 'vos et quilibet vestrum, in vestris civitatibus et diocesibus, per vos et quosvis religiosos et seculares quos ad hoc ydoneos duxeritis deputandos, litteras hujusmodi [apostolicas], quotiens eas vobis exhiberi et presentari contigerit, reverenter recipere, ac illas et indulgentias ac remissiones et alia in eis contenta publice coram populo propter hoc convocando specialiter, cum expediens visum fuerit, diligenter legere et per verbum predicationis, juxta vobis a Deo prudentiam prestitam, publicare et vulgarisare curetis'.
203 Tyerman, *The Invention of the Crusades*, 71.
204 Harold E. Butler, trans., *The Autobiography of Gerald of Wales* (Woodbridge: The Boydell Press, 2005), 102.
205 Tyerman, *The Invention of the Crusades*, 70–71.
206 John XXII, *Lettres Communes*, nos. 18089–18092, 18141–18149, 18174–18175.
207 Housley, 'The Franco-Papal Crusade Negotiations', 171.
208 John XXII, *Lettres ... Relatives à la France*, no. 1683: 'nos, dictis periculis occurrere et predictorum regnorum securitati, et ne per mare eisdem infidelibus deferantur, ad impugnandum christianos, arma, ferrum, lig[n]amina, et pueri christiani quos, pro dolor, ad Christi fidem susceptam abnegandam et impugnandam, aliqui perfidi christiani venales exponunt, providere volentes, certum versus partes illas ob predicta, navium, galearum, et lignorum atque gentium numerum circa instantem mensem madii decrevimus destinare et dilectum atque fidelem militem consiliarium ac familiarem nostrum Amalricum, dominum et vicecomitem Narbonensem, quem etiam ad hoc propria accendit devotio, tanquam discretione preditum, in armis strenuum et expertum, zelo fidei accensum, fidelem et ydoneum capitaneum constituimus in predictis eique dilectum ac fidelem Berengarium Blanchi, admirallum nostrum maris, ad promptiorem et feliciorem expeditionem et executionem tradidimus predictorum'; Housley, 'The Franco-Papal Crusade Negotiations', 171.
209 John XXII, *Lettres ... Relatives à la France*, no. 1685; Housley, 'The Franco-Papal Crusade Negotiations', 171–172.
210 John XXII, *Lettres ... Relatives à la France*, nos. 1683, 1685.

211 John XXII, *Lettres ... Relatives à la France*, nos. 1684, 1710–1711; Housley, 'The Franco-Papal Crusade Negotiations', 171.
212 John XXII, *Lettres ... Relatives à la France*, nos. 1684, 1685; Housley, 'The Franco-Papal Crusade Negotiations', 173.
213 John XXII, *Lettres ... Relatives à la France*, nos. 1693–1709; for detailed analysis on the context of the cardinals' *consilia* on crusade see Housley, 'The Franco-Papal Crusade Negotiations', 173–178.
214 John XXII, *Lettres ... Relatives à la France*, nos. 1693–1709; Housley, 'The Franco-Papal Crusade Negotiations', 174.
215 John XXII, *Lettres ... Relatives à la France*, nos. 1693–1709; Housley, 'The Franco-Papal Crusade Negotiations', 178.
216 John XXII, *Lettres ... Relatives à la France*, no. 1686; Housley, 'The Franco-Papal Crusade Negotiations', 177.
217 John XXII, *Lettres ... Relatives à la France*, nos. 1687–1689; Housley, 'The Franco-Papal Crusade Negotiations', 178.
218 John XXII, *Lettres ... Relatives à la France*, nos. 1710–1711.
219 Housley, 'The Franco-Papal Crusade Negotiations', 179.
220 For Charles IV's economic considerations at that time see Norman Housley, 'Costing the Crusade: Budgeting for Crusading Activity in the Fourteenth Century', in *The Experience of Crusading I: Western Approaches*, eds. N. Housley and M. Bull (Cambridge: Cambridge University Press, 2003), 45–59, 48–50.
221 John XXII, *Lettres ... Relatives à la France*, nos. 1848, 1850; Housley, 'The Franco-Papal Crusade Negotiations', 181.
222 John XXII, *Lettres ... Relatives à la France*, no. 1894: 'Ludovico, comiti Clarimontis ... Hinc est quod, ut in primo generali vel particulari transmarino passagio pro dicte Terre sancte negotio per Sedem Apostolicam indicendo, possis convenientius ac honorabilius transfretare, xxv^m florenorum auri, colligenda de [h]elemosinis et legatis factis vel faciendis in regno Francie, certo tamen modo ipsa persolvendi in ipsis nequaquam habito, tibi liberabiter largimur'.
223 John XXII, *Lettres ... Relatives à la France*, no. 1895.
224 John XXII, *Lettres ... Relatives à la France*, nos. 2308–2310; John XXII, *Lettres Communes*, no. 22117; Carr, *Merchant Crusaders*, 95, 108. For the war of St Sardos see Giovanni Villani, *Cronica*, ii, 307; 'Adae Murimuth Continuatio Chronicarum', in *RBMAS*, 42; 'Thomae Walsingham quondam monachi S. Albani historia Anglicana', in *RBMAS*, 174–176; *Les Grandes chroniques de France*, ix, 31–37, 41–43.
225 'Continuatio chronici Guillelmi de Nangiano', in *RHGF*, xx, 641–643.
226 Norman Housley, *The Later Crusades: From Lyon to Alcazar 1274–1580* (Oxford: Oxford University Press, 1992), 33; For the Franco-Papal Crusade Negotiations of 1332–1333 see John XXII, *Lettres Communes*, nos. 61324–61327, 61299, 63871.
227 'Continuatio chronici Guillelmi de Nangiano', in *RHGF*, xx, 630.
228 John XXII, *Lettres ... Relatives à la France*, no. 2739; Christopher Tyerman, 'Philip VI and the Recovery of the Holy Land', *The English Historical Review*, 100.394 (1985), 25–52, 25–27; Housley, *The Avignon Papacy*, 23.
229 *Annales Ecclesiastici*, xxiiii, 478–480; Golubovich, *Biblioteca Bio–Bibliografica*, iii, 362–363; Jean Dunbabin, *A Hound of God: Pierre de la Palud and the Fourteenth–Century Church* (Oxford: Clarendon Press, 1991), 164–172; Housley, *The Avignon Papacy*, 23–24; Housley, *The Later Crusades*, 34; Tyerman, 'Philip VI and the Holy Land', 27.
230 *Chronique Latin de Guillaume de Nangis*, ii, 130–131: 'Hoc anno [1331] frater Petrus de Palude patriarcha Jerusalem, qui missus fuerat ad Soldanum ad sciendum utrum via posset inveniri qua Terra Sancta recuperaretur, rediens ad Johannem papam, deinde Philippo, regi Francie, in praesentia multorum praelatorum et baronum, relationem suam de obstinatione Soldani faciens, nimium voluntatem regis et baronum commo-

vit, ut quasi unanimiter concordarent pro recuperatione Terrae Sanctae transfretare'; *Les Grandes Chroniques de France*, ix, 130.
231 Tyerman, 'Philip VI and the Holy Land', 27, note 5.
232 John XXII, *Lettres ... Relatives à la France*, no. 4685; Eugène Déprez, *Le préliminaires de la Guerre de Cent Ans: La Papauté, la France et l'Angleterre (1328–1342)* (Paris: Albert Fontemoing, 1902), 85.
233 ASV, Reg. Aven. 40, fols. 88^r–89^r; ASV, Reg. Aven. 41, fols. 223^r–224^r; ASV, Reg. Vat. 101, fols. 2^v–3^r, ep. 6; John XXII, *Lettres Communes*, no. 58207; *Bullarium Ordinis Fratrum Praedicatorum*, eds. T. Ripoll and A. Brémond, 8 vols. (Rome: Ex Typographia Hieronymi Mainardi, 1728–1740), ii, 194–195.
234 John XXII, *Lettres Communes*, no. 58207: 'Petro, patriarche Ierosolimitano, ac universis archiepiscopis et episcopis per regnum Francie constitutis mandatur ut in singulis suis civitatibus et diocesibus verbum crucis publicare curent'; Housley, *The Avignon Papacy*, 23; Housley, *The Later Crusades*, 34; Joseph Delaville le Roulx, *La France en Orient au XIVe siècle: Expéditions du Maréchal Boucicaut* (Paris: Ernest Thorin, 1886), 86; Tyerman, 'Philip VI and the Holy Land', 27.
235 Déprez, *La Papauté, la France et l'Angleterre*, 83–88; Tyerman, 'Philip VI and the Holy Land', 28.
236 For details on the Franco-papal crusade negotiations of 1332–1333 see John XXII, *Lettres Communes*, nos. 61299, 61324–61327, 63871, 61455.
237 Tyerman, 'Philip VI and the Holy Land', 28.
238 Déprez, *La Papauté, la France et l'Angleterre*, 86; Tyerman, 'Philip VI and the Holy Land', 29.
239 John XXII, *Lettres Communes*, no. 61324; Tyerman, 'Philip VI and the Holy Land', 29.
240 John XXII, *Lettres Communes*, no. 61299; Tyerman, 'Philip VI and the Holy Land', 29.
241 'Quinta Vita Joannis XXII', in *VPA*, i, 174.
242 Paris, Bibliothèque Sainte Genevieve, MS 240, fols. 298^v–308^v; Paris, Bibliothèque nationale de France, MS lat. 3293, fols. 161rb–168rb; *Repertorium der Lateinischen Sermones des Mittelalters fur Die Zeit von 1150–1350*, ed. J. B. Schneyer, 11 vols. (Munster–Westfalen: Aschendorffsche Verlagsbuchhandlung, 1973–1995), iv, 766.
243 John XXII, *Lettres ... Relatives à la France*, no. 5207: 'cum igitur, fili carissime, ultramarinum generale passagium ad supplicem precum tuarum intantiam nuper de fratrum nostrorum consilio indicendum duxerimus, et te illius ac totius exercitus christiani qui auctore Domino transfretabit in ipso rectorem constituerimus et capitaneum generalem', nos. 5208–5227; John XXII, *Lettres Communes*, nos. 60792–60797, 61205, 61208, 61211–61212, 61241, 61234–61235, 61247.
244 John XXII, *Lettres ... Relatives à la France*, nos. 5210–5220: 'ac per universas mundi partes decimam ecclesiasticorum reddituum imposuimus sexannalem, colligendam sub certis modis et formis ac in utilitatem dicti passagii, Terre Sancte subsidium et alias contra infideles ac inimicos fidei convertendam'.
245 John XXII, *Lettres ... Relatives à la France*, nos. 5210, 5214, 5226–5227; John XXII, *Lettres Communes*, nos. 60781, 61241, 61234–61235, 61247; Golubovich, *Biblioteca Bio–Bibliografica*, iii, 364.
246 John XXII, *Lettres ... Relatives à la France*, no. 5210: 'quotienscunque populis ad hoc specialiter convocatis proposueritis verbum crucis unius anni et quadraginta dierum, hec non fidelibus ipsis qui ad verbum huiusmodi audiendum devote convenerint centum dierum, vere tamen penitentibus et confessis, indulgentiam elargimur. Volumus autem quod omnes qui signum crucis huiusmodi hactenus in dicte Terre subsidium receperunt ... et cum dicto rege huiusmodi passagium personaliter prosequente in eiusdem Terre Sancte succursum ad recuperationem ipsius transfretaverint plenam suorum peccaminum indulgemus', nos. 5211–5216, 5224–5227; John XXII, *Lettres Communes*, nos. 61205, 61208, 61211–61212, 61241, 61234–61235, 61247; Riley-Smith, *What Were the Crusades?*, 60–65.

247 John XXII, *Lettres ... Relatives à la France*, no. 5269: 'Verum quia, sicut accepimus, prefatus rex et cum eo multi duces, comites, barones et nobiles pluresque alie diversorum conditionum persone intendunt breviter et intense desiderant pretextu dicti passagii Crucis caractere insigniri, nos, considerantes personam tuam gratam existere ipsi regi, et indubitanter sperantes quod sermonem tuum et ministerium idem rex et alii supradicti ad fructum devotionis et gratiam seu effectum exauditionis admittent, auctoritate tibi presentium committimus et mandamus quatinus quando et ubi per regem ipsum super hoc fueris requisitus, sibi et aliis supradictis verbum Crucis juxta datam tibi a Deo prudentiam ferventer proponas et eorum humeris ipsius Crucis signaculum imponas, nichilominus quoque per totum regnum predictum generaliter tibi committimus predicande concedendeque Crucis officium per temetipsum dumtaxat extra tuam diocesim exequendum'.

248 *Les Grandes chroniques de France*, ix, 133–134; *Chronique Latin de Guillaume de Nangis*, i, 135; *Chronique Parisienne anonyme*, 154; *Chronique des quatre premiers Valois (1327–1393)*, ed. S. Luce (Paris: Société de l'histoire de France, 1862), 6; *Chronographia regum Francorum*, ii, 19; 'Quinta Vita Joannis XXII', in *VPA*, i, 174; Déprez, *La Papauté, la France et l'Angleterre*, 99; Delaville le Roulx, *La France en Orient*, 87; Housley, *The Avignon Papacy*, 24; Housley, *The Later Crusades*, 33; Dunbabin, *A Hound of God*, 177; Tyerman, 'Philip VI and the Holy Land', 30. For the 1333 preaching of the crusade in Cyprus see Nicholas Coureas, *The Latin Church in Cyprus, 1313–1378* (Nicosia: Cyprus Research Center, 2010), 98–99.

249 Tyerman, 'Philip VI and the Holy Land', 34–35.

250 For the negotiations, the agreement for the formation of the naval league of 1334 and the events that followed its creation between May–September 1334, see John XXII, *Lettres ... Relatives à la France*, nos. 5247, 5276, 5324; Delaville le Roulx, *La France en Orient*, 88–102; Déprez, *La Papauté, la France et l'Angleterre*, 100–106; Paul Lemerle, *L'Émirat d'Aydin, Byzance et l'Occident. Recherches sur 'La Geste d'Umur Pacha'* (Paris: Bibliothèque Byzantine, 1957), 74–101; Kenneth M. Setton, *The Papacy and the Levant (1204–1571)*, 4 vols. (Philadelphia: The American Philosophical Society, 1976–1984), i, 178–182; Elizabeth A. Zachariadou, *Trade and Crusade: Venetian Crete and the Emirates of Menteshe and Aydin (1300–1415)* (Venice: Hellenic Institute of Byzantine and Post–Byzantine Studies, 1983); Housley, *The Avignon Papacy*, 25–27; Housley, *The Later Crusades*, 34, 57–59; Carr, *Merchant Crusaders*, 127–155; Angeliki Laiou, 'Marino Sanudo Torsello, Byzantium and the Turks: The Background to the Anti–Turkish League of 1332–1334', *Speculum*, 45.3 (1970), 374–392; Norman Housley, 'Angevin Naples and the Defense of the Latin East: Robert the Wise and the Naval League of 1334', *Byzantion*, 51.2 (1981), 548–556; Christopher Tyerman, 'Marino Sanudo Torsello and the Lost Crusade: Lobbying in the Fourteenth Century', *Transactions of the Royal Historical Society*, 32 (1982), 57–73; Tyerman, 'Philip VI and the Holy Land', 34–38; Nicholas Coureas, 'Cyprus and the Naval Leagues 1333–1358', in *Cyprus and the Crusades*, eds. N. Coureas and J. Riley–Smith (Nicosia: Cyprus Research Center, 1995), 107–124.

251 John XXII, *Lettres ... Relatives à la France*, no. 5210; Tyerman, 'Philip VI and the Holy Land', 30–31, 39.

252 The anonymous continuator of the Latin chronicle of William of Nangis characterized Pierre Roger as 'vir eloquentissimus'; *Chronique Latin de Guillaume de Nangis*, ii, 121.

253 John XXII, *Lettres ... Relatives à la France*, no. 5261.

2 Organising and implementing preaching campaigns under Benedict XII and Clement VI

Contra Agarenos verbum crucis predicari: The continuation of the 1334 naval league and the promotion of Philip VI's crusade – from initial support to final abandonment

The death of Pope John XXII on 4 December 1334 stalled both a second naval expedition in the Aegean, after the Christian victory at Adramyttion, and the promotion of Philip VI's crusade to the Holy Land. John's death deprived the crusade of an ardent proponent and a competent diplomat who had devoted significant resources and time to negotiations with the French Crown for the organization of a general crusade. On 20 December 1334, Jacques Fournier succeeded John XXII as Pope Benedict XII. Benedict was an entirely different sort of man than John and pursued different policies than his predecessor.[1] Benedict, an ascetic Cistercian, came from a rigorous monastic background, and on assuming the papacy his priorities were the eradication of heresy and the spiritual reform of the Church, rather than crusading.[2] Even before his elevation to the papal throne, Fournier put himself at the disposal of the Church against heresy, following the example of the prominent Cistercians of the thirteenth century.[3] While Bishop of Pamiers (1317–1326), Fournier had been strenuously engaged, as inquisitor, against the Cathars in Southern France.[4] Fournier became a member of the committee of theologians and canonists delegated to consider the heretical nature of practices resembling magic, and he was engaged by the papacy in the principal theological disputes against key figures of the 1320s.[5] Pope John XXII rewarded Fournier for his anti-heretical eagerness by consecrating him Cardinal-priest of Santa Prisca on 20 December 1327.[6] Such experiences significantly influenced Benedict's papacy and created a strong interconnection, for the pope, between crusading with Byzantium against the Turks in the Aegean, the union of the Churches and the unconditional acceptance of the principles and tenets of the Roman Church.[7] The papal registers provide clear evidence of Benedict's frequent interventions and efforts to eradicate such phenomena.[8] Like his predecessor, much of Benedict XII's pontificate was devoted to a battle against sorcery, necromancy and the invocation of the devil.

Immediately after his elevation to the Holy See, Pope Benedict XII had to contend with two outstanding issues pertaining to the crusade in the Eastern

Mediterranean. First, following the Christian victory at Adramyttion, the papacy had to participate in the continuation of the Christian league and the second phase of the anti-Turkish naval expedition, as John XXII had planned this offensive during the spring of 1334;[9] second, Benedict had to address the advanced Franco-papal crusade negotiations for the organization of the general passage of Philip VI to the Holy Land. For this reason, according to the historiographers of the French kings, the new pope summoned Philip VI to Avignon shortly after his election for counsel and deliberation.[10] In March 1336, Philip VI made direct contact with Benedict during his *tournée* in Southern France, when he visited Avignon.[11]

Benedict XII continued to support his predecessor's crusading policy. On 31 January 1335, with the bull *Ad eripiendum Terram Sanctam*, Benedict addressed all Christianity *pro passagio transmarino*, reaffirming what Pope John XXII had ordained, with the bull *Ad commemorandum recentius* on 26 July 1332, for Philip's crusade to the Holy Land.[12] From the very beginning of his papacy, Benedict assented to John's crusade planning and honouring the terms his predecessor had negotiated with Philip VI.[13] Benedict agreed with the College of Cardinals, which had assigned the king as rector and captain general of the Christian army; Philip had expressed his desire to go on crusade himself and had announced the *passagium generale*. Moreover, the pope confirmed the general levies on all ecclesiastical incomes and revenues for the crusade and ordered all archbishops and their suffragan bishops 'to preach to all believers of Christ the words of the cross against the Hagarenes with certain graces and the accustomed indulgences'.[14] Benedict commanded the high secular clergy to continue preaching the cross in their dioceses.

Despite Benedict XII's renewed commands to the secular clergy for the continuation of crusade preaching in February and April 1335, the priesthood presumably never reached the level of enthusiasm and intensity it needed to conduct a successful campaign.[15] The response to crusade preaching was tepid, and some prelates were indifferent to the celebration of Holy Land Masses *in promovendo passagio transmarino*.[16] At the provincial council held at the abbey of Notre-Dame-du-Pré near Rouen in September 1335, Archbishop Pierre Roger, who was responsible for the conduct of crusade preaching in France, denounced the secular clergy for its lack of enthusiasm and for its disinterest in the promotion of the crusade. Addressing his suffragan bishops, the Archbishop of Rouen stressed:

> Again, now the majority of the prelates, chapters, and rectors of churches render themselves negligent in the promotion of the urgent holy overseas passage, which the lord king of the French assumed, neither performing the Masses assigned by the Apostolic See to be celebrated once a week for the pursuit of the same holy passage, nor exhorting the people to pray and to offer assistance as was enjoined by apostolic letters.

The council urged the diocesan bishops 'to manifest, they themselves or by others, the penalties and indulgences granted for the same holy passage, and more often to preach over this'.[17] Apart from the failure of the major part of the clergy to carry out their crusade preaching duties and the dearth of passion and excitement for its conduct, Benedict XII had to face still another impediment to his effort to continue his predecessor's crusade planning. In June 1335 the pope made a slight indication of clerical opposition to the payment of the crusade tenth imposed by John XXII;[18] this opposition slowed the flow of money for Philip's general passage, making the August 1336 date of its dispatch seem even more challenging.

Alarmed by clerical disobedience, on 17 December 1335, Benedict issued new commands directing the attention of all patriarchs, archbishops and bishops to Philip's crusade.[19] Benedict XII reminded the high clergy of Philip VI's assignment as rector and captain general of the Christian army, an assignment that had been made after Philip informed Pope John XXII of his intention to personally rescue the Holy Land. Once again Benedict referred to the designation of 1 August 1336 as the terminus designated by the King for crossing the sea, along with the other crusaders, and those who, by then, were to take the cross.[20] The pope stressed the need for more frequent and fruitful conduct of crusade preaching and the granting of indulgences.[21] In December 1335, following the orders commanded by Pope John XXII, Benedict wrote:

> By the counsel of his brothers, through apostolic writings [Pope John XXII] commissioned and ordered our reverend brothers the patriarchs, archbishops, and certain bishops in every part of the world ... by themselves and other ecclesiastical persons, secular and regular of all Orders, whom they know to be suitable for this, to preach publicly the word of the cross to all Christ's faithful in their cities and dioceses according to the prudence granted to them by God, and to grant the venerable sign of the cross to those believers who are devotedly willing to take it, whom they believe to be useful to this, placing it upon their shoulders.[22]

With the disinclination of the local clergy in mind, Benedict decided that all preachers '*fideliter laborantibus ad predicationem crucis*' would be granted partial indulgences.[23] The papacy was clearly dependent on the willingness of the clergy to propagate the crusade, and any clerical recalcitrance would impede such a task.[24] In its effort to induce the churchmen to take their place at the pulpit, the papacy made use of indulgences for preaching. Crusade indulgences for those tasked with preaching were first introduced in 1252 by Pope Innocent IV during the preaching campaign for the crusade against Alphonse of Poitiers.[25] This became general practice after Innocent IV's death and especially during the preaching of the crusades to the Holy Land under Urban IV in the early 1260s and during the reign of Clement IV at the end of the decade.[26] Thomas Aquinas argued that crusade preaching, as a form of action, had a purely spiritual nature, and that anyone who took on this duty deserved indulgences.[27] To promote Philip VI's crusading plans, Benedict XII, according to John's bull, *Ad commemorantum recentius*, granted one-year and forty-day indulgences – partial remission of penalties as a consequence of sin – to all crusade preachers as spiritual reward for their contribution; to attract audiences, the pope gave crusade preachers the power to grant 100-days indulgence for attending a crusade sermon, a practice initiated during the papacy of Pope Innocent III, while plenary remission of sins was granted to those ready to cross the sea for the East.[28] Having been granted indulgences and the power to grant indulgences to their audiences, the secular and regular clergy began to preach the crusade in and beyond the French kingdom.

The pope urged the clergy to give the cross only to those who would be appropriate participants in a crusade to the Holy Land, which is rather odd, since the papal orders pertained to a preaching campaign for a *passagium generale*.[29] The papacy normally impeded general participation in the crusade by forbidding people from setting off during the planning of a *passagium particulare*, a small-scale crusading expedition for which expertise in warfare was required, but even in such cases the papacy made it possible for those without military experience to contribute. Even so, Benedict did not announce any liturgical measures for the clergy during their crusade preaching that might forbid those the Church deemed inappropriate from following Philip VI across the sea.

It is likely the pope wanted to exclude general participation in a general passage because of popular reaction to previous papal summonses for crusading. The Avignon papacy twice experienced great eruptions of popular crusading zeal following proclamations of general crusade preaching, in 1309 and in 1320.[30] In both instances, the zeal evolved into frenzy, which was deleterious to normal crusade preparations, and Benedict most probably wanted to avoid a similar reaction to the preaching for Philip VI's crusade. The papacy would find, however, that it could not control people's crusading sentiments, a lesson it learned quite painfully a decade later during the preaching for the Smyrna crusade.

In tandem with the propagation of Philip VI's crusade, Pope Benedict proceeded with arrangements for the implementation of the second phase of the anti-Turkish naval league, which had been founded with the consent and assistance of Pope John XXII in May 1334.[31] On 20 March 1335, Benedict informed King Robert of Naples that France, Venice and the Hospitallers, who had already sent agents to the papal curia, wished to continue their maritime cooperation for the defence of the '*Christicolis partium Romanie*'.[32] Soon thereafter, the pope announced the hiring of four galleys at Marseilles with complete arms for the needs of the league; in early April he wrote to William of Bos, provost in the diocese of Friuli and clerk in the apostolic camera, requesting 6,900 gold florins for the squadron's expenses;[33] a month later he offered another 4,600 gold florins for the same purpose.[34]

On 20 April 1335, the pope granted indulgences and other privileges to the crusaders, and offered a plenary remission of sins '*in articulo mortis*'. As Housley suggests, these kinds of plenary indulgences were regularly conceded by the papacy as a form of spiritual reward for military service against infidels and heretics and even against Avignon's lay rivals in Italy.[35] According to Benedict XII, the indulgence '*in articulo mortis*' would be granted at the moment of death after the recipient had demonstrated his loyalty and devotion to the mother Church and a priest had heard his confession;[36] when papal pleas for military action were urgent, and circumstances did not permit prolonged, full-scale crusade preaching campaigns, the curia made such spiritual concessions. Although the concession of these spiritual rewards became particularly frequent following the death of John XXII, the Church limited the concession of this kind indulgences to the systematic recruitment of crusaders;[37] thus indulgences for fighting the infidels in the East should be examined in the context of Benedict's willingness to promote Philip VI's crusade at the outset of his papacy.

The papal galleys, supplemented by five French warships, were to embark from Marseilles in mid-May to patrol the Aegean through October.[38] From Benedict's letters, dated 14 May 1335, to William of Bos and to the four owners of the galleys engaged in the service of the papacy, it became apparent, however, that the Franco-papal fleet was still docked at Marseilles as of the fourteenth.[39] In February 1336, Philip VI commanded his captain, Hugh Quiéret, to lead the French fleet, including the papal galleys, in a naval battle against the English in support of the Scots, which confirms that the fleet never embarked for the East.[40] There is no evidence that explains why the fleet's five-month service in the Aegean never took place, and the 1336 diversion of the French galleys to the war against Edward III was a decisive blow to the hopes of the West, after the success at Adramyttion, for the reconstitution of the anti-Turkish Christian armada in the Aegean.

Aware of the precarious situation between England and France, Pierre Roger, while preaching the crusade at the royal court before Philip VI and a great many Parisians in July 1335, told the assemblage that any French attack upon England would delay the departure of the crusade.[41] Philip's decision to divert the galleys to the war against England hurt Benedict XII's efforts to pacify Europe, one of the chief objectives of his overall policy, and stalled the preparatory stage of the *passagium generale*. At the beginning of his reign, Benedict had adopted a conciliatory attitude towards the different lay rulers of Europe to help them reach a clear consensus and bring peace to the region.[42] In March 1335, the pope exhorted Edward III of England to send John Stratford, Archbishop of Canterbury, to the royal court at Paris for the arrangement of peace between the two kingdoms.[43] Considering that peace among the European powers was a *sine qua non* for the crusade's implementation, Benedict had every reason to continue pursuing peace in Europe. Once Benedict realized the lay powers of Europe were not disposed to set aside their rivalries for the crusade to the East, he had little reason to insist: on 13 March 1336, the pope informed the French king of his dispensation from his crusade vows and any associated obligations, and he announced the cancellation of all preparations for the *passagium generale*.[44] The pope justified his decision thus:

> Because the aforesaid passage would be happily pursued with harmony among all the Christians, so that for the said passage all should abstain from wars and hostilities through the way of peace and harmony or truces, ceasing the commotions of wars and hostilities among the fellows of the Christian faith and it would be possible to propitiate more conveniently and more easily the favour of God against the enemies of the cross with which it would succeed in averting the enemy of the human race, the rival of peace and the inciter of vileness in [gaining] little and insignificant profit. Thus, as the evidence shows, England

and Scotland are divided from each other, also the dangerous situation in Germany is not devoid of wars, similarly the situation is hazardous in Tuscany and Lombardy, more threatening in Apulia and Sicily, with serious and almost continuous war flourishing between them, and several other hidden hostilities against you and your kingdom.[45]

The passage illustrates Benedict's failure to create harmony among the Western courts, a precondition for crusading in the East. That the pacification of Christianity was closed linked with the implementation of crusading was attested to even more clearly in Iberia where, in 1339, Benedict mediated to abate the conflict between Portugal and Castile; the pope urged them to reconcile, arguing that the strife prevented further Christian expansion in the peninsula and threatened the equilibrium of the border with Muslim Granada.[46] Beyond the seeming impossibility of peace in Europe, Benedict had to face the opposition of some of the French clergy to the preaching of the crusade and the collection of clerical tithes in the kingdom. The appropriation of crusading funds and the diversion of the French galleys originally destined for the East to the war against England proved that the French Crown had other priorities than the crusade; Benedict's suspicion that Philip VI would use crusade funds for his own purposes had been confirmed, and the curia was left to pursue its crusade to the East on its own. Without lay involvement the papacy was incapable of initiating a general crusade expedition to the East, and this prompted Benedict, with good reason, to annul the crusade and exempt Philip VI from his crusade oath.

Nevertheless, Benedict found other ways to support crusading. Shortly after cancelling Philip's crusade, the pope worked hard on behalf of Cilician Armenia: in May 1336, Benedict granted plenary indulgences for a period of two years to those Christians in the kingdoms of Cyprus and Naples, and on Negroponte and Rhodes, who were willing to go *in propriis personis* to Armenia and remain there continuously for a year to protect the kingdom from Mamluk assault; he also commanded the preaching of the cross in these kingdoms.[47] In addition to Armenia, Benedict continued to support crusading in the Iberian Peninsula, where he proclaimed a crusade and secured a triennial tithe in Castile, Leon, Aragon, Navarre and Majorca in 1340 and 1341,[48] and in Bohemia, Hungary and Poland, where he sought to defend the faith against the Tartars.[49]

The pope remained favourably inclined towards other secular rulers who were willing to confront the Muslims on other Eastern Mediterranean fronts. In late 1335, Benedict heeded the request of King Hugh IV to halt the preaching of the *passagium generale* in the Kingdom of Cyprus, because he believed it incited Muslim hatred against Cyprus:[50] in early January 1336, Benedict instructed Hugh IV and the secular clergy on the island to end the crusade preaching as, 'bearing in mind that by the preaching of the cross in the foresaid kingdom [of Cyprus] performed at the present time there is no utility for the general crusade'.[51] Benedict's management of this affair enabled Hugh to continue his campaigns against the Turks in the Aegean and enabled Avignon to resume activity in different theatres. Hugh IV was victorious over the Turks in 1337, which pleased Benedict who, despite the cancellation of Philip VI's crusade, planned to continue to wage war against the enemies of the faith,[52] and he provided support to crusades in the Baltic, in Iberia and in the Aegean until the last months of his reign.[53]

The election of an ascetic Cistercian to the papal throne certainly affected the planning of a crusade to the Holy Land. At the beginning of his papacy, Benedict had to examine and respond to the crusading legacy of his predecessor: the crusade negotiations between the papal curia and France had reached an advanced stage which, combined with Christian naval successes in the Aegean, meant the new pope would have to proceed with the organization of Philip's *passagium generale* and with the anti-Turkish naval league. Benedict backed these projects from the first moments of his papacy, but in the bulk of his correspondence he was less enthusiastic about these projects than Clement V and John XXII had been.

While perhaps not as impassioned as his predecessors, Benedict remained committed to crusading and provided assistance on several occasions to secular rulers willing to fight against the infidels and the enemies of the Church. The pope did not hesitate to cancel Philip's crusade, however, when Philip commanded the galleys destined for the East to attack the English in the Channel and confirmed papal suspicions the King might misappropriate crusade resources. Philip himself provided the pope with reason enough to abandon the *passagium generale*, but Benedict did not withdraw his support for crusading in continental Europe and in the Aegean; realizing the unwillingness of European leaders to crusade to the Holy Land, Benedict aligned his eastern crusading strategy with the appeals of the Christians in the East. The planning and execution of the crusade in the Aegean completely changed, however, after Benedict's death in late April 1342 and the election, in early May, of Pierre Roger as Pope Clement VI.

Ad succurendum Christianis in Romanie partibus: Pope Clement VI, the preaching for the anti-Turkish league and the capture of Smyrna, 1342–1344

Clement VI was generous and active in crusading affairs. The new pope had been at the head of the French royal delegation to Avignon in the early 1330s to secure papal assistance for Philip VI's crusade plans, and he preached the crusade several times during the negotiations. As pope he continued to refer to the crusade in his sermons, as he did on Cardinal William Court's return to Avignon from Italy in 1343 and on the assignment of Humbert II of Viennois as rector and captain-general of the Christian armada against the Turks in 1345.[54] Clement VI summoned the western clergy to conduct crusade preaching more frequently than any other Avignon pope;[55] he also received the full allotment of funds from the apostolic *camera*, thanks to church reforms instituted during the papacy of Benedict XII.[56] More importantly, the new pope made enlisting lay leadership for the crusade to the East one of his chief priorities, and he was progressive in unshackling the crusade to the East from the French Crown. Unlike his predecessors, who relented after fruitless efforts to engage the French King in the crusade, Clement turned to other, more dedicated Christian powers.

At the time of Clement VI's election to the papal throne, various Turkish groups threatened the Christian dominions in the Eastern Mediterranean. The Mamluks had seized possession of Syria-Palestine and Egypt, while several Turcoman warlords and sea raiders had established principalities in Asia Minor: their rapid advance, and the unification of Turkish Anatolia under the Ottomans, would soon bring them to the gates of Constantinople.[57] In 1342, Umur, the most powerful of the emirs in Asia Minor, increased his piratical activities in the Aegean, and urgent calls to suppress this maritime menace reached the papal curia from Romania and other Christian territories in the Eastern Mediterranean.[58] In July of 1342, Clement responded to these appeals by sending the Cistercian William Court, Cardinal-priest of Santi Quattro Coronati, to Venice to help create an anti-Turkish naval league.[59] The pope also wrote letters outlining the necessity of contributing to the naval league to a number of key personages: Hugh IV, King of Cyprus; Robert II Anjou, Prince of Taranto; the Grand Master of the Hospitallers; John I Sanudo, Duke of the Archipelago, to Genoa and to Venice and the other maritime republics of Italy.[60] In August 1343, Henry of Asti, the Latin Patriarch of Constantinople, was made papal legate in Romania and leader of the Christian fleet.[61] Aside from the Holy See and Venice, Cyprus and the Knights Hospitaller were to make the most significant contributions to the realization of the league.[62]

On 30 September 1343, the pope issued the bull, *Insurgentibus contra fidem*, in which he directed the attention of the regular and secular clergy to crusade preaching. The pope summoned the high clergy to choose the appropriate members of the priesthood to preach the crusade everywhere, and to place the mark of the cross on the arms of those who wished to take the cross and to grant them indulgences. The pope also commanded that chests be placed in all churches for the collection of alms, and that the remission of sins be offered to those who contributed.[63]

On the return of Cardinal William Court to Avignon from Italy in late October 1343, Clement VI delivered a triumphant *collatio*. Clement praised the office of the apostolic legate and discussed the tripartite aim of the Cardinal's mission in Italy:[64] Cardinal Court had to conclude truces or make peace among the different cities in Lombardy, unite the people of Lombardy against an invasion by the forces of Louis of Bavaria, and induce Venice and others to race to the aid of the Christians in Romania.[65] With regard to Court's efforts on behalf of the Christians of Romania, Clement said, 'he brought back a gracious and beneficial response from the Venetians' and announced the revival of the Christian naval league.[66] On 1 December 1343, Clement imposed a three-year tenth on all ecclesiastical revenue and benefices to support the Christians against the Turks.[67]

On 4 January 1344, Clement made the Italian Dominican, Venturino of Bergamo, responsible for the conduct of crusade preaching in Lombardy and other parts of Italy.[68] Venturino had acquired fame as a formidable, popular preacher in Northern Italy during the mid-1330s: of Venturino's preaching tour in Florence, Giovanni Villani said the Old Square of Santa Maria Novella was always crowded and 'his preaching was very efficacious and of good eloquence and of Holy words'.[69] In 1335, Venturino made a pilgrimage to Rome at the head of an itinerant movement of flagellants and pilgrims in support of captives; Pope

Benedict XII had suspended Venturino and placed him under the papal sanction of abstinence from preaching,[70] but Pope Clement VI returned Venturino to favour in 1343.[71] Clement wrote to John Visconti, Archbishop of Milan: 'considering the skill and eloquence and the zeal and fervour of the beloved son Venturino of Bergamo, of the Dominican Order', and he offered Venturino the *ministerium predicationis crucis* in the city, diocese and province of Milan;[72] Clement also commanded the Archbishop and his suffragan bishops to facilitate Venturino's mission.[73] The success of Venturino's crusade preaching in Northern Italy was remarkable for the popular excitement it fomented. Venturino ultimately followed Humbert II of Viennois to Smyrna, where he died in late March 1346.

The united Christian fleet finally gathered at Negroponte in the spring of 1344, and in May the fleet inflicted heavy losses on the enemy at Longos on Pallene, the western prong of the Chalcidice peninsula.[74] On 25 July 1344, Clement VI wrote to Hélion of Villeneuve, Grand Master of the Hospitallers, and to Henry of Asti, the papal legate and leader of the Christian fleet, congratulating them on their success and urging them to remain firmly committed to their oaths.[75] On 28 October 1344, the Christian fleet took Smyrna, Umur Pasha's chief port, although the acropolis remained in enemy hands.[76] On 23 December 1344, the pope congratulated Doge Andrea Dandolo and informed Philip VI of France of the *gloriosa victoria* of the crusaders over the Turks and the '*captione triumphali illius castri de Smirnis*'.[77] In January 1345, Clement conveyed the news of the capture of Smyrna to other concerned parties in the West.[78]

The crusaders' victory at Smyrna was, beyond question, Western Christianity's greatest victory in the East since the capture of Rhodes by the Hospitallers in 1309; it was also a personal triumph for Clement VI, who had been indefatigable in his efforts on behalf of the crusade. The Christian victories of 1334 and 1344 were clear manifestations of the transfer of the theatre of crusading activity from the Holy Land to the Aegean Sea, where Western Christianity sought to protect the region's Latin dominions from the Turks. Excitement and crusading enthusiasm spread throughout the West following this naval conquest, which demonstrated that united Christian forces could still confront and defeat the enemy at sea. Smyrna also proved the papacy could plan and undertake a successful crusade in the East without any contribution from the major royal houses in Europe, especially the French Crown. After the loss of the leader of his crusade, Henry of Asti, however, on 17 January 1345, Clement once again sought royal support in his effort to retain Smyrna. Once Clement realized French royal priorities did not include Eastern affairs, he turned his attention to other lay powers.

Filium Imbertum Dalphinum Viennensem, ducem et capitaneum exercitus contra Turcos deputandum: Dauphin Humbert II of Viennois' leadership of the Christian armada against the Turks, 1345

On 17 January 1345, St Anthony's Day, Umur himself led a sudden sally from the acropolis and slaughtered the leaders of the crusade. News of the disaster reached

Avignon in late February 1345, prompting Pope Clement VI to send reinforcements and find new leaders to hold and defend lower Smyrna.[79] On 17 March 1345, the pope informed Doge Andrea Dandolo and the Grand Master of the Hospital that he had appointed Raymond, Archbishop of Thérouanne, as then new papal legate, and Bertrand of Beaux, Lord of Courthezon, as captain of the papal galleys at Smyrna;[80] on 18 March 1345 he wrote to Edward III about the disturbing news from Smyrna.[81] Archbishop Raymond and Bertrand of Beaux were never to set sail for Smyrna, however, as Clement cancelled their assignment on 11 May 1345 at the request of Philip VI; Clement then postponed the offering of crusade indulgences in the French kingdom because of the war with England.[82] Once again, the French King had concerns other than the crusade in the East, and his unwillingness to participate in a renewed effort in Smyrna proved crusading was mainly dependent on the cooperation of Europe's lay rulers. As both local clergy and secular nobility were subject to royal power, their activities were dictated to a great degree by their overlords' priorities, and if these priorities had nothing to do with crusading, then neither local clergy nor the nobility could support papal crusade plans. The pope selected Francesco Michiel, Archbishop of Crete, as vice-legate in the East, and John of Biandrate, Prior of the Hospital in Lombardy, as captain-general of the Christian fleet at Smyrna.[83]

Clement VI wrote to the French and English kings, Philip VI and Edward III, requesting that they put a stop to their hostilities and actively contribute to the crusade. In the months following the St Anthony's Day disaster, Clement made a tremendous effort to capitalize on what the crusaders had achieved in Smyrna so as to gain secular support for his plans, but his attempts were in vain.[84] In the wake of his unsuccessful bid for support from European rulers, and with the situation in Smyrna growing ever more urgent, on 23 May 1345, Clement named Humbert II of Viennois captain-general of the expedition to Smyrna.[85] Humbert II was the dauphin of Viennois from 1333 to 1349, the son of Dauphin John II and Beatrice of Hungary and the last dauphin before the title went to the French Crown and was, thenceforth, bestowed upon its heir. Humbert had signed away his estates and title to the house of Valois in a treaty to take effect should he remain without an heir.

Humbert had already expressed his determination to support the crusade. In response to a letter from the pope dated 15 January 1345 informing Humbert of the Christian victory over the Turks at Smyrna, Humbert sent an embassy to Avignon to announce his willingness to pursue and support the crusade should the pope name him captain-general of the naval expedition.[86] In his *Memorabilia*, however, Humbert's secretary, Humbert Pilati, asserts that both the pope and the College of Cardinals were sceptical about Humbert's ability to command the crusade,[87] and Humbert's reputation in the West perhaps delayed Clement's ultimate designation of the dauphin of Viennois as captain-general.[88] Not long after Humbert's death, in 1355, the Florentine chronicler, Matteo Villani, wrote of Humbert: 'The dauphin of Viennois was a weak man of little virtue and firmness. This man had an effeminate and lascivious life, full of delights'.[89]

It was not only Villani who was of this opinion, some modern historians claim Humbert, as captain-general, was 'more harmful than useful' to the crusade.[90]

Diana Wood alleges Humbert was unable to lead the Christian fleet on account of his military and political incompetence and because he was under ecclesiastical censure after a quarrel with his archbishop.[91] Various scholars have charged Humbert with ineptitude following the regrettable outcome of his stay in the East, and he failed to meet Western expectations of further victories over the Turks in the Aegean (though it is hard to predict how Humbert's reputation would have evolved had his crusade been successful). Mike Carr points to many factors beyond Humbert's indecisiveness and military incompetence that doomed his efforts but, regardless of his alleged character flaws, Humbert was indeed willing to lead the crusade.[92]

But why did Clement VI choose Humbert as captain-general of the Christian fleet given his initial hesitation? Humbert did have the status of the ruler of Dauphiné, and he possessed the economic resources the league needed.[93] The Dauphiné of Viennois in the time of Humbert II included extensive lands east of the Rhône, between Avignon to the south and Lyon to the north. Even if Clement VI initially doubted Humbert's capacity to take the office of captain-general, such doubts had to be put aside following the pope's fruitless efforts to engage Philip VI of France and Edward III of England in the crusade. Unlike these two reluctant kings, Humbert was dedicated to the cause of crusade. In the sermon he delivered on the dauphin's leadership of the Christian armada, Clement VI stated, 'among the other princes, [Humbert] beseeched respectfully' for his office[94] and, at the end of April 1345, a few weeks before his appointment, Humbert arrived at the papal court to discuss the crusade with the pope.[95] Following his meeting with Humbert, Clement was probably convinced of the dauphin's determination to take command of the naval league.

Pope Clement VI delivered an inspirational sermon during Humbert's stay in Avignon, and the text of this sermon is contained in two manuscripts preserved in Paris.[96] The exact day on which the sermon was preached is not indicated in either manuscript, but a cross reference of scattered traces from other sources helps us more or less determine the date of the sermon. Our *terminus ante quem* is 26 May 1345, when Clement issued a series of letters announcing Humbert's taking of the cross and his official designation as captain and leader of the Christian army against the Turks.[97] According to an unnamed Bolognese chronicler, the pope appointed the Dauphin of Viennois as leader and captain of all Christians against the Turks on the feast day of Pentecost, 23 May 1345, during the public celebration of Mass.[98] Moreover, the account of the papal camera for the year 1345 indicates that from 23 to 29 May 'there was a great feast, because the dauphin received the cross'.[99] It is noteworthy that the two sources agree on the date of Humbert's *crucesignatio* as 23 May. Bearing in mind that Clement preached his sermon on the occasion of Humbert's *crucesignatio*, as he had on 1 October 1333 at Pré-aux-Clercs, when his rousing sermon convinced Philip VI of France and other nobles to take the cross, we can fix the date of his sermon as 23 May 1345.[100]

The main objective of this sermon was to convince the audience of Humbert's irreproachable character and of his suitability as captain-general of the Holy League. Its structure follows the 'modern' sermon style developed in the schools of Paris in the late twelfth century.[101] As his point of departure, Clement uses the biblical verse, 'Whilst he fulfilled the Word, he was made leader in Israel', from the first book of Maccabees, as the theme (*thema*) of his sermon. The selection of this verse is quite shrewd, as it seems to be the most appropriate verse for the objective of this particular sermon:[102] Humbert II of Viennois was to be made leader of the Christian army as Judas Maccabeus had been made leader in Israel, and the choice of a passage from the first book of Maccabees, wherein Judas Maccabeus is exalted for his valour and military talent, qualities that made him a natural choice for commander, was purposeful. Since Clement was arguing for the dauphin as an ideal captain-general for the Holy League, he devotes the greatest part of his sermon to praising Humbert's character and military worth.

An introductory section, a *prothema*, immediately follows the announcement of the theme and delineates the sacred dimensions of each individual preaching event.[103] In his *prothema*, the pope asserts the righteousness of a new naval league and discusses the seriousness of the situation in the East. The *prothema* opens with an excerpt from the Old Testament in which the priest, Mattathias, laments the destruction of Israel by the gentiles; Mattathias suffers for the loss of the Holy City, which was dishonoured at the hands of its enemies, and he cries for the children of Israel, who were led into captivity. The *prothema* is based on this particular biblical passage from Maccabees and requires little interpretation to convey its message. Much as Mattathias had, the pope expresses concern for and deep grief over the situation in the East. He reminds his listeners that Jerusalem, and the other places consecrated with the blood of Christ, were still in the hands of the Saracens, and he beseeches his audience to consider the great Turkish danger facing the Christians in Romania.[104] The allusion underlines the pope's fear of the Turkish menace and proves the Turkish emirates in Asia Minor were, in the 1340s, the most serious peril the Latins faced in the East.[105]

Clement's *prothema* quotes the last words of the dying Mattathias to his sons: the priest urges them to be zealous about the Law and to devote their lives to defending the Covenant of their ancestors, so they, too, might earn glory and everlasting fame. In this way, Clement urges his sons, the faithful, to be courageous and to fulfil their obligation to Christ by fighting the Turks. To make his message more concrete, Clement makes use of an *exemplum*: he refers to nine biblical personages who, in times of great difficulty, maintained their faith, their zeal and their devotion to God and who were eventually rewarded with divine grace on earth for their perseverance.[106] Clement then implores his audience to consider that in any generation those who trust in God are never defeated, while the impious man exalted today shall perish tomorrow; thus they should be courageous, and for their courage they will win glory.

The main part of the sermon follows with the announcement, 'I have arranged the armada of the Holy Union'.[107] Here the pope declares he has established a naval league for the defence of the Christians in Romania, and he commemorates the achievements and heroism of the former captain-legate at Smyrna, Henry of Asti, Latin patriarch of Constantinople. The difficult situation facing the Christians in the East demanded the appointment of a new leader and captain of the Christian fleet, and for this reason the papal consistory designated Humbert II of Viennois as captain-general. Clement tells his audience that Humbert humbly besought the pope to grant him this office, generously offering himself for papal service:

> Because among the other princes I have found the beloved son Humbert, dauphin of Viennois, to be more frequently eager [to go on crusade], more humbly beseeching, more zealously desiring, more generously offering, therefore, with the advice of our brothers, we have decided to appoint him, who is here present, leader and captain of the army against the Turks.[108]

This confirms the assumption that during his stay in Avignon Humbert managed to gain the favour of the pope and his cardinals, despite their initial reservations.

Next, with a repetition of his theme, Clement VI again emphasizes Humbert's suitability for the office; here Clement references a passage from Judges to persuade his audience. Just as Judah became leader of the Israelites after the death of Moses, taking his people to the 'Promised Land', similarly Humbert has been appointed leader of the Christians against the Turks after the death of Patriarch Henry. The argument that follows employs powerful symbolism to support Humbert's assumption of the captaincy: Clement argues that the virtues of the nine people from the Old Testament mentioned could justly be applied to Humbert himself:[109] these biblical personages represent the values that make Humbert brave, faithful, honest, just, pious and an experienced, chivalrous warrior.

Clement then opines that the Dauphin could most fittingly be compared with Joshua, a great warrior of Jewish history, and he reinforces his argument with the rhetorical scheme of *rationes*: Humbert recalls Joshua by reason of *successio*, of similar *pronunciatio*, of *interpretatio* and of similar *operatio*.[110] Humbert II of Viennois succeeds Patriarch Henry as Joshua succeeded Moses. To explain the second *ratio*, Clement draws upon numerous scriptural citations from the Numbers and from Deuteronomy. Clement praises the courage Judas shows when the Israelites have to fight the Canaanites: his soldiers are gripped with fear because of the multitude of Canaanites and because of their gigantic physical stature – the Israelites seem the size of locusts in comparison. Similarly, there were various Christian princes who believed the crusade against the Turks was useless and, moreover, that it would be deleterious to all Christendom.[111]

Clement then repeats the words he had written to Philip VI on 11 May 1345.[112] After assenting to the cancellation of the preaching of indulgences in the French kingdom, as Philip demanded, Clement voiced his displeasure with this demand. The pope claimed the King believed the crusade of 1344 was harmful to the Christians in the Aegean, and that Philip had relied on 'rumours lacking any basis of truth'.[113] Clement ended his letter admonishing Philip to trust only those who had been informed first-hand about events in the East.[114] Clement then made clear his determination to support the crusade and Smyrna with or without the contribution of the French Crown.

Clement continues by describing how, in time of crisis, Joshua urged his people not to be afraid because the Lord was with them – the idea of divine assistance thus stems from Joshua. The pope closes the second *ratio* with an *exemplum* from the first book of Maccabees to strengthen his argument against his contemporaries, who were discouraging people from going on crusade because of the moderate size of the Christian fleet as compared to the great number of enemy ships. When Seron, the captain of the Syrians, marched against the Israelites with a great army, Joshua told his soldiers that success in war was not due to the multitude of an army but to a heavenly strength. Clement exalts Humbert's courage in taking on the burden of leading the fleet and declares the divine character of the expedition.

According to the third *ratio*, Joshua's name was interpreted as 'salvation' or 'saviour', the one who would save the people of Israel; Humbert, similarly, would strive for the salvation of the Christians in the East. In the end, according to the fourth *ratio*, with God's grace the dauphin would capture and distribute lands to the 'true Israelites', the defenders of the Christian name, just as Joshua had for the sons of Israel.[115] It is evident that Clement relied extensively on Joshua's exemplar to justify his decision to appoint Humbert as captain-general of the Holy League. But how can Joshua be interpreted in the context of Clement VI's preaching? Roland Bainton initially expressed the view that the Book of Joshua, along with Numbers and Judges, explicates the ideal of conquest and the taking of the Promised Land. Thus Joshua, a warlike account praising the process of conquering and holy war, offers an explicit model of divine promise for military victory, and legitimizes crusading.[116] More recently, Cecilia Gaposchkin, in her study of the stained-glass windows in the upper chapel of the Sainte-Chapelle featuring episodes from the story of Joshua, offers a different image of Joshua as a link to the crusades. The figure of Joshua was an ideal crusading prince and an inspiration for Louis IX of France in the late 1240s, when he was preparing for his first crusade and had commanded the installation of the stained-glass windows at the Sainte-Chapelle.[117] Thus, the image of Joshua in this context could be interpreted as the prototype of a religious warrior in a holy war, rather than as a statement of conquest or crusading itself.

Although the visual evidence from Sainte-Chapelle permits such an interpretation, the textual traces from the twelfth and thirteenth centuries engender a 'spiritual' reading of Joshua in the context of religious military spirit. Douglas Earl's examination of a variety of crusading texts, sermons and manuals for crusade preachers, demonstrates that the appeals to Joshua are scanty; different propagandists built upon Joshua to legitimize crusading and conquest.[118] Apart from Urban II, who linked Joshua to the leaders of the First Crusade, Joshua is portrayed as a natural crusade leader only twice before pope Clement VI's sermon: in the first case, Eudes of Châteauroux, in one of the sermons he preached for the crusade of Charles of Anjou against the Muslim colony of Lucera in 1268/1269, drew upon Joshua 7 to compare Charles to Joshua and the land of Apulia to the Promised Land;[119] in the second case, the Franciscan Bertrand de la Tour, in one of his *ad crucesignatos vel crucesignandos sermones* compiled around 1300, drew upon

Joshua 8 to argue that he who would be assigned to lead the crusaders' army would be a new Joshua.[120]

In the same way, Pope Clement VI relied on Joshua to praise the military valour of Humbert of Viennois and to fashion him as the ideal warrior to become the new captain-general of the Christian fleet. For Clement, whether he was aware of the Eudes and Bertrand sermons or not, he used the story of Joshua as his source to support his choice of Humbert as the new crusade leader; he did not use the example of Joshua to support crusading *per se*. The pope compares Humbert to Joshua and declares that both embody the ideals of love of God, devotion and sacrifice. As God commanded Joshua to lead the Israelites to the Promised Land, so this earthly vicar appoints Humbert to guide the Christian army to the Holy Land.

The pope again reiterates the sermon's theme by indicating the beginning of a *divisio*, where several symbolic meanings are given for each section of the theme; in this sermon Clement divides the principal theme into two parts, with each part separated into different *subdivisiones*. The use of such divisions enabled the preacher to memorize the main parts and structure of the sermon and helped the audience follow the discourse.[121] In the first part of the *divisio*, which is subdivided into three parts, Clement declares the supreme character of Humbert's mission and his virtuous devotion to fulfil it.[122] To reinforce and support his arguments, and to persuade his audience, the pope derived material (*auctoritates*) from the Bible, the fundamental source for all Christian preaching. In effect, the pope urges all Christians to imitate the dauphin who, fervently and with great joy, has assumed leadership of the Christian army against the infidels: everyone was obliged to help accomplish 'the business of the Holy Land' with great delight and desire. Here Clement manifests his determination to continue his crusading endeavour in the East and his urgent wish to provide immediate support to the Christian garrison at Smyrna. The ideal of the extraordinary and redemptive nature of crusading is also apparent, since the *verbum*, Humbert's mission, is described as angelic, apostolic, divine, evangelic, marvellous, Mosaic, prophetic and salvific.

In the second *divisio*, Clement progresses to the second part of his theme, the glorious exaltation of Joshua as the leader of Israel. The pope explains that Humbert has been promoted to the captain-general on account of his name and noble title, Imbertus the Dauphin. He then divides Humbert's name into its two elements, *imber* and *thus*, 'rain' and 'incense'. As Wood rightly observes, by changing the dauphin's name from Humbert into Imbert during his sermon, Clement stresses the transformation brought about by Humbert's assignation. Clement addressed him as Humbert before his appointment and as Imbert from then on.[123] As captain-general, Humbert will be as beneficial for the Christians in the East as is the rain for earth when it falls from Heaven, whilst Humbert's burning devotion is like glowing incense, its aroma as pleasing as frankincense.[124]

In the absence of a more powerful secular ruler, Clement exalts Humbert's title as the leader of Dauphiné, which grants him the nobility and prestige required for the expedition the dauphin was of superior status, noble, virtuous, glorious, highly regarded and beloved. In closing, Clement makes use of a *simile*, emphasising the resemblance of the dauphin to the animal whence his title originally derived, the dolphin, literally *dauphin* in French, which adorned Humbert's coat of arms. The dauphin of Viennois was worthy of comparison to dolphins, with whom he shared many distinctive virtues: the dauphin was large, maritime, distinguished, honest and powerful, all of which qualified him to assume leadership of the crusade armada.[125]

To compose this *moyen oratoire* and the charming description of dolphins, Clement VI did not rely on Scripture but on classical literature, particularly on natural history and treatises on animals. Works such as the *Historia Animalium* and *Historia Naturalis*, of Aristotle and Pliny, respectively, were highly esteemed by the Parisian masters of the late thirteenth and early fourteenth centuries, and they frequently used such works as their source for the composition of *moralitates* in their sermons.[126] Clement VI himself was quite familiar with Aristotelian works, thanks to his education as a bright Benedictine monk and as a university professor in Paris. During his studies at Paris he transcribed a series of extracts from philosophical works for personal use and wrote seven commentaries on Aristotle; these commentaries can be found in two surviving manuscripts.[127]

Pope Clement VI hoped to build on the Christian success at Smyrna in 1344 and continue the struggle against the infidels, but the catastrophe on St Anthony's Day in 1345 made the defence of Smyrna an absolute priority. The pope tried to secure royal leadership for the reestablishment of the naval league against the Turks but, in the absence of a more powerful commander, he was forced to appoint Humbert II of Viennois as captain-general of the Christian fleet. On the occasion of Humbert's designation, Clement delivered a sermon that, with rhetorical eloquence, justified his choice, exalting Humbert's military valour and the mission he had been assigned.

Pro efficatiori succursu Christianorum verbum crucis vivifice mandavimus predicari: The preaching of the second phase of the Smyrna Crusade

After Humbert's designation as the leader of the Christian fleet, Clement turned to the transmission of the message for the upcoming crusade. On 28 July 1345, the pope ordered Archbishop Philip of Mytilene to preach the cross for the defence of the Christian inhabitants of Romania on his way to his diocese;[128] two days later Clement sent instructions to the head of each mendicant Order – Augustinians, Carmelites, Dominicans and Franciscans – for a general preaching for Humbert's crusade.[129] Clement writes the minister general of the Franciscan Order:

> From your Order and the Orders of our beloved sons the Preachers, the Hermits of St Augustine, and of Blessed Mary of Mount Carmel, we want four or more or fewer suitable friars from each of these Orders to be assigned, namely in each province established by those Orders, according to how large or small these provinces are and to what will seem expedient. [These friars] shall solemnly, diligently and faithfully perform the aforesaid preaching and proclamation in abundantly populated and conspicuous places in those provinces. Therefore, with apostolic writings we are ordering your discretion to

have and arrange quickly through your Order that, as mentioned, said friars be received in each separate province. Having zeal for God, [these friars] shall strive to carry out and accomplish this preaching and proclamation fervently and devoutly, showing faithful diligence and solicitude. But so that dissent cannot arise or scandal be encouraged on account of competition among the friars of the aforesaid Orders, who shall be received for the aforesaid [purposes], as was mentioned above, we therefore wish to arrange that, in each of these populous and conspicuous places, on Sundays and feast days, just as these friars go before and follow each other in processions, they shall proceed one-by-one and successively with this preaching and proclamation, namely one friar from these Orders on one Sunday and feast day, second another [friar] of another Order, and third and fourth others from the other Orders on Sundays and feast days until they accomplish the aforesaid solemnly and devoutly. But so that the more skillfully and devoutly these friars work with respect to this duty that they assume, the greater the fruit of their labours they know they will receive, we wish and grant that those who share and participate in this be furnished with the aforesaid indulgences in accordance with the quantity of their labour and devotion.[130]

In addition to the Dominicans and the Franciscans, Pope Clement VI summoned the Augustinians and the Carmelite friars to preach the crusade. Unlike the brothers of the Dominican and Franciscan Orders, who played a dominant role in crusade preaching beginning in the late 1220s, the Carmelites had no such tradition: surprisingly, the Carmelites were absent from crusading throughout the thirteenth century, and if they were active as crusade preachers at the close of the century, little evidence of such survives.[131] As the fourteenth century dawned, the nature of the Order began to change. In 1308, Clement V commanded the prior general of the Carmelites to involve the Order in the preaching campaign for the Hospitaller crusade, and the Carmelite friar, John Boukhil, was among the advisors to Edward II of England when the King took the cross on Pentecost 1313.[132] By 1315, the Carmelites had risen to remarkable theological heights, and around this time they began to adopt the disciplines of the Dominicans and Franciscans and became less inclined to the decrees of religious contemplative life.[133] This change increased Carmelite interest in the university instruction their brothers had received, leading, in 1310s and 1320s, to the emergence of Carmelite scholars with a more 'sophisticated ecclesiology', and the papacy employed these scholars in the preaching of the crusade.[134] The assignment of William of Hokyton, the prior of the Order in England, to preach the crusade in 1346 was significant, as was the preaching of the Alexandria crusade in 1365 by Peter Thomas, papal legate in the East.[135] Indicative of Pope Clement VI's confidence in the Carmelites' skill at preaching the crusade is his January 1346 command to the Carmelite prior provincial of England to preach the crusade in London, Colchester, Canterbury, Winchester and Rochester;[136] in February 1346, in a letter to the Carmelite prior of Germany, the pope grants the prior a two-year extension of the license for preaching the cross against the Turks in the territories under his jurisdiction.[137]

In this letter, Clement informs the prior that he is worried the simultaneous preaching of the crusade by brothers from different Orders might provoke quarrels amongst them and cause public scandal. In fact, quarrels amongst Franciscan and Dominican preachers began quite soon after the establishment of these Orders.[138] The papacy often summoned the Dominicans and the Franciscans to combine their crusade preaching campaigns, and competition and antagonism among the friars inevitably resulted in lively quarrels, largely due to their mutual rivalry, and the pope had to intervene to solve several disputes. In 1266, acrimony arose between the Dominicans and a Franciscan inquisitor in Marseilles – it soon spread throughout most of Southern France, as the friars preached against each other in public.[139] Similar conflicts erupted in Verona in 1290 – where, after a rather tense year, Pope Nicholas IV was forced to mediate between the Orders – and in Ravenna in 1311.[140] Anxious to avoid such disputes amongst the mendicant Orders, Clement sharply defined their respective competencies. He urged all crusade preachers to be diligent, devoted and watchful, and he promised to grant them indulgences in proportion to their contributions, which certainly induced the brothers to preach as effectively as they could.[141]

Clement sent directions to the diocesan clergy in December 1345 and to the heads of the mendicant Orders in February 1346 for the conduct of general crusade preaching.[142] The pope informed both the secular and regular clergy of the concession of a three-year crusade tithe for the defence of the Christians in Romania, adding:

> Nonetheless for the more effective assistance of the aforesaid Christians we commanded to be preached the word of the vivifying cross against the same pagans together with the accustomed indulgences and remissions, in the Kingdom of Cyprus and also in the aforementioned [parts of] Romania and Italy, and in all other parts.[143]

As indicated in papal letters, the preaching of Humbert's crusade was expanded primarily in the Latin lands in the East; preaching activity in Europe was concentrated in Northern Italy, following the crusade preaching of Venturino of Bergamo in Lombardy, which commenced in January 1344. This charismatic preacher's sermons had a stirring impact on public opinion, so Clement decided to make Northern Italy the main propaganda front. If naval warfare was to be of utmost importance, then it made sense that Northern Italy would be a focus of the dissemination of crusade propaganda.[144] The great number of devotees of Venturino's *peregrinatio* to Rome a decade earlier proved his rhetorical flair and the outstanding influence he exerted on his audiences; the preaching he began in Italy in early 1344, coupled with news of the capture of Smyrna at the end of the year, triggered immense popular enthusiasm for the crusade.[145]

In the northern regions of Italy, particularly in Lombardy and Tuscany, the preaching for the Smyrna crusade received the greatest response this was the result of papacy's decision to expand its preaching efforts mainly in these regions. While the initial concentration of preaching in Lombardy and Tuscany seems peculiar, a closer look at Clement's strategic preparation for the crusade proves this was a wise choice. In October 1343, when Clement outlined the objectives of the delegation of Cardinal William Court in Italy, the most important were the restoration of peace in Lombardy and the conclusion of truces among the region's rulers.[146] Clement first prepared the ground in Lombardy, then appointed Venturino, known for his eloquence, to disseminate the crusading message. The peace in the area helped inspire a positive popular response to Venturino's message.

In the middle of March 1345, Pope Clement VI feared that news of the deaths of Hélion of Villeneuve and Henry of Asti would have a detrimental impact on popular support for the crusade,[147] so he avoided prolonged negotiations with the French king and in May appointed Humbert II of Viennois to lead the Christian fleet in the Aegean. Despite his relatively low stature, Humbert inspired confidence in Christians throughout Western Europe, and the presence of Humbert himself in Northern Italy, beginning on 15 September 1345, stoked popular enthusiasm for the crusade.[148] In early November 1345, Humbert left Venice at the head of the Christian fleet; just before Christmas he reached Negroponte, where his forces joined the six galleys from the Holy See, Venice and the Hospitallers.[149] Unfortunately for Humbert, papal negotiations with potential allies and events in the East proved a crucial hindrance to his crusading aims and deprived him of any decisive military victories.[150] Humbert was forced to withdraw from Smyrna to Rhodes, in September, and finally returned to the West in November 1346.

On 28 November 1346, Clement VI informed the Holy Roman emperor and the kings of France, England and Naples that Humbert II of Viennois and the Turks had reached a truce, which meant the end of the Smyrna crusade.[151] Nonetheless, the pope anxiously continued to seek support for the defence of Smyrna, permitting unhindered crusade preaching in all areas other than Cyprus; on 31 July 1346 the pope had urged the Archbishop of Nicosia and his suffragan bishops to abstain from preaching in the Kingdom of Cyprus.[152] As stated, the pope informed the clergy in Cyprus this decision was made at the behest of King Hugh IV because, if the preaching continued, 'it would be the greatest danger for the people and the faithful inhabitants in the kingdom'.[153] In June 1349, however, the pope informed Hugh of the Mamluk sultan's intentions and reminded the king of his vow to take up arms against the sultan when conditions were favourable. In September 1350, Clement demanded that Hugh ratify the agreement between him, Doge Andrea Dandolo and the Grand Master of the Hospital that each would contribute one-fourth of his treasury to the defence of Smyrna.[154] In March 1348, Clement sent letters to *universis Christi fidelibus* describing the depressing situation in the East, and in 1349 he granted 35,000 gold florins to the Grand Master of the Hospitallers to arm four galleys for the defence of Smyrna and '*aliarum partium ultramarinarum*'.[155]

Clement, who of all the Avignon popes was the greatest proponent of the crusade, was finally forced to officially end the universal conduct of crusade preaching in early September 1351, as the Black Death was decimating Europe.[156] When he died the following year, war between Genoa and Venice, the depopulation of Europe, and the culmination of hostility between France and England were all serious obstacles to further crusading in the Aegean. Pope Innocent VI (1352–1362),

Clement's successor, was responsible for the defence of Smyrna, but he confined himself to tepid efforts to revive the anti-Turkish league; it was not until 1359 that Innocent commanded a general crusade preaching, levied a crusade tithe and appointed Carmelite Peter Thomas as papal legate in the East.[157]

During the mid-1360s, Peter I of Cyprus revived the idea of the *passagium generale*, and his attack on Alexandria, as an advance party, and temporary capture of the city in June 1365 was the last remnant of St Louis IX's crusade expeditions, as the remaining Christian powers in the Eastern Mediterranean were forced to fight a continuous war of defence against the neighbouring Turks. The small-scale crusading expedition of Amadeus VI, Count of Savoy, against the Ottomans at Gallipoli in 1366, marked a gradual shift of the crusade theatre to the Northern Aegean. Shortly thereafter, the crusade theatre again shifted, this time to mainland Europe, as Western Christians began to worry about the Ottoman threat to the Continent,[158] and from here the papacy and the Christian kingdoms of Europe were preoccupied with deterring further Ottoman advances in Europe. Allied Christian forces were unsuccessful in their confrontations with the Ottomans at Nicopolis in 1396 and again at Varna in 1444. The rise of Ottoman power became insurmountable, and up until the last quarter of the sixteenth century the Ottomans controlled the Eastern Mediterranean and Romania and increasingly threatened Central Europe.

Notes

1 'Prima Vita Benedicti XII', in *Vitae Paparum Avenionensium*, ed. G. Mollat, 4 vols. (Paris: Librairie Letouzey et Ané, 1916–1928), i, 195 [hereafter *VPA*]; *Chronographia regum Francorum*, ed. H. Moranvillé, 3 vols. (Paris: Société de l'histoire de France, 1891–1897), ii, 22; *Les Grandes chroniques de France*, ed. J. Viard, 10 vols. (Paris: Société de l'histoire de France, 1920–1953), ix, 146; *Chronique des quatre premiers Valois (1327–1393)*, ed. S. Luce (Paris: Société de l'histoire de France, 1862), 6; *Chronique Latin de Guillaume de Nangis de 1113 a 1300 avec les continuations de cette chronique de 1300 a 1368*, ed. H. Géraud, 2 vols. (Paris: Imprimerie de Crapelet, 1843), ii, 143.

2 Clément Schmitt, *Un pape réformateur et un défenseur de l'unité de l'Église: Benoît XII et l'ordre des Frères Mineurs, 1334–1342* (Quaracchi: College Saint Bonaventure, 1959); Mike Carr, *Merchant Crusaders in the Aegean, 1291–1352* (Woodbridge: The Boydell Press, 2015), 100–101.

3 Beverly M. Kienzle, *Cistercians Heresy and Crusade in Occitania, 1145–1229: Preaching in the Lord's Vineyard* (Rochester, New York: York Medieval Press/Boydell Press, 2001).

4 For Jacques Fournier as inquisitor see Lutz Kaelber, *Schools of Asceticism: Ideology and Organization in Medieval Religious Communities* (Pennsylvania: The Pennsylvania State University Press, 1998), 219; Irene Bueno, 'False Prophets and Ravening Wolves: Biblical Exegesis as a Tool Against Heretics in Jacques Fournier's *Postilla* on Matthew', *Speculum*, 89.1 (2014), 35–65. A surviving transcript found in the Vatican (Biblioteca Apostolica Vaticana, Vat. lat. 4030) contains a detailed record of Jacques Fournier's interrogations against the Cathars in Southern France.

5 Sylvain Pyron, 'Censures et condamnation de Pierre de Jean Olivi: enquête dans les marges du Vatican', *Mélanges de l'École française de Rome*, 118.2 (2006), 313–373; Auguste Pelzer, 'Les 51 articles de Guillaume Occam censurés à Avignon en 1326', *Revue d'histoires ecclésiastique*, 18 (1922), 240–270; Irene Bueno, *Defining Heresy: Inquisition, Heresy, and Papal Policy in the Time of Jacques Fournier* (Leiden: Boston, 2015), 151–156.

6 John XXII, *Lettres secrètes & curiales du pape Jean XXII (1316–1334) relatives à la France*, eds. A. Coulon and S. Clémencet, 3 vols. (Paris: Bibliothèque des Écoles françaises d'Athènes et de Rome, 3ᵉ séries, 1900–1967), i, no. 3439.
7 Bueno, *Defining Heresy*, 306–312 (see especially the argumentation during negotiations between Pope Benedict XII and the Calabrese monk, Barlaam).
8 Bueno, *Defining Heresy*, 289–295.
9 John XXII, *Lettres ... Relatives à la France*, nos. 5406, 5412, 5485.
10 *Les Grandes chroniques de France*, ix, 147; *Annales Ecclesiastici ab anno 1198 usque ad annum 1565*, eds. O. Raynaldi and J. Laderchi, 37 vols. (Paris-Freiburg-Bar le Duc, 1864–1867), xxv, 32–35 [hereafter *Annales Ecclesiastici*].
11 Jules Viard, 'Itinéraire de Philippe VI de Valois', *Bibliothèque de l'École des Chartes*, 74 (1913), 74–128, 120; *Les Grandes chroniques de France*, ix, 152–153; *Chronique Latin de Guillaume de Nangis*, ii, 144; Christopher Tyerman, 'Philip VI and the Recovery of the Holy Land', *The English Historical Review*, 100.394 (1985), 25–52, 39.
12 John XXII, *Lettres ... Relatives à la France*, nos. 5210–5216, 5224–5227; Benedict XII, *Lettres closes, patentes et curiales du pape Benoît XII (1334–1342) se rapportant à la France*, ed. G. Daumet (Paris: Bibliothèque des Écoles françaises d'Athènes et de Rome, 3ᵉ séries, 1899–1920), no. 19 [hereafter *Lettres ... Rapportant à la France*]; Benedict XII, *Lettres communes du pape Benoît XII*, ed. J. M. Vidal, 3 vols. (Paris: Bibliothèque des Écoles françaises d'Athènes et de Rome, 3ᵉ séries, 1903–1911), no. 2425 [hereafter *Lettres Communes*].
13 In this epistle, Benedict XII emphatically repeats his consent to John XXII's crusade plans. For details, see ASV, Reg. Vat. 120, fol. 1ʳ⁻ᵛ, ep. 1; Benedict XII, *Lettres Communes*, no. 2425 (summary).
14 Benedict XII, *Lettres ... Rapportant à la France*, no. 19: 'omnium Ecclesiarum reddituum et proventuum decimam per universas mundi partes, ordinibus militaribus et certis aliis personis exceptis, duxit usque ad certi temporis spatium imponendam... et inter illa videlicet contra eosdem Agarenos verbum crucis cum certis gratiis et indulgentiis consuetis cunctis Christi fidelibus predicari'.
15 Benedict XII, *Lettres Communes*, nos. 2466, 2469.
16 'Concilium Rotomagense', in *Sacrorum Conciliorum nova et amplissima collectio*, ed. G. D. Mansi, 31 vols. (Florence, Venice, 1757–1798), xxv, col. 1043 (New edition with supplements L. Petit and J. M. Martin, 60 vols. (Paris, Leipzig, Arnheim, 1899–1927); Tyerman, 'Philip VI and the Holy Land', 39.
17 'Concilium Rotomagense', in *Sacrorum Conciliorum*, xxv, col. 1043: 'item quod ecclesiarum prelati, capitula, et ecclesiarum rectores, in promotione instantis sancti ultramarini passagii, quod dominus rex Francorum assumpsit, se reddant plerique modo negligentes, non celebrando Missas pro prosecutione sancti eiusdem passagii, per sedem apostolicam septimanis singulis ad celebrandum deputatas, neque populum ad orandum et subveniendum, prout per apostolicas litteras injunctum est, exhortando ... exponendo poenas et indulgentias concessas ipso sancto passagio, et super hoc saepius predicando, per se vel alios'.
18 Benedict XII, *Lettres ... Rapportant à la France*, no. 66; Tyerman, 'Philip VI and the Holy Land', 40.
19 Benedict XII, *Lettres Communes*, no. 2453 (summary); for full text see ASV, Reg. Aven. 48, fols. 373ᵛ–376ʳ, ep. 33.
20 ASV, Reg. Aven. 48, fol. 374ʳ: 'ipse rex in kalendas Augusti que essent anno Domini millesimo trecenstesimo tricesimo sexto quas tam eidem regi quam ceteris crucesignatis et crucesignandis pro termino ad transfretandum in dicto passagio assignavit'.
21 ASV, Reg. Aven. 48, fol. 373ᵛ: 'pro pleniori dicte Terre succursu passagium generale indicere, ac pro illo celebrius et utilius peragendo verbum crucis cunctis Christi fidelibus cum indulgentiis consuetis predicari, mandare eiusque passagii et totius exercitus Christiani qui in illo inspirante domino transfretabit prefatum regem generalem rec-

88 Preaching: Benedict XII and Clement VI

torem et capitaneum constituere, ac pro huiusmodi faciendo passagio certa concedere subsidia dignaretur'.

22 ASV, Reg. Aven. 48, fol. 374^r: 'Ac venerabilibus fratribus nostris patriarchis, archiepiscopis, et certis episcopis in universis mundi partibus, de dictorum fratrum suorum consilio per apostolica scripta commisit et mandavit ... in suis civitatibus et diocesis, per se et alias personas ecclesiasticas seculares et regulares ordinum quorumcumque quas ad hoc ydoneas fore cognoscerent, cunctis Christi fidelibus iuxta datam eis a Deo prudentiam proponerent publice verbum crucis et venerabile signum eius quibusvis fidelibus illud suscipere devote volentibus, quos ad hoc utiles fore crederent, concederent ipsorumque humeris imponerent'.

23 ASV, Reg. Aven. 48, fol. 374^v.

24 This point is made in Norman Housley, *The Avignon Papacy and the Crusades, 1305–1378* (Oxford: Oxford Clarendon Press, 1986), 84.

25 Maureen Purcell, *Papal Crusading Policy, The Chief Instruments of Papal Crusading Policy and Crusade to the Holy Land from the Final Loss of Jerusalem to the Fall of Acre, 1244–1291* (Leiden: Brill, 1975), 60.

26 Purcell, *Papal Crusading Policy*, 61–62.

27 Purcell, *Papal Crusading Policy*, 61.

28 For the bull *Ad commemorantum recentius* issued on 26 July 1333 see chapter 1, note 244; ASV, Reg. Aven. 48, fol. 374^v: 'ac insuper quia dignus erat operarius mercede sua singulis eorumdem patriarcharum, archiepiscoporum, et episcoporum, et eis quos ad predicationem crucis, ut dictum est, ipsi ducerent assumendos in hoc divino fideliter laborantibus opere, preter mercedem eternam, quam merito sperare poterant, quotiescunque populus ad hoc specialiter convocatis proponerent verbum crucis unius anni et quadraginta dierum, necnon fidelibus ipsis qui ad verbum huiusmodi audiendum devote convenirent centum dierum, vere tamen penitentibus et confessis indulgentiam extitit'. Pope Innocent III had first established the right to crusade preachers to grant lesser indulgences for attendance at sermons. For details see Christoph T. Maier, *Preaching the Crusades: Mendicant Friars and the Cross in the Thirteenth Century* (Cambridge: Cambridge University Press, 1994), 107.

29 ASV, Reg. Aven. 48, fol. 374^v.

30 See Chapter 3.

31 John XXII, *Lettres ... Relatives à la France*, nos. 5406, 5412, 5485. For details about John XXII's instructions to the parties involved regarding the continuation of the anti–Turkish naval league see Mike Carr, *Merchant Crusaders*, 104–106; Nicholas Coureas, 'Cyprus and the Naval Leagues 1333–1358', in *Cyprus and the Crusades*, eds. N. Coureas and J. Riley-Smith (Nicosia: Cyprus Research Center, 1995), 107–124, 120–124.

32 Benedict XII, *Lettres ... Rapportant à la France*, no. 28.

33 Benedict XII, *Lettres ... Rapportant à la France*, no. 40.

34 Benedict XII, *Lettres ... Rapportant à la France*, no. 54; Benedict XII, *Lettres Communes*, nos. 2247–2250.

35 Housley, *The Avignon Papacy*, 112–113; Carr, *Merchant Crusaders*, 8, 109–113.

36 ASV, Reg. Vat. 119, fol. 132^v, ep. 343; Reg. Vat. 130, fol. 146^v, ep. 749: 'hinc est quod tuis supplicationibus inclinati ut confessor tuus que duxeris eligendum omnium peccatorum tuorum, de quibus corde contritus et ore confessus fueris semel tantum, in mortis articulo plenam remissionem tibi in sinceritate fidei et devotione sancte matris ecclesie persistenti auctoritate apostolica concedente valeat devotioni tue tenore presentium indulgemus'; Housley, *The Avignon Papacy*, 132–133.

37 At this point I will agree with Timothy Guard's opinion that though there was a high demand for indulgences *in articulo mortis* among knights embarking against the infidel, the papacy did not concede these in a systematic way. Timothy Guard, *Chivalry, Kingship and Crusade: The English Experience in the Fourteenth Century* (Woodbridge: The Boydell Press, 2013), 46.

38 Benedict XII, *Lettres ... Rapportant à la France*, no. 40: 'in medio mensis maii proximo futuri in quo dicte galee debent de Massilia recedere inchoandis, satisfacere non postponas'.
39 Benedict XII, *Lettres ... Rapportant à la France*, no. 54; Benedict XII, *Lettres Communes*, no. 2467; Carr, *Merchant Crusaders*, 100.
40 *Les Grandes chroniques de France*, ix, 364; Tyerman, 'Philip VI and the Holy Land', 47. Carr, *Mercahant Crusaders*, 101.
41 *Chronique Parisienne anonyme du XIVe siècle*, ed. A. Hellot (Nogent-Le-Rotrou: Société de l'Histoire de Paris, 1884), 164–165: 'si comme le dist archevesque disoin en son sermon, que se fust contre le roy d'Engleterre ne que le passaige d'oultremer en fût retardé'.
42 Helen Jenkins, 'Papal Efforts for Peace under Benedict XII: 1334–1342' (PhD diss., Philadelphia, University of Pennsylvania, 1933), 22–25; Carr, *Merchant Crusaders*, 107. For Benedict XII's attitude towards Louis of Bavaria see Guillaume Mollat, *The Popes at Avignon: 1305–1378* (London: Thomas Nelson and Sons, 1963), 110–119, 221–224; for Benedict's peace efforts with the Italian Ghibellines and Robert of Naples see Norman Housley, *The Italian Crusades: The Papal-Angevin Alliance and the Crusades Against Christian Lay Powers, 1254–1343* (Oxford: Clarendon Press, 1982), 84–85.
43 Benedict XII, *Lettres closes et patentes du pape Benoît XII intéressant les pays autres que la France*, eds. J. M. Vidal and G. Mollat (Paris: Bibliothèque des Écoles françaises d'Athènes et de Rome, 3ᵉ séries, 1913–1950), no. 801 [hereafter *Lettres ... Intéressant les pays Autres que la France*]; *Chronographia regum Francorum*, ii, 23–24.
44 Benedict XII, *Lettres ... Intéressant les pays Autres que la France*, no. 786.
45 Benedict XII, *Lettres ... Intéressant les pays Autres que la France*, no. 786: 'cum dictum passagium cum universali Christianorum concordia esset feliciter prosequendum, per viam pacis et concordie seu treugarum omnes a guerris et hostilitatibus abstinerent ut dictum passagium, cessantibus guerrarum commotionibus, et bellorum inter Christiane fidei professores posset favente Deo adversus hostes crucis commodius et facilius prosperari, ex quibus, hoste humani generis pacis emulo et incentore nequicie procurante, parvus vel nullus profectus resultaret. Nam, sicut evidentia facti docet, Anglia et Scotia invicem dissident, periculosus etiam et guerris non vacuus est status Germanie, periculosus status similiter Tuscie et etiam Lombardie, periculosior Apulie et Sicilie, guerra vigente gravi et quasi continua inter eas, ut de nonnullis aliis latentibus odiis adversus te regnumque tuum'.
46 Bueno, *Defining Heresy*, 299.
47 Benedict XII, *Lettres ... Rapportant à la France*, nos. 175–176: 'omnibus vere penitentibus et confessis crucis signo suscepto infra biennium a data presentium computandum, contra predictos hostes fidei in Armenorum succursum in propriis personis accesserint et exponerent ibidem per unum annum continuum ... plenam peccatorum suorum de quibus corde contriti et ore confessi fuerint veniam indulgemus'; Benedict XII, *Lettres Communes*, no. 3971.
48 Bueno, *Defining Heresy*, 301.
49 Benedict XII, *Lettres Communes*, nos. 8124–8125, 9139, 9141; Benedict XII, *Lettres ... Intéressant les pays Autres que la France*, no. 3137.
50 Benedict XII, *Lettres Communes*, nos. 8124–8125, 9139, 9141; Benedict XII, *Lettres ... Intéressant les pays Autres que la France*, no. 3137; Nicholas Coureas, *The Latin Church in Cyprus, 1313–1378* (Nicosia: Cyprus Research Centre, 2010), 99–100.
51 Benedict XII, *Lettres ... Intéressant les pays Autres que la France*, nos. 732–733: 'attento quod ex predicatione crucis in dicto regno presentialiter facienda nulla passagio generali utilitas'.
52 Benedict XII, *Lettres ... Intéressant les pays Autres que la France*, no. 1673; Peter Edbury, *The Kingdom of Cyprus and the Crusades, 1191–1374* (Cambridge: Cambridge University Press, 1991), 158.

53 On 18 July 1341 Benedict assented to the crusading plans of the Teutonic Knights in Poland, and he ordered the preaching of the cross and offered several dispensations for the crusaders. See Benedict XII, *Lettres ... Intéressant les pays Autres que la France*, no. 3137.
54 Discussion about these two sermons follows in Chapter 4. For the Latin text see Appendix V; Paris, Bibliothèque Sainte Geneviève, MS 240, fols. 247^v–251^r, 521^r–523^v; Paris, Bibliothèque Nationale de France, MS lat. 3293, fols. 299^v–302^r.
55 Between September 1343 and February 1346, on eight separate occasions Clement VI ordered the general preaching of the crusade against the Turks in the Aegean. See Clement VI, *Lettres closes, patentes et curiales du pape Clément VI se rapportant à la France*, eds. E. Déprez, *et al.*, 3 vols. (Paris: Bibliothèque des Écoles françaises d'Athènes et de Rome, 3e séries, 1901–1961), nos. 433, 591, 1704, 1855–1856, 2341 [hereafter *Lettres Rapportant à la France*]; Clement VI, *Lettres closes, patentes et curiales du pape Clément VI intéressant les Pays autre que la France*, eds. E. Déprez and G. Mollat (Paris: Bibliothèque des Écoles françaises d'Athènes et de Rome, 3e séries, 1960–1961), nos. 735, 1081.
56 Housley, *The Avignon Papacy*, 31–32.
57 Peter M. Holt, *The Age of the Crusades: The Near East from the Eleventh Century to 1517* (London: Longman, 1986), 114–121, 167–177; Carr, *Merchant Crusaders*, 144.
58 Clement VI, *Lettres Rapportant à la France*, no. 311; Housley, *The Avignon Papacy*, 33; Edbury, *The Kingdom of Cyprus*, 158; For details on the history of the emirate of Aydin under Umur, see Paul Lemerle, *L'Emirat d'Aydin, Byzance et l'Occident: Recherches sur 'La Geste d'Umur Pacha'* (Paris: Presses Universitaires de France, 1957).
59 *Annales Ecclesiastici ab anno 1198 usque ad annum 1565*, eds. O. Raynaldi and J. Laderchi, *et al.*, 37 vols. (Paris-Freiburg-Bar le Duc, 1864–1867), xxv, 284–285 [hereafter *Annales Ecclesiastici*].
60 Clement VI, *Lettres Rapportant à la France*, nos. 332–338, 341, 416–417.
61 Clement VI, *Lettres Rapportant à la France*, nos. 340–341.
62 For the preparatory negotiations between the contracting parties see Jules Gay, *Le pape Clément VI et les affaires d'Orient (1342–1352)* (Paris: Société Nouvelle de Librairie et d'Édition, 1904), 32–34; Kenneth M. Setton, *The Papacy and the Levant (1204–1571)*, 4 vols. (Philadelphia: The American Philosophical Society, 1976–1984), i, 182–190; Carr, *Merchant Crusaders*, 105; Housley, *The Avignon Papacy*, 33; Nicholas Coureas, 'Cyprus and the Naval Leagues 1333–1358', 118.
63 ASV, Reg. Vat. 157, fol. 7^{r-v}, ep. 35: 'Quocirca fraternitati vestre per apostolica scripta comittimus et mandamus quatenus statum miserabilem christianorum dictarum partium attendentes tanquam precones fideles et fortes athlete fidei contra infideles eosdem singuli videlicet in suis civitatibus et diocesibus per vos et alias personas ecclesiasticas seculares et regulares ordinum quorumcunque quas ad hoc ydoneos fore noveritis Christi fidelibus iuxta detam vobis et eis a Deo prudentiam proponetis publice verbum crucis et venerabile signum eius quibusvis fidelibus illud suscipere volentibus concedatis…Ceterum ut huiusmodi negotium fidei felicius prosperetur volumus ut in singulis ecclesiis vestrarum civitatum et diocesium singuli trunci concavi ponantur'; ASV, Reg. Vat. 161, fols. 2^v–3^r, ep. 15; Clement VI, *Lettres Rapportant à la France*, no. 433 (summary).
64 Sainte Geneviève, MS 240, fols. 247^v–251^r: 'Collatio facta per dominum Clementem quando venit dominus cardinalis Albus de Ytalia'. Cardinal William Court was called 'Blanc Cardinal' because of his white Cistercian habit. For more details on his career see Lützelschwab Ralf, 'Cardinalis Albus. On the Career of the Cistercian Monk Guillaume Court (†1361), *Cistercian Studies Quarterly*, 45 (2010), 141–167; For the sermon see Diana Wood, *Clement VI: The Pontificate and Ideas of an Avignon Pope* (Cambridge: Cambridge University Press, 1989), 184, Appendix 3, no. 42.

65 Sainte Geneviève, MS 240, fol. 249r: 'Ad literam enim ipsum preter negotia que officium legati incumbent misimus ad tria opera specialiter expetienda: primo ad faciendum pacem seu treugas in Lombardia que erat variis bellis et multiplicibus afflicta mirabiliter et concussa. Secundo ad uniendum omnes de illis partibus ad resistendum Bavaro si vellet Lombardiam intrare. Tertio ad inducendum Venetos et alios ad succurendum Christianis in Romanie partibus contra Turcos'.
66 Sainte Geneviève, MS 240, fol. 249r: 'Tertium etiam unde super facto Turcorum a Venetis responsionem gratam et utilem reportavit'.
67 Clement VI, *Lettres Rapportant à la France*, no. 559; Housley, *The Avignon Papacy*, 33.
68 ASV, Reg. Vat. 137, fol. 166v, ep. 584; Clement VI, *Lettres Rapportant à la France*, no. 591 (summary).
69 Giovanni Villani, *Cronica di Giovanni Villani a miglior lezione ridotta*, ed. G. F. Dragomanni, 8 vols. (Florence: Per il Magheri, 1823), iii, 240–241: 'Le dette sue prediche erano molto efficacy e d'una buona loquela e di sante parole'.
70 Benedict XII, *Lettres ... Rapportant à la France*, nos. 150–151; *Scriptores Ordinis Praedicatorum recensiti notisque historicis et criticis illustrati*, eds. J. Quétif and J. Échard, 2 vols. (Lutèce–Paris, 1719–1721), i, 620–623; Thomas Kaeppeli, *Scriptores Ordinis Praedicatorum*, 4 vols. (Rome: Ad S. Sabinae, 1970–1993), iv, 427–433; Gay, *Le pape Clément VI*, 67.
71 Kaeppeli, *Scriptores Ordinis Praedicatorum*, iv, 228; Domenico Corsi, 'La crociata di Venturino da Bergamo nella crisi spirituale di metà trecento', *Archivio storico Italiano*, 147 (1989), 697–747.
72 ASV, Reg. Vat. 137, fol. 166v, ep. 584: 'Nos attendentes scientiam, et eloquentiam, zelumque ferventem dilecti filii Venturini de Pergamo ordinis fratrum Praedicatorum'; Setton, *The Papacy and the Levant*, i, 190.
73 ASV, Reg. Vat. 137, fol. 166v, ep. 584: 'Quocirca fraternitati tue per apostolica scripta mandamus quatenus eundem Venturinum ad huiusmodi predicationis officium in prefatis civitate, diocesi, et provincia Mediolenense ut premittitur exequendum admittas libere, et admitti a suffraganeis facias antedictis'.
74 Setton, *The Papacy and the Levant*, i, 190; Lemerle, *L'Emirat d'Aydin*, 187–188; Carr, *Merchant Crusaders*, 75.
75 Clement VI, *Lettres Rapportant à la France*, nos. 987–988; Setton, *The Papacy and the Levant*, i,191.
76 Setton, *The Papacy and the Levant*, i, 190–194; Gay, *Le pape Clément VI*, 34–43; Housley, *The Avignon Papacy*, 32–33; Wood, *Clement VI*, 184–186; Norman Housley, *The Later Crusades. From Lyons to Alcazar 1274–1580* (Oxford: Oxford Clarendon Press, 1992), 60; Carr, *Merchant Crusaders*, 75–76.
77 Clement VI, *Lettres Rapportant à la France*, nos. 1350–1351.
78 Clement VI, *Lettres Rapportant à la France*, nos. 1395, 1397.
79 For details on the events of 17 January 1345 see John Kantakouzenos, 'Historia', in *Ioannis Cantacuzeni eximperatoris historiarum libri IV*, ed. L. Schopen, 3 vols. (Bonn: Übersetzung, 1828–1832), ii, 582–583; Giovanni Villani, *Cronica*, iii, 389–390; John of Winterthur, 'Chronicon', in *MGH:S*, ed. G. H. Pertz (Hanover: Impensis Bibliopolii Avlici Hahniani, 1939), iii, 252–253; Peter Giustinian, *Venetiarum historia vulgo Petro Iustiniano Iustiniani filio adiudicata*, ed. R. Cessi (Venice, 1964), 225–226.
80 Clement VI, *Lettres Rapportant à la France*, nos. 1570–1571; Carr, *Merchant Crusaders*, 79.
81 Clement VI, *Lettres Rapportant à la France*, no. 1582.
82 Clement VI, *Lettres Rapportant à la France*, no. 1704; Carr, *Merchant Crusaders*, 79.
83 Setton, *The Papacy and the Levant*, i, 194; Housley, *The Avignon Papacy*, 290; Carr, *Merchant Crusaders*, 79–80.

84 Clement VI, *Lettres rapportant à la France*, nos. 1704, 1844; Gay, *Le pape Clément VI*, 60–61; Wood, *Clement VI*, 185; Carr, *Merchant Crusaders*, 76.
85 For more details, see Wood, *Clement VI*, 186–187. I am also drawing information, for the rest of this section, from my own work: Constantinos Georgiou, '*Ordinavi armatam sancte unionis*: Clement VI's Sermon on the Dauphin Humbert II of Viennois' Leadership of the Christian Armada Against the Turks, 1345', *Crusades*, 15 (2016), 157–175.
86 For more details see ASV, Reg. Vat. 169, fols. 1^r–2^r; Clement VI, *Lettres Rapportant à la France*, no. 1397; full text of the letter no. 1397 in, *Histoire de Dauphiné et des princes qui ont porté le nom de dauphins*, ed. J.-P. de Valbonnais, 2 vols. (Geneva: Chez Fabri & Barrillot, 1721–1722), ii, 507–508; Gay, *Le Pape Clément VI*, 62; Claude Faure, 'Le Dauphin Humbert II à Venice et en Orient (1345–1347)', *Mélanges d'archéologie et d'histoire* 27 (1907), 509–562, 540–541; Carr, *Merchant Crusaders*, 53.
87 Valbonnais, *Histoire de Dauphiné*, ii, 289, 623: 'et licet D. nostro papae et D. cardinalibus displiceret ultra modum obtinuit'; Faure, 'Le dauphin Humbert II', 512; Gay, *Le pape Clément VI*, 62–63; Setton, *The Papacy and the Levant*, i, 195; Wood, *Pope Clement VI*, 186.
88 For Humbert's contemporary reputation, see Faure, 'Le dauphin Humbert II', 540–542; Gay, *Le Pape Clément VI*, 77.
89 Matteo Villani continued the writing of his brother Giovanni Villani's *Cronica* after his death in 1348. Filippo Villani, Matteo's son, continued the account from 1363 when his father died from bubonic plaque. Matteo Villani, *Chronica*, i, 33: 'Era in que' di il Dalfino di Vienna uomo molle, e di poca virtù e fermezza. Costui alcuno tempo tenne vita femminile e lasciva, vivendo in mollizie'.
90 Gay, *Le Pape Clément VI*, 77: 'plus nuisible qu'utile'; Housley, *The Avignon Papacy*, 253; Faure, 'Le Dauphin Humbert II', 540; Nicolae Jorga, *Philippe de Mézières 1327–1405, et la croisade au XIVe siècle* (Paris: É. Bouillon, 1896), 48, 50; Joseph Marie Delaville le Roulx, *Le France en Orient au XIVe siècle, expéditions du maréchal Boucicaut*, 2 vols. (Paris: E. Thorin,1886), i, 107–108.
91 Wood, *Pope Clement VI*, 186–187.
92 Mike Carr, 'Humbert of Viennois and the Crusade of Smyrna: A Reconsideration', *Crusades*, 13 (2014), 237–251, 245–251.
93 Setton, *The Papacy and the Levant*, i, 195; Housley, *The Avignon Papacy*, 34.
94 Appendix V, § 4.
95 According to the papal kitchen accounts, Humbert was among the nobles and cardinals banqueting in the presence of Clement VI from 2 to 8 May. For more details, see *Die Ausgaben der Apostolischen Kammer unter Benedikt XII., Klemens VI., und Innocenz VI. (1335–1362.)*, ed. K. H. Schäfer (Paderborn: F. Schöningh, 1914), 284.
96 Bibliothèque Nationale de France, MS lat. 3293, fols. 299^v–302^r; Bibliothèque Sainte Geneviève, MS 240, fols. 521^r–523^v; Philibert Schmitz, 'Les sermons et discours de Clément VI, O.S.B.', *Revue Bénédictine*, 41 (1929), 15–34, 22; Guillaume Mollat, 'L'oeuvre oratoire de Clément VI', *Archives d'histoire doctrinale et littéraire du moyen age*, 3 (1928), 239–274, 254; *Repertorium der Lateinischen Sermones des Mittelalters für Die Zeit von 1150–1350*, ed. J. B. Schneyer, 11 vols. (Munster–Westfalen: Aschendorff, 1973–1995), iv, 760; Wood, *Pope Clement VI*, 212. Schneyer does not make any reference to manuscript Paris, Bibliothèque nationale de France, lat. 3293, however, while Wood is not accurate when stating the sermon lies in folios 279^v–282^r. The examination of the manuscript shows the correct numeration is 299^v–302^r.
97 Clement VI, *Lettres Rapportant à la France*, nos. 1747–1750 (summaries); Valbonnais, *Histoire de dauphiné*, ii, 211, 511; *Annales Ecclesiastici*, xxv, 358–359; Housley, *The Avignon Papacy*, 253; Faure, 'Le Dauphin Humbert II', 545–548; Setton, *The Papacy and the Levant*, i, 195; Wood, *Pope Clement VI*, 186–187.
98 'Corpus Chronicorum Bononiensium', in *Rerum Italicarum Scriptores: Raccolta degli storici italiani dal cinquecento al millecinquecento*, ed. A. Sorbelli (Città di

Castello–Bologna: Ex Typographia Societatis Palatinae in Regia Curia, 1923), xviii, 536 [hereafter *RIS*]: 'Nella festa de la Pentechoste el papa Clemente cantoe publicamente la messa in Avignone, nella quale egli confirmoe el Dalfino de Viena duse e capitanio de tuti gli christiani li quali volesseno andare oltra mare contra li infideli Turchi a conquistare la Terra Sancta'.
 99 Schäfer, *Die Ausgaben der Apostolischen Kammer*, 284: 'fuit magnum festum, quia Dalphinus recepit crucem'.
100 Jean Dunbabin, *The Hound of God: Pierre de la Palud and the Fourteenth-Century Church* (Oxford: Oxford Clarendon Press, 1991), 177; John Wrigley, 'Clement VI Before his Pontificate: The Early Life of Pierre Roger, 1290/91–1342', *Catholic Historical Review*, 56.3 (1970), 432–473, 458–459.
101 Suzanne Paul, 'An Edition and Study of Selected Sermons of Robert Grosseteste', 2 vols. (PhD diss., University of Leeds: Centre for Medieval Studies, 2002), ii, 75–80; David L. d'Avray, *The Preaching of the Friars: Sermon Diffused from Paris Before 1300* (Oxford: Oxford Clarendon, 1985), 13–29, 180–203.
102 For more details on the *thema* of the medieval sermons, see Mark Zier, 'Sermons of the Twelfth Century Schoolmasters and Canons', in *The Sermon*, ed. B. M. Kienzle (Turnhout: Brepols, 2000), 325–362, 336; Nicole Bériou, 'Les Sermon Latins Après 1200', in *The Sermon*, 363–447, 370–372; Suzanne Paul, 'An Edition and Study of Selected Sermons of Robert Grosseteste', i, 76.
103 Bériou, 'Les Sermon Latins Après 1200', 397–398; Paul, 'An Edition and Study of Selected Sermons of Robert Grosseteste', i, 78.
104 Appendix V, §3.
105 Carr, *Merchant Crusaders*, 50, 119.
106 Appendix V, § 2.
107 Appendix V, § 4.
108 Appendix V, § 4.
109 Appendix V, § 6.
110 Appendix V, § 6.
111 Appendix V, § 9.
112 Clement VI, *Lettres Rapportant à la France*, no. 1704.
113 Clement VI, *Lettres Rapportant à la France*, no. 1704; Carr, *Merchant Crusaders*, 120.
114 Clement VI, *Lettres Rapportant à la France*, no. 1704; Carr, *Merchant Crusaders*, 120–121.
115 Appendix V, § 10.
116 Roland H. Bainton, *Christian Attitudes toward War and Peace: A Historical Survey and Critical Re-evaluation* (New York: Abingdon Press, 1960), 46–48.
117 Cecilia M. Gaposchkin, 'Louis IX, crusade and the promise of Joshua in the Holy Land', *Journal of Medieval History*, 34 (2008), 245–274, 246–255.
118 Douglas S. Earl, 'Joshua and the Crusades', in *Holy War in the Bible: Christian Morality and an Old Testament Problem,* eds. H. Thomas, J. Evans and P. Copan (Illinois: Inter Varsity Press, 2013), 19–43, 26–38.
119 Christoph T. Maier, 'Crusade and Rhetoric Against the Muslim Colony of Lucera: Eudes of Châteauroux's *Sermones de Rebellione Sarracenorum Lucherie in Apulia*', *Journal of Medieval History*, 21.4 (1995), 343–385; Gaposchkin, 'Louis IX, crusade and the promise of Joshua', 258; Earl, 'Joshua and the Crusades', 32–33.
120 Christoph T. Maier, *Crusade Propaganda and Ideology* (Cambridge: Cambridge University Press, 2000), 242–249; Gaposchkin, 'Louis IX, crusade and the promise of Joshua', 257–258; Earl, 'Joshua and the Crusades' 36–37; For further on Bertrand, see Patrick Nold, 'Bertrand de la Tour OMin.: Life and Works', *Archivum Franciscanum Historicum*, 94 (2001), 275–323.
121 d'Avray, *The Preaching of the Friars*, 172–174; Paul, 'An Edition and Study of Selected Sermons of Robert Grosseteste', i, 81–85.

122 Appendix V, § 12.
123 Wood, *Clement VI*, 188.
124 Appendix V, § 15.
125 Appendix V, § 17.
126 Beryl Smalley, *English Friars and Antiquity in the Early Fourteenth Century* (Oxford: Oxford University Press, 1960), 79–85; Edwin D. Craun, *Lies, Slander and Obscenity in Medieval English Literature, Pastoral Rhetoric and the Deviant Speaker* (Cambridge: Cambridge University Press,1997), 194; Claude Bremond, Jacques Le Goff, Jean Claude Schmitt, *L'*'Exemplum'* (Turnhout: Brepols, 1982), 63–64.
127 For more details on Roger's education see Thomas Sullivan, *Benedictine Monks at the University of Paris, A.D. 1229–1500* (Leiden: Brill, 1995), 296–299. For the education of Benedictines see Jean Leclercq, *The Love of Learning and the Desire for God: A Study of Monastic Culture* (New York: Fordham University Press, 1961), 49; James G. Clark, *The Benedictines in the Middle Ages* (Woodbridge: Boydell Press, 2011); Wood, *Pope Clement VI*, 7, 9.
128 ASV, Reg. Vat. 170, fol. 1^v, ep. 3: 'cum nostre gratia benedictionis accedas fraternitati tue per apostolica scripta committimus et mandamus quatenus statum miserabilem Christianorum dictarum partium [Romanie] accedens tanquam preco fidelis et fortis athleta fidei contra infideles eosdem [Turchos] per civitates, torras, et loca insignia fidelium quorumcumque per que eundo ad partes predictas transitum facere te contingit, necnon cum ad partes eosdem duce Deo perveneris in tuis civitate et diocesi ac tota sua provincia Metillinensi in singulis civitatibus et diocesibus eiusdem provincie, per te et alias personas ecclesiasticas, seculares et regulares ordinum quorumcumque quas ad hoc ydoneas fore cognoveris Christi fidelibus, iuxta datam tibi et eis a Deo prudentiam, auctoritate nostra proponas publice verbum crucis et venerabile signum eius quibusvis fidelibus ipsum suscipere devote volentibus eadem auctoritate concedas ipsorumque humeris illud imponas. Fideles eosdem quod ad audiendum propositionem ipsam quotiens experierit possis ad loca ydonea convocare solicitis exhortationibus et opportunis instantiis inducendo ut ipsi suscipientes cum reverentia signum crucis ipsumque suis cordibus inprimentes contra infidelium predictorum perfidiam insurgant viriliter et negotium ipsum ferventer assumant, et ferventius prosequantur'. Clement VI, *Lettres ... Intéressant les Pays Autre que la France*, no. 735.
129 ASV, Reg. Vat. 139, fols. 55^v–56^v, eps. 173–176; Clement VI, *Lettres Rapportant à la France*, nos. 1855–1856.
130 Clement VI, *Lettres rapportant à la France*, no. 1855: 'volumus quod de tuo ac dilectorum filiorum Predicatorum, Heremitarum S. Augustini et Beate Marie de Montecarmelo ordinibus, de singulis eisdem ordinibus, videlicet in singulis provinciis per ordines ipsos destinatis, quatuor vel plures seu pauciores fratres ydonei, prout ipse provincie ampliores seu strictiores fuerint et expedire videbitur, deputentur, qui solemniter in locis populosis et insignibus provinciarum ipsarum predicationem et publicationem faciant solemniter, diligenter et fideliter supradictas. Quocirca discretioni tue per apostolica scripta mandamus quatenus in singulis provinciis per eundem tuum ordinem, ut prefertur, distinctis assumi facias et ordines celeriter dictos fratres, qui zelum Dei habentes ferventer et devote predicationem et publicationem hujusmodi exequi fideli adhibita diligentia et solicitudine studeant et complere. Ne autem propter concurrentiam fratrum predictorum ordinum, qui ad premissa, sicut premittitur, assumentur, oriri valeat dissensio vel scandalum suscitari, sic volumus ordinari quod in singulis eisdem locis populosis et insignibus fratres ipsi diebus dominicis et festivis gradatim et successive, sicut precedunt et subsecuntur in processionibus, ad hujusmodi predicationem et publicationem procedant, scilicet unus frater ex eisdem ordinibus uno die dominico et festivo, secundo alius alterius ordinis, et tertio ac quarto alii ordinum aliorum subsequentibus diebus dominicis et festivis, quousque premissa compleverint solemniter et devote. Ut autem fratres ipsi ad hujusmodi officium assumendum tanto laborent circa illud solertius et devotius, quanto ampliorem fructum ex

suis laboribus hujusmodi se cognoverint percepturos, eos juxta quantitatem laboris et devotionis affectum predictarum indulgentiarum esse volumus et concedimus participes et consortes'.

131 Andrew Jotischky, *The Carmelites and Antiquity: Mendicants and their Pasts in the Middle Ages* (Oxford: Oxford University Press, 2002), 36–37.
132 Guard, *Chivalry, Kingship and Crusade*, 31.
133 Jotischky, *The Carmelites*, 22–31; Nicholas Coureas, 'Philippe de Mézières' Portrait of Peter Thomas as a Preacher', *Carmelus*, 57.1 (2010), 63–80, 64–65. On Carmelite theologians of the fourteenth century see Chris Schabel, 'Early Carmelites Between Giants: Questions on Future Contingents by Gerard of Bologna and Guy Terrena', *Recherches de théologie et philosophie médiévales*, 70.1 (2003), 139–205; Chris Schabel, 'Carmelite *Quodlibeta*', in *Theological Quodlibeta in the Middle Ages. The Fourteenth Century*, ed. C. Schabel (Leiden-Boston: Brill, 2007), 493–543.
134 Jotischky, *The Carmelites*, 27–29.
135 For the appointment of William Hokyton as crusade preacher in England, see Keith J. Egan, 'Aylesford's Medieval Library', *Aylesford Review*, 4 (1962), 231–307, 234; Jotischky, *The Carmelites*, 36. For Peter Thomas as crusade preacher see Coureas, 'Peter Thomas as a Preacher', 63–80.
136 Clement VI, *Lettres Rapportant à la France*, nos. 1462, 1704; Guard, *Chivalry, Kingship and Crusade*, 37.
137 ASV, Reg. Vat. 170, fol. 14^r, ep. 23; Clement VI, *Lettres ... Intéressant les Pays Autre que la France*, no. 920.
138 Henry Charles Lea, *A History of the Inquisition of the Middle Ages*, 3 vols. (New York: Harper and Brothers, 1887–1888), i, 302–303.
139 Lea, *Inquisition*, i, 302.
140 Lea, *Inquisition*, i, 303; For disputes and quarrels among the Franciscans in Cambridge see John Moorman, *The Grey Friars in Cambridge* (Cambridge: Cambridge University Press, 1952), 10, 88, 93, 110.
141 Clement VI, *Lettres rapportant à la France*, no. 1855: 'Ne autem propter concurrentiam fratrum predictorum ordinum, qui ad premissa, sicut premittitur, assumentur, oriri valeat dissensio vel scandalum suscitari, sic volumus ordinari quod in singulis eisdem locis populosis et insignibus fratres ipsi diebus dominicis et festivis gradatim et successive, sicut precedunt et subsecuntur in processionibus, ad hujusmodi predicationem et publicationem procedant, scilicet unus frater ex eisdem ordinibus uno die dominico et festivo, secundo alius alterius ordinis, et tertio ac quarto alii ordinum aliorum subsequentibus diebus dominicis et festivis, quousque premissa compleverint solemniter et devote'.
142 ASV, Reg. Vat. 170, fols. 4^v–6^r, 13^v–14^r, eps. 11, 23; ASV, Reg. Vat. 169, fols. 2^v–3^r, ep. 8; Clement VI, *Lettres... Intéressant les Pays Autre que la France*, nos. 844, 920 (summaries); Clement VI, *Lettres Rapportant à la France*, nos. 2203–2206, 2341 (summaries).
143 ASV, Reg. Vat. 170, fols. 5^r, 13^v, eps. 11, 23: 'et nichilominus pro efficatiori succursu Christianorum predictorum verbum crucis vivifice cum consuetis indulgentiis et remissionibus adversus paganos eosdem in regno Cipri, necnon predictis Romanie et Italie, aliisque universis partibus mandavimus predicari'.
144 I would like to thank Professor Christopher Schabel for this observation.
145 Gay, *Le Pape Clément VI*, 65.
146 Sainte Geneviève, MS 240, fol. 249^r: 'Ad literam enim ipsum preter negotia que officium legati incumbent misimus ad tria opera specialiter expetienda: primo ad faciendum pacem seu treugas in Lombardia que erat variis bellis et multiplicibus afflicta mirabiliter et concussa'.
147 Clement VI, *Lettres Rapportant à la France*, nos. 1569–1570, 1582.
148 For Humbert's itinerary from Genoa to Venice between 15 September and 24 October 1345, see Setton, *The Papacy and the Levant*, i, 199–201.
149 Carr, 'Humbert of Viennois and the Crusade of Smyrna', 240.
150 Carr, 'Humbert of Viennois and the Crusade of Smyrna', 241–250.

151 Clement VI, *Lettres Rapportant à la France*, no. 2957.
152 Clement VI, *Lettres ... Intéressant les Pays Autre que la France*, no. 1081; *Bullarium Cyprium 3*, eds. C. Perrat and J. Richard (in collaboration with Chris Schabel) (Nicosia: Cyprus Research Centre, 2012), iii, 216, no. t–188.
153 Clement VI, *Lettres ... Intéressant les Pays Autre que la France*, no. 1081: 'quod esset maximum periculum pro regnicolis et habitatoribus fidelibus in regno'.
154 Clement VI, *Lettres ... Intéressant les Pays Autre que la France*, nos. 2015, 2300; *Bullarium Cyprium III*, 262, no. t–434, 289, no. t–579.
155 Clement VI, *Lettres ... Intéressant les pays Autre que la France*, no. 1605; Clement VI, *Lettres Rapportant à la France*, no. 4130.
156 Clement VI, *Lettres ... Intéressant les Pays Autre que la France*, no. 2496.
157 Jonathan Riley-Smith, *The Crusades: A Short History* (London: Athlone, 1987), 268.
158 Riley-Smith, *The Crusades*, 269–271.

3   Preaching the crusades

Propaganda, liturgy and popular reaction in the early fourteenth century

Crusade propaganda and liturgy: Preaching testimonies in the chronicles of the early fourteenth century. The liturgy for the liberation of the Holy Land as a component of crusade propaganda

The correspondence of the Avignon popes between 1305 and 1352 includes numerous appeals for the conduct of preaching and the adoption of liturgical measures for the crusade, but data pertaining to the corresponding clerical reaction to those calls is extremely scarce. Apart from some indications that Clement V, in 1309, and Benedict XII, in 1335, were disappointed with what each considered dispassionate preaching, it is difficult to say without further research in the diocesan registers if the local clergy obeyed papal calls. Indeed, the registers of the Avignon popes constitute an accurate representation of the curia's efforts to organize preaching and liturgical campaigns for the crusade; they do not include reports of the clergy's response to papal calls or accounts of actual preaching events.

Some of the preserved crusade sermons provide us with the preacher's name, the liturgical day and the place of preaching, the audience and, most importantly, adequate knowledge of the preacher's real voice. Such examples are the sermons of Pierre de la Palud and Pierre Roger/Clement VI. That sermons with crusade appeals are normally organized in manuscript collections according to the Church's liturgical calendar makes it difficult to identify each sermon with its actual preaching event.

Nevertheless, the chroniclers, especially those from France, provide more details of crusade preaching occurrences and cross-taking ceremonies. The narratives from England, France, Germany and Italy are good sources of information about crusade preaching events and popular reaction to the preaching. These narratives, though, are notable for their lack of any trace of what the preachers said in their sermons. The case of the chronicler of St Florian, who referred to the exact words he heard as an eyewitness during the sermon of a preacher-priest in the city of Enns in 1309, is unfortunately unique.[1]

A number of accounts from beyond France, though concise, complement the crusade preaching imagery of the early fourteenth century. The chronicles of the reigns of Edward I and Edward II of England refer to the preaching mission of the Bishop of Nazareth, in London, on 25 January 1309, for the Hospitallers' crusade.[2] The chronicler particularly stressed the right granted by Clement V to the Bishop for the support of the Holy Land; some accounts from Italy mention the preaching of Venturino of Bergamo in the cities of Northern Italy between early 1344 and late 1345.[3]

A number of accounts testify to Pope Clement V's preaching during the second session of the Council of Vienne on 3 April 1312.[4] These sources also provide information about the *thema* of Clement's sermon, the audience and the liturgical ritual that took place following the close of the pope's sermon. The annalists are more generous in their descriptions of Cardinal Nicholas of Fréauville, papal legate in France, and his preaching during the French royal family's cross-taking ceremony. After Clement V made Nicholas responsible for the organization of the preaching campaign in France in February 1313, the legate's preaching efforts culminated four months later. According to various French narratives, in a ceremony that took place on Pentecost 1313 (3 June) on the Île-de-la-Cité, the legate delivered a stimulating sermon, after which Philip IV took the cross from his hands.[5] The King's three sons, his two brothers, Edward II of England (his son-in-law) and many French barons and nobles were also signed with the cross.[6] Many middle-class French subjects and many nobles came to see the royal family take the cross, and all of them expressed their shared enthusiasm for the King's decision to go on crusade and their willingness to join him. The splendid feasts accompanying this ceremony lasted an entire week. The nobles were arrayed in new garments with rich adornments, either on foot or on horseback, and everywhere there was joy and noise from different musical instruments, and from games.[7]

The sermons Peter of Pleine Chassagne and Peter of Courpalay delivered constitute examples of crusade preaching occasions that are accompanied by testimonies. On Friday, 23 July 1316, at a crowded ceremony in the Sainte-Chapelle, Peter of Pleine Chassagne, now Latin Patriarch of Jerusalem, and Peter of Courpalay, the Abbot of Saint-Germain-des-Prés, preached the crusade.[8] The two prelates delivered their sermons in the presence of the members of the French royal family, including Philip the Tall, son of Philip IV, Robert, the sixth son of Louis IX and count of Clermont; his sons Louis and John, members of the nobility and the high clergy, and many Parisians. After the sermons Louis of Clermont, Count of Clermont from birth, and his brother, John, Count of Soissons, assumed the cross from the hands of Peter of Pleine Chassagne and promised to make all necessary preparations for the departure of the crusade on the feast day of Pentecost 1317.[9] Peter of Pleine Chassagne stressed the necessity of securing the Holy Land, though the narrative sources offer no trace of what the Patriarch and the Abbot actually said in their sermons.[10] In addition, Golubovich quotes an encyclical letter from Peter of Pleine Chassagne, issued 23 July 1316, the same day as Peter's preaching of the crusade at Paris;[11] unfortunately, the preceding letters sent by Peter concerning the crusade have been lost.[12] In his letter, Peter discusses the preparations for the crusade, which was to depart under the leadership of Louis of Clermont. The choice of Louis as the head of the preliminary *passagium* was made in response to Louis's stated interest and eagerness, which he had expressed in June, when he presented a crusade plan; this plan was formalized with his *crucesignatio* in July 1316.[13]

Once again, Peter of Pleine Chassagne emphasized the necessity for prompt action for the crusade to the Holy Land. Since crusading issues had to be considered with diligence and providence, Peter needed to convene an assembly of prelates and men experienced in crusading.[14] Such an assembly has not been confirmed by other sources. There is mention in some accounts of a great gathering of prelates and nobles at the royal chapelle in Paris during the cross-taking ceremony for Louis and the reaffirmation of Philip V's devotion to the crusade.[15] This was a diplomatic manoeuvre, however as, after assuming the regency of the infant King, John I, on 15 November 1316, Philip needed to safeguard his position by maintaining the Capetian role as *Rex Christianissimus* and champion of the crusade.[16] By presenting himself as such, Philip secured papal support in different ways. Jacques Duèze, once elected as Pope John XXII, called upon Philip to undertake an initiative for the Holy Land; the pope gave great grants to Philip and acted on behalf of the French during the conflict with Flanders.[17]

After that, Peter of Pleine Chassagne gives some general directions for the conduct of preaching:

> First of all, you, lord prelates, shall command all the curates of your dioceses and the Friars Minor and Preacher, when they preach the word of God to the clergy and populace on Sundays and feast days, to induce the crusaders and others who wish to assume [the cross] to make preparations in such a way that they can depart on their journey one year from the next feast of Pentecost, and to induce others who will not go so that they are willing to grant some of the goods conferred on them by God for the aforesaid passage and to shower God with prayers for the same purpose, so that it may be accomplished in His honour and for the cure of souls.[18]

The Patriarch of Jerusalem urged the high-ranking members of the secular clergy, the local bishops, to commission the ecclesiastics in their dioceses to preach the crusade, and to send word to members of the regular clergy, the Franciscan and Dominicans friars, that they should assist in this endeavour. This pattern of organizing crusade propaganda had been established in the middle of the thirteenth century, and it had provided the Church with effective results. The employment of *curati*, members of the parochial clergy responsible for the spiritual guidance of the parish, to broadcast the crusade made it so the Church could instantly transmit the crusade message, given the direct contact of the *curati* with its audience. Moreover, the mendicant friars furnished a body of proficient preachers with great channels of communication in urban areas and, because of the itinerant character of their mission, they conveyed crusade propaganda far and wide.[19]

In his letter, Peter of Pleine Chassagne asked for two forms of contribution to the crusade from those unable to participate personally: first, he invited the congregation to say intercessory prayers to God to prompt the intervention of Divine Providence for the crusade's favourable outcome; second, the faithful were to offer financial support to the crusade as compensation for their inability to participate actively. Peter of Pleine Chassagne followed Clement V's model to promote the crusade. A Franciscan himself had presumably developed crusade preaching skills during his tenure as papal legate in the East during and after the Hospitallers' *passagium*.[20] Peter received the papal command to promote the Hospitallers' crusade in the East, and he engaged both the friars and members of the secular clergy in his effort.[21] Satisfied with Peter's fervour and the successful outcome of his mission, Pope Clement V rewarded him with the Patriarchate of Jerusalem in 1314, a post that placed him in proximity to crusade affairs until his death in 1318.[22]

Neither the employment of secular and regular clergy, nor the use of liturgical measures during crusade campaigns, were innovations in the early fourteenth century, but the intensive use of preaching and liturgy in combination during the Hospitallers' *passagium* campaign was unparalleled. Peter of Pleine Chassagne was in charge of the successful conduct of the campaign. He discussed a number of practical issues pertaining to the preparations to be undertaken:

> Again, in every diocese, namely in the cities, two persons should be elected to whom the curates of the churches shall report the names of whose who wish to go and by what form and the aid that they find and receive from those who remain and do not go on the aforesaid passage. Again, these two persons chosen in the cities shall report or send to Paris in writing, by eight days before the next coming feast of Pentecost, the names of those who wish to go and the aid that has been reported to them, so that, when the names and other things are known, there can be foresight concerning the ships and other necessities for the aforesaid passage.[23]

Peter of Pleine Chassagne proposed the election of two people in each city to whom the curates of the churches should report the names of those who wished to crusade; these provincial officials were also obliged to dispatch letters to Paris with the names of all potential crusaders shortly before Pentecost 1317, over a year before departure. As expected, Peter emphasized the role of Paris in the preparation and launch of the crusade; the recovery of Jerusalem was primarily the duty of the French Crown, and thus Peter placed particular emphasis on French leadership of the crusade.

Philip IV had died in 1314, however, and France was in the grip of a succession crisis until the late 1320s. The crisis, combined with a renewal of the conflict with Flanders and a shift of papal crusade initiatives to Italy, dampened the once lively interest of the French Crown in Eastern affairs. Despite Louis of Clermont's preparation for a *passagium particulare*, which he began in September 1318, the organization of several assemblies for the crusade and the proclamation of general preaching in June 1321, the conduct of a crusade to the East was not a priority. The lack of official French crusading enthusiasm is reflected in the absence of any reports of preaching events in the French accounts until the early 1330s.

A certain number of French chroniclers report the preaching of the Latin Patriarch of Jerusalem, Pierre de la Palud, in September 1331, which rekindled Philip VI's crusading fervour and led to the renewal of his crusading oaths, along with other French prelates, nobles and barons, following Pierre Roger's sermon in the Prés-aux-Clercs on 1 October 1333.[24]

The frequent hints in the papal letters for special Masses and prayers, along with the secured chests placed in churches for the collection of alms for the crusade, indicate that the liturgy for the Holy Land was an integral part of the Church's liturgical scheme and had become part of the papacy's crusade financing effort in the early fourteenth century, and this liturgy was continuously renovated with new psalms, prayers and hymns. Beyond preaching, the papacy regularly demanded the clergy, secular and monastic, enhance its propaganda efforts with the celebration of Masses, special prayers, psalms and clamours for the Holy Land. The necessities of the crusade could not be confined to raising arms; they required a significant home front contribution.

Thus, in 1308 and 1309, Clement V did not limit his efforts exclusively to crusade preaching; he also placed special emphasis on the development of an elaborate liturgical apparatus to raise funds for the Hospital's crusade. Liturgical measures for the intercessory support of warfare or of individual combatants had been in use for a long time. Thus, shortly after the fall of Jerusalem to Saladin in 1187, the celebration of Holy Land Masses, special prayers and fasts, processions and the singing of psalms, as well as the Holy Land clamours, became basic elements of crusade propaganda. Pope Clement III first introduced this policy in 1188, when he decreed that special prayers must be said during Mass throughout Christendom for divine forgiveness and to help Christians retake Jerusalem, and his successors continued this policy.[25] By the end of Innocent III's papacy, the liturgical context of crusade preaching was finally institutionalized.[26] Innocent, in his bull, *Quia Maior* of 1212, decreed that psalms be sung and prayers be said during Mass for the cause of the crusade.[27] Such practices were in place during the Albigensian crusade of 1226, thanks to the French theologian and lyric poet, Philip the Chancellor, and Eudes of Châteauroux, the future chancellor of the University of Paris and papal legate for the crusade of St Louis in 1248.[28] After Innocent's papacy, liturgical support for preaching became the core of crusading propaganda, and Amnon Linder emphasizes this: 'Liturgy was one of the main forms of action that Europe embraced in its endeavour to liberate the Holy Land'.[29]

With Clement V the liturgical measures were organized centrally and were given a prominent position in his crusading policy, though they were not innovative.[30] The pope skilfully linked the liturgy to the preaching of the cross to secure the best possible outcome for the papal-Hospitaller crusade. On 11 August 1308, the secular clergy received mandates to perform daily liturgies, to hear confessions and to commemorate the master and the brothers of the Hospital in their prayers.[31] The unknown author of *Sancti Martialis Chronicon* affirms that in 1309 'the lord Pope Clement V established the saying of two prayers every day, during Mass, for the support of the Christians against the Saracens, and he ordered chests placed in all churches for offerings for the benefit of the Holy Land'.[32]

On 11 June 1309, Clement sent a new bull entirely devoted to the liturgical aspects of the Hospitallers' *passagium* to a great many recipients.[33]

A special role was assigned to the members of the monastic orders, especially the Cistercians, for the performance of intercessory liturgies. As early as 1307, the Cistercian General Chapter, which had much experience in such matters, obeyed Clement's request and adopted the daily celebration of Masses in favour of the Holy Land.[34] At this time the support given to the crusade by the monastic orders was not a novelty. The Cistercians played a significant role in preaching the crusades during the twelfth century: prominent Cistercians such as Bernard of Clairvaux had been commissioned by Pope Eugene III to preach the Second Crusade, while in 1178 and 1181, Henry of Clairvaux was assigned the anti-heretical preaching that inspired the campaign against the Waldensians.[35] The Order also played a significant role in the promotion of the anti-heretical crusades, mainly against Albigensians, in the early thirteenth century.[36] Nevertheless, the establishment of the principal mendicant orders, the Franciscans and the Dominicans, had gradually relieved the Cistercians of preaching the crusades outside the monastery.[37] Their offering to the crusade, made along with the Carthusians in 1223,[38] had become intercessory, entreating God on behalf of all Christians fighting the infidels. Moreover, the papacy engaged the Dominicans in the performance of the liturgy for Louis IX's crusades in 1248 and 1270.

Writing in 1309 to all Cistercian abbots and the brothers and sisters of the Order, Clement V requested the celebration of Masses and the recitation of *suffragia* (prayers) on Sundays or feast days to invoke the intercessory boon of the Holy Virgin Mary, '*quinquies orationem Dominicam et septies Salutationem Beate Marie*'.[39] A further and significant contribution by Clement V was the extensive use of the triple set of prayers against the infidels, namely *Omnipotens Sempiterne Deus*, *Sacrificium Domine* and *Protector*, to be said during Mass for the greatest benefit of the crusade. These three prayers constituted the *Missa Contra Paganos*,[40] which was not Clement's invention;[41] the earliest *Contra Paganos* triple set is found in a late eleventh-century manuscript from Central Italy. In thirteenth-century sources we see triple sets of Mass prayers strictly associated with the Holy Land for the first time, though with limited expansion;[42] during Clement's papacy, the *Missa Contra Paganos* occupied a central position in the liturgical crusade propaganda ritual.[43] Linder asserts that 'the pope practically converted all Masses into Holy Land Masses, mobilising liturgy in the cause of the crusade to a degree unknown before … The extraordinary expansion of this *Contra Paganos* Mass was due to Clement V'.[44]

At this point, the Hospitallers' *passagium* might also have been against the Greeks on Rhodes, so the *Missa Contra Paganos* is problematic. Anthony Luttrell believes the Turks had already established a beachhead on Rhodes in 1303, occupying part of the island following an earthquake.[45] The scarcity of source evidence, however, makes the situation on the island before 1306 obscure. By 1306, Rhodes was probably inhabited by a number of Turks; according to Giovanni Villani, 'their master [the Hospitallers] started his passage from Naples and seized the island of Rhodes in Turkey'.[46] Looking closer at Clement's liturgical policy, it is obvious the pope converted all Masses into Holy Land Masses, organizing the liturgical apparatus for the purpose of the Holy Land:[47] Clement thus placed the liturgical campaign for the Hospitallers' *passagium particulare* in the context of his general crusading propaganda machinery. In his letter to Fulk of Villaret on 5 September 1307, Clement confirmed the partial conquest of *insula Rhodi*, which formerly *schismaticorum Grecorum infidelitas detinebat*.[48] Nevertheless, the pope wisely refrained from mentioning Rhodes after the crusade's proclamation. In his bulls, *Exurgat Deus* and *Exaurientes Indesinenter*, wherein Clement outlined the extensive preaching and the liturgical practices for the crusade of the Knights of St John, he made no reference to Rhodes; instead, he announced a '*passagium particulare ad Terre Sancte, Cipri et Armenie regnorum defensionem*'.[49] So the pope, looking further, did not decree these liturgical measures be said explicitly against the Greeks; instead, he initiated liturgical activities on behalf of the Hospitallers as part of the liturgy, which took shape over several years, until the departure of the general crusade. The Clementine, *Missa Contra Paganos*, remained popular until at least the middle of the fifteenth century when, in 1456, Calixtus III (1455–1458) renewed the Clementine set of prayers for the crusade against the Turks, the *Missa Contra Turcos*.[50]

We must see how these three prayers functioned in the liturgy. The core of the *Missa Contra Paganos* was the *Omnipotens Deus*, which was said just before the celebrant priest began the consecration of the Eucharist, followed by the second prayer, the *Sacrificium Domine*. The climax of the liturgy was the third prayer, the *Protector*, which followed Communion.[51] The recitation of the prayers for the crusade after the first half of the Mass had particular significance for the laity, as this was when the congregation prayed for the whole of Christianity.[52] With the Eucharist, the Church commemorated the redemptive sacrifice of Christ on humanity's behalf,[53] and the cross became a symbol of both release from sin and the means of redemption. At the same time, the crusade, through the ritual of the taking of the cross, came to symbolize salvation, in the form of the plenary indulgences granted to the crusaders.

Clement paid careful attention to the organization of crusading propaganda, which he bolstered with liturgical means. By placing special emphasis on the penitential nature of the *Missa Contra Paganos* prayers, the Church provided its flock with an opportunity for divine forgiveness and salvation. Clement supported the crusade preaching with an elaborate liturgical apparatus to guarantee alms giving for the crusade. He gave the *Missa Contra Paganos* a dominant position in the crusade liturgy and expanded it extensively, reminding Western Christendom on a daily basis of its dearest objective, the recapture of the Holy Land.

Further elaboration of the liturgical apparatus for the crusade: The Franco-papal crusade negotiations, 1322–1328

The use of the liturgy for the Holy Land as propaganda and as part of the effort to finance the crusade was continued by Clement's successor, John XXII (1316–1334). John announced the propaganda campaign for Philip V's crusade on

5 June 1321 but only charged the clergy with placing trunks for collections in all churches,[54] which implies that the Clementine liturgical apparatus was still in use as it had been in 1308 and 1309.

On 20 December 1322, however, Pope John issued a series of bulls that provided the French secular clergy with detailed instructions for the performance of the Holy Land liturgy and the versicles and prayers to be adapted during the celebration of Mass.[55] The pope precisely defined the prayers to be said, the psalms and hymns to be sung and the Masses to be celebrated, placing great emphasis on the development of the crusade liturgy as a vital element of the crusade's propaganda machinery, which would safeguard funds for the expedition.

Once again, the pope commanded the high prelates in France to place chests in all churches under their jurisdiction for alms. In late December 1322, with the bull, *Ad pie matris communis*, John XXII sent the Archbishop of Toulouse and his suffragan bishops a collection of liturgical measures that he believed would generate the most revenue for the crusade:

> Both in the cathedrals and in every single church in your cities and dioceses you shall have placed a hollow chest sealed with three keys, in which the said faithful, according to how God inspires their minds, shall be admonished to deposit their alms in support of the defense of the said kingdoms [of Armenia and Cyprus] and the fight against the enemies of the Crucified One and for the remission of their sins. And so that these things are obtained more easily from Him from Whom all good things come, once a week in these churches, on a fixed day that the priest will announce to the people, a Mass shall be said publicly with devotion and reverence, namely one week a Mass for the Holy Trinity, the second for the Blessed Virgin, the third for the holy angels, and so on.[56]

In this way, the pope defined the Masses to be celebrated and underlined the significance of the Holy Land liturgy as a great stimulus for the eleemosynary devotion of the faithful. The pope then instructed the clergy as to which psalms and hymns would supplement the celebration of the three Holy Land Masses:

> Now in each of these Masses, after the *Agnus Dei* and before the reception of the body of the Lord (Eucharist), we command and we decree to be said with every devotion the psalm mentioned below, namely: *Deus, venerunt gentes in hereditatem tuam*, with the: *Gloria patri* and the versicles that follow: *Salvos fac servos tuos*, Responsory: *Deus meus sperantes in te*, Vers.: *Esto, nobis Domine, turris fortitudinis* – Resp.: *A facie inimici* – Vers.: *Nichil proficiat inimicus in nobis* – Resp.: *Et filius iniquitatis non apponat nocere nobis* – Vers.: *Exurge, Domine, adjura nos* – Resp.: *Et libera nos propter nomen tuum*.[57]

John XXII commanded the clergy to chant the appropriate psalms and hymns, and he ordered them to chant them during the liturgy to emphasize their symbolism as it pertained to the crusade. The *Deus, venerunt gentes in hereditatem tuam*

(O God, the heathen has come in your inheritance) is actually the first verse of Psalm 78, which was to be read during the sacrament of the Eucharist, when the celebrant priest prays for the transubstantiation of the bread and wine into the body and blood of Christ. This biblical psalm is a lamentation for the destruction of the holy city of Jerusalem and an invocation for the pardon of sins and for divine assistance in taking vengeance against the gentiles. Following the disaster of Hattin in 1187, Psalm 78 became the standard biblical text for Christian lament and repentance to inspire God to mediate for the liberation of Jerusalem. Penny Cole emphasizes that Psalm 78 had been evoked in crusade preaching earlier than 1187 as an expression of Christian grief over the Muslim pollution of the Holy Sepulcher.[58]

During the rite of consecration, the kneeling congregation, with remorse, prays for God's mercy. It was precisely at this moment, one of reverence and piety, while the faithful pray for the salvation of souls, that the words of the psalm-lamentation for the recapture of Jerusalem would reach them. This would excite crusading ardour and the eleemosynary devotion of the faithful, delivering both alms and the general involvement of the congregation in the crusade. This consecration ritual also reflects the redemptory nature of the crusade: the faithful, through the penitential process of consecration, attain salvation by receiving the Eucharist. In a similar manner, the crusaders, through the penitential act of taking the cross, achieve the remission of sins by accepting crusade indulgences and ultimately achieve redemption by fighting the infidels.

The pope commanded the clergy to chant the hymn *Gloria Patri*, a short hymn of praise to God, also known as the 'Minor' or 'Lesser Doxology', after the psalm, followed by part of an intensely invocative prayer for God's extraordinary intervention in human life. These versicles were actually part of the Litany of the Saints (*Litania Sanctorum*), an invocation for the intercession of the Triune God, of the Blessed Virgin Mary, and of the holy angels and all martyrs and saints. The Litany of the Saints was the most suitable choice of prayer for John XXII, since the crusade Masses he wanted performed once a week were respectively dedicated to the Holy Trinity, to the Virgin Mary and to the angels. Through this sequence of Masses and prayers for the crusade, the pope hoped to secure the intercessory boon, not only of God and the Virgin Mary, but also of the whole army of angels and the saints. Surprisingly, however, John did not request the monastic orders' contribution, especially that of the Cistercians, whom Clement V had employed principally to obtain the mediation of the Virgin Mary, to recite prayers for the liberation of the Holy Land.

The verses from the Litany of the Saints, once inserted into the crusade liturgy, became a petition for divine retribution for the enemies of Christianity, a petition enhanced by Psalm 69, *Deus in adjutorium meum intende*, which was to be said before the Eucharist.[59] This psalm refers to David's life, when he was in flight from numerous enemies: David called for justice and for God's vengeance upon his adversaries, and the excerpt from the psalm included in the crusade liturgy – 'O my God, save your servants who trust in you. Be unto us, Lord, a tower of strength, from the face of the enemies. Let the enemy to accomplish nothing against us, and nor to the son of wickedness to proceed to harm us. Arise, Lord, help us and redeem us for your name's sake'[60] – is a plea from the faithful for God's help and protection. The congregation called for divine punishment of Christ's opponents and asked for God's assistance in Christianity's attempt to liberate Jerusalem.

To inflame anti-gentile sentiment, John XXII commanded the clergy to make use of another prayer to be said, verbatim, during the celebration of Mass every week, a prayer traditionally made against the Church's persecutors and in time of war: 'we beseech you Lord to suppress the pride of our enemies, and prostrate their insolence by the power of your right hand, through Christ our Lord'.[61]

Finally, each of the three Masses for the Holy Trinity, for the Holy Virgin Mary and for the holy angels was augmented by the *Omnipotens Sempiterne Deus in cuius manu* prayer; the first part, from the triple set of prayers, constituted the *Missa Contra Paganos* widely used by Pope Clement V against the infidels from 1309 onwards.[62] After the recitation of the liturgical measures on behalf of the crusade, John XXII believed that the Church could garner money and legacies for the crusade from the faithful.[63]

Once again, the pope stressed the financial needs of the crusade, which were at the core of Franco-papal negotiations between 1322 and 1324. The use of liturgical measures for raising money, in lieu of recruiting crusaders, was an integral component of fourteenth-century crusade propaganda. The more crucial funding became to the realization of any expedition to the East, the more the liturgy became a constituent element of papal crusade propaganda.

New supplements of liturgy performance, 1331–1352

With the encyclical *Gaudemus et exultamus in Domino*, issued on 5 December 1331, Pope John XXII once again assigned Pierre de la Palud the execution of crusade preaching throughout France; he also notified the French clergy of the supplementary Masses and prayers to be performed for the liberation of the Holy Land.

In fact, the greater part of the bull pertains to the Masses to be celebrated, the prayers to be said and the placement of chests for gathering contributions during the liturgical process for Philip VI's crusade.[64] The pope ordered both the regular and secular clergy in the Kingdom of France to celebrate a Mass for the 'liberation of the Holy Land from the hands of the enemies' on a specific day each week.[65] The priesthood was ordered to celebrate successive Masses: the first week for the Holy Trinity, the second week for the Holy Cross and the third week for the Holy Virgin. At this point, and contrary to the bull *Ad pie matris communis* of 1322, John XXII replaced the Mass to the holy angels with the Mass to the Holy Cross, perhaps because of the central place the sign of the cross came to occupy in the crusading propagandistic phraseology of the fourteenth century. Pierre de la Palud's crusade sermon unfolds around the story of the discovery of the Holy Cross; Pierre Roger, Archbishop of Rouen, delivered a sermon in late July 1333 wherein the True Cross occupies a central position.[66] Moreover, the Dominican

William Bernard of Narbonne (†1336), chancellor of Notre-Dame of Paris, inaugurated a sermon on the *Sancta Cruce* by glorifying the reviving sign of the cross (*lignum vite*) and urging the Church militant to offer the mark of the cross to those ready to receive it favourably.[67] The pope also granted ten days' indulgence to all those who truly repented by confessing their sins and who devoutly prayed to God for the crusade's favourable outcome.[68] After that, John XXII identified the set of triple prayers to accompany the celebration of the Holy Land Masses. In contrast to *Ad pie matris communis*, the pope eliminated the *Omnipotens Sempiterne Deus in cuius manu* prayer and introduced a new Holy Land triple set based on the *Deus qui admirabili providentia* prayer, to which he attached the *Sacrificium Domine* at the end of the offertory, and the post-communion *Protector Noster*.[69] The pope paid special attention to crusade liturgy as a core component of the crusading propaganda campaign. He developed the Holy Land Mass and redesigned the Clementine Holy Land Clamour anchored to the *Deus qui admirabili providentia* set of prayers. Finally, John ordered the French clergy to place chests for the collection of crusade donations in every cathedral and parochial or collegiate church in the kingdom.[70]

Almost two years later, on 26 July 1333, the pope sent new mandates to all archbishops and their suffragan bishops in France with specific details about the preaching and liturgical campaign.[71] With the bull, *Ad commemorandum recentius*, John XXII specified the liturgical measures for Philip VI's crusade, but without deviating from what he had already decreed in his bull, *Gaudemus et exultamus in Domino* of 1331.[72]

John emphasized the liturgy as a basic element of crusade propaganda: he renewed the triple set of prayers with the *Deus, qui admirabili providentia* clamour; he decreed that Masses to the Holy Trinity, the Holy Virgin, the holy angels and, later, the Holy Cross, be celebrated once a week, and he augmented the Holy Land Masses with the *Litania Sanctorum*. It seems the same liturgical rite remained in use after John XXII's death in December 1334. On 31 January 1335, with the bull, *Ad eripiendum Terram Sanctam*, Pope Benedict XII called all Christianity to crusade, reiterating John's bull, *Ad commemorandum recentius* of 26 July 1333. Benedict commanded Christians to preach the cross but, unlike John XXII, he made no reference to any liturgical measures to be initiated in tandem with the preaching campaign.[73] The complaints regarding the high clergy's lack of enthusiasm in their performance of Holy Land Masses, made by Pierre Roger, Benedict's successor as Pope Clement VI, during the provincial council at the abbey of Notre-Dame-du-Pré in September 1335, suggest the liturgical directives of 1333 were still in force.[74]

In a similar way, on 30 September 1343, Pope Clement VI, with the bull, *Insurgentibus contra fidem*, followed his preaching command with an order for the placement of chests in all churches for the collection of alms for the crusade,[75] which was in concordance with *Ad commemorandum recentius*. Writing to Edward III in 1344, Clement urged the clergy and the people of England to perform processions and to chant prayers to thank God for the Christian victory over the Turks at Smyrna that year.[76]

Between 1305 and 1352, the papacy, as has been shown, embedded the liturgy for the Holy Land in the crusade propaganda machinery, offering the opportunity to the entire Christian community, through alms, to participate in the crusade. The combination, however, of intensive preaching with a liturgical apparatus on behalf of the crusade resulted in three massive popular reactions; these rapidly evolved into harmful turmoil that the papacy was called upon to quell. These uprisings raised the question as to what degree the Church could control popular pro-crusade sentiment.

Popular responses to preaching

The 'Peoples' Crusade' in 1309

The progressive transition of crusading from large-scale operations to the smaller military expeditions (*passagia particularia*) of the fourteenth century has led to the notion that later crusades were an aristocratic affair with diminished levels of popular enthusiasm or participation. Sylvia Schein insists that there was diminished popular enthusiasm for crusading in the early fourteenth century, and that the *passagium particulare* proclaimed on the Hospitallers' behalf appealed to the upper classes only.[77] It can be argued that the limited number of participants in such a restricted crusade should necessarily be equipped with explicit knowledge of military matters and also possess a certain economic power. From a propagandistic point of view, however, the necessities of the *passagium particulare* could not be confined to the raising of arms; they required a significant home front contribution. Clement V did not limit crusade deliberations to the papal curia and the Hospitallers' grand master; instead, he asked for help from a certain number of lay rulers.[78] Despite the inconsistency of the French Crown and the impediments presented by James II of Aragon, as a study of primary sources illustrates, the pope did not deviate from an intensive crusade propaganda campaign;[79] on the contrary, propaganda for the crusade was widespread in England.[80]

In 1309, the papal request for contributions to the Hospitallers' *passagium* brought together a great number of people from different parts of Western Europe who demanded to participate personally in the Hospitallers' crusade. The 1309 crusade, which remained known as the 'Peoples' Crusade' or 'Crusade of the Poor' because of the low social status of the majority of its participants, has always had a relatively insignificant position in the historiography of the later crusades. The 'Peoples' Crusade' lacked the splendour of the crusades of the twelfth and thirteen centuries and, perhaps more importantly, the inadequacy of documentary sources have so far discouraged scholars from exploring it in depth. While Sylvia Schein has given more emphasis to the 'Peoples' Crusade' than other historians, she has not examined the preaching on behalf of the Hospitallers' crusade which inspired the 'Peoples' Crusade'. Like other scholars, Schein asserts that all those who wished to join the Hospitallers' crusade were poor peasants unable to offer military aid; they took the cross because they misunderstood the papal crusade propaganda for a limited crusade.[81] A more sociological approach reveals that the popular uprising of 1309 was a sort of public manifestation of discontent with high food prices and the famines afflicting the lower rungs of society.[82] As Barber has argued, the 'Peoples' Crusade', like the *Pastoureaux* or 'Shepherds' Crusade' in 1320, was in some aspects driven by social revolt.[83] Such popular excitement, however, both in 1309 and again in 1320, was preceded by intensive crusade preaching. Our understanding of this phenomenon will therefore be incomplete as long as its preaching remains unexplored.

A number of narrative sources provide details on the outburst of popular enthusiasm in response to the preaching for the Hospitallers' *passagium*, but such details give rise to a series of questions.[84] For example, as some chroniclers argued, was the popular paroxysm of 1309 the outcome of crusade preaching? Why were some of the chroniclers ill-disposed towards the participants? Did Clement V expect this kind of popular reaction? What was his response?

The continuator of the chronicle of St Florian Abbey and the author of the *Annales Colbazienses* mention that those who took part in the 'Peoples' Crusade' signed themselves with the cross without papal command, *cruce se signaverunt sine iussu pappe*.[85] In England, several groups of people from the main cities signed themselves with the cross and demanded passage to the Holy Land.[86] The continuator of the Acts of the Abbots of St Trond asserts:

> In the same year [1309] a multitude of common people, both men and women, from the towns and villages and country estates, advancing from the parts across the Rhine and Lorraine, have been signed with the cross of their own accord but without anyone preaching.[87]

According to some narrative sources, the great popular excitement of 1309 was a response to general crusade preaching, and the *Annales Lubicenses* affirm this:

> Pope Clement V ordered the cross to be preached for the overseas expedition through the regions; because of that [preaching] an endless crowd [consisting] of different nations and people of both sexes marked with the cross, arranged to cross the sea for the recovery of the Holy Land.[88]

The Florentine chronicler, Giovanni Villani, confirms the general preaching of the cross in Italy. This was followed, according to Villani, by an astonishing phenomenon: the march of innumerable people, men and women with children, leaving their jobs, carrying crosses, advancing from Piedmont to Lombardy, and along the coast of Liguria, to Genoa and then to Tuscany, across almost all of Italy.[89]

The argument derived from a number of chroniclers that people spontaneously took the cross in the absence of a crusade preaching campaign is unconvincing, while the contention that the mass movement of 1309 was purely a social revolt against the difficult economic circumstances menacing the poor of Western society is not persuasive. Apart from the impoverished, the peasants and the urban poor, the movement had participants of higher social standing – Clement V refers to *crucesignati*, thus confirming the reputable status of these crusaders.[90] Some chroniclers assert that among those who travelled to the papal curia at Avignon in 1309, were knights or professional warriors, men with arms and many Teutonic Knights who, as *crucesignati*, demanded transportation to the Holy Land.[91] Moreover, the *crucesignatio* of thousands of people from Austria, Brabant, England, Flanders, Italy, and from Pomerania and Silesia in Poland, all requesting transportation for the recovery of the Holy Land, could not have been unrelated to rigorous crusade preaching and liturgical measures. The social status and the provenance of the participants indicate that the papal propaganda machinery had reached both rural and urban parochial churches.[92] The magnitude of popular response to the preaching demonstrates that the words 'for the cross' had a strong resonance with the populace, that they evoked powerful religious emotions. Obviously, all those who joined the movement of 1309 regarded it as a crusade, with a clear desire for the conquest of the Holy Land and the salvation of their souls.[93] In fact, the great indulgences offered by the papacy to those attending the preaching for the Hospitallers' *passagium* convinced the crowds to take the cross, and it was in this same manner that the papacy met the storm of congregants who reached Avignon, with an offer of even more indulgences, each to last 100 years.[94]

The outburst of popular enthusiasm in Italy was probably further stimulated by the preaching of the crusade against Venice, which Clement V commanded on 28 June 1309.[95] The pope proclaimed a crusade against Venice to recover papal rights to Ferrara after the Venetian invasion of 1308. In April 1309, the pope sent his nephew, Arnaud of Pellegrue, as Cardinal-legate to lead the papal army against Venice; in June, after the crusade's declaration, Arnaud preached the crusade throughout Italy.[96] The papal concession of indulgences and privileges was similar to that offered to the crusaders fighting for the liberation of Jerusalem, and the preaching campaign for the crusade against Venice and that on behalf of the Hospitallers were launched simultaneously; this most likely inspired the outbreak of crusading zeal in Italy.

It is believed that 12,000 men attacked the fortress of the duke of Brabant, and that those who finally gathered at Avignon from all parts of Europe numbered 30,000; the movement gradually grew in number, as more people suffering from economic hardship and famine joined the *crucesignati*.[97] There is no doubt the movement attracted criminal elements as well – some of these people were simply rambling for alms, while others committed acts of cruelty and violence against wealthy clerics, Jews and the laity.[98] Giovanni Villani asserts, 'the Florentines and other cities forbade to them entrance to their lands, and they were expelling them saying that it was an evil sign for the land that they would enter'.[99]

The excess of popular zeal in 1309 impeded the regular preparation of the crusade. Poor people were unable to sustain the Hospitallers' crusade, while their enormous number made their control impossible and created fertile conditions for violence. This unexpected social turmoil distressed the local clergy in Central Europe, which is apparent in the majority of accounts from German ecclesiastical chroniclers, who were ill-disposed towards the participants in the 'Peoples' Crusade'.[100]

A number of different accusations can be extracted from German accounts of the events. Some chroniclers claim that the wave of *crucesignati* was a rampant crowd without leaders, rambling from place to place; these accounts omit the wide-ranging preaching campaign that paved the way for the outburst of a great range of crusading zeal.[101] The ecclesiastical chroniclers also stress the low social standing of the participants but neglect any mention of the respectable members cited in other accounts. Some accounts take a more pejorative tone than others, portraying the participants as 'innumerable common people'[102] who were 'parasites, pursuers of idleness, they have squandered their property ... all miserable, beggars and weak'.[103]

The chronicles emphasize the crimes that the moving crowd perpetrated against the clergy on its way to Avignon.[104] The author of the chronicle of St Florian Abbey in Upper Austria describes the tortures the clergy suffered at the hands of the 'bothersome' mob:

> They have rapidly grown in numbers, living in a lascivious way from alms, to the scandal of all observers. Ultimately, they rose to such rashness that in some places they seized offerings to clerics from the altars, beating the clerics and threatening those who did not receive them with death, flaying, expulsion from the church, and other dreadful and horrible things.[105]

Such ferocity against the clergy was most likely the main reason for the animosity toward the mob in some of the narrative sources. The German ecclesiastical chronicles were rife with hostility, while ecclesiastical and secular authors outside German territory were more moderate in their accounts. The chronicler of St Florian in Upper Austria also blamed the priests who joined the crowd in 1309 and 'who were preaching such ridiculous and erroneous things that were not consonant with the Catholic faith that they brought horror to prudent ears'.[106] This chronicler cites the words he heard from the mouth of a preacher-priest in the city of Enns in Upper Austria:

> See, beloved, in what manner our affair is directed by the divine will. To those who receive us, an abundance of goods and the solace of health are attributed by God. The houses of those who do not receive us shall be burnt down entirely by fire sent from Heaven. Many of us have already come to the Holy Land who, fighting against the Saracens in a war, have ended their life in glorious martyrdom. And among many thousands of our dead there was not a corpse that was not dressed in a black clothing with a woven gold cross on it miraculously sent from Heaven. Therefore there is no difference for us to perish either here or beyond the sea, because the sepulchre of our Lord is everywhere, and opposing those who put obstacles to our affair and even dying on account of this in any place prepare the eternal reward for us.[107]

The chronicler's report of the anonymous sermon at Enns, albeit very brief, is the only account we possess of the content of a live sermon on behalf of the

Hospitallers' crusade.[108] The chronicler blames the preacher-priest, since he has joined the crowd, but his reporting provides valuable knowledge as to the rhetoric this anonymous crusade preacher used. The preacher describes the spiritual character of the crusade as directed by divine will and adduces the temporal benefits that accrue to those who take the cross. The preacher expresses himself in terms appropriate to military service, exhorting everyone to personally participate in the crusade and declaring that Godly punishment awaits those who stand in the way. The faithful should emulate the pattern of crusaders who journeyed to the Holy Land, devoted soldiers in the war against the Saracens, glorious martyrs. Here the ideal of the penitential and redemptive character of the crusade is singled out: the faithful died in Christ's service, so they are deemed martyrs for God, absolved of every sentence for sin, exalted among military saints. The priest quotes a brief *exemplum*, a moral anecdote, to illustrate this point. The miraculous way whereby all the dead crusaders were found dressed in black garments with the sign of the cross was proof that God had not abandoned them. After Christ's death, the symbol of the cross was the means for all human redemption, and the crusade was a redemptive act. In fact, the appearance of the redemptive symbol of the cross on the corpses of crusaders proves that their sacrifice earned them the reward of eternal life. The audience is finally summoned to join the crusade; all the *crucesignati* zealously opposing those who disturb their business are worthy of eternal reward.

It seems, however, that such initiatives on the part of the local clergy, which could only incite uncontrollable crowds and introduce unmanageable problems for the conduct of the crusade, were reprehensible to the Church. This was another reason for the rejection of the 'People's Crusade' of 1309, a reason clearly delineated in the ecclesiastical accounts. The great popular crusading enthusiasm of 1309 was met with dismay and distaste by the ecclesiastical hierarchy. The *Annales Londonienses* say of the many people who came in support of the Holy Land, 'they set off to go across the sea quickly and without foresight'.[109] Understandably this vast gathering of people seeking transportation to the Holy Land alarmed the clergy and inspired its concern, disapproval and hostility.

In the summer of 1309, the movement reached a decisive stage when a great number of people arrived at the papal curia in order to depart from there for the Holy Land. On 25 July 1309, Pope Clement V accepted the crowd at Avignon, but their transportation was not feasible *propter defectum navigii*.[110] Clement absolved them all of their crusading vows and commanded them to return home, granting them more indulgences.[111] Beyond this point, the fate of the 'People's Crusade' of 1309 remains unknown, as the chroniclers conclude their narratives here. The *Annales Londonienses*, however, report that the English crusaders returned home.[112]

The 'People's Crusade' of 1309 originated in a complex set of circumstances in Europe but was, nevertheless, very closely linked with the rigorous crusade preaching for the Hospitallers' *passagium*. The explosion of crusading zeal in 1309, which followed the crusade preaching commanded by the papacy on 11 August 1308, clearly indicates the impact live preaching and liturgy had on the masses. In combination with prevailing social circumstances, the movement grew too rapidly to make any feasible contribution to the crusade.[113] The events of 1309 unexpectedly took an awkward final turn for both Clement V and the local clergy, who related preaching and liturgical measures with financial contribution to the Hospitallers' crusade, rather than to personal participation.[114]

The pope soon found himself confronted, albeit to a lesser degree, with the peoples' pro-crusade fervour and their misunderstanding of his appeals for contributions for the Holy Land. The episode followed the preaching of papal legate, Nicholas of Fréauville, on Pentecost of 1313, on 3 June, on the Île-de-la-Cité and the cross-taking by the French king and the royal family.[115] Many nobles and barons arrived to see the royal family, and all of them expressed enthusiasm for the king's taking of the cross and their willingness to join him on the crusade.

Crusading delirium was not confined to the nobles of Paris; it also seeped into the lower ranks of French society. The anonymous author of a French chronicle, written in the first years of Philip V's reign (1316–1322), states, according to Schein:

> There was a great gathering of people from all the other cities and towns of France, and it was a great wonder of devotion and of good will that all the people wanted to visit the Holy Sepulcher of our Lord and the other Holy places where Jesus Christ lived on earth. They [the people] had great grief in their souls because the Holy Land was in the hands of the enemies of our savior Jesus Christ, and they appeared ready to shed their blood for the love of Jesus Christ and for the reconquest of his heritage, just as our Lord shed his blood for our sake to conquer paradise.[116]

This passage testifies to the popular crusade enthusiasm which had taken hold in 1309. It is not clear whether such popular reaction was the effect of the general crusade preaching in the French kingdom or the consequence of the king's *crucesignatio*, but it is certain that Nicholas of Fréauville had preached the cross in France, as many narrative sources attest, granting crusade indulgences to those ready to contribute. And with his *crucesignatio*, Philip IV provided the crusade with an ideal leader and a laudable example for his subjects. It was not certain, however, that his leadership would inspire another 'People's Crusade' as was the case four years earlier.

The great popular reaction was the direct effect of the papal summons for crusade contributions. Clement V was unable to foresee the outburst of popular crusading zeal that resulted from his efforts, including the enormous upheaval endured by the local clergy, which might have brought about the failure of the crusade; the pope confronted the crowd at Avignon, granting indulgences and promising them personal participation in a future crusade.

The Pastoureaux, 1320

In the early 1320s, the papacy experienced a new outburst of popular pro-crusade frenzy. A certain number of chronicles, all from France and England, report the rise in 1320 of the Shepherds' Crusade, widely known as the 'Pastoureaux'.[117] Eleven years after the outburst of the 'People's Crusade', the papacy and the French Crown were now confronted by this new phenomenon. As in 1309, the 'Pastoureaux' participants sought 'to proceed overseas against the enemies of the faith' and fight 'for the recovery of the Holy Land'.[118] The majority of French narrative accounts concur that the movement mainly comprised 'shepherd boys of fourteen and sixteen years old, guardians of goats and pigs, who against their parents' will abandoned their flocks in the fields, flew together with shepherd crooks and without money'.[119] An unknown English chronicler states that there were some older boys among the young shepherds, but these were not yet even twenty years old.[120] Similarly, Bishop of Lodève Bernard Gui, eyewitness to the events in Languedoc, thanks to his tenure as papal inquisitor in Toulouse, wrote that the *pastorelli* 'were increased in number and multiply daily little by little, and there were added to them other poor people and vagrant men and women'.[121] According to narrative accounts from France the 'Pastoureaux' surged in May 1320 in Normandy and soon reached Paris,[122] while two English accounts assert, 'many shepherds and other people among them and women from England and other parts of the world assembled, wishing to acquire the Holy Land and to kill the enemies of Christ'.[123] It is obvious that by this time the 'Pastoureaux' participants had increased in number, but nevertheless the only reference to their multitude is found in the *Chronographia regum Francorum*, which states that 10 or nearly 10,000 *pastorelli* from different places entered Paris.[124] Perhaps the chronicler overestimated the overall number of participants, as the movement was at its very early stage, but their bulk made them feel strong enough to fight with the authorities in Paris.[125]

The 'Pastoureaux' then moved *de loco ad locum* and towards Carcassonne, then on to Cahors, Albi and Toulouse. As it progressed the 'Pastoureaux' ravaged local communities, committing acts of atrocious cruelty against Jews and violently attacking rich clerics and laypersons.[126] The movement's itinerant character helped to 'sound their fame upon the whole kingdom of France and elsewhere beyond the realm', which attracted many people who were already seeking alms.[127] But the low social standing of its participants, one of the principal characteristics of the Shepherd's Crusade, doomed it to a brief, failed existence, as 'it turned in nothing and in nothing it ended'.[128]

These events alarmed Pope John XXII and the cardinals in Avignon, and they sent the papal chamberlain to preach against them.[129] Specific mandates were delivered to the Archbishop of Toulouse and his suffragan bishops for general preaching against the shepherds and the imposition of spiritual penalties.[130] Between 19 June and 7 July 1320, the pope dispatched a number of letters in which his distress over the dimensions of the 'Pastoureaux' is more than obvious: he commanded both the regular clergy and the secular authorities in Southern France to vanquish this danger to Philip V's peaceful crusade preparations, and he called on all of the faithful to protect the Jews from savagery.[131]

Despite the initial proliferation of the Shepherds' Crusade participants, by late June or early July 1320, the movement had faded, particularly after local authorities in Southern France assembled an army and quickly dissolved the 'Pastoureaux'. Many of the participants were executed, while the rest dispersed; some managed to reach Bordeaux and move southward from there.[132]

The Latin chronicles of the monks of St-Denis Abbey near Paris and their French translation, *Les Grandes chroniques de France*, and the account of Bernard Gui, the papal inquisitor in Toulouse, describe the 'Pastoureaux' as a rampant band of young shepherds and simple men without money who had 'no leader or commander upon them'.[133] The continuator of William of Nangis, who meticulously described the early stages of the 'Pastoureaux', refers to a certain clerk who led the movement's participants, while John of St Victor tells us, 'among them was a certain priest who, because of his misdeeds, had impoverished his parish and someone else apostate from the order of St Benedict, by whose exhortation many senselessly joined them'.[134] Both John of St Victor and the anonymous continuator of William of Nangis were unsympathetic to the clergymen who led the 'Pastoureaux'. The monastic background of the chroniclers may explain this, as it reflects the consistent ecclesiastical disdain for such movements.[135] Both monastic chroniclers blamed their fellow clergymen for playing a leading role in the 'Pastoureaux', as the movement caused great agitation in France, included attacks on churches and some members of the clergy and threatened preparations for Philip V's crusade. Additionally, both chroniclers were from Northern France and as such possessed particular knowledge of the movement's early phase, when the 'Pastoureaux' were quite possibly guided by the two aforementioned clergymen.

The participants in the 'Pastoureaux' increased in number and, during their journey from Paris, they became an uncontrollable mass, obeying no commands, terrifying local communities and massacring Jews. Inevitably, Bernard Gui was most probably influenced by the course of events in Toulouse when he declared that the 'Pastoureaux' had no leaders while 'some among them were more fiercer in malice and cunning'.[136] It is likely the Shepherds' Crusade had the guidance of clergymen as it began, and as their fame spread widely their followers increased in number, quite quickly and without military leadership, which ultimately resulted in a violent, roiling, uncontrollable crowd.

What was the motive for the outburst of the 'Pastoureaux' in 1320? Did the crusade preaching stimulate the rise of the Shepherds' Crusade? Were difficult economic and social circumstances the movement's efficient cause? All narrative accounts of the Shepherds' Crusade also make reference to the great famine in Europe, but Bernard Gui is the only chronicler who argues that the outbreak of the 'Pastoureaux' was a direct consequence of the arduous economic and social situation in France.[137] He mentions that in 1320 a pestilence appeared in France, causing calamity throughout the kingdom and spurring a certain gathering of simple people of both genders who called themselves '*pastorellos*'.[138] Gui gives the impression that the Shepherds' uprising of 1320 was a sort of manifestation of discontent by the lower ranks of the French society over the ongoing famine and pestilence. It was exactly for this reason that the Shepherds' Crusade, unlike the 'People's Crusade' in 1309, attracted recruits only from the lower classes of society, and these participants turned against wealthy Jews and municipal officials.

The participants in the 'Pastoureaux' wanted to join the overseas passage for the liberation of the Holy Land, and references in the narrative accounts to their appearance align them with traditional crusaders. The unknown authors of *Chronographia regum Francorum* and of the *Chronique parisienne anonyme* assert that the followers of the 'Pastoureaux' wore tight clothing signed with small crosses, and that they carried both banners and plaques painted with scenes of the Crucifixion and the coat of arms of Louis, Count of Clermont.[139] The timing of the movement evokes a connection with the emergence of popular crusading fervour.[140] The period preceding the emergence of the 'Pastoureaux' was Lent and Easter (30 March 1320), a particularly holy season of the ecclesiastical year and one favoured by crusade preachers to deliver their sermons because of the season's strong symbolism: Lent is a period of repentance for Christians and an opportunity for them to purify their souls and, through the Lord's Passion during Holy Week, to finally reach redemption through the Resurrection. In the same way, the penitential processions in Chartres incited the mobilization of the *pueri* in 1212, while the performance of weekly sermons of exhortation and liturgy led to the *crucesignatio pastorellorum* in 1251.[141] The crusading was an act of penitence, and the taking of the cross had a redemptory nature for the crusaders, who were conceded indulgences upon taking their vows.

The anonymous Parisian chronicler mentions that the first great gathering of the Shepherds in Paris took place at the abbey of St-Martin-des-Champs on 3 May 1320, the feast day of the Invention of the Holy Cross.[142] The feast days of the Invention and the Exaltation of the Holy Cross favoured crusade preaching occasions; they were linked directly with the cross, a central theme of many crusade sermons and the *signum victoriale* for those fighting to liberate the Holy Land. Though there is no evidence that crusade preaching was performed on 3 May 1320, it is almost certain a preaching campaign for Louis of Clermont's crusade was underway in France by late July 1316. That the 'Pastoureaux' appeared in Paris bearing banners with Clermont's coat of arms and marked with the sign of the cross indicates that the crusade preaching performed during Lent and on the Easter day of 1320 had set the movement in motion. Crusade preaching, as was the case with the 'People's Crusade' in 1309, triggered the 'Pastoureaux', while the dire economic and social situation in France accelerated its consolidation. The suffering of its participants in the face of famine and poverty inspired their hatred for anyone in possession of wealth, including Jews and rich townspeople. The revival of crusade activity in France in February 1320, following the assemblies convened by Philip V to plan the crusade, sparked the crusade fervour of the masses and, in tandem with the preaching campaign, incited the shepherds in the spring of that year to undertake the crusade themselves.[143]

To sum up, the 'Pastoureaux' of 1320 originated in France in circumstances of economic and social depression; it was inspired by the preaching for the Louis of Clermont crusade and by royal deliberation on crusading. The movement originated in France but did not swell beyond its borders, although there are a few sketchy references to the gathering of shepherds in England. That the Shepherds' Crusade was confined to France underlines France's predominant role in organizing and launching a crusade in the fourteenth century. In combination with brutal social circumstances, the Shepherds' movement, a second 'People's Crusade', became disruptive and violent. It made any contribution to the crusade of Philip and Pope John XXII impossible, and the pope was forced to openly oppose it.

Popular reaction to the preaching of the second phase of the Smyrna Crusade, 1345

Following his 4 January 1344 assignment as the head of preaching for the crusade of Humbert II of Viennois, the Dominican, Venturino of Bergamo, passed through all of the cities in Lombardy and other parts of Northern Italy.[144] The success of Venturino's preaching mission in Northern Italy was remarkable for the popular excitement it fomented in late 1344 and 1345.

A number of narrative accounts from Italy attest to the outburst of crusade enthusiasm in Northern Italy at the beginning of 1345; this enthusiasm increased after July of that year, once the secular clergy began cooperating with the preaching. The Florentine chronicler, Giovanni Villani, reports a gathering of 400 *crucesignati* from Florence, 350 from Siena and a great number from other parts of Tuscany and Lombardy who sought to join the fleet at Venice.[145] In the records from the convent of Santa Maria Novella at Florence are listed the names of six Dominicans who assumed the cross for the anti-Turkish crusade and died after becoming *crucesignati*.[146] The *Corpus chronicorum bononensium* describes how the preaching of Venturino of Bergamo inspired a great number of people from Bologna, the March of Ancona, and the regions of Tuscany and Romagna, all marked with red crosses, '*va de soa propria volontà*' against the Turks,[147] while the anonymous compiler of the *Storie Pistoresi* recounts a number of miracles that sparked an explosion of crusading enthusiasm in Italy.[148] Finally, according to a sixteenth-century account, a great multitude of people, men and women with children, and members of the regular and secular clergy, took the cross[149] – thousands of people from every town and village put their furniture and utensils up for sale so they could set off with the crusaders.[150] The chronicler also describes the deluge of 'itinerant crusaders' who wished to sail for the defence of Smyrna in the streets and squares of the towns.[151] Though this account is relatively unreliable, as it exaggerates the overall number of the *crucesignati*, Clement's assertion of 'their innumerable multitude' in July 1345 reveals that thousands took the cross with the hope of travelling to Smyrna.[152]

The marching bands of *crucesignati* in Northern Italy comprised people from various social strata. The *Historiae romanae fragmenta* identify peasants from different villages and poor bourgeoisie of both sexes from the towns, children and adults from the lower levels of society, and local secular and regular clergy;[153] the participation of the regular clergy is also confirmed by the necrology of Santa Maria Novella.[154] Unlike the popular movements of 1309 and 1320, the Smyrna *crucesignati* from Northern Italy did not commit atrocities and other acts of violence against Jews and against ecclesiastical property, as they were led by some people of high rank. The Bolognese chronicler, Matthew of Griffonibus, refers to two knights from Bologna, while the *Corpus chronicorum bononensium* lists twenty-one Bolognese nobles who took the cross to follow Humbert II of Viennois to Smyrna.[155]

Giovanni Villani referred to the appearance of numerous *crucesignati* from Florence when Humbert passed through the city in early October 1345,[156] and the chronicles from Bologna list twenty-one nobles, as mentioned, from the city who took the cross to follow Humbert to Smyrna on his departure from Bologna on 18 October 1345.[157] Another important contribution to crusade fervour in Northern Italy was Venturino of Bergamo's decision to sail with Humbert to Smyrna, which inspired many Italians to follow him.[158]

Popular crusade excitement was also stirred by widespread reports of miraculous events in a variety of locations. In his 21 July 1345 letter to Edward III, Clement refers to the miraculous appearance in many places of shining crosses that relieved the faithful from sickness.[159] The pope considered it worthy to declare his approbation of these *stupendis miraculis*, which had been widely reported in the West, and to express his pleasure over the popular crusading excitement these miracles of God had incited in Italy.[160] According to papal rhetoric, the present crusading enthusiasm, which derived from God through His miracles, was proof of His intervention on behalf of the 'defense and extension of the Christian faith'.[161]

In addition to Clement's letter, an anonymous fourteenth-century prose chronicler from the Tuscan city of Pistoia writes of a different miracle at Aquila in August 1345 – an appearance of the Virgin Mary with the young Christ holding a cross in His hand on the altar of a small church. This marvellous event inspired great wonder and was regarded as God's portent of a future Christian victory over the infidels, and many people from the town of Aquila and the surrounding countryside took the cross and set out '*a combattere contra l'infideli*'.[162] The chronicler's references to a vision of the Virgin Mary with the young Christ can easily be associated with the crusade's redemptive character as Mary, the Mother of Christ, is directly connected to the Passion of Christ on the cross, the ultimate act of redemption for the sake of mankind.[163]

Reports of miracles attributed to the Virgin Mary multiplied exponentially during the later Middle Ages, while devotion to Mary increased as part of growing consideration of the human nature of Christ.[164] From the late thirteenth century onwards, innumerable miracles attributed to Mary were linked to Christendom's most important pilgrimages, such as the Holy Sepulchre of Christ,[165] and the papacy exhorted the monks of the monastic orders to pray daily for the intercessory boon of the Virgin Mary for the benefit of the crusade.

The chronicler of Pistoia recounts the events of the battle fought between the small Christian force led by Peter, the son of Hugh IV, King of Cyprus, against 1 million Turkish cavalry and infantry:[166] the disheartened crusaders invoked divine assistance and, miraculously, there appeared before them a man of great stature, bestride a white horse, waving a white banner emblazoned with a vermillion cross. He urged the crusaders to fight bravely and to be unafraid, because they would be victorious. The crusaders fought vigorously and achieved a staggering victory over the Turks. The following day, the great number of infidel corpses upon the battlefield made it impossible to retrieve Christian bodies; the crusaders celebrated a Mass devoted to the Holy Trinity and to the Virgin Mary, during which they prayed to God to help them find the dead bodies of their fellow crusaders. After the celebration of the Mass, the horseman appeared again and told them, '*Ecce agnus Dei, ecce qui tollit peccata mundi*', and a pleasant aroma floated above the battlefield. This was followed by a third miracle: flowering grasses erupted from the ground beside the dead crusaders, and the word 'Christian' appeared on the petals of the flowers.[167] According to the chronicler, and confirming the impact the circulation of such stories had on pro-crusade sentiment, after reports of this episode, a great multitude of Italian Christians set out to defend the faith against the Turks.

To a great extent, the narratives of miracles from the *Storie Pistoresi* follow earlier fourteenth-century models or similar narratives in the accounts of the First Crusade.[168] The warrior bestride a white horse and brandishing a shining red cross, sent from Heaven to instil courage in the crusaders before battle, was cited in the sermon preached in September 1331 by the Dominican, Pierre de la Palud.[169] As James MacGregor explains, the use of exemplars of saint-warriors as suitable and efficacious models for setting contemporary knights to action began in the 1070s.[170] The ideal of militant, knightly piety in the narratives of the First Crusade had already been developed by some clerics on the eve of the crusade. In the late 1070s, Gerold d'Avranches, a learned cleric in the household of Hugh d'Avranches, the Earl of Chester, used examples of humble warrior-saints in his preaching to convince contemporary warriors to renounce the world and become monks. Gerold also counselled great lords, knights and noble youths to imitate the deeds of several biblical personages and holy knights from the past. He drew vivid stories from the Bible and from the battles of Demetrius and George, of Theodore and Sebastian, all of whom received the crown of martyrdom in paradise.[171] Such allusions to military saints as a source of inspiration for knightly nobility seem the starting point for marvellous miracle stories of military saints fighting on behalf of the crusaders. The origins of the miracle story in the *Storie Pistoresi* and in Palud's crusade sermon are found in the narratives of the First Crusade, particularly in the accounts of the Battle of Antioch in 1098. The anonymous author of the *Gesta Francorum* and Peter of Tudebode attributed the Christian victory at Antioch to the miraculous appearance of knights on white horses with white banners, sent by Christ and led by the military saints George, Mercurius and Demetrius.[172] As Elizabeth Lapina explains, the same miracle story of Antioch appears, in various versions, in a number of twelfth-century accounts of the Battle of Antioch.[173] This is the same miracle story included in the *Storie Pistoresi* and used as an *exemplum* by Pierre de la Palud in his sermon on the Exaltation of the Cross.

The appearance of a divine sign on the crusaders' corpses after battle against the infidel is largely reminiscent of the *exemplum* of the preacher-priest in the city of Enns during his preaching for the Hospitallers' *passagium* in 1309.[174] This illustrates the wide circulation of such miracle stories among believers and the adaptation of these miracles as moral *exempla* by crusade preachers. These miracle stories animated crusaders in the battlefield and inspired congregants to take the cross. As a common point of reference, these miracles always included divine interference in favour of the crusaders at a crucial juncture or god-sent signs believed to portend the crusade's favourable outcome. The moral of the miracle stories emphasized divine or saintly protection of the fighting class; many miracle stories recount the help of Christ or a saint in battle.[175] It was Clement VI who first perceived how beneficial the circulation of miraculous stories could be for the crusade, and the dissemination of these miracle stories, via the Church's propaganda machinery, offered convincing evidence to the faithful of God's approval of the crusades, which in turn inspired a positive response to crusade preaching.

The great success of crusade preaching, in combination with the wide circulation of reports of miracles in Italy, drove the first waves of *crucesignati* to Venice in the spring of 1345, and their number increased rapidly once Humbert II of Viennois, the leader of the crusade, set foot in Italy. This situation troubled Pope Clement VI who, in May 1345, wrote to Bertucio Acontado, a layperson from Venice, requesting that Acontado take all necessary measures for the departure of the great gathering of pilgrims in Venice, so as 'to evade any dissension and rancor hatred' among them.[176] The arrival of so many pilgrims, even those who had enough money to pay the cost of conveyance to Smyrna, meant that the section of the city held by the crusaders was excessively crowded. Disease and famine killed many of those who travelled to Smyrna, but little is known of the fate of those who remained in Italy.[177]

The enormity of the popular response to the preaching of the Smyrna crusade, which was similar to the popular response to crusade preaching campaigns in 1309 and 1320, revealed the incredible impact of crusading messages. The extreme scale of the outburst proved that there was no diminution of crusading zeal among the masses, as compared to the waning crusade sentiment in the royal houses of Western Christianity. The spiritual salvation crusading offered, inspired a favourable reaction among the more helpless members of society, many of whom chose to take the cross and, ultimately, attain eternal life. Conversely, the degeneration of chivalrous ideals and the gradual development of nation-states meant that Western rulers turned away from crusading toward domestic issues and international political conflicts.

Anxious to secure the necessary economic resources for a crusading expedition to the East, Popes Clement V, John XXII and Clement VI did not restrict general preaching of the crusade. The massive, unmanageable reaction to crusade preaching, however, proved that they were unable to anticipate the effect this unrestrained preaching would have on the popular consciousness, or perhaps their desperation for funds blinded them to the consequences of intensive, widespread crusade preaching. Regardless, in 1346, Clement again assented to further crusade preaching.[178]

Notes

1 'Continuatio Florianensis', in *Monumenta Germaniae Historica: Scriptores Rerum Germanicarum. Nova Series,* eds. G. H. Pertz, *et al.*, 38 vols. (Hanover: Anton Hiersemann Reprint, 1983–), ix, 753 [hereafter MGH:S].

2 'Annales Londonienses', in *Chronicles of the Reigns of Edward I and Edward II: Annales Londonienses and Annales Paulini Edited from Mss. in the British Museum and in the Archiepiscopal Library at Lambeth*, ed. W. Stubbs, 2 vols. (London: Longman, 1882–1883), ii, 266: 'Hoc anno [1308] papa fecit predicare per totam Christianitatem profectionem fidelium in subsidium regum Cypri et Armenie contra saracenos ... Eodem anno [1309], die Conversionis beati Pauli, venit Londonias episcopus Nazareth cum privilegio domini papae in subsidium terrae sanctae'.

3 'Corpus chronicorum bononensium', in *Rerum Italicarum scriptores: Raccolta degli storici italiani dal cinquecento al millecinquecento*, ed. A. Sorbelli (Città di Castello-Bologna: Ex Typographia Societatis Palatinae in Regia Curia, 1923), xviii, cols. 530–533 [hereafter *RIS*]; 'Storie Pistoresi', in *RIS*, xi.5, 214–216.

4 *Les Grandes chroniques de France*, ed. J. Viard, 10 vols. (Paris: Société de l'histoire de France, 1920–1953), viii, 285–287; 'Continuatio chronici Girardi de Fracheto', in *Recueil des historiens des Gaules et de la France*, eds. M. Bouquet, *et al.*, 24 vols. (Paris: Imprimerie Impériale, 1737–1904) xxi, 37 [hereafter RHGF]; *Chronique Latin de Guillaume de Nangis de 1113 a 1300 avec les continuations de cette chronique de 1300 a 1368*, ed. H. Géraud, 2 vols. (Paris: Imprimerie de Crapelet, 1843), i, 389–392; 'Prima Vita Clementis V', in *Vitae Paparum Avenionensium*, ed. G. Mollat, 4 vols. (Paris: Librairie Letouzey et Ané, 1916–1928), i, 19–20 [hereafter VPA]; *Chronique métrique de Godefroy de Paris*, ed. J. A. Buchon (Paris: Imprimerie d'Hippolyte Tilliard, 1827), 171–175; Franz Ehrle, 'Zur Geschichte des Päpsteichen Hofceremoniells im 14 Jahrhundert', *Archiv Für Literatur und Kirchengeschichte des Mittelalters*, 5 (1889), 565–603.

5 *Continuatio chronici Guillelmi de Nangiano*, i, 396: 'Philippus rex Francie, una cum tribus filiis suis prefatis novis militibus jam effectis, necnon rex Anglie Eduardus et regni Anglie potentes, de manu cardinalis Nicolai, ad hoc summo pontifice destinati, crucem pro transfretando in Terre Sancte subsidium assumserunt'.

6 *Les Grandes chroniques de France*, viii, 287–290; *Continuatio chronici Girardi de Fracheto*, in *RHGF*, xxi, 38; *Continuatio chronici Guillelmi de Nangiano*, i, 396; 'Prima Vita Clementis V', in *VPA*, i, 21–22; *Chronique métrique de Godefroy de Paris*, 188; *Auctore Bernardo Guidonis e floribus chronicorum*, in *RHGF*, xxi, 723; *Excerpta e Memoriali Historiarum Johannis a Sancto Victore*, in *RHGF*, xxi, 657; *Fragmenta d'une chronique anonyme finnisant en M.CCC.XXVIII*, in *RHGF*, xxi, 150; Sophia Menache, *Clement V* (Cambridge: Cambridge University Press, 1998), 115; Sylvia Schein, *Fideles Crucis: The Papacy, the West, and the Recovery of the Holy Land 1274–1314* (Oxford: Oxford Clarendon Press, 1998), 255.

7 *Les Grandes chroniques de France*, viii, 288–289: 'Touz les bourgois et maistres de Paris firent très belle feste, et vindrent les uns en paremens riches et de noble euvre fais, les autres en robes neuves, à pié et à cheval, chacun mestier par soy ordené, ou dessus de ille de Nostre Dame, a trompes, tabours, buisines, timbres et nacaires, a grant joie et a grant noise demenant et de tres biaus jeux jouant'; Menache, *Clement V*, 115; Schein, *Fideles Crucis*, 255.

8 'Continuatio chronici Guillelmi de Nangiano', in *RHGF*, xx, 615–616; 'Chroniques de Saint-Denis depuis 1285 jusqu'en 1328', in *RHGF*, xx, 698–699; *Chronique Parisienne anonyme du XIVe siècle*, ed. A. Hellot (Nogent-Le-Rotrou: Société de l'Histoire de Paris, 1884), 25–26; Paul Lehugeur, *Histoire de Philippe le Long, Roi de France*, 2 vols. (Paris: Imprimerie Lahure, 1897), i, 196; Christopher Tyerman, 'Philip V of France, the Assemblies of 1319–20 and the Crusade', *Bulletin of the Institute of Historical Research*, 57 (1984), 15–34, 16, 22; Norman Housley, *The Avignon Papacy and the Crusades, 1305–1378* (Oxford: Oxford Clarendon Press, 1986), 108–110.

9 'Continuatio chronici Guillelmi de Nangiano', in *RHGF*, xx, 616; 'Chroniques de Saint-Denis depuis 1285 jusqu'en 1328', in *RHGF*, xx, 699; *Chronique Parisienne anonyme*, 26.

10 Unfortunately, I did not manage to detect any manuscript with a collection of sermons attributed to Peter of Pleine Chassagne or Peter of Courpalay.
11 Girolamo Golubovich, *Biblioteca Bio-Bibliografica della Terra Santa e dell'Oriente Francescano*, 5 vols. (Florence: Quaracchi, 1906–1927), iii, 147–148. Golubovich found Peter's letter in the first edition of the *Spicilegium sive Collectio aeterum aliquot scriptorum qui in Galliae bibliothecis delituerant*, ed. L. D'Achery, 13 vols. (Paris: Montalant, 1655–1677), viii, 276–277.
12 In his letter of 23 July 1316, Peter of Pleine Chassagne referred to other letters previously sent 'per litteras alias vobis missas': Golubovich, *Biblioteca Bio-Bibliografica*, iii, 147.
13 Arthur de Boislisle, 'Projet de Croisade du Premier Duc de Bourbon, 1316–1333', *Extrait de l'Annuaire Bulletin de la Société de l'histoire de France*, 9 (1872), 230–255, 246–255; Tyerman, 'Philip V and the Crusade', 21.
14 Golubovich, *Biblioteca Bio–Bibliografica*, iii, 147: 'Quia tempus quo debent arripere iter suum illustres viri dominus de Claromonte ... satis breve videtur esse ... maior diligentia et providentia est adhibenda. Propter quod, habito consilio peritorum ... pro felici expeditione passagii Terrae Sanctae ita extitit ordinatum'.
15 'Continuatio chronici Guillelmi de Nangiano', in *RHGF*, xx, 616: 'congregatis praelatis quamplurimis, Parisius solemniter assumpserunt, proclamatumque fuit ex parte comitis Pictavensis, qui jamdudum patre vivente acceperat, ut qui tunc vel etiam ante crucem acceperat, ad transfretandum cum ipsis in festo Pentecostes ab eodem festo immediate post annum futurum totis se viribus praepararet'; 'Chroniques de Saint-Denis depuis 1285 jusqu'en 1328', in *RHGF*, xx, 699; *Chronique Parisienne anonyme*, 26.
16 Tyerman, 'Philip V and the Crusade', 17.
17 John XXII, *Lettres ... Relatives à la France*, nos. 505, 512–513; Charles H. Taylor, 'French Assemblies and Subsidy in 1321', *Speculum*, 43.2 (1968), 217–244, 221.
18 Golubovich, *Biblioteca Bio-Bibliografica*, iii, 147: 'In primis, quod vos domini Praelati mandetis omnibus curatis vestrarum diocesium, et fratribus Minoribus et Praedicatoribus, quod ipsi, dominicis diebus et festivis, quando clero et populo praedicant verbum Dei, inducant Crucesignatos et alios qui sumere voluerint, quod sibi taliter provideant, quod possint a proximo festo Pentecostes venturo in uno anno arripere iter suum: et alios qui non ibunt inducant ut velint de bonis sibi a Deo collatis elargiri pro passagio antedicto, et preces apud Deum effundere pro eodem, ut possit fieri ad honorem ipsius et remedium animarum'.
19 Christoph T. Maier, *Preaching the Crusades: Mendicant Friars and the Cross in the Thirteenth Century* (Cambridge: Cambridge University Press, 1994), 61, 95.
20 Golubovich, *Biblioteca Bio-Bibliografica*, iii, 131–146.
21 See Chapter 1, note 81.
22 Housley, *The Avignon Papacy*, 244–245.
23 Golubovich, *Biblioteca Bio-Bibliografica*, iii, 147–148: 'Item, quod in qualibet dioecesi, videlicet in civitatibus, duae personae eligantur, quibus curati ecclesiarum reportent nomina illorum qui ire voluerint, et qua forma, et auxilium quod invenerint et receperint a remanentibus et non euntibus ad passagium antedictum. Item, quod illae duae personae electae in civitatibus, reportent aut mittant Parisius in scriptis, per octo dies ante festum Pentecostes proxime venturum, nomina illorum qui ire voluerint, et auxilium quod eis fuerat reportatum. Ita quod, scitis nominibus et aliis, possit fieri providentia de navibus et de aliis necessariis ad passagium antedictum'.
24 *Les Grandes chroniques de France*, ix, 130, 133–134; *Chronique Latin de Guillaume de Nangis*, ii, 130–131, 135; *Chronique Parisienne anonyme*, 154; *Chronique des quatre premiers Valois (1327–1393)*, ed. S. Luce (Paris: Société de l'histoire de France, 1862), 6; *Chronographia regum Francorum*, ii, 19; 'Quinta Vita Joannis XXII', in *VPA*, i, 174; Déprez, *La Papauté, la France et l'Angleterre*, 99; Delaville le Roulx, *La France en Orient*, 87; Housley, *The Avignon Papacy*, 24; Norman Housley, *The Later Crusades: From Lyon to Alcazar, 1274–1580* (Oxford: Oxford University Press,

1992), 33; Dunbabin, *A Hound of God: Pierre de la Palud and the Fourteenth-Century Church* (Oxford: Clarendon Press, 1991), 177; Tyerman, 'Philip VI and the Holy Land', 30. For the 1333 preaching of the crusade in Cyprus, see Nicholas Coureas, *The Latin Church in Cyprus, 1313–1378* (Nicosia: Cyprus Research Center, 2010), 98–99.
25 Cecilia M. Gaposchkin, *Invisible Weapons: Liturgy and the Making of Crusade Ideology* (Ithaca and London: Cornell University Press, 2017), 195–197.
26 Amnon Linder, *Raising Arms: Liturgy in the Struggle to Liberate Jerusalem in the Late Middle Ages* (Turnhout: Brepols Publishers, 2003), 1–3; Penny J. Cole, *The Preaching of the Crusades to the Holy Land, 1095–1270* (Cambridge, Massachusetts: The Medieval Academy of America, 1991), 106–107; Christoph T. Maier, 'Crisis, Liturgy and the Crusade in the Twelfth and Thirteenth Centuries', *Journal of Ecclesiastical History*, 48.4 (1997), 625–658, 629.
27 Gaposchkin, *Invisible Weapons*, 201–208.
28 Maier, 'Crisis, Liturgy', 641–657; Christoph T. Maier, 'Mass, the Eucharist and the Cross: Innocent III and the Relocation of the Crusade', in *Pope Innocent III and his World*, ed. J. C. Moore (Aldershot: Ashgate, 1999), 351–360, 354; Charansonnet Alexis, 'L'Évolution de la Predication du Cardinal Eudes de Châteauroux (1190?–1273): Un Approache Statistique', in *De l'homélie au sermon: Histoire de la predication medieval*, eds. J. Hamesse and X. Hermand (Louvain-la-Neuve: Fédération Internationale des institus d'études médiévales, 1993), 103–142.
29 Linder, *Raising Arms*, 114.
30 Janus M. Jensen, *Denmark and the Crusades, 1400–1650* (Leiden-Boston: Brill, 2007), 115.
31 Clement V, *Regestum Clementis papae V: Ex Vaticanis archetypis sanctissimi domini nostri Leonis XIII pontificis maximi iussu et munificentia*, ed. Cura et Studio Monarchorum Ordinis S. Benedicti, 10 vols. (Rome: Typografia Vaticana, 1885–1892), nos. 2989–2990 [hereafter *Regestum*]; *Cartulaire*, no. 4864; Riley-Smith, *The Knights of St John*, 224.
32 'Anonymum S. Martialis chronicon ad annum MCCCXX continuatum', in *RHGF*, xxi, 813: 'dominus Clemens papa quintus instituit dicere ad missas, qualibet die, duas orationes pro subsidio Christianorum contra Sarracenos, et fecit poni archas in ecclesias ad reponendas oblationes ad opus subsidii Terrae Sanctae transmarine'.
33 ASV, Reg. Vat. 56, fols. 198^v–199^r; Linder, *Raising Arms*, 118–119; Gaposchkin, *Invisible Weapons*, 223, 232.
34 The decrees of the annual Cistercian Chapter for the years 1193–1197 prove special intercessory prayers for the Holy Land were said by the Cistercians before 1193. Jensen, *Denmark and the Crusades*, 114–115; Linder, *Raising Arms*, 200–233. More recently, Cecilia Gaposchkin argued that the Cistercians had already begun to perform special prayers for the Holy Land in 1188. Gaposchkin, *Invisible Weapons*, 221.
35 For full account on Bernard of Clairvaux's preaching tour, see Cole, *Preaching the Crusades to the Holy Land*, 41–50; For Henry of Clairvaux see Beverly M. Kienzle, *Cistercians, Heresy and Crusade in Occitania, 1145–1229: Preaching in the Lord's Vineyard* (Rochester, New York: York Medieval Press/Boydell Press, 2001), 109–134.
36 Kienzle, *Preaching in the Lord's Vineyard*.
37 Maier, *Preaching the Crusades*, 8–95; Moorman, *A History of the Franciscan Order*, 300–302; Hinnebusch, *The History of the Dominican Order* (especially the first volume, which deals with the order's origins and growth).
38 Gaposchkin, *Invisible Weapons*, 221.
39 ASV, Reg. Vat. 56, fol. 140^v, ep. 682: 'universitatem vestram rogamus et hortamur in Domino in remissione vobis pecceminum, iniungentes quatenus pro salute vestra et felici consumatione passagii per nos ordinati in subsidium Terre sancte ac aliorum que vobis imminent agendorum pias apud Deum preces effundere studeatis, nos enim de ipsius omnipotentis Dei misericordia et beatorum Petri et Pauli auctoritate, confisi

singulis vestrum vere penitentibus et confessis, qui singulis diebus donec vixerimus, quinquies orationem dominicam et septies salutationem beate Marie virginis huius gratiis a Domino facilius obtinendis dixerint reverenter'.

40 The *'Missa Contra Paganos'* prayers: Clement V, *Regestum*, nos. 2989, 4769; *Cartulaire*, no. 4864; 1. 'Omnipotens Sempiterne Deus, in cuius manu sunt omnium potestates et omnia iura regnorum, respice in auxilium christianorum, ut gentes paganorum, que in sua feritate confidunt, dextere tue potentia conterantur'; 2. 'Sacrificium Domine, quod immolamus intende, et propugnatores tuos ab omni exuas paganorum nequitia et in tue protectionis securitate constituas'; 3. 'Protector noster aspice Deus et propugnatores tuos a paganorum defende periculis, ut ab omnibus perturbationis summoti, liberis tibi mentibus serviant'; Menache, *Clement V*, 108; Schein, *Fideles Crucis*, 222.

41 Linder, *Raising Arms*, 103.

42 Throughout the thirteenth century the triple set of prayers *Missa Contra Paganos* had limited use in the Liturgy for the Holy Land, see Linder, *Raising Arms*, 103–118; Gaposchkin, *Invisible Weapons*, 223–225.

43 For information on the Clementine *Missa Contra Paganos* I was based on my article Constantinos Georgiou, 'Propagating the Hospitallers' Passagium: Crusade Preaching and Liturgy in 1308–1309', in *Islands and Military Orders, c.1291–c.1798*, eds. E. Buttigieg and S. Philips (Famham: Ashgate, 2013), 53–64.

44 Linder, *Raising Arms*, 118, 120; Jensen, *Denmark and the Crusades*, 115, 349–351.

45 Anthony Luttrell, 'The Hospitallers at Rhodes, 1306–1421', in *A History of the Crusades: The Fourteenth and Fifteenth Centuries*, ed. H. W. Hazard, 6 vols. (Madison: The University of Wisconsin Press, 1969–1989), iii, 283.

46 Giovanni Villani, *Cronica*, ix, 137: 'Il loro Maestro de Napoli fece suo passagio, e presono l'isola di Rodi in Turchia'.

47 Linder, *Raising Arms*, 120.

48 Clement V, *Regestum*, no. 2148: 'Dilectis filiis Fulconi magistro et fratribus hospitalis sancti Iohannis Ierosolimitani ... Sane dilecti in Domino filii exhibita nobis nuper vestra petitio continebat, quod dextera Domini vobiscum faciente virtutem insula Rodi, quam scismaticorum Grecorum infidelitas detinebat, non sine magnis laboribus, sumptibus et expensis in potenti brachio accepistis, quam etiam hodie per Dei gratiam retinetis evulsis inde prorsus scismaticis et infidelibus omnino deiectis'.

49 Clement V, *Regestum*, no. 2148.

50 Gaposchkin, *Invisible Weapons*, 240–242; Linder, *Raising Arms*, 119; Jensen, *Denmark and the Crusades*, 350.

51 Clement V, *Regestum*, nos. 2989, 4769: 'Orationes contra paganorum perfidiam per ecclesiam ordinatas, quarum prima Omnipotens Sempiterne Deus, secundo deputata specialiter ad secretam Sacrificium Domine et tertia dici post comunionem precipue consuetam Protector incipiunt'; *Cartulaire*, no. 4864.

52 Maier, 'Crisis, Liturgy', 638.

53 Maier, 'The Eucharist and the Cross', 356–359.

54 John XXII, *Lettres secrètes & curiales du pape Jean XXII (1316–1334) relatives à la France*, eds. A. Coulon and S. Clémencet, 3 vols. (Paris: Bibliothèque des Écoles françaises d'Athènes et de Rome, 3e séries, 1900–1967), no. 1262 [hereafter *Lettres ... Relatives à la France*].

55 John XXII, *Lettres ... Relatives à la France*, nos. 1571–1573; Gaposchkin, *Invisible Weapons*, 234.

56 John XXII, *Lettres ... Relatives à la France*, no. 1571: 'tam in cathedralibus quam in singulis vestrarum civitatum et diocesum ecclesiis poni truncum concavum faciatis, tribus clavibus consignatum, in quo dicti fideles, juxta quod Dominus eorum mentibus inspiraverit, suas helemosinas deponere in dictorum regnorum [Armenie et Cipri] defensionis subdicium ac impugnationem hostium nominis crucifixi suorumque remissionemque peccaminum moneantur. Et ut hec ab illo a quo bona cuncta

procedunt facilius impetrentur, in ipsis ecclesiis semel in ebdomada certa die quam sacerdos pronunciet populo, missa publice, una videlicet epdomada, missa de sancta Trinitate, secunda de beata Virgine, tertia de sanctis Angelis et sic deinceps cum devotione et reverentia decantetur'; Amnon Linder, *Raising Arms: Liturgy in the Struggle to Liberate Jerusalem in the Late Middle Ages* (Turnhout: Brepols, 2003), 27, 100; Guillaume Mollat, 'Jean XXII et Charles IV le Bel (1322–1328)', *Journal des Sevants*, 2 (1967), 92–106, 99.

57 John XXII, *Lettres ... Relatives à la France*, no. 1571: 'in qualibet autem missarum hujusmodi, cum omni devotione post Agnus Dei, ante susceptionem corporis Domini, psalmum dici mandamus et decernimus infrascriptum, videlicet: Deus, venerunt gentes in heretitatem tuam, cum: Gloria patri; et versiculis qui secuntur: versiculus: Salvos fac servos tuos – Responsio: Deus meus sperantes in te – Vers.: Esto, nobis Domine, turris fortitudinis – Resp.: A facie inimici – Vers.: Nichil proficiat inimicus in nobis – Resp.: Et filius iniquitatis non apponat nocere nobis – Vers.: Exurge, Domine, adjura nos – Resp.: Et libera nos propter nomen tuum'.

58 Penny Cole, '"O God, the Heathen Have Come into Your Inheritance" (Ps. 78.1): The Theme of Religious Pollution in Crusade Documents, 1095–1188', in *Crusaders and Muslims in Twelfth-Century Syria*, ed. M. Shatzmiller (Leiden: Brill, 1993), 84–112, 95–97.

59 Linder, *Raising Arms*, 100–101.

60 John XXII, *Lettres ... Relatives à la France*, no. 1571: 'Salvos fac servos tuos – Responsio: Deus meus sperantes in te – Vers.: Esto, nobis Domine, turris fortitudinis – Resp.: A facie inimici – Vers.: Nichil proficiat inimicus in nobis – Resp.: Et filius iniquitatis non apponat nocere nobis – Vers.: Exurge, Domine, adjura nos – Resp.: Et libera nos propter nomen tuum'.

61 John XXII, *Lettres ... Relatives à la France*, no. 1571: 'Hostium nostrorum, quesumus Domine, elide superbiam, et eorum contumaciam dextere tue virtute prosterne, per Christum Dominum nostrum, Amen'.

62 John XXII, *Lettres ... Relatives à la France*, no. 1571: 'Omnipotens sempiterne Deus in cuius manu sunt potestates et omnium iura regnorum, respice ad populum christianorum tuum, nomen sacratissimum invocationem, ut gentes que in sua feritate confidunt potentie tue dextera comprimantur'; Linder, *Raising Arms*, 27.

63 John XXII, *Lettres ... Relatives à la France*, no. 1571: 'hujusmodi vero elemosine et oblationes in truncis mittentur seu deponentur'.

64 ASV, Reg. Aven. 40, fols. 88^v–89^r; ASV, Reg. Aven. 41, fols. 223^r–224^r; ASV, Reg. Vat. 101, fols. 2^v–3^r, ep. 6; John XXII, *Lettres Communes du Pape Jean XXII Analysées d'Après les Registres dits d'Avignon et du Vatican*, ed. G. Mollat, 16 vols. (Paris: Bibliothèque des Écoles Françaises d'Athènes et de Rome, 3e séries, 1904–1947), no. 58207 [hereafter John XXII, *Lettres Communes*]; *Bullarium Ordinis Fratrum Praedicatorum*, ii, 194–195.

65 ASV, Reg. Vat. 101, fols. 2^v–3^r, ep. 6: 'volumus et auctoritate presentium ordinamus, ut singulis predictis et aliis et regularibus ecclesiis dicti regni, qualibet ebdomada semel certa die providentia populo una missa pro liberatione Terre sancte de manibus hostium predictorum prefata prosecutione durante cum infra scriptis orationibus solemniter celebretur, ita quod in prima de Trinitate, in secunda de cruce, ac in tertia ebdomadis de Beata Maria virgine et sic deinceps misse huiusmodi debeant celebrari'.

66 Clermont-Ferrand, Bibliothèque Municipale, MS 46, fols. 215^r–220^v; Paris, Bibliothèque Nationale de France, MS lat. 3293, fols. 161^r–169^r.

67 Paris, Bibliothèque Nationale de France, MS lat. 14965, fols. 331^v–333^r.

68 ASV, Reg. Aven. 40, fols. 88^v–89^r: 'Cunctis quoque fidelibus vere penitentibus et confessis, qui durante prosecutione dicti negotii pro ipsius consummatione felici devote ad Dominum preces effunderint, decem dies, singulis videlicet diebus, quibus oraverint, de injunctis eis penitentiis misericorditer relaxamus'; ASV, Reg. Vat. 101, fol. 3^r, ep. 6; *Bullarium Ordinis Fratrum Praedicatorum*, ii, 195.

69 ASV, Reg. Aven. 40, fols. 88ᵛ–89ʳ: 'Orationes sunt iste: Deus, qui admirabili providentia cuncta disponis; te supliciter exoramus, ut terram, quam Unigenitus tuus proprio sanguine consecravit, de manibus inimicorum crucis eripias, et eam in Christiana religione tuo nomini servire concedes. Per eundem, et oratio secreta: Sacrificium Domine ... Alia oratio post communionem: Protector noster aspice Deus'; ASV, Reg. Vat. 101, fol. 3ʳ, ep. 6; Linder, *Raising Arms*, 146–147.

70 ASV, Reg. Aven. 41, fol. 224ʳ: 'Ut autem huiusmodi sanctum negotium felicius prosperetur volumus ut in singulis cathedralibus collegiatis et parochialibus ecclesiis regni predicti, singuli trunci concavi ponantur'.

71 John XXII, *Lettres ... Relatives à la France*, nos. 5210, 5214, 5226–5227; John XXII, *Lettres Communes*, nos. 60781, 61241, 61234–61235, 61247; Golubovich, *Biblioteca Bio–Bibliografica*, iii, 364.

72 John XXII, *Lettres ... Relatives à la France*, nos. 5210: 'Porro desiderantes intense quod huiusmodi negotium optatum sortiatur effectum et eiusdem regis ac aliorum Christi fidelium prosecutionem dicti negotii efficacius roboretur, auctoritate presentium ordinamus ut in singulis supradictis et aliis etiam regularibus ecclesiis dicti regni qualibet ebdomada semel certa die pronuntianda populo una missa pro libertate dicte Terre de manibus hostium prefata prosecutione durante cum infrascriptis orationibus solemniter celebratur, ita quod in prima de Trinitate, in secunda de Cruce et in tertia ebdomadis de Beata Maria Virgine ... Predicte autem orationes sunt iste: 'Deus qui admirabili providentia etc ...'. Oratio secunda 'Sacrificium, Domine, quod immolamus etc ...'. Alia oratio post communionem 'Protector noster aspice Deus etc ...'".

73 Benedict XII, *Lettres closes, patentes et curiales du pape Benoît XII (1334–1342) se rapportant à la France*, ed. G. Daumet (Paris: Bibliothèque des Écoles Françaises d'Athènes et de Rome, 3ᵉ séries, 1899–1920), no. 19 [hereafter *Lettres ... Rapportant à la France*]; Benedict XII, *Lettres Communes du Pape Benoît XII*, ed. J. M. Vidal, 3 vols. (Paris: Bibliothèque des Écoles Françaises d'Athènes et de Rome, 3ᵉ séries, 1903–1911), no. 2425 [hereafter *Lettres Communes*].

74 'Concilium Rotomagense', in *Sacrorum Conciliorum Nova et Amplissima Collectio*, ed. G. D. Mansi, 31 vols. (Florence, Venice, 1757–1798), xxv, col. 1043 (New edition with supplements L. Petit and J. M. Martin, 60 vols. (Paris-Leipzig-Arnheim, 1899–1927).

75 ASV, Reg. Vat. 157, fol. 7ʳ⁻ᵛ, ep. 35: 'Ceterum ut huiusmodi negotium fidei felicius prosperetur volumus ut in singulis ecclesiis vestrarum civitatum et diocesium singuli trunci concavi ponantur'; ASV, Reg. Vat. 161, fols. 2ᵛ–3ʳ, ep. 15; Clement VI, *Lettres Rapportant à la France*, no. 433 (summary).

76 *Annales Ecclesiastici ab anno 1198 usque ad annum 1565*, eds. A. Theiner, *et al.*, 37 vols. (Paris-Freiburg-Bar le Duc, 1864–1867), xxv, 328: 'et tam per processiones quam sermones ad clerum et populum laudes fecimus solemniter Domino decantari' [hereafter *Annales Ecclesiastici*]; Gaposchkin, *Invisible Weapons*, Appendix 3, 320.

77 Sylvia Schein, *Fideles Crucis: The Papacy, the West, and the Recovery of the Holy Land 1274–1314* (Oxford: Oxford Clarendon Press, 1998), 17.

78 Clement V, *Regestum*, nos. 1248, 2986, 2988, 2990.

79 For Phillip IV's and James II's of Aragon obstacles to the Hospitallers *passagium* see *Cartulaire general de l'Ordre des Hospitaliers de St Jean de Jerusalem 1100–1310*, ed. J. Delaville Le Roulx, 4 vols. (Paris: Leroux, 1894–1906), nos. 4831, 4841, 4860; Clement V, *Regestum*, nos. 3988–3991; Norman Housley, 'Pope Clement V and the Crusades of 1309–1310', *Journal of Medieval History*, 8 (1982), 33–41; Anthony Luttrell, 'The Hospitallers and the Papacy, 1305–1314', in *Studies on the Hospitallers after 1306: Rhodes and the West* (Aldershot: Ashgate Variorum, 2007), 595; Allan Forey, 'The Military Orders in the Crusading Proposals of the Late 13th and Early 14th Centuries', in *Military Orders and Crusades* (Aldershot: Ashgate Variorum, 1994), 325–342; Schein, *Fideles Crucis*, 190–193, 226.

80 Timothy Guard, *Chivalry, Kingship and Crusade: The English Experience in the Fourteenth Century* (Woodbridge: The Boydell Press, 2013), 23–24. See, especially, the list of diocesan registers examined by the author in note 7.
81 Schein, *Fideles Crucis*, 238; Luttrell, 'The Hospitallers and the Papacy', 608; Tyerman, *England and the Crusades* (Chicago-London: The University of Chicago Press, 1988), 241; Housley, *The Later Crusades*, 407–408; Antony Leopold, *How to Recover the Holy Land: The Crusade Proposals of the Late Thirteenth and Early Fourteenth Centuries* (Aldershot: Ashgate, 2000); Menache, *Clement V*, 62–63.
82 Housley, *The Avignon Papacy*, 145; Schein, *Fideles Crucis*, 236.
83 Malcolm Barber, 'The Pastoureaux of 1320', *Journal of Ecclesiastical History*, 32 (1981), 143–166.
84 'Continuatio Florianensis', in *MGH:S*, ix, 747–753; 'Gestorum Abbatum Trudonensium Continuatio Tertia', in *MGH:S*, x, 361–448; 'Chronicon Elwacense', in *MGH:S*, x, 34–51; 'Annales Lubicenses', in *MGH:S*, xvi, 411–429; 'Annales Gandenses', in *MGH:S*, xvi, 555–597; 'Annales Sancti Blasii Brunsvicenses' in *MGH:S*, xxiv, 825; 'Annales Tielenenses', in *MGH:S*, xxiv, 26; 'Annales Cisterciensium in Heinrichow', in *MGH:S*, xix, 545; 'Annales Colbazenses', in *MGH:S*, xix, 717; 'Annales Terrae Prussicae', in *MGH:S*, xix, 691–693; Giovanni Villani, *Cronica*, ii, 145; 'Annales Londonienses', 156; 'Secunda Vita Clementis V', in *VPA*, i, 34; 'Collectio Actorum Veterum, in *VPA*, iii, 89–90; *Annales Ecclesiastici*, xxiii, 381, 448.
85 'Continuatio Florianensis', in *MGH:S*, ix, 752–753; 'Annales Colbazenses', in *MGH:S*, xix, 717.
86 'Annales Londonienses', 156; Guard, *Chivalry, Kingship and Crusade*, 137.
87 'Gestorum Abbatum Trudonensium continuatio tertia', in *MGH:S*, x, 412: 'Anno eodem multitudo communis plebis, tam virorum quam mulierum, de partibus Lotharingie et trans Renum, ex civitatibus, castellis et villis progrediens, nullo predicante, sed sua sponte cruce signantur'; 'Annales Gandenses', in *MGH:S*, xvi, 596: 'innumerabiles vulgares ... se ipsos sine prelatorum consilio cruce signantes'.
88 'Annales Lubicenses' in *MGH: S*, xvi, 421: 'Clemens papa ad expeditionem ultramarinam fecit per regiones praedicari crucem; propter quod diversarum nationum populus infinitus utriusque sexus, cruce signatus, putabat transfretare mare ad recuperandam sanctam terram'.
89 Giovanni Villani, *Cronica*, ii, 137, 145: 'appari grande maraviglia, che si comminciò in Piemonte, e venne per Lombardia, e per la Riviera di Genova, e poi per Toscana, e poi quasi per tutta Italia, che molta gente minuta, uomini e femmine e fanciulli sanza numero, lasciavano il loro mestieri e bisogne, e colle croci s'andavano battendo di luogo in luogo'.
90 Clement V, *Regestum*, no. 4400: 'Cum plurimi de regno Alamanie signo vivifice crucis assumpto voventes Terre sancte subsidium proficisci'.
91 'Gestorum Abbatum Trudonensium Continuatio Tertia', in *MGH:S*, x, 412: 'Annales Cisterciensium in Heinrichow', in *MGH:S*, xix, 545; 'Secunda Vita Clementis V', in *VPA*, i, 34: '40 milibus hominum ad Romanam curiam accedentes ... multi viri cum armis ... de Theutonicis plures, spectantes transfretare cum Hospitalariis'; Housley, *The Avignon Papacy*, 145, note 99.
92 The chroniclers described them as farmers, shoemakers, tanners, poor artisans and common people. 'Continuatio Florianensis', in *MGH:S*, ix, 752: 'agricultores, sutores, pelliperarii et alii manuales operarii'; 'Annales Gandenses', in *MGH:S*, xvi, 596: 'innumerabiles vulgares'.
93 Schein, *Fideles Crucis*, 235.
94 Clement V, *Regestum*, no. 4400: 'nos volentes, quod tam his, qui venerunt, quam eis, qui miserunt, devotio, quam ex hoc ad Redemptorem nostrum gerere comprobantur, eterne salutis pariat incrementum, de omnipotentis Dei misericordia et beatorum Petri et Pauli apostolorum eius auctoritate confisi omnibus peregrinis eisdem, qui venerunt, et illis etiam, qui miserunt aliquos ex eisdem, vere penitentibus et confessis

centum annos de iniunctis eis penitentiis misericorditer relaxamus'; 'Continuatio Canonicorum Sancti Rudberti Salisburgensis', in *MGH:S*, ix, 819: 'multe gratie et indulgentie maxime conceduntur'; 'Annales Paulini', 266. For details on crusading indulgences see: Jonathan Riley-Smith, *What Were the Crusades?* (London: Macmillan, 1977), 60–65.

95 Clement V, *Regestum*, nos. 5081–5082, 5084.
96 Clement V, *Regestum*, nos. 5081–5082, 5084; 'Chronicon Parmense ab anno 1038 usque ad annum 1338', in *RIS*, ix.9, 113; 'Quarta Vita Clementis V', in *VPA*, i, 66; Housley, *The Italian Crusades*, 24; Guillaume Mollat, *The Popes at Avignon: 1305–1378* (London: Thomas Nelson and Sons, 1963), 70–76.
97 'Gestorum abbatum Trudonensium continuatio tertia', in *MGH:S*, x, 412; 'Annales Colbazenses', in *MGH:S*, xix, 717; 'Continuatio Florianensis', in *MGH:S*, ix, 752–753; 'Secunda Vita Clementis V', in *VPA*, i, 34: 'Eodem anno [1309], circa idem tempus, venerunt ad curiam circa XXX milia inter Anglicos et Theutonicos, sed de Theutonicis plures, spectantes posse transfretare cum Hospitalariis'; Schein, *Fideles Crucis*, 236.
98 'Continuatio Florianensis', in *MGH:S*, ix, 752; Giovanni Villani, *Cronica*, ii, 145; Guard, *Chivalry, Kingship and Crusade*, 24.
99 Giovanni Villani, *Cronica*, ii, 145: 'I Fiorentini e più altre cittá non gli lasciarono entrare in loro terre, ma gli scacciavano dicendo, ch'era male segnale nella terra ove entrassero'.
100 'Annales Sancti Blasii Brunsvicenses', in *MGH:S*, xxiv, 825; 'Annales Tielenenses', in *MGH:S*, xxiv, 26; 'Chronicon Elwacense', in *MGH:S*, x, 39; 'Annales Gandenses', in *MGH:S*, xvi, 596; 'Continuatio Florianensis', in *MGH:S*, ix, 752–753; 'Annales Colbazenses', in *MGH:S*, xix, 717; 'Annales terrae Prussiae', in *MGH:S*, 691–693; 'Gestorum abbatum Trudonensium continuatio tertia', in *MGH:S*, x, 412.
101 'Annales Colbazenses', in *MGH:S*, xix, 717: 'cucurrit gens sine capite per mundum'. 'Annales Terrae Prussiae', in *MGH:S*, xix, 693: 'viri et mulieris per terram discurentes'; 'Annales Lubicenses', in *MGH:S*, xvi, 421: 'populum sine capite discurrentem'.
102 'Gestorum Abbatum Trudonensium Continuatio Tertia', in *MGH:S*, 412: 'multitudo communis plebis'; 'Annales Gandenses', in *MGH:S*, xvi, 596: 'innumerabilis vulgares'.
103 'Continuatio Florianensis', in *MGH:S*, ix, 752: 'parassiti, sectatores otii, post dilapidates substantias ... omnes miseri et mendici et invalidi'.
104 Schein, *Fideles Crucis*, 236.
105 'Continuatio Florianensis', in *MGH:S*, ix, 753: 'Illi igitur ... multiplicati super numerum, et de elemosinis cum scandalo omnium intuentium lascive viventes, tandem in talem temeritatem excreverunt, quod alicubi clericis oblationes de altaribus rapiebant, verberantes ipsos, et non recipientibus se mortes, excoriationes, expulsiones de ecclesiis et alia dira et horribilia comminantes'.
106 'Continuatio Florianensis' in *MGH:S*, ix, 753: 'quibus se coniunxerant clerici questuarii; qui quidem clerici questus gratia tam ridiculosa et erronea nec fidei katholice consona predicabant, quod horrorem discretis auribus inferebant'.
107 'Continuatio Florianensis' in *MGH:S*, ix, 753: 'Audivi ego unum in Anaso predicantem in hec verba: Videte, karissimi, quomodo negocium nostrum nutu divino dirigitur. Recipientibus nos rerum ubertas, solatium sanitatis a Deo tribuitur. Domus non recipientium igne misso celitus concremantur. Multi nostrum iam venerunt ad Terram Sanctam, qui dimicantes cum Sarracenis uno bello campestri vitam glorioso martyrio finiverunt. Et inter multa milia occisorum de nostris non erat unum corpus quod non nigro cendato aurea cruce intexta desuper de celo misso miraculose esset vestitum. Unde indifferenter nobis est vel hic vel ultra mare occidi, quia sepulchrum Domini nobis ubique est, et resistere turbatoribus negotii nostri et propter hoc etiam mori, in omni loco coronam nobis preparant sempiternam'.

108 An earlier example from the thirteenth century is the extensive report on Abbot Martin's sermon at Basel in the *Historia captae a latinis Constantinopoleos* of Gunther of Pairs; for details see Cole, *The Preaching of the Crusades*, 92–97.
109 'Annales Londonienses', 156: 'trans mare iter arripuerunt celerimme et improvise'.
110 Clement V, *Regestum*, no. 4400: 'Cum plurimi de regno Alamanie signo vivifice crucis assumpto voventes Terre sancte subsidium proficisci nuper ea intentione accesserint ad sedem apostolicam peregrini, ut exinde in prefate Terre subsidium transfretarent, quorum aliquos nonnulli de dicto regno in eorum expensis ob Crucifixi reverentiam transmiserunt, nec possint ad presens iidem peregrini propter defectum navigii exequi votum suum'.
111 Clement V, *Regestum*, no. 4400; 'Gestorum abbattum Trudonensium continuatio tertia', in *MGH:S*, x, 412; 'Annales Lubicenss', in *MGH:S*, xvi, 421; 'Annales Cisterciensium in Heinrichow', in *MGH:S*, xix, 545; 'Annales Londonienses', 156; 'Secunda Vita Clementis V', in *Vitae Paparum Avenionensium*, i, 34; Annales Ecclesiastici, xxiii, 448.
112 'Annales Londonienses', 156: 'unde gentes Angliae revertebantur in terram suam, et per diversas nationes dispersi'.
113 Housley, *The Avignon Papacy*, 144.
114 Clement V, *Regestum*, no. 2988; Housley, *The Avignon Papacy*, 144.
115 *Continuatio Chronici Guillelmi de Nangiano*, i, 396.
116 *Chronique anonyme finnisant en M.CCC.XXVIII*, in *RHGF*, xxi, 150: 'et fut faicte si grant croiserie par toutes les autres citez et villes de France, que c'estoit une grant merveille de la dévocion et de la bonne voulenté que tout le people avoit de visiter le saint sépulchre de Nostre-Seigneur et les autres lieux sainctz où Jhesu Crist conversa en terre; et avoient grant dueil au cuer de ce que la Terre Saincte estoit en la main des ennemis à Nostre Sauveur Jhesu Crist; et estoient appareilliez d'espandre leur sang pour l'amour de Jhesu Crist et pour conquerre son héritage, aussy comme Nostre-Seigneur espandi le sien sanc pour nous conquerre paradis'; The translation I quoted in the text is from Schein, *Fideles Crucis*, 255–256.
117 *Les Grandes chroniques de France*, viii, 352–354; *Chronique Parisienne anonyme*, 46–48; 'Chroniques de Saint-Denis depuis 1285 jusqu'en 1328', in *RHGF*, xx, 703–704; 'Excerpta e Memoriali Historiarum', in *RHGF*, xxi, 671–672; 'Continuatio chronici Guillelmi de Nangiano', in *RHGF*, xx, 625–626; 'Chronicon auctore Bernardo Guidonis, Episcopo Lodovensi', in *RHGF*, xxi, 730–731; 'Continuatio chronici Girardi de Fracheto', in *RHGF*, xxi, 54–55; 'Fragment d'une chronique anonyme finnisant en M.CCC.XXVIII', in *RHGF*, xxi, 152; 'Adae Murimuth continuatio chronicarum', in *Rerum Britannicarum medii aevi scriptores*, ed. H. R. Thomas, 2 vols. (London: Longman, 1863–1864), i, 31–32 [hereafter *RBMAS*]; 'Thomae Walsingham Quondam Monachi S. Albani Historia Anglicana', in *RBMAS*, i, 157; 'Annales Paulini', 288–289; *Chronographia regum Francorum*, ii, 250–252; 'Prima Vita Joannis XXII', in *VPA*, i, 128–130; 'Tertia Vita Joannis XXII', in *VPA*, i, 161–163; 'Quarta Vita Joannis XXII', in *VPA*, i, 171; 'Sexta Vita Joannis XXII', in *VPA*, i, 191–193; Barber, 'The Pastoureaux of 1320', 143–166.
118 'Continuatio Chronici Guillelmi de Nangiano', in *RHGF*, xx, 625: 'ultramare procedere contra fidei inimicos'; 'Chronicon Auctore Bernardo Guidonis, Episcopo Lodovensi', in *RHGF*, xxi, 730: 'ad recuperandum Terram Sanctam'.
119 'Excerpta e Memoriali Historiarum', in *RHGF*, xxi, 671: 'pueri sexdecim annorum et quatuordecim, custodes ovium et porcorum, dimissis pecoribus in campis et invitis parentibus, cum baculis et sine pecunia confluebant'; *Les Grandes chroniques de France*, viii, 353; *Chronique Parisienne anonyme*, 47; 'Chroniques de Saint-Denis depuis 1285 jusqu'en 1328', in *RHGF*, xx, 703; 'Continuatio chronici Guillelmi de Nangiano', in *RHGF*, xx, 625–626; 'Chronicon auctore Bernardo Guidonis, Episcopo Lodovensi', in *RHGF*, xxi, 730; 'Continuatio chronici Girardi de Fracheto', in *RHGF*, xxi, 54; 'Fragment d'une chronique anonyme finnisant en M.CCC.XXVIII', in *RHGF*, xxi, 152; 'Excerpta e Memoriali Historiarum', in *RHGF*, xxi, 671–672.

130 *Crusade preaching, liturgy and reaction*

120 'Annales Paulini', 288–289: 'hominum juveneum, qui eorum majorem aetatem habuit non attingebant vicesimum annum'.
121 'Chronicon auctore Bernardo Guidonis, Episcopo Lodovensi', in *RHGF*, xxi, 730: 'crescebantque numero et multiplicabantur quotidie paulatim, addebanturque ad eos inopes et alii vagi viri et mulieres'.
122 'Excerpta e Memoriali Historiarum', in *RHGF*, xxi, 671; *Les Grandes Chroniques de France*, viii, 353; *Chronique Parisienne anonyme*, 47; 'Chroniques de Saint-Denis depuis 1285 jusqu'en 1328', in *RHGF*, xx, 703; 'Continuatio chronici Guillelmi de Nangiano', in *RHGF*, xx, 625–626; 'Chronicon auctore Bernardo Guidonis, Episcopo Lodovensi', in *RHGF*, xxi, 730; 'Continuatio chronici Girardi de Fracheto', in *RHGF*, xxi, 54; 'Fragment d'une chronique anonyme finnisant en M.CCC.XXVIII', in *RHGF*, xxi, 152; 'Excerpta e Memoriali Historiarum', in *RHGF*, xxi, 671–672.
123 'Adae Murimuth continuatio chronicarum', in *RBMAS*, i, 31: 'Hoc anno multi pastores, et quidam alii, ac mulieris de Anglia et aliis mundi partibus, collegerunt se, volentes adquirere Terram Sanctam et inimicos Christi interficere'; 'Thomae Walsingham quondam monachi S. Albani historia Anglicana', in *RBMAS*, i, 157.
124 *Chronographia regum Francorum*, i, 251.
125 For details on the acts of violence committed by the 'Pastoureaux' in Paris, see Barber, 'The Pastoureaux of 1320', 145–146.
126 *Les Grandes chroniques de France*, viii, 353; *Chronique Parisienne anonyme*, 47; 'Chroniques de Saint-Denis depuis 1285 jusqu'en 1328', in *RHGF*, xx, 703: 'et tous les Juifs quil trouvoient il occioient sans merci'; 'Chronicon Auctore Bernardo Guidonis, Episcopo Lodovensi', in *RHGF*, xxi, 730.
127 'Chronicon auctore Bernardo Guidonis, Episcopo Lodovensi', in *RHGF*, xxi, 730: 'insonuitque rumore eorum in toto regno Francie et alibi extra regnum'; 'Tertia Vita Joannis XXII', in *VPA*, i, 161.
128 'Adae Murimuth continuatio chronicarum', in *RBMAS*, 32; 'Thomae Walsingham quondam monachi S. Albani historia Anglicana', in *RBMAS*, 157: 'vertitur in nihilum, quod fuit ante nihil'.
129 'Quarta Vita Joannis XXII', in *VPA*, i, 171: 'et cum dicerentur versus Avinionem declinare, camerarius domini pape contra eos eorumque fautores per religiosos predicari mandavit'; Barber, 'The Pastoureaux of 1320', 146.
130 John XXII, *Lettres ... Relatives à la France*, no. 1114.
131 John XXII, *Lettres ... Relatives à la France*, nos. 1104–1107, 1114–1115: 'graves et enormes excessus per illos qui se nominant Pastorellos in personas et bona Judeorum ipsarum partium ... petens contra eos per providentiam apostolice Sedis de congruo remedio provideri ... tu vero ac senescalli, officiales et nobiles supradicti per temporales penas curaretis Pastorellos eosdem ab eorum congregationibus cohibere'; John XXII, *Lettres Communes*, no. 11765.
132 'Chronicon auctore Bernardo Guidonis, Episcopo Lodovensi', in *RHGF*, xxi, 731; Barber, 'The Pastoureaux of 1320', 147.
133 *Les Grandes chroniques de France*, viii, 353; 'Chroniques de Saint-Denis depuis 1285 jusqu'en 1328', in *RHGF*, xx, 703: 'sans denier et sans maille'; 'Chronicon auctore Bernardo Guidonis, Episcopo Lodovensi', in *RHGF*, xxi, 730: 'nullum habentes super se ducem aut principem'.
134 'Excerpta e Memoriali Historiarum', in *RHGF*, xxi, 671: 'inter quos erat quidam presbyter qui propter maleficia sua fuerat parrochia sua spoliatus, et quidam alius apostata a Sancti Benedicti ordine; ad quorum exhortationem multi irrationabiliter concurrentes'; 'Continuatio chronici Guillelmi de Nangiano', in *RHGF*, xx, 625; 'Tertia Vita Joannis XXII', in *VPA*, i, 161; Barber, 'The Pastoureaux of 1320', 144.
135 John XXII, *Lettres ... Relatives à la France*, no. 1114: 'ac multis scandalis variis que periculis que frequenter in diversis partibus ex inordinatis congregationibus talium'.

136 'Chronicon auctore Bernardo Guidonis, Episcopo Lodovensi', in *RHGF*, xxi, 731: 'fueruntque inter eos nonnulli in militia et astutia acriores'.
137 Barber, 'The Pastoureaux of 1320', 147.
138 'Chronicon auctore Bernardo Guidonis, Episcopo Lodovensi', in *RHGF*, xxi, 730; 'Tertia Vita Joannis XXII', in *VPA*, i, 161: 'Anno verbi incarnati MCCCXX, nova quedam pestis in regno Francie est exorta ... subito siquidem insurrexit quedam congregatio hominum simplicium promiscui sexus, qui se Pastorellos vocare ceperunt'.
139 *Chronographia regum Francorum*, ii, 252: 'erant induti strictis vestibus lineis, que gallice dicuntur: sarros, et supersignati parvis crucibus'; *Chroniques Parisienne anonyme*, 47: 'à banieres et pennonceaux ès quieux le crucifiement Nostre Seigneur estoit pourtrait et les armez au conte Louys de Clermont'; Barber, 'The Pastoureaux of 1320', 148, 155.
140 Barber, 'The Pastoureaux of 1320', 155.
141 Gaposchkin, *Invisible Weapons*, 205; Gary Dickson, 'The Advent of the Pastores', *Revue Belge de philologie et d'histoire*, 66.2 (1988), 249–267.
142 *Chroniques Parisienne anonyme*, 47.
143 Barber, 'The Pastoureaux of 1320', 158.
144 ASV, Reg. Vat. 137, fol. 166^v, ep. 584; Clement VI, *Lettres closes, patentes et curiales du pape Clément VI se rapportant à la France*, eds. E. Déprez, *et al.*, 3 vols. (Paris: Bibliothèque des Écoles françaises d'Athènes et de Rome, 3e séries, 1901–1961), no. 591 [hereafter *Lettres Rapportant à la France*].
145 Giovanni Villani, *Cronica*, iv, 70: 'e andaronvi di Firenze di loro volontà, e che ci furono mandati alle spese di chi volle il perdono, da quattrocento uomini segnati di croce con tutte armi con soprasberghe bianche con giglio e croce vermiglia, e per loro medesimi ordinatisi con conestabili e bandiere. E di Siena ve n'andarono bene trecentociquanta, e cosi di molte altre terre di Toscana, e di Lombardia, e di quali pochi, e di quali assai per loro medesimi, sanza ordine di comune, faccendo la via di Vinegia, perocchè la era ordinato il passo e I navilii alle spese della Chiesa, e del papa'.
146 Housley, *The Avignon Papacy*, 146–147.
147 'Corpus chronicorum Bononensium', in *RIS*, xviii, cols. 530–533: 'de che gran gente se misse a tore la croce in Bologna et altro, che inanzi la soa venute, grande gente de la Toscana et de la Marcha et de Romagne sig li andava; ma per la soa venuta troppo più gli andono. Ancora sappiete che il perdono si era de pena et de colpa a chi andava per stare uno anno; et questo se predicò per fra Venturino de Berghamo, fra predicatore, de voluntà de misser lo papa et de suo comandamendo'.
148 'Storie Pistoresi', in *RIS*, xi.5, 214–216: 'Nell'anno del nostro signore Iddio MCCCXLIIII e MCCCXLV furono molte battaglie tra li Christiani et Saracini. E molti miracoli apparavono in quello tempo. E spezial n'aparre uno nella città del l'Aquila, ovevo allato alla città di fuori, e fue cosi: che in una picciola chiesa aparre in su l'altare la nostra Donna col Figliuolo in collo e avea uno croce i' mano. A questo miracolo trassono indiferemente tutti l'uomini e le femine dell'Aquila; e stetevi infine a ora di terza, sic he chiunche v'andava li potea vedere: ella era più rispediente e più bell ache 'l sole. E sappi che tutti li fanciulli che nacquono in quell di nell'Aquila tutti aveano una imagine d'una crocetta in sulla spalla diritta. Onde per questo miracolo molti Aquillani e altri del paese assai presono la croce e andarono a combattere contra l'infideli'.
149 'Historiae romanae fragmenta', in *Antiquitates Italicae Medii Aevi*, ed. L. A. Muratori, 25 vols. (Milan: Typis Michaelis Bellotti, 1723–1896), vii, cols. 664–668 [hereafter *AIME*].
150 'Historiae romanae fragmenta', in *AIME*, vii, col. 664–668: 'Nunc gentium multitudo pro Christi nomine mortem subitura ad crucem amplectendam se apparat. Viri, mulieres, rugularium Ordinum religiosi, Ecclesiastici seculares, iter arripiunt. Hi praedia pretio distrabunt, illi utensilia et superlectiles vendunt. Quibus pecunia irat, ad exercitum se conferebant ... Ex una civitate ducenti, ex alia trecenti, ex hac quingenti, ex

illa mille convenerunt. Hinc potes perpendere, Lector, quam ingens crucesignatorum coetus ille fuerit. Per urbium for a et plateas, qui eiusmodi amictu contegebantur. Viae omnes hominibus in hunc modum indutis replebantur, aliisque supervenientibus renovabantur'.

151 'Historiae romanae fragmenta', in *AIME*, vii, col. 668: 'Crucesignati itinerantes Anconam procedebant. Ibi eorum quilibet mare intrabat, et ad Smyrnensem civitatem transfretabat'.

152 Clement VI, *Lettres Rapportant à la France*, no. 1844: 'Ex quibus intelligentes multi nobiles et potentes se per hoc ad vindicandas crucifixi redemptoris injurias, invitari, multitudo eorum innumerabilis, et specialiter de partibus Italie nonnullis ex eis, videlicet, commissa patricidia, fratricidia, et alia delicta gravia, pro reverentia Redemptoris, in diversis locis, sibi ad invicem remittentibus pacemque reformantibus, ad partes ultramarinas contra Turchos predictas cum armorum potentia se accinxerunt hactenus et accinguntur'.

153 'Historiae romanae fragmenta', in *AIME*, vii, col. 664.

154 Housley, *The Avignon Papacy*, 146–147.

155 'Memoriale Historicum Matthei de Griffonibus', in *RIS*, xviii.2, 56; 'Corpus Chronicorum Bononensium', in *RIS*, xviii, cols. 533–534: 'In lo dicto millesimo lo sopradicto misser lo Dalphino si fe cavalieri li figlio li del nostro signore misser Tadeo, misser Iacomo, misser Zohanne, fratelli et figlioli del nostro signore, a luogho de' fra predicatori, a lo altro de misser santo Nicolò, et questo fu domenegha adi xvi de Ottobre. Facti che funo quisti dui per mano de misser lo Dalphino, li predicti misser Zohanne si feno cavalieri xxi de Bologna, lo nome di quali sono quisti: …'.

156 Giovanni Villani, *Cronica*, iv, 70.

157 'Corpus chronicorum bononensium', in *RIS*, xviii, cols. 533–534.

158 Venturino set sail with Humbert of Viennois to Smyrna where he stayed to his death on 28 March 1346.

159 Clement VI, *Lettres Rapportant à la France*, no. 1844: 'Habet, nempe, ipsa relatio quod cruces fulgentes in plerisque apparuerunt partibus, ad quas concurrentes fideles multa sanitatis beneficia illi, videlicet, qui gravabantur infirmitatibus reportarunt'; Housley, *The Avignon Papacy*, 146.

160 Clement VI, *Lettres Rapportant à la France*, no. 1844: 'Ex quibus intelligentes multi nobiles et potentes se per hoc ad vindicandas crucifixi redemptoris injurias, invitari, multitudo eorum innumerabilis, et specialiter de partibus Italie nonnullis ex eis, videlicet, commissa patricidia, fratricidia, et alia delicta gravia, pro reverentia Redemptoris, in diversis locis, sibi ad invicem remittentibus pacemque reformantibus, ad partes ultramarinas contra Turchos predictas cum armorum potentia se accinxerunt hactenus et accinguntur'.

161 Clement VI, *Lettres Rapportant à la France*, no. 1844: 'claret stupendis miraculis, que divine pietatis clementia, in diversis partibus, pro dicto negotio, sicut ad nos fidedigna, tam verbalis, quam litteralis, relatio pertulit, operatur'; Housley, *The Avignon Papacy*, 147.

162 'Storie Pistoresi', in *RIS*, xi.5, 214; Housley, *The Avignon Papacy*, 146.

163 Benedicta Ward, *Miracles and the Medieval Mind: Theory, Record and Event 1000–1215* (Aldershot: Wildwood House, 1982), 132–137.

164 Benedicta Ward, 'Miracles in the Middle Ages', in *The Cambridge Companion to Miracles*, ed. G. H. Twelftree (Cambridge: Cambridge University Press, 2011), 149–165, 154–155.

165 Ward, 'Miracles in the Middle Ages', 154.

166 'Storie Pistoresi', in *RIS*, xi.5, 215: 'Molti re e signori v'andarono: in fra' quali fue lo figliuolo del re di Cipri. Li Christiani combaterrono con li Turchi presso alla citta di Tebe: li Turchi erano piu d'uno milione tra da cavallo e da pie'.

167 'Storie Pistoresi', in *RIS*, xi.5, 216: 'Li cristiani si missono a cercare de' corpi delli altri cristiani morti; e trovarone infinita moltitudine tra de' cristiani e de' turchi; ma

non poteano riconoscere di loro se no a guesto segno: che in sul capo d'ogni cristiano era uno festuco senza foglie, ed in capo del festuco era uno fiore bianco ritondo a modo d'ostia; nel quale fiore si leggeano lettore che diceano "cristiano"'.
168 Elizabeth Lapina, *Warfare and the Miraculous in the Chronicles of the First Crusade* (Pennsylvania: Penn State University Press, 2015).
169 See Chapter 4, note 68.
170 James B. MacGregor, 'The Ministry of Gerold d'Avranches: Warrior-Saints and Knightly Piety on the Eve of the First Crusade', *Journal of Medieval Studies*, 29.3 (2003), 219–237.
171 Macgregor, 'Gerold d'Avranches', 219–220.
172 Elizabeth Lapina, 'Demetrius of Thessaloniki: Patron Saint of Crusaders', *Viator*, 40.2 (2009), 93–112, 94.
173 Elizabeth Labina examined the transformation of the military saints of the miracle at the Battle of Antioch into the patron saints of crusaders. Lapina, 'Demetrius of Thessaloniki', 93–112.
174 See Chapter 3, note 107.
175 For several miracle stories see Lapina, *Warfare and the Miraculous*, 23–34; Ward, *Miracles and the Medieval Mind*, 110–121; William Purkis, 'Stigmata on the First Crusade', in *Signs, Wonders, Miracles: Representations of Divine Power in the Life of the Church*, eds. K. Cooper and J. Gregory (Woodbridge: Boydell and Brewer, 2005), 99–108; Jaap J. Van Moolenbroek, 'Signs in the Heavens in Groningen and Friesland in 1214: Oliver of Cologne and Crusading Propaganda', *Journal of Medieval History*, 13 (1987), 251–272.
176 Extracts from the registers of the Vatican, ASV, Vat. Reg. 138, ep. 1025: 'vitatis quibusvis dissensionum et rancorum odiis'. A full transcription is provided in Gay, *Le Pape Clément VI*, 175, Appendix II.
177 Gay, *Le Pape Clément VI*, 175: 'Expediens ad modum reputamus ut illi qui zelo Dei et fervore accensi fidei contra Turchos prosecutores et hostes crudeles nominis christiani ad partes se conferunt transmarinas, vitatis quibusvis dissensionum et rancorum odiis, in pacis et caritatis vinculo persistentes invicem sue peregrinationis salutifere perficiant ceptum iter. Sane cum sicut intelleximus quandoque contingat quod aliqui ex peregrinis eisdem ad partes accedendo predictas et Veneтiis Castellanensis diocesis applicants, hoste illo humamni generis procurante qui saluti hominum invidet et callidis fraudibus eis sui laboris conatur auferre mercedem, ad rixas, raucores et odia invicem seu cum aliis provocantur, nes de tue devotionis sinceritate, quam te habere ad talia sedanda dampna et scandala fidedignis assertionibus percepimus, in domino confidentes, ut talium Veneтiis existentium rixas, dissensiones et discordias sedare, ipsosque ad concordiam viis et modis honestis et licitis revocare'.
178 Clement VI, *Lettres Rapportant à la France*, no. 2341; Clement VI, *Lettres ... Intéressant les Pays Autre que la France*, nos. 920, 980.

4 University trained clergy and the preaching of the crusade, 1305–1333

In its effort to disseminate the crusade messages, the papacy employed the friars of the mendicant orders extensively; the contribution of individual preachers, prominent members of the secular or regular clergy, was also significant. These preachers were mostly distinguished Parisian scholars serving as papal legates who preached on special recruitment occasions: notable examples include the Cardinal-priest of Sant'Eusebio, Nicholas of Fréauville (1313, Ordo Praedicatorum – OP), the Latin patriarchs of Jerusalem, Peter of Pleine Chassagne (1316, Ordo Fratrum Minorum – OFM) and Pierre de la Palud (1331, OP), and Pierre Roger, the Archbishop of Rouen (1331–1333, – Ordo Sancti Benedicti – OSB), all of whom preached the crusade *coram papa* or in the presence of the French king. These examples are evidence of the effort undertaken by individual preachers to secure French royal involvement in crusading affairs. Unfortunately, beyond scattered references in documentary or narrative sources to preaching occasions, the preacher's name, the audience and the location, further knowledge is unobtainable due to the absence of sermon texts, particularly those of Nicholas of Fréauville, Peter of Pleine Chassagne and the abbot of Saint-Germain-des-Prés, Peter of Courpalay. All preserved fourteenth-century crusade sermons form part of manuscript collections containing numerous sermons. Apart from some substantial remnants of a preacher's address to his audience, it is hard to argue that the preserved crusade sermon texts are facsimiles of preachers' speeches. The sermons in these collections are organized according to the liturgical day of the ecclesiastical calendar (*sermones de tempore*), or the feast day of individual saints (*sermones de sanctis*), or for special liturgical periods such as Advent and Lent, and this makes the identification of sermons with crusade appeals a difficult task. Nevertheless, the complicated work of matching the surviving crusade sermon text with its actual preaching occasion occasionally becomes feasible through cross-references with other sources, but in the absence of any evidence in other sources, or within the sermon itself, knowledge of anything beyond the sermon's content is impossible; this is the case with the sermons for the Fourth Sunday in Lent (*Laetare Jerusalem*) with crusade appeals, which are presented in this chapter.[1] In the existing crusade sermons, preached by Pierre de la Palud and Pierre Roger/Clement VI, however, the abundance of cross-references in documentary and narrative sources allows us to identify the sermons' exact dates and match these sermons with their actual preaching event.[2]

Crux penitentie predicatur et imponitur volentibus transfretare de Egypto in Jerusalem: The crusade sermons for the Fourth Sunday in Lent (*Laetare Jerusalem*)

Penitence was an essential component of the Lenten season, and it fit ably with the theme of crusading. The cycle of Sunday liturgies during Lent summoned the faithful for sincere remorse, and crusading, as the highest form of penance, was an excellent means for release from sin and salvation. Thus, Lent was the ideal period for promoting crusading. The preachers drew on the evocative language of the Lenten liturgies to call for participation in the crusade and for imitation of Christ on the cross. As Jessalyn Bird recently demonstrated, during the twelfth and thirteenth centuries the canons of St Victor and the masters of Paris often used the imagery in the readings and liturgy of Christ's triumphal entry into Jerusalem to compile crusade sermons for Palm Sunday.[3] Other crusade sermons for a specific feast day in Lent were those for the Fourth Sunday in Lent (*Laetare Jerusalem*), when preachers drew on the penitential thrust of the day to stress the sincere repentance required for the *crucesignati* in their journey from the earthly to heavenly Jerusalem – this was one of the main themes of the *Laetare* sermons.

The sermons for the Fourth Sunday in Lent, with crusade appeals, were well known and much used, judging from various versions in preserved exemplars and the number of surviving manuscripts.[4] The main body of such sermons derives from the late thirteenth century, while certain later examples define the Fourth Sunday in Lent as a regular day for crusade preaching in the late Middle Ages. Moreover, as part of the liturgical Sunday sermon collections, the *Laetare Jerusalem* sermons provide connections between regular preaching and crusade propaganda. The Dominican James of Lausanne gives us a good example of a fourteenth-century *Laetare Jerusalem* crusade sermon.

James was a native of Lausanne and entered the local Dominican convent while in his youth. He was in Paris in 1303, and on 26 June that year he was 'among the most known friars' who attended the Dominican Chapter at St Jacques, the Dominican convent in Paris, an exceptional assembly for deliberation on the royal summons for the convergence of a general assembly in France.[5] At the General Chapter of the Dominican Order held at Naples in May 1311, James was assigned to lecture on the Bible at the University of Paris.[6] According to the statute of the Order's General Chapter at Metz in June 1313, it was decreed that James would read the *Sentences* the following year at Paris; in May 1314, the Dominican minister general, Berengar of Landorra, confirmed James's assignment.[7] On 3 July 1314, James of Lausanne, Pierre de la Palud and John of Naples, as members of the committee of theologians, which was set up in 1313, were charged with the examination of heretical or erroneous concepts in the commentary on the *Sentences* of Durand of St-Pourçain, issued a list of articles wherein James was referred to as *baccalaureus biblicus*.[8] James's designation among other significant Dominican theologians to critique Durand, one of the greatest figures of his age and whose ideas shook the Dominican Order during the 1310s and 1320s, makes it clear he was highly regarded among the Order of Preachers. On 3 July 1317, Pope John XXII wrote to the chancellor of Paris, Thomas of Bailly, to make James of Lausanne *magister* in theology, and, in 1318, James succeeded Hervaeus Natalis as prior of the Dominican province of France, following the latter's appointment as the order's master general.[9] James held the office of the prior provincial until his death in late 1321 or early January 1322, when Hugh of Vaucemain assumed James's duties.[10]

Above all, James of Lausanne made himself useful in the Dominican Order, chiefly as a preacher and administrator, rather than as a man of letters. He became especially known as '*predicator gratissimus et copiosus, sicut patet in collationibus et sermonibus quos conflavit*' during his tenure at Paris.[11] Indeed, in his voluminous repertory of Medieval Latin sermons, Schneyer lists 1,042 *incipits* of James's sermons and *collationes* from more than 100 manuscript collections of sermons found in more than thirty-five different libraries.[12]

Among the mass of James of Lausanne's preaching material, in two cases the researcher can identify a sermon devoted to the crusade, including some references to the notion of the crusade as a pilgrimage, and to the *crucesignatio* as a means for salvation.[13] The first sermon is contained in Paris, Bibliothèque nationale de France, MS lat. 17516, fols. 84ra–85vb.[14] The codex, produced probably in the fourteenth century, is a collection of sermons (*varii sermones*) written and preached by James of Lausanne. Nevertheless, the sermon's text is incomplete, as the scribe omitted the development of the third part of its main division. The sermon's rubric, 'The Fourth Sunday of Lent',[15] is likely indicative of the day of the liturgical calendar James preached the sermon or when it was intended to have been delivered by other preachers. Nevertheless, the complete lack of references in other sources and the fact that the sermon was written to serve a dual purpose – for the recruitment of crusaders and for preaching on the Fourth Sunday in Lent – makes its exact dating difficult. The only evidence to the exact preaching year comes after considering the rubrical indication that James's sermon was Lenten: during Lent 1320, two crusade assemblies, at which nobles and prelates from France gathered to discuss future crusading plans, were held in Paris,[16] and during this year James was provincial of France.

James of Lausanne chose as *thema* for his sermon the biblical verse *Illa que sursum est Jerusalem, libera est* (Galatians 4.26), which forms part of the epistle read during the celebration of Mass on the Fourth Sunday of Lent (*Dominica Laetare*); its powerful symbolism is the foundation of the sermon, and this verse is the root from which the entire discourse arises.[17] The heavenly Jerusalem, the True Church, in comparison with the worldly Jerusalem, is a state of freedom and offers protection to all devotees. The compilers of the *Laetare Jerusalem* crusade sermons use this verse as the embarkation point for their discourse. One of the *Laetare Jerusalem* crusade sermons in Avignon, Bibliothèque Municipale MS 295, however, might be the only instance of the use of a different biblical verse as *thema*.[18] The anonymous scribe drew on the Gospel of the day to open his sermon (*Abiit Ihesus trans mare Galilee, quod est Tiberiadis,* John 6.1). With this particular verse the anonymous compiler describes the crusaders' passage to Jerusalem as analogous to Christ's walking over the Sea of Galilee:[19] His miracle drew a great multitude after Him; similarly the granting of crusade indulgences and the leadership of the crusade by a man of great power, such as the King of France, convinced many to follow.[20]

The Holy City of Jerusalem is the core element of the liturgy of the Fourth Sunday of Lent Mass, also known as *Laetare Jerusalem* (Rejoice Jerusalem), from the *incipit* of the introit (Isaiah 66.10), which was read at Mass of the day. Following crusading phraseology, the sacred city was the most saintly destination for all crusaders, its liberation and protection their ultimate objective.

Additionally, the Fourth Sunday of Lent is associated with the *statio ad crucem in Jerusalem*, the Stational liturgy of the cross in Jerusalem and its accompanying procession – the display of the sign of the cross, a devotional commemoration of Jesus carrying the cross. This exact liturgical day was linked with pilgrimages by early Christians to Jerusalem and thus served as a harbinger of the crusaders' pending pilgrimage to the sacred city.[21] The cost of travel and the growing Muslim threat prevented many Western Christians from going on pilgrimage to Jerusalem, so different locations in Europe, especially churches and shrines with relics from the True Cross and the Instruments of the Passion, emerged as holy stations of particular moral and religious significance. On specified days of the liturgical year in designated holy stations the Church defined the celebration of Stational liturgies in remembrance of the Stations of the cross as a 'symbolism of place-Jerusalem' where it was appropriate to perform the liturgy:[22] during the Fourth Sunday of Lent especially, the Stational liturgy was celebrated at the *statio ad crucem in Jerusalem* in Rome; in the fourteenth century it was transferred with the papacy to Avignon.[23]

The choice of the Fourth Sunday in Lent for the preaching of this particular crusade sermon was not random, as its ritual is closely associated with Jerusalem and with the cross. Likewise, with the crucifixion of Christ, the cross became the symbol for the salvation of mankind and its redemption from sin. The vestment of the crusaders with the salvatory sign of the cross gave the *crucesignati* divine protection and courage in their struggle against the infidels and the enemies of the Church. Among the feast days of the cross, the penitential nature of Lent offered the crusade propagandists the most suitable liturgical period for disseminating the redemptive message of the crusade and inspiring the faithful to take the cross.[24]

In opening his sermon, James of Lausanne alleges that it was customary at the time of a general passage or during the recruitment of crusaders (*crucesignatio*) to send some preachers to offer the cross to all those who wished to accept it and set out for Jerusalem, and to organize the preaching campaign during Lent.[25] At this point, James likened those who were signed with the cross of penitence to those elected by God to be imprinted with the mark of Thau, according to the vision of prophet Ezekiel (9.4). God ordered one of His angels to 'go all through the midst of the city [of Jerusalem] and mark a Thau on the foreheads of the men who groan and grieve over all the abominations which happen'.[26]

The monogram Thau, the last letter of the Phoenician and Old Hebrew alphabets, was later interpreted as a cross and, according to the Bible, was put on the foreheads of those who lamented their sins for the purpose of their salvation from execution. The cross as the symbol of Christ's suffering, marked on the crusaders' arms, afforded them deliverance by redemption from the power of sin to the 'ladder to heaven'.[27] As the mark of Thau represents God's choice to preserve all those who wept for their sins from destruction, likewise the sign of the cross ought to be imprinted not only outwardly on the crusaders' shoulders but inwardly, through the imitation of Jesus' passion on the cross. The same theme appears in another fourteenth-century exemplar of *Laetare Jerusalem* crusade sermon contained in the manuscript from Avignon.[28] While it remains unknown which sermon preceded or followed the other, the Avignon one or James of Lausanne's, the two sermons have the same *thema* and refer to the same reasons all impious people claim for not going on crusade.[29] This theme appears in these two *Laetare* sermons only.

It is extremely difficult to argue how people felt about the crusade in the fourteenth century, as public opinion and criticism of the crusades beyond 1291 remains unexplored. Although it is important that both sermonists were aware of their contemporaries' sentiment toward the crusade, there is just fragmental evidence of popular opposition. The prevailing idea regarding criticism of the crusades in the twelfth and thirteenth centuries is derived from Palmer Allan Throop's study of public opinion and propaganda; this study has, in turn, been adopted more or less by a certain number of historians.[30] According to Throop, after a brief period of crusade enthusiasm between the years 1095–1145, inspired by the victorious outcome of the First Crusade, the crusading idea was constantly challenged following the fiasco of the Second Crusade; Norman Housley alleges that opposition to crusade 'went on increasing in the fourteenth century'.[31] This statement may be partially true, but some episodes in the fourteenth century demonstrate that neither secular rulers nor the Avignon papacy could foresee the extent of popular reaction to summons for taking up arms against the infidels. Those who chose not to take the cross were fearful, impious and voluptuous, and it was the words of the Apostle Paul in the epistle of the day (Galatians 4.21–31) that excited audiences to take the cross and set out for Jerusalem.[32] That those who refused to take the cross were characterized as voluptuous could be evidence that James of Lausanne was addressing the knightly class at one of the 1320 assemblies, where he chastized them for their luxurious way of life and disinterest in crusading.

Both sermons developed the same argumentative structure to criticise those who chose not to depart for Jerusalem, and both referred to the various spiritual and temporal privileges and liberties offered by the Church to the crusaders, privileges divided into those pertaining to worldly life, those pertaining to temporal privileges, and those pertaining to the Church and to God (spiritual privileges).[33] Crusaders were granted such privileges as early as the twelfth century, but these privileges were not instituted until the papacy of Innocent III. The duration of these privileges was determined by the fulfilment of the crusader's obligation, by absolution or death.[34]

Unlike the Avignon sermon, James of Lausanne insisted on papal supremacy with regard to spiritual and temporal affairs and relied on the patristic tradition for strengthening his arguments. James depended on St Augustine and demonstrated a considerable degree of knowledge about St Bernard, which added validity and legitimacy to his positions.[35] When James discussed the Christian tenet that Jesus lives within those who honestly believe in Him and His presence among the Christian community, he underlined this discussion by quoting Bernardine authorities.[36]

The preference for this the Fourth Sunday in Lent for the preaching of the sermon has strong connections with the sermon's *thema* and with crusading ideology. Christoph Maier believes that this specific sermon was based on the *Laetare* Sunday sermon of William Peyraut, the Dominican prior of Lyon, who wrote his sermon sometime before his death in 1271.[37] Peyraut's *Laetare* sermon was widely circulated: it appears in various versions in more than 100 manuscripts.[38] A close comparison between Peyraut's sermon and that of James of Lausanne, however, reveals little resemblance between the two. The ideal of the crusade as a pilgrimage, the *crucesignatio* during Lent, the Christian's redemption from sin through the cross of penitence, the imitation of Jesus' Passion, and the spiritual journey to heavenly Jerusalem are the main themes in both sermons. The direct references to crusading and themes such as the reasons people refused to assume the cross, the Church's consolation for those who chose to crusade and the spiritual rewards the crusaders enjoyed distinguish James of Lausanne's sermon from Peyraut's.

That Peyraut's *Laetare* sermon was not the standard for the compilation of all *Laetare* sermons is even more obvious in another *Laetare* Sunday sermon, preached in 1283 at the Benedictine nunnery of Elstow in south-eastern England.[39] The Elstow sermon's principal subject is the cross of Penitence and penance as a superior form of pilgrimage.[40] The theme of the crusade as penance, offering to all *crucesignati* a journey to the heavenly Jerusalem (*que sursum est*), is common to both sermons. The compiler of the Elstow sermon also exhorted his listeners to assume the cross of penitence with tears, sighs and sorrow for their sins.[41] Similarly, James of Lausanne warned those who took the cross that they needed to express a sincere remorse for their offenses.[42]

Another theme of James of Lausanne's sermon was the emergence of the pilgrimage to Jerusalem as a symbol of salvation for the Christians and as the most charismatic of all penances. Pope Urban II had first associated the traditional pilgrimage to Jerusalem with the journey of the crusaders to the Holy City, and it had become a foundation of crusade phraseology – the penitential value of the crusade is one of the principal ideas in many thirteenth-century *ad status* crusade sermons.[43] Similarly, the theme of Jerusalem as the highest form of spiritual pilgrimage appears in another fourteenth-century *Laetare* sermon. The Augustinian Hermit, Henry of Friemar (1285–1354), declared in this sermon that as the crusaders set forth for and remained in Jerusalem, so all Christians who assume the cross of penitence during Lent have to rejoice in heavenly Jerusalem.[44]

In a sermon for the first Sunday after the Epiphany, James of Lausanne also describes the crusade to the Holy Land as a superior form of penitential pilgrimage, and the taking of the cross as a means of eternal salvation for crusaders.[45] In this sermon, James explains that a man who has not assumed the cross of penitence will not be lifted from earth to Heaven: 'just as the man who desires to go on pilgrimage to the Holy Land commonly receives the cross, in this way the man who desires to go to Heaven has to receive penance'.[46] James closed his argument with a simile from nature – that a man who chooses not to assume the cross of penitence is like a bird that cannot fly from the earth to the sky.[47]

The difference between this particular sermon of James of Lausanne's and respective contemporary or earlier sermons is his reliance on classical learning. According to the tradition of Parisian scholars, James follows a more complicated argumentative structure and meditative treatment, furnishing his sermon with highly sophisticated elements. When James developed a logical argument to rebuke the three different categories of people who were reluctant to join the crusade, he constructed a harmonious blend of classical philosophy and theology that reconciles Aristotle with Christian doctrine. Throughout the sermon, James employs a plethora of Aristotelian, biblical and patristic excerpts, and makes use of a simile by likening human beings to horses.[48] He derived this simile from Aristotle's works on the study of animals, mainly the *Historia animalium* and the *De motu animalium*, and his theory of cognition and perception and their effect on human will and action. In both works Aristotle examined in detail the anatomy of horses and of many other animal species.[49] In his treatise, *On the Movement of Animals*, Aristotle poses a question: 'How does it happen that thinking is sometimes followed by action and sometimes not, sometimes by motion and sometimes not?' The Philosopher concludes that creatures have two generic faculties, the cognitive (*cognitio* or *nous*) and the appetitive (*appetitus* or *orexis*);[50] thus it follows that sometimes a human being has both the desire to reach a goal and the cognition of what must be done to achieve it, but sometimes not.[51]

James also relied on Thomas Aquinas, who divided human behaviour into two categories: the cognitive, which is how we actually know the world, and affective, which is how we comprehend the world – through our emotions.[52] An educated Dominican trained in science and theology, James would have known the works of Aristotle and Aquinas very well. James argued that a horse whose front legs are notably faster than its hind legs is unsafe as it descends, extremely dangerous as it runs and secure as it ascends; such a horse is man, whose 'legs' are his mental knowledge (*cognitio*) and his affection (*affectus*). Similarly, the front legs of horses are their sensitive cognition (*cognitio sensitiva*) and akin to the knowledge of the world acquired by human beings through observation and experience, empirical knowledge, sensory appetite (*appetitus sensitivus*), natural appetite, desires and passions.[53] In moral philosophy, the sensory appetite is a cluster of passions to which mankind is subject by its animal nature (*appetitus animalis*); these passions exert a strong influence on human cognitive faculties and the function of the parts of the body and, consequently, control human will and action.[54]

The theory of appetite had strong applications in medieval theology. In the *Summa theologiae*, Thomas Aquinas maintains that cognitive rational appetite, or volition, acts as a counterbalance to sensory appetite, which impedes human beings from behaving like animals by controlling their external senses – the governing power of the soul over corporeal desires.[55] Intellective cognition (*cognitio intellectus*), the power of rationality which distinguishes humankind from other animals, activates our rational faculties, so we can control our external senses – according to Aquinas, this is the source of man's desire for God: intelligent creatures possess a congenital inclination to gaze at God.[56]

James of Lausanne, evidently affected by Aquinas's legacy, explains that as the rear legs of the horse extend further than its front legs, so does *intellectus* exceed *voluntas*, intellective cognition and will, the higher appetite in humans.[57] James characterized those who chose not to crusade because of the dangers inherent in the journey as irrational and subservient to their appetites. This subservience was very dangerous: seeking only worldly goods, they cannot help but fall into moral offences; it is only intention and *affectus*, heavenly goods, which make moral ascension possible.[58] For emphasis, James once again relied on scriptural testimony, the verse in which Paul exhorts the Colossians to 'lift their thoughts above, where Christ is present'.[59]

The number of preserved late thirteenth- and early fourteenth-century crusade sermons for the Fourth Sunday in Lent demonstrate the increased conduct of crusade preaching on this Lenten feast day during this period. Connecting regular preaching and crusade propaganda made crusading a prominent element within the pastoral mission of the late medieval Church. The crusade sermons for the Fourth Sunday in Lent demonstrate how the powerful devotional character of Lent helped induce the faithful to the spiritual passage to the heavenly Jerusalem. The preachers, as they did with Palm Sunday, clearly chose to address the crusade on another Lenten feast day because of the dominance of penitential themes in the Church's liturgy during Lent; the commemoration of the Passion of Christ on the cross suited the redemptory character of the crusade as a *Via Dolorosa*. Penance and the cross of penitence were the sermon's core messages, and both dovetailed with the penitential character of Lent, a liturgical experience and a route, through the death of Christ on the cross, to Christian salvation. The crusade, as a reference to Christ's final journey to the cross, was a war of penitence that illuminated the path to redemption and salvation.

Stimulating Philip VI to assume the cross: Pierre de la Palud's sermon on the feast of the Exaltation of the Holy Cross, 1331

Another group of liturgical sermons in which the preachers included appeals to crusading were, as it has been shown before, the *de cruce* sermons (for preaching on the feast days of the cross), because of the symbolic connection of the particular day on which they were intended to be delivered with crusading. The sermon delivered by the Latin Patriarch of Jerusalem, Pierre de la Palud, on the feast day of the Exaltation of the Cross consists a notable example of a fourteenth-century *de cruce* sermon with references to the crusade.

Pierre was the youngest son of the knight, Gerard de la Palud, Lord of Verembon and ruler of the lands largely situated in the area of Dombes, in

Burgundy. He was born around 1275–1280, and early on his parents decided to send him for instruction in the fundamentals of the liberal arts. Pierre's higher education included assiduous studies in canon and civil law until circa 1300, when he became a Dominican friar and devoted himself to theology.[60] Between 1310–1311, Pierre began lecturing on the *Sentences* at Paris, and, in 1314, he incepted as Master of Theology.[61] It was during Pierre's studies that Paris witnessed one of the bitterest disputes within Dominican circles, a dispute over Durand of St-Pourçain's commentary on *Sentences*. In 1313, Pierre de la Palud, along with fellow Dominicans, James of Lausanne and John of Naples, was commissioned to enquire into Durand's commentary.[62]

In 1317, Pierre was appointed vicar of the Dominican province of France. Sometime between 1319 and 1329, thanks to his rhetorical skills, he acceded to the office of Dominican preacher general in the same province; his questions on the *Sentences* along with the numerous surviving sermons and the compilation of the 'Liber Bellorum Domini', a collection of chronicles that includes the history of crusades to the East and those against the Albigensians in Southern France, 'are probably his greatest achievement'.[63] His ultimate elevation to the patriarchal see of Jerusalem, in March 1329, brought him into direct involvement with the recovery of the Holy Land and the preaching of the crusade.[64] The Dominicans had already employed Palud, one of their best preachers, in the preaching campaign in Paris for the crusade against the Visconti of Milan in 1325.[65]

Soon after his appointment, the new patriarch set sail for the East. In the autumn of 1329, Pierre de la Palud accompanied Marie, daughter of Louis of Clermont, to Cyprus for her marriage to Guy of Lusignan, son of King Hugh IV of Cyprus. The convoy of four galleys arrived safely in Cyprus, and the royal marriage was held in Nicosia in January 1330. Afterwards, Pierre proceeded to the most important commission of his Levantine mission, the diplomatic journey to the court of al-Nazir Muhammed, the Mamluk Sultan of Egypt. In the spring of 1330, Pierre de la Palud and Bishop William Durand of Mende set out for Acre; from Acre they travelled along the Syro-Palestinian littoral zone into Egypt and to the sultan's court in Cairo.[66] The patriarch negotiated for some sort of Christian control over the Holy Land and for the right of Christians to make undisturbed pilgrimages to Jerusalem[67] but, despite Pierre's diplomatic efforts to re-establish Christian authority in Palestine, his mission ended in failure. Deeply frustrated by the outcome of his reconciliatory efforts in Egypt, Pierre de la Palud returned to Cyprus, where he presided over the trial against Peter of Castro, the Vicar of the Dominican Province of Holy Land, and soon thereafter departed for Avignon.[68]

We might presume that Pierre's frustration with his failure in Cairo triggered his intense personal involvement in preaching the crusade in France in late 1330 until 1332, that it sparked his desire to take immediate action against the Mamluks and prompted his criticism of Philip VI's sluggishness;[69] we can only presume, though, as there is no documentation, with regard to his involvement in crusade preaching in France, for the period he spent at Avignon, from the autumn of 1330 until September 1331. Beginning in September 1331, French chroniclers testify that Pierre's involvement in crusading affairs was a catalyst for a crusading propaganda campaign throughout the French kingdom. According to narrative accounts, in September 1331, Pierre de la Palud preached the crusade in the presence of Philip VI of France and a great many French barons and prelates.[70] A short while later, on 5 December 1331, Pope John XXII made Pierre responsible for the conduct of crusade preaching in the Kingdom of France.[71] Pierre's sermon of 1331 aroused an enthusiastic response from the French nobles and initiated a period of major crusade activity that continued until 1336.

Despite Pierre's personal commitment, none of the surviving sermons attributed to him are entirely devoted to the crusade. Nevertheless, a close study of the sermon corpus in manuscript Clermont-Ferrand, Bibliothèque Municipale, MS 46, which contains seventy of Pierre's sermons, reveals three sermons in which the patriarch partially alluded to the crusade. That the body of Palud's sermons is preserved in a number of different manuscript collections, all arranged according to the feast days of the church calendar (*sermones de sanctis*) or Lent (*sermones quadragesimales*), makes it necessary to conduct a separate, systematic search of each collection for the identification of sermons that address or mention the crusade.[72] Between the doctrinal principles and the religious symbolism of the feast days to which each of these sermons was devoted, Palud's texts are filled with anxiety over the Muslim domination of the Holy Land and exhortations for immediate action on the part of Western Christianity.[73] There is strong supporting evidence in the sermons that they were all delivered after Palud's return from his eastern mission in late 1330.

The most interesting case is the fifty-seventh sermon of the Clermont-Ferrand manuscript which, according to the rubric, was delivered on the feast day of the Exaltation of the Cross.[74] The date of the *de cruce* sermon was the fourteenth of September: there is no mention of the year, but references in the sermon itself, in combination with allusions in other sources, permit us to determine the precise preaching date. Pierre's reference to the Egyptian fig tree as the most fertile of all species of fig tree, and the repetition of this reference throughout the sermon, indicates a vivid remembrance of his mission in Egypt, most likely indicating that the sermon was delivered after his return to Europe in late 1330. Apart from this, in his admonition to all *crucesignatos* and *crucesignandos*, Palud says:

> But against the enemies of the cross of Christ, who are above all infidels and most of all and particularly the Saracens, they must be like a ferocious and wild bull brandishing its horns at Syria and Egypt and destroying the treacherous Mohammed and entirely extirpating his abominable people.[75]

Pierre's hatred of the Mamluks in Syria and Egypt was most likely inflamed during the compilation of the 'Liber Bellorum Domini' in 1329 and culminated after the dispiriting outcome of his negotiations in the court of the Mamluk sultan in April 1330. Though it is difficult to determine with certainty the year of the sermon, this reference obviously dates the sermon to the period after Palud's experience in the Mamluk court, while references elsewhere in the sermon to 'the flowers of the regal lilies of France, the most noble of all flowers' and 'for the royal blood of

France' imply that the sermon was preached in the presence of the King of France to revive French royal interest for the crusade.[76] From other sources, we know that in September 1331 Pierre de la Palud delivered an inspirational sermon in Paris before Philip VI of France to induce French royal participation in a crusade to the Holy Land.[77] This sermon has been confirmed by narrative accounts and from references in a sermon preached in 1332 by Pierre Roger, Archbishop of Rouen. In February of that year, Pierre Roger was the head of a delegation of prelates and nobles from the Kingdom of France to the papal court in Avignon to present and discuss the French King's crusade plans.[78] Allusions in the crusade sermon he delivered before Pope John XXII and the consistory of cardinals at Avignon make logical connections to Palud's sermon on the Exaltation of the Cross and its actual preaching occasion.[79] In his sermon, Pierre Roger states:

> For when on a certain Friday the lord king had summoned his prelates and barons at Paris and elsewhere for various arduous affairs of his kingdom, the patriarch of Jerusalem was present and he insistently asked the king if he would grant him an audience concerning the business of Christ before so many valiant men. And he proposed many reasons why the king was obliged to take up the passage. Consequently all the prelates, twenty-six in number, showed him the same thing with many arguments, and the barons similarly implored him to take up the aforesaid passage, on which they were prepared to follow him and risk themselves and their goods.[80]

In this excerpt, Pierre Roger specified the occasion, the audience, the place and the weekday of the Patriarch of Jerusalem's preaching of the crusade. A certain number of different sources confirm Roger's allusions to Palud in this excerpt. First, regarding the occasion, the attendants and the place of Palud's sermon, some narrative accounts confirm that Pierre de la Palud delivered a tirade before the French king and a great many barons and prelates.[81] Second, a French manuscript in the Bibliothèque nationale at Paris catalogues the participants of a French royal assembly at Paris in September 1331, and Pierre de la Palud is listed in the series of names of French nobles, barons and high prelates.[82] Third, as Roger remarks that Friday was the day of the royal meeting at Paris, we can identify the preserved text as Palud's Exaltation of the Cross sermon preached at the baronial assembly of 1331. According to the 1331 calendar, the feast of the Exaltation of the Cross, the liturgical day of the sermon, according to its rubric, was indeed the day of the convocation in Paris. Thus the sermon's date was 14 September 1331.[83]

Even though the sermon text is preserved in Latin, it can be argued it was originally delivered in French, particularly if we take into account both its French-speaking audience and the author's French translation of a phrase first written in Latin.[84] Beginning in the thirteenth century, there is already explicit evidence that many sermons from France were preached to lay congregations in the vernacular but written down, for posterity, in Latin. Only some segments remained in French, such as some proverbs or translations of the Latin *divisiones*, as we see in this *de cruce* sermon.[85]

The character of the text makes it difficult to determine what exactly Pierre de la Palud said on the occasion, as it seems it has been thoroughly reworked, with very little of the 'original voice' surviving. The sermon is quite long, which testifies to a reconstruction of the text. In essence the sermon breaks the rigid framework of scholastic textual organization, drawing extensively from James of Voragine's *Legenda Aurea* and including only a few substantial remnants of Pierre's address to Philip VI. Two different hands are discernible in the text: Palud's sermon on the Exaltation of the Cross is found on the folios 215r–220v in the Clermont-Ferrand corpus but, from folio 219r to the sermon's end, a second hand appears to complete the sermon,[86] intervening to fill this gap after these folios were lost or destroyed. Most probably the second scribe completed the Clermont-Ferrand manuscript from another manuscript at his disposal, one either lost or awaiting discovery.

The feast day chosen by Pierre de la Palud for his crusade sermon might not have been coincidental, since some individual liturgical days, in addition to the penitential seasons of Advent and Lent, were very popular for crusade preaching. The feast days of the Invention (3 May) and the Exaltation of the Cross (14 September) were very attractive to crusade preachers because of the intense symbolism in the cult of the cross, and the feast of the Exaltation of the Cross became a sort of 'crusaders' festival day'.[87] Even in several late twelfth-century examples of *sermones de cruce* (model sermons meant for preaching on the feast days of the cross), there is a clear connection to crusading.[88] These sermons were not designated as crusade sermons, like Palud's sermon, though they include several passages pertaining to the crusade.

The discovery of an additional sermon on the *Sancta Cruce*, linked to crusade issues in a manuscript collection of sermons from the abbey of St Victor in Paris, reveals the need for more systematic research into fourteenth-century *de cruce* sermons to identify any similar pattern.[89] The great mass of sermon manuscript collections, however, is spread across a considerable number of European libraries, which makes this objective unfeasible for the purposes of this study. The manuscript from St Victor, now in the Bibliothèque nationale, contains a collection of various sermons attributed to the Dominican William Bernard of Narbonne (†1336), chancellor of Notre-Dame of Paris.[90] Bernard inaugurated his sermon on the *Sancta Cruce* by glorifying the reviving sign of the cross (*lignum vite*) and urging the Church militant to offer the mark of the cross to those ready to receive it.[91] According to Bernard, those who wish to fight against the enemies of the faith because of their love for Christ shall receive the cross and set off for the *passagium generale*, and they shall receive eternal life for their devotion and service.[92] The cult of the sign of the cross and the religious zeal for Christ on the cross provided a common theme to crusade preachers. The cross Christ carried on His shoulders to Golgotha was marked on crusaders' arms, while the death of Christ on the cross, which literally rescued men from their sins, was used as a metaphor for the journey of the crusaders to Jerusalem.

For the subject of his sermon, Pierre de la Palud praises the cross's tree because of the feast day on which the sermon was preached. The Patriarch's objective was not limited to a liturgical sermon exclusively for the feast days of the cross, but to warn the French nobility of the danger from Egypt and the urgent need for a new *passagium generale* following his distressing experience in the Mamluk court. Pierre opened his sermon with the biblical verse, 'I have exalted the low tree', taken from Ezekiel's parable for the cedar of Christ and His Church, wherein the prophet referred to the divine promise of the rebuilding of the Holy City and the restoration of the house of David to power.[93] Palud implores his audience to recapture Jerusalem and restore the Temple of the Lord.

Pierre chose to begin this *de cruce* sermon with the glorification of the cross-making with a specific reference to the fig tree of Egypt (*figus Egyptiaca*) as the Tree of the Cross – the figus Egyptiaca is actually more fertile than other trees and the most fruitful of any fig tree:

> But the tree of the cross is the most fertile among all trees, because there is no other single tree in the world or in the terrestrial paradise whose the fruit suffices for the restoration of one people for many years. The fruit which hung one time on the tree of the cross is sufficient for the restoration of all Christians every year on the day of Easter during Holy Communion.[94]

Furthermore, the line 'the fruit of the tree of the cross feeds not only humans on earth but also the angels in Heaven', which relies on Psalm 77, 'the man has eaten from the bread of the angels',[95] refers to a thematic similarity amongst Palm Sunday crusade sermons, that of believers climbing on the palm tree to grasp its fruit.[96] The Tree of the Cross and its fruits is an allusion to the crucifixion and resurrection of Christ, whereby the sign of the cross became the symbol of life and prosperity and the means for redemption from sin. The use of the fig tree, the most fertile of trees, as the Tree of the Cross, and the use of its fruit as symbol of Christ on the cross, served to summon all Christians to protect the cross of Christ.[97] The leitmotif of the fig tree in the sermon has a dual aim: the celebration of the symbol of the cross as the core theme in the liturgy of the feast day of the Exaltation of the Cross, and the sign of the cross, an intense crusading symbol; both served to bring the author's crusading ideas to life.

The sermon is also coloured by appeals to knightly elites. Bearing in mind that the sermon was preached before the King of France and his barons, Pierre inveighed against the luxurious and superfluous lifestyle of the nobility of Western Europe, arguing that emperors, kings and princes, unlike the *pugiles Christi*, spent their life in vanity and injustice: they consumed their fortunes and those of others, undertook unjust wars, cruelly killed other Christians while devastating and plundering their lands and ignoring the business of the cross. According to Pierre de la Palud they were '*veri milites et pugiles Antichristi*', ruining themselves by jousting in tournaments and in other delights, paying for elaborate and expensive vestments and only concerned about their splendid appearance. When the time came to join the *militia Christi* and depart for the sacred passage, these prodigal men would remain impotent and powerless, oblivious to the *exempla* of Godfrey of Bouillon and Raymond, Count of Toulouse and St-Gilles.[98] Palud reserved much space for protests against the lavish lifestyle of the elites of the period as ignoble and opposition of their system of values, which required too great a part of the king's treasury. Such criticism reflects the disinterest of the knightly classes in Europe for crusading in the East. Similarly, James of Lausanne loathed those who chose to enjoy the prosperity and the delights of their homeland rather than depart for Jerusalem.

After 1316, when Pope John XXII lifted the 1312 ban on tournaments that his predecessor had imposed, 'the staging of court pageants, feasts and tournaments was becoming progressively more and more elaborate and princely households were growing in size and in elaborateness of their organization'.[99] The greatest part of royal household outlay was for lavish feasts comprising banquets, tournaments, jousting and pageantry. The jousts and tournaments were a favourite occasion for noble combatants to engage in contests of bravery and heroism, and their atmosphere was one of chivalrous magnificence. These extravagant feasts and pageants also created special opportunities for young noblemen dressed in fashionable and magnificent costumes to impress women – after all, it was through splendour and luxury that the nobility sought acceptance and reassurance.[100] For a clergyman and a noble like Pierre de la Palud, whose churches and lands, subordinated to his patriarchate, had been under Muslim dominion since 1291, these spectacles were an excessive extravagance that distracted princely attention from crusading matters and burdened royal treasuries at a time when the clergy was overtaxed by its mandate to secure funds for the crusade. Even though Philip VI of France expressed his intention, after Palud's sermon, to go on crusade himself, any censure of costly entertainments fell on deaf ears. Less than a year after Palud's sermon, the French king made overgenerous arrangements for knighting his eldest son and future French king John II; wealth and plush living were, for the nobility, a *sine qua non* condition for maintaining the loyalty, service and support of their noble subjects, and for their dignity and pride.[101]

As a contrast to the idleness of the contemporary nobility and similar to previous sermons, Pierre recounts the examples of Godfrey of Bouillon and of Raymond IV, Count of Toulouse and St-Gilles, noblemen who sold their patrimonies to personally crusade and who earned perpetual inheritance in Heaven. Godfrey of Bouillon and Raymond of Toulouse were zealous Christians who eagerly responded to Pope Urban II's summons to go to war for the liberation of Jerusalem and the Holy Sepulchre from the Muslims. Both emerged as leading figures of the First Crusade; contemporary accounts of the First Crusade praised their accomplishments, and they became figures of legend.[102] According to Dunbabin, the appearance of Raymond of Toulouse among the legendary, heroic personages of the crusading movement should be attributed to Pierre's compilation of 'Liber Bellorum Domini' in 1329.[103] Godfrey of Bouillon, the first Latin ruler of the Kingdom of Jerusalem, was portrayed as the most valiant and devout of all crusaders; he was truly pious, the perfect Christian king.[104] In the *Chansons de Geste*, a collection of French epic poems written between the eleventh and fourteenth centuries, Godfrey of Bouillon was the central figure in the crusade cycle of poems: like Charlemagne and Roland, his heroic deeds were glorified;

he became a legendary personage believed to be descended from the 'King of the Swan', a mythic figure.[105]

The sermon's aristocratic audience was exhorted to take the cross and go on crusade, as 'in all Christian armies against the infidels, and specially the Saracens, the principal banner is the cross of Christ'.[106] The assembled were urged to demonstrate their courage by imitating different examples of Christian courage throughout history, and to have faith:

> And so the soldiers and champions of Christ in the army of Charlemagne and of the noble Duke Godfrey always confessed, took communion devoutly, and heard the divine service before fighting, and thus they tasted beforehand the fruit which hung on the cross and thereby armed themselves, just as the weasel eats the rue and thus intrepid attacks and kills the basilisk.[107]

References to liturgical practices and to acts of devotion are included in the sermon to convince the audience to prepare spiritually for taking the cross and for battle through remorse, through the act of confession and through communion with Christ. The cycle of the celebration of the Mass, the confession of sins and the taking of the Eucharist were already common practices for the armies of the First Crusade.[108] These liturgical practices of religious devotion were necessary for an undertaking of such holy character; they also demonstrated the close rapport of the *milites et pugiles Christi* with God and served as the medium for the spiritual and moral exaltation of the crusaders.[109] The reference to the armies of Charlemagne directs the audience's attention to the Carolingian era, during Charlemagne's campaigns for the defence of Christianity against the infidels, when the earliest reported patterns of liturgical rites and practices of war were developed.[110] The ideology of the liturgical practices undertaken in the ninth century during war perfectly suited the general character of crusade as holy war.

To enhance the mental vigour of his audience, and to make his discourse more amusing, Pierre included a lively recounting of the legend of the basilisk and the weasel. In medieval imagery, the basilisk was a birdlike lizard with a snake's tail and a curious topknot on its head: it was the king of serpents, a deadly animal of great strength that could destroy humans with a single glance or even with just its scent.[111] According to legend, only the weasel could kill this fabulous animal. References to the basilisk are found in the *Pharsalia* and *Historia Naturalis* of Lucan and Pliny the Elder, respectively, from the first century, and they appear in the Middle Ages.[112] The prominent Parisian scholar, theologian and particularly gifted preacher, Eudes of Châteauroux, makes use of the basilisk legend in his 1268 sermon for the crusade against the Muslims of Lucera. Pope Innocent IV appointed him papal legate to the East, and in 1248 he accompanied the French king, Louis IX, on crusade to Egypt. Sometime after his arrival at the papal curia in 1254, Eudes compiled two sermons on the anniversary of the death of Robert, Count of Artois, and other French nobles at the battle of Massura in 1250.[113] Eudes of Châteauroux passed the last decade of his life deeply devoted to the preaching of the crusade and to producing numerous collections of model sermons:[114] among his voluminous body of work are three sermons he preached for the promotion of the crusade against the Muslim colony of Lucera in Apulia and various *ad status* crusade sermons.[115] Eudes compares Frederick II Hohenstaufen's venomous and malicious offspring, who would come to devour the clerics and antagonize the Church, with the basilisk, which would greedily swallow all animals.[116] In our case, the basilisk and the weasel serve to admonish Pierre's audience quite well. The allegory provides Pierre with strong didactic elements that easily connect the physical characteristics of the basilisk, and the wizard, with the habits of his audience.[117] According to Church moralists, the basilisk was a symbol of the devil, the enemy of humanity.[118] The basilisk served as a representation of immorality, which poisons man and prevents him from being righteous. In the sermon, the basilisk is interpreted as the opulence and vanity that impede European nobility from committing to crusade; the weasel, whose intrepid attacks kill the basilisk, symbolizes courage, moral excellence and virtue. The moral values attributed to the weasel are equivalent to the spirituality and ethos necessary for the conduct of a holy war; thus Palud urges his listeners to look to the cross, to taste the body and blood of Christ and to then fearlessly, as crusaders, expose themselves to the danger of death. If they died in a holy war for the sake of Christ they would eat the fruit of the cross of satiety in Heaven.[119]

Elsewhere, while exhorting all Christians to fight the infidels, specifically the Saracens in Syria and Egypt, Pierre de la Palud incorporated, with great force and energy, another exemplar of bestial imagery. The *moralitates*, with their strong moral and allegorical symbolism, presented the preacher's message in a pleasant way and provided moral instruction. Palud cited the story of a unicorn, tamed by a maiden and trapped in her lap, as a symbol of the Incarnation; the beast was ultimately slaughtered by hunters in the wood, and this moral tale served as an allegory for the Immaculate Conception and the Passion of Christ. The choice of this particular instructive story, wherein the unicorn represents the source of all morality, was very appropriate. The message of the *moralitas*, which recalls the Passion, Resurrection and Ascension of Christ, may have been an anamnesis for Pierre and his mission in Egypt, during which he certainly saw a number of exotic beasts, including crocodiles, elephants, giraffes, leopards and unicorns (rhinoceroses), most likely at the sultan's menagerie in Cairo. The Dominican friar Humbert of Dijon, who had been on pilgrimage to the Holy Land around the time Palud visited Cairo, testified: 'In this same city there are many and diverse foreign animals, astonishing to see, such as leopards, elephants, unicorns, crocodiles ...'.[120] Such foreign animals from the Orient, unseen and unknown in Europe, astonished Western travellers and pilgrims, who recalled them in accounts of their journeys.

In the Middle Ages, the circulation of such legends and other tales about birds and animals, real or mythical, was very common, and the wealth of illuminated manuscript bestiaries in different libraries confirms the popularity of bestiary lore. Church fathers such as Isidore of Seville and the Venerable Bede, in their efforts to reconcile and combine philosophy with Christian doctrine, acquainted themselves with natural history and introduced animal stories to their oeuvres.[121] A number of books with moralising collections of descriptions, and often illustrations, of real and mythical animals were produced in medieval Europe. The fables found in these bestiaries became very popular especially among the Parisian preachers as the allegorical essence of the animal descriptions increased their instructive efficiency.[122] The symbolism and metaphors in tales about animals and beasts served as moral and religious instruction for Christian congregations; their use gradually increased in the late thirteenth and early fourteenth centuries, mainly at the centre of theology in Paris.[123] Indeed, during this period the *moralitates* became very popular 'moyen oratoire' among the Parisian friar-doctors.[124] The source of these tales (generally folktales or legends) was not scriptural – it was often pagan, based on natural history and bestiary lore.[125] The *Historia Animalium* of Aristotle, translated into Latin by Michael Scot; Pliny's *Historia Naturalis*; the work of Gaius Julius Solinus, *De Mirabilibus Mundi*; and the treatises *De Animalibus* and *De Vegetabilibus et Plantis* by the Christian theologian and scientist Albert the Great were highly esteemed by the *moralitates* compilers,[126] who also collected material about animals from bestiaries and from the writings of Avicenna and Averroes.[127] James of Lausanne in particular loved to use stories from natural history, especially beast fables, to make comparisons between men and beasts to interpret human behaviour; he usually supplemented his moralities with personal anecdotes and observations on everyday life, which made his discourses livelier and more amusing.[128] Beyond their instructive role, such stories helped preachers hold the attention of their audience and were also a means of direct propagation. Pierre called upon Christians to be generous to their persecutors, to follow the example of Jesus who, at the time of His Passion, like a tamed lamb, forgave those who tortured, humiliated and crucified Him. Pierre also urged his audiences to be as ferocious and wild as a bull against the enemies of the cross of the Christ, as Jesus was against the demons, the enemies of humanity.[129]

At the same time, biblical authorities and other *exempla* with strong narratives and powerful interpretations described noble personages and models of human action to be imitated by their audiences. Such an example comes from the Gospel of Luke, in which Jesus commended the apostles for their faithfulness to Him during the Last Supper: 'you are they who persisted with me in my temptations. And I dispose to you a kingdom as my Father disposed to me, that you may eat and drink at my table, in my kingdom'.[130] These verses served to inspire audiences to imitate the disciples of Jesus who continued to be with Him to the end. Likewise, Christians have to renounce the temptations of opulence and follow Christ in Jerusalem. Stories from non-scriptural sources were also used in sermons, such as the moral story of the martyrdom of a certain Templar or Hospitaller knight who, in the war against the Saracens, was lanced on his right and left sides by the enemy and mortally wounded. Acclaimed as a martyr, that very night he dined at the table of Christ in Heaven, while another knight who had chosen not to participate in the crusade spent the evening in tears, on earth, eating his meal over his cloak.[131] This *exemplum* illustrated the spiritual rewards earned by crusaders who sacrificed themselves on the battlefield against the infidels: the Church honours these crusaders, placing them amongst the martyrs, with God in heaven, where they taste the fruits on the Tree of the Cross.

Portrayals of heroic acts and knightly glory attributed to the main military orders in the Holy Land appeared widely in the narratives of crusade propagandists and the sermons of preachers in the West until the fall of Acre.[132] Several illustrative stories and *exempla* in thirteenth-century collections recount different instances of the heroism of Templar knights in the battlefield against the infidels and acclaim the knights' martyrdom.[133] Nevertheless, Pierre de la Palud's reference to the Knights of the Temple two decades after the suppression of the Order seems paradoxical. It might have been that the patriarch wanted to acknowledge the order's significant contribution to the struggle against the Saracens: during interrogations at the Templars' trial in Paris, Pierre de la Palud never declared his support for the charges against the Knights; it seems he was more sympathetic than polemical.[134] References to the Templars, especially in the presence of the French king, might have been an allusion to the part played by the French Crown in the dissolution of the Order.

More space is reserved for the apposition of different and quite extensive stories of Christian history, all closely linked to the cult of the cross and all recited in chapters pertaining to the discovery and Exaltation of the Holy Cross in the *Legenda Aurea* of James of Voragine.[135] Palud presented the episodes of Seth and the Queen of Sheba, the legends of the heavenly vision of Emperor Constantine the Great and the cross (*In hoc signo vinces*) and that of Helena, Constantine's mother, in the discovery of the True Cross in Jerusalem; he also recounted episodes from the life of Chosroes, King of Persia, including the capture of Jerusalem in 615, the humiliation of the True Cross, the demolition of the Holy Sepulchre and, finally, the Exaltation of the Holy Cross after Emperor Heraclius entered Jerusalem and liberated the Holy City.[136] Such legends fit very well with the message of the feast days of the cross and with the depiction of crusading as a perpetual battle against Christ's enemies.

Pierre de la Palud quoted extensively from Voragine's compilation, and sections of the *Legenda Aurea* make up almost half of his sermon: this implies that the preserved sermon is an elaborated textual version of Pierre's September 1331 sermon, and surely reflects little of what was actually said during the preaching event. The frequent use of biblical and patristic authorities and the quotations from the *Legenda Aurea* would have made it difficult for an audience to follow the preacher's argumentation, and the sermon's overall length makes it unsuitable for live preaching.

But why did Pierre copy so much from the *Legenda Aurea*? That Jacobus intended the *Legenda Aurea* to serve as a preaching manual, particularly for friars in the Dominican houses, leads us to believe that Pierre copied from the *Legenda* for exactly this reason.[137] The addendum in one of the preserved manuscripts of the *Legenda Aurea* of two tables/indexes of legends included in the *Legenda*, whose composition, according to a note written in 1349, is attributed to Pierre de la Palud, reinforces this assumption.[138] That Pierre read all of the legends in the *Legenda Aurea* closely and listed all of them by content to facilitate their study by his fellow Dominicans – so they could easily find *exempla* and illustrative stories from the lives of the saints – explains why, in this *de cruce* sermon, Palud reproduced so much of the *Legenda Aurea*.

152 *University trained clergy*

As in other contemporary crusade sermons, Pierre expressed his grief over the critical state of affairs in the Holy Land; from here on he continues his conclusion in a more hortatory tone, drawing on a Maccabean exemplar to convey his sorrow for the Muslim occupation of the Holy Land. The priest Mattathias in this passage (I Machabaeorum 2.7–13) laments the destruction of Israel by the gentiles. This excerpt creates a link between the suffering of Mattathias and that of the Christians for the loss of Jerusalem. In the same way as Mattathias, the Patriarch expresses his deep grief and concern over the situation in the East. He reminds his listeners that Jerusalem and the other places consecrated with the blood of Christ were still in the hands of the Saracens, and that immediate action '*pro recuperatione et defensione Terre Sancte*' was necessary.[139] The life of the bad king, Nebuchadnezzar, was an example not to be followed: the princely nobility and magnates were instructed to follow the example of St Louis, who built churches, monasteries and hospitals during his reign and, as a pious and zealous Christian, devoted himself to the liberation of Jerusalem.[140] Thus, Pierre exhorted Philip VI to follow the example of his father-in-law, to take the cross and personally participate in the crusade. Pierre enhanced his argument for taking the cross and travelling to the East by declaring that the wood of the cross would sustain all those who travelled to the Holy Land, and that the sign of the cross on a crusader's shoulder would protect him from potential danger at sea. He likens the cross to an omnipotent shield:

> For if anyone were covered with such a shield that he could not be killed, or mortally wounded, or captured bearing it, or if he were captured if captivity would be worth more to him than his ransom would cost, and if he were wounded he would heal quickly and better [than before], such a man would have to be very courageous in war. But the crusaders are protected by such an invincible shield in every war that they fight for the name of the Crucified One.[141]

A more meditative treatment was introduced with respect to the spiritual rewards following a crusader's demise. Pierre drew on eschatology and apocalyptic literature to stir the spiritually of those who vowed to fight for the cross. The crusaders who might lose their lives in the war for Christ would be absolved of the fear of hell, since their deaths would be considered penitential acts and confessions of faith.[142] For this they would rank among the martyrs of Christ and receive plenary remission of sins; as champions of Christ who sacrificed their mortal bodies at the last judgment, they would receive immortal and glorious bodies.[143]

The use of moral stories just before the conclusion of a sermon had a mental and emotional impact on an audience. With a didactic *exemplum*, Palud promises the miraculous interference of God on behalf of the crusaders, the divine providence granted them throughout their journey to the Holy Land. Such a didactic *exemplum* recounted by the Patriarch is the episode of a fleet of pilgrims and crusaders driven ashore by the wind near a Saracen fortress on the Spanish coast, al-Kazez. Captured by the Moorish sultan, the Christians were informed that they owed the sultan a tribute of 100 heads per annum. The Christian inhabitants of al-Kazez asked the crusaders to participate in a battle against their infidel overlord, to which the crusaders agreed; it was winter, and the sea route to the Holy Land was risky, and all of the crusaders agreed to enter into the service of Christ.

Following their victory, the crusaders sailed to the Holy Land, where they joined a Christian army, swelling it to 7,000 men. They besieged the fortress and defeated the 100,000 mounted soldiers in the sultan's army. After the Christian victory, one of the captives asked the Christians what happened to the white-clad knights with red crosses on their armour and shoulders.[144] The miraculous appearance of the knights during the battle is emblematic of the divine protection the *milites Christi* enjoyed when fighting the gentiles. The crusade, as a just war for the protection of the Church and the liberation of the Holy Land, was a meritorious act, and its participants enjoyed Christ's protection and assistance. Therefore, all Christians who were willing to fight for the sake of Christ and the defence of the Church would be fight without fear.

In this *de cruce* sermon, delivered a year after the arrival of Pierre de la Palud from Cyprus on the feast day of the Exaltation of the Cross, the Patriarch praised the Tree of the Cross. The intense crusading symbolism in his sermon, which corresponds with the feast days of the cross, helps Pierre organize and convey his feelings about the crusade. During the first part of the sermon, Pierre is quite critical, presumably highly charged, emotionally, as he considers the failure of his Egyptian mission: he inveighs against the extravagant lifestyle of the nobility and their indifference towards the critical situation in the Holy Land, and he draws Philip VI's attention to the danger Egypt presents. In the second part of the sermon, the Latin patriarch of Jerusalem, in a hortatory tone, proclaims the Christian duty to fight for Christ and tries to convince his audience of the crusade's penitential value, explaining how it would give them sure access to Heaven. The devotion of the crusaders to their cause and their sacrifice in the battlefield was regarded as a meritorious act by the Church, which rewarded them with plenary remission of their sins.

Crusaders were compensated for their sacrifice with martyrdom. Pierre's message was in effect the same as that which had circulated throughout Western Christianity after Pope Urban II preached the First Crusade at Clermont, but the Latin Patriarch invigorated his appeal with a host of different illustrations and allegories, some from sources other than the Bible, giving his sermon an array of exotic animal symbolism. The adaptation of the sermon to his own style, to the needs of his audience and to the occasion, is the hallmark of Pierre's preaching, as the form of sermons followed is almost entirely from standardized models. Pierre's preaching reinvigorated Philip VI's interest and aroused the enthusiastic reaction of the French nobility for the business of the cross to the East, and initiated a period of major crusade activity that continued until 1336.

Crusade propaganda and diplomacy in the framework of the Franco-papal crusade negotiations, 1332–1333: The sermons of Pierre Roger, Archbishop of Rouen

The positive outcome of Pierre de la Palud's sermon in stimulating French royal interest for the crusade resulted in the beginning of the Franco-papal crusade negotiations, which took place from early 1332 to late 1333. During the negotiations, the French king sent three embassies at Avignon for deliberation on crusade. The Archbishop of Rouen, Pierre Roger, as the head of the royal envoys, preached the crusade in Avignon in the presence of Pope John XXII at several times, and this section will examine these preserved sermons.

Pierre Roger was born at Maumont in Corrèze sometime in 1290 or 1291. He was the second son of William Roger, a man of the lesser nobility and Lord of Maumont.[145] In 1301, at the age of ten, Pierre, a child of unusual promise, entered the Benedictine abbey of la Chaise-Dieu of the diocese of Clermont in the Auvergne. He resided at la Chaise-Dieu for six years, then left the monastery for the University of Paris,[146] where he studied arts, philosophy and theology. His great knowledge and outstanding rhetorical skills distinguished him as a prominent theologian, canonist and orator, and his gifts attracted papal attention: in 1323, Pope John XXII commanded the chancellor of Paris to confer on Pierre the master's degree in theology.[147]

Pierre was involved in theological disputes during his time at the university. In the academic year 1320–1321, he was engaged in a theological debate with the Franciscan, François of Meyronnes, over the *Sentences* of Peter Lombard, and in 1325 he attacked Marsilius of Padua. In 1324, Marsilius, an Italian scholar and political theorist, published the 'Defensor Pacis', which was written in the context of a power struggle between Pope John XXII and Louis of Bavaria; 'Defensor Pacis' disputes the Church's temporal power, especially papal policy concerning the crusades, indulgences, vows, excommunication and some doctrinal issues, and Marsilius supports imperial supremacy over the Church. Pope John XXII, with the *Quia quorumdam mentes* in 1325, justified the right of the Church and clergy to own property.[148] Pierre's performance in scholastic disputations revealed his abilities as a formidable public speaker, and his fame spread among religious and royal circles in France. The general appreciation the clergy had for Pierre Roger is proven by his rapid rise through the Benedictine ranks. John Chandorat, abbot of la Chaise-Dieu, granted Pierre the expectation of the priory of St Pantaléon in 1322 and the conventual priory of Savigneaux in the diocese of Lyon in late 1323. The prior of Savigneaux was an important member of the abbatial council, representing the monastic community outside Chaise-Dieu. Soon after, with papal support, Pierre Roger was beneficed with the priory of St Baudil in Nîmes and, in 1325, the provision of the abbey of St Germain-des-Près. In June 1326, Roger assumed the abbacy of Fécamp in the diocese of Rouen, one of the three most significant abbeys in France.[149] In early 1329, he joined the secular clergy after he was appointed Bishop of Arras and consecrated that March. Before the end of 1329, Pierre Roger was promoted to the archbishopric of Sens; in 1330, he took possession of the major see of the archbishopric of Rouen.[150]

As Archbishop of Rouen, Pierre Roger had a prominent role in every major ecclesiastical and royal affair in France, and he was in continual communication with Pope John XXII concerning both ecclesiastical and lay affairs in the realm of Philip VI. In 1328, he acted as an intermediary in the conflict between the kings Philip VI of France and Edward III of England, gaining French royal favour and earning an appointment as counsellor to the king of France.[151] Chiefly engaged in the diplomatic and ecclesiastical affairs of France and in royal administration, in February 1332, Pierre Roger led an embassy from Philip VI to the papal court in Avignon to present French royal plans for a crusade to the Holy Land and to make further arrangements with the pope.[152] During the negotiations between Avignon and Paris, from February 1332 to October 1333, Pierre Roger emerged as a leading figure, a prominent diplomat and a crusade propagandist. On 19 February 1332, the Archbishop of Rouen, while at Avignon, announced these plans before the pope and the College of Cardinals, after which he delivered a suppliant sermon to achieve papal confirmation and support; this preserved sermon was followed by a second on the First Sunday in Lent 1332, just before the end of Pierre Roger's first diplomatic mission at Avignon. His allusion, in the sermon he delivered at the papal chapel at Avignon on 16 July 1333, that he had been sent to the pope on a third occasion, indicates there was a second embassy between Lent 1332 and July 1333, but its date remains unknown.[153] On the occasion of this third diplomatic mission, on 16 July 1333, Pierre Roger preached the crusade in front of a populous consistory in the papal chapel at Avignon,[154] and on 1 October 1333, Pierre Roger preached the crusade in the Prés-aux-Clercs for the last time in the context of the 1332–1333 Franco-papal crusade negotiations.[155] As we have seen, Pierre Roger delivered four sermons during his diplomatic missions at the papal curia on behalf of the French King, three at Avignon and one at Paris, but only three survive. I present the two sermons delivered on 19 February 1332 and 16 July 1333, as the sermon preached on the First Sunday in Lent 1332 makes no references to the crusade; I did not manage to identify the final sermon of the four, which Pierre Roger preached on 1 October 1333.

In his sermons, the Archbishop presents himself to his fellow ecclesiastics as a royal representative, rather than as a prominent theologian and man of the cloth. Addressing an exclusively ecclesiastical audience, Pierre Roger limits his discussion of some of the spiritual aspects of the crusade, choosing instead to build his discourse around the practical issues pertaining to Philip VI's crusade plans. He delineates the King's crusade aspirations, praising the king and attributing to Philip all of the vital qualities of a great soldier, declaring him the best of all secular rulers to lead the crusade. Lastly, Pierre Roger pays special attention to securing papal financial aid for Philip's crusade, the ultimate objective of his mission to Avignon.

Pierre Roger addressed the pope on both occasions, clearly imparting the principal objective of his visit to Avignon at the head of the French royal embassy. Using his sermon of 19 February 1332 [hereafter app. III] as his point of departure, Pierre Roger made the biblical verse, 'He made His decision to set out for Jerusalem and He sent messengers', from the Gospel of Luke, the theme of his sermon.[156] The choice of this particular verse announced the main objective of Pierre's discourse, that the French king had decided to set out for the Holy Land, and that he had sent envoys to the pope to negotiate the implementation of the crusade. Pierre Roger commended Philip VI's desire to perform such a great and virtuous service, and he offered evidence of his patron's commitment:

Now, most Holy Father, your most devout son the king of France has appointed us his envoys at the feet of your sanctity, servants of the same holiness. Stimulated by the Holy Spirit, and confident of divine assistance, not dubious of your and the Church's counsel, support and patronage, stirred by devotion, admonished by your healthy exhortation, agitated by the insistence of his prelates and barons and also of the lord patriarch [Pierre de la Palud], whether appropriate or not, and also bound by his [crusading] vow and obligation and the taking of the cross, following in the footsteps of his predecessors, as he [the king] wrote to your holiness at another time, he has taken on a great task, a meritorious task, a very virtuous task, a task most worthy of all praise, namely to go personally to Jerusalem and to the Holy Land consecrated with the blood of Christ and to liberate the Sepulchre of the Lord from the hands of the impious blasphemers.[157]

Pierre Roger referred to the tirade delivered by the Patriarch of Jerusalem, Pierre de la Palud, on 14 September 1331, and the exhortations by the high clergy and the barons in the French Kingdom, which stimulated royal crusading enthusiasm and prompted the King to appeal for papal assistance.[158]

In his sermon on 16 July 1333 [hereafter app. IV], Pierre Roger begins with a brief *prothema*, beseeching the pope to designate Philip VI of France leader and captain of the planned general passage for the recovery of the Holy Land. In the sermon's *thema*,[159] Pierre Roger likens Philip VI to Esdras, the Jewish priest and scribe who is closely connected with the restoration of Israel.[160] The symbolic meaning of this comparison would have been evident to the sermon's audience, the pope and the College of Cardinals. As Esdras called on his compatriots, the priests and the Levites, who wished to follow him on his journey from Babylon to Jerusalem, so did Philip VI similarly summon his fellow Christians to accompany him to liberate Jerusalem. In app. IV, Pierre Roger declares Philip VI's desire to personally crusade in the East, and the Archbishop asks the Church to support this effort by granting indulgences, exemption from taxes and other privileges to the French King.[161]

The French royal hunger for crusading to Jerusalem was declared in a more scholarly manner in app. III. The sermon's theme is divided into three parts, each part corresponding to each concept – *intellectus, affectus, effectus* – of his triple cluster.[162] These formulae of divisions, first appearing in the schools of Paris in the late twelfth century, proved crucial in scholastic preaching as a means for delineating ideas bound together by similar elements; with the *distinctiones*, these formulae of divisions were the most common topoi of the Parisian theologians' sermons.[163] For *intellectus*, which requires observance and understanding, Roger explains that Philip VI sees the crusade as a virtuous act of praise for God and of moral excellence, and that he was sincere in his desire and prepared to assume such a burden. With *affectus*, which requires delight and satisfaction, the King, because of his fiery affection, has devoted himself to pursuing the business of the Holy Land. With *effectus*, which requires enforcement and vigilance, or providence, the King needs aid and fruitful counsel to ensure the exigency and the advantageous timing of a *passagium*.[164] Pierre Roger tells the pope and the College of Cardinals that Philip VI was 'to go to Jerusalem not only for a pilgrimage but to liberate the entire Holy Land'.[165]

One of the main objectives of Pierre Roger's missions to Avignon was to safeguard the Church's financial support. As the King's envoy to the papal court, he appealed to the papacy for assistance in putting French crusade plans into practical effect. In app. III the Archbishop informs the pope and his cardinals that the King has insufficient economic resources to prepare, implement and sustain the crusade on his own, and that he is in need of the Church's financial contribution and counsel:

> Thus, the lord king for the recovery of the Holy Sepulchre and the other Holy Places and of the whole Holy Land has sent us, servants of your sanctity, to beg at the feet of your beatitude and to obtain opportune support.[166]

Pierre Roger reiterates that Philip VI is earnestly seeking papal financial support, as the royal treasury could not meet the tremendous expenses necessary for such a costly project as the crusade, and 'most especially now when we have no city or place in Outremer where we can rest our feet'.[167] To achieve his purpose, the French king humbly beseeched Pope John XXII for his support. Like Esdras, who was favoured by the Persian king and thus received royal support and funds to rebuild Jerusalem and restore the Temple, so Philip VI asked for papal support for his most holy crusading proposal. To this end, Roger petitions Pope John XXII, as the head of the entire Church 'to call in general upon everyone in his kingdom, that is, the whole Christianity, to come in support of such a king for such a pious and necessary affair, to open the treasures of the Church for him, to grant indulgences, privileges, and immunities universally'.[168]

In app. III, this plea is bolstered by the words of Pope Clement V from his address at the Council of Vienne, in which he reminds his audience to have in mind that the cities and the other places their ancestors acquired in the Holy Land had been devastated by the aggressive madness of the enemies. Pierre Roger continues:

> Because of this, the promotion of the mentioned business requires greater expenses than it formerly required, when some of the ancestors of the same king and certain other Christian princes passed over the sea in support of the same land [Holy Land], when the aforesaid cities and places remained in a state of prosperity, in which cities and places catholic warriors were able to be received and to refresh themseves – so it is not surprising if they ask much for so great an affair. Nor are they asking for uncustomary things, but for what have been granted at other times for similar affairs or for not so reasonable [affairs]. Not are they asking for things without advice, but with the counsel of many and great prelates from the kingdom of France.[169]

This demonstrates the general anxiety of both royal and ecclesiastical powers with regard to funding crusades. The guarantee and grant of extra funds for the crusade was a necessary means and a prerequisite for the papacy to achieve secular participation in the crusade. The Avignon papacy worried about securing money for the crusade beyond crusade tithes on revenue from ecclesiastical incomes; to generate crusade funds, the papacy had combined crusade preaching to the laity with an intense liturgical apparatus, to an unprecedented degree, from the reign of Clement V. Such measures guaranteed an economic contribution from more of the faithful.

To garner papal support and funds for the French crusade project, Pierre Roger employs a scholastic style and his rhetorical ability and literacy to the utmost; he reminds the pope of the papal *plenitudinem potestatis et auctoritatis* to inaugurate a crusade. No one other than the pope could judge and decide over crusading affairs, and no one in the entire Church, other than St Peter and his successors, has the right to make crusade decrees.

Pierre Roger intensifies the emotional pressure on John XXII and adds validity to his argument regarding papal supremacy over spiritual and temporal issues by citing in both sermons the same passage (book 2, chapters 7–8) from Bernard's *De Consideratione ad Eugenium Papam*.[170] The *De Consideratione*, dedicated to Pope Eugene III, is an apologia for the fiasco of the Second Crusade: Bernard of Clairvaux discusses the status of the universal church and the sovereignty of the Roman Pontiff over all human subjects, among other ecclesiological issues. As the head of the universal Church and the supreme lord of all Christian subjects, the pope has the duty to protect and support his flock.[171] Thus, with the use of the *auctoritas* from Bernard of Clairvaux, whose words were indisputably valid at Avignon, Pierre made an urgent argument on behalf of his mission. The particular passage from *De Consideratione* quoted in app. III and app. IV was very popular; it was frequently cited by other medieval thinkers, and became a commonplace for the exposition of the papal 'fullness of power'.[172]

The *plenitudo potestatis* doctrine and the claim of the vicariate of Christ had special relevance to papal authority over bishops and also to the pope's power over emperors and kings; hence, the defence of the Church and the faith against infidels and heretics fell under papal jurisdiction. This rhetoric had been folded into papal terminology by the fifth century and was established by the middle of the twelfth century in the theological writings of Bernard of Clairvaux and in Gratian's *Decretum*, and it was Pope Innocent III who, at the close of the twelfth century, had become its most zealous enthusiast.[173] It is arguable that Roger's intention, by including his discourse the theological doctrine about papal 'fullness of power', was to stress the necessity of papal authorization of Philip's crusading plans and of the relinquishment of ecclesiastical money to the French royal treasury. According to Roger, only the pope could announce a general passage to the Holy Land; no one else on earth could compel those who were bound by oath to pass over the sea.[174]

To obtain papal acquiescence, Pierre Roger describes the harmonious relationship between the Holy See and the French royal house, a relationship from which have emerged reciprocal obligations for the fruitful accomplishment of the crusade. Pierre Roger reminisces here about the concrete and ancient bonds between the papacy and the French Crown, the most Christian of kingdoms, and reminds John XXII that '*de corde regni Francie traxistis originem*'.[175] He addresses the pope:

> The king of France is sending [us] to you our lord, his father. It is clear from the chronicles how great the affection of the French Crown for the Holy Roman Church has always been and conversely of the Holy Roman Church for the French Crown. There has been such great affection, so great a bond, so great confederation, so great love that at no time did one abandon the other, so that it would not be present in all prosperities and adversities, and in aids and counsels, and opportune favours.[176]

Philip VI has sent his envoys to Avignon with royal obedience to and filial reverence for the pope. The French King

> does not exactly seek this aid for the enrichment of his kingdom, for the payment of debts or testaments, for the improvement of the currency, but for the sake of Christ, for revenge for His injuries, for the cleansing of the Holy Land and the Holy Places, for the recovery of our legacy, for the augmentation of the cult of Christ.[177]

No one seemed more determined to usefully carry out the *negotium Christi*, without any flattery or pretence, than the French King. In app. III, Pierre Roger emphasizes eight of Philip VI's distinguishing characteristics, each greatly requisite for the advantageous execution of the crusade, each a quality that makes him its appropriate leader.[178] The French King possessed the ardour of inward piety, necessary for whoever wished to wage such a war; moreover, like the warriors before him, Philip had a natural love of God, an indispensable affection for a prince who had to be fearless, 'Nor is there any wonder, because the soul of man is generous, for he is easier led than dragged'.[179]

Pierre Roger then lists the other characteristic qualities that made Philip the appropriate leader of the crusade. The French King had been vigorously trained in arms, an essential attribute for a prince, since in war a small number of skilled men are worth more than a multitude of ignorant men, and in support of this assertion Pierre quotes a passage from Vegetius, *On military affairs* or *Epitome of military science*, a late Latin technical work on military affairs written by Publius Flavius Vegetius Renatus sometime in the late fourth or the early fifth century: 'The courage of a fighter is heightened by the knowledge of his profession, and he only wants an opportunity to do what he is convinced he has been perfectly taught'.[180] The *Epitoma rei militaris* had been characterized as the 'handbook of chivalry', and it enjoyed great popularity in the Middle Ages, as the various manuscripts and the number of translations into vernacular languages testify.[181] With his quote from Vegetius, Pierre Roger sought to convince the pope and the Cardinals of Philip VI's capability in warfare and his rightful position as the leader of the crusade, particularly as Philip was in the bloom of lifetime and in robust physical condition: he had significant experience, unlike many of the younger men who would accompany him on the crusade, but there was no deficiency in his physical vigour, as there was in many of the older men who would follow him. According to Pierre Roger, the French king was of an age when, in a man, knowledge and corporeal strength flourish, and he possessed both discretion in deliberation and the splendour of wisdom.[182]

In app. IV, Pierre Roger reminds his audience of the distinctive characteristics of Philip VI that rendered him 'the more suitable and the more appropriate among all the Christian princes' to assume leadership of the crusade.[183] From the very beginning of app. IV and in other sections of his discourse the Archbishop makes clear the assignment of the French King at the head of the Christian army is the dominant objective of his last diplomatic mission to Avignon in 1333.[184] Further, Philip VI's comparison to Joshua, the ideal of crusading prince, bolsters this assertion.[185] Pierre Roger declares that nothing would be more advantageous than permitting Philip and his company to duly carry out the crusade, that there is no one more splendid or honest, and that there is no one else who rules with more probity or who could coordinate and execute the crusade more profitably.[186] The Archbishop once again extols Philip VI's vivacity and his skill in arms, lauds the power of his realm and the obedience of his vassals, praises his prudence and brightness in consultation, exalts his sagacity and foreknowledge in difficult circumstances, acclaims the sanctity and integrity of his deeds and commends his religious devotion, faithfulness and piety; these were all necessary attributes for the commander and rector of the Christian army and, when compared to all other Christian princes of Europe, they were excellently present in the King of France.[187] Philip VI of France, a faithful Christian, an excellent warrior and a good king, was therefore the best choice to lead all Christians in the struggle against the infidels. Roger enthusiastically praises Philip VI as *Rex Christianissimus* and as a superior warrior: Philip was devoted to the *opus Christi* for the recapture of the lands formerly belonging to Christians and for the protection of the Church from its enemies; for his devotion and piety, Philip would receive the favour and assistance of *Divina Clementia*.

As royal representative, Pierre Roger attempted to convince his audience of the French King's determination to advance the cause of crusading, and in app. IV he presents, in a more apologetic tone, argumentation in defence of Philip VI against charges of unconcern and delay.[188] The Archbishop of Rouen draws his audience's attention to evidence of the King's persistence in carrying out his crusading plans by describing Philip's interest in fighting the enemies of the faith, which was present even before he assumed the throne of France:

> When somebody persists continuously in his intention it is sign that he is firm in this purpose. Certainly, for a long time, even before he took over the kingdom, the lord king thought of testing his forces against the enemies of the faith, as your holiness also knows, and he persevered continuously in this purpose so much that he begged your holiness so that all those who would withdraw from such a holy purpose, directly or indirectly, publicly or secretly, in word or deed, would be bound by the chain of excommunication.[189]

Philip had taken the cross in 1313 and, by 1326, had expressed his willingness to join the crusade of the Christian kings against the Moors in Iberia:[190]

> If anyone assumes some task where he does [not] make the necessary preparation, this is a sign that he was not firm in this, but when he prepares the necessary means for this, it is a sign that he was firm. Now the lord king is preparing, as much as he can, the appropriate means for that work the dukes, counts and other powerful men, who are not from his kingdom, are about to retain themselves for this holy passage and they will distribute generously their own goods for the sake of this [passage]. Note here regarding the provision he made both in ships and in equipment and in so many more things that it would need a long time to narrate each one separately. Thus this is a sign that he was firm.[191]

Nevertheless, such preparations were impossible without funding. In 1332, money was a pressing need for the royal treasury, and the collection of the tithe did not add sufficient crusade funds to the royal coffers until late 1335.[192] So Pierre Roger's allusions to crusade preparations by the French Crown, especially those pertaining to ships, were a misleading story designed to garner extra papal financial commitment. In app. IV, the Archbishop has to excuse Philip to Pope John XXII, because '*non videmus quod unam galeam fecerit fieri*'.[193]

Pierre Roger's desire to secure papal financial support for his crusade plans is obvious, but mention of the French king's intention to use this money solely for the crusade, rather than for royal purposes, reveals that there were papal doubts about the expenditure of crusade funds by the French royal house, and that Pope John XXII remained hesitant about granting Philip a new crusade tithe; as early as the outset of his reign, Pope John had expressed his disapproval of the financial policies of the French monarchy and had accused it of wasting crusade money.

Pierre Roger argues that since his accession to the throne, Philip VI has demonstrated remarkable leadership and excellent character; this entitled him to paternal support, and thus he had sent a legation to his father, the pope. Philip VI was determined to go *in propria persona* on crusade and, therefore, many *milites Christiani* were ready to follow him to Jerusalem. Hoping to banish any doubt as to Philip's sincere crusade intentions, Roger refers to the crusade vow sworn in public by French royal agents at the papal court in the place of their master:[194] on 16 July 1333, shortly before Roger's preaching of app. IV, French envoys Pierre Roger, Hugh Bandeti – Bishop of Thérouanne and also Dean of Paris – and the noblemen Henry Avaugour and Peter Trousseau, in the presence of Pope John XXII and on behalf of their king, renewed Philip's promise to go on crusade.[195] With the rhetorical question 'who can think that a king so devoted, so Catholic, created by so holy ancestors shall come against things promised in this way, indeed thus strenghtened by an oath [sworn] solemnly and publicly before the eyes of so many people? Certainly nobody', Roger again affirms the earnestness of the king's crusading aims, to assuage any doubts the pope might have.[196] Roger informs the pope that Philip needs three years for his preparations, designating 28 July 1336 as the date of Philip's departure, and he asks the pope to advise the other Christian kings who were to accompany Philip that they must be ready by July of 1336. The Archbishop also informs the pope that Philip has pledged to restore, without further delay, the crusade funds he had used for other purposes, and that Philip's eldest son and successor, John, Duke of Normandy, has consented to the expenditure of these funds only '*in usum passagii vel negotii Terre Sancte*'.[197] Philip VI has also agreed to the appointment of four prelates from the Kingdom of France, two selected by the pope and two selected by the king himself, who would be charged with safeguarding the funds conceded for the crusade.[198]

Pierre Roger reminds the pope and the Cardinals of Philip's crusading zeal, of his wish to lead his men against the Saracens and other enemies of the faith, and of his intention to go *personaliter* in Jerusalem; it was this pronounced, continuous crusade enthusiasm that had inspired Philip to send prelates to the pope to request papal assistance and to summon the nobles in his kingdom and elsewhere to follow him, and he had already begun spending money for the preparations necessary for the *passagium*.

Beyond the diplomatic aspect of Pierre Roger's preaching, in its greatest part the 'real voice' in the sermon texts, the Archbishop also introduces a cluster of crusade-friendly themes typically exploited by the crusade preachers. The passionate and effusive expression of grief over the pollution of the Holy Sepulchre and other Holy Places was a core component of crusade discourse, and Pierre Roger proclaims the magnificence and importance of the Holy Sepulchre, 'of which the glory was greater than the Temple of Solomon, where the desire of all nations existed'.[199] In a great dramatic tone, he describes the untenable possession of the Lord's Sepulchre by the vicious Saracens to evoke an emotional response from his audience. He laments the current miserable situation in the Holy Land and expresses his grief over the pollution and the destruction of the places where Jesus passed his life on earth for the salvation of humanity, and he reminds his audience that Jerusalem is still in Muslim hands. Pierre Roger draws on the Maccabean passage (I Machabeorum 2.7–13) in which the priest Mattathias laments the destruction of Israel by the gentiles.[200] Crusade propagandists between the twelfth and early fourteenth centuries considered the Maccabean Wars parallel to the crusades and an excellent means of conveying, alongside Deuteronomy, the magnitude of the Christian victories in the East; references to these wars evoked a positive response to crusade appeals, with Mattathias and mainly Judas Maccabeus representing ideal crusade leaders.[201] The image of a mourning Mattathias as an emblem of Christian anguish over an aversion to the Muslim pollution and destruction of the Holy Places is noteworthy. The common use of this episode from the Book of Maccabees (I Machabeorum 2.7–13) by Pierre de la Palud in 1331 and by Pierre Roger/Clement VI in 1332–1333 and 1345 (see Appendices III, IV, V) in this context suggests another remarkable development in the use of Maccabean allusions from the fourth decade of the fourteenth century. This episode served the need of crusade propagandists to warn Western Europe of the critical situation facing their fellow Christians in the East and to motivate French royal interest in crusading to the Mediterranean. In app. IV, in a critical tone, Pierre Roger expresses the need for immediate action by Western Christians to relieve their brothers in the kingdoms of Armenia and Cyprus, and in Rhodes, from Turkish attacks; Roger stresses the urgency of repelling these attacks and of halting further Turkish advances in Greece.[202]

In fact, in the early 1330s, the fear of Ottoman expansion made Westerners anxious about the fate of the Latin presence in the East: in addition to the rapacious activity of the Turkish emirs of Mentesche and Aydin, the Christians in the East had to face the appearance of a new and even more serious danger in north-western Anatolia. Soon after his first important victory over the Byzantines, at Nicaea in 1302, Osman I, the founder of the Ottoman state, and his successor, Orhan, pushed the frontiers of Ottoman settlement to the edge of the Byzantine Empire, and, by 1331, the nascent Ottoman Empire had conquered a number of important Byzantine cities, including Ephesos, Bursa and Nicaea. The Western fear of further Ottoman expansion would be realized in 1354, when the Ottomans travelled by sea to seize the city of Gallipoli on the European mainland.[203]

Another theme particularly common in crusade sermons is crusading to Jerusalem as a redemptive act for salvation of humans from corruption. In both sermons (app. III and app. IV), Pierre Roger develops the reasons why Christians must take up arms against the enemies of the faith, and he summons all Christianity to fight the infidels. [204] Pierre Roger explains in both sermons why everyone should set out for Jerusalem and why this *passagium* to the Holy Land must be undertaken:

> What is more holy than this task [the crusade], what more glorious, what more honorable, what more splendid for any Christian than to go to Jerusalem? This task is purgative of our corruption, it removes our disorder, it ignites our holy emotions, it incites our devotion, it is imitative of the paternal tradition, it completes our perfection, it is conductive and promotes our salvation.[205]

As Judas Maccabeus summons his men to take up arms against the gentiles coming to conquer Jerusalem, so Pierre Roger urges his fellow Christians to hasten to support their brothers in the East. The invocation of Judas Maccabeus, along with the use of passages from St Bernard's *De laude nove Militie Templi*, indicates that Maccabean imagery continued to serve themes in crusade preaching, particularly the association of crusaders with the Maccabees. Pierre Roger cites a biblical *exemplum* from the second book of Maccabees: at the front of the column of those willingly proceeding toward Jerusalem with Judas there appears a knight dressed in white on horseback, shaking a spear, and Judas's men praised merciful God and courageously rushed forward and fell upon the enemy like lions, killing thousands as many others fled.[206] Similarly, in addressing the moral value of Philip VI's army, Pierre Roger assures the pope and the Cardinals that his soldiers behave with the sweetness of lambs in the company of friends, but against their enemies they fight like lions. Pierre cites an extract from Pope John XXII's letter to Philip VI in which John advises the King 'to get in action the warriors of the kingdom of France, vigorous men and very skilled in warfare'.[207]

The message of this anecdote is that God would be the patron of all crusaders who in *prompto animo* sail to Jerusalem, and divine providence would miraculously come to the crusader army. The crusade, as service, would lead to and promote the crusaders' salvation, the remission of sins and open access to Heaven: should the crusade be victorious, each crusader will enjoy *peccatorum indulgentiam* and the glory of his victory; if the crusade fails, each crusader will fly directly to the kingdom of Heaven.[208]

At this point, Pierre Roger combines two themes, crusading as an act of penitence, one that offers its participants spiritual rewards, and crusade as a form of salvation and martyrdom.[209] The Church, Christ and the Holy Places all summoned the Christians to pass over the sea, and the spiritual and temporal rewards granted by the Church to crusaders appealed to the faithful. At this point, Pierre Roger emphasizes the rewards crusaders would receive should they die in battle: those who died in the war for Christ would be recompensed with heavenly rewards and eternal beatitude. For all those who would assume the cross for the same *negotio* 'the treasures of the Church will be rendered accessible':

> With all fear and terror [put aside], strive to act faithfully against the enemies of the holy faith. If any of your men should die, the Almighty knows that, he has died for the truth of the faith and the salvation of the fatherland, and for the defense of the Christians; for that reason he will obtain a heavenly reward from God. It is not only general recompense for the future, on the contrary for the present too, [since] for this business the treasures of the Church are opened: generally plenary remission of sins, relaxation of penalties and effusion of many other rewards shall be granted to all. Therefore come all thirsty to the waters and be in haste you who do not have money.[210]

To strengthen his argument, Roger quotes a passage from Pope Leo IV's 853 appeal to the Frankish army to attack the Saracens who had pillaged Rome in 846.[211] Pope Leo called on the Franks to fight the enemies of the faith: he promised that those who died for the truth of the faith, for the salvation of the homeland and for the defence of Christians would be recompensed by God in Heaven. As Brundage observes, although Leo's letter was not a proclamation of doctrine, the pope made a 'fundamental link between the act of fighting against the infidel in defense of the faith and the prospect of salvation'.[212] Obviously death in battle for the defence of the Holy Land, the fatherland of all Christians, was considered martyrdom and, as a meritorious act, a means for the personal salvation of each fallen crusader.

Pierre Roger saw the crusade as a catharsis, a release from the corruption of sins into which Christians had fallen, a way for them to realise how the enemies of their faith had usurped their inheritance, how the '*impious Hagarenes*' had profaned the Holy Places. At this point the audience was further excited to hear a personal testimony to the Muslim attitude toward the occupation of the Holy Sepulchre: 'I heard the sultan to have declared that if the sepulchre of the perfidious Mohammed was in our possession in the way that the Sepulchre of Christ is in their possession, they would never rest until they had recovered it'.[213] It is unknown if Roger ever visited the Mamluk court at Cairo or heard the Sultan speaking anywhere else, so it may be supposed this testimony was not a personal anecdote of Roger's but a quote from someone else.

The crusaders, by fighting so strenuously against the infidels, honoured paternal tradition, following not only the examples of the Fathers in the Old Testament but also of previous (*exempla precedentium*) illustrious men who fought valorously for the recuperation of the Holy Land, great men who remain in memory, who are praised, whose history serves as a lesson to all who would give it their attention.[214] Once again, the Maccabean exemplar served as a beacon for crusading to the Holy Land. Along with allusions to Zachariah and *De laude nove Militie Templi*, Pierre Roger constructs his most powerful exemplar.

In app. IV, Pierre Roger discusses the different forms of contribution to the crusade and how each offers an opportunity to the whole of Christendom to participate, a theme present in many earlier crusade sermons and in papal letters. Pierre Roger asserts that anyone can contribute to the crusade: some could give corporeal support to the crusade by choosing to go, while others could contribute spiritually by praying and offering advice[215] – no Christian was excluded from going on crusade or from contributing financially. The redemptive character of the crusade offered Christians a prospect for salvation, so the Church, the only path for the rescue of souls, had no right to prevent any Christian from such expectation. Therefore, when new weapons and military practices meant crusading required fewer participants, most with experience in arms, the Church devised other ways for those who could not go to contribute. The offering of alms for the crusade secured the general contribution of money for the crusade and, when financing a crusade became a prerequisite, the Avignon papacy added special daily prayers and psalms for the Holy Land to its liturgical calendar. The liturgical apparatus, in tandem with the general preaching campaigns, guaranteed universal participation in the crusade.

Taking as his starting point the *thema* in app. IV, Pierre Roger develops a syllogism to prove that all Christians must crusade against the infidels. As Artaxerxes decreed in his letter to Esdras, 'any of the Israelites in my kingdom, including the priests and Levites, who desire to go to Jerusalem, may follow you', there is also a particularity, as Artaxerxes summoned only those people 'in his kingdom', the Kingdom of Israel.[216] Roger continues: 'For the entire Christianity must pursue this affair and be invoked in support of the Holy Land in such a way that all Jewish treachery, all general idolatry, and all other infidelity are excluded'.[217] It is noteworthy that among the perfidious Jews, the pagans, the idolaters, the infidel Saracens and all other enemies of the faith, Pierre Roger does not include the schismatic Greeks. The omission might have been intentional, reflecting ongoing negotiations for the realization, with the participation of the Byzantine emperor, of a Christian, anti-Turkish naval league. In fact, in response to Byzantine appeals, in July 1332, the Baillie of Negroponte had been sent to Constantinople to secure the cooperation of Emperor Andronicus III in a Christian alliance against the Turks.[218] The discussions resulted in a Christian naval union of forty galleys that was victorious against the Turks at Adramyttion in September 1334. Thus, we might assume that the formerly schismatic Greeks, at the time of Pierre Roger's sermon, on 16 July 1333, had become potential allies in the papacy's effort to defeat the Turks in the Aegean.

In both sermons, Pierre Roger highly commends Jerusalem, the city of God and the glory of the Christian people. According to the approach to Jerusalem as 'the mother-city', the image of the Holy City and the Lord's Sepulchre had become dominant themes in the preaching of the crusades during the two preceding centuries. The pilgrimage to and the defence of Jerusalem, 'because of its place in the life of Christ and its subsequent sanctity', was the ultimate goal of every crusader.[219] The centrality of Jerusalem in crusade phraseology obviously continued in the fourteenth century. Pierre Roger went a step further, though, emphasising the significance not only of Jerusalem but also of the entirety of the Holy Places where Jesus lived on earth,[220] and his sermon travels from Jesus' birthplace to the homes in which he resided as a child to the locales where he lived and taught, finally arriving at his crucifixion and burial:

> And the glorious Sepulchre of the Lord and the Holy City of Bethlehem where Christ was born, Nazareth where He was nourished, the Valley of Josaphat where Saint Mary was buried and where Jesus will judge us all, in fact all that land where He lived so agreeably with humans, where He suffered harsh words, harder whippings, the hardest torments of the cross for our sake, and the name of the Christian religion has been brought under the servitude of blasphemers.[221]

Pierre Roger declared, 'they have to decide to fight bravely and to prefer to die rather than see so great evils', underlining the importance of the Holy Land and the need to fight for its liberation as the best way to protect and preserve Christianity.[222] Crusade in the Holy Land, as a form of pilgrimage, enabled Christians to share the Passion of Christ and to fight to defend their faith.[223]

Pierre Roger explains in his discourse why Christians had failed to retain possession of the Holy Places. He refers to Pope Urban II's words about *peccatis nostris exigentibus* at the Council of Clermont, when he declared that the sins of Christians were the primary reason for the loss of the Holy Land and for Muslim dominion over its Holy Places.[224] Urban II stated that *peccatis nostris exigentibus* was the main reason Christianity had lost the Holy Land to the Muslims, while St Bernard, some fifty years later, reiterates Urban's assertion as '*Dominus provocatus peccatis nostris*' in a letter to Pope Eugene III about the failure of the Second Crusade.[225] Similarly, John of Abbeville, in the early thirteenth century, draws on St Bernard and Lamentations 5 to portray the loss of Jerusalem and part of the Holy Land as God's punishment for the sins of all Christians.[226] Throughout the thirteenth century, crusade apologists repeat the *peccatis nostris exigentibus* in their explanations of the recurrent disasters of crusading in the Holy Land.[227] Pierre Roger does the same in the fourteenth century by describing the regrettable state of the Holy Land in the Bernadine spirit of the *De laude*.

Further in app. III, in an effort to evoke guilt and regret in his audience, Pierre Roger inveighs the miserable state of the Muslim-occupied Holy Land and calls upon the prelates of the Church to make a contribution for the realization of the crusade. For this particular call to action, Pierre uses a *simile* from the biblical verse, 'Behold the envoys of peace cry and weep bitterly', from the book of Isaiah (33.7), in which the prophet recounts the treachery of the Assyrians, who broke their treaty of peace with Judah's messengers by attacking his cities.[228] The messengers who concluded the treaty, valiant men, lament the destruction and the despoliation of their lands. Here, Pierre Roger likened the pope, the Cardinals and the other prelates to these lamenting angels of peace, so as to clarify their responsibility to the crusade:

> The angels of peace are our lord the supreme angel in the ecclesiastical hierarchy, and you my lord cardinals and other prelates of the churches, who indeed ought to be like angels because of purity in life, because of clarity in understanding, because of fertility and utility in teaching, because of felicity in the protection of flock of the Lord, because of constancy in divine praise and contemplation, because of firmness in moral perseverance. Hence these angels *seeing [the Holy City] will cry out in the markets and they will weep bitterly*, rather, most bitterly. For they will weep by reason of love, they will weep by reason of grief, they will weep by reason of suffering, they will weep by reason of fear, which are the four reasons for weeping.[229]

Much like Judah's angels of peace, Pierre's audience had to lament the devastation of the Holy Places in the Levant and the City of Jerusalem, which lay abandoned, desolated and humiliated. Drawing on Wisdom 5.18, Pierre argues that Philip VI has heeded the summons from the East: 'his zeal will take armour, and he will arm the creature for the revenge of the enemies, and various reasons confirmed his determination in accomplishing such a task'.[230] The Holy Spirit had compelled the French king to take up the *negotium Terre Sancte*. The 14 September 1331 preaching of the Latin Patriarch of Jerusalem, Pierre de la Palud, incited all prelates of the Kingdom of France and inspired the king's barons to declare they would follow their king to Jerusalem, and all of them demanded, vehemently, that the king not delay his departure. So, the king offered himself to the crusade with great passion and love, meriting more than those who only assumed the cross after much inducement to do so.

According to Pierre Roger, it was the right time for direct military action against the infidels: first, everyone had the fervent desire for the *negotium*; second, there was scriptural testimony supporting such an operation; third, there was a prophecy that conveyed the truth about the treacherous Hagarenes.[231] As Bernard of Clairvaux did during his preaching tour in 1146 on behalf of the Second Crusade, Roger based his promotion of the French crusade on eschatological themes inspired by the so-called 'Sibylline Oracles', collections of oracular prophecies emanating from Sibyl or the sibyls (divinely inspired seeresses), which were widely circulated in antiquity, and the *tempus acceptabile*.[232] In reality, Roger argues, people of every age, social status and gender were convinced that God had ordained the present time as the appropriate moment. Roger then presents evidence from the prophets, Daniel and Ezekiel, that the present day was the *tempus acceptabile*: the verse, 'blessed is he who waits, and comes to the one thousand three hundred and thirty-five days', is taken from Daniel's visions of the coming of the Christ and the destruction of the Antichrist.[233] Roger continues with the words of Ezekiel: 'I have assigned to you a day corresponding to a year', claiming that the year 1335 was within the time, according to the Scriptures, when the Christians would defeat the Muslims with God's mercy and aid.[234] Roger concludes his presentation of biblical evidence with a verse from Paul: 'behold, now is the acceptable time; behold, now is the day of salvation', reminding his audience, 'the Lord in this time would restore the Kingdom of Israel'.[235] He then tells of a prophecy that predicted that the diabolic law of Muhammed, which contravened the true law, was due to perish in the year 1335, and this was why Philip VI had selected this particular year for his departure.[236]

So, drawing on Luke 9.23 and on John Chrisostomos's sermon *De Santa Cruce*, Pierre Roger summons the Christians to bear the cross and follow the footsteps of Christ on earth.[237] The bearing of Christ's Cross by the crusader and his journey to the Holy Places to liberate his fellow Christians was actually considered a direct *imitatio* of Christ's last journey on the cross for the salvation of mankind.[238]

Pierre Roger's preaching was completely successful: he succeeded in expunging any papal doubts about the sincerity of Philip's crusading aims. The pope had good reason to be cautious about Philip, since the French king had not always used crusading money honestly and efficiently. Pope John XXII designated Philip VI rector and captain general of the Christian army and granted him a sexennial crusade tithe. On 26 July 1333, ten days after the archbishop's sermon, Pope John XXII issued a series of bulls announcing Philip's appointment, addressing other issues pertaining to the planned *passagium generale* and commanding the conduct of general preaching.[239]

The crusade sermons in the first half of the fourteenth century: An overview

The study of identified crusade sermons during the reign of Pope John XXII (1316–1334) raises a number of questions. How do the fourteenth-century crusade sermons compare to the model crusade sermons of the thirteenth? Or, to what extent were fourteenth-century crusade propagandists affected by the Humbert of Romans' treatise on the preaching of the Holy Cross, a handbook that provides specific instructions to crusade preachers? Furthermore, is the study of fourteenth-century crusade sermons so important?

Close comparison of thirteenth- and fourteenth-century crusade sermons reveals that earlier sermon texts were used as models for the compilation of fourteenth-century crusade sermons. The fourteenth-century crusade preachers took advantage of the wealth of preaching aids from the thirteenth century – including treatises on preaching, *summae*, collections of model sermons and *exempla* – for their crusade sermons.[240] The fourteenth-century crusade sermonists often borrowed themes from earlier models to develop their own work, adopting certain elements to scheme the argumentative structure of their sermons. The sharing of ideas and techniques among preachers is observed in preserved crusade model sermons as early as the thirteenth century. Such developments appear to have happened because the majority of the mendicant friar-preachers shared common experiences during their university training, especially those at Paris, and they drew upon the same resources, biblical commentaries and preaching aids. The uniformity of the crusading message also meant that fourteenth-century crusade preachers could use earlier models for inspiration.

But what, specifically, are the similarities between thirteenth- and fourteenth-century sermons, and to what extent did the earlier models affect the latter? I have compared twenty-seven edited crusade recruitment sermons, *ad status* and other sermons, all preached in different occasions throughout the thirteenth century, to the eleven crusade sermons from the fourteenth century, which are presented in Chapters 3 and 4 of this book. Excluding James of Lausanne's Lenten sermon, in no other case did an identified fourteenth-century crusade sermon have the same *thema* as a thirteenth-century sermon. James seems to have been inspired by earlier versions of sermons for the Fourth Sunday in Lent with crusade appeals: he used the cross of penance as a theme, alongside the spiritual elevation of Christians to the heavenly Jerusalem, as the core of his sermon.[241] The salvatory nature of the cross, the crusaders' redemption from sin through their *crucesignatio* and the penitential character of crusading were a common place for all crusade sermons in the thirteenth and fourteenth centuries. The significance of the cross for the crusader on the battlefield was explained in the early thirteenth century in two crusading appeals from St Victor at Paris and in the fourteenth century by Pierre de la Palud:[242] the Victorines and Palud assured their audiences that the sign of the cross protected the soldiers of Christ from harm during battle. In a sermon to those already bearing the sign of the cross (*ad crucesignatos*), James of Vitry provides them with moral instruction with regard to the significance of their undertaking, emphasising that 'the cross arms them so they may not be hurt by enemies'.[243]

All preserved sermons for the recruitment of the Fifth Crusade, except that of John of Abbeville, Cardinal-bishop of Sabina, list the reasons some gave for refusing to take the cross; these sermons seem to have influenced both James of Lausanne and Pierre de la Palud.[244] The same theme was also considered by Roger of Salisbury, Bishop of Bath and Wells, in his mid-thirteenth-century (1244–1247) crusade sermon, which was meant to be preached on either Good Friday or on the fourth Sunday after the octave of Epiphany.[245] In his *Laetare* sermon, James refers to three reasons given by people who refused to set sail for the Holy Land, while Palud decries the negligence of the French with regard to the business of the cross.[246] James of Lausanne, however, differs from earlier propagandists in his contention with these issues: he hurls epithets at the unwilling so as to injure their reputations. James presumably found material in Humbert of Romans's treatise on the preaching of the cross. Humbert had been master general of the Dominican Order between 1254 and 1263; after he resigned he devoted the rest of his life to writing, specifically to compiling preaching guides. Sometime between 1265 and 1266, or perhaps between 1266 and 1268, according to a recent study, Humbert compiled the *Liber sive tractatus de predicatione crucis contra Sarracenos infideles et paganos*, a manual for preaching the crusade.[247] Humbert's oeuvre provided future crusade preachers with a wide range of preaching material, including *exempla*, biblical passages upon which a crusade sermon might be preached, a variety of themes suitable for crusade sermons, advice for the compilation of new crusade sermons and recommendations as to how preachers could accomplish their task more effectively.[248] For example, for those who chose not to take the cross, Humbert suggested a number of comparisons intended to shame them publicly. James most probably profited from Humbert's proposal.

An examination of Eudes of Châteauroux's crusade sermons confirms that some fourteenth-century preachers exploited his preaching material for the compilation of their sermons. A comparison of his crusade sermons and those compiled by fourteenth-century authors reveals certain similarities in content; it seems that Pierre de la Palud and Pierre Roger were both aware of Eudes's model crusade sermons, as both made use of themes raised extensively therein. Pierre de la Palud, as we have seen, in his sermon on the Exaltation of the Holy Cross, refers to the legend of the basilisk, a moral story found nowhere else, in this context, except in the sermons of Eudes of Châteauroux.

Eudes larded his crusade sermons with biblical prophecies, especially those from the book of Revelation, as did Oliver of Paderborn before him; in a similar manner, Pierre Roger made extensive use of biblical prophecies regarding the final prevalence of Christians in the Holy Land and, while writing about Philip VI's army, he employed a similar *simile* found in Eudes of Châteauroux's sermon for the deceased French nobles at Massura in Egypt: Eudes likens the French nobles, who fought with strength and courage against the Saracens at Massoura, to lions.[249] In a clear reference to Eudes, Pierre Roger compares Philip VI's soldiers to lions, inspiring terror in their enemies and declaring them stronger than lions in conflict.[250]

Other themes suitable for the preaching of the crusade found in the sermons of Eudes of Châteauroux and in those written during the fourteenth century are also found in Humbert of Romans's handbook for the preaching of the cross, and the extant form of Eudes's sermons is contemporaneous with Humbert's manual for crusade preachers: Eudes of Châteauroux revised all of his sermon collections, changing the text and adding new material during the late 1260s.

With these facts in mind, it becomes difficult to say with certainty which of their predecessors had the greatest influence on the fourteenth-century crusade propagandists. An inscription in a manuscript from the Vatican Library that includes the works *Vita Sancti Thomae* by Bernard Gui and *De predicatione sancte crucis* by Humbert of Romans indicates that the codex was presented to Pierre Roger in 1324 when he was master of theology at Paris.[251] If the Vatican codex (Vat lat. 3847) remained in Roger's possession, perhaps he used *De predicatione sancte crucis* as a source to compile his own crusade sermons.

Throughout their discourses, James of Lausanne, Pierre de la Palud and Pierre Roger all repeat subjects suggested by Humbert of Romans – Roger to a greater extent than James and Palud. In addition to the use of shameful comparisons to change the minds of those determined not to crusade, James of Lausanne refers to four of the seven graces that would be offered as rewards to the crusaders, according to Humbert. James writes about the absolution of the *crucesignatus* from excommunication, the relaxation of penalties for sin, the granting of a plenary indulgence and the ecclesiastical protection enjoyed by those who set sail for Jerusalem;[252] Pierre Roger and Palud also make reference to the plenary indulgence not granted by the Church for any pilgrimage other than the crusade. In his sermon on the Exaltation of the Cross, Palud aspired to write a memorial sermon suitable for preaching the crusade during the feast days for the cross, and in his sermon he cites a series of episodes closely associated with the cycle of the True Cross. Following the advice of Humbert of Romans, Palud used the *Historia Tripartita* as his authority, and he includes in his sermon the illustrative stories of the discovery of the True Cross by Helena, of the vision of Constantine the night before his battle against Maxentius, and of the efforts of emperors, Julianus and Theodosius, to restore the True Cross.[253] The source of these illustrative stories and legends connected with the cross that Palud compiled in his sermon, was James of Voragine's *Legenda Aurea*; indeed, Palud inserted large verbatim passages from these stories, all of them derived from Voragine's work. As Humbert of Romans urged crusade preachers to call on their listeners to imitate the *exempla* of eminent figures form the history of the fight against the infidels,[254] so Palud refers to the *exempla* of prominent ancestors such as Charlemagne and Godfrey of Bouillon who, motivated by their zeal for God, displayed unparalleled courage in the struggle against the enemies of the faith.

Pierre Roger, however, borrows extensively from Humbert of Romans's tract for his sermons, more than any other fourteenth-century crusade propagandist. He integrates a multitude of themes from *De predicatione crucis* – almost impossible to use for an individual preaching event – into each of his crusade sermons. Roger intended to bequeath comprehensive models for preaching the cross to future preachers, and this was more important to him than impressing his spiritual descendants with his vast knowledge, though it made his crusade sermons rather lengthy. Pierre Roger, one of the most charismatic preachers of his age, masterfully incorporated all of the citations from Humbert of Romans into his crusade sermons. Thus, when Roger attempted to convince Pope John XXII of Philip VI's ardour for the recovery the Holy Land, he followed Humbert's advice and referred to the *exempla* of the priests, Mattathias Maccabeus, Eli and Phineas, three biblical personages known for their morality and zealous service to the Lord's law.[255] In late May 1345, after he had become Pope Clement VI, Roger delivered a sermon to convince the College of Cardinals of the suitability of Humbert II, dauphin of Viennois, to lead the Christian fleet to Smyrna; describing Humbert II's military valour, he compares the Dauphin with Judas Maccabeus and Joshua, the greatest warriors in Jewish history.[256]

Pierre Roger quotes extensively from biblical episodes that mention or pertain to the 'Promised Land' in his crusade sermons, something Humbert of Romans had suggested preachers do. When Humbert classified the six kinds of expertise necessary for preachers of the cross, he assigned first place to knowledge of biblical events associated with the 'Promised Land, which is known as the Holy Land now'.[257] Pierre Roger also emphasized the voluntary nature of the crusade by citing different biblical *themata* recommended by Humbert of Romans, such as devotion to the Holy Land, zeal for the law of Christ and fraternal love for the Eastern Christians.[258] Roger urged Westerners to sail for the East in support of their fellow Christians in Armenia, Cyprus, Rhodes and Romania, all of whom were in great danger.[259]

Roger's description of the crusade as a pious enterprise because of the sanctity of the Holy Land, likewise seems derived from Humbert of Romans.[260] As Humbert suggested, Roger refers in his sermons to Bethlehem, Nazareth, the Valley of Joshaphat, the Holy Sepulchre and Jerusalem,[261] though he also includes in his discourse a number of issues pertaining to the crusade originally found in Pope Urban II's sermon at Clermont and in the writings of St Bernard.[262]

All of this clearly demonstrates to what extent thirteenth-century crusade sermonists influenced the compilation of crusade sermons during the first five decades of the Avignon papacy, but it is obvious that the *De predicatione sancte crucis* of the Dominican, Humbert of Romans, exerted the greatest influence on later preachers, providing more preaching material and guidance than any other source. There is much evidence especially in the crusade sermons of Pierre Roger that testifies to his familiarity with the material provided by Humbert of Romans in the *De predicatione crucis*. This confirms the assumption that Pierre Roger owned the Vatican text of Humbert's manual, which presumably found a home in the papal library following his death.[263] Roger did not base his sermons solely on Humbert, however, as there is material from the papal written legacy concerning the crusades in his sermons: not only did Roger use text from Pope Urban II's sermon at Clermont to describe the desolate and damaged state of the Holy Land following its Muslim conquest, but he also employed the *exemplum* of Clement V at the Council of Vienne in 1311–1312.[264]

Despite these loans from earlier models, the 'original voice' in fourteenth-century crusade sermons proclaims their authors' preoccupations with the fate of the crusade, reflects contemporary social and moral ills and mirrors the emergence of new political and economic priorities that were deleterious to the cause of crusade. Similar to previous models, in their entirety, the Avignon crusade sermons comprise carefully arranged scholastic texts; the authorities upon which they were constructed, though different audiences, different aims and different authors, make each crusade sermon unique. Despite their dependence on earlier sermonists, the Avignon crusade preachers tried to enrich their texts with new *exempla* (the Templar and the Hospitaller in Palud's sermon) and new *auctoritates* (passages from Clement V's sermon at the Council of Vienne). In fact, the abundance of crusade preaching aids accessible to fourteenth-century crusade preachers did not derail the development of preaching in the fourteenth century, nor did it impede the production of new material.[265]

Notes

1 For the full text of James of Lausanne's *Laetare Jerusalem* sermon, see Appendix II; *Repertorium der Lateinischen Sermones des Mittelalters fur Die Zeit von 1150–1350*, ed. J. B. Schneyer, 11 vols. (Munster-Westfalen: Aschendorffsche Verlagsbuchhandlung, 1973–1995), iii, 66 [hereafter *Repertorium 1150–1350*].

2 For the manuscripts with Pierre de la Palud's and Pierre Roger's collections of sermons, see Schneyer, *Repertorium 1150–1350*, iv, 718, 757–769; for the works of Pierre de la Palud, see Thomas Kaeppeli, *Scriptores Ordinis Praedicatorum*, 4 vols. (Rome: Ad S. Sabinae, 1970–1993), iii, 243–249.

3 Jessalynn Bird, 'Preaching the Crusades and the Liturgical Year: The Palm Sunday Sermons', *Essays in Medieval Studies*, 30 (2015), 11–36.

4 Schneyer, *Repertorium 1150–1350*, i, 255, 310; ii, 546, 643; iii, 66; iv, 129; v, 552, vi, 617; vii, 127; viii, 59, ix, 62; Christoph T. Maier, *Preaching the Crusades: Mendicant Friars and the Cross in the Thirteenth Century* (Cambridge: Cambridge University Press, 1994), 113; Penny J. Cole, *The Preaching of the Crusades to the Holy Land, 1095–1270* (Cambridge, Massachusetts: The Medieval Academy of America, 1991), appendix C, 232–234.

5 *Chartularium Universitatis Parisiensis sub auspiciis consilii generalis facultatum Parisiensium*, eds. H. Denifle and A. Chatelain, 4 vols. (Paris: Ex Typis Fratrum Delalain, 1889–1897), ii, 102: 'inter fratres conventus hi sunt celebriores'; *Histoire littéraire de la France*, eds. Religieux Bénédictins de la Congrégation de Saint-Maur, *et al.*, 43 vols. (Paris: Imprimerie Nationale, 1733–), xxxiii, 459–460.

6 *Chartularium Universitatis Parisiensis*, ii, 148: 'Assignamus ad legendum Sententias Parisius fratrem Thedericum de Provincia Saxonie. Item, providemus eidem studio pro Biblia legenda de fratre Jacobo de Lausania'.

7 *Chartularium Universitatis Parisiensis*, ii, 167: 'providemus quantum nostra interest de fratre Jacobo de Lausana quod legat Sententias Parisius anno sequenti'; 172: 'assignamus ad legendum Sententias Parisius isto anno fratrem Jacobum de Lausana'; *Histoire littéraire de la France*, xxxiii, 460; For details on the academic career of theology students in the fourteenth century, see William J. Courtenay, 'The Bible in the Fourteenth Century: Some Observations', *Church History*, 54.2 (1985), 178–181.

8 *Histoire littéraire de la France*, 460; Beryl Smalley, *English Friars and Antiquity in the Early Fourteenth Century* (Oxford: Basil Blackwell, 1960), 248–249; Chris Schabel, Russell L. Friedman, Irene Balcoyiannopoulou, 'Peter of Palude and the Parisian Reaction to Durand of St. Pourçain's on Foreknowledge and Future Contingents', *Archivum Fratrum Praedicatorum*, 71 (2001), 183–300; Jean Céleyrette and Jean-Luc Solère, 'Jacques de Lausanne, censeur et plagiaire de Durand de Saint-Pourçain: Édition de la Q. 2, Dist. 17 du L. I de son Commentaire des Sentences', in *Philosophy and Theology in the Long Middle Ages: A Tribute to Stephen F. Brown*, eds. K. Emery, R. Friedman and A. Speer (Leiden: Brill, 2011), 855–891.

9 *Histoire littéraire de la France*, 461; *Chartularium Universitatis Parisiensis*, ii, 206; *Scriptores Ordinis Praedicatorum*, ii, 323–324.

10 *Histoire littéraire de la France*, 461; Rosalie Galbraith, *The Constitution of the Dominican Order, 1216–1320* (Manchester: Publications of the University of Manchester, 1925), 260.

11 *Histoire littéraire de la France*, 473; Smalley, *English Friars*, 250.

12 Schneyer, *Repertorium 1150–1350*, iii, 54–157.

13 James of Lausanne also made occasional references to the crusade in a *collatio* after the preaching for the Fourth Sunday in Lent, and in a sermon intended for the preaching on the eighth Sunday after the Epiphany. For the full text, see Jacobus de Laosanna [O.P.], *Sermones Dominicales et Festivales per totum anni circulum per reverendum patrem fratrem Jacobum de Laosana [O.P.], ... Declamati, impressioni*

mandati per quendam patrem professorem Ordinis Minorum regularis observantie (Paris: Ambrosii Girault, 1530), fols. 35ᵛ–37ʳ, 76ᵛ–78ᵛ.
14 See Appendix II for full textual edition.
15 Paris, BnF, MS lat. 17516, fol. 84ʳ: 'Dominica quarta in Quadragessima'.
16 For the French crusade assemblies in 1320, see Chapter 1, note 179.
17 Daniel MacCarthy, *The Epistles and Gospels of the Sundays Throughout the Year: With Notes* (Dublin-London: John Mulleny, 1866), 182–188.
18 Avignon, Bibliothèque Municipale, MS 295, fol. 52ʳᵇ. The manuscript includes two sermons for the Fourth Sunday in Lent with crusade appeals.
19 Avignon, Bibliothèque Municipale, MS 295, fol. 52ᵛᵃ: 'passagium nostrum est ut transeamus mare Galilee'.
20 Avignon, Bibliothèque Municipale, MS 295, fol. 52ʳᵇ: 'quando ille qui est caput passagii est magne potentie, ut rex Francie et cetera, et probus in armis et expertus in negotiis bellicis'.
21 Herbert Thurston, *The Stations of the Cross: An Account of Their History and Devotional Purpose* (London: Burns and Oates, 1914), 2–3.
22 Helen Gittos, *Liturgy, Architecture, and Sacred Places in Anglo-Saxon England* (Oxford: Oxford University Press, 2013), 143–144.
23 Thurston, *The Stations of the Cross*, 21.
24 For the preferred individual feast days for preaching the crusade see Christoph Maier, *Crusade Propaganda and Ideology: Model Sermons for the Preaching of the Cross* (Cambridge: Cambridge University Press, 2000), 4.
25 Appendix II, §1.
26 Appendix II, §1.
27 For a complete account on the ideological aspect and symbolism of the crusaders' cross, see Giles Constable, *Crusaders and Crusading in the Twelfth Century* (Farnham: Ashgate, 2008), especially chapter 2, 45–92.
28 Avignon, Bibliothèque Municipale, MS 295, fols. 50ᵛᵃ–52ʳᵇ.
29 Appendix II, §2; Avignon, Bibliothèque Municipale, MS 295, fol. 51ʳᵃ.
30 Palmer Allan Throop, *Criticism of the Crusade: A Study of Public Opinion and Crusade Propaganda* (Amsterdam: N. V. Swets and Zeitlinger, 1940); Maureen Purcell, *Papal Crusading Policy: The Chief Instruments of Papal Crusading Policy and Crusade to the Holy Land from the Final Loss of Jerusalem to the Fall of Acre, 1244–1291* (Leiden: Brill, 1975); Elizabeth Siberry, *Criticism of Crusading, 1095–1274* (Oxford: Clarendon Press, 1985).
31 Norman Housley, *The Avignon Papacy and the Crusades 1305–1378* (Oxford: Clarendon Press, 1986), 230.
32 Appendix II, §2.
33 Appendix II, §7–10; Avignon, Bibliothèque Municipale, MS 295, fols. 51ᵛᵇ–52ʳᵃ.
34 Christopher Tyerman, *The Crusades: A Very Short Introduction* (Oxford: Oxford University Press, 2004), 14–16; Riley-Smith, *What Were the Crusades?*, 67.
35 Appendix II, § 5–7.
36 Appendix II, § 6. James of Lausanne, like St Bernard, held that Christ did not arrive on earth without anointment, advocating the divine nature of Christ's interference on earth for the salvation of humankind. For the text of Bernard's sermon 'In vigilia nativitatis Domini' see *Sancti Bernardi abbatis primi Claraevallensis opera genuina*, 3 vols. (Paris: The Monks of Saint Bernard, 1833–1835), ii, 142–144.
37 Maier, *Preaching the Crusades*, 113–114; full text of Peyraut's *Laetare* sermon is available in a Tübingen incunabulum, a collection of *de tempore* sermons compiled by William Peyraut: see Guilelmus Peraldus, *Sermones Dominicales ex epistolis et Evangelys atque de sanctis secundum ecclesie ordinem Wilhelmi cancellary Parisiensis* (Tübingen: Friedrich Meynberger, 1499), sermon no. 39.
38 Peyraut's sermons are preserved in more than 100 manuscripts from the fourteenth and fifteenth centuries and in fifteen later editions until the mid-seventeenth century. For more details, see Schneyer, *Repertorium 1150–1350*, ii, 555–556.

39 The Elstow sermon is preserved today in a manuscript in Oxford (Oxford, Bodleian Library, MS Laud. Misc. 511, fol. 93^{r-v}) and was published in Cole, *The Preaching of the Crusades*, 232–234.
40 Cole, *The Preaching of the Crusades*, 174–176.
41 Cole, *The Preaching of the Crusades*: 'Ista cruce signati sunt quotque cum lacrimis, dolore et suspiriis peccata sua precogitarunt postmodum ea integer ... Beati sunt omnes illi qui isto modo crucem penitentie assumpserunt'.
42 Appendix II, §1.
43 Jonathan Riley-Smith, *What Were the Crusades?* (London: Macmillan, 1977), 57–58.
44 München, Bayerische StaatsBibliothek, MS Clm 18732, fols. 71^v–73^r. For details on Henry of Friemar's career as theologian, see: Chris Schabel and William J. Courtenay, 'Augustinian *Quodlibeta* after Giles of Rome', in *Theological Quodlibeta in the Middle Ages: The Fourteenth Century*, ed. C. Schabel, 2 vols. (Leiden: Brill, 2007), i, 545–568, 550–552; Adolar Zumkeller, *Theology and History of the Augustinian School in the Middle Ages*, ed. J. Rotelle (Villanova: Augustinian Press, 1996), 31, 111.
45 The sermon is contained in an early printed corpus of James of Lausanne's sermons for all Sundays and feast days of the ecclesiastical calendar. See Jacobus de Laosanna (O.P.), *Sermones Dominicales et festivales*, fols. 35^v–37^r.
46 Jacobus de Laosanna (O.P.), *Sermones Dominicales et festivales*, fol. 36^r: 'sicut homo volens peregrinari in terram sanctam communiter accipit crucem, sic homo volens ire ad paradisum debet accipere penitentiam'.
47 Jacobus de Laosanna (O.P.), *Sermones Dominicales et festivales*, fol. 36^r: 'exemplum in natura avis qui non potest elevari a terra nisi volando, nec potest volare, nisi ponendo se in modum crucis'.
48 Appendix II, §3.
49 Αριστοτέλης, *Αριστοτέλους Περί Ζώων Μορίων, βιβλ. δ. Περί Ζώων Πορείας: βιβλ. α. Περί Ζώων Κινήσεως, βιβλ. β. Περί Ζώων Γενέσεως, βιβλ. γ. Περί Πνεύματος, βιβλ. δ, Ο Νόθον Είναι Λέγεται. Aristotelis De Animalium Partibus, Lib. IIII., etc.*, ed. F. Sylburgius, 4 vols. (Francofurdi: Apud heredes A. Wecheli, 1585).
50 Aristotle was arguing: 'And all of these can be reduced to thought and desire', see *De Motu Animalium*, ed. and trans., M. C. Nussbaum (Princeton: Princeton University Press, 1978), 38–39, 185–188, 234, 237.
51 *De Motu Animalium*, 185.
52 For the theory of knowledge and the human behaviour according to Aristotle and Thomas Aquinas see Norman Kretzmann and Eleonore Stump, 'Thomas Aquinas', in *Routledge Encyclopedia of Philosophy*, ed. E. Craig, 9 vols. (London-New York: Routledge, 1998), i, 326–350, 336–338.
53 'Thomas Aquinas', in *Routledge Encyclopedia of Philosophy*, i, 338.
54 'Thomas Aquinas', in *Routledge Encyclopedia of Philosophy*, i, 337–338.
55 'Thomas Aquinas', in *Routledge Encyclopedia of Philosophy*, i, 338–339; *Philosophy in the Middle Ages, the Christian, Islamic, and Jewish Traditions*, eds. A. Hyman and J. J. Walsh (Indianapolis-Cambridge: Hackett Publishing Company, 1973), 503–569, 548: James J. Walsh (trans.): 'Question LXXXII: The Will, Second article, *Objection I*: It would seem that the will desires of necessity all that it desires. For Dionysius says that *evil is outside the scope of the will*. Therefore the will tends of necessity to the good which is proposed to it. *Objection II*: Further, the object of the will is compared to the will as the mover to the movable thing. But the movement of the movable necessarily follows the mover. Therefore it seems that the will's object moves it of necessity. *Objection IIII*: Further, just as the thing apprehended by sense is the object of the sensitive appetite, so the thing apprehended by the intellect is the object of the intellectual appetite, which is called the will. But what is apprehended by the sense moves the sensitive appetite of necessity, for Augustine says the *animals are moved by things seen*. Therefore it seems that whatever is apprehended by the intellect moves the will of necessity.'

56 *Philosophy in the Middle Ages*, 548: James J. Walsh (trans): '*Objection III*: There are certain particular goods which have not a necessary connection with happiness, because without them a man can be happy; and to such the will does not adhere of necessity. But there are some things which have a necessary connection with happiness, namely, those by means of which man adheres to God, in Whom alone true happiness consists. Nevertheless, until through the certitude produced by seeing God the necessity of such a connection be shown, the will does not adhere to God of necessity, nor to those things which are of God. But the will of the man who sees God in His essence of necessity adheres to God, just as now we desire of necessity to be happy. It is therefore clear that the will does not desire of necessity whatever it desires.'
57 Appendix II, §3.
58 Appendix II, §3.
59 Colossenses 3.1: 'Que sursum sunt querite ubi Christus est'.
60 Jean Dunbabin, *A Hound of God: Pierre de la Palud and the Fourteenth–Century Church* (Oxford: Clarendon Press, 1991), 1–15.
61 Dunbabin, *A Hound of God*, 31, 52.
62 See Chapter 1, note 223. For John of Naples see Peter Biller, 'John of Naples, Quodlibets and Medieval Theological Concern with the Body', in *Medieval Theology and the Natural Body*, eds. P. Biller and A. J. Minnis (Woodbridge: York Medieval Press, 1997), 3–13; Russell L. Friedman, 'Dominican Quodlibetan Literature, ca. 1260–1330', in *Theological Quolibeta in the Middle Ages: The Fourteenth Century*, ed. C. Schabel, 2 vols. (Leiden: Brill, 2007), ii, 401–492.
63 Dunbabin, *A Hound of God*, 123, 139; Galbraith, *The Constitution of the Dominican Order*, 149–151; *Repertorium Medii Aevi*, ed. F. Stegmüller, 8 vols. (Madrid: Consejo Superior de Investigaciones Cientificas, 1940–), iv, 356–361; Schneyer, *Repertorium 1150–1350*, iv, 718; Kaeppeli, *Scriptores Ordinis Praedicatorum*, iii, 243–249.
64 Dunbabin, *A Hound of God*, 127–132, 164, 174; Joseph Delaville le Roulx, *La France en Orient au XIVe siècle: Expéditions du maréchal Boucicaut* (Paris: Ernest Thorin, 1886), 78; John F. Benton, 'Theocratic in Fourteenth-Century France: The *Liber Bellorum Domini* by Pierre de la Palu', in *The Library Chronicle: Bibliographical Studies in Honor of Rudolf Hirsch*, eds. W. Miller and T. Waldman (Philadelphia: University of Pennsylvania Library, 1975), 38–55.
65 Norman Housley, *The Italian Crusades: The Papal-Angevin Alliance and the Crusades Against Lay Powers, 1254–1343* (Oxford: Oxford Clarendon Press, 1982), 122–123.
66 Thomas Kaeppeli and Benoit Pierre, 'Un Pèlerinage Dominicain inédit du XIVe siècle: Le Liber de locis et conditionibus Terrae Sanctae et Sepulcro d'Humbert de Dijon O.P. (1332)', *Revue Biblique*, 62.1 (1955), 513–540, at 518–519; Dunbabin, *A Hound of God*, 169.
67 Girolamo Golubovich, *Biblioteca Bio-Bibliografica della Terra Santa e dell'Oriente Francescano*, 5 vols. (Florence: Quaracchi, 1906–1927), iii, 362–363; *Chronique latin de Guillaume de Nangis de 1113 a 1300 avec les continuations de cette chronique de 1300 a 1368*, ed. H. Géraud, 2 vols. (Paris: Imprimerie de Crapelet, 1843), ii, 130–131; Dunbabin, *A Hound of God*, 169–171; Housley, *The Avignon Papacy*, 23–24; Norman Housley, *The Later Crusades: From Lyon to Alcazar 1274–1580* (Oxford: Oxford University Press, 1992), 33; Christopher Tyerman, 'Philip VI and the Recovery of the Holy Land', *The English Historical Review*, 100.394 (1985), 25–52, 27.
68 For details over the trial, see Christina Kaoulla and Chris Schabel, 'The Inquisition against Peter de Castro: Vicar of the Dominican Province of the Holy Land', *Archivum Fratrum Praedicatorum*, 77 (2007), 121–198.
69 Clermont-Ferrand, Bibliothèque Municipale, MS 46, fol. 140^v; Dunbabin, *A Hound of God*, 152–153.
70 *Chronique latin de Guillaume de Nangis*, ii, 130–131; *Les Grandes chroniques de France*, ed. J. Viard, 10 vols. (Paris: Société de l'Histoire de France, 1920–1953), ix,

130; Dunbabin, *A Hound of God*, 172; Christopher Tyerman, 'Philip VI and the Holy Land', 27, note.5.
71 John XXII, *Lettres communes du pape Jean XXII analysées d'après les registres dits d'Avignon et du Vatican*, ed. G. Mollat, 16 vols. (Paris: Bibliothèque des Écoles françaises d'Athènes et de Rome, 3ᵉ série, 1904–1947), no. 58207.
72 Schneyer, *Repertorium 1150–1350*, iv, 718; Kaeppeli, *Scriptores Ordinis Praedicatorum*, iii, 243–249; *Histoire littéraire de la France*, xxxvii, 74–80.
73 The three sermons with addresses to the crusade were preached on the feast days of Corpus Christi, St Gregory, and the Exaltation of the Cross. See Clermont-Ferrand, MS 46, fols. 137ᵛ–141ʳ, 71ʳ–77ʳ, 215ʳ–220ᵛ; Dunbabin, *A Hound of God*, 152–153.
74 Clermont-Ferrand, MS 46, fol. 215ʳ: 'In exaltatione sancte crucis, sermo lvii'.
75 Clermont-Ferrand, MS 46, fol. 216ʳ: 'Sed contra inimicos crucis Christi qui sunt super omnes infideles et maxime et specialiter Sarraceni, debent esse thaurus ferox et indomitus ad ventilandum cornibus Syriam et Egyptum, et destruendum perfidum Machometum et eius nephandum populum totaliter extirpandum'.
76 Clermont-Ferrand, MS 46, fol. 218ʳ: 'quod maxime decet regales Francie lyliacas, cum enim flos lylii nobilissimus florum'; Dunbabin, *A Hound of God*, 174.
77 See note 70.
78 The French embassy to Avignon in February 1332 consisted of Pierre Roger, Archbishop of Rouen, the Bishop of Thérouanne, the Lord of Avaugour and Pierre Troussel. On 19 February 1322 Pierre Roger presented the French royal plans for the implementation of the crusade in the East. For further details see John XXII, *Lettres Communes*, no. 61324.
79 Paris, Bibliothèque Sainte Geneviève, MS 240, fols. 290ᵛ–298ᵛ.
80 Appendix III, §13: 'cum enim quadam die Veneris dominus rex prelatos et barones suos Parisius et alibi pro arduis regni sui negotiis convocasset, dominus patriarcha Iherosolimitanus affuit, et regem obnixe rogavit ut coram tot valentibus vellet sibi dare audientiam super negotio Christi. Qui ibidem proposuit multa, propter que rex tenebatur ad passagium assumendum. Consequenter omnes prelati numero xxvi hoc idem multis rationibus ostenderunt baronesque consimiliter, ipsum obsecrantes ut predictum negotium assumeret, in quo parati erant eum sequi et exponere se et sua'; Baluze in *Vitae Paparum Avenionensium*, ii, 288–289, has wrongly indicated 298ᵛ as the folio for this specific sermon. In fact, the folio 298v of the Sainte Genevieve manuscript marks the end of this February 1332 sermon and the beginning of another crusade sermon delivered by Pierre Roger presumably in July 1333.
81 *Chronique Latin de Guillaume de Nangis*, ii, 130–131; *Les Grandes Chroniques de France*, ix, 130.
82 Paris, Bibliothèque nationale de France, Nouvelles Acquisitions Françaises, MS 7603, fols. 44ʳ–45ᵛ; Tyerman, 'Philip VI and the Holy Land', 27 (note 5).
83 Jean Dunbabin dates this particular sermon in 1332. Dunbabin, *A Hound of God*, 174.
84 Clermont-Ferrand, MS 46, fol. 217ᵛ: 'In quibus verbis tria tanguntur propter que sancta crux fuit et est merito exaltanda. Primo quia est fundamentum et documentum omnis virtutis, *humile*. Secundo quia sustentamentum et audacie fulcimentum ire in bellis, *lignum*. Tertio quia accelerationem et complementum vere salutis, *exaltavi*. Gallice: Fundament enseignement de tote virtu sonstennement e estu que lau ne puet estre vencu avancement et acomplissement de brave salu'; Dunbabin, *A Hound of God*, 143.
85 d'Avray, *The Preaching of the Friars*, 95 (especially see note 3); Larissa Taylor, *Soldiers of Christ: Preaching in Late Medieval and Reformation France* (Oxford: Oxford University Press, 1992), 55–56. Louis-Jacques Bataillon, 'Approaches to the Study of Medieval Sermons', *Leeds Studies in English*, 11 (1980), 19–35, 22–24.
86 For further details on the Clermont-Ferrand, MS 46 codex see *Histoire littéraire de la France*, xxxvii, 75; Dunbabin, *A Hound of God*, 143.

87 Christopher Tyerman, *England and the Crusades, 1095–1588* (Chicago-London: The University of Chicago Press, 1988), 159, 168, Maier, *Crusade Propaganda and Ideology*, 4.
88 Maier lists several models of *de cruce* sermons from the late twelfth and thirteenth centuries in *Preaching the Crusades*, 112–113.
89 Gilbert Ouy, *Les Manuscrits de l'Abbaye de Saint-Victor: Catalogue établi sur la base du répertoire de Claude de Grandrue (1514)*, 2 vols. (Turnhout: Brepols, 1999), i, 112, 197.
90 For details on Bernardi's ecclesiastical career see William J. Courtenay, *Parisian Scholars in the Early Fourteenth Century: A Social Portrait* (Cambridge: Cambridge University Press, 1999), 4, 16–17, 152–153; For the *de sancta cruce* sermon see Paris, Bibliothèque nationale de France, MS lat. 14965, fols. 331^v–333^r.
91 Paris, BnF, MS lat. 14965, fol. 331^v: 'et generale ideo posuit eam demonstratio in medio ecclesie militantis sicut in loco accessibile, *quia lignum vite in medio*, ut ex omni parte et omnis homo possit ad eam accedere pro fructu gratie colligendo'.
92 Paris, BnF, MS lat. 14965, fols. 331^v–332^r: 'Qui apprehenderint eam, sic crucem Christi, cuius ratio est quando debet fieri passagium generale, illi qui volunt amore Christi pugnare contra hostes fidei accipiunt crucem insignum, quod volunt vitam corporis exponere ut possint vitam eternam habere'.
93 Ezekiel 17.24: 'Exaltavi lignum humile'. Prophet Ezekiel in this chapter tells of God's promise of salvation to his exiled people in Babylon, the punishment of the persecutors of Israel and the planting of a cedar on the high mountains of Israel. This cedar would become a great tree and would bear fruit and under its branches all birds and animals would find protection. Nebuchadnezzar II, the Babylonian king who in 592 B.C. sacked Jerusalem, forced Ezekiel's family, along with 3,000 other Jews, into exile in Babylon. For details on the prophecy of the 'Cedar of Lebanon' see Robert E. Lerner, *The Power of Prophecy: The Cedar of Lebanon Vision from the Mongol Onslaught to the Dawn of the Enlightenment* (Berkeley: University of California Press, 1983).
94 Clermont-Ferrand, MS 46, fol. 215^r: 'Arbor autem crucis fertilissima est inter omnes quia non sit alia una arbor in mundo, nec in paradiso terrestri cuius fructus sufficiat ad refectionem unius gentis per multos annos, fructus qui in arbore crucis semel pependit sufficit ad refectionem omnium Christianorum singulis annis in die Paschatis in sacra communione'.
95 Clermont-Ferrand, MS 46, fol. 215^{r-v}: 'et non solum fructus arboris crucis pascit homines in terra sed etiam angelos in cello cum sit verus Deus et homo, unde in psalmo: *panem angelorum manducavit homo*, <psalmus 77.25>'.
96 Bird, 'Preaching the Crusades and the Liturgical Year', 18, 22.
97 Dunbabin, *A Hound of God*, 175.
98 Clermont-Ferrand, MS 46, fol. 215^v: 'Sunt enim alii milites et pugiles verbi gratia antichristus totam vitam suam consumet in vanitate et iniquitate. Ipse enim <II Thessalonicenses 2.4>: *Vir vanus in superbiam erigitur et extollitur super omne*, quod dicitur, *Aut colitur Deus*. Unde super omnes reges et imperatores et principes preteritos presentes et futuros in pompis et superfluis plura sua et aliena consumet, et ipse ille iniquus iniquitati vacans injusta bella christianis maxima indicet terras eorum vastando, destruendo, predando, corpora occidendo. Unde illi sunt veri milites et pugiles antichristi, qui sua et aliena in pompis et vanitatibus mundi consument torneando, hastiludiando, vestes curiosas, sumptuosas, diversificatas communia pompatica facie se sua et aliena in talibus consumendo, per quod remanent impotentes ad militiam Christi in viagio Sancto pro quo faciendo Godofridus et comes sancti Egidii sua patrimonia vendiderunt, ut in celestibus hereditatem perpetuam possiderint, de vanis militibus antichristi psalmus <78.33>: *Defecerunt in vanitate dies eorum*. Peiores autem milites antichristi sunt illi qui iniquitati vacantes ut antichristiani iniusta bella suscitant christianis vastando, predando et cetera. Christianos Christi sanguine redemptos

crudeliter occidendo quibus Sanctus Paulus consulit ut dimittentes militiam antichristi subeant militiam Ihesu Christi, dicens Romanos 6<.19>: *Sicut exhibuistis membra nostra servire immunditie et iniquitati ad iniquitatem,* quod pertinet ad militiam antichristi, *ita nunc exhibete membra nostra servire iustitie in sanctificationem,* quod pertinet ad militiam Christi. Milites ergo et pugiles Christi implentes istud et illud, Romanos 12<.1>: *Exhibeatis corpora vestra hostiam viventem sanctam Deo placentem,* et illud Ysaie 40<.31>: *Qui sperant in Domino mutabunt fortitudinem,* quia sicut fortiter servierunt antichristo fortius serviant Christo, dicentes cum David <psalmus 59.10>: *Fortitudinem meam ad te custodiam,* isti, *commedunt fructum eius et qui custos est Domini sui glorificabitur'.*

99 Richard Barber and Juliet Barker, *Tournaments: Jousts, Chivalry and Pageants in the Middle Ages* (Woodbridge: Boydell, 1989), 86.
100 Maurice Keen, 'Chivalry and the Aristocracy', in *The New Cambridge Medieval History,* ed. M. Jones, *et al.*, 7 vols. (Cambridge: Cambridge University Press, 1995–), vi, 214, 218.
101 Dunbabin, *A Hound of God,* 174; Keen, 'Chivalry and Aristocracy', 218.
102 Conor Kostick, *The Social Structure of the First Crusade* (Leiden: Brill, 2008), 159–243.
103 Dunbabin, *A Hound of God,* 175, note 45.
104 For further details, see Raymond of Aquiler, 'Historia Francorum qui Ceperunt Iherusalem', in *Recueil des historiens des croisades: Historiens Occidentaux,* 5 vols. (Paris: Académie Imperiale des Inscriptions et Belles–Lettres, 1862–1866), iii, 235–309. Robert the Monk portrayed Godfrey as 'Hic vultu elegans, statura procerus, dulcis eloquio, moribue egregious, et in tantum militibus lenis, ut magis in se monachum quam militem figuraret'; Robert the Monk, 'Roberti Monachi Historia Ierosolimitana', in *RHC: HO,* iii, 731; John France, 'The Election and Title of Godfrey de Bouillon', *Canadian Journal of History,* 18 (1983), 321–329; Jonathan Riley-Smith, 'The Title of Godfrey de Bouillon', *Bulletin of the Institute of Historical Research,* 52 (1979), 83–96; Alan Murray, 'The Title of Godfrey of Bouillon as Ruler of Jerusalem', *Interdisciplinary Journal of Medieval Research,* 3 (1990), 163–178.
105 John Simon, *Godfrey of Bouillon: Duke of Lower Lotharingia, Ruler of Latin Jerusalem, c.1060–1100* (London: Routledge, 2018); John Simon, 'Godfrey of Bouillon and the Swan Knight', in *Crusading and Warfare in the Middle Ages: Realities and Representations. Essays in Honour of John France,* eds. S. John and N. Morton (Farnham: Ashgate, 2014), 129–142; Urban T. Holmes, *A History of the Old French Literature: From the Origins to 1300* (New York: F. S. Crofts, 1937), 124–126; Joachim Bumke, *Courtly Culture: Literature and Society in the High Middle Ages* (Berkeley-Los Angeles-Oxford: University of California Press, 1991), 92–99.
106 Clermont-Ferrand, MS 46, fol. 215^v: 'In omnibus autem exercitibus Christianis contra infideles et specialiter Sarracenos vexillum principale est crux Christi'.
107 Clermont-Ferrand, MS 46, fols. 215^v–216^r: 'Et ita milites et pugiles Christi in exercitu Karoli Magni et ducis nobilis Godefridi pugnati semper prius confitebantur et comunicabant devote divinum servitium audiebant, et sic fructum qui in cruce pependit prelibabant et eo se armabant sicut mustela commedit rutam, et sic intrepida basiliscum aggreditur et occidit'.
108 See Jonathan Riley-Smith, *The First Crusade and the Idea of Crusading* (London: Athlone, 1986), 83–84.
109 Christoph T. Maier, 'Crisis, Liturgy and the Crusade in Twelfth and Thirteenth Centuries', *Journal of Ecclesiastical History,* 48.4 (1997), 628–657, 628.
110 Michael McCormick, 'The Liturgy of War in the Early Middle Ages', *Viator,* 15 (1984), 1–23; Maier, 'Crisis, Liturgy and the Crusade', 629.
111 *The Book of Beasts: Being a Translation from a Latin Bestiary of the Twelfth Century,* ed. and trans. T. H. White (London: Cope, 1954), 168–169.
112 For the origins of the legend see Robert McNeill Alexander, 'The Evolution of the Basilisk', *Greece and Rome,* 10.2 (1963), 170–181.

113 Penny Cole, David d'Avray, Jonathan Riley-Smith, 'Application of Theology to Current Affairs: Memorial Sermons on the Dead of Mansurah and on Innocent IV', in *Modern Questions about Medieval Sermons: Essays on Marriage, Death, History and Sanctity*. eds. N. Bériou and D. d'Avray (Spoleto: Centro Italiano di Studi sull'Alto Medioevo, 1994), 217–245. For the edition of these sermons, see Penny Cole, *The Preaching of the Crusades*, 235–243, appendix D.

114 For more details on the life and the *ad status* crusade sermons of Eudes of Châteauroux, see Maier, *Crusade Propaganda and Ideology*, 9–10, 128–175. For Eudes' preaching against the Albigensians and his view of heresy, see Nicole Bériou, 'La prédication de Croisade de Philippe le Chancelier et d'Eudes de Châteauroux en 1226', in *La prédication en pays d'Oc (XIIe– début XVe siècle)*, Cahiers de Fanjeaux 32, (Toulouse: Privat, 1997), 85–109.

115 The three sermons against the Muslims at Lucera, preached between 1268–1269, have been transcribed and analysed by Christoph Maier in 'Crusade and Rhetoric Against the Muslim Colony of Lucera: Eudes of Châteauroux's *Sermones de rebellione Sarracenorum Lucherie in Apulia*', *Journal of Medieval History*, 21.4 (1995), 343–385. Eudes of Châteauroux wrote more *ad status* crusade sermons that any other author in the thirteenth century.

116 Maier, 'Crusade against Lucera', 367.

117 Natasha Hodgson, 'Lions, Tigers, and Bears: Encounters with Wild Animals and Bestial Imagery in the Context of Crusading to the Latin East', *Viator*, 44.1 (2013), 68.

118 Collins, *Symbolism of Animals*, 35–36.

119 Clermont-Ferrand, MS 46, fol. 216^r: 'Nam ante occulos habentes et gustantes corpus Christi in cruce suspensum et sanguinem in ea expansum, exponunt se audacius mortis periculo propter eum et si in bello moriuntur propter Christum in paradiso comedunt fructum satiativum'.

120 Humbert of Dijon, 'Un Pèlerinage Dominicain Inédit du 14e siècle: Le Liber de Locis et Conditionibus Terrae Sanctae et Sepulcro d'Humbert de Dijon O.P. (1332)', eds. T. Kaeppeli and P. Benoit, *Revue Biblique*, 62.4 (1955), 513–540, 520; Thierry Buquet, '"*Animalia Extranea et Stupenda ad Vivendum*". Describing and Naming Exotic Beasts in Cairo Sultan's Menagerie', in *Animals and Otherness in the Middle Ages: Perspectives Across Disciplines*, eds. F. de Asis Garcia, M. Ann-Walker, and M. V. Picaza (Oxford: Archaeopress, 2013), 25–35, 27: 'In eadem etiam civitate sunt multa et diversa animalia stupenda et extranea ad vivendum, ut puta leopardi, elephantes, unicornia, crocodilli …'.

121 Arthur A. Collins, *Symbolism of Animals and Birds Represented in English Church Architecture* (New York: McBride, Nast and Company, 1913), 2–3; The Venerable Bede in his commentary on the book of Isaiah and Isidore of Seville in his *Etymologies* among other animal stories referred also to the legend of Basilisk.

122 Hodgson, 'Lions, Tigers, and Bears', 68–70.

123 The thirteenth-century scholar, Bartholomew Anglicus, in his *De proprietatibus rerum* made use of the legend of Basilisk and the weasel; Smalley, *English Friars*, 240.

124 Smalley, *English Friars*, 240.

125 Smalley, *English Friars*, 79–85; Edwin D. Craun, *Lies, Slander and Obscenity in Medieval English Literature, Pastoral Rhetoric and the Deviant Speaker* (Cambridge: Cambridge University Press, 1997), 194.

126 Claude Bremond, Jacques Le Goff, Jean Claude Schmitt, *L'"Exemplum'* (Turnhout: Brepols, 1982), 63–64; Smalley, *English Friars*, 84; Craun, *Pastoral Rhetoric*, 194.

127 Buquet, *Animals and Otherness*, 27–29.

128 Smalley, *English Friars*, 249.

129 Clermont-Ferrand, MS 46, fol. 216^r: 'Rinoceros amore virginitatis illectus in gremio puelle super proposite accedens ad eam capud reclinat et obdormit, et qui alias sua

ferocitate, nec vi nec arte, capere se permittit in gremio puelle ut facit ovis et agnus ita mansuescit. Ut venatores ipsum ad libitum capiant et si volunt vulnerant et occidant. Ita et Christus dominus prius hominibus taquam unicornis ferox et ferus qui non solum capi, sed nec videri se ab hominibus permittebat dicens <Exodi 33.20>: *Non videbit me homo et vivet.* Per hoc quod inclinavit celos et descendit in uterum virginis ubi capud sue divitatis pedibus humanitatis convinxit, 2.9. Mensibus requievit ita mansuetus factus est quod <Actuum Apostolorum 8.32> *Tanquam ovis ad occisionem ductus est, et quasi agnus coram tondente se obmutuit*, unde Deuteronomiorum 33<.17>: *Cornua rinoferontis cornua illius.* Et in psalmo <78.69>: *Edificavit sicut unicornium sanctificium suum.* In passione vero se habuit sicut thaurus quia aligatus ad calumpnam flagellandus postea, ad stipitem crucis quasi ficulnee manibus et pedibus clavis affixus mansuevit ut ovis et agnus ex ea parte qua *cum pateretur, non comminabatur, cum malediceretur non maledicebat*, prima Petri 2<.23>. Proprie injurie enim memor erat illis qui se exspoliaverant, crucifixerant et occidebant, condonabat et pro eis orabat dicens: *Pater ignosce illud, illis quia nesciunt quid faciunt*, unde Luce 23<.34>, *primogenita Thauri pulchritudo illius* <Deuteronomiorum 33.17>. Sed contra demones populi hostes fuit Thaurus ferox non mansuetus quia cornua in manibus eius, unde dicit Bernardus super illud: *Dominus fortis et potens in prelio, illo nimirum prelio, in quo debellavit aeras potestates*, non equo residens sed in cruce pendens non manu armata sed clavis affixa. Quamvis ergo omnis Christianus debeat esse devotione et compassione crucis arbori alligatus, dicens cum Paulo <Galatas 2.19>: *Christo confixus sum cruci*, hoc tamen specialius convenit crucesignatis et signandis quibus consumitur super humeros signum crucis. Unde dicit Chrisostomus <Homiliae super Mattheum 28>: *In propris iniuriis esse quempiam patientem, laudabile est, iniurias vero Dei dissimulare nimis est impium*, unde cruci alligatus ut agnus mansuetus Christianis sibi iniuriam facientibus in persona propria vel in rebus non guerram facere, nec malum pro malo reddere, sed amore et exemplo Christi omnia condonare. Sed contra inimicos crucis Christi qui sunt super omnes infideles, et maxime et specialiter Sarraceni, debet esse Thaurus ferox, et indomitus ad ventilandum cornibus Syriam et Egyptum, et destruendum perfidum Machometum et eius nephandum populum totaliter extirpandum'.

130 Clermont-Ferrand, MS 46, fol. 216[r]: '<Luce 22<.28–30>: Vos estis qui permansistis mecum in temptationibus meis, et ego dispono vobis sicut disposuit mihi pater meus regnum, ut edatis et bibatis super mensam meam in regno meo'.

131 Clermont-Ferrand, MS 46, fol. 216[r]: 'Unde cum miles quidam Templarius vel Hospitelarius in bello quodam contra Sarracenos de acie in qua erat ordinatus exiret et hostes invaderet, quodam alio sibi clamante quod ad terram super clamidem suam commederet, nocte illa respondit quod ymmo in cello commederet in Christi mensa quod et factum est. Nam percutiens a dextris et sinistris finaliter occisus est ab hostibus martyr factus'.

132 For the references to the Military Orders in Western sources during the twelfth and thirteenth centuries, see Helen Nicholson, '"*Martyrum collegio sociandus haberet*": Depictions of the Military Orders' Martyrs in the Holy Land, 1187–1291', in *Crusading and Warfare in the Middle Ages: Realities and Representations. Essays in Honour of John France*, eds. S. John and N. Morton (Farnham: Ashgate, 2014), 101–118.

133 For a certain number of thirteenth-century *exempla* about the Templar knights see *The Exempla or Illustrative Stories from the Sermones Vulgares of Jacques de Vitry*, ed. T. F. Crane (London: The Folklore Society, 1890), 38–42 (nos. LXXXV–XCI exempla for the Templars), 54–57 (nos. CXIX–CXXIV exempla for the crucesignatos and crucesignandos also referring to the Templars); *Anecdotes historiques, légendes et apologues tirés du recueil inédit d'Étienne de Bourbon*, ed. A. Lecoy de la Marche (Paris: Société de l'histoire de France, 1877), 85–92.

134 For the role of Pierre de la Palud in the procedures against the Templars, see Dunbabin, *A Hound of God*, 21–25.

182 *University trained clergy*

135 A comparison between the sermon and the text of *Legenda Aurea* shows that Palud has accurately copied verbatim from the Voragine's chapter on the history of the Invention of the Cross. For the Latin text of the 'Golden Legend' see *Jacobi a Voragine Legenda Aurea Vulgo Historia Lombardica Dicta*, ed. T. Graesse (Lipsiae: Impensis Librariae Arnoldiane, 1801), 303–311, 605–611. For an English translation and introduction, see *The Golden Legend: Reading on the Saints*, trans. W. Granger Ryan, 2 vols. (Princeton: Princeton University Press, 1993), i, 277–284; ii, 168–173.
136 Clermont-Ferrand, MS 46, fols. 216^v–217^v; *The Golden Legend*, i, 277–282; ii, 168–172.
137 Alain Boureau, *La Légende Dorée: Le Système Narratif de Jacques de Voragine († 1298)* (Paris: Editions du Cerf, 1984), 21–25.
138 The two tables which actually list all legends included in the text of the *Legenda Aurea* appear in a manuscript from the Dominican convent in Auxerre kept today in Amiens. For the tables and the note see Amiens, Bibliothèque Municipale, MS 462, fols. 208^r, 212^v: 'Explicit tabula super legendas sanctorum, edita a quodam fratre Ordinis Praedicatorum, et creditur fuisse dominus frater Petrus de Palude, patriarcha Ierosolimitanus. Deo gratias consumata fuit hec scriptura anno Domini MCCCLIX, XVI die Octobris, hora prime'; *Histoire Littéraire de la France*, xxxvii, 80.
139 Clermont-Ferrand, MS 46, fol. 217^v.
140 Clermont-Ferrand, MS 46, fol. 218^r: 'Vero humiles reges principes et magnates quando sunt humiles et bone voluntatis sic plus possunt quam subditi ita et plura et maiora bona faciunt. Et plura et maiora mala impediunt et puniunt quam subdici eorum faciant nec facere valeant. Sic manifestum est quod sanctus Ludovicus quamdiu regnavit plura et maiora bona fecit quam aliquis de regno suo fecerit nec facere potuerit, ut patet in ecclesiis, monasteriis et hospitalibus que fundavit'.
141 Clermont-Ferrand, MS 46, fol. 219^r: 'Si quis enim tali scuto cooperiretur quod non posset occidi, nec ad mortem vulnerari, nec capi sub eo, aut si caperetur plus valeret sibi captio quam constaret redemptio, e[t] si vulneraretur cito et melius sanaretur, talis deberet in bello esse audacissimus. Tali autem scuto inexpugnabile proteguntur crucesignati in omni bello in quo pugnant pro nomine crucifixi'.
142 Clermont-Ferrand, MS 46, fol. 219^r: 'De morte inferni summe terribili quia mors peccatorum pessima, illam non habent timore morientes in bello Christi'.
143 Clermont-Ferrand, MS 46, fol. 219^{r-v}: 'morientes pro Christo consequentes plenissimam indulgendiam peccatorum falce martirii purgati ascententes in celum ... et sic est de corpore mortali pro Christo occiso, pro quo pugil Christi in die iudicii recipiet corpus gloriosum et imperiale seu immortale'.
144 Clermont-Ferrand, MS 46, fol. 220^r: 'Bona tamen narro quam habuerunt peregrini navigantes per mare ad terram sanctam vi ventorum repulsi ad quadam frontariam in Hispania, prope castrum Alkazez Sarracenorum, quod dabat singulis annis Soldano centum Christianorum capita pro tributto. Unde rogati a militaribus, secularibus et regularibus, Christianis qui illic aderant ad defensionem terre cum eis castrum huius obsidere assumserunt quia per tunc obstante hyeme ad terram sanctam ad quam erat principalis eorum intentio proficisci non poterant bene acqueverunt, ut non essent interim ottiosi sed occupaverunt in servitio Ihesu Christi, obsidione itaque ponita supervenerunt in auxilium obsessorum quatuor reges Sarracenorum cum centum milibus bellatorum cum quibus vestri vix cum septem milibus pugnatorum confligentes, habuerunt Deo auxiliante triumphum hostibus omnibus aut fugatis aut occisis aut captiantis. Captianti vero querebant a captiantibus unde venisset et quo abiiset acies candidatorum super arma alba crucibus rubeis in humeris signatorum que se vestris adiungens et inde in paganos se mergens omnes exterruit et victoriam nostris dedit'; Dunbabin, *A Hound of God*, 175–176.
145 'Prima Vita Clementis VI, in *Vitae Paparum Avenionensium*, ed. G. Mollat, 4 vols. (Paris: Librairie Letouzey et Ané, 1916–1928), i, 241 [hereafter *VPA*]; *Histoire littéraire de la France*, xxxvii, 209–210; Diana Wood, *Clement VI: The Pontificate*

and Ideas of an Avignon Pope (Cambridge: Cambridge University Press, 1989), 7; John E. Wrigley, 'Clement VI Before his Pontificate. The Early Life of Pierre Roger, 1290/91–1342', *The Catholic Historical Review*, 56.3 (1970), 433–473, 433–434.
146 Thomas Sullivan, *Benedictine Monks at the University of Paris, A.D. 1229–1500* (Leiden: Brill, 1995), 296–299; Wood, *Pope Clement VI*, 7; Wrigley, 'Clement VI Before his Pontificate', 437.
147 John XXII, *Lettres Communes*, no. 17738; *Histoire littéraire de la France*, xxxvii, 210; Wood, *Pope Clement VI*, 8–9; Wrigley, 'Clement VI Before his Pontificate', 439.
148 Wrigley, 'Clement VI Before his Pontificate', 441–443.
149 Wrigley, 'Clement VI Before his Pontificate', 442.
150 For details on the continuous ascendance of Pierre Roger through the ecclesiastical ranks see Wrigley, 'Clement VI before his Pontificate', 438–451.
151 Wrigley, 'Clement VI Before his Pontificate', 456–457.
152 John XXII, *Lettres Communes*, no. 61324; *VPA*, ii, 288–289; *Chronique latin de Guillaume de Nangis*, ii, 130–131; *Les Grandes chroniques de France*, ix, 130.
153 Appendix IV, § 1.
154 Sainte Geneviève, MS 240, fols. 298^v–308^v; BnF, MS lat. 3293, fols. 240^r–249^r; Schneyer, *Repertorium 1150–1350*, iv, 766; Tyerman, 'Philip VI and the Holy Land', 29–30.
155 *Les Grandes Chroniques de France*, ix, 133–134; *Chronique latin de Guillaume de Nangis*, ii, 135; *Chronique Parisienne anonyme*, 154; *Chronique des quatre premiers Valois (1327–1393)*, ed. S. Luce (Paris: Société de l'histoire de France, 1862), 6; *Chronographia regum Francorum*, ii, 19; 'Quinta Vita Joannis XXII', in *VPA*, i, 174; Déprez, *La papauté, la France et l'Angleterre*, 99; Delaville le Roulx, *La France en Orient*, 87; Housley, *The Avignon Papacy*, 24; Housley, *The Later Crusades*, 33; Dunbabin, *A Hound of God*, 177; Tyerman, 'Philip VI and the Holy Land', 30.
156 Luke 9.51: 'Faciem suam firmavit ut iret Iherusalem et misit nuncios'.
157 Appendix III, § 2.
158 Appendix III, § 14–15, 24, 30–38.
159 Ezrae 7.13: 'A me decretum est ut cuicumque placuerit in regno meo de populo Israhel, et de sacertotibus eius, et de Levitis ire in Iherusalem tecum vadat'.
160 Appendix IV, § 1–3.
161 Appendix IV, § 3.
162 Appendix III, § 4–5, 12, 30.
163 The *distinctiones* in the late twelfth century were lists (there are some alphabetical *distinctio* collections) of different meanings of a word contained in the Bible. Each word offers four meanings of Biblical interpretation. The *intellectus, affectus, effectus* cluster, however, does not form a *distinctio* on a word. They nevertheless correspond to the distinctions mentality. An outstanding analysis of the mendicant formulae of divisions in sermons is given in d'Avray, *The Preaching of the Friars*, 72–75, 248–249.
164 Appendix III, § 4.
165 Appendix III, § 6.
166 Appendix III, § 30.
167 Appendix III, § 38.
168 Appendix IV, § 3.
169 Appendix III, § 38.
170 'De consideratione ad Eugenium papam', in *Sancti Bernardi Opera*, eds. J. Leclercq and H.-M. Rochais, 8 vols. (Rome: Editiones Cistercienses, 1957–1977), 3: 379–493, 423, Lib.II, cap.7–8; For an English translation see James Brundage, *The Crusades: A Documentary History* (Milwaukee: Marquette University Press, 1962), 115–121; Appendix III, § 35; Appendix IV, § 7,9–10.
171 For further evidences on Bernard's concept of papal temporal and spiritual superiority in the *De Consideratione* see Elizabeth Kennan, 'The 'De Consideratione' of

St. Bernard of Clairvaux and the Papacy in the Mid–Twelfth Century: A Review of Scholarship', *Traditio*, 23 (1967), 73–115.
172 Evan F. Kuehn, 'Melchizedek as Exemplar for Kingship in Twelfth–Century Political Thought', *History of Political Thought*, 31.4 (2010), 557–575, 565–567.
173 J. A. Watt, 'The Papacy', in *The New Cambridge Medieval History*, v, 107–164, 117–118.
174 Appendix IV, § 9.
175 Appendix III, § 32; Appendix IV, § 44.
176 Appendix III, § 32; Appendix IV, § 44.
177 Appendix III, § 34.
178 Appendix III, § 16–23.
179 Appendix III, § 17.
180 Appendix III, §18; Flavius Vegetius Renatus, *Epitoma rei militaris*, ed. C. Lang (Leipzig: Bibliotheca Scriptorum Graecorum et Romanorum Teubneriana, 1885), lib.I, 1.6.; *Vegetius: Epitoma rei militaris*, ed. Michael D. Reeve (Oxford: Oxford Classical Texts, 2004), I, c.1, n.7, 6.
181 For more details about the Epitome's authorship, dating, comments and an English translation of the Latin text, see *Vegetius: Epitome of Military Science*, trans. N. P. Milner (Liverpool: Liverpool University Press, 1993).
182 Appendix III, §18–19.
183 Appendix IV, § 5.
184 Appendix IV, §5–6, 22, 34, 37.
185 Appendix IV, § 41.
186 Appendix IV, § 6.
187 Appendix IV, § 34.
188 Appendix III, § 14–15, 25; Appendix IV, § 34, 37–43.
189 Appendix III, § 24.
190 Tyerman, 'Philip VI and the Holy Land', 26–27.
191 Appendix III, § 25.
192 Elizabeth A. R. Brown, 'Customary Aids and Royal Fiscal Policy Under Philip VI of Valois', *Traditio*, 39 (1974), 191–258, 191–205; Tyerman, 'Philip VI and the Holy Land', 39–40.
193 Appendix IV, § 43.
194 Appendix IV, § 37.
195 Appendix IV, § 37; The papal chaplain at Avignon, Henry of Diessenhofen, in his 'Quinta Vita Joannis XXII' did not include the nobleman Peter Trousseau among the French royal envoys. See: 'Quinta Vita Joannis XXII', in *VPA*, i, 174: 'In predicto etiam consistorio Petrus, archiepiscopus Rothomagensis, et Johannes, episcopus Morinensis et decanus Parisiensis, et Henricus, miles, dictus de Analgoria, habentes procuratorium sufficiens, in animam predicti regis juraverunt ut iret in propria persona ultra mare'; Tyerman, 'Philip VI and the Holy Land', 29.
196 Appendix IV, § 37.
197 Appendix IV, § 40.
198 Appendix IV, § 41.
199 Appendix III, § 8.
200 Appendix III, § 7–8; Appendix IV, § 3, 19.
201 Nicholas Morton, 'The Defence of the Holy Land and the Memory of the Maccabees', *Journal of Medieval History*, 36 (2010), 275–293.
202 Appendix IV, § 32.
203 Donald E. Pitcher, *An Historical Geography of the Ottoman Empire: From Earliest Times to the End of the Sixteenth Century* (Leiden: Brill, 1968), 35–40.
204 Appendix III, § 14–15; Appendix IV, § 30–32.
205 Appendix IV, § 25.
206 Appendix IV, § 32.

207 Appendix III, § 21; Margaret Haist, 'The Lion, Bloodline and Kingship', in *The Mark of the Beast: The Medieval Bestiary in Art, Life and Literature*, ed. D. Hassig (New York-London: Garland Publishing, 1999), 3–22.
208 Appendix IV, § 33.
209 Appendix IV, § 22, 25–26, 33.
210 Appendix IV, § 22.
211 'Leonis Papae IV: Epistolae et Decreta', in *Patrologia Latina*, ed. J.-P. Migne, 115:655–675, 657, epist. I (Ad exercitum Francorum).
212 James A. Brundage, *Medieval Canon Law and the Crusader* (Madison-Milwaukee-London: The University of Wisconsin Press, 1969), 22–23.
213 Appendix IV, § 27.
214 Appendix IV, § 33.
215 Appendix IV, § 23.
216 Appendix IV, § 12.
217 Appendix IV, § 12.
218 Donald M. Nicol, *Byzantium and Venice: A Study in Diplomatic and Cultural Relations* (Cambridge: Cambridge University Press, 1988), 253–254.
219 Norman Housley, 'Jerusalem and Development of the Crusade Idea, 1095–1128', in *The Horns of Hattin*, ed. B. Z. Kedar (Jerusalem: Yad Izhak Ben–Zvi; London: Variorum, 1992), 27–40, 29–31.
220 Appendix III, § 8; Appendix IV, § 21.
221 Appendix III, § 8.
222 Appendix III, § 8.
223 Malcolm Barber, *The New Knighthood: A History of the Order of the Temple* (Cambridge: Cambridge University Press, 1994), 45–47.
224 Appendix III, § 9; Appendix IV, § 27.
225 For the debate on the exact nature and content of the sermon of Pope Urban II at Clermont see Dana C. Munro, 'The Speech of Pope Urban II at Clermont, 1095', *American Historical Review*, 11 (1906), 231–242; H. E. J. Cowdrey, 'Pope Urban II's Preaching of the First Crusade', *History*, 55 (1990), 177–188; John France, 'Les Origines de la première croisade: Un Nouvel Examen', in *Autour de la première croisade*, ed. M. Balard (Paris: Publications de la Sorbonne, 1996), 43–56; For the explanation of St Bernard for the result of the second crusade, see St Bernard, 'De Consideratione Libri quinque ad Eugenium Tertium', in *Patrologia Latina*, ed. J.-P. Paul Migne, 221 vols. (Paris, 1841–1855), clxxxii, cols. 727–808, col. 742.
226 Jessalynn Bird, 'Crusade and Reform: The Sermons of Bibliothèque Nationale, MS nouv. acq. lat. 999', in *The Fifth Crusade in Context: The Crusading Movement in the Early Thirteenth Century*, eds. E. Mylod, G. Perry, T. W. Smith, and J. Vandeburie (London: Routledge, 2017), 92–113.
227 Palmer A. Throop, 'Criticism of Papal Crusade Policy in Old French and Provençal', *Speculum*, 13.4 (1938), 379–412.
228 Appendix III, § 10.
229 Appendix III, § 10.
230 Appendix III, § 10.
231 Appendix III, § 26.
232 Iben Fonnesberg-Schmidt, *The Popes and the Baltic Crusades, 1147–1254* (Leiden: Brill, 2007), 28.
233 Appendix III, § 28.
234 Appendix III, § 28.
235 Appendix III, § 28.
236 Appendix III, § 29; *VPA*, ii, 289; Dunbabin, *A Hound of God*, 173.
237 Appendix IV, § 44.
238 Denis H. Green, *The Millstatter Exodus: A Crusading Epic* (Cambridge: Cambridge University Press, 1966), 419–422.

239 John XXII, *Lettres ... Relatives á la France*, nos. 5207–5227.
240 Maier, *Crusade Propaganda and Ideology*, 6; Maier, *Preaching the Crusades*, 111–122; d'Avray, *The Preaching of the Friars*, 64–90; Louis-Jacques Bataillon, 'Les instruments de travail des prédicateurs au XIIIe siècle', in *Culture et travail intellectuel dans l'Occident Medieval*, eds. G. Hasenohr and J. Longere (Paris: Editions du CNRS, 1981), 197–209.
241 Maier, *The Preaching of the Friars*, 113; Appendix II (BnF, MS lat. 17516, fols. 84ra–85vb).
242 For the two anonymous crusade appeals in the miscellany from St Victor at Paris, both written for the recruitment of the Fifth Crusade, see Jessalynn Lea Bird, 'The Victorines, Peter the Chanter's Circle, and the Crusade: Two Unpublished Crusading Appeals in Paris, Bibliothèque Nationale, MS. Latin 14470', *Medieval Sermon Studies*, 48 (2004), 5–28, 22–28; Clermont-Ferrand, MS 46, fol. 218^v.
243 Maier, *Crusade Propaganda and Ideology*, 86–99.
244 Bird, 'The Victorines, Peter the Chanter's Circle', 22–28. For the preaching of Oliver of Paderborn of the Fifth Crusade in Germany see Jaap J. Van Moolenbroek, 'Signs in the Heavens in Groningen and Friesland in 1214: Oliver of Cologne and Crusading Propaganda', *Journal of Medieval History*, 13 (1987), 251–272. For the sermons of James of Vitry see Maier, *Crusade Propaganda and Ideology*, 83–100. For John of Abbeville see Cole, *The Preaching of the Crusades*, Appendix A, 222–226.
245 Cole, *Preaching the Crusades*, Appendix B, 227–231. For the sermon's content analysis see in the same book, 167–173.
246 Appendix II; Clermont-Ferrand, MS 46, fol. 215^v.
247 Humbert of Romans, *Tractatus Solemnis Fratris Humberti quondam Magistri Generalis Ordinis Praedicatorum: De predicatione sancte crucis* (Nuremberg: Peter Wagner, 1495); Valentin L. Portnykh, 'Le Traité d'Humbert de Romans, O.P., De la Prédication de la Sainte Croix Contre les Sarrasins (XIIIe Siècle). Analyse Historique et Édition du Texte' (PhD diss., Novosibirsk, Novosibirsk State University, 2011); For details on the preserved shorter version of Humbert of Romans' treatise and textual edition see Valentin Portnykh, 'The Short Version of Humbert of Romans' Treatise on the Preaching of the cross: An edition of the Latin Text', *Crusades*, 15 (2016), 55–115; Valentin Portnykh, 'An Unknown Short Version of the Treatise *De predicatione sancte crucis* by Humbert of Romans', *Studi Medievali*, 2 (2015), 721–738; For the use of the *De predicatione* in the fifteenth century see: Valentin Portnykh, 'Le traité d' Humbert de Romans (OP) 'De la prédication de la sainte croix'. Une hypothèse sur son utilisation dans les guerres saintes du XV siècle', *Revue d' histoire ecclésiastique*, 109.3–4 (2014), 588–624.
248 Cole, *The Preaching of the Crusades*, 202–217; Penny Cole, 'Humbert of Romans and the Crusade', in *The Experience of Crusading: Western Approaches*, eds. N. Housley and M. Bull (Cambridge: Cambridge University Press, 2003), 157–174. Valentin Portnykh in his recent completed PhD thesis provided a historical analysis and a critical edition of Humbert's *De Predicatione Crucis* text, based on the examination of two manuscript resemblances from Madrid (Madrid, Biblioteca Nacional, MS 19423) and from the Vatican (BAV, Vat. lat. MS 3847).
249 Cole, *The Preaching of the Crusades*, 237, appendix D: 'antedicti nobiles leones fuerunt nobilitate, fortitudine atque audacia'.
250 Appendix III, § 21.
251 Cole, *The Preaching of the Crusades*, 202, note 88. For more details on the codex from the Vatican Library and thoughts over when possibly the works in the codex were brought together, see Cole, 'Humbert of Romans and the Crusade', 156–160.
252 BnF, MS lat. 17516, fols. 84^r–85^v; Humbert of Romans, *De predicatione sancte crucis*, capitulum xvii, 'De gratiis ecclesie datis ad idem [ad bellum contra saracenos]'.
253 Humbert of Romans, *De predicatione sancte crucis*, capitulum x, 'De Primaria Crucesignationis Inventione', and capitulum xxxi, 'De Historia Tripertita',

capitulum xxx, 'De diversis narrationibus ex ecclesiastica historia utilibus predicantibus crucem'.
254 Humbert of Romans, *De predicatione sancte crucis*, capitulum xvi, 'De exemplis antiquorum que inducunt ad bellum contra saracenos'.
255 Appendix III, § 7.
256 Srr Appendix V
257 Humbert of Romans, *De predicationis sancte crucis*, capitulo xxix, 'De sex generibus scientie que sunt necessaria de predicatoribus crucis'.
258 Humbert of Romans, *De predicationis crucis*, capitulo iii, 'De triplici suffragio fiendo Terre Sancte', capitulo xxvii, 'Themata ex tota Biblia ad predicantum crucem', capitulo xi, 'De zelo divini amoris qui movere debet ad crucis assumptione', capitulo xii, 'De Fraterna charitate que movere debet ad crucis assumptione'.
259 Appendix IV, § 32.
260 Humbert of Romans, *De predicatione crucis*, capitulo xiv, 'De devotione habenda ad Terram Sanctam'.
261 Appendix III, § 8; Appendix IV, § 21.
262 Humbert of Romans, *De predicatione crucis*, capitulo xxxix, 'De verbis Urbani pape'. Pierre quoted and discussed crusade ideas coming from Urban II's inspirational speech at Clermont, and from the works of Bernard of Clairvaux 'De Consideratione', and 'De Nova militia Templi'.
263 Cole, 'Humbert of Romans and the Crusade', 159.
264 Appendix III, § 38.
265 A characteristic example of such developments in the fourteenth-century crusade preaching is the *Summa Predicantium*, compiled by the English Dominican, John of Bromyard, sometime between 1330 and 1348. Bromyard devoted a whole chapter in his *Summa*, a model sermon suitable for the preaching of the crusade, which it also could be adapted for preaching on the feast days of the cross. Bromyard's *Crux* model sermon consists one of the few examples of fully extant crusade sermon compiled by a non-French friar or Paris theologian in the fourteenth century. For more details, see John of Bromyard, *Summa Predicantium Doctissimi Viri Fratris Johannis Bromyard, Ordinis Predicatorum* (Basel, 1485). For the period of its compilation, see Leonard Boyle, 'The Date of the Summa Praedicantium of John Bromyard', *Speculum*, 48.3 (1973), 533–537; Guard, Timothy, 'Pulpit and Cross: Preaching the Crusade in Fourteenth-century England', *English Historical Review*, 129.541 (2014), 1319–1345.

Conclusion

This study examines papal efforts to organize crusade preaching campaigns, the evolving use of the liturgy for the crusade and preserved crusade sermon texts – and their preachers – from the pontificate of Clement V to the European outbreak of the Black Death. These years were marked by a series of intensive efforts instigated by the papacy to launch crusades to the Holy Land and the Aegean. Such efforts were undertaken up until the outbreak of the Black Death in Western Europe.

The letters of the first four Avignon popes reveal detailed information as to the organization of crusade preaching, including those on whom the papacy relied to conduct the preaching, its frequency, its geographic extent, the preaching responsibilities assigned to individual preachers and the hindrances to its normal conduct. Unlike their predecessors from the twelfth to the late-thirteenth century, the Avignon popes, in their crusade bulls, omitted instructions to potential preachers as to what was appropriate for pronouncement. The formulaic language of the papal letters is very repetitive with regard to instructions to the clergy, and the correspondence from the beginning of John XXII's reign increasingly summarizes instructions for the conduct of preaching. Apart from the Hospitaller preaching campaign, papal correspondence in the early fourteenth century progressively pays more attention to the liturgical measures that were to accompany the preaching campaign, rather than to the preaching itself. This is quite possibly related to the greater attention given from the end of the thirteenth century to securing all Christianity's participation in the crusade and financial resources for its undertaking. Even though the early fourteenth-century Avignon popes drew on the liturgy for the Holy Land which had been developed during the previous centuries, they continued to enrich the liturgical apparatus. Pope Clement V made extensive use of the liturgy for the Holy Land as propaganda for the Hospitaller crusade and also introduced the *Missa Contra Paganos*. This Clementine triple set of prayers, which remained popular until the mid-fifteenth century, augmented the already existing liturgical apparatus and allowed the pope to place the Hospitaller expedition to Rhodes under his general crusading plans in support of the kingdoms of Armenia and Cyprus. These liturgical measures remained in use after the Pontiff's death in 1314, and his successor, John XXII, expanded the liturgical rite for the crusade with new psalms, hymns and litanies. This same liturgical apparatus remained in use under Popes Benedict XII and Clement VI.

The combination of preaching with liturgical measures to raise money in lieu of recruitment was an integral part of fourteenth-century crusade propaganda. The more funds became crucial for any expedition to the East, the more the liturgy became a constituent element of the papal crusade propaganda network. The papacy wisely embedded the liturgy for the Holy Land in the crusade propaganda machinery, offering the opportunity to all Christians to contribute financially to the crusade. With Clement V and John XXII, the liturgical measures were centrally organized and made central to their crusading policies: both popes connected the liturgy with the preaching of the cross to secure funding. In the first half of the fourteenth century, financing emerged as a principal prerequisite for the implementation of any expedition to the East. The Avignon popes were desperate to secure money for the crusade, and this compelled the papacy to intensify its propagandistic efforts, despite papal opposition to general participation in crusading as the new form of crusading in the East demanded small-scale military enterprises and expertize in warfare. Nonetheless, intensive crusade preaching, in combination with the liturgical apparatus, inspired three cases of massive popular reaction in less than forty years: in 1309, in 1320 and in 1344. This phenomenon revealed the papacy's deficiencies in maintaining control over crusade preaching: they were unable to anticipate the effect fervent crusade preaching had on popular consciousness, and its harmful consequences.

The first Avignon popes relied on earlier established patterns for organising crusading propaganda, but they adjusted their strategies to meet the challenges of the early fourteenth century. The thirteenth century provided the crucial background for the organization of crusade preaching campaigns in the fourteenth century, with regard to those whom the papacy designated as responsible for the preaching. The popes employed Franciscan and Dominican friars extensively to carry out crusade preaching; from the mid-1340s, the papacy employed mendicants from the Carmelite Order and the Order of the Augustinian Hermits on a regular basis – the Carmelites in particular played a prominent role in the preaching campaign for the second phase of the Smyrna Crusade in 1345. Following the Smyrna Crusade and throughout the remainder of the fourteenth century, the Carmelites continued to build their reputation as effective crusade preachers.

Papal correspondence with the high secular clergy demonstrates that the Avignon papacy trusted the diocesan clergy to assist the mendicants in the dissemination of crusade propaganda more than their thirteenth century predecessors had. This indicates the enhanced educational level achieved by the secular diocesan clergy in the fourteenth century, especially the level achieved by the high prelates, as the majority of them began their ecclesiastical careers as members of the mendicant or monastic orders, often studying at universities.

The papal summons to friar-preachers from four different mendicant orders to join together in crusade preaching campaigns inflamed the existing competition and antagonism among the friars, and the concurrent preaching by brothers from different orders provoked sometimes quarrels between them and concomitant public scandals; their rivalries embroiled the Church in conflict and impeded the normal conduct of crusade preaching, even necessitating papal intervention. To circumvent such disputes, the papacy, particularly Clement VI, sharply defined the friars' respective preaching responsibilities.

It was also during the first half of the fourteenth century that the Avignon popes had to face another obstacle to the effectiveness of crusade preaching in recruiting crusaders and securing financial resources, the failure of a great part of the clergy to carry out their crusade preaching duties; some members of the parish clergy were illiterate, while others were simply negligent. As this book shows, the Avignon Popes' crusade bulls are full of harsh criticism for those friars and secular clergymen who preached without passion or excitement. In an effort to induce the churchmen to take their place at the pulpit with vigour and passion, the papacy granted indulgences for preaching.

Another more serious impediment to the consistent conduct of crusade preaching was the emergence, in the fourteenth century, of powerful Western monarchs. These rulers were efficient both in resisting papal authority and in controlling their subjects. Both the crusaders and the clergy – especially the secular clergy, which had been responsible for the execution of crusade preaching – were under the influence of powerful lay rulers. The exercise of the papal summons for preaching the cross depended on the cooperation of secular rulers; if a powerful monarch thought that the crusade-preaching campaign in his kingdom did not serve his purposes, he impeded the clergy in his kingdom from participating in the campaign. Indeed, a thorough study of the first half of the fourteenth century provides several examples of lay discontent and opposition to crusade preaching. In early 1309, in their respective kingdoms, Philip IV and James II of Aragon obstructed preparations and prevented the preaching for the Hospitallers' *passagium*. Likewise, in 1335, Pope Benedict XII, at the behest of King Hugh IV, halted the preaching of the crusade in the Kingdom of Cyprus; ten years later, in May 1345, Philip VI of France forced Pope Clement VI to postpone the preaching of indulgences in France because of Philip's war with England.

Despite such difficulties, the Church paid special attention to the way in which the preaching would be conducted. The success of crusading propaganda depended on the preachers' quality, morality and charisma, as well on their enthusiasm and overall number: the popes urged all crusade preachers to work hard, to be devoted to their duty and watchful during preaching performance. During general crusade preaching campaigns, the papacy ordered friar-preachers and the secular clergy to conduct intensive crusade preaching and to hear confessions during Mass in every episcopal or parish church on Sundays and feast days. In some cases, mostly in urban centres, the papacy wanted the preaching to take place on a daily basis outside churches, wherever there was a great gathering of people.

The involvement of a number of brilliant individual preachers, secular and regular clerics, in crusading diplomacy and in the dissemination of the message of the cross, resulted in the writing of several sermon texts, all of them important testaments to the development of crusading and crusade policy in the early fourteenth century. The identification of five crusade sermon exemplars for the

Fourth Sunday in Lent, *Laetare Jerusalem*, from the early fourteenth century, demonstrate that crusade preachers drew on the penitential thrust of the day to stress the sincere repentance required for the *crucesignati* and established this particular Sunday as a regular day for crusade preaching. The thematic development of crusade appeals in the *Laetare Jerusalem* sermons also make it possible to connect regular preaching and crusade propaganda in the later Middle Ages.

The rhetoric of some preserved crusade sermons was crafted for purposes other than recruitment; these texts mirror the attitude of the French Crown to the crusade and rail against the moral and social ills that either slowed the implementation of the crusade or contravened its purpose. The two sermons preached by the Archbishop of Rouen, Pierre Roger, royal representative at Avignon, in the context of Franco-papal crusade negotiations in 1332–1333, are the ideal examples of such texts. Pierre Roger's sermons contain numerous arguments to support French royal requirements for the crusade ensconced in crusade-friendly themes. The argumentative structure and content arrangement of these sermons makes them fine models of diplomatic intelligence, philosophical and theological knowledge in the later Middle Ages. The personality, educational background and tenets of faith held by the author are reflected in these crusade sermons, and they should be assessed as tools for pastoral and political missions rather than as presentations of original crusading ideas.

This study focuses on the organization of the preaching of the crusades to the Holy Land during the first half of the fourteenth century. The examination of papal initiatives for the organization of crusade preaching in other geographical areas, such as the Iberian Peninsula or the Baltic region, lies beyond the scope of this book. Moreover, investigation of the diocesan registers in France, Germany and Spain will provide further knowledge of secular clergy's reaction to papal commands for crusade preaching, as Timothy Guard's work for England demonstrates.[1] Finally, the different sermons for the feast days of the cross that include crusade appeals – preserved in a number of different manuscript collections, all arranged according to the feast days of the church calendar (*sermones de sanctis*) or Lent (*sermones quadragesimales*) – make it necessary to conduct a separate, systematic search of each collection for the identification of more such examples.

Note

1 Timothy Guard, *Chivalry Kingship and Crusade: The English Experience in the Fourteenth Century* (Woodbridge: The Boydell Press, 2013), 149–153; Timothy Guard, 'Pulpit and Cross: Preaching the Crusade in Fourteenth-century England', *English Historical Review*, 129.541 (2014), 1328–1345.

Appendix I
A list of crusade sermons from the first half of the fourteenth century

William Bernard of Narbonne, O.P.

1. Sermon *De Sancta Cruce*
   Paris, Bibliothèque nationale de France, MS lat. 14965, fols. 331v–333r.
   Incipit: *Lignum vite in medio* [Genesis 2.7]; Arbor posita in medio orti...
   Reference: Schneyer, *Repertorium 1150–1350*, ii, 447, no. 351.

2. *Collatio in Quadragessima*
   Incipit: *Convertentur ad Dominum universi fines terre* [Psalmus 21.28]; Videtur communiter quod uno rege accipiente crucem multi ad exemplum eius accipiunt...
   Reference: Schneyer, *Repertorium 1150–1350*, ii, 435, no. 185.[1]

Henry of Friemar, O.E.S.A.

1. Sermon on the *Dominica quarta in Quadragessima*
   München, Bayerischen Staatsbibliothek, Clm 18732, fols. 71va–73rb
   Incipit: *Illa que sursum est Iherusalem*, [Galates 4.26]; Quando aliquis crucem transmarinam assumit et proponit in terra sancta manere...
   Reference: Schneyer, *Repertorium 1150–1350*, ii, 642, no.53; viii, 790, no. 74.

James of Lausanne, O.P.

1. Sermon on the *Dominica quarta in Quadragessima*
   Paris, Bibliothèque nationale de France, MS lat. 17516, fols. 84ra–85vb
   Incipit: *Illa que sursum est Iherusalem, libera est* [Galates 4.26]; Consuetum est quod tempore generalis passagii...
   Reference: Schneyer, *Repertorium 1150–1350*, iii, 66, no. 152.

2. Sermon on the *Dominica prima post Octavas Epiphanie*
   Jacobus de Laosanna (O.P.), *Sermones dominicales et festivales per totum anni circulum per reverendum patrem fratrem Jacobum de Laosana,... declamati, impressioni mandati per quendam patrem professorem*

---

[1] Unfortunately, I did not manage to locate the sermon's text to any of the manuscripts listed by Schneyer in *Repertorium 1150–1350*.

ordinis minorum regularis observantie (Paris: Ambrosii Girault, 1530), fols. 35v–37r

Incipit: *Dolentes querebamus te* [Luce 2.48]; Tempus flendi et tempus ridendi…

Reference: Schneyer, *Repertorium 1150–1350*, iii, 61, no. 87.

Pierre de la Palud, O.P.

1. Sermon *In Exaltatione Sancte Crucis*
   Clermont-Ferrand, Bibliothèque Municipale, MS 46, fols. 215r–220v.
   Incipit: *Exaltavi lignum humile* [Ezechiel 17.24]; Ficus egyptiaca est talis nature…
   Reference: Dunbabin, *A Hound of God*, 152.

Pierre Roger/Pope Clement VI, O.S.B.

1. *Collatio facta per dominum Clementem Sextum pro passagio faciendo*
   Paris, Bibliothèque nationale de France, MS lat. 3293, fols. 161r–169r; Paris, Bibliothèque Sainte Geneviève, MS 240, fols. 290v–298v.
   Incipit: *Faciem suam firmavit ut iret Jerusalem,* [Luce 9.51] Videtur mihi, quod ad hoc quod aliquis opus…
   Reference: Schneyer, iv, 761, no. 36; Wood, *Clement VI*, 213.

2. Sermon *In indictione passagii generalis*
   Paris, Bibliothèque nationale de France, MS lat. 3293, fols. 240r–249r; Paris, Bibliothèque Sainte Geneviève, MS 240, fols. 298v–308v.
   Incipit: Sanctissime pater et domine reverentissime missi ex parte devotissimi filii vestri regis Francie… *A me decretum est ut cuicumque placuerit* [Ezrae 7.13]
   Reference: Schneyer, iv, 766, no.80; Wood, *Clement VI*, 211, no. 2.

3. *Sermo factus per dominum Clementem papam VI quando Dalphinus fuit factus capitaneus passagii contra Thurcos.*
   Paris, Bibliothèque nationale de France, MS lat. 3293, fols. 299v–302r; Paris, Bibliothèque Sainte Geneviève, MS 240, fols. 521r–523v.
   Incipit: *Dum implet verbum, factus est dux in Israhel* [I Machabeorum 2.55]; Textus refert ad litteram in eodem libro…
   Reference: Schneyer, *Repertorium 1150–1350*, iv, 760, no. 27; Wood, *Clement VI*, 212, no. 16; Schmitz, 'Les Sermons et Discours de Clément VI, O.S.B.', 22; Mollat, 'L'Oeuvre Oratoire de Clément VI', 254; Constantinos Georgiou, 'Ordinavi armatam sancte unionis, Clement VI's Sermon on the Dauphin Humbert II of Viennois' Leadership of the Christian Armada Against the Turks, 1345', *Crusades*, 15 (2016), 157–175.

Sermo Anonymus

1. Sermon on the *Dominica quarta in Quadragessima*
   Avignon, Bibliothèque Municipale, MS 295, fols. 50va–52rb.
   Incipit: *Illa que sursum est Iherusalem* [Galates 4.26]; Consuetum est, quod tempus passagium...
   Reference: Schneyer, viii, 59, no. 46.
2. Sermon on the *Dominica quarta in Quadragessima*
   Avignon, Bibliothèque Municipale, MS 295, fols. 52rb–52rb.
   Incipit: *Abiit Ihesus trans mare Galilee quod est Tiberiadis* [Johannes 6.1]...
   Reference: Schneyer, viii, 59, no. 47.

Appendix II
James of Lausanne's sermon on the Fourth Sunday in Lent

P = Paris, Bibliothèque nationale, MS Latin 17516, fols. 84ra–85vb

Dominica quarta in Quadragessima

[1] *Illa que sursum est Iherusalem, libera est*, Galatas 4.[1] Consuetum est quod tempore generalis passagii vel crucesignationis mittuntur aliqui predicatores qui crucem hominibus eam accipere volentibus inponant et volentes ad eam suscipiendam moveant et disponant. Karissimi, tempus crucesignationis e<s>t tempus quadragessime, maxime modo. Tunc enim crux penitentie predicatur et imponitur volentibus transfretare de Egypto in Ierusalem, de servitute peccati in libertatem gratie. Istud figuratum fuit Ezechiel 9:[2] *Transi per mediam civitatem, et signa Thau super frontes virorum gementium et dolentium super cunctis abhominationibus que fiunt Thau*. Que habet figuram crucis, sed inperfecte, designat penitentiam, que est valde imperfecta crux respectu crucis et passionis Christi. Hic significatur modo super frontes virorum gementium et dolentium de peccatis suis, et est signum quod sic[3] significati volunt transfretare de Egypto in Ierusalem, id est de servitute peccati in libertatem gratie.

[2] Qui autem non sunt ad hoc voluntarii inducendi sunt et movendi. Et ecce quomodo quidam ad literam retrahuntur ne transfretent in Terram Sanctam propter periculum vie, qui enim navigant mare enarrent pericula eius; alii propter defectum indulgentie, quando non datur plena indulgentia; alii propter incommoditatem patrie, quia est inquieta propter bella et intemperata.[4] Primi sunt timidi, secundi sunt indevoti, tertii sunt delicati. In opposita autem istorum habent allicere. Et ideo beatus Paulus in epistola hodierna et in verbis assumptis exprimit opposita predictorum ut alliciat quemlibet ad accipiendum crucem penitentie, ut [P 84rb] transeat de Egypto in Ierusalem, de servitute peccati in libertatem gratie, dicens: *Illa que sunt sursum*, et cetera. Ubi secundum predicta facit tria: quia

---

1 Galates 4.26.
2 Ezechiel 9.4.
3 sic] sit P
4 intemperata] intempata P

primo timidis explicat securitatem vie, *que sursum est*; indevotis immensitatem indulgentie, *libera est*; delicatis commoditatem patrie, *Ierusalem*.

[3] Quantum ad primum, sciendum est quod equus[5] qui habet pedes anteriores notabiliter breviores posterioribus nunquam secure descendit, sed valde periculose maxime si currat. Talis tamen equus secure ascendit. Talis equus est homo. Pedes enim quibus homo moraliter fertur sunt cognitio et affectus. Et pedes quidam anteriores sunt cognitio sensitiva et appetitus sensitivus, posteriores vero sunt intellectus et voluntas. Et constat quod anteriores sunt breviores posterioribus, quia ad plura se extendit intellectus et voluntas quam sensus et appetitus sensitivus. Et ideo periculosum est homini descendere deorsum propter precipitium, sed securum est ei ascendere sursum. Descendit autem homo quando intentio eius et affectus tendit in bona temporalia, que sunt infra hominem. Ascendit autem sursum quando intentio eius et affectus tendunt in bona eterna et spiritualia. Et ideo periculosum valde est homini descendere per affectum in temporalia, quia pedes eius anteriores, scilicet sensus et appetitus sensitivus, qui sunt breviores, descendunt ad talia cum impetu. Propter quod vix potest homo evadere casum et precipitationem in peccatum. Sed securum est homini ascendere per intentionem et affectionem ad superna et spiritualia. Ideo dicit apostolus, Colossenses 3:[6] *Que sursum sunt querite ubi Christus est*. Et tan[P 84va]guntur tria de isto ascensu: primo sollicitudo exercitii, *querite*; celsitudo domicilii, *que sursum sunt*; gratitudo consortii, *ubi Christus est*.

[4] Quantum ad primum, notandum quod circa difficiliora et utiliora consuevit adhiberi amplior sollicitudo. Difficillimum est homini in hoc mortali corpore existenti ascendere ad spiritualia et eterna, ymmo impossibile, nisi aliunde iuvetur. Gravia enim de se non ascendunt, *corpus autem quod corrumpitur adgravat animam*, Sapientie 9.[7] Et ideo homo de se non potest ad eterna et spiritualia ascendere. Debet ergo cum omni sollicitudine querere ea que iuvant ad ascensum, que sunt duo: pulsus ab inferiori et tractus a superiori. Quando enim aliquis ab inferiori pellitur et a superiori trahitur, faciliter conscendit. Pellitur <quidem>[8] homo ab inferiori timore gehenne, per quem multi abstinent a peccatis et faciunt quedam bona. Et istud non sufficeret ad ascendendum in paradisum, quia gravia quantumcumque pellantur sursum, nisi sit ibi aliquid ea retinens, iterato descendunt. Sic quantumcumque homo timore gehenne pellatur sursum deserendo mala et faciendo aliqua bona, tamen sursum non stat, sed iterato cadit, nisi amore celestium retineatur et attrahatur. Aliter querere nihil valet· *Delusa est sollicitudo querentis*, Genesis 31.[9] Sed quando homo trahitur amore celestis patrie, tunc bene ascendit, nec cadit, quia fortissimum est vinculum amoris quo ligatur et trahitur. Et ideo Dominus movet nos querere modum ascensus, Luce 12:[10] *Querite*

---

5   equus] equs P
6   Colossenses 3.1.
7   Sapientie 9.15.
8   quidem] quod P
9   Genesis 31.35.
10 Lucas 12.31.

primum regnum Dei. Talibus enim solum porriget Deus manum ad eos trahendum et levandum ad se. [P 84vb] Qui enim ascenderet versa facie deorsum at dorso sursum nec convenienter ascendet, nec mereretur quod existens sursum porrigeret ei manum. Sic est de illo qui dimittit peccare solo timore seu ex consideratione gehenne. Talis enim habet faciem versam deorsum. Solum enim aspicit ad gehennam, cuius timore obmittit peccare. Et per consequens habet dorsum sursum, et ideo non[11] meretur <quod> Deus det ei manum ad levandum eum sursum. Sed quando ex dilectione Dei et ex desiderio paradisi homo dimittit, tunc ascendit versa facie sursum, et ideo meretur quod Deus porrigat ei manum adiutorii sui ad levandum eum ad se. Quod figuratum fuit <II Regum>[12] 10,[13] ubi legitur quod Hieu dixit ad Ionadab: *Numquid est cor tuum cum corde meo, sicut cor meum est cum corde tuo? Qui ait est.* At ille: *Si est, inquit, da manum tuam. Qui dedit ei manum suam. At ille levavit eum ad se.* Hieu qui inter ipse est, est Christus, qui dixit Exodi 3:[14] *Ego sum qui sum. Qui est, misit me ad vos.* Ionadab, qui inter obediens Domino signat penitentem qui habet rectum cor cum Deo, quando detestatur peccatum amore Dei et celestis patrie, huic Deus porrigit manum et levat eum ad se. De hoc Deuteronomiorum 33:[15] *Ascensor celi, auxiliator tuus, habitaculum eius sursum.*

[5] In quo innuitur secundum, scilicet celsitudo domicilii, de quo facit sapiens Ecclesiasticus tertio[16] talem questionem: *Quis novit si spiritus filiorum Adam ascendat sursum?* Cui respondeo quod filii Adam per ymitationem culpe non ascendunt. Si enim ipse propter culpam eiectus est de sursum, hoc est de [P 85ra] paradiso terrestri, imittatores eius illuc non ascendunt, et multo minus ad celestem. Et quamvis omnes peccantes in hoc sint eis similes, tamen specialiter non ieiunantes. Unde Augustinus: 'Qui hoc ieiunium non observat, cibum vetitum manducat'. Et tales sunt filii Adam per ymitationem,[17] qui non ascendunt sursum, sed remanent deorsum, similes illi mulieri de qua dicit Luce 13[18] quod: *Non poterat sursum respicere.* Sed filii Adam per naturam et non per ymitationem in culpa ascendunt sursum, et isti sunt pauci et abiecti in hoc mundo. Et iustum est quod Deus illos plus elevet sursum qui in hoc[19] mundo magis deprimuntur et abiecti fiunt propter ipsum.

[6] *Quia reliquum fuerit, de Juda mittet*[20] *radices deorsum et faciet fructum sursum,*[21] ubi Christus est: ecce gratitudo consortii. Christus enim inter unctus et

---

11 non *supralin.* P
12 <ii regum>] *lacuna* P
13 II Regum 10.15.
14 Exodi 3.14.
15 Deuteronomiorum 33.26, 27.
16 Ecclesiasticus 3.21.
17 ymitationem] qua dixit Luce 13 *add. et del. per homoioteleuton* P
18 Lucas 13.11.
19 in hoc] inhoc P
20 mittet] mitcet P
21 Isaie 37.31.

beatus Bernardus dicit quod: *Non sine²² unctione venit Christus*.²³ Ipse enim est in quo est omnis gratia qui ita transfert affectum eorum qui cum eo sunt in se ipsum, ut quasi non meminerit sui, sed Christi. Unde Apostolus Galatas secundo:²⁴ *Vivo ego, iam non ego, vivit vero in me Christus*. Unusquisque autem vitam suam reputat illud in quo maxime delectatur. Si ergo existens cum Christo vitam suam reputat vitam Christi, planum est quod talis in Christo maxime delectatur et consolatur, Corinthios primo:²⁵ *Per Christum habundat consolatio nostra*.

[7] Secundo indevotis explicat indulgentiam, *libera est*. Ad litteram crucesignati²⁶ gaudent multis li[P 85rb]bertatibus quibus alii non gaudent. Sic accipientes crucem penitentie gaudent multis libertatibus quibus peccatores impenitentes non gaudent. Et sunt tres libertates seu tria privilegia: primum est quod spurius legittimatur; secundum est quod deffenditur citatus; tertium est quod absolvitur²⁷ excommunicatus.

[8] Quantum ad primum, sciendum quod peccator quasi spurius est. Spurius enim proprie est qui extante matrimonio et vivente uxore legittima generatur ex alia. Talis secundum rigorem iuris non debet ali<mentari>²⁸ de bonis patris, nec habet actionem ad hoc. Quamvis de benignitate canonis paternis bonis sustentetur, secundum autem omnia iura paterna hereditate privatur. Sic peccator qui peccando non sequitur rationem, que debet esse vera domina in toto homine, sed concupiscentiam, que debet esse ancilla, spurius est. Nec debet secundum rigorem iuris nutriri bonis que Deus creavit, quia secundum Augustinum peccator non est dignus pane quo nescitur, et privatur²⁹ hereditate celesti. *Non enim erit heres filius ancille*, Galatas 4.³⁰ Sed per crucem penitentie legittimatur ut sit heres hereditatis celestis, Mathei:³¹ *Penitentiam agite, appropinquabit enim regnum celorum*. Unde possunt dicere illud Galatas 4:³² *Iam non sumus filii ancille, sed libere, qua libertate Christus nos liberavit*. Sed notandum quod papa³³ legittimans aliquem in spiritualibus videtur eum legittimare in temporalibus, saltem in terris iuriditioni sue subiectis. Sic Christus legittimans peccatorem per penitentiam legittimat ipsum in spiritualibus, sed in temporalibus non in presenti, quia hic non est [P 85va] terra Christo subiecta, Iohannis 19:³⁴ *Regnum meum non est de hoc*

---

22 sine *add. in mg.* P
23 Sermo in vigilia Nativitatis Domini, see Sancti Bernardi, Abbatis Primi Cleraevallensis, Opera Genuina, 3 vols. (Paris: Monks of Saint Benedict, 1833–1835), ii, 141–144.
24 Galatas 2.20.
25 II Corinthios 1.5.
26 crucesignati] cruce signati P
27 absolvitur] ab solvitur P
28 ali<mentari>] ali + *lacuna* P
29 et privatur *inv.* P
30 Galatas 4.30.
31 Mathei 3.2.
32 Galatas 4.31.
33 papa] ipsa *a.c.* P
34 Johannes 18.36.

mundo, sed in terra[35] *viventium, in qua creatura liberabitur a servitute corruptionis*[36] *in libertatem glorie filii Dei*, Romanos 8.[37]

[9] Secunda libertas seu secundum privilegium accipientium crucem penitentie est quod citatus deffenditur. Quandoque datur crucesignatis privilegium quod coram quocumque citentur non teneantur respondere, dum tamen compareant coram ordinario suo et sattisfaciant[38] ad arbitrium eius. Omnes peccatores citati sunt ad tribunal Christi, nec recipiant sentenciam dampnationis ad instantiam pessimi adversarii dyaboli, *qui vocatur accusator fratrum*, Apocalypsis 12.[39] Ab ista citatione liberantur accipientes crucem penitentie, dummodo satti<s>faciant ad arbitrium sui ordinarii, scilicet conscientie sue, Corinthios 11:[40] *Si nosmet ipsos diiudicaremus, non utique iudicaremur*, vel ad arbitrium sacerdotis, Proverbiorum 6:[41] *Fac quod dico et libera animam tuam*.

[10] Tertia libertas seu tertium privilegium est quod excomunicatus absolvitur. Omnis qui facit contra caritatem peccando mortaliter excommunicatus est iure divino, Corinthios ultimo:[42] *Si quis*[43] *non amat Dominum nostrum Ihesum Christum, sit anathema*. Accipientes autem crucem penitentie absolvuntur ab isto anathemate. Unde Job 33[44] dicit de peccatore sed penitente: *Dicet: peccavi et vere deliqui, et ut dignus eram, non accepi. Liberavit enim animam suam, ne pergeret in interitum*. De hoc eodem dicitur Iohannis 8:[45] *Si manseritis in sermone meo, vere liberi eritis*, illa libertate de qua dicitur Romanos 6:[46] *Liberati a peccato*, [P 85vb] *servi autem facti Deo, habetis fructum vestrum in sanctificationem, finem vero vitam eternam*, Amen.

---

35 in terra] interra P
36 corruptionis *corr.e* correctionis P
37 Romanos 8.21.
38 sattisfaciant] satcifaciant P
39 Apocalypsis 12.10.
40 I Corinthios 11.31.
41 Proverbiorum 6.3.
42 I Corinthios 16.22.
43 si quis] siquis P
44 Job 33.27.
45 Johannes 8.31.
46 Romanos 6.22.

Appendix III
Pierre Roger's crusade sermon at the papal chapel in Avignon, 19 February 1332

G = Paris, Bibliothèque Sainte Geneviéve, MS 240, fols. 290vb–298va
F = Paris, Bibliothèque nationale de France, MS lat. 3293, fols. 161rb–168rb
Rubric in G 290vb: **Collatio facta per dominum Clementem sextum pro passagio faciendo.**
Rubric in F 161rb: **Sermo de passagio regis Francie.**

[1] *Faciem suam firmavit ut iret Iherusalem*[1] *et misit nuncios*, [G 291ra] Luce 9.[2] Videtur michi quod, ad hoc quod aliquis opus [F 161va] aliquod[3] virtuose exerceat, requiruntur tria: clara cognitio ad consiliandum, recta electio ad acceptandum, firma immobilitatio ad perseverandum. Et quod[4] hec tria requirantur[5] dicit Philosophus secundo *Ethicorum*,[6] ostendens quod, ad hoc quod aliquis ex habitu operetur, oportet quod sit[7] sciens et eligens et firmiter et immobiliter operetur. Unde et prima duo satis probantur per primam diffinitionem virtutis,[8] quam ibi ponit dicens:[9] 'Virtus est habitus electivus in medietate consistens, prout sapiens et recta ratio determinabunt'. Tercium satis probatur per secundam diffinitionem ibi datam de virtute,[10] que est quod 'virtus est que[11] habentem perficit, et eius opus bonum reddit'. Unde ante acquisitionem virtutis, et si agit bona, non tamen bene, quia vero firmiter et immutabiliter,[12] delectabiliter et faciliter. Et quod hec conditio tercia requiratur patet etiam per sanctos. Unde Gregorius, primo *Moralium*:[13]

---

1 Iherusalem] Ierusalem F
2 Lucas 9.51.; Luce *add. in mg.* G
3 aliquod] opus virtuose *add. in mg.* F, G
4 quod *s.l.* F
5 requirantur] requiruntur F; philosophus *add. in mg.* G
6 Ethicorum] Heticorum F
7 sit *om.* F
8 virtutis] q *add. et del.* G
9 Aristoteles Latinus: Ethica Nicomachea, ed. R. A. Gauthier, 5 vols. (Leiden: Brill, 1972–1974), 3:167, Lib.II, §6.
10 ibi datam de virtute *inv.* G; Aristotelis, Eth. Nic., II.5.1106a, 15–17
11 est que *om.* F
12 immutabiliter] et immobiliter *add.* G
13 *Sancti Gregorii Magni Moralia in Iob*, ed. M. Adriaen, 3 vols. (Turnhout: Brepols, 1979–1985), 1:55, Lib.I, §37; Gregorius *add. in mg.* G

'Incassum[14] bene agitur si ante vite terminum deseratur; frustra enim velociter currit, qui prius quam[15] ad metas venerit,[16] deficit.' Et Bernardus, in quadam epistola, dicit:[17]

> Sive perseverantia nec qui pugnat victoriam, nec palmam victor consequitur. Hec est nutrix ad[18] meritum, mediatrix ad premium. Soror patientie, filia constantie, amica pacis, amicitiarum nodus, unanimitatis vinculum, sanctitatis propugnaculum.[19] Tolle perseve[G 291rb]rantiam, nec obsequium mercedem habet, nec beneficium gratiam, nec laudem fortitudo. Perseverantia sola est cui eternitas redditur, vel que potius eternitati hominem reddit, dicente Domino: *qui perseveraverit usque in finem hic salvus erit.*[20]

Ideo sapiens Ecclesiastici 5:[21] *Esto firmus in via Domini*, et illa sancta Iudith, octavo capitulo, dicebat:[22] *Orate ut firmum faci*[F 161vb]*at consilium meum Deus.*

[2] Modo, pater sanctissime, devotissimus filius vester rex Francie, qui nos, sanctitatis vestre servos, ad pedes eiusdem[23] sanctitudinis suos nuncios destinavit, Spiritu Sancto instigatus, de[24] divino auxilio confisus, de vestro et Ecclesie consilio, adiutorio et patrocinio non dubius, devotione motus, vestra salubri exhortatione admonitus, prelatorum et baronum suorum et etiam domini patriarche instantia oportune et importune pulsatus, et[25] etiam voto et obligatione et crucis assumptione astrictus, predecessorum suorum inherendo vestigiis, sicut alias[26] sanctitati vestre scripsit, opus grande, opus meritorium, opus valde virtuosum, opus omni laude dignissimum assumpsit,[27] videlicet[28] ire[29] personaliter in Iherusalem et Terram Sanctam[30] Christi sanguine consecratam sepulchrumque[31] dominicum de impiorum et blasphemorum manibus liberare.

---

14 incassum] in cassum G
15 prius quam] antequam F
16 venerit] pervenerit F
17 'Epistolae: Corpus Epistolarum', in *Sancti Bernardi Opera*, eds. Jean Leclercq and Henri-Marie Rochais, 8 vols. (Rome: Editiones Cistercienses, 1957–1977), 7:323, epist.129.2; Bernardus *add. in mg.* G
18 ad] pre *del.* G
19 sanctitatis propugnaculum *om.* G
20 Mattheus 24.13.
21 Ecclesiasticus 5.12.; Ecclesiasticus *add in mg.* G
22 Iudith 8.31.; Iudith *add in mg.* G
23 eiusdem] sanctitatis sive *add* G
24 de] et G
25 et] est G
26 alias] g *add. et del.* G
27 dignissimum assumpsit *inv.* F
28 videlicet *om.* F
29 ire *om.* G
30 sanctam] et *add.* G
31 sepulchrumque] sepulchrum que F

[3] Quod quidem opus tanto virtuosius ostenditur quanto ex ipso opere difficilius esse censetur. Difficultas enim in opere auget rationem [G 291va] virtutis, ut dicit Philosophus[32] secundo *Ethicorum*. Unde potest dici illud primo[33] Paralipomenon 29:[34] *Opus grande est nec enim homini preparatur habitatio, sed Deo*, et Neemie 4:[35] *Opus grande est et latum*; Et sequitur paucis interpositis:[36] *Deus noster pugnabit pro nobis. Et nos ipsi*[37] *faciemus opus*, ut dicat dominus rex[38] divino fretus auxilio illud Exodi 34:[39] *Cernat populus iste in cuius es medio opus domini terribile quod facturus sum*; Et sequitur:[40] *ego ipse eiciam*[41] *ante faciem tuam Amorreum et Chananeum*,[42] *Etheum et Frerezeum*,[43] *Eveum et Iebuseum*; Ad litteram isti tenebant tunc Terram Sanctam occupatam. Opus ergo tam grande et tam virtuosum assumpsit.

[4] Sed quia, ut supra [F 162ra] dictum est, ad hoc quod opus fiat virtuose, requiritur firmitas et immobilitatio, ideo non solum assumpsit, non solum concepit, quia sicut dicitur Proverbiorum 11:[44] *Impius facit opus instabile*, sed firmavit immutabiliter, dicens cum Apostolo, ad Philippenses primo:[45] *Confidens hoc ipsum, quod*[46] *qui cepit opus bonum ipse perficiet*. Et hoc dicunt verba thematis preassumpta: *Faciem suam firmavit ut iret*[47] *Iherusalem et misit nuncios*. In quibus verbis tanguntur tria que in bona assumptione[48] cuiuslibet negotii requiruntur. Requiritur[49] enim aliquid ex parte intellectus, aliquid ex parte affectus, aliquid ex parte effectus. [G 291vb] Ex parte intellectus requiritur consideratio et intelligentia evidens, que in negotio conspiciat bonitatis preconium virtuosum. Ex parte affectus requiritur delectatio et complacentia demulcens, alliciens, vinciens, que in negotio adiciat[50] caritatis incendium copiosum. Ex parte effectus[51] requiritur executio et vigilantia seu providentia diligens, que pro negotio compariat oportunitatis auxilium et consilium fructuosum.

32 philosophus] in *add.* F; Philosophus *add in mg.* G
33 primo] primi G
34 29] 19 *a.c.* G; I Paralipomenon 29.1.; Paralipomenon *add in mg.* G
35 Neemie 4.19.; Neemie *add. in mg.* G
36 II Ezra 4.20–21.
37 nos ipsi] nosipsi G
38 rex] domino *add.* G
39 Exodus 34.10.; Exodus *add. in mg.* G
40 Exodus 34.11.
41 eiciam] etiam G
42 Chananeum] Cananeum F
43 Frerezeum] Ferezeum F
44 Proverbia 11.18.; Proverbiorum *add in mg.* G
45 Philippenses 1.6.
46 quod *om.* G
47 iret] in *add. et del.* G
48 assumptione] assuptione G
49 requiritur] tria *add.* F
50 adiciat] addiciat G
51 effectus] affectus *a.c.* G

204 Appendix III

[5] Modo videtur michi quod, ut dicunt verba thematis preassumpta, in negotio per dominum regem assumpto[52] ista tria reperimus evidenter. Primo enim ex parte intellectus conspicitur in negotii assumptione[53] sanctitatis et iustitie irrefragabile fundamentum, quia[54] *ut iret Iherusalem*. Secundo ex parte affectus adicitur[55] in negotii prosecutione firmitatis et constantie immutabile seu invariabile[56] fulcimentum, [F 162rb] quia *faciem suam firmavit*. Tertio ex parte effectus petitur necessitatis seu oportunitatis et exigentie indefectibile iuvamentum, quia ideo *misit nuncios*.

[6] Dico ergo primo quod in virtuosa cuiuslibet negotii assumptione requiritur ex parte intellectus consideratio et intelligentia evidens, que in negotio conspiciat bonitatis preconium virtuosum. Ideo hic primo conspicitur in negotii assumptione sanctitatis et iustitie irrefragabile fundamentum, quia *ut iret*[57] *Iherusalem*. Ad litteram hoc[58] negotium quod assump[G 292ra]sit est ut vadat in Iherusalem non ad peregrinandum[59] solum, sed ad ipsam et totam Terram[60] Sanctam liberandum. De nobilitate cuius civitatis loquitur[61] pulchre beatus[62] Bernardus in libello suo *De laude nove*[63] *militie Templi*, dicens[64] sic:[65]

> Salve civitas Sancta, quam ipse sanctificavit sibi tabernaculum suum Altissimus, quo tanta in te et per te generatio salvaretur. Salve civitas[66] Regis magni, ex qua nova et iocunda mundo miracula nullis pene ab initio defuere temporibus. Salve domina gentium, princeps provinciarum, Patriarcharum, Prophetarum mater et Apostolorum, initiatrix fidei, gloria populi Christiani, quam Deus semper a principio propterea passus est[67] oppugnari, ut viris fortibus sicut virtutis, ita foret occasio et[68] salutis. Salve terra promissionis, que olim fluens lac et mel tuis dumtaxat habitatoribus, nunc universo orbi remedia salutis, vite porrigis alimenta. Terra, inquam, bona et optima, que in fecundissimo illo sinu tuo ex archa paterni cordis celeste granum suscipiens,

---

52 assumpto] assupto G; divisio thematis *add. in mg.* G
53 assumptione] assuptione G
54 quia] q *add. et del.* F
55 adicitur] addicitur G
56 invariabile] inevariabile *a.c.* G
57 iret] in *add. et del.* G
58 hoc *om.* F
59 non ad peregrinandum] ad peregrinandum non G
60 terram] civitas Iherusalem *add. in mg.* F
61 loquitur] dicit G; Bernardus *add. in mg.* G
62 pulchre beatus *om.* G
63 nove] Caritas Iherusalem *add. in mg.* G
64 dicens *om.* G
65 'Liber ad Milites Templi: De laude nove Militie', in *Sancti Bernardi Opera*, eds. Jean Leclercq and Henri-Marie Rochais, 8 vols. (Rome: Editiones Cistercienses, 1957–1977), 3:223–224, cap.v, §11.
66 civitas] s *add. et del.* G
67 propterea passus est *inv.* G
68 et *om.* G

tantas ex superno semine martirum segetes protulisti, et nichilominus ex omni reliquo fidelium genere fructum fertilis [F 162va] gleba tricesimum, et sexagesimum, et centesimum, super omnem terram multipliciter procreasti. Unde et de magna multitudine dulcedinis tue iocundissime[69] satiati et opulentissime saginati, memoriam suavitatis tue ubique eructuant[70] qui te viderunt, et usque ad extremum terre magnificentiam glorie tue loquuntur[71] [G 292rb] eis qui te non viderunt,[72] et enarrant mirabilia que in te fuint. *Gloriosa dicta sunt de te, civitas Dei.*

[7] Sed tunc,[73] propter peccata[74] nostra et in magnum improperium totius populi Christiani, tanta nobilitas conversa est in ignominiam. Unde verificatur illud Trenorum primo:[75] *Peccatum peccavit*[76] *Iherusalem; propterea instabilis facta est. Omnes qui glorificabant eam spreverunt eam quia viderunt ignominiam eius.* Ideo lamentando dicebat Jeremias in principio 'Libri Trenorum':[77] *Quomodo sedet sola civitas plena populo, facta est quasi vidua domina gentium, princeps provinciarum*[78] *facta est sub tributo,* et cetera. Unde dicere possumus – proch dolor– quod scribitur ibidem in ultimo capitulo:[79] *Defecit gaudium cordis nostri, versus est in luctum chorus noster. Cecidit*[80] *corona capitis*[81] *nostri, ve nobis, quia peccavimus,*[82] *propterea mestum factum est cor nostrum, ideo contenebrati*[83] *sunt oculi nostri propter montem Syon quia disperiit, vulpes ambulaverunt in eo*, vulpes ille ad litteram de quibus dicitur Canticorum 2:[84] *Capite nobis*[85] *vulpes parvulas que demoliuntur vineas*. Unde tantam ignominiam populi sui videns, ille sanctus Mathathias primo Machabeorum 2 dicebat:[86] *Ecce sancta*[87] *nostra,*[88] *ecce*[89] *pulchritudo nostra,*[90] *ecce claritas nostra desolata est,*

69 iocundissime] saginati et *add. et del.* G
70 eructuant] eructant G; eructavit *a.c.* G
71 loquuntur] locuntur G
72 non viderunt *inv.* G
73 tunc] nunc F; semper *add.* F
74 peccata] pecata G
75 Lamentationes 1.8.; Trenorum *add. in mg.* G
76 peccavit] pecavit G
77 Lamentationes 1.1.; Trenorum *add. in mg.* G
78 provinciarum] proviciarum G
79 ibidem in ultimo capitulo] in ultimo capitulo ibidem G; Lamentationes 5.15–18.
80 cecidit] uccidit G
81 capitis] n *add. et del.* F
82 peccavimus] et *add.* G
83 contenebrati] obtenebrati G
84 Canticum Canticorum 2.15.; Canticorum *add. in mg.* G
85 nobis] vobis G
86 I Machabeorum 2.12–13.; Machabeorum *add.in mg.* G
87 sancta] sanctitas G
88 nostra] vestra F
89 ecce] ecclesie F
90 nostra] vestra F

206   Appendix III

et coinquinabant eam gentes. Quid ergo nobis adhuc[91] *vivere? Quoniam dicat melius est mori* [F 162vb] *quam vivere, melius est enim mori in bello, quam videre* [G 292 va] *mala gentis nostre*[92] *et sanctorum,* primo Machabeorum 3.[93] Unde ista videntes[94] illi[95] fortissimi Machabei,[96] sicut dicitur II Machabeorum 15:[97] *Statuerunt dimicare fortiter eo quod civitas Sancta periclitabatur. Erat enim pro uxoribus et filiis, itemque quod fratribus et*[98] *cognatis, minor solicitudo, maximus vero et primus pro*[99] *sanctitate timor erat templi.* Unde videte quod, ut apparet ex textu, magis statuerunt dimicare pro templi et locorum sanctorum conservatione et maior erat[100] de hoc sollicitudo et timor quam de perditione uxorum et filiorum, fratrum et cognatorum. Nec mirum,[101] quia, sicut etiam[102] dicitur primo[103] Regum 4,[104] Hely sacerdos, audita morte duorum filiorum suorum et captione arche Dei, et etiam uxor Phinees,[105] audita morte[106] mariti et soceri, plus de captione arche doluerunt quam ille de morte filiorum et illa de morte mariti et soceri.[107] Unde[108] dixit illa:[109] *Translata est*[110] *gloria de Israhel, quia capta est archa Dei.*

[8] Quid ergo debemus facere nos Christiani, qui videmus et templum Domini– cuius gloria fuit maior quam templi Salomonis, non ex edificatione murorum aut ornatu seu apparatu scutorum aureorum, sed pro eo quod illud intravit desideratus cunctis gentibus, sicut dicitur Aggei 2:[111] *Veniet desideratus cunctis gentibus et implebo domum istam gloria,* et sequitur,[112] *magna erit domus istius novissime plus quam*[113] *prime*– gloriosumque sepulchrum do[G 292 vb]minicum et sanctam civitatem Vethleem in qua Christus natus est, in qua nutritus est, Vallem Iosaphat in qua Beata Maria [F 163ra] sepulta est et in qua Christus nos omnes iudicaturus

---

91   adhuc] ad huc F
92   nostre] vestre F
93   primo] primi G; I Machabeorum 3.59.; Machabeorum *add in mg.* G
94   videntes] vidente G
95   illi] isti G
96   Machabei] templum bellare *add. in mg.* F
97   II Machabeorum 15.17–18.; Machabeorum *add. in mg.* G
98   et *s.l.* F
99   pro] bellare pro templo *add. in mg.* G
100 erat *om.* F
101 mirum] virum *a.c. in mg.* F
102 etiam] Regum *add. in mg.* G
103 primo] primi G
104 I Samuelis 4.19.
105 Phinees] Finees F
106 morte] m *add. et del.* F
107 mariti et soceri *inv.* G
108 unde] Christiani preliari pro Iherusalem G
109 I Samuelis 4.21.
110 est] Christiani/ Terra Sancta *add in mg.* F
111 Aggeus 2.8.; Aggeus *add in mg.* G
112 Aggeus 2.10.
113 plus quam] plusquam F

est, quinymmo totam terram illam in qua tam dulciter cum hominibus conversatus est, in qua dura verba, duriora verbera, durissima crucis tormenta pro nobis passus est, esse reducta sub servitute blasphemantium[114] nominenque[115] Christiane religionis[116] substracta?[117] Certe multo fortius debemus statuere, dimicare fortiter et eligere mori potius quam tanta mala videre. Ideo dicebat propheta Jeremias 51 capitulo sic:[118] *Recordamini procul Domini, et Iherusalem*[119] *ascendat super cor vestrum. Confusi sumus quoniam audivimus opprobrium,*[120] *et operuit*[121] *ignominia facies nostras, quia venerunt alieni super sanctificationem domus Domini.*

[9] Unde Urbanus[122] papa in Concilio Claromontensi in quodam sermone quem fecit dicebat sic:[123]

> Iherusalem,[124] ipsa civitas, in qua, Christus ipse pro nobis passus est, peccatis nostris exigentibus, sub potentia Sarracenorum redacta, divine servituti ad ignominiam totius populi Christiani subducta est. Cui servit nunc ecclesia beate Marie, in qua ipsa sepulta fuit in valle Josaphat. Sed quid de templo Salomonis, ymmo Domini dicemus[125] cum testante propheta: *Ultio domini sit, ultio templi sui,* Jeremie 51,[126] quid, inquam, dicemus[127] nisi, *Deus, venerunt gentes in hereditatem tuam,* [G 293 ra] *polluerunt templum sanctum tuum, posuerunt*[128] *Iherusalem,*[129] et cetera.[130] Cogitantibus autem nobis de sepulchro[131] dominico magis libet flere quam aliquid dicere. In eo enim requievit Deus, in eo mortuus est, in eo sepultus est. O quam preciosus locus sepulchri[132] dominici, locus, inquam,[133] concupiscibilis, locus incomparabilis, in [F 163rb] quo adhuc Deus annuum non pretermittit facere miraculum, cum in die passionis sue, extinctis omnibus

---

114 blasphemantium] blasphematium G
115 nomineque] nomenque G; et *add*. F, G
116 christiane religionis] christiana religio G
117 substracta] substrata F
118 Jieremias 51.50–51.; Jeremias *add. in mg*. G
119 Iherusalem] Ierusalem F
120 opprobrium] obproprium F
121 operuit] opperuit F
122 Urbanus] Urbanus *add. in mg*. G
123 'Baldrici, Episcopis Dolensis, Historia Jerosolimitana', in *Recueil des Historiens des Croisades: Historiens Occidentaux. Tome quatrième* (Paris: Imprimerie Nationale, 1844–1895), 13–14.
124 Iherusalem] Ierusalem F
125 dicemus] c *add. et del*. G
126 Jieremias 51.11.; Jeremie *add. in mg*. G
127 dicemus *in mg*. F
128 posuerunt] ieh *add. et del*. F
129 Psalmi 79.1.; Iherusalem] Ierusalem F
130 et cetera *s.l*. F
131 sepulchro] sepulcro F
132 sepulchri] sepulcri F
133 inquam] in quam F

et in sepulchro et in ecclesia circumcirca luminibus, iubare divino lampade extincte[134] reaccenduntur. Sed quid de tota Terra Sancta dicemus nisi quod scriptum est primo[135] Machabeorum 2:[136] *Sancta in manu extraneorum facta sunt, templum eius sicut homo ignobilis?*[137] Terram autem[138] Sanctam merito dixerimus in qua[139] non est etiam passus pedis quem non illustraverit et sanctificaverit vel corpus vel umbra salvatoris, vel gloriosa presentia Sancte Dei genitricis, vel amplectendus apostolorum cetus, vel martirum ebibendus[140] sanguis effusus.

[10] Et[141] certe, licet omnes Christiani ad hoc debeant merito animari,[142] tamen viri ecclesiastici multo fortius, Ysaie 33:[143] *Ecce*[144] *videntes clamabunt angeli pacis amare flebunt.* Angeli[145] pacis sunt[146] dominus noster supremus angelus in ecclesiastica ierarchia, vosque[147] domini[148] mei domini cardinales et ceteri prelati ecclesiarum, qui quidem debent esse sicut angeli propter puritatem in vita, propter claritatem in intelligentia, propter fecundi[G 293 rb]tatem et utilitatem in doctrina, propter felicitatem in gregis dominici custodia, propter assiduitatem in laude et contemplatione divina, propter firmitatem in bona[149] perseverantia. Isti ergo angeli *videntes clamabunt foris*[150] *et flebunt amare*,[151] ymmo amarissime. Flebunt enim ex amore, flebunt ex dolore, flebunt ex labore,[152] flebunt ex timore, que sunt quatuor cause fletus. Unde rationem istius fletus Ysaias subjungit statim dicens:[153] *Angeli pacis amare flebunt. Dis*[F 163va]*sipate sunt vie, cessavit transiens per semitam,*[154] *irritum factum est pactum, proiecit civitates, non reputavit homines. Luxit et clanguit terram,*[155] *confusus est Libanus et absorbuit et factus est Saron*

---

134 extincte] ex tincte F
135 primo] primi G
136 I Machabeorum 2.8.; Machabeorum *add. in mg.* G
137 ignobilis] ingnobilis F
138 autem] etiam G
139 qua] et *add.* F
140 ebibendus] obediens G
141 et] in *add. et del.* F
142 animari] annuere G, *a.c. in mg.* F
143 Isaias 33.7.; Isaie *add. in mg.* G
144 ecce] cla *add. et del.* G
145 angeli] prelati angeli *add. in mg.* G
146 sunt *in mg.* F
147 vosque] vos que F
148 domini] mei domini *add. et del.* F, *add.* G; prelati angeli *add. in mg.* F
149 bona] boni F
150 foris] fortiter F
151 Isaias 33.7.
152 labore] flebunt ex labore *om. per homoioteleuton* F; flebunt ex labore *a.m. add. in mg.* F
153 Isaias 33.7–10.
154 semitam] sentatam *a.c. in mg.* F
155 terram] terra F

sicut desertum, et concussa est Basan, et Carmelus, sed,[156] *nunc*[157] *exurgam dicit dominus, rex nunc exultabor,*[158] *et nunc sublimabor.*[159] Unde potest dicere idem rex illud Zachariae primo:[160] *Zelatus sum Iherusalem*[161] *et Syon zelo magno, et ira magna ego irascor super*[162] *gentes opulentas*; et in Psalmo:[163] *Zelus domus tue comedit me, et opprobria*[164] *exprobrantium tibi ceciderunt super me*; ut de eo accipiamus illud Sapientie quinto:[165] *Accipiat*[166] *armaturam zelus illius,*[167] *et armabit creaturam ad ultionem inimicorum,* ut cum divino auxilio possit dicere civitati Iherusalem[168] sic desolate[169] et derelicte illud quod scribitur Ysaie 62:[170] *Non vocaberis ultra derelicta, et terra tua non vocabitur amplius desolata,* [G 293 va] *sed vocaberis voluntas mea in ea, et terra tua inhabitabitur, quia complacuit Domino in te et terra tua inhabitabitur.*[171] *Inhabitabit enim iuvenis cum virgine, et habitabunt in te filii tui, et gaudebit sponsus super sponsam, et gaudebit super te Deus tuus. Super muros tuos Ierusalem constitui custodes,*[172] *tota die et tota nocte perpetuo non tacebunt. Qui reminiscimini*[173] *Deum, ne taceatis, et ne detis silentium ei, donec stabiliat et donec ponat Iherusalem*[174] *laudem in terra*; et sequitur in fine capituli:[175] *tu vocaberis civitas quesita et non derelicta.*

[11] Patet ergo quomodo in negotii istius assumptione est[176] sanctitatis et iustitie irrefragabile fundamentum, quia *firmavit faciem suam ut iret Iherusalem,*[177] [F 163vb] ut dicamus de domino rege quod ibidem scriptum est, scilicet, Luce 9:[178] *Facies eius erat*[179] *euntis in Iherusalem.* Quod autem istud negotium habeat sanctitatis et iustitie irrefragabile fundamentum posset persuaderi una ratione que talis est: illud negotium habet sanctitatis et iustitie irrefragabile fundamentum quod

---

156 sed] tu *add. et del.* G
157 nunc] nimis *a.c. in mg.* F
158 exultabor] exaltabor F
159 Psalmi 11.6.; Isaias 33.11.
160 Zacharias 1.14–15.; Zacharie *add. in mg.* G
161 Iherusalem] Ierusalem F
162 super] supra F
163 Psalmi 69.10.
164 opprobria] obprobria F
165 quinto] vero *a.c. in mg.* F; Sapientia 5.18.; Sapientie *add. in mg.* G
166 accipiat] accipiet F
167 illius] illo *a.c.* F
168 Iherusalem] Ierusalem F
169 desolate] desolute G
170 Isaias 62.4–7.; Isaie *add in mg.* G
171 quia complacuit...inhabitabitur *om. per homoioteleuton* G
172 constitui custodes *inv.* G
173 reminiscimini] reminiscemini G
174 Iherusalem] Ierusalem F
175 Isaias 62.12.
176 est] fuit G
177 Iherusalem] Ierusalem F
178 Lucas 9.53.; Luce *add in mg.* G
179 erat] scilicet *add.* G

habet bonitatis preconium virtuosum, quod imperat fidei sinceritas, spei soliditas, Dei et proximi caritas, sani consilii veritas, recti iudicii equitas, virilis animi strenuitas, cordis et corporis sobrii puritas; negotium assumptum per dominum regem est huiusmodi; ergo, et cetera. Maior est evidens, quia actus imperatus a virtutibus theologicis et cardinalibus est totus virtuosus, totus bonus, et to[G 293 vb]tus sanctus. Sed minor habet septem partes secundum septem virtutes[180] a quibus actus iste dicitur imperatus – quam possem[181] probare inducendo in qualibet virtute, sed quia in per[182] se notis non est insistendum, et[183] causa brevitatis, ista sufficiunt de primo membro principali.

[12] Dico secundo quod,[184] quia in virtuosa alicuius negotii assumptione ex parte affectus requiritur delectatio et complacentia demulciens, alliciens, vinciens, que in negotio adiciat caritatis incendium copiosum, ideo hic[185] adicitur pro negotii ipsius[186] prosecutione firmitatis et constantie[187] invariabile et immutabile fulcimentum, quia[188] dicitur in themate, *firmavit*. Quod autem *firmavit* habeo quinque argumenta vel signa satis clara:[189] primum est Spiritus Sancti urgens stimulatio ad assumendum faciliter. Secundum est subiecti patens dispositio ad exequendum utiliter. Tertium est concepti propositi perseverans con[F 164ra]tinuatio ad prosequendum viriliter. Quartum est medii conveniens preparatio ad exequendum feliciter. Quintum est temporis congrui interpellatio[190] ad insistendum celeriter.

[13] Dico ergo primo quod probat firmitatem istius negotii Spiritus Sancti urgens stimulatio[191] ad assumendum faciliter. Differentia est inter opera hominum et Dei, quia opera hominum sunt variabilia, sed opera Dei sunt firma et stabilia. Unde Actuum 5 dixit ille Gamaliel doctor legis:[192] *Si ex hominibus est hoc consilium aut opus dissolvetur, si vero* [G 294 ra] *ex Deo est, non poteritis dissolvere, ne forte et Deo repugnare videamini*. Modo istud negotium fecit faciliter assumere dominum regem Spiritus Sancti urgens stimulatio. Nota modum: cum enim quadam die Veneris dominus rex prelatos et barones suos[193] Parisius et alibi pro arduis regni sui negotiis[194] convocasset, dominus patriarcha Iherosolimitanus affuit, et regem obnixe rogavit ut coram tot valentibus vellet sibi dare audientiam

180 septem virtutes *inv.* G
181 possem] possum G
182 per *om.* F
183 et *om.* G
184 quod] quid F
185 hic] hoc *a.c.* G
186 ipsius *om.* F
187 constantie] argumenta firmari *add. in mg.* F
188 quia] quod F
189 clara] firmitas argumenta *add. in mg.* G
190 interpellatio] interpalatio G
191 stimulatio] stipulo *a.c. in mg.* F
192 Recte Actus 5.38–39.; Actuum *add. in mg.* G
193 prelatos et barones suos] prelatos suos et barones G
194 pro...negotiis] pro diversis regni sui negotiis arduis G

Appendix III 211

super negotio Christi. Qui ibidem proposuit multa, propter que[195] rex tenebatur ad passagium assumendum. Consequenter[196] omnes prelati numero xxvi hoc idem multis rationibus ostenderunt baronesque consimiliter, ipsum obsecrantes ut predictum negotium assumeret, in quo parati erant eum sequi et exponere se et sua. Unde in veritate cuilibet loquenti poterat[197] dici illud Matthei 10:[198] *Non enim vos estis qui loquimini, sed Spiritus Patris, verbi qui loquitur in vobis.* Unde ex verbis omnium exterius pulsantium et a Spiritu[199] Sancto intus pungente[200] factum est cor eius tamquam[201] cera liquescens in medio [F 164rb] ventris sui, ut compelleretur dicere 'ego assumam'. Nec mirum, quia Proverbiorum 21 dicitur:[202] *Cor regis in manu Domini,*[203] *quocumque voluerit, inclinabit illud,* et non solum quocumque[204] sed quandocumque 'nescit enim tarda molimina Spiritus Sancti gratia'.[205] Unde Gregorius *super Ezekielem*:[206]

> Considero patres novi et veteris testamenti, David, Danielem, Amos, Petrum et Paulum, et Mattheum et apertis oculis fidei intueor. [G 294 rb] Implet namque subito Spiritus Sancti gratia puerum citharedum, et psalmistam facit; implet abstinentem puerum, et iudicem senum facit; implet pastorem armentarium, et prophetam facit; implet piscatorem, et principem apostolorum facit; implet etiam subito[207] persecutorem, et doctorem gentium facit; implet publicanum, et primum evvangelistam facit.

Et ita possum dicere quod subito implevit Spiritus Sancti gratia illustrem regem[208] et militem Christi[209] fecit, Jeremie[210] 51: rex contra Babilonem a Domino suscitatus est. Unde potest dici de rege illud Actuum 8:[211] *Spiritus Domini rapuit Philippum,*[212] et sequitur, *Philippus autem inventus est in Azoto.*[213]

---

195 que *add. in col.* F
196 consequenter] consequenterque F
197 poterat] poterant *a.c.* F
198 Mattheus 10.20.; Matthei *add. in mg.* G
199 a Spiritu] aSpiritu F
200 pungente] pungete F
201 tamquam] tanquam F
202 Proverbia 21.1.
203 domini] quocumque *add. et del.* F
204 quocumque] sed quandocumque *add. et del.* F
205 'Sancti Ambrosii Mediolanensis Episcopi Expositio Evangelii Secundum Lucam: Libris X Comprehensa', in *Patrologia Latina*, ed. J.-P. Migne, 15: 1560, Lib.II, §19.
206 'Homelia XXX: Lectio sancti evangelii secundum Iohannem', in *Corpus Christianorum, Series Latina, Gregorius Magnus: Homiliae in Evangelia,* ed. Raymond Étaix (Turnhout: Brepols, 1999), 141: 253–268, 265; Patrologia Latina, 76:1225–1226; Gregorius *add. in mg.* G
207 subito] docto *add. et del.* G
208 regem *mg.* F, *om.* G
209 militem Christi *inv.* G
210 Jeremie] Jeremie *add. in mg.* G
211 Recte Actus 8.39, 40.; Actuum *add. in mg.* G
212 Philippum] Pphilippum F
213 Azoto] Azato G

212 *Appendix III*

[14] Unde videtur michi quod, sicut angelus, postquam et factum et modum conceptionis Christi Beate Virgini nunciaverat, sollicite requirebat et expectabat responsum nec patiebatur dilationis terminum ut Virgo diceret *ecce ancilla Domini*,[214] et cetera, sicut pulchre deducit Bernardus omelia quarta[215] super *Missus est*, sic omnes prelati et barones regis responsum,[216] recusantes omnis dilationis diffugium, cum omni instantia postulabant, dicentes verbis competenter mutatis et aliquibus commissis quod [F 164va] dicit idem Bernardus:[217]

> Audiamus a te responsum letitie quod desideramus ut iam exultent *ossa humiliata*.[218] Expectat Dominus tuum responsum. Expectamus et nos verbum miserationis quos mirabiliter premit imperium[219] magne confusionis. Ecce offertur [G 294 va] tibi negotium tante virtutis: statim liberabimur,[220] si consentis. Hoc supplicat a te Pater, Adam cum misera sobole sua, hoc Abraham, hoc David, hoc ceteri flagitant sancti patres tui, hoc totus mundus, tuis genibus provolutus,[221] expectat: nec immerito,[222] quoniam ex ore tuo pendet consolatio miserorum, redemptio captivorum, liberatio dampnatorum,[223] salus denique universorum filiorum Adam, totius generis tui. Responde ergo verbum, quod terra, quod inferi quod expectant et superi.[224] Ipse quoque omnium rex tuum desiderat responsionis assensum, et cui complacuisti in silentio iam magis placebis in verbo, cum ipse clamet de[225] cello: 'fac me audire vocem tuam'. Si ergo tu eum facis audire vocem tuam, ipse te faciet videre salutem nostram. Tu es cui hoc[226] promissum est, an alium expectamus? Tu utique es per quem ipse Deus Rex[227] noster ante secula disposuit operari[228] salutem in medio terre. Responde ergo verbum quid tardas,[229] quid trepidas? Surge, curre, aperi, surge per fidem, curre per devotionem, aperi per confessionem.

---

214 Lucas 1.28.
215 quarta] iiiia F
216 responsum] regis *add.* G
217 Bernardus *add. in mg.* G; 'Sermones in laudibus Virginis Matris [Homiliae super Missus est in laudibus Virginis Matris, Homilia IV', in *Sancti Bernardi Opera Omnia*, ed. J. Mabillon (Paris: Gaume Fratres, 1839), 1.1: 1701–1702.
218 Psalmi 50.10.
219 imperium] improperiumi F
220 liberabimur] liberamur F
221 provolutus] pro volutus F
222 immerito] in merito F
223 dampnatorum] at *s.l.* F
224 superi] superbi G
225 clamet de] clamat est G
226 cui hoc] hic cui G
227 ipse Deus Rex] Rex ipse Deus G
228 operari] comperari F
229 tardas] tocedas G

Dic:[230] *Ego*[231] *servus tuus, ego servus tuus et filius ancille tue. Dirupisti*[232] *vincula mea*[233] *tibi sacrificabo hostiam laudis, et nomen Domini invocabo. Vota mea Domino reddam in conspectu omnis populi eius; in atriis domus Domini, in medio tui, Iherusalem.*[234]

[15] Bene ergo fuit hic spiritus sancti urgens [F 164vb] stimulatio, II ad Corinthios[235] 5:[236] *Caritas Christi urget nos*. Et ideo apparet quod firmavit in Psalmo:[237] *Confir*[G 294 vb]*ma hoc, Deus, quod operatus es in nobis*, et cetera, ut dicat rex Spiritui Sancto[238] quod dicit Augustinus in quadam epistola:[239] 'Sanctum opus in me spira ut cogitem,[240] compelle ut faciam, suade ut diligam, confirma ut teneam, custodi me,[241] ne perdam', Ecclesiastici 4:[242] *Firmabit illum,*[243] *et iter directum adducet, et letificabit illum*. Nota hic quomodo Ysaias propheta qui se obtulit dicens Ysaie 6:[244] *Domine mitte me*, non fuit minoris meriti quam Jeremias propheta[245] excusans[246] se et dicens:[247] *Domine nescio loqui, quia puer ego sum*, cum ille se obtulerit ex magno ardore caritatis, alius se excusavit[248] ex amore humilitatis. Ergo non minus dominus noster[249] rex plus[250] meritur qui sic se obtulit[251] quam illi qui assumpserunt post[252] multas inductiones, et cetera.

[16] Dico secundo quod probat firmitatem istius negotii subiecti patens dispositio ad exequendum utiliter: 'Actus activorum sunt in patiente disposito'.[253]

---

230 Psalmi 115.7–10.
231 ego] ergo *a.c.* G
232 dirupisti] disrupisti G
233 mea] et *add.* G
234 Iherusalem] Ierusalem F
235 Corinthios] Timotheum F
236 II Corinthios 5.14.; ad Corinthios *add. in mg.* G
237 Psalmi 67.29.
238 rex spiritui sancto] spiritui sancto rex G
239 Augustinus Hipponensis, 'Liber Exhortationis, vulgo de salutaribus documentis ad quemdam comitem - Carnis Mala. Oratio Animae ad Deum', in *Sancti Aurelii Augustini Hipponensis Episcopi Opera Omnia* (Paris: Opera et Studio monachorum ordinis sancti Benedicti, 1837), 6:1564–1568, 1565, §65; Augustinus *add. in mg.* G
240 cogitem] cogidem F
241 me *om.* F
242 Ecclesiasticus 4.20.
243 illum] illam *a.c.* G
244 Isaias 6.8.
245 propheta] et dixit *add.* G
246 excusans] excusas G
247 Jeremias 1.6.
248 excusavit] excusabat G
249 noster *om.* F
250 plus *om.* F
251 obtulit] obstulit *a.c.* G
252 post] rex passagium *add. in mg.* F
253 Aristoteles, De Anima, II, 2, 414a 25–27.; Aristoteles *add. in mg.* F

214 *Appendix III*

Modo, absque omni adulatione et fictione ad[254] executionem utilem istius[255] negotii nullus videtur magis dispositus domino rege. Unde sibi dictum videtur Josue primo:[256] *Confortare, et esto robustus tu enim divides populo huic terram, de qua iuravi patribus tuis, ut darem eam eis.* Et ratio videtur michi esse[257] quia dominus rex habet octo que sunt valde necessaria ad hoc quod aliquis sit dispositus[258] ad exequendum utiliter tantum factum. Primo habet quo ad Deum fervorem interne[259] devotionis. Que dispo[F 165ra]sitio est valde[260] necessaria quia, sicut dicitur [G 295 ra] primo Machabeorum 3:[261] *Non in multitudine exercitus victoria belli, sed de celo fortitudo est.* Unde quilibet volens bene[262] in isto bello procedere debet dicere quod dicebat David Golie Philisteo: *Tu venis ad*[263] *me cum gladio, hasta,*[264] *et*[265] *clippeo, ego autem venio ad te in nomine Domini exercituum, agminum Dei Israhel*, primo Regum 17.[266]

[17] Secundo habet quo ad milites amorem mutue dilectionis. Que dispositio est etiam multum[267] necessaria quia princeps debet studere plus diligi quam timeri. Nec mirum quia generosus[268] est hominis animus, facilius enim[269] ducitur quam trahitur.[270] Unde dicebat David de Jonatha, probo milite, quod erat *amabilis super amorem mulierum*,[271] II Regum primo.[272]

[18] Tertio quia quo ad arma habet vigorem virtuose[273] operationis sive[274] exercitationis.[275] Et hoc est etiam necessarium quia, sicut dicit Vegetius *De re militari*:[276] plus valet docta paucitas in bello quam 'indocta multitudo exposita

---

254 ad] ex *add. et del.* F
255 istius] huius F
256 Josue 1.7.; Josue *add. in mg.* G
257 esse *om.* G
258 dispositus] necessarie conditiones passagii *add. in mg.* G
259 interne] eterne *a.c.* G
260 valde] bene F
261 I Machabeorum 3.19.; Machabeorum *add. in mg.* G
262 bene *om.* G
263 ad] ii *add. et del.* F
264 hasta *om.* G
265 et *s.l.* F
266 I Samuelis 17.45.; Regum *add. in mg.* G
267 etiam multum *inv.* G
268 generosus] generosius *a.c.* F
269 enim] dici *a.c. in mg.* F, *om.* G
270 trahitur] trahatur F
271 mulierum] mulieris F
272 II Samuelis 1.26.; Regum add. in mg. G
273 virtuose] victoriose F
274 operationis sive *om.* F
275 exercitationis] excercitationis G
276 *Vegetius: Epitoma rei militaris*, ed. Michael D. Reeve (Oxford: Oxford Classical Texts, 2004), I, c.1, n.7, 6.

semper ad cedem' 'scientia enim rei bellice dimicandi[277] nutrit audaciam; nemo enim facere metuit quod se bene didicisse[278] confidit'.

[19] Quarto quia quo ad etatem habet florem robuste complexionis. Que conditio est etiam bene[279] necessaria quia in iuvenibus non est prudentia, in senibus deficit virtus et potentia, sed in etate virili utrumque viget[280] et prudentia[281] et fortitudo. Unde potest dici regi illud Judicum 8:[282] *Juxta etatem et robur es hominis.*

[20] Quinto quo ad [G 295 rb] consilium habet splendorem sapientie et discretionis. Sicut enim dicitur Ecclesiastes 9:[283] *Melior est sapientia quam arma bellica*, quia Proverbiorum 20:[284] *Cogitationes* [F 165rb] *consiliis*[285] *roborantur, et gubernaculis*[286] *tractanda sunt bella.*

[21] Sexto habet quo ad militum numerum et meritum conditionem bifurcatam. Habent enim milites sui in ordine ad amicos dulcorem agnine conversationis,[287] sed in ordine ad inimicos terrorem leonine concertationis seu invasionis. Unde[288] milites[289] regni[290] Francie pre ceteris sunt in convictu agnis mitiores sed in conflictu leonibus fortiores. Unde potest dici de eis illud II Regum primo:[291] *Aquilis velociores,*[292] *leonibus fortiores.* Unde et vos, pater sanctissime, in epistola novissime[293] eis directa sic inter alia dicebatis:[294]

> Exurgant viri ad bella doctissimi, strenui[295] regni Francie bellatores; accingantur viri fortes, nec sub corporis ignavia mala dissimulent supradicta. Prodeant in publicum eorum signa victricia, quorum potentiam[296] specialiter

---

277 dimicandi] dimicando G
278 didicisse] didisscisse F
279 est etiam bene] etiam bene est G
280 viget] et prudentia *add. et del.* G
281 sed in etate…prudentia *om. per homoioteleuton* F
282 Iudicum 8.21.; Iudicum *add. in mg.* G
283 Ecclesiasticus 9.18.; Ecclesiastes *add. in mg.* G
284 Proverbia 20.18.
285 consiliis] Proverbiorum *add. in mg.* G
286 gubernaculis] tractatur *add. et del.* F
287 conversationis] conservationis G
288 unde *s.l.* G
289 milites] reni *add. et del.* F
290 regni *add. et del.* F
291 II Samuelis 1.23.; Regum *add. in mg.* G
292 velociores] volcciores F
293 in epistola novissime *bis scr. et del.* F
294 This passage is a verbatim record from Pope Clement IV's directions sent on 10 August 1265 to the Dominican provincial priors and the Franciscan ministers in France for the planned crusade of Louis IX. See *Annales Ecclesiastici ab anno 1198 usque ad annum 1565*, eds. A. Theiner, et al., 37 vols. (Paris-Freiburg-Bar le Duc, 1864–1867), 22: 161; *Bullarium Franciscanum*, ed. D. A. Rossi (Rome, 1765), 3:26. Unfortunately, the identification of John XXII's letter to which Pierre Roger makes reference here was not possible.
295 strenui] strennui G
296 potentiam] potentia F

expectat,[297] et expetit terra illa. Eis debetur huiusmodi belli[298] victoria, eis hoc paratur ad gloriam, eis ad meritum reservatur. Non desit ad hoc opus suo capiti virtus strenuitatis ipsorum, inter ceteras nationes eis specialius ab ipso redemptore nostro concessa; non patiantur equanimiter eterni regis[299] iniurias, qui cuiusvis eorum domino iniuriam etiam inferri procul dubio nequaquam cum patientia supporta[G 295 va]rent. Absit, ut in hoc casu solvant militie cingulum regni eiusdem, milites gloriosi. Absit, ut[300] in bello domini per desidiam reddantur inglorii,[301] qui per virtutis exercitium solent in[302] bellis ceteris gloriosi[F 165va]ores haberi.

[22] Septimo habet quo ad subditos decorem pacifice et prompte obeditionis. Sedet enim populus regni[303] Francie *in pulchritudine pacis, in tabernaculis fiducie, in requie opulenta*, Ysaie 32,[304] et specialiter rex noster[305] videtur esse[306] alter[307] Salomon cui Deus dedit[308] pacem per circuitum.

[23] Octavo habet quo ad potentiam honorem precelse dominationis. Unde potest dici de eo illud Ecclesiastici 48:[309] *Potentia nemo vicit illum*. Non ergo mirum si firmatus sit in isto proposito quia sermo eius potestate plenus est[310] ut dicat illud Ecclesiastici 24:[311] *In Syon firmata sum*, et cetera, *in Iherusalem[312] potestas mea*. Proverbiorum 15:[313] *Sermo purus firmabitur ab eo*. Nec mirum quia propter devotionem ei non deerit[314] auxiliatrix divina clementia, adest suorum amicitia, armorum industria, virium potentia,[315] peritorum copia, militum audacia, subditorum obedientia, super omnes seculares principes excellentia.

[24] Dico tertio quod hanc firmitatem probat concepti propositi perseverans[316] continuatio ad prosequendum viriliter. Ad litteram quando aliquis in suo proposito continue perseverat signum est quod in illo [G 295 vb] proposito firmatus est. Certe dominus rex a multis temporibus etiam antequam perveniret ad regnum

---

297 expectat] spectat G
298 belli] bella G
299 regis] regni F
300 ut *om.* G
301 inglorii] in glorii F
302 in] fo *add. et del.* F
303 regni] Frangi *add. et del.* F
304 Isaias 32.18.; Ysaie *add. in mg.* G
305 noster *om.* F
306 esse] est G
307 alter] so *add. et del.* F
308 Deus dedit *inv.* G
309 48] xviii G, F; Ecclesiasticus 48.13.; Ecclesiastici *add. in mg.* G
310 est] Ecclesiastes *add.* F
311 24] xxiii G; Ecclesiasticus 24.15.; Ecclesiastici *add. in mg.* G
312 Iherusalem] Ierusalem F
313 15] xx G, F; Proverbia 15.26.; Proverbiorum *add. in mg.* G
314 deerit] de erit F
315 potentia] parvorum *add.* G
316 perseverans] perseveras G

concepit vires suas contra[317] inimicos fidei experiri, sicut etiam sanctitas vestra novit, et in isto proposito continue perseveravit in tantum quod etiam[318] eidem sanctitati vestre supplicavit quod quicumque ipsum[319] a tam sancto proposito, publice vel occulte, di[F 165vb]recte vel indirecte,[320] verbo vel facto retraherent,[321] excommunicationis vinculo innodati essent.[322] Bene est ergo argumentum quod in isto proposito perseverat ut dicatur de eo illud Ecclesiastici 15:[323] *Firmabitur*[324] *in illo et non flectetur.*

[25] Dico quarto quod hanc firmitatem probat medii conveniens preparatio ad exequendum feliciter. Si aliquis[325] aliquod opus assumat et nullum[326] apparatum ad illud faciat, signum est quod non firmavit, sed quando preparat media ad hoc necessaria, signum est quod firmavit. Modo dominus[327] rex convenientia media ad istud[328] opus preparat[329] quantum potest, duces, comites et alios potentes, et qui non sunt de regno suo, pro isto sancto passagio retinendo et eis sua liberaliter propter hoc[330] distribuendo. Nota hic de apparatu quem facit tam[331] in navibus quam armaturis et aliis quam[332] pluribus quod longum esset per singula enarrare. Ergo signum est quod firmavit ut dicat dominus rex illud 3 Regum 6:[333] *Firmabo sermonem meum quem*[334] *locutus sum,* ut sibi videatur profetice dictum illud Psalmus:[335] *Thabor et Hermon exultabunt tuum brachium cum potentia. Firmetur* [G 296 ra] *manus tua, et exaltetur*[336] *dextera tua, iustitia et iudicium preparatio sedis tue, misericordia et veritas precedent faciem tuam. Beatus populus qui scit iubilationem: Domine, in lumine vultus tui ambulabunt, et in nomine tuo exultabunt, et in*[337] *iustitia tua exaltabuntur.*[338] *Quia gloria virtutis eorum tu es,*

---

317 contra *om.* G; imicos *add. et del.* F
318 etiam *om.* G
319 ipsum *mg.* F
320 publice vel…indirecte] directe vel indirecte, publice vel occulte G
321 retraherent] essent *add.* G
322 essent *mg.* F
323 Ecclesiasticus 15.3.; Ecclesiastici *add. in mg.* G
324 firmabitur] firmabit F
325 aliquis *bis scr. et del.* F
326 et nullum *om.* G
327 dominus *om.* G
328 istud] illud G
329 media ad illud opus preparat *a.m.* G
330 liberaliter propter hoc] propter hoc liberaliter G
331 facit tam *a.m.* G
332 quam] aliis *add.* F
333 III Reges 6.12.; Regum *add. in mg.* G
334 quem] quod F
335 Psalmi 89.13–19.; Psalmus *add. in mg.* G
336 exaltetur] ex altetur F
337 in *om.* G
338 exaltabuntur] exultabuntur G; passagium tempus *add. in mg.* F

et in beneplacito tuo exaltabitur cornu nostrum. Quia[339] *Domini est*[340] *assumptio nostra, et sancti Israel regis nostri.*

[26] Dico quinto quod istam firmitatem probat temporis congrui evidens in[F 166ra]terpellatio ad insistendum celeriter, sicut dicitur Ecclesiastici 8:[341] *Cum negotio tempus est*[342] *et oportunitas.* Videtur michi ex duobus vel tribus quod tempus presens ad insistendum celeriter huic tam sancto negotio interpellare.[343] Videtur ex tribus, scilicet, ex[344] ferventi omnium ad hoc negotium desiderio, ex scripture testimonio, ex perfidorum Agarenorum utinam[345] veraci vaticinio.

[27] Primo quod interpellat[346] tempus videtur ex ferventi omnium ad hoc negotium desiderio. In veritate omnis etas, omnis[347] sexus, omnis status videtur esse a Deo ad hoc accensus quod quasi impossibile videtur quin hoc tempus sit ad hoc ordinatum a Deo. Unde videtur verificari[348] illud Psalmus:[349] *Tu exurgens misereberis Syon,*[350] *quia*[351] *tempus miserendi eius, quia venit tempus*, et sequitur[352] in eodem Psalmo:[353] *ut annunciant*[354] *in Syon nomen*[355] *Domini, et laudem eius in Iherusalem,*[356] in conveniendo populos in unum et reges ut serviant Domino.

[28] Secundo videtur [G 296 rb] interpellare ex scripture testimonio.[357] Scriptum est enim Danielis 12:[358] *Beatus qui expectat, et pervenit ad dies mille trecentos triginta quinque*, ut accipiamus diem pro anno iuxta illud Ezekielis 4:[359] *Diem*[360] *pro anno dedi tibi.* Et licet in scripturis[361] frequenter accipiatur tempus determinatum pro indeterminato, sicut forsitan hic, tamen non est dubium quod frequenter etiam[362] assumitur[363] tempus ipsum etiam[364] determinatum. Quia ergo occulta sunt

---

339 quia] u *add. et del.* F
340 est *s.l.* G
341 Ecclesiastici] Ecclesiastes F || Ecclesiasticus 8.6.; Ecclesiastici *add. in mg.* G
342 est] et orptumitas *add. et del.* F
343 interpellare] interpallare G
344 ex] tempus pro passagio *add. in mg.* G
345 utinam] ut *a.c. in mg.* F; ut G
346 interpellat] interpellet F
347 omnis *om.* G
348 videtur verificari *inv.* F; videtur *add. in mg.* F
349 Psalmi 102.14.; Psalmus *add. in mg.* G
350 Syon *add. in mg.* F
351 quia] venit *add.* F
352 sequitur] ut a *add. et del.* G
353 Psalmi 102.22.; Psalmus *add. in mg.* G
354 annunciant] annuncietur F
355 nomen] tuum *add. et del.* G
356 Iherusalem] Ierusalem F
357 testimonio] S *add. et del.* G
358 Daniel 12.12.; Danielis *add. in mg.* G
359 Ezekiel 4.6.; Ezekielis *add. in mg.* G
360 diem *mg.* F
361 scripturis] scriptura F
362 etiam *om.* F
363 assumitur] i *s.l.* F
364 etiam *om.* F

iudicia Dei et³⁶⁵ incomprehensibilia³⁶⁶ a nobis, subiciamus nos misericordie Dei in hoc accepto tempore, quia hoc saltem certum est quod non sine [F 166rb] misterio tempus illud a propheta positum est, ut dicamus, confisi de misericordia et adiutorio Dei,³⁶⁷ illud II ad Corinthios 6:³⁶⁸ *Ecce nunc tempus acceptabile, ecce nunc dies salutis.* Utinam enim Dominus hoc tempore restituat regnum Israhel.

[29] Tertio videtur interpellare tempus ex perfidorum Agarenorum utinam veraci vaticinio. Dicunt enim viri multum³⁶⁹ solemnes quod prophete eorum predixerunt legem illam diabolicam et contra omnem³⁷⁰ rationem datam illius pessimi et sceleratissimi Machometi in anno xxxv proximo finiendo quod vaticinium eis magnum³⁷¹ timorem incutit. Et sicut nostis, Deus frequenter per malos³⁷² multa vera predicit, sicut per Balaam,³⁷³ et³⁷⁴ Caypham et multos alios, quia donum prophetie non est donum gratie gratum facientis sed gratie gratis date. Et [G 296 va] satis istud videtur³⁷⁵ credibile, quynnimo mirum est quo occulto Dei iudicio legem tam iniquam Deus tanto tempore permisit durare. Sed nunc largiente Domino verificabitur illud Deuteronomii 32:³⁷⁶ *Foris vastabit eos gladius, et intus pavor, iuvenem simul et virginem, lactantem cum homine sene*, et sequitur:³⁷⁷ *mea est ultio, et ego retribuam eis in tempore, ut labatur pes eorum: iuxta est dies perditionis, et adesse³⁷⁸ festinant tempora.* Patet ergo quomodo tempus interpellat³⁷⁹ ad insistendum celeriter. Et forsan hoc divino nutu factum est quod dominus rex tale tempus elegit, licet videatur³⁸⁰ aliquibus nimis breve.³⁸¹ Unde iudicio meo proprie potest dici regi illud Hester 4:³⁸² *Quis novit utrum* [F 166va] *idcirco ad regnum Veneris, ut³⁸³ in tali tempore parareris?*³⁸⁴ Et talis interpellatio temporis arguit firmitatem in Psalmo:³⁸⁵ *Auxit populum suum vehementer, et firmavit eum super inimicos eius.* Et sic patet secundum.

---

365 et *om.* G
366 incomprehensibilia] in comprehensibilia F
367 de misericordia…Dei] de misericordia Dei et adiutorio eius G
368 Corinthios] Chorinthios F; II Corinthios 6.2.; ad Corinthios *add. in mg.* G
369 multum] multi F
370 omnem] dominem *a.c.* G
371 eis magnum *inv.* F
372 malos] m *add. et del.* F
373 Balaam] Balam G
374 et] per F
375 istud videtur] videt istud G
376 32] xxvii G, F; Deuteronomii *add. in mg.* G; De Uteronomii F; Deuteronomium 32.25.
377 Deuteronomium 32.35.
378 adesse] ad esse F
379 interpellat] interpelat G
380 videatur] videat G
381 nimis breve *a.m.* G
382 Hester 4.14.; Hester *add. in mg.* G
383 ut] et G
384 parareris] pareris F
385 Psalmi 105.24.; Psalmus *add. in mg.* G

220   *Appendix III*

[30] Dico tertio quod in virtuosa sui[386] negotii assumptione ex parte effectus requiritur executio et vigilantia seu providentia[387] diligens, que pro negotio comperiat oportunitatis[388] auxilium et consilium fructuosum. Et ideo hic pro negotii consummatione petitur necessitatis seu oportunitatis et exigentie indefectibile iuvamentum, quia ideo sequitur in themate, *misit nuncios*. Ad litteram enim duo prima non sufficerent sine[389] tertio. Modo clarum est quod ad [G 296 vb] istud[390] tertium rex et facultates[391] regni sui non sufficiunt, quinymmo sibi dici potest quod dicebat ille Ietro Moysi Exodi 18:[392] *Supra vires tuas, est negotium solus sustinere non poteris.* Unde sicut Salomon pro edificatione templi ad Yram[393] regem ut eum iuvaret misit nuncios et ille eum iuvit, sicut apparet I[394] Regum 5, sic dominus rex pro templi recuperatione et aliorum locorum[395] sanctorum et totius Terre Sancte misit nos, sanctitatis vestre servos, ad pedes vestre beatitudinis pro petendo et obtinendo auxilio oportuno ut dicat rex[396] illud Genesis 32:[397] *Mitto nunc legationem ad Dominum, ut inveniam gratiam.*

[31] Et videte quod iudicio meo quatuor vel quinque concurrunt[398] in ista legatione que inducunt[399] ut id quod petitur[400] faciliter concedatur, sicut innuunt verba predicta: primum est mittentis et eius ad quem mittit et econtra affectio et bene[F 166vb]volentia[401] visceralis. Secundum est missorum ad eum ad quem mittit subiectio et reverentia filialis. Tertium est negotii pro[402] quo mittit devotio et sanctimonia[403] specialis. Quartum est eius ad quem mittit sublimatio et excellentia singularis cum qua concurrit obligatio et exigentia paternalis. Quintum est modi petendi humiliatio et convenientia salutaris.

[32] Dico ergo quod primum quod debet inducere ad concedendum petita faciliter est mittentis ad eum ad quem mittit et econtra affectio et benivolentia visceralis. Mittit enim[404] rex Francie ad vos, dominum [G 297 ra] nostrum,[405] patrem

---

386   sui *om.* F
387   providentia] pro videntia F
388   oportunitatis] auxit *add. et del.* F
389   sine *om.* G
390   istud *om.* G
391   facultates] facultatis F
392   18] xxiii G; Exodus 18.18.; Exodi *add. in. mg.* G
393   Yram] Ysram F
394   I] 3 G, F; Regum *add. in mg.* G
395   locorum] sanctum *add. et del.* F
396   rex] nuncius impetrare *add. in mg.* F
397   32] xxvii G, F; Genesis 32.4.; Genesis *add. in mg.* G
398   concurrunt] concurrut G; quatuor…concurrunt] quatuor concurrunt vel quinque F
399   inducunt] inducut G
400   petitur] nuncii impetrare *add. in mg.* G
401   benevolentia] benivolentia F
402   pro] in F
403   sanctimonia] sanctimonialis *a.c.* F
404   enim *mg.* F
405   nostrum] rex Francie – Ecclesia romana *add. in mg.* G

suum. Patet autem ex cronicis quanta semper fuit[406] affectio corone Francie ad Sanctam Romanam Ecclesiam et econtra Sancte Romane Ecclesie ad coronam Francie. Unde tanta fuit affectio, tanta colligatio, tanta confederatio, tantus amor quod[407] nunquam unus alteri defuit quin adesset in omnibus prosperitatibus[408] et adversitatibus,[409] et auxiliis, et consiliis gratiis, et favoribus oportunis. Unde semper dixit quilibet Romanus pontifex specialiter inter ceteros reges regi Francie illud Apostoli ad Hebreos primo:[410] *Ego ero illi in patrem, et ipse erit michi in filium.* Sed certe hodie singulariter ista affectio[411] viget sanctitatis vestre ad regem, de cuius regno traxistis originem, et econtra domini regis ad beatitudinem vestram. Unde singulariter sibi dicitis illud Psalmus:[412] *Ipse invocavit me, Pater meus es tu*, et sequitur:[413] *et ego primogenitum*[414] *ponam illum, excelsum*[415] *pre regibus terre. In eternum servabo illi misericordiam meam*,[416] et cetera. Ergo [F 167ra] bene ista conditio[417] movet ad faciliter concedendum ut dicatis sibi illud 3 Regum 2: [418] *Pete quod vis nec enim fas est ut avertam faciem meam*, quia,[419] *certe fili tu semper mecum es*, Luce 15.[420] Et ideo dicitur in auctoritate assumpta 'mitto ego rex filius tuus' primo[421] Paralipomenon 19:[422] *Misit rex David nuncios.*

[33] Dico secundo quod secundum quod debet inducere ad concedendum petita faciliter est nunciorum [G 297 rb] missorum ad eum ad quem mittuntur subiectio et reverentia filialis. Si enim secundum Gregorium:[423] 'Cum is qui ad intercedendum[424] mittitur displicet, irati animus ad deteriora provocatur', cum mittitur ille qui est servus devotus et filius, debet ad concedendum facilius inclinari, quia si oppositum est causa oppositi,[425] propositum est causa propositi. Modo dominus rex non misit quoscumque, sed nos, creaturas vestras, servos vestros.

---

406 semper fuit *inv.* G
407 quod] contra *add. et del.* G
408 prosperitatibus] pro speritatibus F
409 adversitatibus] ad versitatibus F
410 Hebreos 1.5.; ad Hebreos *add. in mg.* G
411 affectio] videt *add. et del.* F
412 Psalmi 89.27.
413 Psalmi 89.28–29.
414 primogenitum] meum *add.* G
415 excelsum] excellum F
416 misericordiam meam *inv.* F
417 bene ista conditio] ista conditio bene G
418 III Reges 2.20.; Regum *add. in mg.* G
419 quia *om.* G
420 Luce 15.31.
421 primo] primi G
422 I Paralipomenon 19.2.; Paralipomenon *add. in mg.* G
423 'Sancti Gregorii Magni: Regulae Pastoralis liber - Pars Prima', in *Patrologia Latina*, ed. J.-P. Migne 77: 23, cap.x; Gregorius *add. in mg.* G
424 intercedendum] intercodendum G
425 oppositi] u *add. et del.* F

Unde verificatur illud Luce 14:[426] *Servus nuntiavit domino suo.* Ergo[427] hoc[428] debet inducere ad facilius concedendum.

[34] Dico tertio quod tertium quod debet inducere ad concedendum[429] faciliter[430] et cetera est negotii pro quo mittit[431] devotio et sanctimonia specialis. Res enim pro qua petitur auxilium adeo sancta est quod non potest peti pro negotio[432] sanctiori, sicut tactum est in primo articulo. Unde in auctoritate assumpta sequitur 'mitto legationem'. Ad litteram enim non petitur istud auxilium pro regni ditatione, pro debitorum aut testamentorum solutione, pro monete melioratione, sed pro Christo, pro iniurie sue vindicatione, pro Terre Sancte et locorum sanctorum mundatione, pro hereditatis nostre recuperatione, pro [F 167rb] Christi cultus augmentatione, *pro Christo enim fungimur legatione,*[433] II ad Corinthios[434] 5.

[35] Dico quarto quod quartum quod debet inducere ad concedendum faciliter est sanctitatis vestre ad quam mittit sublimatio et excellentia singularis cum qua concurrit obligatio et exigentia paterna[G 297 va]lis. Et ideo sequitur in auctoritate quod legationem[435] mittit non ad quemcumque, sed ad dominum, ad vos, ad litteram, qui universorum bonorum ecclesiasticorum dominus estis. Potest enim vobis dici, 'Dominus universorum tu es'.[436] Vos enim estis assumptus ad plenitudinem potestatis ut possitis de bonis ecclesiasticis disponere secundum quod vobis videtur[437] expedire. Unde de auctoritate vestra loquitur Bernardus II *De consideratione ad Eugenium papam* dicens sic:[438]

> Indagemus diligentius quis sis, quam geris personam in Ecclesia Dei. Quis es?[439] Sacerdos magnus, summus pontifex. Tu princeps episcoporum, tu heres apostolorum,[440] tu primatu Abel, gubernatu Noe, patriarchatu Abraham, ordine Melchisedech, dignitate Aaron, auctoritate Moyses, iudicatu Samuel, potestate Petrus, unctione Christus. Tu es cui claves tradite, cui oves credite

---

426 Luce 14.21.; Luce *add. in mg.* G
427 ergo] ad *add. et del.* G; r *s.l.* F; et *add.* F
428 hoc] hic F
429 concedendum] fide *add. et del.* G
430 faciliter *om.* F
431 mittit] mittitur G
432 negotio *a.m.* G
433 fungimur legatione *inv.* F
434 Corinthios] Timotheo G, Chorinthios F; II Corinthios 5.20.
435 legationem] legatione G
436 Esther 24.21.: 'Dominus Omnium tu es'. This biblical verse has been paraphrased and substantially adjusted in the sermon text.
437 videtur] videbitur G
438 'De consideratione ad Eugenium papam', in *Sancti Bernardi Opera*, eds. Jean Leclercq and Henri-Marie Rochais, 8 vols. (Rome: Editiones Cistercienses, 1957–1977), 3:423, Lib.II, cap.8.15.; Bernardus *add. in mg.* G
439 es] tu es *add. in mg.* F
440 tu princeps…apostolorum] Tu princeps apostolorum, episcoporum heres apostolorum G

Appendix III 223

<sunt>. Sunt quidem[441] et [si] alii[442] celi ianitores et gregum pastores; tamen tu, tanto gloriosius, quanto[443] differentius, pre illis nomen hereditasti. Habent illi sibi assignatos greges,[444] singuli singulos; tibi universi crediti, unus uni. Non modo ovium, sed pastorum tu unus omnium pastor.[445]

Et sequitur:[446]

Igitur iuxta canones tuos, alii in partem sollicitu[F 167va]dinis, tu in plenitudinem potestatis vocatus[447] es. Aliorum potestas certis artatur limitibus; tua extenditur etiam in ipsos, qui potestatem super [G 297 vb] alios acceperunt.[448] Nonne,[449] si causa extiterit,[450] tu episcopo celum potes[451] claudere, tu ab episcopatu illum deponere, et tradere Sathane potes?[452] Sicut ergo inconcusse privilegium tuum tibi, tam in datis clavibus quam in omnibus commendatis concessum est.[453]

Et subdit in fine:[454]

Itaque, cum quisque[455] ceterorum habeat[456] suam, tibi una comissa est gratissima [BC: grandissima] navis, facta ex omnibus ipsam universalis Ecclesia, toto orbe diffusa.

[36] Unde de quolibet summo pontifice dicitur in Psalmo:[457] Constituit eum dominum domus sue, et principem omnis possessionis[458] sue, in talibus enim subest domino nostro pape cum voluit posse.

[37] Bene ergo in vobis est ad quem mittitur sublimatio et excellentia singularis, sed, sicut dicebam, cum hac[459] concurrit obligatio et exigentia paternalis. Ad vos

---

441 quidem *a.c. col.* F
442 alii] cui *add. et del.* F
443 quanto] et *add.* F
444 assignatos greges *inv.* G
445 non modo…pastor] non omni sed pastor tu unus omnium pastorum G
446 'De consideratione ad Eugenium papam', 3:424, Lib. II, cap.8.16.
447 vocatus] vocatis F
448 acceperunt] receperunt G
449 nonne] none G
450 extiterit] ca *add. et del.* F
451 potes] ii *add.* F
452 tradere Sathane potes] Sathane potes tradere G
453 est] in *mg.* F; *om.* G
454 'De consideratione ad Eugenium papam', 3:424, Lib. II, cap.8.16.
455 quisque] quilibet G
456 habeat] herebat F
457 Psalmi 105.21.; Psalmus *add. in mg.* G
458 possessionis] possessiones *a.c.* F
459 hac] talibus G

enim, pater sanctissime, istud negotium sicut ad patrem et caput[460] totius Ecclesie et omnium fidelium specialius noscitur pertinere. Ad quem enim magis pertinet ut populus Deo serviens et numero et merito[461] augeatur, ut Christiana religio vigeat, in terra illa specialiter quam Christus proprio sanguine consecravit et singulariter[462] adamavit, quam ad sanctitatem vestram? Certe, pater sanctissime, res vestra nunc agitur, quem posuit[463] Dominus caput[464] super Ecclesiam sanctam suam.[465] Unde dominus Martinus papa scribens universis prelatis inter cetera dicit sic:[466]

> Et si Terre Sancte negotium, quod cunctis Christi fidelibus [F 167vb] cordi non immerito esse debet,[467] olim, [G 298ra] dum minor status[468] nobis adesset,[469] affectuose fuerimus prosecuti, nunc tamen, pastoralis officii debito exigente, tanto magis ad illud afficimur, quanto[470] ad nos specialius noscitur idem negotium pertinere, ideoque summo desiderio ducimur ut negotii eiusdem impedimentis quibuslibet[471] congruis remediis occurratur.

[38] Dico quinto[472] quod debet movere ad concedendum petita faciliter modi petendi humiliatio et convenientia salutaris. Quandoque aliquid petitur, quantumcumque iustum et rationabile, per talem modum quod iuste ab eo a quo petitur denegatur quia vel[473] petitur ex debito, vel alio modo superbo, vel ex alia causa minus rationabili.[474] Et ideo filiis Zebedei dictum est illud Mathei 20:[475] *Nescitis quid petatis*.[476] Sed, pater sanctissime, dominus rex petit illud[477] auxilium[478] non ex debito, non modo superbo,[479] sed ex dono gratuito, quia in propositione assumpta sequitur:[480] *mitto legationem ad dominum ut inveniam gratiam, ut dica-*

---

460 caput] capud F
461 numero et merito] merito, numero et F
462 singulariter *a.m.* G
463 posuit] possuit *a.c.* F
464 caput] capud F
465 sanctam suam *inv.* G
466 Pope Martin IV, *Les Registres de Martin IV (1281–1285): Recueil des bulles de ce pape publiées ou analysées d'après les manuscrits originaux des archives du Vatican*, ed. F. Olivier-Martin (Paris: École Française de Rome, 1901), no.248.
467 debet] debent *a.c.* F
468 status] statue G
469 adesset] ad esset F
470 quanto] quante F
471 quibuslibet] quibuscumque G
472 dico quinto *inv.* F
473 quia vel *inv.* G
474 denegatur vel…minus rationabili *a.m.* G
475 20] xv G, F; Matthei 20.22.; Matheus *add. in mg.* G
476 petatis] petitis G
477 illud] istud F
478 auxilium] non *add. et del.* F
479 non ex debito, non modo superbo *inv.* F
480 Genesis 32.5.

mus quod scribitur ad Hebreos 4:[481] *Adeamus cum fiducia ad thronum gratie eius, ut*[482] *misericordiam consequamur, et gratiam inveniamus in auxilio oportuno.* Et videtur quod signanter dicit 'in auxilio oportuno'. Non enim sufficeret auxilium nisi esset, secundum rei exigentiam, oportunum. Unde pro minimis minimum, pro parvis[483] parvum, pro mediocribus mediocre, pro magnis magnum, pro maximis[484] maximum est auxilium oportunum. Cum ergo istud negotium sit [F168ra] maximum et nunc maxime, cum [G 298 rb] nullam ultra mare civitatem[485] vel locum habeamus in quo possit requiescere pes noster – unde hoc[486] advertens dominus Clemens quintus sacro concilio Viennensi approbante dicebat sic:[487] 'Attendentes quod, civitatibus locisque aliis que fideles olim in illis[488] partibus obtinebant per ipsorum hostium truculentam rabiem devastatis, locus aliquis ibidem ad recipiendum propugnatores fidei non remansit, propter quod negotii memorati promotio maioribus indiget profluis expensis quam indigeret[489] olim, cum aliqui eiusdem regis progenitores et quidam alii Christiani principes, civitatibus et locis predictis in statu prosperitatis[490] manentibus in quibus recreari et recipi poterant catholici bellatores, in eiusdem terre subsidium transfretarunt' – ideo si petuntur magna pro tam magno negotio non est mirum. Et tamen non petuntur insolita, sed alias pro simili negotio vel pro non ita rationabili concessa. Non petuntur etiam inconsulta, sed cum consilio prelatorum multorum et magnorum regni Francie quorum non mediocriter interest[491] cum deliberatione maxima ordinata.

[39] Et certe, pater sanctissime, inter cetera dona virtutum et gratiarum multiplicium[492] quibus personam vestram pre cunctis vestris participibus Dominus insignivit, ex quibus memoria vestra cum laudibus perpetuo permanebit, non mediocriter vestro acrescet[493] nomini si temporibus vestri regiminis terra [F 168rb] illa ad religionem Christiani [G 298 va] cultus reducatur. Et certe credo indubitanter quod pre magno desiderio in corde vestro dicitis quod dicebant sancti patres ante[494] desiderantes adventum Christi: putas ne videbo, putas ne parebo, putas ne videbunt oculi mei. Ego autem de misericordia Dei confisus sanctitati vestre dico

---

481 Hebreos 4.16.; ad Hebreos *add. in mg.* G
482 ut] et G
483 parvis] parvus *a.c.* F
484 maximis] a *s.l.* F
485 civitatem] vel *add. et del.* F
486 hoc] hic F
487 Clement V, *Regestum Clementis papae V: ex vaticanis archetypis sanctissimi domini nostri Leonis XIII pontificis maximi iussu et munificentia*, ed. Cura et Studio Monachorum Ordinis S. Benedicti, 10 vols. (Rome: Typografia Vaticana, 1885–1892), nos. 8986–8987.
488 illis] ipsis G
489 indigeret] indigerent *a.c.* F
490 prosperitatis] prosperitatibus F
491 interest] inest G; pro Deus *add. et del.* G
492 multiplicium] multiplicum F
493 acrescet] ac crescet G; crescit *a.c.* G
494 ante *om.* F

utinam prophetice illud Ysaie 60:[495] *Videbis, et afflues, et mirabitur et dilatabitur cor tuum: quando conversa fuerit ad te multitudo maris; fortitudo gentium venerit tibi.*

[40] Quod ipse Ihesus Christus, Dei Filius, cuius negotium agitur, vobis et nobis videre concedat, qui est benedictus in secula seculorum, Amen.

---

495 Ysaias 60.5.; Ysaie *add. in mg.* G

Appendix IV
Pierre Roger's crusade sermon at the papal chapel in Avignon, 16 July 1333

G = Paris, Bibliothèque Sainte Geneviéve, MS 240, fols. 298va–308vb
F = Paris, Bibliothèque nationale de France, MS lat. 3293, fols. 240ra–249rb
Rubric in F 240ra: **Sermo super passagio Terre Sancte.**

[1] Sanctissime pater et domine reverentissime, missi ex parte devotissimi filii vestri regis Francie iam tertio ad presentiam vestre beatitudinis principaliter supplicamus, et adhuc cum instantia supplicamus, ut pro recuperatione Terre Sancte generale passagium indicatis,[1] regem ipsum constituendo ipsius passagii capitaneum et rectorem, dicentes regi[2] quod primo Esdre 7 dicitur:[3] *A me decretum est ut cuicumque placuerit in regno meo de populo Israel et de sacerdotibus eius et de Levitis ire in Iherusalem[4] tecum vadat.*

[2] Et fuerunt verba ista ad litteram dicta[5] Esdre scribe [G 298vb] quando, post destructionem Iherusalem[6] et templi Salomonis, populo Israel de Iudea eiecto et in Babiloniam captivato, Deus Cyrum[7] regem Persarum taliter illustravit ut Esdram et Neemiam in Iudeam ad civitatis reedificationem et templi restaurationem cum multis donis et muneribus, gratiis, et largitionibus destinavit, sicut patet in loco preallegato per totum, et Neemie[8] 2.

[3] Et videtur michi quod isto tempore – quando videt quilibet quod Iherusalem,[9] que solebat esse domina gentium, facta est sub tributo, et que solebat[10] esse plena populo,[11] sedet sola, quodque vie Syon lugent eo[12] quod non sit qui veniat ad so[F 240rb]lemnitatem, quando facti sunt hostes eius in capite eius, quando loca

---

1 indicatis] inducatis *a.c.* G
2 regi] Esdre *add. in mg.* G
3 dicitur] capitulo F; primo] primi G; Ezra 7.13.
4 Iherusalem] Ierusalem F
5 dicta] dicte *a.c.* G
6 Iherusalem] Ierusalem F
7 Cyrum *om. et lac. a.c.* F, omnipotens *p.c (a.m.)* F
8 Neemie] Neemie *add. in mg.* G; terra sancta *add. in mg.* F
9 Iherusalem] Ierusalem F
10 solebat] obprobria Terre Sancte *add. in mg.* G
11 quando videt…plena populo *a.m.* G
12 eo *s.l. (lacuna)* G

228 *Appendix IV*

sancta prophanata sunt universa, quando sepulchrum domini est ignominiosum quod debebat esse multipliciter gloriosum, quando templum eius factum est sicut homo ignobilis pollutum a gentibus, et ubi colebatur unigenitus Dei filius Ihesus Christus modo colitur perditionis filius Machometus, quando Christiano populo insultant filii alieni[13] et[14] improperant dicentes: 'Confidis in Christo; adiuvet te si potest', quando nobis tantus imminet pudor, tanta confusio, tantum opprobrium[15] quod filii ancille vilissime, matrem nostram, matrem universorum fidelium detinent ancillatam, matrem illam, scilicet, in qua dominus[16] salutem nostrum dignatus est[17] operari – regem, devotissimum filium vestrum, cui Deus dedit in cor ut edi[G 299ra]ficaret domum domini que est in Iherusalem,[18] sicut[19] dicitur primo[20] Esdre 7, in suo sancto proposito confovendo, multiplicibus gratiis et favoribus[21] prosequendo, dictumque[22] pro inspiratione tam sancti propositi collaudando, decet vestram potissime sanctitatem, quam posuit Deus *caput super omnem Ecclesiam, que est corpus eius*, ad Ephesios[23] primo,[24] cunctos[25] de regno vestro, id est, de tota Christianitate, in tanti regis auxilium pro tam pio et necessario negotio generaliter invocare,[26] ei thesauros Ecclesie aperire, indulgentias, privilegia, et immunitates universaliter concedendo, dicentes regi verba thematis pre assumpta:[27] *A me decretum est*, et cetera.

[4] Hoc enim verbum de ore vestro benedicto emanare totis desideriis[28] affectamus. [F 240va] Hoc cum cordis suspiriis postulamus. *Sonet ergo hec vox vestra in auribus nostris*, Canticorum 2.[29] Hec enim erit vox dilecta, vox sonora, vox grata, vox placita,[30] vox totis precordiis expectata, vox letitie et exultationis in tabernaculis iustorum, vox, inquam, ex qua pendet consolatio miserorum, redemptio captivorum, destructio Agarenorum, exultatio Christianorum. Pater ergo sanctissime *fac me audire vocem tuam*, Canticorum 8.[31] *Dabit enim dominus voci tue vocem virtutis*, in Psalmo.[32] Dic ergo verbum *a me decretum est*,[33] et cetera.

13 filii alieni *inv.* G
14 et] qui G
15 opprobrium] obprobrium F
16 dominus] noster *add.* G
17 salutem nostrum dignatus est] dignatus est salutem nostram G
18 Iherusalem] Ierusalem F
19 sicut] Esdre *add. in mg.* G
20 primo] primi G
21 gratiis et favoribus *inv.* G
22 que *a.c. s.l.* G
23 Ephesios 1.22.23.; ad Ephesios *add. in mg.* G
24 primo] primi *a.c.* G
25 cunctos] s *s.l.* F
26 pro invocando ?
27 Ezra 7.13.
28 desideriis] viribus G || emanare totis desideriis *bis scr. et del.* F
29 Canticum Canticorum 2.14.:'sonet vox tua in auribus meis'; Canticorum *add. in mg.* G
30 placita] placida G
31 Canticum Canticorum 8.13.; destructio] Canticorum *add. in mg.* G
32 Psalmi 68.34.; in psalmo *om.* G
33 est *om.* G

[5] In quibus verbis quatuor tanguntur que in indictione generalis passagii attenduntur: requiritur enim [G 299rb] aliquid ex[34] parte indicentis, aliquid ex parte prosequentis, aliquid ex parte operis imminentis,[35] aliquid ex parte assumentis. Ex parte indicentis plenitudo copiosa, ex parte prosequentis multitudo numerosa, ex parte operis imminentis[36] rectitudo virtuosa, ex parte assumentis aptitudo vigorosa. Modo ista quatuor hic concurrunt, ut dicunt verba thematis preassumpta: primo enim in indicente est plenitudo copiosa quia auctoritatis et excellentie tenet fastigium singulare: *A me decretum est*. Secundo in prosequente est multitudo numerosa quia Christianitatis eximie, non infidelitatis et perfidie, affert auxilium et subsidium generale, quia sequitur:[37] *ut cuicumque placuerit in regno meo de populo Israel et de sacerdotibus eius*[38] *et de*[39] *Levitis*. Tertio in opere imminente[40] est rectitudo virtuosa que sanctitatis et glorie profert preconium salutare, quia sequitur in themate: *ire in Iherusalem*,[41] [F 240vb] que est res virtuosa, res gloriosa. Quarto in assumente est aptitudo vigorosa quia ydoneitatis et convenientie profert indicium speciale, quia sequitur: *tecum vadat*, scilicet, cum rege Francie qui est ad hoc ut sit rector istius multitudinis, convenientior et aptior omnibus principibus Christianis.

[6] Videte ergo pater sanctissime,[42] quomodo, ut dicunt verba thematis preassumpta, indicente nil est excellentius potestate ad decernendum, inducendum, et compellendum universaliter, *A me decretum est*. Videte etiam [G 299va] quomodo prosequente nil salubrius sua universitate ad prosequendum utiliter, quia sequitur: *ut cuicumque placuerit*, et cetera. Videte tertio quomodo opere[43] imminente[44] nil splendidius honestate ad assumendum[45] faciliter, quia sequitur: *ire in Iherusalem*.[46] Videte quarto quomodo assumente nil convenientius probitate[47] ad regendum et disponendum salubriter, quia sequitur: *tecum vadat*, scilicet, cum rege.

[7] Dico ergo primo quod hic conspicitur in sanctitate vestra plenitudo[48] copiosa quia auctoritatis et excellentie tenet fastigium singulare, unde ea nil[49] excellentius potestate ad decernendum, indicendum, et compellendum universaliter, quia dicitur in themate: *A me decretum est*. Vos enim ad literam estis assumptus

---

34 ex] a F
35 imminentis] iminentis F
36 imminentis] iminentis F
37 sequitur] in auctoritate *add.* G
38 eius *om.* G
39 de *om.* G
40 imminente] iminente F
41 Iherusalem] Ierusalem F
42 pater sanctissime *inv.* G
43 opere] opera *a.c.* F
44 imminente] pre *add. et del.* G; iminente F
45 assumendum] assupremendum *a.c.* G
46 Iherusalem] Ierusalem F
47 probitate] quia *add. et del.* G
48 plenitudo] potestas pape *add. in mg.* F; pape potestas *add. in mg.* G
49 nil] nichil G

230 Appendix IV

ad plenitudinem potestatis, alii in partem sollicitudinis, ut ad vos solum pertineat universaliter decernere in tota Ecclesia quod fuerit faciendum. Nulli enim alii nisi Petro et eius successoribus dictum est Luce 22:[50] *Et tu aliquando conversus, confirma fratres tuos.* Nulli etiam alii universaliter [F 241 ra] dictum est: *Pasce oves meas*, Johannis ultimo,[51] absque determinatione specialis ovilis. Unde hanc potestatem et auctoritatem attendens, Bernardus II, *De consideratione ad Eugenium* capitulo 7 dicit sic:[52]

> Indagemus diligentius quis sis, quam geris personam in Ecclesiam Dei. Quis es? Sacerdos magnus, summus pontifex. Tu[53] princeps episcoporum, tu heres Apostolorum, tu primatu Abel, [G 299vb] gubernatu Noe, patriarchatu Abraham, ordine Melchisedech, dignitate Aaron, auctoritate Moyses, iudicatu Samuel, potestate Petrus, unctione Christus. Tu es cui claves tradite, cui oves credite sunt. Quidem et si alii celi ianitores, et gregum pastores; tamen de tanto gloriosius, quanto et[54] differentius, pre illis nomen hereditasti. Habent illi sibi assignatos greges, singuli singulos: tibi universi crediti, unus uni. Non modo ovium, sed pastor tu[55] unus omnium pastorum.

Et sequitur:[56]

> Ergo, iuxta canones tuos, alii in partem sollicitudinis, tu in plenitudinem[57] potestatis vocatus es. Aliorum potestas certis artatur limitibus; tua extenditur etiam in ipsos, qui potestatem super alios acceperunt.[58] Nonne, si causa extiterit, tu episcopo celum claudere, tu ab episcopatu illum deponere, et tradere Sathane potes? Stat ergo inconcusse privilegium tuum tibi, tam in datis clavibus quam in ovibus commendatis[59] concessum.

Et subdit in fine:[60]

> Itaque, cum quisque ceterorum habeat suam, tibi una commissa[61] est gratissima navis, facta ex omnibus ipsa universalis Ecclesia, toto orbe diffusa.

---

50 Lucas 22.32.; Luce *add. in mg.* G
51 Johannes 21.17.; Johannes G; Johannes *add. in mg.* G
52 Bernardus *add. in mg.* G; 'De consideratione ad Eugenium papam', in *Sancti Bernardi Opera*, eds. Jean Leclercq and Henri-Marie Rochais, 8 vols. (Rome: Editiones Cistercienses, 1957–1977), 3:423, Lib.II, cap.8.15.
53 tu *om.* G
54 et *om.* G
55 es *add.* G
56 'De consideratione ad Eugenium papam', 3:424, Lib. II, cap.8.16.
57 plenitudinem] plenitudine F
58 acceperunt] receperunt G
59 commendatis] comendatis F
60 'De consideratione ad Eugenium papam', 3:424, Lib. II, cap.8.16.
61 commissa] comissa G

[8] Quia ergo in sanctitate vestra est plenitudo potestatis et auctoritatis, [F 241rb] pertinet ad vos decernere ut dicatis illud primo[62] Esdre 6:[63] *Statui decretum, quod studiose impleri volo*. Vobis enim ad literam dicitur primo[64] Esdre 10:[65] *Tuum est decernere, nos erimus tecum*[66] *confortare* [G 300ra] *et fac*, et dicit scriptura signanter:[67] *Tuum est decernere*.

[9] Est enim negotium istud vestrum specialiter ex duobus: primo ex potestatis plenitudine quia nullus alius potest passagium generale indicere. Nullus alius obligatos ex voto universaliter per totum mundum potest ad transfretandum compellere. Ergo vestrum est decernere. Unde potest de vobis dici illud[68] Ysaie 14:[69] *Decrevit et quis poterit infirmare et manus extenta et quis avertet eam*, quasi dicat 'nullus'. Secundo vestrum est decernere ex paterna cura et sollicitudine quia sicut pius pater habetis omnibus providere et etiam previdere. Unde[70] Bernardus IV, *De consideratione ad Eugenium papam* capitulo ultimo dicebat sic:[71]

> Oportet te esse[72] considera[73] formam iustitie, sanctimonie speculum, pietatis exemplar, assertorem veritatis, fidei defensorem,[74] doctorem gentium, Christianorum ducem, amicum sponsi, sponse paranimphum, cleri ordinatorem, pastorem plebium, magistrum insipientium, refugium oppressorum, pauperum advocatum, miserorum spem, tutorem pupillorum, iudicem viduarum, oculum[75] cecorum, linguam mutorum, baculum senum, ultorem scelerum, malorum metum, bonorum gloriam, virgam potentium,[76] malleum tyrannorum, regum patrem, legum moderatorem, canonum dispensatorem, sal terre, orbis lumen, sacerdotem altissimi, vicarium Christi, Christum domini postremo dominum [F 241va] Pharaonis. Intellige que dico: dabit enim tibi Dominus intellectum, ubi[77] [G 300rb] malitie victa est potentia, aliquid tibi supra hominem presumendum. Vultus tuus super facientes mala. Timeat spiritum ire tue, qui hominem non veretur, gladium tuum[78] non[79] formidat.[80] Qui[81]

---

62 primo] primi G
63 Ezra 6.12.; Esdre *add. in mg.* G
64 primo] primi G
65 Ezra 10.4.
66 erimus tecum *inv.* F
67 Ezra 10.4.
68 illud] Isaie *add. in mg.* G
69 14] xliiii G; Isaias 14.27.
70 unde] Bernardus *add. in mg.* G
71 'De consideratione ad Eugenium papam', 3:466, Lib. IV, cap.7.23.
72 esse *om.* F
73 considera] considerare F
74 defensorem] defenfensorem F
75 oculum] occulum F
76 potentium] potentum G
77 Christi...ubi *a.m.* G
78 tuum *om.* G
79 non *om.* F
80 formidat] formidet F
81 qui] postremo Dominum Pharaonis *add.* G

232 *Appendix IV*

ammonitionem contempsit. Cui irasceris tu, Deum sibi iratum, non hominem putet. Qui te non audierit, audiendum Deum, contra se, paveat.

[10] Unde propter hanc curam et sollicitudinem dicebat dominus Innocentius tertius in sermone quem[82] fecit pro succursu Terre Sancte in concilio[83] Lateranensi:[84]

> Sic ergo fratres dilectissimi,[85] totum me vobis committo,[86] totum me vobis expono, paratus sum iuxta consilium[87] vestrum, si videritis expedire, personalem subire laborem, et transire ad reges, et principes ad populos, et nationes; adhuc autem et ultra, si forte clamore valido eos valeam excitare, ut surgant ad prelium domini preliandum, et vindicandum iniuriam Crucifixi, qui pro peccatis nostris eiectus est de terra[88] sua, quam proprio corporis sanguinem[89] consecravit, et in qua universa redemptionis nostre sacramenta peregit. Quidquid non egerint alii, nos sacerdotes Domini negotium specialiter assumamus, subvenientes et succurrentes, in personis et rebus, ita necessitatibus Terre Sancte, ut nullus omnino remaneat, qui non sit particeps tanti operis, nec sit expers tante incredis. Nam et olim simili modo per sacerdotes fecit Deus salutem in Israhel,[90] quanto [G 300va] per Machabeos, utique sacer[F 241vb]dotes, filios Mathatie, liberavit Iherusalem[91] et templum de manibus impiorum.

[11] Ego tute paratus sum pro hac causa, si dispositum est a Deo, bibere calicem passionis ut addere possim quod addidit Ihesus Christus dicens:[92] *Desiderio desideravi hoc Pascha manducare vobiscum, antequam*[93] *patiar*. Ergo bene, pater sanctissime, ex paterna cura et sollicitudine tuum est decernere. Et certe, pater beatissime, bene ostendistis quod ex paterna cura et sollicitudine[94] istud negotium erat vestrum, quia qui vidit testimonium perhibet quod iam per duos annos isti negotio tam sollicite intendistis quod die ac[95] nocte circa hoc continue laborastis, omnem curam et sollicitudinem circumferentes pro bona ordinatione negotii memorati. Unde bene dicitur in auctoritate:[96] *Tuum est decernere*.

---

82 quem] Innocentius *add. in mg.* G
83 concilio] consilio G
84 'Innocentii III Pape Sermones de Diversis in Concilio Generali Lateranensi Habitus', in *Patrologia Latina*, ed. J.-P. Migne, 217:674–680, 676, sermo vi.
85 dilectissimi] carissimi G
86 committo] comitto F
87 consilium] concilium F
88 terra] et *add.* F
89 sanguinem] sanguine F
90 Israhel] Israel F
91 Iherusalem] Ierusalem F
92 Lucas 22.15.
93 antequam] ante quam F
94 tuum est decernere *add. et del.* F
95 ac] et G
96 Ezra 10.4.

Et sequitur: *nos erimus tecum*, tecum[97] in consilio,[98] tecum[99] in auxilio, tecum[100] in presidio. Confortare ergo et fac ut vobis dicamus quod scribitur Judicum 19:[101] *Ferte*[102] *sententiam, et*[103] *in communi decernite quid facto opus sit*. Et sic patet primum principale.

[12] Secundo dico quod hic attenditur in prosequente multitudo numerosa quia Christianitatis eximie, non infidelitatis et perfidie, affert auxilium et subsidium generale. Unde ea nil salubrius sua universitate[104] ad prosequendum utiliter. Unde sequitur in themate:[105] *ut cuicumque placuerit in regno meo de populo Israel et de*[106] *sa*[G 300vb]*cerdotibus eius et de*[107] *Levitis*, et cetera. [F 242ra] Unde videtur michi quod hic ex parte prosequentis est[108] quedam generalitas et quedam specialitas, generalitas in totius Christianitatis inclusione,[109] specialitas[110] in totius infidelitatis exclusione. Generalitas quidem cum dicitur:[111] *cuicumque placuerit de populo et de sacerdotibus eius et de*[112] *Levitis*, et cetera. Specialitas autem cum dicitur:[113] *in regno meo*, et cum dicitur: *Israhel*.[114] Sic enim debet istud negotium prosequi et in Terre Sancte subsidium tota Christianitas invocari ut omnis tam Iudaica perfidia, quam generalis ydolatria, quam omnis alia infidelitas[115] excludatur.

[13] Causa autem istius generalitatis videtur michi ad presens esse triplex: prima est[116] generalis ratio omnes afficiens,[117] ymmo generalis obligatio omnes[118] vinciens. Secunda est generalis imitatio omnes respiciens. Tertia est generalis remuneratio omnes alliciens.

[14] Prima ergo causa istius generalitatis est generalis ratio omnes afficiens, ymmo generalis obligatio omnes vinciens,[119] ubi[120] enim est eadem ratio, ibi idem ius. Negotium autem Terre Sancte omnes Christianos generaliter tangit

---

97 tecum *om.* G
98 consilio] concilio F
99 tecum *om.* G
100 tecum *om.* G
101 Iudicum 19.30.
102 ferte] forte G
103 et *om.* G
104 sua universitate *inv.* G
105 Ezra 7.13.
106 de *om.* G
107 de *om.* G
108 est] et F
109 inclusione] in conclusione G
110 specialitas] specialitatis *a.c.* G
111 Ezra 7.13.
112 de *om.* F
113 Ezra 7.13.
114 Israhel] Israel F
115 infidelitas] Christiani passagium *add. in mg.* F
116 est *bis. scr.* F
117 afficiens] universitas Christianorum passagium *add. in mg.* G
118 omnes] omnis G
119 vinciens] uniens G
120 ubi] sarraceni bellum *add. in mg.* F

quadruplici ratione, ex quibus merito Sarracenis occupantibus Terram Sanctam indicitur iustum bellum: prima[121] ratione successionis, secunda[122] ratione professionis, tertia[123] ratione sanctificationis, quarta[124] ratione obligationis.

[15] Primo quidem[125] ratione[126] successionis. Terra enim Sancta dicitur [G 301ra] 'Terra Promissionis', fuit enim, Genesis 12, promissa semini Abrahe. Unde dixit sibi Deus:[127] *Semini tuo dabo terram hanc*, et Genesis 13 dictum est ei:[128] *Omnem terram quam conspicis, tibi dabo*[129] *et semini tuo usque in sempiternum*. Que promissio [F 242rb] fuit confirmata per miraculum Genesis 15, quando dixit sibi Deus:[130] *Ego Dominus qui eduxi te de Ur Chaldeorum*[131] *ut darem tibi terram istam, et possideres eam. At ille ait: Domine Deus, unde scire possum quod possessurus sum eam? Et respondit ei*[132] *Dominus: Sume, inquit, michi vaccam*[133] *triennem*, et cetera. Que promissio etiam fuit confirmata Ysaac Genesis 26. Unde dixit sibi Deus:[134] *Tibi et semini tuo dabo universas regiones has*. Que etiam promissio fuit confirmata Jacob Genesis 27. Unde dixit sibi Deus:[135] *Terram, in qua dormis, tibi dabo et semini tuo. Dilataberis*[136] *ad orientem, et occidentem, septentrionem, et meridiem, et benedicentur in te et in semine tuo omnes tribus terre*. Ex quibus patet quod ex promissione divina terra illa debetur Abrahe, Ysaac et Jacob et semini eorum usque[137] in sempiternum; sed semen eorum sunt soli Christiani; ergo eis debetur terra illa.

[16] Quod autem sunt semen Christiani et[138] non alii patet, quia illi sunt filii Abrahe, qui imitantur[139] opera Abrahe, iuxta dictum Salvatoris, Johannis 8:[140] *Si* [G 301rb] *filii Abrahe estis, opera Abrahe facite*. Unde Judeis dicebat Christus:[141] *Vos ex patre dyabolo estis et opera patris vestri vultis facere*. Sed soli Christiani imitantur[142] opera Abrahe et aliorum patriarcharum, eadem enim fides que erat in eis est in nobis. Et ideo Apostolus ad Galatas 4 deduxit quod non qui *secundum*

---

121 prima] primo G
122 secunda] secundo G
123 tertia] tertio G
124 quarta] quarto G
125 quidem] iuste bellare contra sarracenos *add. in mg.* G
126 ratione] succes *add. et del.* F
127 Genesis 12.7.; Genesis *add. in mg.* G
128 Genesis 13.15.; Genesis *add. in mg.* G
129 tibi dabo *inv.* G
130 Genesis 15.7–10.; Genesis *add. in mg.* G
131 chaldeorum] caldeorum F
132 ei *om.* F
133 vaccam] vacam F
134 Genesis 26.3.
135 Genesis 28.13, 14.; Genesis *add. in mg.* G
136 dilataberis] dilataberim *a.c.* G
137 usque *om.* F
138 christiani et] ergo eis…Christiani et *om. per homoeoteleuton* F
139 imitantur] imittantur F
140 Iohannes 8.39.; Iohannis *add. in mg.* G
141 Iohannes 8.44.
142 imitantur] imittantur F

carnem natus est,[143] sed is[144] qui secundum spiritum est filius Abrahe. Unde concludit:[145] *Non enim heres erit*[146] *filius ancille cum filio libere*. Adduceris illud Genesis 21:[147] *Eice ancillam et filium eius, non enim erit heres filius ancille cum filio libere*. Et ideo concludit Apostolus:[148] [F 242va] *Itaque fratres non sumus ancille filii sed libere*; et ad Galatas[149] 3:[150] *Abrahe dicte sunt promissiones et semini eius. Non dicit in seminibus quasi in multis, sed quasi in uno, et semini tuo qui est Christus*.

[17] Patet ergo quod[151] illa terra iure successionis debetur Christianis. Unde possunt dicere Christiani: 'Non aliena petimus, nec aliena vobis[152] vendicamus, sed hereditatem patrum nostrorum'. Et nota quomodo non potest nobis currere prescriptio in hac parte tum quia data est semini in sempiternum, tum quia, postquam[153] fuit promissa sanctis patriarchis, steterunt filii Israhel[154] in Egipto CCCC annis, et tamen non currit eis tempus quin eam iuste acquisierint[155] et occupatores interfecerint[156] universos.

[18] Secunda[157] ratio est ratione professionis. Christianus enim dicitur a Christo. [G 301va] Ut igitur actio[158] nomini respondeat,[159] debet Christianus que Christi sunt agere, defendere, et tueri. Unde Augustinus *De doctrina*[160] *Christiana* dicit sic:[161] 'Si Christianum te esse delectat, que Christi sunt gere et tunc merito tibi nomen Christiani assume'. Sed certum est quod Christus Terram illam Sanctam proprii corporis sanguine comperavit, sicut supra allegatum est. Ergo merito quilibet Christianus debet conari ut Christo restituatur, et maxime quia Christus eam perdidit non propter factum suum sed propter peccata nostra, scilicet, Christianorum. Ergo, cum secundum Philosophum II Ethicorum ex contrariis 'contrario[162] modo' factis 'fit omnis virtus et corrumpitur',[163] sicut propter

---

143 Galates 4.23.; ad Galatas *add. in mg.* G
144 is] hiis G
145 Galates 4.30.
146 heres erit *inv.* G
147 Genesis 21.10.; Genesis *add. in mg.* G
148 Galates 4.31.
149 Galatas] Galathas F
150 Galates 3.16.; ad Galatas *add. in mg.* G
151 quod] quomodo G
152 vobis] nobis G
153 postquam] post G
154 Israhel] Israel F
155 acquisierint] acquisierunt *a.c.* G
156 intefecerint] interfecerat G
157 secunda] christiani passagium *add. in mg.* F
158 actio < > nomini respondeat *lacuna* G
159 nomini respondeat *inv.* G
160 doctrina] Augustinus *add. in mg.* G
161 'Sanctus Augustinus: De vita Christiana', in *Patrologia Latina*, ed. J.-P. Migne, 40:1031–1046, 1033, Lib.I, cap.1.
162 contrario] d add. et del. G
163 *Aristoteles Latinus: Ethica Nicomachea*, ed. R. A. Gauthier, 5 vols. (Leiden: Brill, 1972–1974), 3:167, Lib.II, §6.

peccata nostra Christus eam perdidit, sic per virtutum[164] exercitium debet sibi per Christianos restitui atque[165] reddi. Clamat enim in Psalmo:[166] *Tu es qui restitues*[167] *hereditatem meam michi.* Unde ex ista causa [F 242vb] clamabat propheta[168] in alio Psalmo dicens:[169] *Deus, venerunt gentes in hereditatem tuam, polluerunt templum sanctum tuum, posuerunt Iherusalem*[170] *in pomorum custodiam, posuerunt mortalia servorum tuorum,* et cetera usque ibi: *propitius esto peccatis nostris propter nomen tuum.*[171]

[19] Tertia causa est ratione sanctificationis. Terra enim Sancta tota fuit per aspersionem sanguinis Christi et martirum sanctificata in tantum quod, sicut[172] dicit Urbanus papa in sermone quem fecit in concilio Claromontensi:[173] 'Non est in ea passus pedis, quem non sanctificaverit aut illustraverit vel [G 301vb] corpus vel umbra salvatoris vel gloriosa presentia[174] sancte Dei genitricis vel amplectendus apostolorum cetus, vel martirum ebibendus sanguis effusus'. Unde terram illam Deus specialiter preelegit quia et[175] ibi in mundo conversatus moram traxit,[176] ibi docuit, ibi[177] mortuus fuit, ibi sepultus, ibi venturus est iudicare vivos et mortuos, et reddere unicuique secundum opera sua. Quod ergo loca sic sanctificata possit aliquis catholicus sub dissimulatione[178] videre taliter per istos impios prophanari et pollui, certe non potest, sed debet dicere quod dicebant illi sancti Machabei primo Machabeorum 2:[179] *Ecce sancta nostra, et pulchritudo nostra, et claritas nostra desolata est, et coinquinaverunt eam gentes. Quid ergo nobis adhuc*[180] *vivere?* quasi dicat: 'melius[181] mori quam vivere':[182] *Melius est enim nobis*[183] *mori in bello quam videre mala gentis nostre et sanctorum.* Unde istam rationem tangit propheta Jeremias, Jeremie 51 dicens:[184] *Recordamini* [F 243ra]

164 virtutum] virtutis G
165 atque] Philosophus *add. in mg.* G
166 Psalmi 16.5.
167 restitues] restituins G
168 propheta] Psalmus *add. in mg.* G
169 Psalmi 78.7.
170 Iherusalem] Ierusalem F
171 Psalmi 78.9.
172 sicut] Urbanus *add. in mg.* G
173 Claromontensi] Clarontensi F; 'Baldrici, Episcopis Dolensis, Historia Jerosolimitana', in *Recueil des Historiens des Croisades: Historiens Occidentaux. Tome quatrième* (Paris: Imprimerie Nationale, 1844–1895), 14.
174 presentia] presentia *bis scr. et del.* F
175 et *om.* G
176 ibi in mundo conversatus moram traxit] in mundo conversatus ibi moram traxit G
177 ibi] m *add. et del.* G
178 sanctificata possit aliquis catholicus sub dissimulatione] sanctificata sub dissimulatione possit aliquis catholicus G
179 I Machabeorum 2.12–13; Machabeorum *add. in mg.* G
180 nobis adhuc *inv.* G
181 melius] est *add.* G
182 I Machabeorum 3.59.
183 nobis *om.* G
184 Ieremias 51.50–51.; Ieremie *add. in mg.* G

procul Domini, et Israhel[185] *ascendat supra corpus vestrum. Confusi sumus quoniam audivimus opprobrium:*[186] *et operuit ignominia facies nostras, quia venerunt alieni super sanctificationem domus Domini.*

[20] Quarta ratio est ratione obligationis. Quilibet enim[187] est obligatus Christo sicut vasallus domino. Unde et corpus et quidquid habet[188] a Deo. Quomodo ergo erit fidelis vasallus qui in lo[G 302ra]cis in quibus Christus debet pre ceteris honorari, coli, et adorari videt ipsum blasphemari et multas ei et eius sancto nomini contumelias irrogari, maxime quia, sicut dicit Chrisostomus:[189] 'Licet iniuriam propriam[190] dissimulare pium sit, tamen iniuriam Christi dissimulare iniquum est'. Unde propter hoc clamat Christus in Psalmo:[191] *Apprehende arma et scutum, et exurge in adiutorium michi. Effunde frameam, et conclude adversus eos qui persecuntur*[192] *me*, et cetera. Unde debet dicere quilibet Christianus sicut dicebat ille sanctus[193] puer II Machabeorum 6, *cum ad mortem duceretur*,[194] dicebat enim sic:[195] *E*[196] *celo ista possideo, sed propter Dei leges hec ipsa despicio.* Quia ergo quilibet generaliter se profitetur filium, se profitetur[197] Christianum, se asserit catholicum, se recognoscit vasallum, patet quod hec est generalis ratio omnes afficiens, ymmo generalis[198] obligatio omnes vinciens. Unde generaliter dicitur cuilibet primo[199] Esdre primo:[200] *Quis est in vobis de universo populo Israhel?*[201] *Sit Deus illius cum eo ascendat in Israhel*[202] *que est in Iudea, et edificet domum domini Dei Israhel.*[203] *Ipse enim est Deus qui est in Israhel;*[204] et sequitur:[205] *surrexerunt principes patrum de Iuda et Beniamin,*[206] *et sacerdotes, et Levite, omnis cuius suscitavit Deus spiritum, ut ascen*[F 243rb]*derent ad edificandum templum Domini, quod erat in Iherusalem.*[207]

185 Israhel] Israel F
186 opprobrium] obprobrium F
187 enim] debet *add. et del.* G
188 habet *bis scr.* G
189 Chrisostomus] Crisostomus F; *Johannes Crysostomus super Mattheum*, ed. Johann Koelhoff (Cologne, 1487), 236.
190 propriam] Chrisostomus *add. in mg.* G
191 Psalmi 35.2–3.; Psalmus *add. in mg.* G
192 persecuntur] secuntur G
193 sanctus] Machabeorum *add. in mg.* G
194 Danielis 13.45.
195 II Machabeorum 7.11.
196 e] ex G
197 se profitetur *inv.* F
198 generalis] ratio omnes v *add. et del.* G
199 primo *om.* G
200 I Ezra 1.3.; vasallum patet…dicitur Esdre primo *a.m.* G
201 Israhel] Israel F
202 Israhel] Israel F
203 Israhel] Israel F
204 Israhel] Israel F
205 sequitur] suxe *add. et del.* G; Ezra 1.5
206 Beniamin] Benyamin G
207 Iherusalem] Israel F

238 *Appendix IV*

[21] Secunda[208] causa istius generalitatis est generalis invitatio omnes respiciens. Invitat enim omnes generaliter Christus, dicens illud Psalmi:[209] *Respice in faciem Christi* [G 302rb] *tui*. Invitant enim livores et vulnera, invitant[210] caput, manus,[211] pedes et latera, invitant[212] spine clavi[213] et lancea, invitant[214] sputa, clamant opprobria, invitant[215] innumerabilia genera tormentorum: *O vos omnes qui transitis per viam, attendite, et videte si est dolor*[216] *sicut dolor meus*, Trenorum primo.[217] Invitat Bethleem in qua natus est, invitat Nazareth in qua nutritus est, invitat templum in quo oblatus est,[218] invitat Iherusalem[219] in qua passus est, invitat sepulchrum in quo sepultus est, invitat vallis Iosaphat in qua iudicaturus est, invitant illi sancti montes in quibus oravit, docuit et in celos ascendit, invitat mos etiam ille in quo transfiguratus est et universaliter tota illa[220] terra benedicta in qua cum hominibus tam dulciter conversatus est, Ysaie 62:[221] *Qui reminiscimini Domini, ne taceatis, et ne detis silentium ei, donec stabiliat et donec ponat Iherusalem*[222] *laudem in terra*.

[22] Tertia causa istius generalitatis est generalis remuneratio omnes alliciens. Remuneratio enim que pro[223] tam virtuoso opere[224] debetur generaliter omnes allicit, omnes respicit – et quidem remuneratio in eterna beatitudine cum pro isto opere transit quis de terra ad celum, de exilio ad patriam, de paupertate ad regnum, de morte ad vitam, de labore ad requiem, de dolore ad gaudium, de miseria ad Paradisum. Ideo Leo papa in[225] quadam[226] [F 243va] epistola directa exercitui regis Francie, et causa[227] 23, questione 8,[228] dicit sic:[229] [G 302va] 'Omni timore et terrore[230] deposito, contra inimicos sancte fidei, agere fideliter studete. Novit enim omnipotens, si quilibet vestrorum moriatur, quod pro veritate fidei,

---

208 secunda] invitatio christiani ad passagium *add. in mg.* G
209 Psalmi 84.10.; Psalmus *add. in mg.* G
210 invitant *om.* G
211 caput, manus *inv.* F
212 invitant *om.* G
213 spine clavi *inv.* F
214 invitant *om.* G
215 invitant *om.* G
216 dolor] similis *add.* G
217 Lamentationes 1.12.; Trenorum *add. in mg.* G
218 invitat Nazareth in qua nutritus est, invitat templum in quo oblatus est *inv.* G
219 Iherusalem] Ierusalem F
220 illa] causa *add. et del.* G
221 Isaias 62.6–7.; Ysaie *add. in mg.* G
222 ponat Iherusalem] ponatIherusalem G || Ierusalem F
223 pro *a.m. add. s.l.* F
224 opere] negotio G
225 in] Leo *add. in mg.* G
226 quadam] quodam G
227 causa] est G
228 viiia] viii F
229 'Leonis Papae IV: Epistolae et Decreta', in *Patrologia Latina*, ed. J.-P. Migne, 115:655–675, 657, epist. I (Ad exercitum Francorum).
230 et terrore *om.* F

ac salvatione patrie, et defensione Christianorum mortuus est: ideo a Deo celeste premium consequetur'. Non solum autem est generalis remuneratio in futuro, ymmo etiam in presenti. Pro isto enim negotio thesauri aperiuntur Ecclesie: plena omnibus generaliter concedetur peccatorum remissio, penarum relaxatio, multarum aliarum gratiarum effusio. Ergo omnes sitientes venite ad aquas, et qui non habetis argentum, properate, emite, et comedite. Venite, emite absque argento et absque ulla commutatione vinum et lac. Propter istam ergo causam dicat vestra sanctitas illud quod scribitur II Esdre 2:[231] *Me constituit regem orbis terrarum dominus Israhel,*[232] *dominus excelsus, et significavit michi edificare sibi domum in Iherusalem*[233] *que est in Iudea. Si quis*[234] *est ex genere vestro dominus ipsius,*[235] *ascendat cum eo*[236] *in Iherusalem.*[237]

[23] Patet ergo triplex causa istius generalitatis. Est autem ista generalitas pro generibus singulorum, ut non[238] singuli status, sed de quolibet statu aliqui in passagium istud vadant. Et propter hoc dicit textus:[239] *ut cuicumque placuerit de populo Israel, de sacerdotibus, et de*[240] *Levitis.* Vel posset[241] dici quod est quodammodo distributio et generalitas pro singulis[242] generum. Dicitur enim tripliciter aliquis in passagium istud [G 302vb] ire: quandoque partiendo auxilium corporale, [F 243vb] sicut qui in personis propriis illuc ibunt, quandoque mittendo subsidium temporale vel penitentiale,[243] sicut qui dant[244] de suo, quandoque impertiendo suffragium spirituale, ut orationes[245] et similia.[246] Bene ergo ista generalitas singulos de tota Christianitate concernit, quia puto quod non erit aliquis[247] compos mentis qui aliquo trium predictorum modorum illuc non vadat. Primo[248] Esdre primo dicitur quod Esdras[249] et Neemias et ceteri ascenderunt in Iherusalem:[250] *Universi adiuverunt manus eorum cum vasis argenteis et aureis in substantia, et in supellectili*[251] *exceptis hiis que sponte obtulerant.*[252]

---

231 Ezra 2.3–5.; Esdre *add. in mg.* G
232 Israhel] Israel F
233 Iherusalem] Ierusalem F
234 si quis] siquis F
235 ipsius *om.* F
236 ascendat cum eo *inv.* G
237 Iherusalem] Ierusalem F
238 pro generibus singulorum, ut non *a.m.* G
239 Ezra 7.13.
240 de *om.* G
241 posset] potest G
242 singulis] ire in passagium *add. in mg.* G; passagium *add. in mg.* F
243 penitentiale] spirituale G
244 dant] dat F
245 orationes] rationes G
246 similia] concilia F
247 erit aliquis *inv.* G
248 primo] primi G
249 Esdras *om. (lacuna)* F; Esdre *add. in mg.* G
250 Iherusalem] Ierusalem F; Ezra 1.6.
251 supellectili] superlectili G
252 obtulerant] obtulerat G

240 *Appendix IV*

[24] Patet ergo et generalitas et causa generalitatis. Sed quia dictum est ibi, etiam quedam specialitas est[253] exclusiva. Sicut enim vult textus quod istud generaliter indicatis quantum ad totam Christianitatem ut afferant[254] auxilium et subsidium, quod tamen vult quod ab[255] hoc tota infidelitas[256] et perfidia excludantur,[257] propter quod signanter dicit textus:[258] *in regno meo et de populo Israhel,*[259] et causam istius specialitatis reddit Apostolus secunda ad Corinthios 6, dicens sic:[260] *Nolite iugum ducere cum infidelibus? Que enim participatio iustitie*[261] *cum iniquitate? Aut que societas lucis ad tenebras? Que autem conventio Christi ad Belial? Aut que pars fidelis cum infideli? Quis autem consensus templo Dei cum ydolis?* Unde ad litteram, postquam Iudas Machabeus, fortissimus miles, fedus [G 303ra] inivit cum Romanis, tunc infidelibus, in primo bello quod post fedus[262] initum[263] habuit mortuus est, sicut patet primo[264] Machabeorum 9,[265] licet semper antea de hostibus triumphasset. Et II Esdre ultimo dicitur[266] quod, separatis alienigenis:[267] *Congregati sunt universi filii Israhel*[268] *in Iherusalem*[269] *celebrare* [F 244ra] *letitiam, secundum testamentum Domini Dei Israel*. Et ideo primo[270] Esdre 10:[271] *Et missa est vox in Iuda et in Israhel*[272] *omnibus filiis transmigrationis ut congregarentur in Iherusalem,*[273] non aliis sed filiis. Et sic patet secundum principale.

[25] Dico tertio quod in opere imminente[274] est rectitudo virtuosa que sanctitatis et glorie profert preconium salutare. Dicto enim opere nil splendidius honestate ad assumendum faciliter. Unde sequitur in themate: *ire in Iherusalem*.[275] Quid enim isto opere sanctius, quid gloriosius, quid honestius, quid splendidius cuilibet Christiano quam ire in Iherusalem?[276] Istud est opus purgativum

253 est *om.* F
254 afferant] auferant G
255 ab] ad G
256 infidelitas] fidelitas G
257 excludantur] excludatur G
258 Ezra 7.13.
259 Israhel] Israel F
260 II Corinthios 6.14–16.; ad Corinthios *add. in mg.* G
261 iustitie] iustie F
262 fedus] hedus *a.c.* F
263 initum *om.* G
264 primo] primi G
265 9] Machabeorum *add. in mg.* G
266 dicitur] Esdre *add. in mg.* G
267 II Ezra 3.56.
268 Israhel] Israel F
269 Iherusalem] Ierusalem F
270 primo] primi G
271 Ezra 10.7.; Esdre *add. in mg.* G
272 Israhel] Israel F
273 Iherusalem] Israel F
274 imminente] iminente F
275 Iherusalem] Ierusalem F
276 Iherusalem] Ierusalem F

nostre corruptionis, est exclusivum[277] nostre confusionis, est inflamativum sancte affectionis et[278] incentivum nostre devotionis, est imitativum paterne traditionis, est completivum nostre perfectionis, est directivum et promotivum nostre salvationis. Et potest ex quolibet istorum sumi ratio quare est passagium faciendum.

[26] Dico primo quod istud opus est purgativum nostre corruptionis. Quis enim illuc ibit qui non prius a se omnem feditatem et corruptionem abiciat? Debet [G 303rb] enim attendere totus populus Christianus illud quod dixit ille Achor Judith quinto capitulo, ubi dicitur sic:[279] *Non fuit qui insultaret populo isti nec quando recessit a cultura Domini, Dei sui. Quotienscumque autem preter ipsum Deum suum alterum coluerunt, dati sunt in predam et in gladium et in opprobrium. Quotienscumque autem penituerunt recessisse a cultura Dei, dedit eis Dominus celi virtutem resistendi.* Unde etiam propter peccata nimia totus populus corruit, sicut patet de Achor[280] qui furatus est regulam [F 244rb] auream de anathemate Josue 7.[281] Unde dicitur ibi:[282] *Non poteris stare coram hostibus tuis donec deleatur ex te qui contaminatus est hoc scelere.* Quomodo ergo se quilibet[283] non purgabit ab omni corruptione peccati et ut sit[284] particeps indulgentie, que solum datur penitentibus et confessis, et ut non exponat periculo se et totum exercitum Christianum, ad Romanos 8:[285] *Creatura liberabitur a servitute[286] corruptionis in libertatem glorie filiorum Dei*? Unde ex isto opere transibunt odia in dilectionem, inimicitie convertentur in pacem, tranquillitas extinguet[287] iram, mansuetudo remittet rancorem,[288] convertetur superbia in humilitatem, avaritia in largitatem, luxuria in castitatem, crapula in sobrietatem, invidia in caritatem, ira et bella in pacem, accidia in operositatem, sicut tangit Leo in sermone *de Quadragesima*; unde *hec erit mutatio dextere* [G 303va] *excelsi*.[289] Credo enim quod[290] ex hoc opere subtrahentur dyabolo plus quam centum milia animarum et reddentur Deo. Unde poterit dici Christianis[291] illud I[292] Esdre 4:[293] *Benedixerunt Deum[294] patrum suorum, qui dedit illis remissionem et refrigerium, ut ascenderent et edificarent*

---

277 exclusivum] animatum Christiani ad passagium *add. in mg.* G
278 et] est G
279 Iudith 5.17–19.; Judith *add. in mg.* G
280 Achor] Achior *a.c.* F
281 Iosue 7.21, 24.
282 Iosue 7.13.; Josue *add. in mg.* G
283 se quilibet *inv.* G
284 sit *om.* G
285 Romanos 8.21.; ad Romanos *add. in mg.* G
286 servitute] servitutem G
287 extinguet] extinget F
288 rancorem] iram G
289 Psalmi 77.11.
290 quod *a.m.* G
291 christianis] christianus G
292 I] ii G, F
293 4] capitulo *add.* G; I Ezra 4.62–63.; Esdre *add. in mg.* G
294 Deum] prti *add. et del.* G

Iherusalem[295] *et templum, ubi nominatum est nomen eius in ipso; et exultaverunt cum musicis et letitia*. Debet ergo movere ad hoc passagium purgatio nostre corruptionis.

[27] Secundo dico quod istud opus est exclusivum nostre confusionis. Nunquid enim ad magnam confusionem redundat totius populi Christiani quod nostra hereditas ad alienos[296] sit conversa, quod loca sancta sint[297] per Agarenos impios profanata?[298] [F 244va] Audivi soldanum[299] dixisse quod, si ita penes[300] nos esset sepulchrum[301] perfidi Machometi sicut apud eos est sepulchrum[302] Christi, quod nunquam cessarent quousque ipsum recuperassent. Unde de isto opprobrio loquebatur Jeremias, Trenorum ultimo dicens:[303] *Recordare, Domine,*[304] *quid acciderit nobis; intuere et respice opprobrium nostrum. Hereditas nostra versa est ad alienos, et domus nostre ad extraneos*, et sequitur:[305] *defecit gaudium cordis nostri; versus est in luctum chorus noster. Mestum factum est cor nostrum contenebrati sunt oculi nostri, propter montem Syon quia disperiit;*[306] *vulpes ambulaverunt in eo*. Et primo[307] Machabeorum 2 dicebat ille Mathatias:[308] *Ut quid natus sum videre contritionem populi* [G 303vb] *mei, et contritionem civitatis sancte et sedere illic, cum datur in manibus inimicorum? Sancta in manu*[309] *extraneorum facta sunt,*[310] *templum eius sicut homo ignobilis. Vasa glorie eius captiva ducta sunt.* Et Urbanus papa in sermone quem fecit in concilio Claromontensi[311] dicebat:[312] 'Iherusalem'[313] 'civitas ipsa, in qua, Christus ipse[314] pro nobis passus est, peccatis nostris exigentibus, sub potentia Sarracenorum redacta divine servituti, ad ignominiam totius populi Christiani subducta est'. Unde tantum

---

295 Iherusalem] Ierusalem F
296 ad alienos] adalienos F
297 sint *om*. G
298 profanata] prophanata G
299 soldanum] ita *add*. G
300 penes] apud G
301 sepulchrum] sepulcrum F ‖ nos esset sepulchrum *a.m.* G
302 sepulchrum] sepulcrum F
303 Lamentationes 5.1–2.; Trenorum *add. in mg.* G
304 Domine] et intuere *add*. G
305 Lamentationes 5.15, 17–18.
306 disperiit] deperiit G
307 primo] primi G
308 I Machabeorum 2.7–9.; Machabeorum *add. in mg.* G
309 manu] manibus G
310 sunt] in *add*. G
311 concilio Claromontensi *inv*. G
312 'Sermo Urbani Pape', in *The Historia Ierosolimitana of Baldric of Bourgueil*, ed. S. Biddlecombe (Woodbridge: The Boydell Press, 2014), Book I, 7: 'quoniam ipsa civitas, in qua, prout omnes nostis, Christus ipse pro nobis passus est, peccatis nostris exigentibus, sub spurcitiam paganorum redacta est, Deique servitutui, ad ignominiam nostram dico, subducta est'.
313 Iherusalem] Ierusalem F
314 ipse *om*. G

opprobrium nostrum *videntes angeli pacis amare*[315] *flent*, sicut dicitur Ysaie 33.[316] Ergo ex ista causa:[317] *Venite et edificemus muros Iherusalem*[318] *et non*[319] *simus ultra opprobrium*,[320] Neemie[321] secundo. Est ergo alia causa movens ad passagium exclusio nostre[322] confusionis.

[28] Tertio dico quod istud opus est inflammativum[323] sancte affectionis et incentivum [F 244vb] nostre devotionis. Si enim memoria rei dilecte incendit et inflammat affectionem,[324] multo magis presentia. Unde qui presentialiter intuebitur loca illa sanctissima, quis dubitat quin eius devotio incendatur et eius[325] affectio inflammetur? Ideo dicebat propheta in Psalmo:[326] *Te decet ymnus, Deus*,[327] *in Syon, et tibi reddetur votum in Iherusalem.*[328] *Exaudi orationem meam ad te omnis caro veniet*, et in alio Psalmo:[329] *Letatus sum in hiis que dicta sunt michi: in domum Domini ibimus. Stantes erant pedes*[330] *nostri in atriis*[331] *tuis, Iherusalem.*[332] Unde quo[G 304ra]modo ista devotio fuit accensa ex corporali presentia istorum tam sanctorum locorum bene ostendit Jeronimus fuisse completum in illis sanctis Paula et Eustochio,[333] sed causa brevitatis omitto. Tamen inter cetera dicit sic:[334] 'Ivit illuc Paula per huiusmodi loca discurrens,[335] suam ubique devotionem effudit'. Et vere non mirum. Si enim loca sanctorum visitata corporaliter ad devotionem accendunt, multo magis[336] loca illa in quibus primus homo formatus est, patriarche, prophete, apostoli, fundatores Ecclesie et discipuli nati sunt, ubi tot miracula perpetrata sunt, ubi ecclesiastica sacramenta instituta sunt, ubi angeli frequentissime[337] apparuerunt, ubi triumphi tam nobiles habiti sunt, ubi virgo beatissima nata, conversata et sepulta est,[338] ubi in honore eius fabricate sunt ecclesie

---

315 amare] amore *a.c.* G
316 33] Isaie *add. in mg.* G; Isaias 33.7.
317 Neemias 2.17.
318 Iherusalem] Ierusalem F
319 non *om.* F
320 opprobrium] Jeremie ii *add.* G
321 Neemie] Neemie *add. in mg.* G
322 nostre *bis scr.* G
323 inflammativum] inflamativum G
324 affectionem *om.* G
325 eius *om.* G
326 Psalmi 65.2–3.
327 ymnus Deus *inv.* G; ympnus G
328 Iherusalem] Ierusalem F
329 Psalmi 122.1–3.; Psalmus *add. in mg.* G
330 pedes] tui *add. et del.* G
331 atriis] atrii F
332 Iherusalem] Ierusalem F
333 Paula et Eustochio] Paulo et Eustachio G
334 'Hieronymus: Epistolae secundum ordinem temporum distributae', in *Patrologia Latina*, ed. J.-P. Migne, 22:483–492, epistola XLVI (ad Paulae et Eustochii ad Marcellam – De Sanctis Locis).
335 discurrens] discurres G
336 multo magis] multomagis G
337 tot miracula…frequentissime *a.m.* G
338 conversata et sepulta est] conversata est et sepulta G

244 *Appendix IV*

miro lapideo tabulatu,[339] sicut dicit Jeronimus,[340] ubi ei angelus conceptum filii Dei nunciavit, ubi peperit, ubi nutrivit, ubi ipse Dei filius[341] natus est, nutritus, baptizatus, ubi ieiunavit, ubi cum dyabolo pugnavit, ubi predicavit, ubi miracula multa[342] fecit, ubi passus, ubi sepultus,[343] ubi resurrexit, ubi resurgens discipulis apparuit, unde[344] [F 245ra] ascendit ad celos, ubi Spiritum Sanctum[345] visibiliter misit, ubi venturus est iudicare vivos et mortuos. Dicamus ergo tanta devotione accensi *introibimus in tabernaculum eius, adorabimus in loco ubi steterunt pedes eius*, in Psalmo.[346] Et ista est [G 304rb] alia ratio que debet movere quemlibet[347] ad passagium faciendum.

[29] Dico quarto quod istud opus est imitativum[348] paterne traditionis. Inter cetera que magis solent animare ad strenue[349] bellandum sunt exempla precedentium. Exempla enim efficacius movent quam verba, sed specialiter movent exempla quando[350] in exemplaribus et est numerositas et multitudo, et est claritas et celsitudo, et est exempli virtuositas et magnitudo. Quomodo[351] autem non solum patres veteris testamenti sed etiam[352] viri illustrissimi pro recuperatione illius Terre Sancte viriliter pugnaverunt – unde eorum memoria manet cum laudibus, ut docent historie[353] – cuilibet intuenti, quamque sollicitudinem Romani pontifices adhibuerunt[354] ad nobiles imittandum[355] ad tam sanctum et nobile bellum, patet in eisdem historiis[356] evidenter. Ergo istud factum bene est imitativum[357] paterne traditionis, primo[358] Machabeorum 2:[359] *Mementote operum patrum, que fecerunt in generationibus suis, et accipietis*[360] *gloriam magnam, et nomen*[361] *eternum*, ut dicat sanctitas vestra illud Zacharie 14:[362] *Congregabo omnes gentes ad*

---

339 miro lapideo tabulatu] muro lapideo tabulata G
340 Jeronimus] Hieronymus *add. in mg.* G
341 Dei filius *inv.* G
342 miracula multa *inv.* G
343 ubi passus, ubi sepultus] ubi passus et sepultus G
344 unde] ubi G
345 sanctum *om.* G
346 Psalmi 132.7.; Psalmus *add. in mg.* G
347 quemlibet] quelibet G
348 imitativum] imittativum F
349 strenue] strennue G
350 quando] quandoque *a.c.* G
351 quomodo] am *add. et del.* G
352 etiam *om.* G
353 historie] ystorie F || cum laudibus *add. et del.* F
354 adhibuerunt] adhibuerut F
355 imittandum] invitandum G
356 historiis] ystoriis F
357 imitativum] imittativum F
358 primo] primi G
359 I Machabeorum 2.51.; Machabeorum *add. in mg.* G
360 accipietis] s *s.l.* G
361 nomen] in *add.* G
362 Zacharias 14.2.; Zacharie *add. in mg.* G

Iherusalem[363] *in prelium, et capietur civitas.* Et ista causa videtur sufficere ad tenendum firmiter quod passagium est faciendum. Alias enim tot et tanti sancti[364] Romani pontifices non tantum laborassent pro isto negotio, qui etiam ad hoc sedes proprias frequenti[G 304va]ssime reliquerunt, [F 245rb] Ecclesia etiam principes qui dictum negotium[365] assumpserunt[366] tantis laudibus non extolleret, thesaurum[367] Ecclesie non ita largiter aperiret, Deusque non tanta[368] miracula ostendisset. Sicut referunt hystorie,[369] pugilibus Christi in prosecutione predicti[370] negotii miracula evidentissima et auxilia angelica frequentissime sunt impensa, in tantum quod, sicut dicit Bernardus[371] in libro *De laude nove Militie Templi*, ibi[372] visum est quod:[373] 'unus[374] fugabat[375] mille, et duo decem milia'.

[30] Dico quinto quod istud opus est completivum nostre perfectionis. Si enim perfectio nostra consistit in caritate, iuxta illud Apostoli ad Colossenses 3:[376] *Super omnia hec, caritatem habete, quod est vingulum perfectionis*; ad opus autem istud[377] movent Dei dilectio, legis emulatio, fraterna compassio, que procedunt ex caritate; ergo bene est completivum nostre perfectionis.[378] Movet quidem Dei dilectio clamantis in Psalmo:[379] *Quis consurget michi adversus*[380] *malignantes? Aut quis stabit mecum adversus operantes iniquitatem?* Unde si in veteri testamento Moyses accensus zelo viginti[381] milia interfecit propter *vitulum conflatilem quem erexerant* Exodi 32,[382] et Helyas zelo zelatus pro Domino exercituum quadringentos et L[383] prophetas, Baal fecit interfici, sicut patet III Regum 18. Et[384] ex zelo divini amoris omnes prophetas Baal[385] et servos eius et sacerdotes

---

363 Iherusalem] Ierusalem F
364 sancti *om.* G
365 negotium] passagium G
366 assumpserunt] seu negotium *add.* G
367 thesaurum] thesauros G
368 tanta] tata F
369 hystorie] ystorie F
370 predicti] dicti G
371 Bernardus] Bernardus *add. in mg.* G
372 ibi *a.m.* G
373 decem milia] decemmilia F; 'Liber ad Milites Templi: De laude nove Militie', in *Sancti Bernardi Opera*, eds. Jean Leclercq and Henri-Marie Rochais, 8 vols. (Rome: Editiones Cistercienses, 1957–1977), 3:221, cap.iv, §8.
374 unus] vii F
375 fugabat] fugabant F
376 Colossenses 3.14.; ad Colossenses *add. in mg.* G
377 istud] annuatio passagii *add. in mg.* G
378 perfectionis] compassionis G
379 Psalmi 94.16.; Psalmus *add. in mg.* G
380 adversus] apud G
381 viginti] xx F
382 Exodus 32.8.; Exodi *add. in mg.* G
383 L] quinquaginta G
384 et *lacuna* F <Hieu>
385 fecit interfici...Baal *om. per homoeoteleuton* G

fecit interfici[386] in templo eius, sicut patet[387] IV Regum [G 304vb] 10, quomodo potest dicere se[388] zelum Dei habere qui videt in templo Dei erectum ydolum Machometi, qui falsus propheta[389] plures seduxit, et [F 245va] seducere non cessat plus quam prophete Baal? Certe non habet zelum Domini[390] qui hoc sub dissimulatione pertransit, ymmo debet dicere quilibet illud Psalmus:[391] *Zelus domus tue comedit me, et opprobria exprobrantium tibi ceciderunt super me*, et Zaccharie primo:[392] *Zelatus sum Iherusalem[393] et Syon zelo magno, et ira magna ego irascar super gentes opulentas*, et sequitur:[394] *revertar ad Iherusalem[395] in misericordiis, et[396] domus mea edificabitur in ea*, et sequitur:[397] *adhuc affluent civitates mee bonis, et consolabitur dominus adhuc Syon, et eliget adhuc Iherusalem*.[398]

[31] Movet etiam legis emulatio. Perfidi enim Sarraceni non permittunt legem veram[399] evangelicam[400] predicari. Item peccant contra legem nature peccatum contra naturam flagiciosissime comittendo. Ex quibus duabus causis emulatores legis evangelice[401] et nature arma debent[402] assumere contra eos, primo[403] Machabeorum 2:[404] *Nunc ergo, filii, emulatores estote legis, et date animas vestras pro testamento patrum*; vobis enim dicitur Ysaie 2:[405] *Venite, ascendamus[406] ad montem[407] domini, et ad domum Dei Jacob*, quia de Syon exibit lex et verbum Domini de Ierusalem.[408]

[32] Movet tertio fraterna compassio. Si enim testante [G 305ra] Johane[409] in *canonica* sua prima, tertio capitulo:[410] *Nos debemus pro fratribus animas ponere*, quomodo videntes fratres in regno Armenie, in insula Rodi, et in Cypro[411] expositos

---

386 interfici] Regum *add. in mg.* G
387 patet] dicitur G
388 dicere se *inv.* G
389 propheta] multos et *add.* G
390 domini] Dei G
391 Psalmi 69.10.
392 Zacharias 1.14–15.; Zacharie *add. in mg.* G
393 Iherusalem] Ierusalem F
394 Zacharias 1.16.
395 Iherusalem] Ierusalem F
396 et *om.* F
397 Zacharias 1.17.
398 Iherusalem] Ierusalem F
399 legem veram] legem veram legem G
400 evangelicam] ebbangelicam G
401 evangelice] ebbangelice G
402 arma debent *inv.* G
403 primo] primi G
404 I Machabeorum 2.50.; Machabeorum *add. in mg.* G
405 Isaias 2.3.
406 ascendamus] as cendamus F
407 montem] Isaie *add. in mg.* G
408 verbum domini de Ierusalem] de Iherusalem verbum Dei G
409 Johane] Johannes *add. in mg.* G
410 I Iohannes 3.16.
411 Cypro] Cipro F

tanto periculo non subveniemus[412] eisdem? Videmus hodie Turcos impugnantes in illis partibus Christianos et iam magnam partem[413] Grecie occupasse, et timendum esset quod ultra procede[F 245vb]rent, etenim[414] 'res tua tunc agitur paries cum proximus ardet', sicut[415] dixit ille versificator. Unde credo quod ad convincendum nostram ignaviam Deus permittat eos contra nos insurgere cum et econtra nos contra eos arma sumere deberemus. Unde verificatur illud Judith 14:[416] *Mures egressi de cavernis suis, ausi sunt provocare nos*[417] *ad prelium*. Absit ergo quod fratribus nostris in tanta servitute et periculo constitutis non subveniamus, ymmo faciamus sicut ille sanctus Judas Machabeus, sicut legitur II Machabeorum 11, ubi dicitur quod, cum ipse et qui cum eo erant audissent gentiles ingressos Iudeam ad expugnandum Iherusalem[418] et loca vicina, rogavit ipse:[419] *Et omnis turba dominum cum lacrimis ut ipse bonum angelum mitteret ad salutem Israel, et ipse prius armis, sumptis ceteros adhortatus est*[420] *similiter secum subire periculum et ferre auxilium fratribus. Cumque pariter prompto animo procederent, Iherosolimis apparuit precedens eos eques in veste candida, armis au*[G 305rb]*reis, hastam vibrans. Tunc omnes benedixerunt Dominum, et convaluerunt animis: non solum homines sed bestias fortissimas, supra muros ferreos parati penetrare. Ibant igitur de celo habentes adiutorium et more leonum irruentes in hostes, prostraverunt ex eis quatrodecim milia peditum, et equites mille sexaginta, universos autem in fugam converterunt.* Sperantes autem[421] in auxilio Domini, eamus in Iherusalem,[422] quia sicut dicit[423] propheta in Psalmo:[424] *Qui confidunt in Domino, sicut mons Syon non commovebitur in eternum,*[425] *qui habitat*[426] [F 246ra] *in Iherusalem.*[427] *Montes in circuitu eius, et Dominus in circuitu populi sui, ex hoc nunc et usque in seculum. Quia non relinquet Dominus virgam peccatorum super sortem iustorum, ut non extendant iusti*, et cetera. Ex hoc possunt elici quatuor rationes que movere debent ad passagium faciendum: una ex Dei dilectione, due ex legis emulatione, quarta ex fraterna compassione.

[33] Dico sexto quod istud opus est directivum et promotivum nostre salvationis. Per hoc[428] enim opus peccatum excluditur et celi aditus aperitur. Unde

---

412 subveniemus] subvenimus G
413 partem] hodie *add. et del.* F
414 etenim] et enim F
415 sicut] sicud G
416 14] xv *a.c.* G || d *add. et del.* G; Judith *add. in mg.* G; Iudith 14.12
417 provocare nos *inv.* G
418 Iherusalem] Ierusalem F
419 II Machabeorum 11.6–12.; Machabeorum *add. in mg.* G
420 est *(lacuna)* G
421 autem] ergo G
422 Iherusalem] Ierusalem F
423 dicit] dixit F
424 Psalmi 124.1–3.; Psalmus *add. in mg.* G
425 in eternum] ineternum G
426 habitat] habitant *a.c.* G
427 Iherusalem] Ierusalem F
428 hoc] lucrum passagium *add. in mg.* G, F

248 *Appendix IV*

in isto bello semper quisque lucratur, quia si[429] vincit acquirit et peccatorum indulgentiam et de victoria gloriam, si vincitur statim ad regnum celorum evolat, quod *regnum non est esca et potus sed iustitia et pax et gaudium in Spiritu Sancto*, sicut dicit Apostolus ad Romanos 14.[430] Et ex ista causa pul[G 305 va]cre[431] hortatur[432] beatus Bernardus in libro *De laude nove Militie Templi*[433] ad istud[434] opus assumendum dicens sic:[435]

> Securi procedite, milites, et intrepido animo inimicos Christi propellite, certi quia nec mors, nec vita poterunt vos separare a caritate Dei, que est in Christo Ihesu, illud sane vobiscum in omni periculo replicantes: sive vivimus, sive morimur Domini sumus. Quam gloriosi revertuntur victores de prelio! Quam beati moriuntur martyres in prelio![436] Gaude, fortis[437] athleta, si vivis et vincis in Domino;[438] sed magis exulta et gloriare, si moriaris[439] et iungeris Domino. Vita quidem fructuosa, et victoria[440] [F246rb] gloriosa; sed utraque mors sacra vite preponitur.[441] Nam si beati qui in Domino moriuntur, multo magis qui pro Domino moriuntur? Et quidem sive in lecto, sive in bello quis moritur, preciosa erit sine dubio in conspectu Domini mors sanctorum eius. Ceterum in bello tanto profecto preciosior, quanto et[442] gloriosior. O vita secura, ubi pura conscientia! O, inquam,[443] vita secura, ubi absque formidine mors expectatur, ymmo et exoptatur cum dulcedine, et excipitur cum devotione! O vera sancta et tuta[444] militia, atque a duplici[445] illo periculo prorsus libera, quo id hominum genus solet frequenter periclitari, ubi dumtaxat Christus[446] causa est militandi.[447] Quotiens namque[448] congrederis tu, qui militiam militas

---

429 quia si] quiasi G
430 Romanos 14.17.; ad Romanos *add. in mg.* G
431 pulcre] pulchre G; Bernardus *add. in mg.* G
432 hortatur] ortatur F
433 templi] hortatur enim *add.* G
434 istud] illud G
435 'Liber ad Milites Templi: De laude nove Militie', 3:214–215, cap.i, §1, 2.
436 quam beati moriuntur martyres in prelio *om. per homoeteleuton* G
437 de prelio…fortis *a.m.* G
438 si vivis et vincis in Domino] si vivis et si vincis in prelio alias in Domino F
439 moriaris] morieris G
440 fructuosa et victoria *om. per homoeoteleuton* G
441 preponitur] proponitur G || vite preponitur *inv.* F
442 et *om.* G
443 inquam] in *a.m. add. s.l.* F
444 tuta] letitia *add. et del.* F
445 duplici] dupplici F
446 dumtaxat Christus *inv.* G
447 causa est militandi *bis scr.* F
448 quotiens namque] quotienscumque F

secularem, timendum est, ne aut[449] occidas hostem quidem[450] in corpore, te vero in anima, aut forte occidaris[451] in corpore simul,[452] [G 305vb] et in[453] anima.[454]

Et subdit:[455]

Christi milites secure preliantur prelia Domini, nec[456] aliquod[457] metuentes aut de hostium cede peccatum, aut de sua nece periculum, quandoquidem mors pro Christo vel ferenda, vel inferenda, et nihil[458] habeat criminis, et[459] plurimum glorie mereatur. Hinc quippe Christo, inde Christus acquiritur, qui nimirum et libenter accipit hostis mortem pro ultione, et libentius prebet seipsum militi pro consolatione. Miles, inquam,[460] Christi securus[461] interimit, interit securius. Sibi prestat[462] cum interit, Christo cum interimit. Non enim sine causa gladium portat: Dei enim minister est ad vindictam malefactorum, [F 246va] laudem vero[463] bonorum.

Et multa tangit ibi circa illam materiam sed causa brevitatis omitto. Et ideo talibus militibus in bello Christi militantibus loquitur Dominus per prophetam Ysaiam ultimo:[464] *Quomodo sicut mater blanditur, et ego consolabor vos, in Iherusalem*[465] *consolabimini. Et videbitis, et gaudebit cor vestrum, et ossa vestra ut herba germinabunt.* Et sic patet alia causa quare est istud negotium assumendum. Patet ergo tertium quomodo in isto opere est rectitudo virtuosa.

[34] Dico ultimo quod in assumente inspicitur[466] aptitudo vigorosa quia ydoneitatis et convenientie profert indicium speciale. Unde eo nil convenientius probitate ad regendum et disponendum salubriter, quia sequitur in themate: *tecum vadat,* [G 306ra] tecum, scilicet, cum rege Francie, sicut cum aptiore, convenientiore[467] et magis ydoneo rectore et capitaneo exercitus Christiani. Quod autem

---

449   aut *om.* G
450   quidem] quide G
451   occidaris] occideris G
452   te vero...simul *a.m.* G
453   in *om.* F
454   anima] an *a.m. add. s.l.* F
455   'Liber ad Milites Templi: De laude nove Militie', 3:217, cap.iii, §4.
456   nec] ne G
457   aliquod] aliquid G
458   nihil] nil F
459   et] aut G
460   inquam] enim G
461   securus] securius F
462   prestat] prerat F
463   vero] autem G
464   Isaias 66.13–14.; Ysaie *add. in mg.* G
465   Iherusalem] vos *add. et del.* G; Ierusalem F
466   inspicitur] aspicitur G
467   aptiore, convenientiore] aptiori, convenientiori F

250 *Appendix IV*

sit convenientior rector et capitaneus? Patet ex conditionibus que in rectore et ductore Christiani exercitus requiruntur, que excellenter in rege Francie pre cunctis Christianis principibus respiciuntur adesse. Habet enim pre ceteris in[468] inperiis[469] auctoritatem et obedientiam, in conciliariis et conciliis[470] claritatem et prudentiam, in armorum exercitiis strenuitatem et peritiam, in negotiis sagacitatem[471] et providentiam, in periculis securitatem et fiduciam,[472] in observantiis conformitatem et benivolentiam, in iudiciis inflexibilitatem et iustitiam, in promissis veritatem et [F 246vb] observantiam, in factis sanctitatem et innocentiam, in divinis cultibus sinceritatem, fidelitatem et latriam. Quis enim rege Francie quo ad principes seculares in[473] imperio[474] excellentior,[475] in obedientia suorum subditorum potior, in conciliis et conciliariis[476] prudentior, in armorum exercitiis in se et in suis militibus peritior, in negotiis prudentior, in periculis de auxilio Dei[477] securior, in observantiis militibus conformior, in iudiciis iustior, in promissiis verior, in factis sanctior, in divinis cultibus devotior? Certe audeo dicere quod nullus. Unde in eis omnibus dedit eum Deus[478] excelsiorem[479] cunctis gentibus, sicut [G 306rb] clare probarem sed omitto causa brevitatis. Unde de eo posset bene exponi illud Psalmi:[480] *Posui adiutorium in potente, et exaltavi electum de plebe mea. Inveni David, servum meum; oleo sancto meo unxi eum. Manus enim mea auxiliabitur ei, et brachium meum confortabit eum. Nichil proficiet inimicus in eo, et filius iniquitatis non apponet nocere ei. Et concidam a facie ipsius*[481] *inimicos eius, et odientes eum in fugam convertam. Et veritas mea et misericordia mea cum ipso, et in nomine meo exaltabitur cornu eius. Et ponam in mari manum eius, et in fluminibus dexteram eius. Ipse invocavit me: Pater meus es tu, Deus meus, et susceptor salutis mee. Et ego primogenitum ponam illum,*[482] *excelsum pre regibus terre. In eternum*[483] *servabo illi misericordiam meam, et testamentum meum fidele ipsi. Et ponam* [F 247ra] *in seculum seculi semen eius, et thronum eius sicut dies celi.* Unde de eo potest dici illud Judith 15:[484] *Tu gloria Iherusalem,*[485] *tu letitia Israel, tu honorificentia populi nostri, quia fecisti viriliter, et confortatum*

---

468 in] regis Francie conditiones pre passagio faciendo *add. in mg.* G
469 inperiis] imperiis G
470 concliariis et conciliis] consiliariis et consiliis G
471 sagacitatem] sagacita F
472 fiduciam] fidentiam F
473 in *om.* G
474 imperio] iperio F
475 excellentior] rum *add. et del.* F
476 in conciliis et conciliariis] in consiliis et consiliariis G
477 Dei *om.* G
478 Deus] Dominus G
479 excelsiorem] excellentiorem G
480 illud psalmi] in psalmo illud G; Psalmi 88.20–30.; Psalmus *add. in mg.* G
481 ipsius] eius G
482 illum] et *add.*
483 in eternum] ineternum G
484 Iudith 15.10–11; Judith *add. in mg.* G
485 Iherusalem] Ierusalem F

est cor tuum, fecisti, inquam, viriliter[486] istud negotium[487] assumendo. Cum tali ergo capitaneo surgant milites Christiani et vadant in Iherusalem,[488] non de suis presumentes viribus sed de virtute Domini Sabaoth sperantes victoriam, cui nimirum facile esse confidant iuxta sententiam Machabei:[489] *Concludi multos in manu* [G 306va] *paucorum et non esse differentia in conspectu Dei celi liberari in multis, et in paucis, quia non in multidunine exercitus victoria belli, sed de celo fortitudo est.*

[35] Ergo, pater sanctissime, a finibus terre colligite ministros ex fortissimis Israhel,[490] omnes tenentes gladios et ad bella doctissimos, de quorum profectione cum tanto principe *letetur mons Syon, et exultent filie Iude,*[491] ut concedente Domino impleatur:[492] *Redemit Dominus populum et liberavit eum, et venient*[493] *et exultabunt in monte Syon, et gaudebunt de bonis domini. Letare, Iherusalem,*[494] *et cognosce iam tempus visitationis tue. Gaudete, et laudate*[495] *simul, deserta Iherusalem,*[496] *quia consolatus est dominus populum suum; redimit Iherusalem.*[497] *Paravit Dominus brachium sanctum suum in oculis*[498] *omnium gentium,*[499] ut dicat Terre Sancte:

> Virgo Israel, corrueras, et non erat qui sublevaret te. Surge iam, excutere de pulvere, virgo, captiva filia Syon. Surge, inquam, et sta in excelso, et vide iocundi[F 247rb]tatem, que venit[500] tibi a Deo tuo. Non vocaberis ultra derelicta, et terra tua non vocabitur amplius desolata, quia complacuit domino in te, et terra tua inhabitabitur. Leva in circuitu oculos[501] tuos et vide: omnes isti congregati sunt, venerunt tibi. Hoc tibi auxilium missum de sancto. Omnino per istos tibi iam[502] iamque illa persolvetur antiqua promissio: Ponam te in lucem[503] seculorum, gaudium in generatione et gene[G 306vb]rationem, et suges[504] lac gentium, et mamillas regum lactaberis,

---

486 viriliter] co *add. et del.* G
487 istud negotium *inv.* G
488 Iherusalem] Ierusalem F
489 I Machabeorum 3.18–19.
490 Israhel] Israel F; ex *add. et del.* F
491 Psalmi 48.12.
492 Ieremias 31.11–12.
493 venient] veniet F
494 Iherusalem] Ierusalem F
495 laudate] letate F
496 Iherusalem] Ierusalem F; m *a.m add.* F
497 Iherusalem] Ierusalem F
498 oculis] occulis F
499 Isaias 52.9–10.
500 venit] veniet G
501 oculos] occulos F
502 iam] nam *a.c.* G
503 lucem] liccem *a.c.* G
504 suges] sugges F

sicut deducit Bernardus *De laude nove Militie Templi*.[505] Videntes ergo, pater sanctissime, regem sic convenientem ad regendum et disponendum salubriter, dicatis illud III[506] Esdre 8:[507] *Precepi eis qui desiderant ex gente Iudeorum, sua sponte, et ex sacerdotibus et Levitis, qui sunt in regno meo, comitari tecum in Iherusalem.*[508] *Si qui ergo cupiunt*[509] *ire tecum, conveniant, et proficiscantur, sicut placuit michi*, ut dicat regi quilibet miles Christianus illud Luce 22:[510] *Paratus sum tecum*[511] *in*[512] *carcerem et in mortem ire.*

[36] Sed forte dicet aliquis audacter, 'Paratus sum secum ire',[513] sed ipse nunquam ibit, sed[514] totum hoc fit ficte ad pecuniam extorquendam.[515] Sed salva sic obloquentium reverentia, non dubito quin rex proponat istud passagium tempore ad hoc per sanctitatem vestram statuto personaliter facere, legitimo[516] impedimento cessante. Et quod contrarium tolli debeat de cordibus omnium sic opinantium videtur michi posse apparere ex tribus: [F 247va] primo ex vinculo obligationis, secundo ex modo provisionis, tertio ex zelo devotionis.

[37] Primo quidem patet ex vinculo[517] obligationis. Licet enim obligatio quam rex facturus est ex voto solemniter emittendo deberet sufficere,[518] maxime cum ipsa[519] crucis assumptione solemniter et publice facta – quia scriptum est Deuteronomii 23:[520] *Cum* [G 307ra] *votum voveris domino Deo tuo, non tardabis reddere, quia requiret illud*[521] *Dominus Deus tuus, et si moratus fueris, reputabitur tibi ad peccatum. Si valueris tollere, absque peccato eris. Quod autem, semel egressum est de labiis tuis, observabis, et facies sicut promisisti domino Deo tuo, et propria voluntate et ore tuo locutus es* – ymmo etiam promissio solo verbo, cum reges Francie non consueverint[522] facere irrita que de eorum labiis processerunt, quinymmo eorum verbum firmam contineat veritatem, tamen, ut eius sincera intentio magis clare omnibus elucescat et nulla remaneat materia dubitandi, reverendum patrem dominum Johannem, Dei gratia Morinensem episcopum, et[523]

---

505 'Liber ad Milites Templi: De laude nove Militie', 3:218–219, cap.iii, §6; Bernardus *add. in mg.* G
506 3] ii G, F
507 III Ezra 8.11–12.; Esdre *add. in mg.* G
508 Iherusalem] Ierusalem F
509 cupiunt] cupiant G
510 Lucas 22.33.; Luce *add. in mg.* G
511 tecum *a.m.* G
512 in] passagium *add. in mg.* F
513 secum ire] ire tecum G
514 sed] set F
515 extorquendam] extorquendum G
516 legitimo] personaliter facere passagio *add. in mg.* G
517 vinculo] perfectionis *add. et del.* G
518 sufficere] max *add. et del.* G
519 maxime cum ipsa *inv.* G
520 xxiii] xxii G; Deuteronomium 23.21–23.; Deuteronomii *add. in mg.* G
521 quia requiret illud *a.m.* G
522 consueverint] consueverunt G
523 et] ac G

venerabilem virum dominum Guidonem[524] Bandeti decanum Parisiensem, et nobiles et potentes viros dominos Henricum de Analgoria[525] et Petrum Trosselli de Castellis dominos milites, conciliarios[526] suos, et me, una cum eis quinque, quatuor, tres aut duos ex nobis suos procuratores et nuncios speciales constituit, ad iurandum in animam suam, tactis sacrosanctis evangeliis, in presentia [F 247vb] sanctitatis vestre quod termino per vos statuendo dictum passagium prosequetur realiter et personaliter, legitimo impedimento cessante, sicut in litteris, sigillo suo[527] in cera viridi sigillatis, plenius continetur. Quis ergo potest opinari quod rex tam devotus, tam [G 307rb] catholicus, tam ex sanctis progenitoribus procreatus venire debeat contra sic promissa, ymmo sic solemniter et publice coram tantis iuramento vallata? Certe nullus. Ymmo certe iudicio meo veraciter poterit dici[528] de eo illud[529] Ruth 3:[530] *Non cessabit homo, usque compleverit que locutus est.*

[38] Et quia, pater sanctissime, de tempore locutus sum, licet rex brevitatem temporis totis affectat[531] precordiis, tamen sibi et suo concilio[532] visum fuit quod non poterat[533] ex multis causis – specialiter quia oportebit hoc significari[534] omnibus regibus totius Christianitatis et ut possint se illi qui cum eo transfretaturi sunt melius preparare – brevior terminus assignari quam V kalendas Augusti proximis ad tres annos. Hoc tamen rex in dispositione vestre sanctitatis reliquit.

[39] Secundo patet ex modo provisionis. Providetur enim circa concedenda eidem per sanctitatem vestram taliter, sicut in litteris predictis plenius continetur,[535] quod merito potest excludi[536] de cordibus omnium quod hic[537] nulla fictio habet locum. Primo quidem quia[538] rex etiam predictos socios et collegas meos et me suos constituit procuratores et nuncios ad iurandum etiam in animam suam, tactis sacrosanctis evangeliis, in vestre[539] [F 248ra] presentia sanctitatis quod de concedendo eidem nichil recipiet nec recipi scienter permittet committendum in usus alios quam[540] passagii memorati ac preparatoriorum eiusdem,[541] [G 307va] et si per aliquem recepta fuissent restitui faciet absque dilatione morosa.

---

524 Guidonem] Hugonem G
525 Analgoria] Alnagoria F
526 conciliarios] consiliarios G
527 sigillo suo *inv.* G
528 poterit dici *inv.* G
529 illud] Deuteronomii iii *add. et del.* G
530 Ruth 3.18.; Ruth *add. in mg.* G
531 affectat] affectet G
532 concilio] consilio G
533 poterat] poterit G
534 significari] significare G
535 continetur] contineretur G
536 excludi *om.* G
537 hic] hec *a.c.* G
538 quia] iuramenta regis contra suspectione in avaritie de pecuniis passagii *add. in mg.* G
539 vestre] vestra F
540 quam] quod F
541 eiusdem] passagii *add.* G

254 *Appendix IV*

[40] Secundo voluit idem rex quod dominus Johannes, filius suus[542] primogenitus, dux Normanie, Andegavensis[543] Cenomanensisque[544] comes, collegas meos prenominatos et me simili modo suos constitueret procuratores et nuncios ad iurandum in animam suam, tactis sacrosanctis evangeliis, in presentia vestre beatitudinis quod ipse, ad quemcumque statum ipsum contingeret devenire,[545] etiam si ad successionem vel regimen regni ipsum devenire contingat, nichil recipiet nec recipi permittet de concedendis predictis nisi convertendis in usum[546] passagii vel negotii Terre Sancte.

[41] Tertio quia etiam[547] providetur quod pecunia concedendorum per sanctitatem vestram dicto regi non suis thesaurariis[548] aut receptoribus sed probis viris burgensibus assignetur, qui eam[549] expendant iuxta mandatum quatuor prelatorum regni Francie, quorum duo per sanctitatem vestram et duo per regem deputari debebunt. Qui etiam prelati et burgenses iurabunt quod ea fideliter distribuent pro passagio et preparatoriis ipsius, nec in alios usus convertent nec converti pro posse permittent. Providetur etiam quod, si regem ab arreptione itineris – quod absit – contingeret[550] impediri, pecunia ipsa, galee, vasa, et omnia[551] que restabunt, predictis quatuor [F 248rb] prelatis assignabuntur integre [G 307vb] per eos nomine Sedis Apostolice conservanda pro utilitate passagii generalis vel particularis, si postmodum per Sedem Apostolicam contingat[552] indici, certis modis et formis in dictis litteris contentis. Et certe, pater sanctissime, nunquam alias in quocumque passagio fuit talis modus provisionis servatus, quinymmo semper regi Francie concedebantur[553] talia[554] subsidia in Terre Sancte subsidium iuxta suum arbitrium convertenda. Patet ergo[555] quod quilibet merito[556] opinari potest quod rex completurus est que sic solemniter et sub talibus provisionibus promittit, ut de eo verificetur illud Josue 23:[557] *De omnibus que vobis pollicitus est non preteriit unum incassum. Implevit ergo opere quod promisit, et prospere cuncta venerunt.*

[42] Tertio potest apparere[558] ex zelo devotionis. Rex enim, sicut novit vestra sanctitas, a multis temporibus citra desideravit vires suas contra Sarracenos

---

542   suus] eius G
543   Andegavensis] Andegavensisque F
544   Cenomanensis *om.* F
545   devenire] evenire G
546   usum] usu G
547   quia etiam *inv.* G
548   thesaurariis] thesauris G
549   eam] etiam G
550   contingeret] contigerit G
551   galee, vasa, et omnia] galee et vasa omnia G
552   contingat *om.* F
553   regi Francie concedebantur] concedebatur regi Francie F
554   talia] adventagia seu *add.* G
555   ergo] tunc G
556   merito *a.c in mg.* F || merito opinari potest] opinari potest merito G
557   Iosua 23.14–15.; Josue *add. in mg.* G
558   apparere *om.* F

et inimicos fidei experiri et conceperat ire personaliter in Iherusalem,[559] sed ex magna sui deliberatione concilii[560] ad faciendum istud sanctum passagium[561] suum convertit propositum, quod tanto sanctius esse dinoscitur quanto terra illa nobis iure potiori debetur, sicut patuit in rationibus supra tactis. Zelum autem istum sic firmum et perseverantem habuit quod fere[562] a duobus annis citra circa istud principaliter institit[563] et nos frequenter ad sanctitatem vestram mittendo et pre[G 308ra]latos et nobiles de regno suo et alios ad hoc invitando et multipliciter inducendo, ymmo ab illis de sanguine suo et aliis maioribus regni iuramentum quod cum eo transfretaturi essent [F 248va] exigendo et alia multa salubria que longum esset narrare per singula ordinando.[564]

[43] Sed forte dicet aliquis, sicut dixistis archiepiscopo: 'Iam sunt fere duo anni quod rex istud negotium inchoavit et tamen adhuc non videmus quod unam galeam fecerit fieri aut aliquid ex quo appareat ipsum zelum tantum sicut predicatis ad negotium predictum[565] habere'. Sed hoc non debet[566] animum movere cuiuscumque.[567] Sicut enim dixi supra, ad solam sanctitatem vestram pertinet indicere passagium generale, nec deceret[568] regem quodcumque passagium assumere et realiter prosequi nisi habitis sanctitatis vestre consiliis[569] aut auxiliis oportunis. Et ergo, si[570] rex iam fecisset aliqua preparatoria antequam sanctitas vestra indixit passagium generale, posset notari merito de nimia anticipatione. Debet enim sententia[571] executionem precedere, alias ordo retrogradus censeretur. Sed postquam sanctitas vestra indixerit, manum suam mittet ad fortia et ad preparatoria dicti passagii sollicite et diligenter intendet. Cum hoc[572] etiam,[573] pater sanctissime, rex de suo sine adiutorio Ecclesie non posset passagium perficere supradictum. Et ideo non decebat eum aliquid in predictis facere quousque vestram scivisset [G 308rb] intentionem super subsidiis que eidem facere ordinastis.

[44] Patet ergo ex istis tribus quod hic nichil ficte agitur sed mere et pure secundum Deum et secundum quod in corde regis versatur. Et certe, pater sanctissime, hoc potest liquide apparere. Tanta[574] enim fuit semper Ecclesie Romane ad regem Francie dilectio et regis[575] Francie ad Ecclesiam Romanam [F 248vb]

---

559 Iherusalem] Ierusalem F
560 concilii] consilii G
561 sanctum passagium *inv.* G
562 fere] proferre G
563 institit] instetit G
564 ordinando] rex excusare *add. in mg.* F
565 negotium predictum *inv.* G
566 debet] excusatio regis Francie *add. in mg.* G
567 cuiuscumque] cuiusquam F
568 deceret] decent F
569 consiliis] concilio F
570 si *add. s.l.* G; *om.* F
571 sententia] anticipatior *add. et del.* F || excomunicationis *add. et del.* G
572 hoc] hec G
573 etiam] autem G
574 tanta] rex ecclesia *add. in mg.* F
575 regis] regum F

256 *Appendix IV*

devotio quod nunquam sibi mutuo in suis necessariis defuerunt. Unde et reges Francie[576] summum pontificem de sua sede eiectum ad eandem reduxerunt, romani etiam pontifices innumerabiles gratias regibus Francie in omnibus eorum necessitatibus[577] impenderunt, sicut patet Ystorias intuenti. Et si hoc fuerat[578] alias, multo fortius tempore vestro, qui de corde regni Francie[579] traxistis originem. Quare patet quod rex non habet ad impetrandum a vobis subsidia exquisitos colores querere nec aliquid similare, cum certus sit quod in suis necessitatibus sibi vestre liberalitatis munificentia non deesset, sicut retroacta tempora docuerunt. Patet etiam istud ex alio, quia certe regem latere non potest quin verum sit illud quod scribitur Numerorum 32, ubi dicitur sic:[580] *Si facitis quod promittitis, expedite*[581] *pergite coram Domino ad pugnam: et omnis vir armatus transeat donec subvertat Dominus inimicos suos, et subiciatur ei omnis terra. Tunc eritis*[582] *inculpabiles apud Deum et apud* [G 308va] *Israel, et obtinebitis regiones, quas vultis coram domino. Sin autem quod dicitis, non feceritis, nulli dubium est quin peccetis in dominum: et scitote quoniam peccatum vestrum apprehendet vos.* Quia ergo hoc[583] non ignorat, ideo sollicitus est ut impleat quod promisit. Experientia enim docuit quid aliis contigerit in premissis. Nullus ergo dubitet quin rex istud proponat facere. Dominus[584] enim est cum rege tamquam adiutor fortis sibi promittens quod erit secum quocumque[585] perrexerit. Ideo rex clamat et dicit omnibus Christianis illud Luce 9:[586] *Si quis* [F 249ra] *vult venire post me, abneget semetipsum*, inquam, et tollat crucem suam et sequatur me abneget[587] semetipsum, uxorem, liberos et hereditatem propriam derelinquendo, *et tollat crucem suam et sequatur me.*[588] Quia crux est signum victoriale quod quilibet pro isto passagio debet portare in humeris, et per quam in illis partibus mirabiles triumphi sunt habiti.[589] Nec mirum, quia, sicut dicit Crisostomus in[590] quodam sermone quem fecit *De laude*[591] *Crucis*:[592]

576 Francie] et *add.* F
577 † necessitatibus...et subiciatur † G
578 fuerat] fuit F
579 Francie *om.* F
580 Numeri 32.20–24.; Numerorum *add. in mg.* G
581 expedite] expediti *p.c.* G
582 eritis] s *s.l.* G
583 hoc] hec G
584 dominus] ergo *add. et del.* G
585 quocumque] ubicumque G
586 Lucas 9.23.; Luce *add. in mg.* G
587 et tollat crucem suam et sequatur me abneget *om. per homoeoteleuton* F
588 et sequatur me *om.* G
589 sunt habiti *inv.* G; sunt] nec mirum *add. et del.* G
590 in] Crisostomus *add. in mg.* G
591 laude] laudes crucis *add. in mg.* G
592 'Sermo de Sancta Cruce', in *Patrologia Latina*, ed. J.-P. Migne, 142:1031–1036, 1032, sermo xv.

Crux est spes Christianorum,[593] resurrectio mortuorum,[594] crux[595] cecorum dux, crux[596] desperatorum[597] via, crux[598] claudorum baculus, crux[599] consolatio pauperum, crux[600] reformatio divitum, crux[601] destructio superborum, crux[602] male vinentium pena, crux adversus demones triumphus,[603] crux[604] devictio dyaboli, crux[605] adolescentium pedagogus,[606] crux[607] sustentatio inopum, crux[608] spes desperatorum, crux[609] navigantium gubernator, crux[610] periclitantium portus, [G 308vb] crux[611] obsessorum[612] murus, crux[613] pater orphanorum, crux[614] defensor viduarum, crux[615] iustorum consiliarius,[616] crux[617] tribulatorum requies, crux[618] parvulorum custos, crux[619] virorum caput, crux[620] senum finis, crux[621] lumen in tenebris sedentium, crux[622] Regum magnificentia, crux[623] scutum perpetuum, crux[624] insensatorum sapientia, crux[625] libertas servorum, crux[626] imperitorum philosophia, crux[627] lex impiorum, crux[628]

593 christianorum] Crux istud originale est in isto volumine superius in sermone sancti Andree folio CXXII verso et sunt in isto originali quinquaginta virtutes crucis Domini nostri Ihesu Christi *a.m. add. in mg.* F
594 mortuorum] rum *s.l.* F
595 crux *om.* G
596 crux *om.* G
597 desperatorum] errantium F
598 crux *om.* G
599 crux *om.* G
600 crux *om.* G
601 crux *om.* G
602 crux *om.* G
603 triumphus] ri *s.l.* G
604 crux *om.* G
605 crux *om.* G
606 pedagogus] pedagoga G
607 crux *om.* G
608 crux *om.* G
609 crux *om.* G
610 crux *om.* G
611 crux *om.* G
612 obsessorum] obcessorum F
613 crux *om.* G
614 crux *om.* G
615 crux *om.* G
616 consiliarius] conciliarius F
617 crux *om.* G
618 crux *om.* G
619 crux *om.* G
620 crux *om.* G
621 crux *om.* G
622 crux *om.* G
623 crux *om.* G
624 crux *om.* G
625 crux *om.* G
626 crux *om.* G
627 crux *om.* G
628 crux *om.* G

258 *Appendix IV*

prophetarum preconizatio, crux[629] annunciatio apostolorum, crux[630] martirum gloriatio, crux[631] monachorum abstinentia, crux[632] virginum castitas, crux[633] gaudium sacerdotum, crux[634] Ecclesie fundamentum, crux[635] [F 249rb] orbis terre tutela,[636] crux[637] templorum destructio, crux[638] ydolorum repulsio, crux[639] scandalum Iudeorum, crux[640] perditio impiorum, crux[641] invalidorum virtus, crux[642] egrotantium meditus, crux[643] emundatio leprosorum, crux[644] paraliticorum requies, crux[645] esurientium panis, crux[646] sitientium fons, crux[647] nudorum protectio.

Hanc ergo crucem baiulet et sequatur me, *quia qui sequitur me non ambulat in tenebris, sed habebit lumen vite*,[648] quod nobis concedat qui est benedictus in secula seculorum, Amen.

629 crux *om.* G
630 crux *om.* G
631 crux *om.* G
632 crux *om.* G
633 crux *om.* G
634 crux *om.* G
635 crux *om.* G
636 tutela] cautela F
637 crux *om.* G
638 crux *om.* G
639 crux *om.* G
640 crux *om.* G
641 crux *om.* G
642 crux *om.* G
643 crux *om.* G
644 crux *om.* G
645 crux *om.* G
646 crux *om.* G
647 crux *om.* G
648 Iohannes 8.12.

Appendix V
Clement VI's sermon on the Dauphin Humbert II of Viennois' leadership of the Christian armada against the Turks, 1345

F = Paris, Bibliothèque nationale de France, MS lat. 3293, fols. 299va–302ra.
G = Paris, Bibliothèque Sainte Genevieve, MS 240, fols. 521ra–523va.
Rubric in F 299va: **Sermo factus per dominum Clementem papam sextum super coronatione et missione Delphini.**
Rubric in G 521ra: **Sermo factus per dominum Clementem papam VI quando Dalphinus fuit factus capitaneus passagii contra Thurcos.**

[1] *Dum*[1] *implet*[2] *verbum, factus est dux in Israhel*, I Machabeorum 2.[3] Textus refert ad litteram in eodem libro et capitulo quod[4] [G 521rb] Mathatias sacerdos, videns[5] desolationem factam in populo[6] Israhel per gentiles, compatiens[7] fratribus prorupit in hec verba:[8] *Ve michi, ut quid natus sum videre contritionem populi mei, et contritionem civitatis sancte, et sedere illic, cum datur*[9] *in manibus inimicorum? Sancta in manu*[10] *extraneorum facta sunt, templum eius sicut homo ignobilis.*[11] *Vasa glorie*[12] *eius captiva adducta sunt, trucidati sunt*[13] *senes eius in plateis et* [F 299vb] *iuvenes eius ceciderunt in gladio inimicorum. Que gens non hereditavit regnum eius vel obtinuit spolia eius? Omnis compositio eius ablata est. Que erat libera, facta est ancilla. Et ecce sancta nostra, et pulchritudo*[14] *nostra, et claritas nostra desolata est, et coinquinaverunt eam gentes. Quid ergo nobis adhuc vivere?* Et subdit quod idem sacerdos, ita fratribus compatiens, filios

---

1 dum] dulm *a.c.* F
2 implet] impleret G
3 I Machabaeorum 2.55.
4 quod] ix F
5 sacerdos videns *inv. a.c* F
6 populo *om.* G
7 compatiens] compassus G
8 I Machabaeorum 2.7–13.
9 datur] dantur F
10 manu] manibus G
11 ignobilis] innobilis F
12 glorie] gloria F
13 trucidati sunt *om.* G
14 pulchritudo] pulcritudo F

suos allocutus[15] est in hec verba:[16] *Nunc confortata est superbia et castigatio, et tempus adversionis, et ira indignationis. Nunc ergo, filii, emulatores estote legis, et date animas vestras pro testamento patrum, et mementote operum patrum,*[17] *que fecerunt in generationibus suis, et accipietis gloriam magnam, et nomen eternum.*

[2][18] Et quia magis movent exempla quam verba, adducit exempla novem, dicens sic:[19] *Abraham nonne in temptatione inventus est fidelis, et reputatum est ei ad iustitiam? Joseph in tempore angustie sue custodivit mandatum, et factus est dominus Egipti. Phinees, zelando zelum Dei, accepit testamentum sacerdotii eterni. Josue,*[20] *dum impleret verbum, factus est dux in Israhel. Caleph, dum testificatur in ecclesia, accepit*[21] *hereditatem. David in sua misericordia consecutus est sedem regni in* [G 521va] *secula. Helyas, dum zelat zelum legis, receptus est in celo. Ananias, Azarias, Misahel*[22] *credentes,*[23] *liberati sunt de flamma. Daniel in sua simplicitate liberatus est de ore leonum. Et ita cogitate per generationem et*[24] *generationem: quia omnes qui sperant in eum, non infirmantur.*[25] *Et a verbis viri peccatoris non*[26] *timueritis, quia gloria eius stercus et vermis est, hodie extollitur, et cras* [F 300ra] *non invenietur,*[27] *quia conversus est in terram suam, et cogitatio eius periit. Vos ergo, filii, confortamini, et viriliter agite in lege, quia cum feceritis que vobis precepta sunt in lege a*[28] *Domino Deo vestro*[29] *in ipsa gloriosi eritis.*

[3] Modo videtur michi quod ego, Mathatias sacerdos et summus pontifex, licet immeritus, videns et sanctam civitatem Iherusalem et loca alia Christi sanguine dedicata in manibus spurcidorum[30] Agarenorum, vidensque Turcos[31] inimicos fidei Christiane intantum contra cultum Christiani nominis desevire ut quasi de omnibus partibus Romanie ipsum delere voluerunt,[32] et innumerabiles captivos duxerunt,[33] et abdicaverunt[34] miserabili servituti, hec audiens, tactus dolore cordis intrinsecus, merito potui exclamare, sicut exclamavit[35] Mathatias: 'Ve michi,

15 allocutus] alloqutus F
16 I Machabaeorum 2.49–51.
17 et mementote operum patrum *om. per homoioteleuton* G
18 exempla movent *add. in mg.* F; patrum exempla *add. in mg.* G
19 I Machabaeorum 2.52–64.
20 Josue] Jhosue F
21 accepit] cepit F
22 misahel] misael F
23 credentes] ardentes F
24 per generationem et] de generatione ad G
25 infirmantur] confundantur G
26 non] ne F
27 non invenietur] morietur G
28 a] et G
29 vestro] nostro G
30 spurcidorum] spulcidorum F
31 turcos] turchos F
32 voluerunt] voluerint G
33 duxerunt] adduxerint G
34 abdicaverunt] addicaverunt G
35 exclamavit] clamavit G

quid[36] adhuc michi vivere?', quasi dicam,[37] 'melius erat michi mors quam vita'. *Melius est enim nos mori quam videre mala gentis nostre et sanctorum*, sicut dicitur I Machabeorum 3.[38]

[4] Ordinavi armatam sancte unionis, ut dicatur illud I[39] Machabeorum 5:[40] *Convenit ecclesia magna cogitare quid facerent[41] fratribus suis, qui in tribulatione magna erant et expug*[G 521vb]*nabantur* a gentibus. Cuius constitui capitaneum et legatum bone memorie H<enricum> patriarcham Constantinopolitanum, cui multa prospera succreverunt[42] et cetera. Sed tandem, sicut Domino placuerit,[43] ipso subtracto de medio et ipso vivente in gloria, mortuo autem in carne, non quidem ut[44] solent mori ignavi, sed sicut cadunt coram[45] filiis iniquitatis sancti et iusti, habui de aliquo duce et capitaneo exercitui agminis Domini Dei Israhel providere. Et quia inter ceteros principes[46] repperi instantem sepius, supplicantem humilius, [F 300rb] optantem ardentius, offerentem liberalius dilectum filium Imbertum Dalphinum Viennensem, hic presentem, idcirco ipsum, de fratrum nostrorum concilio,[47] ducem et capitaneum exercitus contra Turcos duximus deputandum, dicentes de eo verba thematis preassumpta:[48] *Dum implet[49] verbum, factus est dux in Israhel.*

[5] Nota primo[50] Paralipomenon 10, II Regum 5:[51] *Qui percusserit Zebezeum[52] et cetera.* Judicum 1:[53] *Quis ascendet ante nos contra Chananeum[54] et erit dux belli? Dixitque[55] dominus: 'Judas ascendet: ecce tradidi terram in manu eius'.* Et 10 capitulo:[56] *Qui primus ex vobis contra filios Israhel ceperit dimicare[57] erit dux populi.*

[6] Et videte quod, licet omnes conditiones illorum novem de quibus exemplificat textus sibi possumus congrue adaptare, videlicet[58] Abrahe fidelitatem,

---

36 quid] michi *add. et del.* G
37 dicam] dicat *a.c.* F; dicat G
38 I Machabaeorum 3.59.
39 i *s.l.* F
40 I Machabaeorum 5.16.
41 facerent] facerint G
42 succreverunt] successerunt F
43 placuerit] placuit G
44 ut] sicut G
45 coram] eorum F
46 principes] habui *add.* F
47 concilio] consilio G
48 preassumpta] preassumpti F
49 implet] impleret G
50 primo] primi G
51 I Paralipomenon 11.6; II Samuelis 2.8.
52 zebezeum] zebudeum G
53 Iudicum 1.1–2.
54 chananeum] cananeum G
55 dixitque] dicitque G
56 Iudicum 10.18.
57 contra filios israhel ceperit dimicare] ceperit dimicare contra filios israhel G
58 videlicet] scilicet G

Joseph castitatem, Phinees sinceritatem, Josue[59] probitatem et bonitatem, Caleph veritatem, David pietatem, Helye caritatem, trium puerorum firmam credulitatem,[60] et Danieli simplicitatem, tamen videtur michi quod, quo ad presens, ratione [G 522ra] ducatus et capitaneatus quem sibi de presenti concedimus, congruentius[61] assumimus verbum quod dictum est de Josue probitate et bonitate, dicentes verba thematis preassumpta: *Dum implet*[62] *verbum, factus est dux in Israhel.*[63] Et ratio videtur michi esse quod[64] iste noster capitaneus recte comparatur Josue, ratione successionis, ratione similis pronunciationis, ratione interpretationis, ratione similis operationis.

[7] Primo quidem ratione successionis. Josue enim successit Moysi. Unde Ecclesiastici 46:[65] *Jesus*[66] *Nave successor Moysi.* Ita iste ad litteram, in ista guberna[F 300va]tione successor patriarche mitissimi, sanctissimi, et Deo carissimi, ut merito dicam sibi illud, Josue 1:[67] *Moyses servus meus mortuus est: surge, et transi Iordanem istum, tu et omnis populus qui tecum est, in terram quam ego dabo filiis Israhel. Nullus poterit tibi resistere, sicut fui*[68] *cum Moyse, ita ero tecum: non dimittam te neque derelinquam te.*[69] *Confortare et esto robustus.*

[8] Secundo ratione similis pronunciationis. Sicut enim habet hystoria[70] Numerorum 13, filii Israhel antequam intrarent terram promissionis, miserunt XII exploratores qui omnes exceptis Josue et Caleph retulerunt terram esse optimam,[71] sed tamen impossibilem ad obtinendum[72] propter habitatores ipsius. Unde dicebant:[73] *Terra*[74] *quam lustravimus devorat*[75] *habitatores suos; populus quem aspeximus procere stature est. Ibi*[76] *vidimus*[77] *monstra quedam filiorum Emaum*[78] *de genere giganteo,*[79] *quibus comparati*[80] *quasi locuste videbamur.* Et paulo

---

59 josue *om.* F
60 trium puerorum firmam credulitatem *om.* G
61 congruentius] concedimus *add et del.* F
62 implet] impleret G
63 verbum factus est dux in israhel] et cetera F; delphinus *add in mg.* F; delphinus josue *add. in mg.* G
64 quod] quia G
65 Ecclesiasticus 46.1.
66 iesus] ihesus F
67 Iosue 1.2, 5–6.
68 fui] sui G
69 te *om.* F
70 hystoria] ystoria F
71 esse optimam *inv.* G
72 obtinendum] optinendum F
73 Numeri 13.33.
74 terra] terram G
75 devorat] devorant G
76 ibi] ubi F
77 vidimus] montes *add. et del.* G
78 Emaum] Emant G
79 giganteo] gigantes G
80 comparati] coparati F

ante:[81] *Nequaquam ad hunc populum valemus ascendere, quia fortior nobis est.* Unde fecerunt murmurare filios Israhel[82] et [G 522rb] dicere:[83] *Utinam mortui essemus in Egipto* et cetera. Sed soli Josue et Caleph compescebant murmur[84] populi, dicentes:[85] *Ascendamus et possideamus terram quoniam poterimus obtinere eam.* Et ideo de istis duobus dicitur Ecclesiastici 46[86] quod *ipsi duo constituti a periculo sunt liberati.*

[9] Ad litteram autem hodie sunt[87] multi principes clamantes et dicentes quod id quod fit contra Turcos[88] non est utile, ymmo magis toti Christianitati dampnosum et inutile. Dicunt enim illorum esse magnam multitudinem et istam armatam esse valde modicam. [F 300vb] Et ideo retrahunt populum, non attendentes quod dixerunt isti duo Josue et Caleph, Numerorum 14:[89] *Nolite rebelles esse contra Dominum, neque timeatis populum terre huius, quia sicut panem ita possumus eos devorare, cum recesserit ab illis omne presidium. Dominus nobiscum est; nolite metuere.* Et ita ad litteram dicit iste, considerans illud Deuteronomii 31:[90] *Viriliter agite, et confortamini. Nolite timere, nec paveatis ad conspectum eorum, quia Dominus Deus tuus ipse est ductor tuus, et non dimittet te, neque derelinquet te.* Nota hic multa exempla. Unde I Machabeorum 3:[91] *Quomodo poterimus pauci pugnare contra multitudinem tantam tam fortem?*[92] Sed respondit[93] ille bonus miles Judas:[94] *Facile est concludi multos in manu paucorum, nec est differentia in conspectu Dei celi*[95] *liberare in multis vel in*[96] *paucis, quia non in multitudine exercitus*[97] et cetera.

[10] Tertio ratione interpretationis. Josue enim interpretatur salus, vel salvatio, seu[98] salvator aut salvaturus. Iste autem ad litteram vadit pro salute Christianorum illarum partium. Unde de isto Jo[G 522va]sue dicitur Ecclesiastici 46:[99] *Fuit magnus secundum nomen suum, maximus in salutem*[100] *electorum Dei, expugnare insurgentes hostes, ut consequeretur hereditatem Israhel. Quam gloriam adeptus*

---

81 Numeri 13.32.
82 fecerunt murmurare filios israhel] ceperunt filii israhel murmurare G
83 Numeri 14.3.
84 murmur *om.* G
85 Numeri 13.31.
86 Ecclesiasticus 46.10.
87 sunt *om.* F
88 Turcos] Turchos G
89 Numeri 14.9.
90 Deuteronomium 31.6.
91 I Machabaeorum 3.17.
92 pugnare *ponitur post* fortem G
93 respondit] respondet G
94 I Machabaeorum 3.18–19.
95 celi *om.* G
96 in *om.* F
97 exercitus *om.* G
98 seu] vel G
99 Ecclesiasticus 46.1–3.
100 salutem] salute G

264 Appendix V

est in tollendo manus suas, et iactando contra civitates rumpheas. Qui ante illum restitit? Nam hostes ipse Dominus percussit.

[11] Quarto ratione similis operationis. Sicut enim Josue fortis in bello terram acquisivit et distribuit filiis Israhel, ita iste utinam et acquirat et distribuat Dei gratia faciente, [F 301ra] ut sibi dicatur illud Josue 1:[101] *Tu sorte divides populo huic terram, pro qua iuravi patribus tuis, ut traderem eam illis. Confortare igitur et esto robustus valde.* Unde sicut Josue duxit filios Israhel, ita[102] iste veros Israhelitas et defensores nominis Christiani. Quia ergo similis est Josue in successione,[103] in exhortatione,[104] et[105] in interpretatione, et erit per Dei gratiam in operatione, idcirco merito de eo assumpsi quod dictum est de Josue: *Dum implet[106] verbum, factus est dux in Israhel.*[107]

[12][108] In quibus verbis tanguntur duo: Primo eius devotio virtuosa, *dum implet[109] verbum*; secundo eius sublimatio gloriosa, quia *factus est dux in Israhel*. Primo quidem eius devotio virtuosa, quia implet verbum. Verbum quidem quod non potest contempni sine improperio, verbum quidem quod[110] debet audiri cum desiderio, verbum quidem[111] quod debet impleri cum magno gaudio, cum magno incendio, cum magno tripudio. Verbum quidem de isto fratrum nostrorum adiutorio non potest quidem contempni sine magno totius Christianitatis improperio. Unde dicebat ille Jeremias Trenorum ultimo:[112] *Recordare, Domine[113] quid accide*[G 522vb]*rit nobis. Intuere et respice opprobrium nostrum* et cetera. Et in Psalmo:[114] *Deus, venerunt gentes in hereditatem tuam* et cetera usque ibi: *Facti sumus opprobrium[115] vicinis nostris, subsannatio et illusio[116]* et cetera. Iste autem non contempnit, ymmo[117] potest dicere illud Psalmi:[118] *Zelus domus tue comedit me, et opprobrium[119] exprobrantium tibi ceciderunt super me.* Nota parabolam de illo[120] *qui exiit seminare semen suum*, quomodo[121] de ultimis dicitur[122] quod[123]

---

101 Iosue 1.6–7.
102 ita] ista *a.c.* F
103 in successione *om.* G
104 exhortatione] exortatione F
105 et *om.* F
106 implet] impleret G
107 verbum factus est dux in israhel] et cetera F
108 verbum viagii contra turchos *add. in mg.* G
109 implet] impleret G
110 quod *om.* F
111 quidem *om.* F
112 Lamentationes 5.1.
113 domine] et vide *add.* G
114 Psalmi 78.1, 4.
115 opprobium] obprobium F
116 vicinis nostris subsannatio et illusio *om.* G
117 ymmo] unde G
118 Psalmi 68.10.
119 opprobrium] opprobria F
120 Lucas 8.5.
121 quomodo] quoniam G
122 Lucas 8.15; cf. Matthaeus 13.23.
123 quod *om.* G

hii sunt[124] *qui corde bono et optimo verbum retinent, et fructum afferunt in patientia,* Mathei 13[125] et Luce 8. [F 301rb]

[13] Secundo istud verbum debet audiri cum desiderio. Unde I Machabeorum 3:[126] *Dixerunt unusquisque ad proximum suum: 'Erigamus deiectionem populi nostri et pugnemus pro populo nostro et sanctis nostris'. Et congregatus est conventus ut essent parati ad prelium*[127] et cetera. Sicut illa que dicebat Luce 1:[128] *Fiat michi secundum verbum tuum;*[129] Job 4:[130] *Ad me missum est*[131] *verbum absconditum*[132] et cetera.

[14] Tertio istud verbum debet impleri cum magno gaudio, cum magno incendio, et cum magno tripudio. Unde I Machabeorum 3 dicitur:[133] *Surrexit Judas, qui vocabatur Machabeus, et adiuvabant eum omnes fratres eius, et universi qui se coniunxerant patri eius, et preliabantur*[134] *prelium Israhel cum letitia.* Implevit ergo verbum, Ecclesiastici 48:[135] *Verbum illius*[136] *quasi facula ardebat*; in Psalmo:[137] *Ignitum eloquium tuum vehementer, et servus tuus dilexit illud.* Verbum quidem divinum et iherarchicum,[138] verbum quidem[139] angelicum, verbum quidem[140] mosaicum, verbum quidem[141] propheticum, verbum quidem[142] evangelicum, verbum quidem[143] apostolicum, verbum quidem[144] mirificum, verbum quidem[145] salvificum, Actuum 15:[146] *Vobis verbum salutis huius*[147] *missum* [G 523ra] *est.* Johannis 6:[148] *Verba que ego loquor vobis, spiritus et vita sunt*; et ibidem: *verba vite eterne habes.*[149] Jeremie 1:[150] *Ecce dedi verba mea in ore tuo. Ecce constitui te super gentes et regna, ut evellas*

---

124 sunt *om.* G
125 13] xii F
126 I Machabaeorum 3.43–44.
127 prelium] populum G
128 Lucas 1.38.
129 verbum tuum *om.* F
130 4 *om. (lacuna)* G || Iob 4.12.
131 est *om.* G
132 absconditum] Domini G
133 I Machabaeorum 3.1–2.
134 preliabantur] prelibantur *a.c. s.l.* G
135 Ecclesiasticus 48.1.
136 illius] illud F
137 Psalmi 118.140.
138 iherarchicum] thearticum F
139 quidem *om.* F
140 quidem *om.* F
141 quidem *om.* F
142 quidem *om.* F
143 quidem *om.* F
144 quidem *om.* F
145 quidem *om.* F
146 Recte Actus 13.26.
147 huius *om.* G
148 6] xvi F || Iohannes 6.64, 69.
149 habes] habet G
150 Ieremias 1.9–10.

266 *Appendix V*

et destruas, et dissipes et perdas, et edifices et plantes et cetera. Illud autem verbum implebit, quia Ruth 3:[151] *Non cessabit homo donec opere compleverit quod*[152] incepit. Verbum enim, quod egressum est *de ore suo, non revertetur ad eum vacuum* et cetera, Ysaie 55.[153] Vel implebit[154] verbum quod aufert timoris formidinem, verbum[155] quod profert [F 301va] valoris magnitudinem,[156] verbum[157] quod offert amoris plenitudinem,[158] verbum[159] quod confert honoris celsitudinem: *Si verba mea in vobis manserint, quodcumque volueritis petetis, et fiet vobis*, Johannis 15.[160]

[15][161] Sequitur secundo eius sublimatio gloriosa, quia *factus est dux in Israhel*, Ysaie 55:[162] *Testem populis*[163] *dedi eum, ducem*[164] *ac preceptorem gentibus*. Et videtur michi quod istud competit sibi et ex nomine et ex dignitate. Ipse enim vocatur Imbertus et est in dignitate Dalphinus. Imbertus idem est quod 'ymber' et 'thus'.[165] Iste autem est ymber refrigerans,[166] imber[167] fecundans, imber[168] delectans. Ad litteram enim ipse erit Christianis[169] in illis partibus degentibus refrigerium in persecutione, auxilium in defensione, solatium in consolatione, ut sit imber[170] et cetera, Ysaie 55:[171] *Quemadmodum descendit imber*[172] *et nix de celo* et cetera; Proverbiorum 16:[173] *Clementia eius quasi imber*[174] *serotinus*, ut dicant fideles illarum partium illud Osee[175] 6:[176] *Veniet quasi ymber* [G 523rb] *nobis temporaneus et serotinus terre*; et Deuteronomii 32:[177] *Quasi ymber super terram et quasi stille super gramina* et cetera.

151 Ruth 3.18
152 quod] impleverit *add. et del.* G
153 Isaias 55.11.
154 implebit] implevit G; ver *add. et del.* G
155 verbum *om.* F
156 valoris magnitudinem] amoris plenitudinem G
157 verbum *om.* F
158 amoris plenitudinem] valoris magnitudinem G
159 verbum *om.* F
160 Iohannes 15.7.
161 delphinus *add. in mg.* F; ducatus delphinus *add. in mg.* G
162 Isaias 55.4.
163 populis] populi G
164 ducem] et videtur *add. et del.* G
165 thus] tus F
166 refrigerans] refrigerativus F
167 imber] ymber G
168 imber] ymber G
169 christianis] christianus G
170 imber] ymber G
171 Isaias 55.10.
172 imber] ymber G
173 Proverbia 16.15.
174 imber] ymber G
175 osee] ozee G
176 6 *om.* G || Osee 6.3.
177 Deuteronomium 32.2.

[16] Sed non solum est imber,[178] sed et thus: thus ardens, thus redolens, thus vigens. Habet enim ardorem devotionis, odorem[179] bone opinionis, vigorem sancte operationis, Canticorum 3:[180] *Ascendit sicut virgula fumi ex aromatibus mirre, et thuris* et cetera. Et 4 capitulo:[181] *Odor vestimentorum tuorum, sicut odor thuris,* ut de eo dicamus illud Ecclesiastici 50:[182] *Quasi stella matutina in medio nebule, et*[183] *quasi luna* [F 301vb] *plena, in diebus suis lucet. Quasi sol refulgens, sic ille effulsit.*[184] *Quasi arcus*[185] *refulgens inter nebulas glorie, et quasi flos*[186] *rosarum in diebus vernis, et quasi lilia que sunt in transitu aque, et quasi thus ardens in diebus estatis, quasi ignis effulgens et thus ardens in igne, quasi vas auri solidum, ornatum omni lapide precioso, quasi oliva pullulans,*[187] *et quasi cypressus in altitudinem se extollens, in accipiendo illam stolam glorie, vestire eum*[188] *in consummatione*[189] *virtutis. In ascensu altaris sancti gloriam dedit sanctitatis amictum.*

[17][190] Sed est[191] ex dignitate Dalphinus. Dalphinus enim piscis est maritimus,[192] piscis crassus, piscis magnus, piscis[193] fortis et probus. Et iste noster est piscis[194] maritimus[195] propter penitentie amaritudinem vel propter prosapie celsitudinem, <piscis> magnus propter potentie magnitudinem,[196] piscis crassus non solum in corpore sed in mente propter benificentie plenitudinem, piscis fortis et probus propter victorie multitudinem, ut propter primum a Deo exaudiatur faciliter, ut[197] propter [G 523va][198] secundum a cunctis timeatur equaliter, ut[199] propter tertium a cunctis diligatur suaviter, <ut> propter quartum a cunctis revereatur et honoretur veraciter. Ut sit dux generosus, ut sit dux virtuosus, ut sit dux gratiosus et amorosus, ut sit dux[200] gloriosus, I Machabeorum 13:[201] *Vidit Symon Iohannem filium suum, quod vir prelii esset, et constituit eum ducem virtutum universarum.*

---

178 imber] ymber G
179 odorem] ardorem F
180 3] iiii F || Canticum Canticorum 3.6.
181 Canticum Canticorum 4.11.
182 Ecclesiasticus 50.6–12.
183 et *om.* G
184 effulsit] refulsit G
185 arcus] ortus G
186 flos] ros G
187 pullulans] pululans F
188 eum] eam F
189 consummatione] consummationem G
190 delphinus *add. in mg.* F
191 est *om.* G
192 maritimus] maritinus F
193 crassus... piscis] est magnus piscis est crassus piscis est G
194 piscis *om.* F
195 maritimos] Delphini piscis condiciones *add. in mg.* G
196 magnus propter potentie magnitudinem *om. per homoioteleuton* G
197 ut *om.* F
198 a deo... ut propter *iter. in folio* 523va G
199 ut *om.* F
200 et amorosus ut sit dux] ut sit dux amorosus et G
201 13] xiiii G || I Machabaeorum 13.54.

268 Appendix V

Ibit enim iste[202] *de virtute in* [F 302ra] *virtutem*, quia[203] *Dominus solus dux eius fuit*, et ideo[204] *videbitur Deus deorum in Syon*, quia Proverbiorum 4:[205] *Ducam te per semitas equitatis, quas cum ingressus fueris, non artabuntur gressus tui, et*[206] *currens non habebis offendiculum. Tene disciplinam,*[207] *nec dimittas eam, et custodi illam, quia ipsa est vita tua*, ut per gratiam hic et in futuro per gloriam quam nobis concedat ille[208] qui est benedictus in secula seculorum, Amen.

202   Psalmi 83.8.
203   Deuteronomium 32.12.
204   Psalmi 83.8.
205   Proverbia 4.11–13.
206   et *om.* F
207   disciplinam *om.* F; offendiculum *a.c. in mg.* G
208   ille *om.* G

Bibliography

Manuscript sources

Amien, Bibliothèque Municipale, MS 462, fols. 208r–212v.
Avignon, Bibliothèque Municipale, MS 295, fols. 50va–52vb.
Clermont-Ferrand, Bibliothèque Municipale, MS 46, fols. 71r–77r, 137v–141r, 215r–220v.
München, Bayerische StaatsBibliothek, MS Clm 18732, fols. 71v–73r.
Paris, Archives de France, JJ 54A, fol. 14r, nos. 191–192.
Paris, Bibliothèque nationale de France, MS lat. 3293, fols. 161r–169r, 299v–302r.
——— MS lat. 14965, fols. 331v–333r.
——— MS lat. 17516, fols. 84ra–85vb.
——— Nouvelles Acquisitions Françaises, MS 7603, fols. 44r–45v
Paris, Bibliothèque Sainte Genevieve, MS 240, fols. 290v–308v, 247v–251r, 521r–523v.
Vatican City, Archivio Segreto Vaticano, MS Reg. Aven. 40, fols. 88r–89r.
——— MS Reg. Aven. 41, fols. 223r–224r.
——— MS Reg. Aven. 48, fols. 373v–376r, 432r–433v.
Vatican City, Archivio Segreto Vaticano, MS Reg. Vat. 52, fols. 42v–43r.
——— MS Reg. Vat. 56, fols. 198v–199r, 140v.
——— MS Reg. Vat. 60, fols. 271v–272r.
——— MS Reg. Vat. 63, fols. 4v–5r.
——— MS Reg. Vat. 72, fols. 51v, 53r.
——— MS Reg. Vat. 74, fols. 3v–5v.
——— MS Reg. Vat. 101, fols. 2v–3r.
——— MS Reg. Vat. 119, fol. 132v.
——— MS Reg. Vat. 120, fol. 1r–v.
——— MS Reg. Vat. 137, fol. 166v.
——— MS Reg. Vat. 139, fols. 55v–56v.
——— MS Reg. Vat. 157, fol. 7r–v.
——— MS Reg. Vat. 161, fols. 2v–3r.
——— MS Reg. Vat. 169, fols. 1r–3r.
——— MS Reg. Vat. 170, fols. 1r–v, 4v–6v, 13r–14r.

Printed primary sources

Acta Aragonensia: Quellen zur Deutschen, Italienischen, Französischen, Spanischen, zur Kirchen–und Kulturgeschichte aus der Diplomatischen Korrespondenz Jaymes 11 (1291–1327), ed. Finke, H., 3 vols. (Berlin-Leipzig, 1908–1922).

'Adae Murimuth continuatio chronicarum', in *Rerum Britannicarum medii aevi scriptores*, ed. Thompson, E. (London: Eyre and Spottiswoode, 1889).

Annales Ecclesiastici ab anno 1198 usque ad annum 1565, eds. Baronio, C., *et al.*, 37 vols. (Paris-Freiburg-Bar le Duc, 1864–1867).

'Annales Cisterciensium in Heinrichow', in *Monumenta Germaniae Historica: Scriptores Rerum Germanicarum. Nova Series*, vol.19, 544–545.

'Annales Colbazenses', in *Monumenta Germaniae Historica: Scriptores Rerum Germanicarum. Nova Series*, vol.19, 711–719.

'Annales Gandenses', in *Monumenta Germaniae Historica: Scriptores Rerum Germanicarum. Nova Series*, vol.16, 555–597.

'Annales Londonienses', in *Chronicles of the Reigns of Edward I and Edward II*, vol.1, 3–251.

'Annales Lubicenses', in *Monumenta Germaniae Historica: Scriptores Rerum Germanicarum. Nova Series*, vol.16, 411–429.

'Annales Paulini', in *Chronicles of the Reigns of Edward I and Edward II*, vol.1, 253–312.

'Annales Sancti Blasii Brunsvicenses' in *Monumenta Germaniae Historica: Scriptores Rerum Germanicarum. Nova Series*, vol.24, 825.

'Annales Terrae Prussiae', in *Monumenta Germaniae Historica: Scriptores Rerum Germanicarum. Nova Series*, vol.19, 691–693.

'Annales Tielenenses', in *Monumenta Germaniae Historica: Scriptores Rerum Germanicarum. Nova Series*, vol.24, 21–27.

'Anonymum S. Martialis Chronicon ad Annum MCCCXX Continuatum', in *Recueil des Historiens des Gaules et de la France*, vol.21, 802–814.

Antiquitates Italicae Medii Aevi, ed. Muratori, L. A., 25 vols. (Milan: Typis Michaelis Bellotti, 1723–1896).

Archives Historiques du Poitou, eds. Guérin, P. and Léonce, C., 14 vols. (Poitiers: Imprimerie Oudin, 1881–1958).

Aristote, Histoire Des Animaux, ed. and trans., Louis, P., 3 vols. (Paris: Les Belles Lettres, 1964–1969).

Aristote, Les Parties Des Animaux, ed. and trans., Louis, P. (Paris: Les Belles Lettres, 1990).

Benedict XI, *Le registre de Benoit XI*, ed. Grandjean C. (Paris: Bibliothèque des Écoles françaises d'Athènes et de Rome, 1903).

Benedict XII, *Lettres closes, patentes et curiales du pape Benoît XII (1334–1342) se rapportant à la France*, ed. Daumet, G. (Paris: Bibliothèque des Écoles Françaises d'Athènes et de Rome, 3ᵉ séries, 1899–1920).

Benedict XII, *Lettres communes du pape Benoît XII*, ed. Vidal, J. M., 3 vols. (Paris: Bibliothèque des Écoles Françaises d'Athènes et de Rome, 3ᵉ séries, 1903–1911).

Benedict XII, *Lettres closes et patentes du pape Benoît XII intéressant les pays autres que la France*, eds. Vidal, J. M. and Mollat, G. (Paris: Bibliothèque des Écoles Françaises d'Athènes et de Rome, 3ᵉ séries, 1913–1950).

Bernard of Clairvaux, 'Liber ad milites Templi de laude Novae Militiae', in *Sancti Bernardi abbatis primi Claraevallensis opera genuina*, 3 vols. (Paris: Monks of Saint Bernard, 1833–1835).

Bernard of Clairvaux, 'De Consideratione libri quinque ad Eugenium tertium', in *Patrologia Latina*, vol.182, cols.727–808.

Bernard of Clairvaux, 'Sancti Bernardi Claraevallensis abbatis de Consideratione Libri V ad Eugenium III', ed. Krabinger, G. (Landshut: Libraria Joseph Thomanni, 1845).

Bibliography 271

Bernard of Clairvaux, *Sancti Bernardi Abbatis Primi Claraevallensis Opera Genuina*, 3 vols. (Paris: The Monks of Saint Bernard, 1833–1835).

Biblioteca Bio-Bibliografica della Terra Santa e dell'Oriente Francescano, ed. Golubovich, G., 5 vols. (Florence: Quaracchi, 1906–1927).

Boniface VIII, *Les régistres de Boniface VIII*, ed. Digard, G. (Paris: Bibliothèque des Écoles Françaises d'Athènes et de Rome, 1884–1939)

Bullarium Cyprium 2: Papal Letters Concerning Cyprus, 1261–1314, ed. Schabel, C. (Nicosia: Cyprus Research Centre, 2010).

Bullarium Cyprium 3: Lettres papales relatives à Chypre 1316–1378, eds. Perrat, C., and Richard, J. (in collaboration with Christopher Schabel) (Nicosia: Cyprus Research Centre, 2012).

Bullarium Ordinis Fratrum Praedicatorum, eds. Ripoll, T., *et al.*, 8 vols. (Rome: Ex Typographia Hieronymi Mainardi, 1728–1740).

Cartulaire General de l'Ordre des Hospitaliers de St Jean de Jerusalem 1100–1310, ed. Delaville Le Roulx, J., 4 vols. (Paris: Leroux, 1894–1906).

Chartularium Universitatis Parisiensis sub auspiciis consilii generalis facultatum Parisiensium, eds. Denifle, H. and Chatelain, A., 4 vols. (Paris: Ex Typis Fratrum Delalain, 1889–1897).

'Chronicon Auctore Bernardo Guidonis, Episcopo Lodovensi', in *Recueil des Historiens des Gaules et de la France*, vol.21, 690–734.

'Chronicon Elwacense', in *Monumenta Germaniae Historica: Scriptores Rerum Germanicarum. Nova Series*, vol.10, 34–51.

Chronicon Galfridi le Baker de Swynebroke, ed. Thompson, M. E. (Oxford: Clarendon Press, 1889).

'Chronicon Parmense ab anno 1038 usque ad annum 1338', in *Rerum Italicarum Scriptores*, vol.9.9, 3–259.

Chronique des quatre premiers Valois (1327–1393), ed. Luce, S. (Paris: Société de l'Histoire de France, 1862).

'Chronique du Templier de Tyr (1242–1310)', in *Les Gestes des Chiprois, Recueil de Chroniques Françaises Écrites en Orient aux XIIe et XIVe Siècles*, 139–334.

Chronique Latin de Guillaume de Nangis de 1113 a 1300 avec les continuations de cette chronique de 1300 a 1368, ed. Géraud, H., 2 vols. (Paris: Imprimerie de Crapelet, 1843).

Chronique métrique de Godefroy de Paris, ed. Buchon, J. A. (Paris: Imprimerie d'Hippolyte Tilliard, 1827).

Chronique Parisienne anonyme du XIVe siècle, ed. Hellot, A. (Nogent-Le-Rotrou: Société de l'Histoire de Paris, 1884).

'Chroniques de Saint-Denis depuis 1285 jusqu'en 1328', in *Recueil des historiens des Gaules et de la France*, vol.20, 654–724.

Chroniques Gréco–Romanes, ed. Hopf, C. (Berlin: Imprimerie Gustave Schade, 1873).

Chronicles of the Reigns of Edward I and Edward II: Annales Londonienses and Annales Paulini, Edited from Mss. in the British Museum and in the Archiepiscopal Library at Lambeth, ed. Stubbs, W., 2 vols. (London: Longman, 1882–1883).

Chronographia regum Francorum, ed. Moranvillé, H., 3 vols. (Paris: Société de l'histoire de France, 1891–1897).

Clement V, *Regestum Clementis papae V: Ex Vaticanis archetypis sanctissimi domini nostri Leonis XIII pontificis maximi iussu et munificentia*, ed. Cura et Studio Monarchorum Ordinis S. Benedicti, 10 vols. (Rome: Typografia Vaticana, 1885–1892).

272 Bibliography

Clement VI, *Lettres closes, patentes et curiales du pape Clément VI se rapportant à la France*, eds. Déprez, E., *et al.*, 3 vols. (Paris: Bibliothèque des Écoles françaises d'Athènes et de Rome, 3ᵉ séries, 1901–1961).

Clement VI, *Lettres closes, patentes et curiales du pape Clément VI intéressant les pays autre que la France*, eds. Déprez, E. and Mollat, G. (Paris: Bibliothèque des Écoles Françaises d'Athènes et de Rome, 3ᵉ séries, 1960–1961).

'Collectio Actorum Veterum', in *Vitae Paparum Avenionensium*, iii, 1–561.

Conciliorum Oecumenicorum Decreta, ed. Alberigo, J. (Bologna: Istituto per le Scienze Religiose, 1972).

'Continuatio Canonicorum Sancti Rudberti Salisburgensis', in *Monumenta Germaniae Historica: Scriptores Rerum Germanicarum. Nova Series*, vol.9, 819.

'Continuatio Chronici Girardi de Fracheto', in *Recueil des Historiens des Gaules et de la France*, vol.21, 6–70.

'Continuatio Florianensis', in *Monumenta Germaniae Historica: Scriptores Rerum Germanicarum. Nova Series*, vol.9, 747–753.

'Corpus Chronicorum Bononiensium', in *Rerum Italicarum Scriptores*, vol.18, cols.520–621.

De Motu Animalium, ed. and trans., Nussbaum, M. C. (Princeton: Princeton University Press, 1978).

Die Ausgaben der Apostolischen Kammer unter Benedikt XII., Klemens VI., und Innocenz VI. (1335–1362.), ed. Schäfer, K. H. (Paderborn: F. Schöningh, 1914).

Diplomatarium Veneto-Levantinum, sive Acta et diplomata res Venetas, Graecas atque Levantis illustrantia a.1300–1454, ed. Thomas, G. M., 2 vols. (Venice: Typis Marci Visentini, 1880–1899).

'Excerpta e memoriali historiarum, auctore Johanne Parisiensi, Sancti Victoris Parisiensis Canonico Regulari', in *Recueil des historiens des Gaules et de la France*, vol.21, 630–676.

Flavius Vegetius Renatus, *Epitoma Rei Militaris*, ed. Lang, C. (Leipzig: Bibliotheca Scriptorum Grecorum et Romanorum Teubneriana, 1885).

'Fragmenta d'une Chronique anonyme Finnisant en M.CCC.XXVIII', in, *Recueil des historiens des Gaules et de la France*, vol.21, 146–158.

'Gestorum abbatum Trudonensium continuatio tertia', in *Monumenta Germaniae Historica: Scriptores Rerum Germanicarum. Nova Series*, vol.10, 361–448.

Giovanni Villani, *Cronica di Giovanni Villani a Miglior Lezione Ridotta*, ed. Dragomanni, G. F., 8 vols. (Florence: Per il Magheri, 1823).

Guilelmus Peraldus, *Sermones Dominicales ex epistolis et Evangelys atque de sanctis secundum ecclesie ordinem Wilhelmi Cancellary Parisiensis* (Tübingen: Friedrich Meynberger, 1499).

Histoire de Dauphiné et des princes qui ont porté le Nom de Dauphins, ed. Valbonnais, J.-P., 2 vols. (Geneva: Chez Fabri & Barrillot, 1721–1722).

'Historiae Romanae Fragmenta', in *Antiquitates Italicae Medii Aevi*, vol.7, cols.443–998.

James of Molay, 'Concilium Super negotio Terre Sancte', in *Vitae Paparum Avenionensium*, vol.3, 150–154.

Humbert of Romans, *Tractatus solemnis Fratris Humberti quondam Magistri Generalis Ordinis Praedicatorum: De predicatione sancte crucis* (Nuremberg: Peter Wagner, 1495).

Jacobus de Laosanna (O.P.), *Sermones Dominicales et festivales per totum anni circulum per reverendum patrem fratrem Jacobum de Laosana, ... Declamati, impressioni mandati per quendam patrem professorem ordinis Minorum regularis observantie* (Paris: Ambrosii Girault, 1530).

Jacobus de Voragine, *Jacobi a Voragine Legenda Aurea vulgo historia Lombardica Dicta*, ed. Graesse, Th. (Lipsiae: Impensis Librariae Arnoldiane, 1801).
John Kantakouzenos, 'Historia', ed. Schopen, L., *Ioannis Cantacuzeni Eximperatoris Historiarum Libri IV*, 3 vols. (Bonn: Übersetzung, 1828–1832).
John XXII, *Lettres communes du pape Jean XXII analysées d'après les registres dits d'Avignon et du Vatican*, ed. Mollat, G., 16 vols. (Paris: Bibliothèque des Écoles françaises d'Athènes et de Rome, 3ᵉ séries, 1904–1947).
―――― *Lettres secrètes & curiales du pape Jean XXII (1316–1334) relatives à la France*, eds. Coulon, A. and Clémencet, S., 3 vols. (Paris: Bibliothèque des Écoles françaises d'Athènes et de Rome, 3ᵉ séries, 1900–1967).
John of Bromyard, *Summa Predicantium doctissimi viri fratris Johannis Bromyard, Ordinis Predicatorum* (Basel, 1485).
John of Winterthur, 'Chronicon', in *Monumenta Germaniae Historica: Scriptores Rerum Germanicarum. Nova Series*, vol.3, 246–267.
Les Gestes des Chiprois, Recueil de chroniques françaises écrites en Orient aux XIIᵉ et XIVᵉ siècles, ed. Raynaud, G. (Geneva: Socièté de l'Orient Latin, 1887).
Les Grandes chroniques de France, ed. Viard, J., 10 vols. (Paris: Société de l'histoire de France, 1920–1953).
'Memoriale Historicum Matthei de Griffonibus', in *Rerum Italicarum Scriptores*, vol.18.2, 3–111.
Monumenta Germaniae Historica: Scriptores Rerum Germanicarum. Nova Series, eds. Pertz, G. H., *et al.*, 38 vols. (Hanover: Anton Hiersemann Reprint, 1983–).
Patrologia Latina, ed. Migne, J.-P., 221 vols. (Paris, 1841–1855).
Peter Giustinian, *Venetiarum historia vulgo Petro Iustiniano Iustiniani filio adiudicata*, ed. Cessi, R. (Venice, 1964).
'Prima Vita Benedicti XII', in *Vitae Paparum Avenionensium*, vol.1, 195–209.
'Prima Vita Clementis V', in *Vitae Paparum Avenionesium*, vol.1, 1–23.
'Prima Vita Joannis XXII', in *Vitae Paparum Avenionensium*, vol.1, 107–136.
'Quarta Vita Clementis V', in *Vitae Paparum Avenionensium*, vol.1, 59–80.
'Quarta Vita Joannis XXII', in *Vitae Paparum Avenionensium*, vol.1, 169–171.
Raymond of Aquiler, 'Historia Francorum qui ceperunt Iherusalem', in *Recueil des historiens des Croisades: Historiens Occidentaux*, vol.3, 235–309.
Recueil des historiens des Croisades: Historiens Occidentaux, 5 vols. (Paris: Académie Imperiale des Inscriptions et Belles-Lettres, 1862–1866).
Recueil des historiens des Gaules et de la France, ed. Bouquet, M., *et al.*, 24 vols. (Paris: Imprimerie Impériale, 1737–1904).
Registrum Simonis de Gandavo Diocesis Saresbiriensis, AD 1297–1315, 2 vols. (Oxford, 1913–1914).
Repertorium medii aevi, ed. Stegmüller, F., 8 vols. (Madrid: Consejo Superior de Investigaciones Cientificas, 1940–).
Rerum Italicarum Scriptores: Raccolta degli Storici Italiani dal Cinquecento al Millecinquecento, ed. Carducci, G., *et al.*, 33 vols. (Città di Castello: Ex Typographia Societatis Palatinae in Regia Curia, 1900–1979).
Sacrorum conciliorum nova et amplissima collectio, ed. Mansi, G. D., 55 vols. (Florence, Venice, Paris, Leipzig: Humberto Welter, 1759–1962).
Scriptores Ordinis Praedicatorum, ed. Kaeppeli, T., 4 vols. (Rome: Ad S. Sabinae, 1970–1993).
Scriptores Ordinis Praedicatorum recensiti notisque historicis etc Criticis illustrati, eds. Quétif, J. and Échard, J., 2 vols. (Lutèce-Paris, 1719–1721).

'Secunda Vita Clementis V', in *Vitae Paparum Avenionensium*, vol.1, 24–53.
'Sexta Vita Clementis V', in *Vitae Paparum Avenionensium*, vol.1, 89–106.
'Sexta Vita Joannis XXII', in *Vitae Paparum Avenionensium*, vol.1, 178–182.
Spicilegium sive collectio veterum aliquot scriptorum qui in Galliae bibliothecis delituerant, ed. D'Achery, L., 13 vols. (Paris: Montalant, 1655–1677).
'Storie Pistoresi', in *Rerum Italicarum Scriptores*, vol.11.5, 3–239.
'Tertia Vita Joannis XXII', in *Vitae Paparum Avenionensium*, vol.1, 152–168.
The Exempla or Illustrative Stories from the Sermones Vulgares of Jacques de Vitry, ed. Crane, T. F. (London: The Folklore Society, 1890).
Titres de l'Ancienne Maison Ducale de Bourbon, ed. Huillard-Bréholles, M., 2 vols. (Paris: Typographie de Henri Plon, 1867–1874).
Vitae Paparum Avenionensium hoc est historia pontificum romanorum ... ab anno 1305 usque ad annum 1394, ed. Mollat, G., 4 vols. (Paris: Librairie Letouzey et Ané, 1916–1928).
William Le Maire, 'Livre de Guillaume le Maire', ed. Célestin–Port, C., in *Mélanges historiques: Choix de documents*, 2 (1877), 206–569.

Secondary works

Alberzoni, M. P. and Montaubin, P., eds., *Legati, delegati e l'impressa d'Oltremare (secoli XII–XIII)/ Papal Legates, Delegates and the Crusades (12th–13th Century)* (Turnhout: Brepols, 2014).
Alexis, C., 'L'Évolution de la Predication du Cardinal Eudes de Châteauroux (1190?–1273): Un Approache Statistique', in *De l'Homélie au Sermon: Histoire de la Predication Medieval*, eds. Hamesse, J. and Hermand, X. (Louvain-la-Neuve: Fédération Internationale des Institus d'Études Médiévales, 1993), 103–142.
Arbel, B., ed., *Intercultural Contacts in the Medieval Mediterranean* (London: Frank Cass, 1996).
Atiya, A. S., *The Crusade in the Later Middle Ages* (London: Methuen, 1938).
Bainton, R. H., *Christian Attitudes toward War and Peace: A Historical Survey and Critical Re-evaluation* (New York: Abingdon Press, 1960).
Baratier, E., 'Une Prédication de la Croisade à Marseille en 1224', in *Economies et Sociétés au Moyen Age: Mélanges Offerts à Édouard Perroy* (Paris: Publications de la Sorbonne, 1973), 690–699.
Barber, M., 'The Pastoureaux of 1320', *Journal of Ecclesiastical History*, 32 (1981), 143–166.
——— *The Trial of the Templars* (Cambridge: Cambridge University Press, 1993).
——— *The New Knighthood: A History of the Order of the Temple* (Cambridge: Cambridge University Press, 1994).
Barber, R. and Barker, J., *Tournaments: Jousts, Chivalry and Pageants in the Middle Ages* (Woodbridge: Boydell, 1989).
Bataillon, L.-J., 'Approaches to the Study of Medieval Sermons', *Leeds Studies in English*, 11 (1980), 19–35.
——— 'Les instruments de travail des prédicateurs au XIIIe Siècle', in *Culture et Travail Intellectuel dans l'Occident Medieval*, eds. Hasenohr, G. and Longere, J. (Paris: Editions du CNRS, 1981), 197–209.
Benton, J. F., 'Theocratic in Fourteenth-Century France: The *Liber Bellorum Domini* by Pierre de la Palu', in *The Library Chronicle: Bibliographical Studies in Honor of Rudolf Hirsch*, eds. Miller, W. and Waldman, T. (Philadelphia: University of Pennsylvania Library, 1975), 38–55.

Bériou, N., 'La reportation des Sermons Parisiens à la Fin du XIIIe Siècle', *Medioevo e Rinascimento*, 3 (1989), 87–124.

—— 'La Prédication de Croisade de Philippe le Chancelier et d'Eudes de Châteauroux en 1226', in *La prédication en Pays d'Oc (XIIe– début XVe siècle)*, Cahiers de Fanjeaux 32, (Toulouse: Privat, 1992), 85–109.

—— *L'Avènement des Maîtres de la Parole. La Prédication à Paris au XIIIe Siècle*, 2 vols. (Paris: Institut d'études Augustiniennes, 1998).

—— 'Les Sermon Latins après 1200', in *The Sermon*, ed. Kienzle, B. M. (Turnhout: Brepols, 2000), 363–447.

Biller, P., 'John of Naples, Quodlibets and Medieval Theological Concern with the Body', in *Medieval Theology and the Natural Body*, eds. Biller, P. and Minnis, A. J. (Woodbridge: York Medieval Press, 1997), 3–13.

Blake, B., 'A Crucial Sermon by Cardinal Bertrand de Poujet', *Medieval Studies*, 67 (2005), 75–98.

Boislisle, A., 'Projet de Croisade du Premier Duc de Bourbon, 1316–1333', *Extrait de l'Annuaire Bulletin de la Société de l'Histoire de France*, 9 (1872), 246–255.

Boureau, A., *La Légende Dorée: Le système Narratif de Jacques de Voragine († 1298)* (Paris: Editions du Cerf, 1984).

Bourel de la Ronière, C., 'Une Escadre Franco-papale (1318–1320)', *Mélanges d'Archéologie et d'Histoire*, 13 (1893), 397–418.

Boyle, L., 'The Date of the Summa Praedicantium of John Bromyard', *Speculum*, 48.3 (1973), 533–537.

Bremond, C., Le Goff, J. and Schmitt, J. C., *L'"Exemplum"* (Turnhout: Brepols, 1982).

Brown, E. A., 'Customary Aids and Royal Fiscal Policy under Philip VI of Valois', *Traditio*, 39 (1974), 191–258.

Browning, O., *Guelph and Ghibellines: A Short History of Medieval Italy from 1250–1409* (London: Methuen and Co, 1893).

Brundage, J., *The Crusades: A Documentary History* (Milwaukee: Marquette University Press, 1962).

—— *Medieval Canon Law and the Crusader* (Madison-Milwaukee-London: The University of Wisconsin Press, 1969).

—— 'Humbert of Romans and the Legitimacy of Crusader Conquests', in *The Horns of Ḥaṭṭīn: Proceedings of the Second Conference of the Society for the Study of the Crusades and the Latin East, Jerusalem and Haifa, 2–6 July 1987*, ed. Kedar, B. (Jerusalem: Yad Izhak Ben-Zvi, 1992), 302–313.

Bueno, I., 'False Prophets and Ravening Wolves: Biblical Exegesis as a Tool Against Heretics in Jacques Fournier's *Postilla* on Matthew', *Speculum*, 89.1 (2014), 35–65.

—— *Defining Heresy: Inquisition, Theology, and Papal Policy in the Time of Jacques Fournier* (Leiden: Brill, 2015).

Bull, M. and Housley, N. (eds.), *The Experience of Crusading I: Western Approaches* (Cambridge: Cambridge University Press, 2003).

Bumke, J., *Courtly Culture: Literature and Society in the High Middle Ages* (Berkeley, Los Angeles, Oxford: University of California Press, 1991).

Buquet, T., '"*Animalia Extranea et Stupenda ad Vivendum*"'. 'Describing and Naming Exotic Beasts in Cairo Sultan's Menagerie', in *Animals and Otherness in the Middle Ages: Perspectives Across Disciplines*, eds. Asis Garcia, F., Ann-Walker, M. and Picaza, M. V. (Oxford: Archaeopress, 2013), 25–35.

Butler, H. E. (trans.), *The Autobiography of Gerald of Wales* (Woodbridge: The Boydell Press, 2005).

Carr, M., *Merchant Crusaders in the Aegean* (Woodbridge: The Boydell Press, 2015).
—— 'Humbert of Viennois and the Crusade of Smyrna: A Reconsideration', *Crusades*, 13 (2014), 237–251.
Cardini, F., 'Nella Presenza del Soldan Superba: Bernardo, Francesco, Bonaventura e il Superamento Spirituale dell'Idea di Crociata', *Studi Francescani*, 71 (1974), 199–250.
—— 'Gilberto di Tournai. Un Francescano Predicatore della Crociata', *Studi Francescani*, 72 (1975), 31–48.
Céleyrette, J. and Solère, J.-L.,'Jacques de Lausanne, Censeur et Plagiaire de Durand de Saint-Pourçain: Édition de la Q. 2, Dist. 17 du L. I de son Commentaire des Sentences', in *Philosophy and Theology in the Long Middle Ages*, eds. Emery, K., Friedman, R., and Speer, A. (Leiden: Brill, 2011), 855–891.
Charles, H., *A History of Auricular Confession and Indulgences in the Latin Church*, 3 vols. (Philadelphia: Lea Brothers, 1896).
Chester, J. W., *The Great Famine: Northern Europe in the Early Fourteenth Century* (Princeton: Princeton University Press, 1996).
—— 'John Pecham on the Crusade', *Crusades*, 9 (2010), 159–171.
—— 'The Great Famine: 1315–1322 Revisited', in *Ecologies and Economies in Medieval and Early Modern Europe: Studies in Environmental History for Richard C. Hoffmann*, ed. Bruce, S. G. (Boston, 2010), 45–62
Chrissis, N. G., *Crusading in Frankish Greece: A Study of Byzantine–Western Relations and Attitudes, 1204–1282* (Turnhout: Brepols, 2012).
—— 'The City and the Cross: The Image of Constantinople and the Latin Empire in Thirteenth-Century Papal Crusading Rhetoric', *Byzantine and Modern Greek Studies*, 36.1 (2012), 20–37.
—— 'New Frontiers: Frankish Greece and the Development of Crusading in the Early Thirteenth Century', in *Contact and Conflict in Frankish Greece and the Aegean*, eds. Chrissis, N. G. and Carr, M. (Farnham: Ashgate, 2014), 17–41.
—— 'Crusades and Crusaders in Medieval Greece', in *A Companion to Latin Greece*, eds. Tsougarakis, N. I. and Lock, P. (Leiden: Brill, 2015), 23–72.
Clark, J. G., *The Benedictines in the Middle Ages* (Woodbridge: Boydell Press, 2011).
Cole, P., d'Avray, D., Riley-Smith, J., 'Application of Theology to Current Affairs: Memorial Sermons on the Dead of Mansurah and on Innocent IV', in *Modern Questions About Medieval Sermons: Essays on Marriage, Death, History and Sanctity*, eds. Bériou, N. and d'Avray, D. (Spoleto: Centro Italiano di Studi sull'Alto Medioevo, 1994), 217–245.
Cole, P. J., '"O God, the Heathen Have Come into Your Inheritance" (Ps. 78.1): The Theme of Religious Pollution in Crusade Documents, 1095–1188', in *Crusaders and Muslims in Twelfth-Century Syria*, ed. Shatzmiller, M. (Leiden: Brill, 1993), 84–112.
—— *The Preaching of the Crusades to the Holy Land, 1095–1270* (Cambridge, Massachusetts: The Medieval Academy of America, 1991).
—— 'Humbert of Romans and the Crusade', in *The Experience of Crusading: Western Approaches*, eds. Housley, N. and Bull, M. (Cambridge: Cambridge University Press, 2003), 157–174.
Collins, A., *Symbolism of Animals and Birds Represented in English Church Architecture* (New York: McBride, Nast and Company, 1913).
Constable, G., 'A Report of a Lost Sermon by St. Bernard on the Failure of the Second Crusade', in *Religious Life and Thought (11th–12th centuries). Collected Essays of Giles Constable* (Variorum Collected Studies Series, 89) (London: Variorum Reprints, 1979), 49–54.

Constable, G., *Crusaders and Crusading in the Twelfth Century* (Farnham: Ashgate, 2008).
────── 'Charter evidence for Pope Urban II's Preaching of the First Crusade', in *Canon Law, Religion, and Politics: Liber Amicorum Robert Somerville*, eds. Blumenthal, U.-R., Winroth, A., and Landau, P. (Washington: Catholic University of America Press, 2012), 228–232.
Corsi, D., 'La Crociata di Venturino da Bergamo nella Crisi Spirituale di Metà Trecento', *Archivio Storico Italiano*, 147 (1989), 697–747.
Costa, M., 'In Praedicatione Crucesignatorum. Estratégias Ducentistas de Incitamento à Cruzada', *Cuadernos de Investigación del Monasterio de Santa María la Real*, 22 (2006), 6–40.
Coupe, M. D., 'Peter the Hermit – a Re-Assessment', *Nottingham Medieval Studies*, 31 (1987), 37–45.
Coureas, N. and Riley-Smith, J. (eds.), *Cyprus and the Crusades: Papers Given at the International Conference 'Cyprus and the Crusades'* (Nicosia: Cyprus Research Centre, 1995).
Coureas, N., 'Cyprus and the Naval Leagues 1333–1358', in *Cyprus and the Crusades*, eds. Coureas, N. and Riley-Smith, J. (Nicosia: Cyprus Research Center, 1995), 107–124.
────── *The Latin Church in Cyprus, 1195–1312* (Aldershot: Ashgate, 1997).
────── *The Latin Church in Cyprus, 1313–1378* (Nicosia: Cyprus Research Center, 2010).
────── '"Philippe de Mézières" Portrait of Peter Thomas as a Preacher', *Carmelus*, 57.1 (2010), 63–80.
Courtenay, W. J., 'The Bible in the Fourteenth Century: Some Observations', *Church History*, 54.2 (1985), 176–187.
────── *Parisian Scholars in the Early Fourteenth Century: A Social Portrait* (Cambridge: Cambridge University Press, 1999).
Cowdrey, J. H., 'Pope Urban II's Preaching of the First Crusade', *History*, 55 (1970), 177–188.
Craig, E. (ed.), *Routledge Encyclopedia of Philosophy*, 9 vols. (London-New York: Routledge, 1998).
Cramer, V., 'Kreuzzugspredigt und Kreuzzugsgedanken von Bernhard von Clairvaux bis Humbert von Romans', *Das Heilige Land in Vergangenheit und Gegenwart*, 1 (1939), 43–204.
Craun, E. D., *Lies, Slander and Obscenity in Medieval English Literature, Pastoral Rhetoric and the Deviant Speaker* (Cambridge: Cambridge University Press, 1997).
d'Avray, D. L., *The Preaching of the Friars: Sermons Diffused from Paris before 1300* (Oxford: Clarendon Press, 1985).
Delaville le Roulx, J., *La France en Orient au XIVe Siècle: Expéditions du Maréchal Boucicaut* (Paris: Ernest Thorin, 1886).
Delcorno, C., 'Medieval Preaching in Italy (1200–1500)', in *The Sermon*, ed. Kienzle, B. M. (Turnhout: Brepols, 2000), 449–560.
Delorme, F. M., 'Bulle d'Innocent IV pour la Croisade (6 février 1245)', *Archivum Franciscanum Historicum*, 6 (1913), 386–389.
────── 'Bulle d'Innocent IV en Faveur de l'Empire Latin de Constantinople', *Archivum Franciscanum Historicum*, 8 (1915), 307–310.
────── 'De Praedicatione Cruciate saec. XIII per Fratres Minores', *Archivum Franciscanum Historicum*, 9 (1916), 99–117.
Déprez, E., *Le Préliminaires de la Guerre de Cent Ans: La Papauté, la France et l'Angleterre (1328–1342)* (Paris: Albert Fontemoing, 1902).
Dickson, G., 'The Advent of the Pastores', *Revue Belge de Philologie et d'Histoire*, 66.2 (1988), 249–267.

Dunbabin, J., *A Hound of God: Pierre de la Palud and the Fourteenth-Century Church* (Oxford: Clarendon Press, 1991).
Duby, G., *France in the Middle Ages 987–1460: From Hugh Capet to Joan of Arc* (London: Wiley Blackwell, 1993).
Earl, D. S., *Reading Joshua as Christian Scripture*. Journal of Theological Interpretation Supplement 2 (Winona Lake: Eisenbrauns, 2010).
─── 'Joshua and the Crusades', in *Holy War in the Bible: Christian Morality and an Old Testament Problem*, eds. Thomas, H. A., Evans, J. and Copan, P. (Illinois: Inter Varsity Press, 2014), 19–43.
Edbury, P. W. (ed.), *Crusade and Settlement: Papers Read at the First Conference of the Society for the Study of Crusades and the Latin East* (Cardiff: University College Cardiff Press, 1985).
─── 'Preaching the Crusade in Wales', in *England and Germany and the High Middle Ages*, eds. Haverkamp, A. and Vollrath, H. (Oxford: Oxford University Press, 1996), 221–233.
─── *The Kingdom of Cyprus and the Crusades, 1191–1374* (Cambridge: Cambridge University Press, 1991).
Egan, K. J., 'Aylesford's Medieval Library', *Aylesford Review*, 4 (1962), 231–307.
Ehrle, F., 'Zur Geschichte des Päpsteichen Hofceremoniells im 14. Jahrhundert', *Archiv Für Literatur und Kirchengeschichte des Mittelalters*, 5 (1889), 565–603.
Emery, K., Friedman, R., Speer, A. (eds.), *Philosophy and Theology in the Long Middle Ages* (Leiden: Brill, 2011).
Fasolt, C., *Council and Hierarchy: The Political Thought of William Durant the Younger* (Cambridge: Cambridge University Press, 1991).
Faure, C., 'Le Dauphin Humbert II à Venice et en Orient (1345–1347)', *Mélanges d'Archéologie et d'Histoire* 27 (1907), 509–562.
Flori, J., *Prêcher la croisade, XI–XIII Siècle. Communication et Propaganda* (Paris: Perrin, 2012).
Fonnesberg-Schmidt, I., *The Popes and the Baltic Crusades, 1147–1254* (Leiden: Brill, 2007).
Forey, A., 'The Military Orders in the Crusading Proposals of the Late 13th and Early 14th Centuries', in *Military Orders and Crusades* (Aldershot: Ashgate Variorum, 1994), 318–331.
France, J., 'The Election and Title of Godfrey de Bouillon', *Canadian Journal of History*, 18 (1983), 321–329.
─── 'Les Origines de la Première Croisade: Un Nouvel Examen', in *Autour de la Première Croisade*, ed. Balard, M. (Paris: Publications de la Sorbonne, 1996), 43–56.
Freed, J., *The Friars and German Society in the Thirteenth Century* (Cambridge: The Medieval Academy of America Publications, 1977).
Friedman, R. L, 'Dominican Quodlibetal Literature, ca. 1260–1330', in *Theological Quodlibeta in the Middle Ages: The Fourteenth Century*, ed. Schabel, C., 2 vols. (Leiden: Brill, 2007), ii, 401–492.
Galbraith, R., *The Constitution of the Dominican Order, 1216–1320* (Manchester: Publications of the University of Manchester, 1925).
Gaposchkin, C. M., 'Louis IX, crusade and the promise of Joshua in the Holy Land', *Journal of Medieval History*, 34 (2008), 245–274.
─── *Invisible Weapons: Liturgy and the Making of Crusade Ideology* (Ithaca-London: Cornell University Press, 2017).

Gay, J., *Le Pape Clément VI et les Affaires d'Orient* (1342–1352) (Paris: Société Nouvelle de Librairie et d'Édition, 1904).
Geanakoplos, D. J., *Emperor Michael Palaeologus and the West, 1258–1282: A Study in Byzantine-Latin Relations* (Massachusetts: Harvard University Press, 1959).
—— 'Byzantium and the Crusades, 1261–1354', in *A History of the Crusades: The Fourteenth and Fifteenth Centuries*, vol.3, 27–69.
Georgiou, C., 'Propagating the Hospitallers' Passagium: Crusade Preaching and Liturgy in 1308–1309', in *Islands and Military Orders, c.1291–c.1798*, eds. Buttigieg, E. and Philips, S. (Famham: Ashgate, 2013), 53–64.
—— '*Ordinavi armatam sancte unionis*, Clement VI's Sermon on the Dauphin Humbert II of Viennois' Leadership of the Christian Armada Against the Turks, 1345', *Crusades*, 15 (2016), 157–175.
Gilmour-Bryson, A., '"Vox in excelso" Deconstructed. Exactly What Clement V Say?', in *On the Margins of Crusading: The Military Orders, the Papacy and the Christian World*, ed. Nicholson, H. (Farnham: Ashgate, 2011), 75–88.
Gittos, H., *Liturgy, Architecture, and Sacred Places in Anglo-Saxon England* (Oxford: Oxford University Press, 2013).
Granger, W. R. (trans.), *The Golden Legend: Reading on the Saints*, 2 vols. (Princeton: Princeton University Press, 1993).
Green, D. H., *The Millstatter Exodus: A Crusading Epic* (Cambridge: Cambridge University Press, 1966).
Guard, T., *Chivalry, Kingship and Crusade: The English Experience in the Fourteenth Century* (Woodbridge: The Boydell Press, 2013)
—— 'Pulpit and Cross: Preaching the Crusade in Fourteenth–century England', *English Historical Review*, 129.541 (2014), 1319–1345.
Haist, M., 'The Lion, Bloodline and Kingship', in *The Mark of the Beast: The Medieval Bestiary in Art, Life and Literature*, ed. Hassig, D. (New York-London: Garland Publishing, 1999), 3–22.
Hallam, E. and Everard, J., *Capetian France, 987–1328* (London-New York, 2001).
Hamesse, J. and Hermand, X. (eds.), *De l'Homélie au Sermon: Histoire de la Predication Medieval* (Louvain-la-Neuve: Fédération Internationale des Instituts d'Études Médiévales, 1993).
Herde, P., 'From Adolf of Nassau to Lewis of Bavaria, 1292–1347', in *The New Cambridge Medieval History*, ed. Jones, M., et al., vol.6, 515–551.
Hillgarth, J. N., *Ramon Lull and Lullism in Fourteenth Century France* (Oxford: Clarendon Press, 1971).
Hinnebusch, W. A., *The History of the Dominican Order*, 2 vols. (New York: Alba House, 1965–1973).
Hodgson, N., 'Lions, Tigers, and Bears: Encounters with Wild Animals and Bestial Imagery in the Context of Crusading to the Latin East', *Viator*, 44.1 (2013), 65–94.
Holmes, U. T., *A History of the Old French Literature: From the Origins to 1300* (New York: F. S. Crofts, 1937).
Holsinger, B. W., 'The Color of Salvation: Desire, Death, and the Second Crusade in Bertrand of Clairvaux's Sermons on the Song of Songs', in *The Tongue of the Fathers: Gender and Ideology in Twelfth–Century Latin*, eds. Townsend, D. and Taylor, A. (Philadelphia: University of Pennsylvania Press, 1997), 156–186.
Holt, P. M., *The Age of the Crusades: The Near East from the Eleventh Century to 1517* (London: Longman, 1986).

Horner, P. J. (ed. and trans.), *A Macaronic Sermon Collection from Late Medieval England, Oxford MS Bodley 649* (Toronto: Pontifical Institute of Medieval Studies, 2006).

Horowitz, J., 'Les *Exempla* au Service de la Prédication de la Croisade au 13e Siècle', *Revue d'Histoire Ecclésiastique*, 92.2 (1997), 367–394.

Housley, N., 'The Franco-Papal Crusade Negotiations of 1322–23', *Papers of the British School at Rome*, 48 (1980), 166–185.

—— 'Angevin Naples and the Defense of the Latin East: Robert the Wise and the Naval League of 1334', *Byzantion*, 51.2 (1981), 548–556.

—— *The Italian Crusades: The Papal-Angevin Alliance and the Crusades Against Christian Lay Powers, 1254–1343* (Oxford: Clarendon Press, 1982).

—— 'Pope Clement V and the Crusades of 1309–1310', *Journal of Medieval History*, 8 (1982), 29–43.

—— *The Avignon Papacy and the Crusades, 1305–1378* (Oxford: Clarendon Press, 1986).

—— *The Later Crusades, 1274–1580: From Lyons to Alcazar* (Oxford: Oxford University Press, 1992).

—— 'Jerusalem and Development of the Crusade Idea, 1095–1128', in *The Horns of Hattin*, ed. Kedar, B. (Jerusalem: Yad Izhak Ben-Zvi; London: Variorum, 1992), 27–40.

—— 'Cyprus and the Crusades, 1291–1571', in *Cyprus and the Crusades*, eds. Coureas, N. and Riley-Smith, J. (Nicosia: Cyprus Research Centre, 1995), 187–206.

—— (trans.), *Documents on the Later Crusades, 1274–1580* (Basingstoke: Macmillan, 1996).

—— 'Frontier Societies and Crusading in the Late Middle Ages', in *Intercultural Contacts in the Medieval Mediterranean*, ed. Arbel, B. (London: Frank Cass, 1996), 104–106.

—— 'Costing the Crusade: Budgeting for Crusading Activity in the Fourteenth Century', in *The Experience of Crusading I: Western Approaches*, eds. Bull, M. and Housley, N. (Cambridge: Cambridge University Press, 2003), 45–59.

Hurlock, K., 'Power, Preaching and the Crusades in Pura Wallia c.1180–1280', in *Thirteenth Century England*, eds. Bjorn, W., Janet, B. and Schofield, P. (Woodbridge: Boydell, 2007), 94–108.

Hyman, A. and Walsh, J. J. (eds.), *Philosophy in the Middle Ages, the Christian, Islamic, and Jewish Traditions* (Indianapolis-Cambridge: Hackett Publishing Company, 1973).

Jenkins, H., 'Papal Efforts for Peace under Benedict XII: 1334–1342', (PhD diss., Philadelphia, University of Pennsylvania, 1933).

Jensen, J. M., *Denmark and the Crusades, 1400–1650* (Leiden, Boston: Brill, 2007).

Jones, A., 'Fulk of Neuilly, Innocent III, and the Preaching of the Fourth Crusade', *Comitatus*, 41 (2010), 119–148.

Jones, M., et al., (eds.), *The New Cambridge Medieval History*, 7 vols. (Cambridge: Cambridge University Press, 1995).

—— 'The Last Capetians and Early Valois Kings, 1314–1364', in *The New Cambridge Medieval History*, vol.6, 388–422.

Jotischky, A., *The Carmelites and Antiquity: Mendicants and their Pasts in the Middle Ages* (Oxford: Oxford University Press, 2002).

Jorga, N., *Philippe de Mézières 1327–1405, et la Croisade au XIVe Siècle* (Paris: É. Bouillon, 1896).

Kaelber, L., *Schools of Asceticism: Ideology and Organization in Medieval Religious Communities* (Pennsylvania: The Pennsylvania State University Press, 1998).

Kaeppeli, T. and Pierre, B., 'Un Pèlerinage Dominicain Inédit du XIVe Siècle: Le Liber de Locis et Conditionibus Terrae Sanctae et Sepulcro d'Humbert de Dijon O.P. (1332)', *Revue Biblique*, 62.1 (1955), 513–540.

Kedar, B. and Schein, S., 'Un Projet de Passage Particulier Proposé par l'Ordre de l'Hôpital 1306–1307', *Bibliotheque de l'Ecole des Chartes*, 137 (1979), 211–226.

Kedar, B., *Crusade and Mission: European Approaches Toward the Muslims* (New Jersey-Princeton: Princeton University Press, 1988).

——— (ed.), *The Horns of Ḥaṭṭīn: Proceedings of the Second Conference of the Society for the Study of the Crusades and the Latin East, Jerusalem and Haifa, 2–6 July 1987* (Jerusalem: Yad Izhak Ben-Zvi, 1992).

Keen, M., 'Chivalry and the Aristocracy', in *The New Cambridge Medieval History*, vol.6, 209–222.

Kennan, E., 'The "De Consideratione" of St. Bernard of Clairvaux and the Papacy in the Mid-Twelfth Century: A Review of Scholarship', *Traditio*, 23 (1967), 73–115.

Kienzle, B. M. (ed.), *The Sermon* (Turnhout: Brepols, 2000).

——— *Cistercians, Heresy and Crusade in Occitania, 1145–1229: Preaching in the Lord's Vineyard* (Rochester, New York: York Medieval Press/Boydell Press, 2001).

——— 'Preaching the Cross: Liturgy and Crusade Propaganda', *Medieval Sermon Studies*, 53 (2009), 11–32.

Kostick, C., *The Social Structure of the First Crusade* (Leiden: Brill, 2008).

Kuehn, E. F., 'Melchizedek as Exemplar for Kingship in Twelfth–Century Political Thought', *History of Political Thought*, 31.4 (2010), 557–575.

Laiou, A., 'Marino Sanudo Torsello, Byzantium and the Turks: The Background to the Anti-Turkish League of 1332–1334', *Speculum*, 45.3 (1970), 374–392.

Constantinople and the Latins: The Foreign Policy of Andronicus II 1282–1328 (Massachusetts: Harvard University Press, 1972).

Lapina, E., 'Demetrius of Thessaloniki: Patron Saint of Crusaders', *Viator*, 40.2 (2009), 93–112.

——— 'The Maccabees and the Battle of Antioch', in *Dying for the Faith, Killing for the Faith: Old Testament Faith-Warriors (1 and 2 Maccabees) in Historical Perspective*, ed. Signori, G. (Leiden: Brill, 2012), 147–159.

——— *Warfare and the Miraculous in the Chronicles of the First Crusade* (Pennsylvania: Penn State University Press, 2015).

Lapina, E. and Morton, N., eds., *The Uses of the Bible in Crusader Sources* (Leiden: Brill, 2017).

Lea, H. C., *A History of the Inquisition of the Middle Ages*, 3 vols. (New York: Harper and Brothers, 1887–1888).

Lea Bird, J., 'Reform or Crusade? Anti–usury and Crusade Preaching During the Pontificate of Innocent III', in *Pope Innocent III and his World*, ed. Moore, J. C. (Aldershot: Ashgate, 1999), 165–185.

——— 'The Victorines, Peter the Chanter's Circle, and the Crusade: Two Unpublished Crusading Appeals in Paris, Bibliothèque Nationale, MS. Latin 14470', *Medieval Sermon Studies*, 48 (2004), 5–28.

——— 'Parisian Masters and the Justification of the Albigensian Crusade', *Crusades*, 6 (2007), 117–156.

——— 'Preaching the Crusades and the Liturgical Year: The Palm Sunday Sermons', *Essays in Medieval Studies*, 30 (2015), 11–36.

——— 'Crusade and Reform: The Sermons of Bibliothèque Nationale, MS noun. acq. lat. 999', in *The Fifth Crusade in Context: The Crusading Movement in the Early*

Thirteenth Century, eds. Mylod, E. J., Perry, G., Smith, T. W. and Vanderburie, J. (London: Routledge, 2017), 92–113.

────── 'Preaching and Crusading Memory', in *Remembering the Crusades and Crusading*, ed. Megan, C.-W. (London: Routledge, 2017), 13–33.

────── 'Preaching and Narrating the Fifth Crusade: Bible, Sermons and the History of a Campaign', in *The Uses of the Bible in Crusader Sources*, eds. Lapina, E. and Morton, N. (Leiden: Brill, 2017), 316–340.

Leclercq, J., *The Love of Learning and the Desire for God: A Study of Monastic Culture* (New York: Fordham University Press, 1961).

Lecoy de la, A. (ed.), Anecdotes Historiques, Légendes et Apologues tirés du Recueil Inédit d'Étienne de Bourbon (Paris: Société de l'Histoire de France, 1877).

────── 'La Prédication de la Croisade au Treizième Siècle', *Revue des Questions Historiques*, 48 (1890), 5–28.

Lehugeur, P., *Histoire de Philippe le Long, Roi de France*, 2 vols. (Paris: Imprimerie Lahure, 1897).

Lemerle, P., *L'Émirat d'Aydin, Byzance et l'Occident. Recherches sur 'La Geste d'Umur Pacha* (Paris: Bibliothèque Byzantine, 1957).

Lerner, R. E., *The Power of Prophecy: The Cedar of Lebanon Vision from the Mongol Onslaught to the Dawn of the Enlightment* (Berkeley: University of California Press, 1983).

Linder, A., *Raising Arms: Liturgy in the Struggle to Liberate Jerusalem in the Late Middle Ages* (Turnhout: Brepols Publishers, 2003).

Linehan, P., '"Quedam de quibus dubitans" on Preaching the Crusade in Alfonso X's Castile', in P. Linehan, *Historical Memory and Clerical Activity in Medieval Spain and Portugal* (Farnham: Ashgate, 2014), 129–154.

Lizerand, G., *Clément V et Philippe IV le Bel* (Paris: Librairie Hachette, 1910).

Longère, J., *Iacobus de Vitriaco. Sermones Vulgares uel ad Status* (Turnhout: Brepols, 2013).

Luttrell, A., 'The Aragonese Crown and the Knights Hospitallers of Rhodes: 1291–1350', *The English Historical Review*, 76 (1961), 1–19.

────── 'The Hospitallers and the Papacy, 1305–1314', in *Studies on the Hospitallers after 1306: Rhodes and the West* (Aldershot: Ashgate Variorum, 2007), 595–622.

────── 'The Hospitallers at Rhodes, 1306–1421', in *A History of the Crusades*, vol.3, 278–314.

Leopold, A., *How to Recover the Holy Land: The Crusade Proposals of the Late Thirteenth and Early Fourteeenth Centuries* (Aldershot: Ashgate, 2000).

Lützelschwab, R., 'Cardinalis Albus. On the Career of the Cistercian Monk Guillaume Court (†1361), *Cistercian Studies Quarterly*, 45 (2010), 141–167.

MacCarthy, D., *The Epistles and Gospels of the Sundays Throughout the Year: With Notes* (Dublin-London: John Mulleny, 1866).

McCormick, M., 'The Liturgy of War in the Early Middle Ages', *Viator*, 15 (1984), 1–23.

Macgregor, J. B., 'The Ministry of Gerold d'Avranches: Warrior-Saints and Knightly Piety on the Eve of the First Crusade', *Journal of Medieval Studies*, 29.3 (2003), 219–237.

────── 'The First Crusade in Late Medieval "Exempla"', *The Historian*, 68.1 (2006), 29–48.

McNeill, R. A., 'The Evolution of the Basilisk', *Greece and Rome*, 10.2 (1963), 170–181.

Maggioni, G. P., 'Between Hagiography and Preaching: The Holy Cross in the Works of James de Voragine', *Hagiographica*, 20 (2013), 183–218.

Maier, C. T., *Preaching the Crusades: Mendicant Friars and the Cross in the Thirteenth Century* (Cambridge: Cambridge University Press, 1994).

────── Christoph Maier, 'Crusade and Rhetoric Against the Muslim Colony of Lucera: Eudes of Châteauroux's *Sermones de Rebellione Sarracenorum Lucherie in Apulia*', *Journal of Medieval History*, 21.4 (1995), 343–385.

────── 'Crisis, Liturgy and the Crusade in the Twelfth and Thirteenth Centuries', *Journal of Ecclesiastical History*, 48.4 (1997), 628–657.

────── 'Mass, the Eucharist and the Cross: Innocent III and the Relocation of the Crusade', in *Pope Innocent III and his World*, ed. Moore, J. C. (Aldershot: Ashgate, 1999), 351–360.

────── *Crusade Propaganda and Ideology: Model Sermons for the Preaching of the Cross* (Cambridge: Cambridge University Press, 2000).

────── '*Civilis ac pia Regis Francorum deceptio*: Louis IX as Crusade Preacher', in *Dei Gesta per Francos: Etudes sur les Croisades Dédiées à Jean Richard*, eds. Balard, M., Kedar, B. Z., Riley-Smith, J. (Aldershot: Ashgate, 2001), 57–63.

Mégier, E., 'Christian Historical Fulfilments of Old Testament Prophecies in Latin Commentaries on the Book of Isaiah (ca. 400 to ca. 1150)', *Journal of Medieval Latin*, 17 (2007), 87–100.

Menache, S., 'The Failure of John XXII's Policy Towards France and England: Reasons and Outcomes, 1316–1334', *Church History*, 55.5 (1986), 423–437.

────── 'The Communication Challenge of the Early Crusades, 1099–1187', in *Autour de la Première Croisade: Actes du Colloque de la Society for the Study of the Crusades and the Latin East (Clermont-Ferrand, 22–25 juin* 1995), ed. Balard, M. (Paris: Publications de la Sorbonne, 1996), 293–314.

────── *Clement V* (Cambridge: Cambridge University Press, 1998).

────── 'The Hospitallers During Clement V's Pontificate: The Spoiled Sons of the Papacy?', in *The Military Orders: Welfare and Warfare*, eds. Barber, M. and Nicholson, H. (Aldershot: Ashgate, 2000), vol.2, 153–162.

Milner, N. P. (trans.), *Vegetius: Epitome of Military Science* (Liverpool: Liverpool University Press, 1993).

Mollat, G., 'L'Oeuvre Oratoire de Clément VI', *Archives d'Histoire Doctrinale et Littéraire du Moyen Age*, 3 (1928), 239–274.

────── *The Popes at Avignon: 1305–1378* (London: Thomas Nelson and Sons, 1963).

────── 'Jean XXII et Charles IV le Bel (1322–1328)', *Journal des Sevants*, 2 (1967), 92–106.

Moore, J. C. (ed.), *Pope Innocent III and his World* (Aldershot: Ashgate, 1999).

Moorman, J., *The Grey Friars in Cambridge* (Cambridge: Cambridge University Press, 1952).

────── *A History of the Franciscan Order from its Origins to the Year 1517* (Oxford: Clarendon Press, 1968).

Moranvillé, H., 'Les Projets de Charles de Valois sur l'Empire de Constantinople', *Bibliothèque de l École des Chartes*, 51(1890), 63–86.

Morris, C., 'Propaganda for War: The Dissemination of the Crusading Ideal in the Twelfth Century', in *The Church and War*, ed. Shiels, W. J. (Oxford: Oxford University Press, 1983), 79–101.

Morton, N., 'The Defence of the Holy Land and the Memory of the Maccabees', *Journal of Medieval History*, 36 (2010), 275–293.

Muessig, C., 'Les sermons de Jacques de Vitry sur les Cathares', *La Prédication en Pays d'Oc (XIIe– début XVe siècle)*, Cahiers de Fanjeaux 32, (Toulouse: Privat, 1992), 69–83.

Mula, S., 'Twelfth- and Thirteenth-Century Cistercian Exempla Collections: Role, Diffusion, and Evolution', *History Compass*, 8.8 (2010), 903–912.

Munro, D. C., 'The Speech of Pope Urban II at Clermont, 1095', *American Historical Review*, 11 (1906), 231–242.

Murray, A., 'The Title of Godfrey of Bouillon as Ruler of Jerusalem', *Interdisciplinary Journal of Medieval Research*, 3 (1990), 163–178.

Nicholas, D., *The Evolution of the Medieval World: Society, Government and Thought in Europe, 312–1500* (London-New York: Longman, 1992).

Nicholson, H., '"*Martyrum collegio sociandus haberet*": Depictions of the Military Orders' Martyrs in the Holy Land, 1187–1291', in *Crusading and Warfare in the Middle Ages: Realities and Representations. Essays in Honour of John France*, eds. John, S. and Morton, N. (Farnham: Ashgate, 2014), 101–118.

Niall, C. and Gerish, D., 'Parallel Preachings: Urban II and al-Sulamī', *Islam and the Medieval Mediterranean*, 15.2 (2003), 139–148.

Nicol, D. M., *Byzantium and Venice: A Study in Diplomatic and Cultural Relations* (Cambridge: Cambridge University Press, 1988).

Nold, P., 'Bertrand de la Tour OMin.: Life and Works', *Archivum Franciscanum Historicum*, 94 (2001), 275–323.

Ouy, G., *Les Manuscrits de l'Abbaye de Saint-Victor: Catalogue Établi sur la Base du Répertoire de Claude de Grandrue (1514)*, 2 vols. (Turnhout: Brepols, 1999).

Paul, S., 'An Edition and Study of Selected Sermons of Robert Grosseteste', 2 vols. (PhD diss., University of Leeds: Centre for Medieval Studies, 2002).

Paulet, L., *Recherches sur Pierre L'Hermite et la croisade* (Paris-Brussels: Vve J. Renouard, 1856).

Pelzer, A., 'Les 51 articles de Guillaume Occam censurés à Avignon en 1326', *Revue d'histoires ecclésiastique*, 18 (1922), 240–270.

Petit, J., 'Memoire de Foulques de Villaret sur la Croisade', *Bibliotheque de l'École des Chartes*, 60 (1899), 602–610.

Phillips, J., 'St Bernard of Clairvaux, the Low Countries and the Lisbon Letter of the Second Crusade', *Journal of Ecclesiastical History*, 48.3 (1997), 485–497.

Phillips, M., 'The Thief's Cross: Crusade and Penance in Allan of Lille's *Sermo de Cruce Domini*', *Crusades*, 5 (2006), 143–156.

Pitcher, D. E., *A Historical Geography of the Ottoman Empire: From Earliest Times to the End of the Sixteenth Century* (Leiden: Brill, 1968).

Portnykh, V.L., 'Le Traité d'Humbert de Romans, O.P., De la Prédication de la Sainte Croix Contre les Sarrasins (XIIIe Siècle). Analyse Historique et Édition du Texte', (PhD diss., Novosibirsk, Novosibirsk State University University, 2011).

——— 'Le traité d' Humbert de Romans (OP) "De la prédication de la sainte croix". Une hypothèse sur son utilisation dans les guerres saintes du XV siècle', *Revue d' histoire ecclésiastique*, 109.3–4 (2014), 588–624.

——— 'An Unknown Short Version of the Treatise *De predicatione sancte crucis* by Humbert of Romans', *Studi Medievali*, 2 (2015), 721–738.

——— 'The Short Version of Humbert of Romans' Treatise on the Preaching of the Cross: An edition of the Latin Text', *Crusades*, 15 (2016), 55–115.

Purcell, M., *Papal Crusading Policy: The Chief Instruments of Papal Crusading Policy and Crusade to the Holy Land from the Final Loss of Jerusalem to the Fall of Acre, 1244–1291* (Leiden: Brill, 1975).

Purkis, W., 'Stigmata on the First Crusade', in *Signs, Wonders, Miracles: Representations of Divine Power in the Life of the Church*, eds. Cooper, K. and Gregory, J. (Woodbridge: Boydell and Brewer, 2005), 99–108.

―――― 'Memories of the Preaching for the Fifth Crusade in Caesarius Heisterbach's Dialogus Miraculorum', *Journal of Medieval History*, 40 (2014), 329–345.
Pyron, S., 'Censures et condamnation de Pierre de Jean Olivi: Enquête dans les marges du Vatican', *Mélanges de l'École française de Rome*, 118.2 (2006), 313–373.
Religieux Bénédictins de la Congrégation de Saint-Maur, *et al.* (eds.), *Histoire Littéraire de la France*, 43 vols. (Paris: Imprimerie Nationale, 1733).
Riley-Smith, J., *The Knights of St John of Jerusalem and Cyprus, 1050–1310* (London: Macmillan, 1967).
―――― *What Were the Crusades?* (London: Macmillan, 1977).
―――― 'The Title of Godfrey de Bouillon', *Bulletin of the Institute of Historical Research*, 52 (1979), 83–96.
―――― *The First Crusade and the Idea of Crusading* (London: Athlone, 1986).
―――― *The Crusades: A Short History* (London: Athlone, 1987).
Röhricht, R., 'Die Kreuzpredigten Gegen den Islam: Ein Beitrag zur Geschichte der Christlichen Predigt im 12. und 13. Jahrhundert', *Zeitschrift für Kirchengeschichte*, 6 (1884), 550–572.
Ruddick, A., *English Identity and Political Culture in the Fourteenth Century* (Cambridge: Cambridge University Press, 2013).
Schabel, C., Friedman, R. L. and Balcoyiannopoulou, I., 'Peter of Palude and the Writing and Reception of Durand of St. Pourçain's *Sentences* Commentaries', *Archivum Fratrum Praedicatorum*, 71 (2001), 183–300.
Schabel, C., 'Early Carmelites Between Giants: Questions on Future Contingents by Gerard of Bologna and Guy Terrena', *Recherches de Théologie et Philosophie Médiévales*, 70.1 (2003), 139–205.
―――― 'Carmelite *Quodlibeta*', in *Theological Quodlibeta in the Middle Ages. The Fourteenth Century*, ed. Schabel, C., 2 vols. (Leiden-Boston: Brill, 2007), 493–543.
Schabel, C. and Courtenay, W. J., 'Augustinian *Quodlibeta* after Giles of Rome', in *Theological Quodlibeta in the Middle Ages: The Fourteenth Century*, ed. Schabel, C., 2 vols. (Leiden: Brill, 2007).
Schein, S., 'Philip IV and the Crusade: A Reconsideration', in *Crusade and Settlement: Papers Read at the First Conference of the Society for the Study of Crusades and the Latin East*, ed. Edbury, P. W. (Cardiff: University College Cardiff Press, 1985), 121–126.
―――― *Fideles Crucis: The Papacy, the West, and the Recovery of the Holy Land 1274–1314* (Oxford: Oxford Clarendon Press, 1998).
―――― 'Bernard of Clairvaux's Preaching of the Second Crusade and Orality', in *Oral History of the Middle Ages: The Spoken Word in Context*, eds. Jaritz, G. and Richter, M. (Budapest: Central European University, Department of Medieval Studies, 2001), 188–195.
Schmitt, C., *Un Pape Réformateur et un Défenseur de l'Unité de l'Église: Benoît XII et l'Ordre des Frères Mineurs, 1334–1342* (Quaracchi: College Saint Bonaventure, 1959).
Schmitz, P., 'Les Sermons et Discours de Clément VI, O.S.B.', *Revue Bénédictine*, 41 (1929), 15–34.
Schneyer, J. B. (ed.), *Repertorium der Lateinischen Sermones des Mittelalters für Die Zeit von 1150–1350*, 11 vols. (Munster-Westfalen: Aschendorffsche Verlagsbuchhandlung, 1973–1995).
Setton, K. (ed.), *A History of the Crusades: The Fourteenth and Fifteenth Centuries*, 6 vols. (Madison: The University of Wisconsin Press, 1969–1989).

––––––– *The Papacy and the Levant* (1204–1571), 4 vols. (Philadelphia: The American Philosophical Society, 1976–1984).

Shepkaru, S., 'The Preaching of the First Crusade and the Persecution of the Jews', *Medieval Encounters*, 18 (2012), 93–135.

Siberry, E., *Criticism of Crusading, 1095–1274* (Oxford: Clarendon Press, 1985).

Simon, J., 'Godfrey of Bouillon and the Swan Knight', in *Crusading and Warfare in the Middle Ages: Realities and Representations. Essays in Honour of John France*, eds. John, S. and Morton, N. (Farnham: Ashgate, 2014), 129–142.

––––––– *Godfrey of Bouillon: Duke of Lower Lotharingia, Ruler of Latin Jerusalem, c.1060–1100* (London: Routledge, 2018).

Sini, K., 'A Great Stirring of Hearts or Papal Inspiration? Contesting Popular Authority in the Preaching of the First Crusade', in *Authorities in the Middle Ages: Influence, Legitimacy, and Power in Medieval Society*, eds. Sini, K., Korpiola, M. and Ainomen, T. (Berlin: De Gruyter, 2013), 55–68.

Smalley, B., *The Study of the Bible in the Middle Ages* (Oxford: Oxford University Press, 1941).

––––––– *English Friars and Antiquity in the Early Fourteenth Century* (Oxford: Basil Blackwell, 1960).

Smith, T. W., 'The Use of the Bible in the *Arengae* of Pope Gregory IX's Crusade Calls', in *The Uses of the Bible in Crusader Sources*, eds. Lapina, E. and Morton, N. (Leiden: Brill, 2017), 206–236.

Sommerfeldt, J. R., 'The Bernandine Reform and the Crusading Spirit', *Catholic Historical Review*, 86.4 (2000), 567–578.

Sullivan, T., *Benedictine Monks at the University of Paris, A.D. 1229–1500* (Leiden: Brill, 1995).

Taylor, C. H., 'The Composition of the Baronial Assemblies in France, 1315–1320', *Speculum*, 29.2 (1954), 433–459.

––––––– 'French Assemblies and Subsidy in 1321', *Speculum*, 43.2 (1968), 217–244.

Taylor, L., *Soldiers of Christ: Preaching in Late Medieval and Reformation France* (Oxford: Oxford University Press, 1992).

Throop, P. A., 'Criticism of Papal Crusade Policy in Old French and Provençal', *Speculum*, 13.4 (1938), 379–412.

––––––– *Criticism of the Crusade: A Study of Public Opinion and Crusade Propaganda* (Amsterdam: N. V. Swets and Zeitlinger, 1940).

Thurston, H., *The Stations of the Cross: An Account of their History and Devotional Purpose* (London: Burns and Oates, 1914).

Tugwell, S., *Early Dominicans: Selected Writings* (New York: Paulist Press, 1982).

Tyerman, C., 'Marino Sanudo Torsello and the Lost Crusade: Lobbying in the Fourteenth Century', *Transactions of the Royal Historical Society*, 32 (1982), 57–73.

––––––– 'Philip V of France, the Assemblies of 1319–20 and the Crusade', *Bulletin of the Institute of Historical Research*, 57 (1984), 15–34.

––––––– 'Philip VI and the Recovery of the Holy Land', *The English Historical Review*, 100.394 (1985), 25–52.

––––––– *England and the Crusades* (Chicago-London: The University of Chicago Press, 1988).

––––––– *The Invention of the Crusades* (London: Palgrave Macmillan, 1998).

––––––– *The Crusades: A Very Short Introduction* (Oxford: Oxford University Press, 2004).

Van den Wyngaert, A., 'Frère Guillaume de Cordelle O.F.M.', *La France Franciscaine*, 4 (1921), 52–71.

Van Moolenbroek, J. J., 'Signs in the Heavens in Groningen and Friesland in 1214: Oliver of Cologne and Crusading Propaganda', *Journal of Medieval History*, 13 (1987), 251–272.

Viard, J., 'Itinéraire de Philippe VI de Valois', *Bibliothèque de l'École des Chartes*, 74 (1913), 74–128.

Walker, L., 'Living in the Penultimate Age: Apocalyptic Thought in James of Vitry's *ad status* Sermons', in *The Uses of the Bible in Crusader Sources*, 297–316.

Ward, B., *Miracles and the Medieval Mind: Theory, Record and Event 1000–1215* (Aldershot: Wildwood House, 1982).

───── 'Miracles in the Middle Ages', in *The Cambridge Companion to Miracles*, ed. Twelftree, G. H. (Cambridge: Cambridge University Press, 2011), 149–165.

Watt, J. A., 'The Papacy', in *The New Cambridge Medieval History*, vol.5, 107–164.

Wenzel, S., *Latin Sermon Collections from Later Medieval England: Orthodox Preaching in the Age of Wyclif* (Cambridge: Cambridge University Press, 2005).

───── *Medieval Artes Praedicandi: A Synthesis of Scholastic Sermon Structure* (Toronto-Buffalo-London: University of Toronto Press, 2015).

White, T. H. (ed. and trans.), *The Book of Beasts: Being a Translation from a Latin Bestiary of the Twelfth Century* (London: Cope, 1954).

Wolfram, G., 'Kreuzzugspredigt und Kreuzlied', *Zeitschrift für Deutsches Altertum*, 30 (1886), 89–132.

Wood, D., *Clement VI: The Pontificate and Ideas of an Avignon Pope* (Cambridge: Cambridge University Press, 1989).

Wrigley, J. E., 'Clement VI Before his Pontificate. The Early Life of Pierre Roger, 1290/91–1342', *The Catholic Historical Review*, 56.3 (1970), 433–473.

Zachariadou, E. A., *Trade and Crusade: Venetian Crete and the Emirates of Menteshe and Aydin (1300–1415)* (Venice: Hellenic Institute of Byzantine and Post-Byzantine Studies, 1983).

Zier, M., 'Sermons of the Twelfth Century Schoolmasters and Canons', in *The Sermon*, ed. Kienzle, B. M. (Turnhout: Brepols, 2000), 325–362.

Zumkeller, A., *Theology and History of the Augustinian School in the Middle Ages*, ed. Rotelle, J. (Villanova: Augustinian Press, 1996).

Index

Acre 22, 32, 142, 151, 284
Ademar of Le Puy 26
Adramyttion 48, 67–68, 71, 166
Aegean Sea 48, 75, 276
al-Kazez (Saracen fortress – Spain) 152
al-Nazir Muhammed (Mamluk Sultan) 142
Albert the Great (theologian) 150
Albigensians 8, 102, 142
Alexandria 83, 86
Allan of Lille (theologian) 2–3, 7
Alphonse of Poitiers 69
Amadeus VI of Savoy 86
Amalric Augerii (prior in St Mary of Aspirano) 26, 32
Amaury (Viscount of Narbonne) 21, 44
Anatolia 74, 163
Ancona (March of) 23, 117
Andrea Dandolo (Doge) 75–76, 85
Andreas of Antioch 48
Andronicus II Palaeologus (Byzantine emperor) 22, 281
Andronicus III Palaeologus (Byzantine emperor) 165
Antioch (battle of) 8, 119, 281
Apulia 6, 72, 80, 149
Aquila 118
Aragon 20, 31, 72, 108, 190
Aristotle 82, 140, 150
Arnaud of Pellegrue (Cardinal-bishop) 110
Arras (bishopric) 154
Asia Minor 20, 48, 74, 78
Assyrians 167
Augustinians (Hermits of St Augustine) 4, 29–30, 82–83, 189, 285, 287; *see also* mendicant friars
Austria 35, 110–111
Averroes 150
Avicenna 150
Ayas (port of) 41
Aydin (emir of) 163

Baldwin of Forde (Archbishop of Canterbury) 43
Baltic 5, 73, 191
Bannockburn (battle of) 35
Baratier, E. 7
Bede (Venerable) 149, 180n121
Benedict XI (Pope) 20, 22
Benedict XII (Pope) 11–12, 39, 48, 67–73, 75, 97, 107, 189–190, 270, 280
Berengar of Landorra (Dominican minister general) 135
Bériou, N. 8, 275–276
Bernard Gui (Bishop of Lodève) 26, 32, 114–115, 170
Bernard of Clairvaux (St) 1, 6–7, 102, 158, 167, 270–271, 281, 284–285
Bertrand de Got *see* Clement V (Pope)
Bertrand de la Tour 80
Bertrand du Pujet 9
Bertucio Acontado 120
Bethlehem 166, 172
Black Death 85, 188
Black Sea 24
Blake, B. 9
Bologna 117–118
Boniface VIII (Pope) 20, 28, 34, 271
Bordeaux 20, 115
Brabant 110
Brindisi 22, 30
Brundage, J. 6, 164
Burgundy (county of) 38, 142
Byzantine empire 23, 163, 276, 279; Byzantine emperor 22, 48, 165; Byzantines 21–22, 163; Byzantium 20, 22–24, 67;

Caesarius Heisterbach 7
Cahors 114
Cairo 46, 142, 149, 165
Caltabelotta (Treaty of) 20

Capetian 28–29, 35, 39–40, 45, 49, 99
Carcassonne 114
Cardini, F. 5, 276
Carmelites 4, 29–30, 82–83, 189, 280, 285; *see also* mendicant friars
Castellana (diocese of) 23
Castile 72, 282
Cathars 67
Catherine of Courtenay (titular empress of Constantinople) 22, 25
Chaise-Dieu (Benedictine abbey) 154
Charlemagne (King of the Franks) 147–148, 171
Charles II of Anjou of Naples 20, 23
Charles IV of France 12, 40–45, 49, 283
Charles of La Marche 37
Charles of Valois (titular emperor of Constantinople) 12, 21–25, 31, 37, 41, 43, 45–46
Chartres 116
Cilician Armenia (kingdom of) 25, 28–29, 38, 41, 43–46, 48, 72, 104, 163, 172, 188
Cistercians 2, 8, 67, 102, 105, 281
Clement III (Pope) 101
Clement V (Pope) 11–12, 20–36, 38, 40, 43, 83, 97–98, 100–102, 105–106, 108–110, 112–113, 120, 157–158, 172, 188–189, 271, 279, 280, 282–283
Clement VI (Pope) 3, 10–13, 30, 67, 73–77, 79–83, 85, 90n55, 97, 107, 120, 134, 162, 171, 189–190, 272, 279, 283, 285, 287
Clermont 5, 7, 26, 116, 153, 172, 284; count of 38, 56, 98; diocese of 154 *see also* Council (ecclesiastical) of Clermont
Colchester 83
Cole, P. 2, 5–6, 8, 276
Constable, G. 6, 276–277
Constantine the Great (Roman emperor) 151, 171
Constantinople 74, 165, 276, 281; church of 23; emperor of 22, 26; Latin empire of 12, 21–25, 33, 277; Latin patriarch of 74, 78; *see also* Crusade against Constantinople
Council (ecclesiastical): of Clermont 1, 5, 7, 26, 166, 172, 284; Fourth Lateran 2, 232; of Lyon (second) 34; of Vienne 12, 32–34, 157, 172, 225
Coureas, N. 9–10, 277, 280
Cowdrey, J. 7, 277

Cramer, V. 5, 277
Crusade/-s: against Constantinople 21–25, 28, 31; First 7–8, 26–27, 80, 119, 138, 147–148, 153, 277, 281–282, 284–286; Fifth 5–9, 127, 169, 281–282, 285; Fourth 2, 7, 23, 280; Hospitaller 12, 24, 29, 98–103; Italian 5, 280; of Nicopolis 86; Peoples' 13, 109–110, 112–117; Second 1, 6–7, 43, 102, 138, 158, 166–167, 276, 279, 284–285; Smyrna 12–13, 70, 82, 84–85, 117, 120, 189; Third 7; Varna 86
Cyprus (Kingdom of) 25, 28, 29, 32–33, 39, 44, 46, 48, 72, 74, 84–86, 104, 118, 142, 153, 163, 172, 188, 190, 271, 277, 280, 285

d'Avray, D. 6, 276–277
Delorme, D. 5, 277
Demetrius (St) 119, 281
Dominicans 3–4, 11, 30, 32, 82–84, 99, 102, 117, 142, 151, 286; Dominican Order 75, 135–136, 170, 278–279; Order of Preachers 30; *see also* mendicant friars
Durand of St Pourçain 135–136, 142, 276, 285

Earl, D. 8, 80, 278
Edbury, P. 7, 278, 285
Edessa (County of) 1
Edward I of England 20, 98, 270–271
Edward II of England 20, 49, 83, 98, 270–271
Edward III of England 71, 76–77, 107, 118, 154
Egypt 33, 39, 43, 48, 74, 135, 142–143, 146, 148–149, 153, 170
Elne (diocese of) 32
Elstow (Benedictine nunnery) 139
England 1–2, 4–6, 9, 13, 20–21, 23, 35–36, 45, 71–72, 76–77, 83, 85, 97–98, 107–110, 113–114, 116, 139, 154, 190–191, 279–280, 286–287
Enns 97, 111, 119
Esdras 156–157, 165
Eudes of Châteauroux 3, 6, 80, 101, 148, 170, 295
Eugene III (Pope) 1, 158, 166
Ezekiel 137, 146, 168

Ferrara 21, 110
Flanders 31, 35–39, 99–100, 110
Flori, J. 6, 278

France 1–2, 5–8, 10–13, 20–24, 28–32, 34–40, 42–43, 45–49, 67–68, 70–71, 73, 75–77, 80, 84–85, 97–98, 100, 104, 106–107, 113–116, 135–137, 142–144, 146–147, 154–157, 159–160, 162–163, 167, 190–191, 269–274, 276–286
Francesco Michiel (Archbishop of Crete) 76
Francis (St) 5
Franciscans 30, 82–84, 102; Franciscan Order 4, 6, 31, 82–83, 283; Minorites 30; *see also* mendicant friars
François of Meyronnes 154
Frederick II of Hohenstaufen (German emperor) 149
Frederick III of Sicily 20, 23–24
Freed, J. 5, 278
Frisia 5, 27
Fulk of Neuilly 7, 9, 280
Fulk of Villaret (Master General of the Hospitallers) 24–31, 38–39, 103, 284

Galeazzo I Visconti (Lord of Milan) 41
Gallipoli 86, 163
Gaposchkin, C. 8, 80, 278
Gascony 20
Genoa 22–24, 38, 48, 74, 85, 109
George (St) 119
Georgiou, C. 279
Gerald of Wales (Archdeacon) 7, 43, 275
Germany 1–2, 5, 13, 72, 83, 97, 191, 278
Gerold d'Avranches 119, 282
Ghibellines 38, 45, 275
Gilbert of Tournai (Franciscan preacher) 5
Giovanni Villani (Florentine chronicler) 74, 102, 109–110, 117–118, 272
Godfrey of Bouillon 146–147, 171, 284, 286
Granada 46, 72
Great Famine 35–36, 115, 276
Gregory IX (Pope) 4, 9, 286
Gregory VIII (Pope) 1
Gregory X (Pope) 29, 33–34, 46
Guard, T. 9, 56n104, 88n37, 191, 279
Guelph 23, 35, 275
Guy of Lusignan 46, 142

Hattin (battle of) 105, 275, 280–281
Helena (Roman empress) 151, 171
Hélion of Villeneuve (Grand Master of the Hospitallers) 75, 85
Henry Avaugour 161
Henry II of Lusignan (King of Cyprus) 28, 33

Henry III of England 6
Henry of Asti (titular Latin patriarch of Constantinople) 13, 74–75, 78, 85
Henry of Clairvaux (abbot) 102
Henry of Friemar (Augustinian theologian) 3, 11, 139, 193
Henry (Cardinal-bishop of Albano) 1, 20
Heraclius (Byzantine emperor) 151
Hervaeus Natalis (Dominican prior of France) 136
Holsinger, B. 7, 279
Holy Cross 106–107, 141, 168, 282; Exaltation of 11, 116, 119, 141, 143–146, 151, 153, 170–171, 194; feast of 3, 116, 137, 143, 145–146, 151, 171, 191; Invention of 116, 145
Holy Land 1, 5, 9–10, 12–13, 20–22, 24, 29, 31–37, 39–42, 46, 48–49, 67–70, 73, 75, 81, 97–99, 101–116, 139–140, 142–144, 149, 151–153, 155–159, 162–167, 169–172, 188–189, 191, 276, 278, 282–286
Honorius III (Pope) 7
Horowitz, J. 8, 280
Hospitallers (knights of St John) 12, 24–26, 28–32, 34, 40, 48, 70, 74–75, 85, 98, 100, 102–103, 108–110, 112–113, 119, 190, 279, 282–283; *see also* Hospitaller Crusade (*passagium*)
Housley, N. 5, 9, 25, 41, 46, 70, 138, 275–276, 280
Hugh Bandeti (Bishop of Thérouanne) 161
Hugh d'Avranches (Earl of Chester) 119
Hugh IV of Lusignan (King of Cyprus) 46, 72, 74, 85, 118, 142, 190
Hugh of Vaucemain (Dominican prior of France) 136
Hugh Quiéret 71
Humbert II of Viennois 3, 12, 13, 73, 75–82, 83–85, 117–118, 120, 194, 259, 279
Humbert of Dijon 149
Humbert of Romans (Dominican master general) 4, 6–8, 27, 168–172, 272, 275–276, 284
Humbert Pilati 76
Hungary 23, 72, 76
Hurlock, K. 7, 280

Iberia (Iberian Peninsula) 8–9, 46, 72–73, 161, 191
Innocent III (Pope) 2–3, 7–8, 70, 101, 138, 158, 232, 280–281, 283
Innocent IV (Pope) 6, 69, 148, 276–277

Innocent VI (Pope) 85–86
Isidore of Seville (St) 149
Israel 78, 152, 156, 162, 165, 168;
   Israelites 78–81, 165
Italy 2, 9–10, 13, 23–24, 35, 37–38, 45,
   70, 73–75, 84–85, 97–98, 100, 102,
   109–110, 117–118, 120, 275, 277

Jacques Duèze *see* John XXII (Pope)
Jacques Fournier *see* Benedict XII (Pope)
James II of Aragon 31, 108, 190
James of Lausanne 3, 11, 13, 135–142,
   147, 150, 169, 171, 173n13, 174n36,
   193, 196
James of Molay (master general of the
   Templars) 25–26, 272
James of Vitry (theologian and crusade
   propagandist) 4, 8–9, 21, 27, 169, 287
James of Voragine 145, 151, 171, 273
Jerusalem 3, 10–11, 13, 21, 37, 46, 78,
   98–101, 105–106, 110, 134–142,
   144–147, 150–153, 155–157, 161–167,
   169, 171–172, 191, 280–282, 284–286
Jesus Christ 3, 24, 27, 44, 68, 70, 78,
   103, 105–106, 112–113, 118–120, 135,
   137–139, 141, 143–146, 148–153, 156,
   158–159, 162, 164, 166, 168, 172,
   285–286
Jews 7, 110, 114–117, 165, 286; Jewish 7,
   79, 156, 165, 171, 280
Joan of Navarre 21
John Chrisostomos (St) 168, 237
John I Sanudo (Duke of Archipelago) 74
John I of France 99, 147
John of Abbeville (Cardinal-bishop of
   Sabina) 166, 169
John of Biandrate (Hospitaller prior in
   Lombardy) 76
John of Bromyard 4, 187n265, 273
John of Naples 135, 142, 275
John Stratford (Archbishop of
   Canterbury) 71
John XXII (Pope) 9, 11–12, 20, 34–49,
   67–71, 73, 99, 103–107, 114, 117, 120,
   136, 143–144, 147, 154, 157–159, 161,
   162, 168, 171, 188–189, 273, 283
John (canon regular of St Victor) 32, 37, 115
Josaphat (Valley of) 166, 207
Joshua 8, 79–81, 160, 171, 278

Kienzle, B. 7–8, 275, 277, 281, 287

Languedoc 114
Lapina, E. 8, 119, 281–282, 286

Latin 7, 10, 13, 20–23, 25, 28, 31, 34,
   36–37, 43–44, 46, 48, 74–75, 78, 84, 98,
   101, 115, 134, 136, 141, 144, 147, 150,
   153, 159, 163, 167, 271, 273, 275–281,
   283–287; Latins 22, 78, 275, 281
Lea, B. J. 8–9, 281–282
Leo IV (Pope) 164, 241
Liguria 109
Limassol 26; *see also* Cyprus (Kingdom of)
Lombardy 35, 41, 72, 74, 76, 84–85,
   109, 117
London 29, 83, 98
Longos 75
Louis IV of Bavaria 35, 45, 74, 154, 279
Louis IX of France (St) 6, 8, 80, 86, 98,
   102, 148, 278, 283
Louis of Bourbon (Count of Clermont)
   38–39, 45, 98, 100, 116, 142
Louis X of France 35, 37
Low Countries 2, 7, 296
Lucan 148
Lucera (Muslim colony of) 6, 80,
   148–149, 283
Lyon 77, 139, 154, 280; *see also* Council
   of Lyon (second)

Maccabees 7, 78, 80, 162–163, 281, 283;
   Judas Maccabeus 78, 162, 163, 171;
   Maccabean 8, 162–163, 165; Mattathias
   Maccabeus (priest), 78, 152, 162, 171
MacGregor, J. 7–8, 119, 282
Maier, C. 3, 6, 31, 139, 283
Mamluks 20, 41, 45, 74, 142–143;
   Mamluk 25, 38, 43, 46, 72, 85,
   142–143, 146, 165
Marino Sanudo Torsello 39, 43, 48,
   281, 286
Marseilles 7, 38, 70–71, 84, 274
Marsilius of Padua 154
Martin IV (Pope) 22, 224
Massoura (battle of) 3, 6, 170
Matthew of Griffonibus (Bolognese
   chronicler) 118, 273
Matthew Paris 6
Maxentius, Roman emperor 171
Mediterranean 25, 28, 31, 43, 48, 68, 72,
   74, 86, 162, 274, 280, 284
Menache, S. 7, 283
mendicant: friars 4–6, 29, 34, 99, 283;
   orders 4, 30, 84, 102, 134, 189
Mentesche (emirate of) 163
Mercurius (St) 119
Moolenbroek, J. V. 5, 287
Moors 46, 161

Morton, N. 8, 281, 282–284, 286
Moses 79
Muessig, C. 8, 283
Muhammed 142, 168
Muslim 5–6, 8, 25, 44, 72, 80, 105, 137, 143, 147, 149, 152, 162, 164, 166–167, 172, 283; Muslims 72, 147–148, 166, 168, 276, 281;
Mytilene 82

Naples 22–25, 70, 72, 85, 102, 135, 142, 275, 280
Narbonne 11, 38, 44, 107, 145
Nazareth 29, 98, 166, 172
Nebuchadnezzar 152, 178n93
Negroponte 48, 72, 75, 85, 165
Nicholas IV (Pope) 84
Nicholas of Fréauville (Cardinal-bishop of Sant' Eusebio) 10, 34, 46, 49, 98, 113, 134
Nîmes 26, 154
Notre-Dame-du-Pré, abbey (Rouen) 68, 107

Oliver of Paderborn (preacher) 5, 27, 107, 170
Orhan 163
Osman I 163
Ottomans 74, 86, 163, 296

Pallene 75
Paris 3, 37–39, 43–44, 46–48, 71, 77–78, 98–100, 113–116, 135–136, 142, 144, 151, 155–156, 161, 169, 170; Bibliothèque nationale 8, 136, 144–145, 193–194, 196, 201, 227, 259, 269, 281; Bibliothèque Sainte Genevieve 194, 201, 227, 259, 269; Île-de-la-Cité 10, 46, 98, 113; Longchamp-en-Lions 38; Notre-Dame 107, 145; Parisian theologians 8, 10, 82, 134–135, 140, 148, 150, 156; Prés-aux-Clercs 48, 155; Sainte-Chapelle 8, 10, 37, 80, 98; St-Denis abbey 115; St-Germain-des-Prés 10, 37, 98, 134; St-Martin-des-Champs 116; St Victor abbey 8, 32, 37, 115, 135, 145, 169; Treaty of 20; University of 3–4, 82, 101, 135, 154
Paschali, M. 9
passagium: Hospitallers' 12, 24–30, 32, 34, 1–100, 102–103, 109–110, 112, 119, 190, 279; *see also* Crusade Hospitaller; *generale* 33, 38, 41, 48, 68, 70–73, 86, 145–146, 168, 231; *particulare* 38, 41, 44–45, 70, 100, 103, 108
Pastoureaux 13, 109, 113–116, 274
Paulet, L. 7, 284
Peter Gauvain (Bishop-elect of Viviers) 41
Peter Lombard 154
Peter of Blois 2
Peter of Castro 142
Peter of Courpalay (Abbot of St-Germain-des-Prés) 10, 37, 98, 122n10, 134
Peter of Pleine Chassagne (Latin patriarch of Jerusalem) 10, 30, 37, 49, 98–100, 122n10, 134
Peter the Chanter 2, 281
Peter the Hermit 7, 9, 26–27, 277
Peter Thomas (papal legate) 83, 86, 277
Peter Trousseau (French royal envoy) 161, 184n195
Philip IV of France 12, 20–24, 29, 31–36, 40, 49, 98, 100, 113, 190, 285
Philip of Taranto 25
Philip V (the Tall) of France 35, 37–41, 49, 103, 113–116, 286
Philip VI of France 12, 39–40, 46–49, 67–73, 75–77, 79, 101, 106–107, 141–145, 147, 152–157, 159–163, 167–168, 170–171, 190, 275, 286
Philip (Archbishop of Mytilene) 82; *see also* Mytilene
Philips, J. 7
Philips, M. 7, 284
Phineas 171
Pierre de la Palud (Latin patriarch of Jerusalem) 3, 11, 13, 46, 49, 97, 101, 106, 119, 134–135, 141–147, 149, 151, 153, 156, 162, 167, 169–171, 193, 278
Pierre Roger 11, 13, 47–49, 68, 71, 73, 97, 101, 106–107, 134, 144, 153–168, 170–172, 191, 194, 201, 227, 287; *see also* Clement VI (Pope)
Pietro Gradonico (Doge) 24
Pliny 82, 150
Pliny the Elder 148
Poitiers 25–27, 29, 34, 69
Poland 23, 72, 110
Portnykh, V. 6, 284
Porto 12, 34, 43
preaching aids 9, 168–169, 172; *artes praedicandi* 3, 287; *distinctiones* 3, 156; *exempla* collections 3–4, 8, 119, 146, 150–151, 165, 169–172, 274, 280, 282, 284; *summae* 3, 169

Index 293

Prussia 5, 270
Purkis, W. 7, 284

Ramon Lull 22, 33, 279
Ravenna 22, 24, 84
Raymond (Archbishop of Thérouanne) 146–147
Rhodes 12, 24–29, 32, 34, 72, 75, 85, 102–103, 163, 172, 188, 282
Riley-Smith, J. 5–6, 276–277, 280, 283, 285
Robert (Count of Artois) 6, 148
Robert (Count of Flanders) 35, 37; *see also* Flanders
Roger of Salisbury (Bishop of Bath and Wells) 169
Romagna 22–24, 117
Roman Church 21–22, 67, 159
Romania 23, 47, 74, 78, 82, 84, 86, 172
Rouen 47, 68, 106, 134, 144, 153–155, 160, 191

St Baudil (priory) 153
St Florian (abbey) 97, 109, 111
Santa Maria Novella (cathedral-Florence) 74, 117
Santa Rufina 12, 34
Saracens 22, 37, 78, 101, 111–112, 143, 148–152, 162, 164–165, 170
Schein, S. 7, 28, 108, 113, 281, 285
Schneyer, J. B. 11, 92n96, 136, 285
Sheba 151
Shepkaru, S. 7, 286
Siena 117
Silesia 110
Smith, T. 9, 286
Smyrna 12–13, 70, 73, 75–76, 78–79, 81–82, 84–86, 107, 117–118, 120, 171, 189, 276
Soissons (Count of) 98
Sommerfeldt, J. 7, 286
Spain 23, 31, 46, 191, 282
Stephen of Bourbon 4, 8; *see also exempla* collections
Syria 20, 28, 74, 80, 143, 149, 276; Syro-Palestinian zone 20, 34, 48, 142

Tartars 72
Templars (knights) 25, 28–29, 31–32, 34, 55n79, 151, 274
Teutonic (knights) 110
Thomas Aquinas 69, 140–141

Thomas of Bailly 136
Toulouse 104, 114–115, 146–147
Turcoman 48, 74
Turks 3, 10, 22, 26, 39, 45, 47, 67, 72–79, 82–83, 85–86, 102–103, 107, 117, 119, 165–166, 259, 279, 281
Tuscany 35, 72, 84, 109, 117
Tyerman, C. 5, 9, 36, 39, 286

Umur Pasha (Turcoman overlord) 74–75, 282
Urban II (Pope) 1, 5, 7, 26, 80, 139, 147, 153, 166, 172, 277, 284
Urban IV (Pope) 69

Valois (dynasty) 46, 49, 76, 271, 275, 280, 283, 287; *see also* Charles of Valois
Vatican 6, 11, 170, 172, 269
Vegetius Renatus 159, 272
Venice 22–24, 31, 48, 70, 74, 85, 110, 117, 120, 278, 284
Venturino of Bergamo 10, 74–75, 84–85, 98, 117–118, 277
Victorines 8, 169, 281; *see also* St Victor abbey
Vincennes 48

Waldensians 102
Walker, L. 9, 287
West 7, 12, 21–22, 75–76, 85, 118, 151
Western: Christianity 1, 21–24, 41, 48, 57, 75, 86, 103, 120, 137, 143, 153, 162; Church 1, 73; Europe 10, 22, 27, 35, 43–44, 48–49, 85, 108–109, 146, 162–163, 188; monarchs 21, 25, 28, 30, 49, 72, 190
William Bernard of Narbonne (chancellor of Notre-Dame of Paris) 3, 11, 107, 145, 193
William Court (Cardinal-priest of Santi Quattro Coronati) 73–74, 85, 90n64
William Durand (Bishop of Mende) 38, 46, 142
William Le Maire (Bishop of Angers) 33–34, 274
William Nogaret 33
William of Nangis 46, 115, 271
William Peyraut 3, 139, 174n37
William Roger (Lord of Maumont) 154
Winchester 83

Zachariah 165